Debbie Cooper

LIFE CONTINGENCIES

LIFE CONTINGENCIES

BY

ALISTAIR NEILL

M.A., M.S., F.F.A., F.I.A., F.C.I.I.

Special edition for sale to members of the
Institute of Actuaries and members or students of the
Faculty of Actuaries

HEINEMANN : LONDON

William Heinemann Ltd
10 Upper Grosvenor Street, London WIX 9PA

LONDON   MELBOURNE   TORONTO
JOHANNESBURG   AUCKLAND

First published 1977
Reprinted 1979
© The Institute of Actuaries and the Faculty of
Actuaries in Scotland 1977

Printed and bound in Great Britain by
REDWOOD BURN LIMITED
Trowbridge & Esher

CONTENTS

PREFACE

The main purpose of this book is to serve as a text-book for students studying for the professional examinations of the Institute of Actuaries and the Faculty of Actuaries. It covers the principal 'basic' specialist tool of an actuary—life contingencies—and its application to the calculation of premiums and contributions, and the valuation, of life assurance contracts and pension funds.

Whereas the previous text book *Life and Other Contingencies* by P. F. Hooker and L. H. Longley-Cook was published in two volumes, this book reverts to the older practice of King and of Spurgeon in being in one volume. At the time that the previous book was published it was thought that only a few solved examples and no exercises for the student should be included in a text-book. There has now been a change of opinion, due partly to the success of the text-book on *Compound Interest and Annuities-Certain* by D. W. A. Donald which included many examples and exercises, and a major part of this new book is the carefully selected series of examples and exercises.

Any author on the subject is bound to be indebted to the authors of the previous text-books and I acknowledge particularly the works of E. F. Spurgeon, C. W. Jordan, and Hooker and Longley-Cook. I would also express appreciation of the help and advice I have received from Mr C. J. Wake and also many other members of the profession from both sides of the border, particularly Miss M. C. Allanach, Mr A. J. Jolliffe and Mr H. J. Price. For assistance in checking the examples and exercises I would thank Mr D. O. Forfar, and also Mr L. J. G. Purdie and Mr R. Garden.

A. N.

INTRODUCTION FOR STUDENTS

Because life contingencies is concerned with probabilities and is an application of compound interest, it is essential that the student have a sound knowledge of elementary probability and compound interest theory before reading this book.

The book has a practical approach to a practical subject and contains many solved examples and exercises for the student. For the reader to gain full advantage he or she should study carefully the solved examples, preferably trying to solve them first including the arithmetic, and consider how the principles discussed in the immediately preceding section have been applied. The exercises should then be attempted and the solution checked with the answers in Appendix I before studying the next section.

The solved examples and exercises have been carefully constructed and are in a logical sequence—the student will not obtain full advantage from his reading unless they are all solved or at least seriously attempted.

Similar attention should be paid to the more difficult examples and exercises covering the work of the whole chapter (many being based on actual examination questions) which should be studied and solved before the next chapter is read.

There is a recent tendency for published mortality tables to include rather more significant figures than would be used in practice; an example is the table known as A1967–70 shown in Appendix III. This is a result of computer technique and in the solved examples fewer significant figures have been taken than shown in the tables.

Although the text-book has been written with the student studying by himself or herself particularly in mind it is hoped that the layout and many exercises should also assist both those teaching and studying by the welcome increasing number of classes and lecture courses.

THE MORTALITY TABLE

1.1 Mortality experience

The subject of Life Contingencies, a knowledge of which is fundamental to the actuary, is an application of mathematics dealing with calculations in respect of payments depending on human survivorship or death. Such calculations, which usually include the element of compound interest as well as mortality, are required in connection with life assurance, pension funds and friendly societies.

Although the rate or rates of interest money will earn in future are not known, problems in compound interest can be solved by making assumptions as to the future rate of interest. Once the assumptions are made, numerical results are obtained with the aid of tables containing functions such as $(1+i)^n$, v^n, etc. Similarly, although the mortality a group of persons will experience in the future is not known, problems in life contingencies can be solved by making assumptions on future mortality and numerical results will be obtained with the aid of tables of functions based on that mortality. The basic table, a mortality table, sometimes referred to as a life table, is strictly confined to the fundamental functions which will be explained in this chapter and which do not involve compound interest. Other functions which are based on the mortality table and which involve compound interest as well as mortality will be described commencing with Chapter 2.

As the best indication of what is likely to happen in the future is often a knowledge of what has happened in the past, mortality tables are usually based, directly or indirectly, on the mortality which has actually been experienced by a suitable group of persons. Before the functions comprised in the mortality table are studied we will first consider how such a mortality experience could be investigated and how the results could be recorded.

If a large number, n_α, of persons attaining the birthday α during a short period of time could be kept under observation from that age until all of them had died, the number of them surviving to each birthday, $x = \alpha + 1$, $x = \alpha + 2$, and so on, would form a non-increasing sequence n_x and ultimately at some value of x equal, say, to ω we should have $n_\omega = 0$, when they have all died.

The number of persons who died between exact age x and exact age $x + 1$ would be $n_x - n_{x+1}$, that is $-\Delta n_x$. The ratio $-\Delta n_x / n_x$ would be the proportion of persons dying between exact age x and exact age $x + 1$ out of a given number (in this case n_x) attaining age x. This proportion forms a useful measure of the mortality at age x and may be referred to as the observed rate of mortality at age x.

If α were a young age, such as 20, or even 0, and ω were in the neighbourhood of 105 or 110, as it might quite well be, it would take nearly a century to carry out such a set of observations. Furthermore, during this period economic, social, sanitary, medical and other conditions, which are likely to have important influences on mortality, would probably have changed very considerably, so that the recorded values of n_x, $-\Delta n_x$ and $-\Delta n_x / n_x$, would provide very little indication of the mortality likely to be experienced by a comparable group of persons in the future. Observations of the mortality of groups of persons are thus not conducted precisely in the manner just described.

In the past 200 years or so, however, observed rates of mortality have been computed for various kinds of groups of persons, in different parts of the world, at all ages, and during different periods of years. The technical processes by which these rates have been obtained is not the subject of this book. It is sufficient for our purpose to say that there exists a large amount of data (usually in the form of rates of mortality) from which it is apparent that mortality varies, not only with regard to age and sex, but also with regard to many other characteristics of the persons concerned and their environment, some of which were mentioned in the previous paragraph. Improvements in many of these conditions have caused rates of mortality in most countries and at most ages to fall for a century, but the information available enables reasonable assumptions to be made on the mortality likely to be experienced in the future by various groups of persons.

Let us now return to the illustrative group of n_x persons observed from age α to age ω. If a sudden change took place in the environmental conditions in the year in which these persons attained age y— such change could on the one hand be an epidemic or a war or some other change which increased rates of mortality or on the other hand might be the introduction of a new drug or a new surgical treatment which reduced rates of mortality—this would cause a break at age y in the progression of the observed rates of mortality, $-\Delta n_x/n_x$, from age to age. Also it is known that in certain parts of the world rates of mortality fluctuate from year to year owing to variations in weather conditions. Apart from influences such as these, which we may refer to briefly as 'sudden changes' and which would produce irregularities in the series $-\Delta n_x/n_x$, we should expect that changing economic, social and other conditions would be gradual in their effect and would not unduly disturb the steady progression of the rates from age to age.

If we divided the n_x persons into a number of sub-groups by some random process, the known features of statistical regularity would lead us to expect that the rates of mortality observed at the same age x in different sub-groups would be approximately the same. There would be variations between the sub-groups but these would have all the characteristics of random variations. If, on the other hand, we were to divide the n_x persons into a number of sub-groups according to some feature likely to affect mortality, for example sex or occupation, we should expect the observed rates of mortality at any age x in these sub-groups to differ to a larger extent than could be explained by random variations.

Statistical considerations also suggest that the irregularities in the progression of the observed rates of mortality, $-\Delta n_x/n_x$, from age to age (apart from irregularities due to 'sudden changes') could be reduced by increasing the number, n_x, of persons observed. This involves the conception of the group of n_x persons as a random sample from some larger group of persons. A less precise way of looking at the matter is to assume that additional persons could be included who would be constituted similarly to the original group n_x with regard to all the characteristics influencing mortality. In practice, however, it would be very unusual to be able precisely to define the population from which n_x was to be regarded as a random sample or to include an additional group of persons similarly constituted, and the possibility of reducing irregularities by increasing n_x is therefore to be regarded from a theoretical standpoint rather than as a practical possibility. Also even if n_x could be made very large, the numbers surviving to very high ages would be small and therefore there would be irregularities in the progression of the observed rate of mortality from age to age at these high ages.

1.2   The mortality table

It follows from what has been said in the previous section that the idea of a group of persons attaining age α and being gradually reduced in numbers, until they are all dead, by the operation of mortality in such a way that the rates of mortality at successive ages form a smooth series is a purely theoretical conception. It is, nevertheless, a very useful conception which forms the basis of the theory of life contingencies and has been shown by long use to be suitable for solving most practical problems in life assurance and similar work. The fundamental function of the mortality table is a function known as l_x. This hypothetical function corresponds to the empirical sequence n_x which has been discussed above. It is a positive non-increasing function representing the number of lives who are expected to survive to age x out of l_α lives who attain age α, this being the youngest age for which l_x is tabulated. For theoretical purposes it is convenient to assume that l_x is a continuous function, having values for all x and not just integers and with unique finite differential coefficients to any required order at all points.

Just as $-\Delta n_x/n_x$ is the observed rate of mortality at age x, so $-\Delta l_x/l_x$ is the rate of mortality at age x assumed in the mortality table. The mortality assumption on which the table is based may take the form of an assumed rate of mortality for each integral age x, since, given such a series of rates and a suitable arbitrary value of l_α, a column of l_x can be constructed for integral values of x. In fact, the l_x column in most mortality tables is constructed in this way. In this event, although l_x will be defined for integral ages only, we can assume that it exists for all values of x, integral and fractional. Sometimes l_x is defined by a mathematical formula, in which event we can obtain the rates of mortality by calculating numerical values of l_x for integral ages. In this case, l_x will be defined for all values of x.

As described, l_x represents the number of lives who, according to the mortality table, are expected to survive to age x out of l_α lives who attain age α. Since the mortality table can start at any age, l_{x+t} may be regarded as representing the number of lives who are expected to survive to age $x+t$ out of l_x lives aged x; both x and $x+t$ not necessarily being integers. Although in the definition of the mortality table nothing was said about the various characteristics of the individual hypothetical lives, the l_x lives in the mortality table, like the n_x persons in the illustrative mortality investigation, are not necessarily to be regarded as all exactly identical from the point of view of the various characteristics which influence mortality. l_{x+t}/l_x is a function which expresses the mortality assumption in the form of the expected proportions surviving to each age and hence it gives the probability relations as applicable to random samples. The ratio l_{x+t}/l_x is the probability of survival to age $x+t$ in respect of an individual life aged x taken at random from an indefinitely large number of lives who are assumed to experience, as a whole, the mortality on which the table is based. It will be seen that $1-l_{x+t}/l_x$ is analogous to the 'cumulative distribution function' of probability theory. In dealing with problems in life contingencies, whenever we refer to a life aged x we imply, unless a specific statement is made to the contrary, that a life taken at random is intended.

If a random sample of m lives aged x is taken, the expected number surviving to age $x+t$ is ml_{x+t}/l_x but the actual number is subject to random variations. For sufficiently large values of m these random variations are small relative to the expected number. Many of the functions developed in this book are similarly subject to random variations. Practical work usually concerns groups of lives which may be regarded as random samples, and these random variations are usually small in relation to the errors involved in the choice of a mortality table, to variations in mortality from year to year and to errors arising from deviations of actual rates of interest and expenses from those assumed. Accordingly they are usually ignored in practice, but the fact that they exist should not be overlooked and some examples are described in Chapter 11.

A possible table of l_x which starts at age 0 and ceases at age 100 is shown in Table 1.1.

We would then have the probability (rounded to four decimal places) of a member of the group at birth, taken at random, living to exact age 1 as 0·9929 and to exact age 2 as 0·9912. If we wished to find the probability of a member aged exactly 1 living to exact age 2 we would divide l_2 by l_1 that is 9,911,725 by 9,929,200 to give ·9982.

It is important to remember that the figures in the l_x column have no meaning individually and are only meaningful when related to each other—thus the probability of a person living from exact age 20 to exact age 30 is $\dfrac{l_{30}}{l_{20}} = \dfrac{9,480,358}{9,664,994} = \cdot9809$. While the table should strictly be interpreted only in this way this ratio is sometimes said

CHAPTER ONE

verbally to be the 'number alive at age 30' divided by the 'number alive at age 20'.

Because the figures in the table have no meaning except when divided by each other, all the figures in a mortality table could be multiplied by a factor and no change would be made in the mortality

TABLE 1.1

Age x	l_x
0	10,000,000
1	9,929,200
2	9,911,725
3	9,896,659
⋮	
10	9,805,870
⋮	
20	9,664,994
⋮	
30	9,480,358
⋮	
40	9,241,359
⋮	
50	8,762,306
⋮	
60	7,698,698
⋮	
70	5,592,012
⋮	
80	2,626,372
⋮	
90	468,174
⋮	
99	6,415
100	0

represented—thus Table 1.2a and b would apart from the rounding of certain of the figures represent the same mortality, the first being the previous table multiplied by $\frac{1}{100}$, and the second by $\frac{1}{2}$.

While the table shown commences at age 0 this is not necessary and, for example, a mortality table intended for use in life assurance offices to show the mortality of annuitants might commence at age 40. Normally the l_x figure for the lowest age is taken as some convenient round number such as 1,000,000, 999,999 or 500,000—this is called the radix of the table. The first age at which the value of l_x becomes negligible is called the limiting age and is denoted by ω, so that $l_\omega = 0$—in the table above $\omega = 100$. Some mortality tables are assumed to conform to a mathematical formula so that the l_x column converges asymptotically to zero and never actually becomes 0. However, for practical purposes, a limiting age such as 100, 105 or 110 is assumed for all mortality tables.

TABLE 1.2a

x	l_x
0	100,000
1	99,292
⋮	
10	98,059
⋮	
20	96,650
⋮	

TABLE 1.2b

x	l_x
0	5,000,000
1	4,964,600
⋮	
10	4,902,935
⋮	
20	4,832,497
⋮	

1.3 Probabilities of living and dying—rate of mortality

Table 1.3 is an extract of a mortality table which will be used to exemplify the notation used in this section. This introduces the symbol d_x which is the difference between successive l_x figures. Thus

$$d_x = l_x - l_{x+1}, \quad \text{or} \quad d_x = -\Delta l_x. \qquad (1.3.1)$$

In the convenient (but strictly incorrect) interpretation of the mortality table mentioned in the previous section d_x represents the 'number dying aged x last birthday'.

TABLE 1.3

x	l_x	d_x
40	80,935	455
41	80,480	481
42	79,999	511
43	79,488	546
44	78,942	585
45	78,357	626
⋮	⋮	⋮
50	74,794	844

Probability of death and survival can be obtained directly from the l_x and d_x columns of the mortality table. The symbol (x) is used to denote 'a person aged x', or 'a life aged x'.

The probability that (x) will survive to age $x+1$, is denoted by p_x, so

$$p_x = \frac{l_{x+1}}{l_x}, \qquad (1.3.2)$$

thus
$$p_{40} = \frac{l_{41}}{l_{40}} = \frac{80,480}{80,935} = \cdot 9944.$$

The probability of a person age x dying during the year, the *rate of mortality*, is given the symbol q_x, so

$$q_x = \frac{d_x}{l_x} = \frac{l_x - l_{x+1}}{l_x} = \frac{-\Delta l_x}{l_x}, \qquad (1.3.3)$$

thus
$$q_{40} = \frac{d_{40}}{l_{40}} = \frac{455}{80,935} = \cdot 0056.$$

The probability of (x) living for a year plus the probability of (x) dying within a year must obviously be 1, so

$$p_x + q_x = 1, \text{ or } p_x = 1 - q_x, \text{ or } q_x = 1 - p_x. \qquad (1.3.4)$$

The probability that (x) will live for n years to age $x+n$ is given the symbol $_np_x$;

$$_np_x = \frac{l_{x+n}}{l_x} \qquad (1.3.5)$$

for example
$$_5p_{40} = \frac{78,357}{80,935} = \cdot 9681.$$

Another way of looking at $_np_x$ is to consider it as the product of successive probabilities of living each year

$$_np_x = \frac{l_{x+1}}{l_x} \cdot \frac{l_{x+2}}{l_{x+1}} \cdot \frac{l_{x+3}}{l_{x+2}} \cdots \frac{l_{x+n}}{l_{x+n-1}}$$

$$= p_x \cdot p_{x+1} \cdot p_{x+2} \cdots p_{x+n-1}.$$

The probability that (x) will die within n years is given the symbol $_nq_x$;

$$_nq_x = \frac{l_x - l_{x+n}}{l_x} = \frac{1}{l_x} \sum_{y=x}^{x+n-1} d_y = 1 - {_np_x} \qquad (1.3.6)$$

so $_5q_{40} = \dfrac{80,935-78,357}{80,935}$ or $\dfrac{455+481+511+546+585}{80,935}$ or $1 - \cdot9681$

all equalling $\cdot0319$.

It can be seen that if no figure prefixes the symbol p or q, 1 is assumed, i.e. $_1p_x \equiv p_x$; $_1q_x \equiv q_x$.

The probability that (x) will live m years but die in the following n years, or that (x) will die between ages $x+m$ and $x+m+n$ is given the symbol

$$_{m|n}q_x = \frac{l_{x+m}-l_{x+m+n}}{l_x} = \frac{l_{x+m}}{l_x} \cdot \frac{l_{x+m}-l_{x+m+n}}{l_{x+m}} \qquad (1.3.7)$$

$$= {_mp_x} \cdot {_nq_{x+m}}.$$

Thus $\quad _{3|2}q_{40} = \dfrac{l_{43}-l_{45}}{l_{40}} = \dfrac{79,488-78,357}{80,935} = \dfrac{1,131}{80,935}$

$$= \cdot0140.$$

When $n = 1$ it may be omitted and the symbol becomes

$$_{m|}q_x = \frac{d_{x+m}}{l_x} = {_mp_x} \cdot q_{x+m},$$

being the probability that (x) will die in a year, deferred m years;

thus $\quad _{2|}q_{42} = \dfrac{d_{44}}{l_{42}} = \dfrac{585}{79,999} = \cdot0073.$

1.4 Mortality tables

It will be seen that a mortality table is defined either by the l_x or q_x (or p_x) columns. If the q_x figures are given, the l_x column will be obtained by choosing a suitable radix (l_0) and successively obtaining the d_x and l_x figures:—

$$d_0 = l_0 \cdot q_0$$

$$l_1 = l_0 - d_0$$

$$d_1 = l_1 \cdot q_1 \quad \text{and generally}$$

$$d_x = l_x \cdot q_x$$

$$l_{x+1} = l_x - d_x.$$

The radix is arbitrary and is chosen so that a suitable degree of accuracy is obtained when the l_x figures are divided. Apart from this point the absolute value of an individual value of l_x is of no consequence. There is no reason why the value of l_x should not be recorded in decimals and this is sometimes done at the high ages of a table in order to obtain a smoother run of figures.

The examples in this book will normally use the tables given in Appendix III—The English Life Table No. 12—Males, the A1967–70 Table for Assured Lives and the $a(55)$ tables for Annuitants.

The English Life Table No. 12—Males is constructed from the mortality rates experienced by the male population in England in the years 1960, 1961 and 1962. The A1967–70 table is based on the experience within these years of lives assured of United Kingdom life assurance companies (and has the unusual radix of 34,489 decided so that the value of the largest function calculated did not exceed the capacity of the computer). The $a(55)$ tables give the rates of mortality separately for males and females and were based on the mortality experience of annuitants of United Kingdom life offices in 1946 to 1948, but projected into the future so that estimated rates were obtained thought to be applicable for annuities purchased in 1955.

Mortality rates have been tending to decrease at most ages and in most countries of the world for more than a hundred years, and published tables thus gradually cease to represent the experienced mortality. The English Life Tables are published at ten-year intervals, being based on the ten-yearly population census, while the assurance and annuitants tables are published at longer intervals. It might be thought that tables would become out of date quickly but is is common practice to adjust published tables, the most usual method being to deduct (or perhaps add) a certain number of years to the actual age before entering the table. One example of this is the common deduction of about four years from the age of a female policyholder in calculating the premiums for a life assurance policy, the published premium rates having been based on male mortality.

Example 1.1

Using the mortality table given in section 1.2, find the probability of a person aged 30,

   (i) surviving to age 40

  (ii) dying before age 40

 (iii) dying between the ages of 60 and 80.

Solution

(i) $\quad {}_{10}p_{30} = \dfrac{l_{40}}{l_{30}} = \dfrac{9,241,359}{9,480,358} = \cdot 9748$

(ii) $\quad {}_{10}q_{30} = \dfrac{l_{30}-l_{40}}{l_{30}} = \dfrac{238,999}{9,480,358} = \cdot 0252$ or,

$\qquad {}_{10}q_{30} = 1 - {}_{10}p_{30} = 1 - \cdot 9748 = \cdot 0252$

(iii) $\quad {}_{30|20}q_{30} = \dfrac{l_{60}-l_{80}}{l_{30}} = \dfrac{5,072,326}{9,480,358} = \cdot 5350.$

Example 1.2

If a mortality table is represented by the function

$$l_x = 1000\sqrt{100-x}$$

find (i) the probability of a life surviving from birth to age 19

(ii) the probability of a life aged 36 dying before age 51.

Solution

(i) $\quad {}_{19}p_0 = \dfrac{l_{19}}{l_0} = \dfrac{1,000\sqrt{100-19}}{1,000\sqrt{100}} = \tfrac{9}{10} = \cdot 9$

(ii) $\quad {}_{15}q_{36} = \dfrac{l_{36}-l_{51}}{l_{36}} = \dfrac{1,000\sqrt{64}-1,000\sqrt{49}}{1,000\sqrt{64}} = \tfrac{1}{8} = \cdot 125.$

Example 1.3

Complete Table 1.4a.

TABLE 1.4a

x	q_x	l_x	d_x
90	$\frac{1}{3}$	3,000	
91	$\frac{2}{5}$		
92	$\frac{1}{2}$		
93	$\frac{2}{3}$		
94	$\frac{4}{5}$		
95	1		

Solution

$$d_{90} = q_{90} \cdot l_{90} = \tfrac{1}{3}(3,000) = 1,000$$
$$\therefore l_{91} = 2,000$$
$$d_{91} = q_{91} \cdot l_{91} = \tfrac{2}{5}(2,000) = 800$$
$$\therefore l_{92} = 1,200$$

and proceeding similarly we obtain Table 1.4b.

TABLE 1.4b

x	q_x	l_x	d_x
90	$\tfrac{1}{3}$	3,000	1,000
91	$\tfrac{2}{5}$	2,000	800
92	$\tfrac{1}{2}$	1,200	600
93	$\tfrac{2}{3}$	600	400
94	$\tfrac{4}{5}$	200	160
95	1	40	40
96		0	

Example 1.4

Prove that $_{m|n}q_x = {}_mp_x - {}_{m+n}p_x.$

Solution

$$_{m|n}q_x = \frac{l_{x+m} - l_{x+m+n}}{l_x}$$

$$= \frac{l_{x+m}}{l_x} - \frac{l_{x+m+n}}{l_x}$$

$$= {}_mp_x - {}_{m+n}p_x.$$

Example 1.5

A life aged 50 is subject to the mortality of the English Life Table No. 12—Males, for 10 years, then the $a(55)$ Male table, for 20 years, then the A1967–70 table with a deduction of 2 years for the remainder of life. Find the probability that the life lives to age 90.

Solution

In this type of question the probabilities in the age ranges should be kept separate so that the l_x figures on one mortality table are always divided by a figure from the same table. Thus the required probability

$$= \left\{ \begin{array}{c} \text{probability of living} \\ \text{for 10 years} \end{array} \right\} \cdot \left\{ \begin{array}{c} \text{probability of living} \\ \text{for further 20 years} \end{array} \right\}$$
$$\cdot \left\{ \begin{array}{c} \text{probability of living} \\ \text{for further 10 years} \end{array} \right\}$$

$$= (_{10}p_{50} \text{ on ELT No. 12—Males}) . (_{20}p_{60} \text{ on } a(55)\text{—Males})$$
$$. (_{10}p_{78} \text{ on A1967-70})$$

$$= \frac{78,924}{90,085} \cdot \frac{363,991}{859,916} \cdot \frac{4012 \cdot 83}{14965 \cdot 5}$$

$$= \cdot 0994.$$

Note. The figures are taken from the l_x column of the tables; an explanation of the $l_{[x]}$ column will follow later in section 1.10.

Exercise 1.1

Using the A1967–70 table, find the values of $_{20}p_{40}, {}_{30}q_{25}, {}_{20|15}q_{42}$.

Exercise 1.2

Using the same mortality as stated in Example 1.5 above, find the probability that the life aged 50 dies between the ages of 70 and 85.

Exercise 1.3

A man aged 56 is subject to the mortality of the English Life Table No. 12—Males, and his brother aged 60 is subject to the mortality of the $a(55)$, Males table. Who is more likely to survive 10 years?

1.5 The graph of l_x

So far consideration has been given mainly to exact integral ages—this being the method by which tables are usually tabulated. If the interpretation of the mortality table as being based on a certain number of lives at an earlier age is considered it might be thought that l_x would be a discontinuous function decreasing by 1 each time one of the lives died during the year. However, this 'number alive' interpretation is only a useful shorthand—the l_x figures are as previously discussed only meaningful when divided by each other to give probabilities, and considered in this way it will be obvious that l_x is a continuous function of x, as has already been mentioned in section 1.2.

Actual determination of l_x at fractional ages when required will mainly be done by some form of interpolation except perhaps where the mortality table is known to have been based on a mathematical expression. The graph of l_x according to the English Life Table No. 12—Males is shown in Figure 1.1. The general shape of the curve should be noted as well as the obvious fact that l_x is always decreasing. In most tables l_x falls steeply at the infantile ages, and there are at least two points of inflexion.

In the symbol (x) for a life aged exactly x, x may thus not necessarily be an integer.

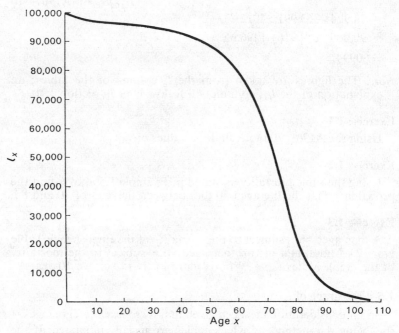

FIGURE 1.1   Graph of l_x—English Life Table No. 12—Males.

1.6   The force of mortality

As l_x is a continuous function it can be differentiated and the ratio that the rate of decrease of l_x at age x bears to the value of l_x at that age is called the force of mortality at age x and is represented by the symbol μ_x.

$$\mu_x = -\frac{1}{l_x}\frac{dl_x}{dx} \quad \text{or} \tag{1.6.1}$$

$$= -\frac{d}{dx}\log_e l_x. \tag{1.6.2}$$

This is a measure of the mortality at the precise moment of attaining age x expressed in the form of an annual rate. The negative sign is introduced so that μ_x will be positive, l_x being a decreasing function. The differential coefficient is divided by l_x because as we have seen the absolute magnitude of the l_x figure is arbitrary and depends on the radix of the table, and by dividing by l_x we obtain a figure which is independent of the radix.

Rewriting formula (1.6.1)

$$\frac{dl_x}{dx} = -l_x\mu_x \qquad (1.6.3)$$

and integrating over the range α to the limiting age of the table, x being written as $\alpha + t$

$$\int_0^{\omega-\alpha} \frac{dl_{\alpha+t}}{dt}\,dt = -\int_0^{\omega-\alpha} l_{\alpha+t}\mu_{\alpha+t}dt$$

i.e.
$$[l_{\alpha+t}]_0^{\omega-\alpha} = -\int_0^{\omega-\alpha} l_{\alpha+t}\mu_{\alpha+t}dt$$

$$\therefore\ l_\omega - l_\alpha = -\int_0^{\omega-\alpha} l_{\alpha+t}\mu_{\alpha+t}dt$$

and as $l_\omega = 0$
$$l_\alpha = \int_0^{\omega-\alpha} l_{\alpha+t}\mu_{\alpha+t}dt.$$

As $l_x = 0$ for all $x > \omega$, ∞ is often substituted for $\omega - \alpha$ in such integrals, and writing x for α we obtain

$$l_x = \int_0^\infty l_{x+t}\mu_{x+t}dt. \qquad (1.6.4)$$

If the limits of integration above had been taken as 0 and 1 we would have obtained

$$[l_{\alpha+t}]_0^1 = -\int_0^1 l_{\alpha+t}\mu_{\alpha+t}dt$$

$$\therefore\ l_{\alpha+1} - l_\alpha = -\int_0^1 l_{\alpha+t}\mu_{\alpha+t}dt$$

and as $l_{\alpha+1} - l_\alpha = -d_\alpha$, we obtain (writing x for α)

$$d_x = \int_0^1 l_{x+t}\mu_{x+t}dt. \qquad (1.6.5)$$

Integrating formula (1.6.2) from age α to $\alpha+n$ again writing $\alpha+t$ for x,

$$\int_0^n \mu_{\alpha+t}\,dt = -\int_0^n \frac{d}{dt}\log_e l_{\alpha+t}\,dt$$

$$= -[\log_e l_{\alpha+t}]_0^n$$

$$= -(\log_e l_{\alpha+n} - \log_e l_\alpha)$$

$$= -\log_e \frac{l_{\alpha+n}}{l_\alpha},$$

i.e.
$$\log_e \frac{l_{\alpha+n}}{l_\alpha} = -\int_0^n \mu_{\alpha+t}\,dt$$

$$\therefore \frac{l_{\alpha+n}}{l_\alpha} = e^{-\int_0^n \mu_{\alpha+t}\,dt}$$

and writing x instead of α

$$_np_x = e^{-\int_0^n \mu_{x+t}\,dt} \tag{1.6.6}$$

and
$$l_x = l_0 e^{-\int_0^x \mu_t\,dt}. \tag{1.6.7}$$

Formula (1.6.6) bears an obvious and important similarity to the compound interest formula:

Present value of 1 due n years hence $= e^{-\int_0^n \delta_t\,dt}$, where δ_t is the varying force of interest; thus the force of mortality is analogous to the force of interest.

The probability $_nq_x$ can then be expressed

$$_nq_x = 1 - e^{-\int_0^n \mu_{x+t}\,dt}. \tag{1.6.8}$$

An alternative formula can be derived by integrating formula (1.6.3) from age α to $\alpha+n$ when x is rewritten $\alpha+t$

$$\therefore [l_{\alpha+t}]_0^n = -\int_0^n l_{\alpha+t}\mu_{\alpha+t}\,dt$$

$$\therefore l_{\alpha+n} - l_\alpha = -\int_0^n l_{\alpha+t}\mu_{\alpha+t}\,dt$$

and rewriting x for α and dividing by l_x

$$_nq_x = \frac{l_x - l_{x+n}}{l_x} = \frac{1}{l_x}\int_0^n l_{x+t}\mu_{x+t}\,dt \tag{1.6.9}$$

or
$$_nq_x = \int_0^n {}_tp_x\mu_{x+t}dt.$$
(1.6.10)

When $n = 1$,
$$q_x = \int_0^1 {}_tp_x\mu_{x+t}dt.$$
(1.6.11)

This form of expression is particularly useful when extended to multiple life functions, and can be roughly described as 'keep the life alive until duration t; kill him off at that instant; then add (i.e. integrate) these probabilities over the required time range'.

Thus the probability $_{n|m}q_x$ may similarly be expressed

$$_{n|m}q_x = \int_n^{n+m} {}_tp_x\mu_{x+t}dt.$$

The graph of the function $\mu_x l_x$ is called the curve of deaths. An example is given in Figure 1.2 using the same table of mortality as

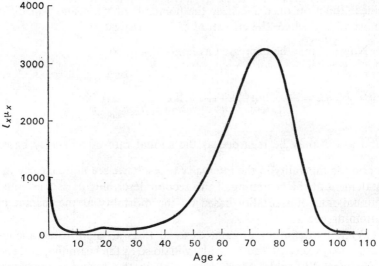

FIGURE 1.2. Graph of $l_x\mu_x$—English Life Table No. 12—Males.

was used to demonstrate the graph of l_x. The maximum and minimum points of the curve will correspond with the points of inflexion on the curve of l_x, as $\dfrac{dl_x}{dx} = -l_x\mu_x$ so that $\dfrac{d^2l_x}{dx^2} = 0$ when $\dfrac{d(l_x\mu_x)}{dx} = 0$.

It will be found from an examination of mortality tables that at some parts of the table $q_x > \mu_x$ and at others $q_x < \mu_x$. From formula (1.6.9)

$$l_x q_x = \int_0^1 l_{x+t}\mu_{x+t}\,dt.$$

If $l_{x+t}\mu_{x+t}$ is increasing, $l_x q_x$ will exceed the value at the start of the interval i.e. $l_x\mu_x$; so that $q_x > \mu_x$ if the graph of $l_x\mu_x$ is increasing. Considering the graph of l_x, as $-\dfrac{dl_x}{dx} = l_x\mu_x$ it follows that if $l_x\mu_x$ is increasing $\dfrac{dl_x}{dx}$ is decreasing, that is the gradient of the tangent to the curve is decreasing and the curve of l_x is concave to the x-axis as demonstrated in Figure 1.3.

So if the curve of l_x is concave to the x-axis $q_x > \mu_x$, and if l_x is convex to the x-axis $q_x < \mu_x$.

Thus μ_x and q_x will be most nearly equal when l_x is most nearly a linear function of x, i.e. near the point of inflexion and will differ most widely where the curvature of l_x is greatest.

Now $\dfrac{dl_x}{dx}$ may be expressed as $\lim\limits_{h\to 0}\dfrac{l_{x+h}-l_x}{h}$, so

$$\mu_x = -\frac{1}{l_x}\lim_{h\to 0}\frac{l_{x+h}-l_x}{h} = \lim_{h\to 0}\frac{l_x - l_{x+h}}{hl_x} = \lim_{h\to 0}\frac{{}_h q_x}{h}$$

and as $\dfrac{{}_h q_x}{h}$ may be regarded as the annual rate of mortality based upon the mortality in the interval x to $x+h$, we see more clearly the statement at the beginning of this section describing μ_x as a nominal annual rate of mortality based on the mortality at the instant of attaining age x.

While by definition q_x cannot exceed 1, as μ_x is an instantaneous rate it may exceed 1 and normally will do so at the beginning and end of a mortality table. Mortality is high in the period immediately following birth and for example in the first hour after birth $\dfrac{1}{(24)(365)}\,q_0$ will considerably exceed $\dfrac{1}{(24)(365)}$ so that the ratio $\dfrac{{}_h q_0}{h}\left(\text{where } h = \dfrac{1}{(24)(365)} \text{ or 1 hour}\right)$ approximating to μ_x will be > 1.

In the last year of the mortality table the rate of mortality is 1 for all $x > \omega - 1$, that is $\omega - x < 1$,

$$\therefore \frac{\omega - x q_x}{\omega - x} = \frac{1}{\omega - x} > 1, \quad \text{so that } \mu_x > 1.$$

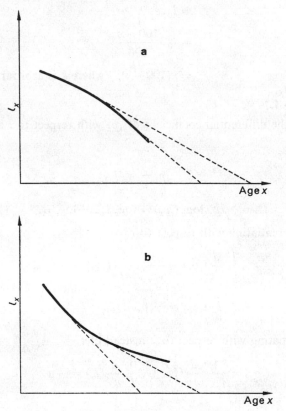

FIGURE 1.3. (a) Graph of l_x concave to x-axis. (b) Graph of l_x convex to x-axis.

Example 1.6

Find l_x if $\mu_x = \dfrac{1}{100 - x}$.

Solution

Using formula (1.6.7) $l_x = l_0 e^{-\int_0^x \mu_t dt}$, where l_0 is the arbitrary radix.

$$\therefore l_x = l_0 \cdot e^{-\int_0^x \frac{1}{100-t} dt}$$

$$= l_0 \cdot e^{[\log_e (100-t)]_0^x}$$

$$= l_0 \cdot e^{\log_e (100-x) - \log_e 100}$$

$$= l_0 \cdot e^{\log_e \frac{100-x}{100}}$$

$$= l_0 \cdot \frac{100-x}{100}$$

$$= k(100-x), \quad \text{where } k \text{ is arbitrary.}$$

Example 1.7

Find the differential coefficient of $_tp_x$ with respect to t and x.

Solution

$$_tp_x = \frac{l_{x+t}}{l_x}$$

$$\therefore \log_e (_tp_x) = \log_e l_{x+t} - \log_e l_x,$$

and differentiating with respect to t

$$\frac{1}{_tp_x} \frac{d}{dt} (_tp_x) = \frac{1}{l_{x+t}} \cdot \frac{d}{dt} (l_{x+t}) = -\mu_{x+t}$$

$$\therefore \frac{d}{dt} (_tp_x) = -_tp_x \cdot \mu_{x+t}. \tag{1.6.12}$$

Differentiating with respect to x instead of t

$$\frac{1}{_tp_x} \frac{d}{dx} (_tp_x) = \frac{1}{l_{x+t}} \frac{d}{dx} (l_{x+t}) - \frac{1}{l_x} \frac{d}{dx} (l_x) = -\mu_{x+t} + \mu_x$$

$$\therefore \frac{d}{dx} (_tp_x) = _tp_x(\mu_x - \mu_{x+t}). \tag{1.6.13}$$

These two formulae are worth remembering.

Example 1.8

A life is subject to a constant force of mortality of ·039221. Find the probability

(a) That he will live 10 years

(b) That he will die within 15 years.

Solution

(a) $_{10}p_x = e^{-\int_0^{10} (.039221)dt}$, and as $.039221$ is δ at 4% interest

$\qquad = v^{10}$ at 4%

$\qquad = .6756$

(b) $_{15}p_x$ similarly is v^{15} at 4% $= .5553$

$\qquad \therefore \ _{15}q_x = 1 - .5553 = .4447.$

Exercise 1.4

Show by integrating formula (1.6.10) using the result (1.6.12) that $_nq_x = 1 - {}_np_x.$

Exercise 1.5

A life aged 50 is subject to a constant force of mortality of $.048790$. Find the probability that he will die between the ages of 70 and 80.

1.7 Estimation of μ_x from the mortality table

When l_x is tabulated and any underlying mathematical formula is not known, values of μ_x can be found only approximately, the formulae demonstrated below being the most useful.

From formula (1.6.6) $\qquad p_x = e^{-\int_0^1 \mu_{x+t}dt}$

$$\therefore \int_0^1 \mu_{x+t}dt = -\log_e p_x, \qquad (1.7.1)$$

sometimes expressed as

$$= \text{colog}_e p_x,$$

where 'colog' is written for '$-\log$'. The integral represents the mean value of μ_{x+t} between x and $x+1$ and if it is assumed that this approximates to $\mu_{x+\frac{1}{2}}$ we have

$$\mu_{x+\frac{1}{2}} \doteqdot -\log_e p_x \qquad (1.7.2)$$

the approximation being closest where μ_{x+t} does not differ much from a linear function in the range.

Alternatively taking the value of $_2p_{x-1}$,

$$_2p_{x-1} = e^{-\int_{-1}^1 \mu_{x+t}dt}$$

so that
$$\int_{-1}^{1} \mu_{x+t}dt = -\log_e(p_{x-1}\cdot p_x)$$

and if the integral is considered as approximately equal to $2\mu_x$ we get

$$2\mu_x \fallingdotseq -(\log_e p_{x-1}+\log_e p_x)$$

$$\therefore \mu_x \fallingdotseq \tfrac{1}{2}(\text{colog}_e p_{x-1}+\text{colog}_e p_x). \tag{1.7.3}$$

Another method of approach is to assume that l_x follows a mathematical form, normally a polynomial, and use the Taylor expansion to obtain a value of $\dfrac{dl_x}{dx}$ (or l'_x) which can be used in the basic formula

$$\mu_x = -\frac{1}{l_x}\frac{dl_x}{dx}.$$

For example, assuming a function of the second degree,

$$l_{x+h} = l_x + hl'_x + \frac{h^2}{2!}l''_x$$

$$\therefore l_{x-1} = l_x - l'_x + \tfrac{1}{2}l''_x$$

and
$$l_{x+1} = l_x + l'_x + \tfrac{1}{2}l''_x.$$

Subtracting
$$l_{x-1} - l_{x+1} = -2l'_x$$

$$\therefore \mu_x = -\frac{1}{l_x}\cdot l'_x = \frac{1}{2l_x}(l_{x-1}-l_{x+1})$$

$$= \frac{1}{2l_x}(d_{x-1}+d_x). \tag{1.7.4}$$

A further method is to use the relationship between the differential and difference operator—that is

$$D = \log(1+\Delta) = \Delta - \frac{\Delta^2}{2} + \frac{\Delta^3}{3} - \ldots$$

so that
$$\mu_x = -\frac{1}{l_x}Dl_x = -\frac{1}{l_x}(\Delta l_x - \tfrac{1}{2}\Delta^2 l_x + \tfrac{1}{3}\Delta^3 l_x \ldots)$$

i.e.
$$\mu_x = \frac{1}{l_x}(d_x - \tfrac{1}{2}\Delta d_x + \tfrac{1}{3}\Delta^2 d_x \ldots). \tag{1.7.5}$$

This formula might be thought to enable the value of μ_0 to be found whereas the other formulae are not applicable l_{-1} having no meaning. However, in actual experience μ_x varies rapidly as x increases from 0 to 1 and it is rarely possible to find a satisfactory value for μ_0 if the only information available is the values of l_x at integral ages.

Example 1.9

Find an expression for μ_x assuming that l_x is a 4th degree polynomial.

Solution

Using the Taylor expansion

$$l_{x+h} = l_x + hl'_x + \frac{h^2}{2!} l''_x + \frac{h^3}{3!} l'''_x + \frac{h^4}{4!} l^{iv}_x,$$

$$l_{x-2} = l_x - 2l'_x + 2l''_x - \tfrac{4}{3}l'''_x + \tfrac{2}{3}l^{iv}_x \tag{1}$$

$$l_{x-1} = l_x - l'_x + \tfrac{1}{2}l''_x - \tfrac{1}{6}l'''_x + \tfrac{1}{24}l^{iv}_x \tag{2}$$

$$l_{x+1} = l_x + l'_x + \tfrac{1}{2}l''_x + \tfrac{1}{6}l'''_x + \tfrac{1}{24}l^{iv}_x \tag{3}$$

$$l_{x+2} = l_x + 2l'_x + 2l''_x + \tfrac{4}{3}l'''_x + \tfrac{2}{3}l^{iv}_x. \tag{4}$$

We wish to eliminate all the derivatives except l'_x. Subtracting formula (4) from (1), and (3) from (2) gives

$$l_{x-2} - l_{x+2} = -(4l'_x + \tfrac{8}{3}l'''_x) \tag{5}$$

$$l_{x-1} - l_{x+1} = -(2l'_x + \tfrac{1}{3}l'''_x). \tag{6}$$

Multiplying formula (6) by 8 and subtracting from (5) gives

$$(l_{x-2} - l_{x+2}) - 8(l_{x-1} - l_{x+1}) = -4l'_x + 16l'_x = 12l'_x$$

$$\therefore \mu_x = -\frac{l'_x}{l_x} \fallingdotseq -\frac{1}{12l_x} ((l_{x-2} - l_{x+2}) - 8(l_{x-1} - l_{x+1}))$$

$$\left. \begin{aligned} &= \frac{1}{12l_x} (8(l_{x-1} - l_{x+1}) - (l_{x-2} - l_{x+2})) \\[2mm] \text{or} \quad &\frac{1}{12l_x} (7(d_{x-1} + d_x) - (d_{x-2} + d_{x+1})) \end{aligned} \right\} \tag{1.7.6}$$

Example 1.10

Find a value for μ_{90} on the A1967–70 table by four different formulae.

Solution

Formula (1.7.3) gives $\mu_{90} \fallingdotseq -\frac{1}{2}(\log_e p_{89} + \log_e p_{90})$

$$= -\frac{1}{2}(\log_e \cdot 79896 + \log_e \cdot 78349)$$

$$= -\frac{1}{2}(-\cdot 22443 - \cdot 24400)$$

$$= \cdot 23422.$$

Formula (1.7.4) gives $\mu_{90} \fallingdotseq \dfrac{1}{2l_{90}}(d_{89} + d_{90})$

$$= \frac{656 \cdot 37 + 564 \cdot 78}{2(2608 \cdot 53)}$$

$$= \cdot 23407.$$

Formula (1.7.5) requires a table of the differences of d_x thus:

x	d_x	Δd_x	$\Delta^2 d_x$	$\Delta^3 d_x$	$\Delta^4 d_x$
90	564·78				
		−88·97			
91	475·81		5·02		
		−83·95		2·06	
92	391·86		7·08		−0·55
		−76·87		1·51	
93	314·99		8·59		
		−68·28			
94	246·71				

$$\mu_{90} \fallingdotseq \frac{1}{2608 \cdot 53}(564 \cdot 78 - \tfrac{1}{2}(-88 \cdot 97) + \tfrac{1}{3}(5 \cdot 02) - \tfrac{1}{4}(2.06) + \tfrac{1}{5}(-0 \cdot 55)...)$$

$$= \frac{1}{2608 \cdot 53}(564 \cdot 78 + 44 \cdot 48 + 1 \cdot 67 - 0 \cdot 52 - 0 \cdot 11)$$

$$= \frac{610 \cdot 30}{2608 \cdot 53}$$

$$= \cdot 23396.$$

Formula (1.7.6) gives $\mu_{90} \fallingdotseq \dfrac{7(d_{89} + d_{90}) - (d_{88} + d_{91})}{12l_{90}}$

$$= \frac{7(656 \cdot 37 + 564 \cdot 78) - (747 \cdot 93 + 475 \cdot 81)}{12(2608 \cdot 53)}$$

$$= \cdot 23399.$$

The tabulated value is ·23398.

Exercise 1.6

Use two approximate formulae to find values of μ_{80} according to the $a(55)$ Male table and compare them with the tabulated value.

Exercise 1.7

If $l_x = 100\sqrt{100-x}$ find μ_{84} exactly and by using an approximate method.

1.8 Interpolation for fractional ages

When a mathematical formula for l_x or one of the other mortality functions is known, normally the values of functions at fractional durations can readily be determined. However if, as is more usual, only the values at integral ages are known interpolation methods must be used. The most commonly used method is linear interpolation, that is, in the case of l_x

$$l_{x+t} \doteqdot (1-t)l_x + t \cdot l_{x+1} = l_x - t \cdot d_x, \tag{1.8.1}$$

for integral x, and $0 \leq t \leq 1$.

This assumption means that the graph of l_x becomes not a smooth curve but a series of straight-line segments. If the same assumption is used for all functions inconsistencies can arise, for example q_x will not equal $\dfrac{d_x}{l_x}$, when q_x, d_x and l_x are all interpolated in this way.

Considering the second form of formula (1.8.1) $l_{x+t} \doteqdot l_x - t \cdot d_x$ it is apparent that a tth part of the total deaths d_x in the year of age are assumed to occur in a tth part of the year—the assumption is therefore that there is a uniform distribution of deaths throughout the year of age. In making the statement that we are assuming a uniform distribution of deaths over a year we must always state whether it is a year of age or a year of time—in this case we are assuming uniformity over the year of age between ages x and $x+1$.

The following relations follow from formula (1.8.1), with $0 \leq t \leq 1$

$$_tp_x = 1 - t \cdot q_x$$

$$_tq_x = t \cdot q_x.$$

At first glance it might be thought that the assumption assumes that the force of mortality is constant over the year, but as

$$\frac{dl_{x+t}}{d(x+t)} = \frac{dl_{x+t}}{dt} = -d_x$$

from differentiating formula (1.8.1), x being treated as a constant age, then

$$\mu_{x+t} = -\frac{1}{l_{x+t}}\frac{dl_{x+t}}{d(x+t)} = \frac{d_x}{l_{x+t}} = \frac{d_x}{l_x} \cdot \frac{l_x}{l_{x+t}} = \frac{q_x}{_tp_x} = \frac{q_x}{1-t.q_x}.$$

It will be seen that this formula gives two different values for μ_x, one from the range $x-1$ to x, and one from the range x to $x+1$.

Example 1.11

Show that the assumption of uniform deaths over each year of age implies

$$d_{x+t} = (1-t)d_x + t.d_{x+1}.$$

Solution

$$d_{x+t} = l_{x+t} - l_{x+t+1}$$
$$= (1-t)l_x + t.l_{x+1} - (1-t)l_{x+1} - t.l_{x+2}, \text{ using formula (1.8.1)}$$
$$= (1-t)(l_x - l_{x+1}) + t(l_{x+1} - l_{x+2})$$
$$= (1-t)d_x + t.d_{x+1}.$$

Example 1.12

If within the range $n \leqq x \leqq m$, l_x takes the form $a+bx+cx^2$ and it is assumed that there is a uniform distribution of deaths within the range, find the value of x for which this assumption gives the maximum error in l_x.

Solution

Write l_x^* for the assumed value of l_x, that is

$$l_{n+t}^* = l_n + \frac{t}{m-n}(l_m - l_n)$$
$$= a+bn+cn^2 + \frac{t}{m-n}(a+bm+cm^2 - a - bn - cn^2)$$

and $\quad l_{n+t} = a+b(n+t)+c(n+t)^2$

$$\therefore \; l_{n+t} - l_{n+t}^* = bt + 2cnt + ct^2 - \frac{t}{m-n}(b(m-n)+c(m^2-n^2))$$

then $\quad \dfrac{d}{dt}(l_{n+t} - l_{n+t}^*) = b + 2cn + 2ct - b - c(m+n)$

and this $= 0$ for a maximum or minimum, where

$$2cn + 2ct - c(m+n) = 0,$$

i.e.
$$t = \frac{m-n}{2}$$

$$\therefore x = n+t = n+ \frac{m-n}{2} = \frac{n+m}{2} \quad \text{be required value of } x.$$

Exercise 1.8

On the English Life Table No. 12—Males find, using the assumption of uniform distribution of deaths over the year of age:

(a) $\frac{3}{4}q_{36\frac{1}{2}}$

(b) $\mu_{70\frac{1}{2}}$.

1.9 Laws of mortality

The term 'law of mortality' is used to describe a mathematical expression for a function of the mortality table such as l_x, q_x or μ_x, the most common being μ_x—an example was given in Example 1.6. Such a law will simplify the calculation of mortality functions but to serve a useful purpose will have to reproduce actual experience closely, and it is now thought that it is unlikely that a law can be found that will represent μ_x over a large range of ages, although some complicated expressions have in recent years been used in the attempt. The most famous laws of mortality are those of Gompertz and Makeham.

Gompertz Law was propounded in 1825 and in modern notation states that

$$\mu_x = Bc^x, \tag{1.9.1}$$

where B and c are constant over the range of ages considered. Integrating formula (1.9.1) with t written for x,

$$\int_0^x \mu_t dt = \int_0^x Bc^t dt$$

$$= \left[\frac{Bc^t}{\log_e c} \right]_0^x$$

$$= \frac{Bc^x}{\log_e c} - \frac{B}{\log_e c}$$

$$= -(c^x-1)\log_e g \quad \text{where} \quad \log_e g = \frac{-B}{\log_e c}$$

$$= -\log_e g^{c^x-1};$$

then
$$l_x = l_0 . e^{-\int_0^x \mu_t dt}$$

$$= l_0 . e^{\log_e g^{c^x - 1}}$$

$$= l_0 . g^{c^x - 1}.$$

This is usually written $\quad l_x = kg^{c^x},\quad$ (1.9.2)

where
$$k = \frac{l_0}{g}.$$

Hence
$$_tp_x = \frac{kg^{c^{x+t}}}{kg^{c^x}},$$

i.e.
$$_tp_x = g^{c^x(c^t - 1)}\qquad (1.9.3)$$

when Gompertz law is assumed.

In 1860 Makeham suggested a modification of the Law, the effect being to assume that

$$\mu_x = A + Bc^x \qquad (1.9.4)$$

and proceeding similarly

$$\int_0^x \mu_t dt = \int_0^x (A + Bc^t) dt$$

$$= Ax + \frac{Bc^x}{\log_e c} - \frac{B}{\log_e c}$$

$$= -\log_e s^x - \log_e g^{c^x - 1},$$

where g is as above and $\log_e s = -A$, then

$$l_x = l_0 . e^{-\int_0^x \mu_t dt}$$

$$= l_0 e^{\ \log s^x + \log_e g^{c^x - 1}}$$

$$= l_0 s^x g^{c^x - 1},$$

usually written $\quad l_x = ks^x g^{c^x},\quad$ (1.9.5)

where
$$k = \frac{l_0}{g}$$

and hence $\quad _tp_x = s^t g^{c^x(c^t - 1)}\qquad$ (1.9.6)

when Makeham's Law is assumed.

One of the important uses of these laws is in the calculation of functions involving more than one life which before the introduction of computers could be an onerous task. It should be noted that each law only defines the form of the force of mortality and not its numerical value until values are chosen for the parameters. The value of these parameters are usually within the ranges

$$\cdot001 < A < \cdot003$$

$$10^{-6} < B < 10^{-3}$$

$$1\cdot08 < c < 1\cdot12.$$

Other Laws of Mortality of importance are:

de Moivre (1725) $\qquad\qquad l_x = k(\omega - x)$—a straight line

Double Geometric Law (1867) $\quad \mu_x = A + Bc^x + Mn^x$

Makeham's Second Law (1889) $\quad \mu_x = A + Hx + Bc^x$

Perk's (1931) $\qquad\qquad\qquad \mu_x = \dfrac{A + Bc^x}{Kc^{-x} + 1 + Dc^x}.$

Example 1.13

Find an expression for μ_x if

$$l_x = ks^x w^{x^2} g^{c^x}.$$

Solution

$$\log_e l_x = \log_e k + x \log_e s + x^2 \log_e w + c^x \log_e g$$

$$\therefore \frac{d}{dx}(\log_e l_x) = \log_e s + 2x \log_e w + c^x \log_e c \log_e g$$

$$\therefore \mu_x = -\frac{d}{dx}(\log_e l_x) = A + Hx + Bc^x,$$

where $\quad \log_e s = -A, \quad H = -2 \log_e w, \quad B = -\log_e c . \log_e g,$

which is Makeham's Second Law of Mortality.

Example 1.14

Assuming that the $a(55)$ Males table of mortality follows a Gompertz formula use the values of $l_{50}, l_{60}...$ to determine the value of c.

Solution

As $l_x = kg^{c^x}$ we will require three values of l_x as there are three 'unknowns' in the formula for l_x, in effect the radix of the table having been added to the two 'real' unknowns.

$$l_{50} = 937,753 = kg^{c^{50}} \tag{1}$$

$$l_{60} = 859,916 = kg^{c^{60}} \tag{2}$$

$$l_{70} = 682,850 = kg^{c^{70}} \tag{3}$$

Dividing (2) by (1), and (3) by (2), gives

$$\frac{l_{60}}{l_{50}} = \frac{859,916}{937,753} = \cdot9170 = g^{c^{50}(c^{10}-1)} \tag{4}$$

$$\frac{l_{70}}{l_{60}} = \frac{682,850}{859,916} = \cdot7941 = g^{c^{60}(c^{10}-1)} \tag{5}$$

$$\therefore \ c^{50}(c^{10}-1)\log_{10} g = \log_{10}(\cdot9170) = -\cdot03763 \tag{6}$$

and $\qquad c^{60}(c^{10}-1)\log_{10} g = \log_{10}(\cdot7941) = -\cdot10012 \tag{7}$

dividing (7) by (6), $\qquad c^{10} = \dfrac{\cdot10012}{\cdot03763} = 2\cdot661$

$$\therefore \ c = 1\cdot103.$$

Exercise 1.9

If $\mu_x = A \log_e x$ find an expression for l_x.

Exercise 1.10

If it is assumed that A1967–70 table of mortality follows Makeham Law, use the values of l_{30}, l_{40}, l_{50}, etc., to find the value of A, B, c.

Exercise 1.11

A mortality table is such that the force of mortality is twice that of a second table for which functions have been tabulated and which follows Gompertz Law. Show that the probability of a life aged x surviving n years on the first table is the same as the probability of a life aged $(x+a)$ surviving n years (where a is a constant) on the second table and find the value of a.

1.10   Select, ultimate and aggregate mortality tables

So far consideration has been given to tables where the rates of mortality depend on the age of a member of the group concerned, the group perhaps being the population of a country, the class of assured lives or the class of annuitant lives. Where attention is paid also to the duration for which a member has been within the group the table is called a 'Select' table. Such a table in the case of a population table might thus take account specially of mortality of immigrant lives, but the more common use is with assured lives and annuitants' tables where it is reasonable to assume that the lives concerned have been 'selected', and are likely to experience lighter mortality than the group as a whole at the same age—the assured lives because of the medical evidence obtained before a life assurance office accepts a proposal, and the annuitant lives because a person who is ill is unlikely to purchase an annuity (this is known as self-selection, being exercised by the lives themselves). While normally select mortality is lighter than ordinary it is possible for the mortality to be heavier, for example, the mortality of ill-health retirals from pension schemes is likely to be particularly heavy for the first few years after retiral, in which case it may be referred to as reversed or negative selection.

A mortality table in which no regard is paid to period of membership in the group, such as a population table, is called an 'aggregate' table.

While some mortality investigations have indicated that the effect of selection may continue indefinitely implying that a different table will be required for each entry age it is nowadays common practice to use a short 'select' period of one or two years. The A1967–70 and $a(55)$ tables have select periods of two and one years respectively. The implication of a select period of two years is that one mortality rate is used at each age for all those who have been in the group for at least two years. This part of the table is referred to as an 'ultimate' mortality table and the normal l_x and other symbols are used. For the functions in the select part of a select and ultimate table square brackets are used, thus $q_{[x]}$ is the rate of mortality for a life aged exactly x who has just joined the group. If the select period is longer than one year further symbols are required and the rate of mortality for a life aged $x+1$ who joined the group one year ago is $q_{[x]+1}$, and similarly the rate of mortality for a life aged $x+r$ who joined the group r years ago is $q_{[x]+r}$ unless the select period is less than r years when the brackets can be omitted.

The l_x columns of a select and ultimate table are set out as shown in Table 1.5 extracted from the A1967–70 table (taking the figures to one decimal place rather than three as published). The figures in heavy type show the table as it relates to a life entering at age 52—the figures are considered on the horizontal line until the ultimate part of the table is reached when the figures then continue downwards. Except in the right-hand column of l's (the ultimate column) figures should never be related in the same vertical column. Tables set out in a similar way are used for the other mortality functions such as $d_{[x]}, p_{[x]}, q_{[x]}, \mu_{[x]}$. When the select period is one year as in $a(55)$ the values for (x) and $[x]$ may however be put on the same line.

TABLE 1.5

Age $[x]$	$l_{[x]}$	$l_{[x]+1}$	l_{x+2}	Age $x+2$
50	32,558·0	32,464·8	32,338·6	52
51	32,383·8	32,282·0	32,143·5	53
52	**32,188·7**	**32,078·0**	**31,926·4**	54
53	31,970·9	31,850·6	**31,685·2**	55
54	31,728·2	31,597·9	**31,417·7**	56
55	31,458·3	31,317·6	**31,121·8**	57

A graph of some of the values of $q_{[x]}$ and q_x on the A1967–70 mortality table is given in Figure 1.4, the select values commencing at ten-year intervals.

It will be seen that the large number of select mortality tables can be represented by one compact select-ultimate table by the choice of the radixes $l_{[x]}$ so that the ultimate portion of each of the tables is identical. Thus in constructing the table $l_{[x]}, l_{[x]+1}$, etc., are calculated in the reverse order from the method of section 1.4. If r is the select period of the table then to find the values commencing at $l_{[x]}, l_{[x]+r-1}$ would first be found from

$$l_{[x]+r-1} = \frac{l_{x+r}}{p_{[x]+r-1}}$$

and $l_{[x]+r-2}$ from

$$l_{[x]+r-2} = \frac{l_{[x]+r-1}}{p_{[x]+r-2}}$$

and so on. The values of $d_{[x]}, d_{[x]+1}, \ldots$ would then be found by subtracting the $l_{[x]}, l_{[x]+1}$, etc.

The normal relationships hold between the various mortality functions for a select-ultimate table, the only difference being that the age suffix is expressed in a different way until the ultimate portion of the table is reached. For example, in the above table with a select period of two years, the mortality rates experienced in the first three years by a life entering the group at age x are

$$q_{[x]} = \frac{d_{[x]}}{l_{[x]}} = \frac{l_{[x]} - l_{[x]+1}}{l_{[x]}},$$

$$q_{[x]+1} = \frac{d_{[x]+1}}{l_{[x]+1}} = \frac{l_{[x]+1} - l_{x+2}}{l_{[x]+1}},$$

$$q_{x+2} = \frac{l_{x+2} - l_{x+3}}{l_{x+2}}.$$

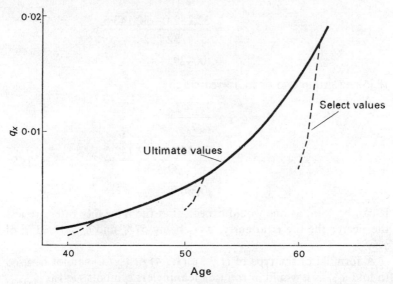

FIGURE 1.4. Graph of $q_{[x]}$ and q_x at selected values on the A1967-70 table of mortality.

For example, for $x = 52$, the rates of mortality subsequently experienced will be (again reducing the number of significant figures when reading from the tables)

$$q_{[52]} = \frac{32,188 \cdot 7 - 32,078 \cdot 0}{32,188 \cdot 7} = \cdot 00344,$$

$$q_{[52]+1} = \frac{32,078 \cdot 0 - 31,926 \cdot 4}{32,078 \cdot 0} = \cdot 00473$$

$$q_{54} = \frac{31{,}926{\cdot}4 - 31{,}685{\cdot}2}{31{,}926{\cdot}4} = {\cdot}00756$$

$$q_{55} = \frac{31{,}685{\cdot}2 - 31{,}417{\cdot}7}{31{,}685{\cdot}2} = {\cdot}00844.$$

It will be seen that there are three different rates of mortality for each age, depending on duration, for example, at age 52 the rates of mortality would be if just joined group $= q_{[52]} = {\cdot}00344$ (as above) if joined group one year ago

$$= q_{[51]+1} = \frac{l_{[51]+1} - l_{53}}{l_{[51]+1}}$$

$$= \frac{32{,}282{\cdot}0 - 32{,}143{\cdot}5}{32{,}282{\cdot}0}$$

$$= {\cdot}00429.$$

If joined group two or more years ago

$$= q_{52} = \frac{l_{52} - l_{53}}{l_{52}}$$

$$= \frac{32{,}338{\cdot}6 - 32{,}143{\cdot}5}{32{,}338{\cdot}6}$$

$$= {\cdot}00603.$$

It can be seen, as one would expect, that the mortality rates are less the nearer the life is to entry, $q_{[52]}$ being 57% and $q_{[51]+1}$ 71% of q_{52}.

A formula of the type of (1.7.3), (1.7.4) or (1.7.6) cannot be used to find $\mu_{[x]}$ as it would introduce meaningless symbols such as $d_{[x]-1}$. Even the use of an advancing difference formula such as (1.7.5) may not give a satisfactory answer because the run of values of $d_{[x]}$, etc., cause the formula to converge only very slowly. Also during the select period the graph of μ_x is likely to be of a different shape from the ultimate giving discontinuity in the curve at the end of the select period—this is also apparent from the graph of $q_{[x]}$ and q_x in Figure 1.4.

Example 1.15

Write in terms of l's an expression for $_{3|4}q_{[40]+2}$, if the select period of the table is six years.

Solution

$$3|4q_{[40]+2} = \frac{l_{[40]+5} - l_{49}}{l_{[40]+2}}.$$

Example 1.16
Find the values of the following using the table in the previous section:

(i) $5p_{[50]}$, (ii) $2q_{[51]}$, (iii) $3p_{[51]+1}$, (iv) $1|3q_{[53]}$.

Solution

(i) $5p_{[50]} = \dfrac{l_{55}}{l_{[50]}} = \dfrac{31,685\cdot2}{32,558\cdot0} = \cdot9732,$

(ii) $2q_{[51]} = \dfrac{l_{[51]} - l_{53}}{l_{[51]}} = \dfrac{32,383\cdot8 - 32,143\cdot5}{32,383\cdot8} = \cdot0074,$

(iii) $3p_{[51]+1} = \dfrac{l_{55}}{l_{[51]+1}} = \dfrac{31,685\cdot2}{32,282\cdot0} = \cdot9815,$

(iv) $1|3q_{[53]} = \dfrac{l_{[53]+1} - l_{57}}{l_{[53]}} = \dfrac{31,850\cdot6 - 31,121\cdot8}{31,970\cdot9}$

$$= \cdot0228.$$

Exercise 1.12
Find the values of the following using the table in the previous section:

(i) $4p_{[50]+1}$, (ii) $3|2q_{[50]}$, (iii) $4q_{[51]+1}$.

Exercise 1.13
It is required to construct a select table with select period two years to be added to the English Life Table No. 12—Males which is to be treated as the ultimate table. If $q_{[x]} = \frac{1}{2}q_x$ and $q_{[x]+1} = \frac{2}{3}q_{x+1}$, find the value of $l_{[60]}$.

EXAMPLE AND EXERCISES ON CHAPTER 1

Example 1.17
A group of lives experience special mortality between ages 50 and 60 which can be represented by an addition to the force of mortality according to the A1967–70 mortality table ultimate of ·01 at age 50

decreasing continuously in arithmetic progression to zero at age 60. Calculate the probability that a life aged 50 will live 10 years.

Solution

Probability required $= e^{-\int_0^{10} (\mu_{50+t} + \cdot 001(10-t))dt}$,

where μ_{50+t} is on A1967-70.

$$= e^{-\int_0^{10} \mu_{50+t} dt} . e^{-\int_0^{10} \cdot 001(10-t)dt}$$

$$= {}_{10}p_{50} \text{ (on A1967-70)} . e^{-\cdot 001 \left[10t - \frac{t^2}{2} \right]_0^{10}}$$

$$= {}_{10}p_{50} . e^{-\cdot 05}$$

$$= \frac{30,039 \cdot 8}{32,669 \cdot 9} \cdot 9513$$

$$= \cdot 8747.$$

Exercise 1.14

If ${}_np_x = \dfrac{x}{x+n}$, find μ_x.

Exercise 1.15

If q_x is treated as a continuous function of x and has a minimum value when $x = y$, show that $\mu_y = \mu_{y+1}$.

Exercise 1.16

If $\mu_x = ab^x + cd^x$, find an expression for l_x.

Exercise 1.17

A group of lives experience mortality which can be represented between ages 80 and 90 by the $a(55)$ Males ultimate table with a deduction from the force of mortality of $\cdot 05$ at age 80 increasing continuously to $\cdot 15$ at age 90. Find the probability of a life aged 80 dying within the next ten years.

Exercise 1.18

A life aged 60 has just retired due to ill-health and is assumed to be subject to a constant force of mortality of $\cdot 024693$ for two years and then will be subject to the mortality of the $a(55)$ Males ultimate table. Find the value of $l_{[60]}$ if $l_{65} = 788,316$.

Exercise 1.19

A company has staff employed in both a tropical country and in the United Kingdom. The mortality experienced by the two groups in a certain age range is connected as follows (accented symbols relating to the mortality in the tropical country):

$$l_x = ks^x g^{c^x}, \quad l'_x = ms^x g^{r^x}$$

Given that $p'_{30} = \frac{3}{4} p_{30}$, c $= 1 \cdot 1$ and $\log_e g = - \cdot 001$, find r.

CHAPTER TWO

ANNUITIES, ASSURANCES, PREMIUMS

2.1 Pure endowments

This chapter will be concerned with formulae for the values of payments which depend on the survival or the death of a person normally referred to as a life. The functions introduced will involve both mortality and interest and are known as monetary functions.

The first formula to be considered is that for a pure endowment, that is a payment made on a certain date in the future, if a life is then alive. The symbol for the present value of a pure endowment of 1 payable if (x) survives n years is $_nE_x$ or $A_{x\,:\,\overline{n|}}^{\,1}$—the first being simpler but the second being consistent with the general notation used in life contingencies.

The value of $A_{x\,:\,\overline{n|}}^{\,1}$ will be the value on the assumption that 1 will certainly be payable (that is discounting at compound interest for n years) multiplied by the probability that it will be paid (that is the probability that (x) lives n years) so

$$A_{x\,:\,\overline{n|}}^{\,1} = v^n \cdot {}_np_x = v^n \frac{l_{x+n}}{l_x},$$

or multiplying both numerator and denominator by v^x,

$$= \frac{v^{x+n}l_{x+n}}{v^x l_x}.$$

This gives symmetry in the numerator and denominator, and if we define a new function

$$D_x = v^x l_x, \tag{2.1.1}$$

$$A_{x\,:\,\overline{n|}}^{\,1} = \frac{D_{x+n}}{D_x}. \tag{2.1.2}$$

The function D_x is the first *commutation* function we meet—that is a function introduced to reduce the computation in calculations and which involves both interest and mortality functions. Commutation functions are calculated and tabulated in columns (called commutation columns) at the main rates of interest, and were invaluable in

life contingency calculations especially before the advent of computers.

$A_{x:\overline{n}|}^{1}$ may also be called the *net single premium* at age x for an
n-year pure endowment of 1. It represents the single premium an
insurer will require in return for the promise to pay the sum of 1 at
the end of n years if he is then alive. The word 'net' indicates that no
provision is made for the life insurance company's expenses.

As an example the net single premium for a 20-year pure endowment of £100 for a life aged 50 will be found on the basis of the
A1967–70 mortality table ultimate and 4% interest. Referring to the
table in Appendix III (but reducing the number of significant figures)

$$\text{Premium} = 100 \, \frac{D_{70}}{D_{50}} = 100 \cdot \frac{1,517 \cdot 00}{4,597 \cdot 06} = 33 \cdot 00,$$

so the premium required is £33·00.

It is interesting to check the result by accumulating the premiums
that would be paid by a large number of persons each of age 50. If
we take the large number to be l_{50}, i.e. 32,670 the total premiums
will be

$$32,670 \times £33 \cdot 00 = £1,078,110$$

which accumulated over 20 years at 4% interest (i.e. multiplying by
$(1 \cdot 04)^{20} = 2 \cdot 19112$) gives £2,362,268. Dividing this total amount
available after 20 years among the $l_{70} = 23,622$ assumed to survive
gives £100 to each of the persons, as expected.

This calculation illustrates what is meant by accumulating a fund
with the benefit of both interest and *survivorship*. The share of each
individual who survives to age 70 includes a portion of the premiums
paid by those who forfeit benefit by not surviving.

If therefore $A_{x:\overline{n}|}^{1}$ is the present value of a sum of 1 payable at the
end of n years to a life aged x, $\dfrac{1}{A_{x:\overline{n}|}^{1}}$ will be the accumulated value of
a payment of 1 made by a life aged x, n years previously, allowing for
both interest and mortality. It is the equivalent of $\dfrac{1}{v^n}$ or $(1+i)^n$
where interest only is involved.

Exercise 2.1

Find the present value at 4% interest of a sum of £1,000 due to a
life aged 30 payable on the survival of 25 years, assuming A1967–70
ultimate mortality.

Exercise 2.2

What does £500 at age 25 accumulate to after 30 years with interest at 4% and with the benefit of survivance on the basis of the A1967–70 ultimate mortality table?

2.2 Annuities

A life annuity, or annuity, is a series of payments made at equal intervals (yearly if not otherwise stated) during the lifetime of a given life. It may be temporary, that is limited to a certain number of years, or payable throughout life, and will be assumed to be the latter if not otherwise stated. It may be deferred, that is commencing some years in the future, or immediate, that is the first payment is made one year (in a yearly annuity) after commencement.

The present value of an immediate yearly annuity of 1 per annum to (x) is denoted by a_x and can be considered as the sum of a series of pure endowments of 1,

i.e.
$$a_x = A_{x:\frac{1}{1|}} + A_{x:\frac{1}{2|}} + A_{x:\frac{1}{3|}} + \ldots + A_{x:\frac{1}{\omega-x-1|}}$$

$$= \frac{D_{x+1}}{D_x} + \frac{D_{x+2}}{D_x} + \frac{D_{x+3}}{D_x} + \ldots + \frac{D_{\omega-1}}{D_x}$$

$$= \frac{1}{D_x} \sum_{t=1}^{\omega-x-1} D_{x+t}.$$

We now define a new commutation function N_x as follows:

$$N_x = \sum_{t=0}^{\omega-x-1} D_{x+t}$$

so
$$a_x = \frac{N_{x+1}}{D_x}. \tag{2.2.1}$$

The commutation columns of N_x are easily obtained by summing the D_x values from the oldest age back to the youngest age, the process being based on

$$N_x = N_{x+1} + D_x.$$

As $D_x = 0$ for $x \geqslant \omega$, N_x can also be defined as

$$N_x = \sum_{t=0}^{\infty} D_{x+t}. \tag{2.2.2}$$

If the annuity has payments limited to a specified maximum period, say n years (the *term* of the annuity) it is given the symbol $a_{x:\overline{n}|}$ and may be expressed as

$$a_{x:\overline{n}|} = \sum_{t=1}^{n} A_{x:\overline{t}|}^{1} = \sum_{t=1}^{n} \frac{D_{x+t}}{D_x}.$$

As $\sum_{t=1}^{n} D_{x+t}$ is the difference between N_{x+1} and N_{x+n+1},

$$a_{x:\overline{n}|} = \frac{N_{x+1} - N_{x+n+1}}{D_x}. \qquad (2.2.3)$$

If an annuity is deferred for m years the payments for the first m years are omitted. Thus a life annuity to (x) deferred m years has the first payment at age $x+m+1$. Its value $_m|a_x$ can be found either by subtracting the first m payments from the life annuity, that is

$$_m|a_x = a_x - a_{x:\overline{m}|}$$

$$= \frac{N_{x+1}}{D_x} - \frac{N_{x+1} - N_{x+m+1}}{D_x} = \frac{N_{x+m+1}}{D_x} \qquad (2.2.4)$$

or directly as

$$_m|a_x = \sum_{t=m+1}^{\infty} A_{x:\overline{t}|}^{1} = \frac{1}{D_x} \sum_{t=m+1}^{\infty} D_{x+t} = \frac{N_{x+m+1}}{D_x}.$$

A third method is to find the value at age $x+m$ and discount to age x using both interest and mortality, that is

$$_m|a_x = A_{x:\overline{m}|}^{1} \cdot a_{x+m} = \frac{D_{x+m}}{D_x} \cdot \frac{N_{x+m+1}}{D_{x+m}} = \frac{N_{x+m+1}}{D_x}.$$

If the deferred annuity has limited payment, say for a maximum of r years, it is given either the symbol $_m|a_{x:\overline{r}|}$ or

$$_m|_r a_x = \frac{1}{D_x} \sum_{t=m+1}^{m+r} D_{x+t}$$

$$= \frac{N_{x+m+1} - N_{x+m+r+1}}{D_x}. \qquad (2.2.5)$$

The annuities discussed so far have the first payment at the end of the payment period, and are called immediate annuities. If the first of the series of payments commences at the beginning of the period the annuity is called an annuity-due and the symbol used is $\ddot{a}$, the double dot (or *trema* or *diaeresis*) above distinguishing it from *a*. The terminology is slightly confusing as the first payment under an immediate annuity is not made immediately, the annuity commencing immediately being called an annuity-due, but the word 'immediate' was originally used to distinguish it from deferred. If the word 'annuity' is used by itself an immediate annuity is assumed unless the context otherwise requires. The reader will already have met the notation and terminology in the study of compound interest.

While the technical terms are *immediate annuity* and *annuity-due*, in dealing with the general public an insurance company may refer to 'annuity in arrears' or 'annuity in advance' respectively.

It will be seen that there will be annuity-dues corresponding to each of the above immediate annuities, as follows, each payment being one year earlier than the immediate annuity;

$$\ddot{a}_x = \sum_{t=0}^{\infty} \frac{D_{x+t}}{D_x} = \frac{N_x}{D_x} \qquad (2.2.6)$$

$$\ddot{a}_{x:\overline{n}|} = \sum_{t=0}^{n-1} \frac{D_{x+t}}{D_x} = \frac{N_x - N_{x+n}}{D_x} \qquad (2.2.7)$$

$$_m|\ddot{a}_x = \frac{N_{x+m}}{D_x} \qquad (2.2.8)$$

$$_m|_r\ddot{a}_x = \frac{N_{x+m} - N_{x+m+r}}{D_x}. \qquad (2.2.9)$$

The difference between $\ddot{a}_x$ and a_x is the payment made immediately so

$$\ddot{a}_x = 1 + a_x. \qquad (2.2.10)$$

For the temporary annuity

$$\ddot{a}_{x:\overline{n}|} = \frac{N_x - N_{x+n}}{D_x}$$

$$= \frac{D_x + N_{x+1} - N_{x+n}}{D_x}$$

$$= 1 + a_{x:\overline{n-1}|}, \qquad (2.2.11)$$

and it should be noted that the term of the annuity is '$n-1$' not 'n' as the first payment of 1 is given separately.

Another relationship between a_x and $\ddot{a}_x$ can be found—

$$a_x = \frac{N_{x+1}}{D_x}$$

$$= \frac{D_{x+1}}{D_x} \cdot \frac{N_{x+1}}{D_{x+1}}$$

$$= \frac{v^{x+1} \cdot l_{x+1}}{v^x l_x} \cdot \ddot{a}_{x+1}$$

$$\therefore a_x = vp_x \cdot \ddot{a}_{x+1}. \tag{2.2.12}$$

It can be shown similarly that

$$a_{x:\overline{n}|} = vp_x \cdot \ddot{a}_{x+1:\overline{n}|}. \tag{2.2.13}$$

Other relations can be proved either by using the commutation functions or by general reasoning, for example

$$_m|\ddot{a}_x = {}_{m-1}|a_x \tag{2.2.14}$$

$$_m|_r\ddot{a}_x = {}_{m-1}|_r a_x \tag{2.2.15}$$

$$a_{x:\overline{n}|} - a_{x:\overline{n-1}|} = \frac{D_{x+n}}{D_x} = A_{x:\frac{1}{\overline{n}|}}. \tag{2.2.16}$$

This last is a useful relationship if the value of $A_{x:\frac{1}{\overline{n}|}}$ is required but is not tabulated, when temporary annuities are tabulated.

If values of pure endowments or annuities are required on select tables then the only difference will be that the commutation functions (which are tabulated in much the same way as are the mortality functions) are calculated using the select mortality functions:

$$D_{[x]} = v^x l_{[x]}$$

$$D_{[x]+t} = v^{x+t} l_{[x]+t}$$

$$N_{[x]} = \sum_{t=0}^{\infty} D_{[x]+t},$$

where $D_{[x]+t} = D_{x+t}$ when t is equal to or greater than the select period of the table.

Most published mortality tables tabulate values of annuities as well as commutation functions. Almost all tables give values of life annuities and some give values of temporary annuities. Care must be taken in referring to tables as sometimes $\ddot{a}$ and sometimes a is tabulated.

Example 2.1

Calculate the value of the following, using the commutation columns of the A1967–70 table at 4% interest:

$$\ddot{a}_{40}, \ a_{40}, \ \ddot{a}_{[40]}, \ a_{[40]}, \ a_{40\,:\,\overline{30|}}, \ \ddot{a}_{[50]\,:\,\overline{10|}}, \ _5|a_{45}, \ _{10}|_{15}\ddot{a}_{[30]}.$$

Solution

$$\ddot{a}_{40} = \frac{N_{40}}{D_{40}} = \frac{132{,}002}{6{,}986{\cdot}50} = 18{\cdot}894.$$

$$a_{40} = \frac{N_{41}}{D_{40}} = \frac{125{,}015}{6{,}986{\cdot}50} = 17{\cdot}894,$$

as expected one less than $\ddot{a}_{40}$.

$$\ddot{a}_{[40]} = \frac{N_{[40]}}{D_{[40]}} = \frac{131{,}995}{6{,}981{\cdot}60} = 18{\cdot}906,$$

slightly greater than a_{40} as the mortality in the first year is lighter.

$$a_{[40]} = \frac{N_{[40]+1}}{D_{[40]}}$$

$$= \frac{N_{[40]} - D_{[40]}}{D_{[40]}}$$

(as $N_{[40]}+1$ is not tabulated; and the select period is two years)

$$= \frac{131{,}995 - 6{,}981{\cdot}60}{6{,}981{\cdot}60}$$

$$= 17{\cdot}906,$$

as expected one less than $\ddot{a}_{[40]}$.

$$a_{40\,:\,\overline{30|}} = \frac{N_{41} - N_{71}}{D_{40}}$$

(the first N suffix being one year more than the starting age as it is an immediate annuity, and the difference between the suffixes being the term)

$$= \frac{125{,}015 - 12{,}070{\cdot}9}{6{,}986{\cdot}50}$$

$$= 16{\cdot}166.$$

$$\ddot{a}_{[50]:\overline{10}|} = \frac{N_{[50]} - N_{60}}{D_{[50]}}$$

(the first N suffix being the starting age as it is an annuity-due, and the difference between the suffixes being the term)

$$= \frac{73,544\cdot8 - 35,841\cdot3}{4,581\cdot32}$$

$$= 8\cdot230.$$

$$_5|a_{45} = \frac{N_{51}}{D_{45}}$$

(the N suffix being the deferred term plus one year (as it is an immediate annuity) more than the entry age)

$$= \frac{68,970\cdot1}{5,689\cdot18} = 12\cdot123.$$

$$_{10}|_{15}\ddot{a}_{[30]} = \frac{N_{40} - N_{55}}{D_{[30]}}$$

(the first N suffix being the deferred term added to the entry age as it is an annuity-due, and the difference between the suffixes is the term)

$$= \frac{132,002 - 52,502\cdot8}{10,430\cdot0}$$

$$= 7\cdot622.$$

Exercise 2.3

Calculate the following on the A1967–70 table of mortality and 4% interest:

$$\ddot{a}_{60}, \; a_{[70]}, \; a_{65:\overline{15}|}, \; \ddot{a}_{65:\overline{15}|}, \; _{20}|_5a_{35}, \; _{10}|_{15}\ddot{a}_{[40]}.$$

Exercise 2.4

A father wishes to provide an annuity of £100 per annum to his son, now aged exactly 10, the first payment being on his 21st birthday. What sum would an insurance company require as a premium assuming A1967–70 select mortality and 4% interest?

Exercise 2.5

Prove that $\ddot{a}_{x:\overline{n}|} - a_{x:\overline{n}|} = 1 - A_{x:\overline{n}|}^{\;1}$.

Exercise 2.6

Prove, and explain by general reasoning

$$a_x = \sum_{t=1}^{\infty} {}_t|q_x \cdot a_{\overline{t}|}.$$

Exercise 2.7

Prove $\dfrac{a_x \cdot a_{x+1} \cdot a_{x+2} \cdots a_{x+n}}{\ddot{a}_{x+1} \cdot \ddot{a}_{x+2} \cdot \ddot{a}_{x+3} \cdots \ddot{a}_{x+n}} = {}_n|a_x.$

Exercise 2.8

The select rate of mortality in a mortality table with a select period of one year is 60% of the ultimate rate. If at $4\frac{1}{4}$% per annum interest $a_{45} = 15 \cdot 719$ and $a_{46} = 15 \cdot 509$, calculate $a_{[45]}$.

2.3 Accumulations

If each member of a large group of lives aged x makes a payment of 1 into a fund at the end of each year, and these payments are accumulated in the fund for n years, the share of each survivor at the end of the n years is given the symbol $s_{x:\overline{n}|}$, in an obvious extension at the compound interest notation; the accumulation being with the benefit both of interest and survivorship.

Each of the payments can be accumulated separately, the first made at age $x+1$ accumulating to $\dfrac{1}{A_{x+1:\overline{n-1}|}^{1}}$, the second to $\dfrac{1}{A_{x+2:\overline{n-2}|}^{1}}$ and the last to 1. Thus the total will be

$$\sum_{t=1}^{n} \frac{1}{A_{x+t:\overline{n-t}|}^{1}}$$

$$= \sum_{t=1}^{n} \frac{D_{x+t}}{D_{x+n}}$$

$$= \frac{N_{x+1} - N_{x+n+1}}{D_{x+n}}.$$

Alternatively $s_{x:\overline{n}|}$ can be considered as the accumulated value at age $x+n$ of the series of payments for which $a_{x:\overline{n}|}$ represents the value of age x, that is

$$s_{x:\overline{n}|} = a_{x:\overline{n}|} \cdot \frac{1}{A_{x:\overline{n}|}^{1}}$$

$$= \frac{N_{x+1} - N_{x+n+1}}{D_x} \cdot \frac{D_x}{D_{x+n}}.$$

i.e.
$$s_{x\,:\,\overline{n}|} = \frac{N_{x+1} - N_{x+n+1}}{D_{x+n}}.$$ (2.3.1)

Similarly, the function $\ddot{s}_{x\,:\,\overline{n}|}$ being the accumulation of the annuity-due can be evaluated

$$\ddot{s}_{x\,:\,\overline{n}|} = \frac{N_x - N_{x+n}}{D_{x+n}}.$$ (2.3.2)

It will be noted that the formulae in section 2.2 and this section are of the form

$$\frac{N_y - N_{y+n}}{D_x},$$ (2.3.3)

where y is the age at which the first payment is due
$\quad n$ is the number of payments, and
$\quad x$ is the age at which the value of the payments is desired.

Individual formulae should therefore not be memorised.

Example 2.2

A group of lives aged 30 pay £10 at the beginning of each year for 20 years into a fund. Find the share of each surviving member of the group at the end of the 20 years if the group experience A1967–70 ultimate mortality and the fund earns 4% per annum interest.

Solution

The accumulation will be

$$10\ddot{s}_{30\,:\,\overline{20}|} = 10\,\frac{N_{30} - N_{50}}{D_{50}}$$

$$= 10\,\frac{219{,}735 - 73{,}567 \cdot 1}{4{,}597 \cdot 06}$$

$$= 317 \cdot 96.$$

That is the share is £317·96 which can be compared to the amount when the accumulation is only at interest, $10\ddot{s}_{\overline{20}|} = 309 \cdot 69$.

Exercise 2.9

A group of lives aged 50 pay £5 at the beginning of each year for 5 years into a fund. Find the share of each surviving member of the group at the end of 15 years if they experience A1967–70 ultimate mortality and the fund earns 4% interest.

Exercise 2.10

Show by calculating numerical values using A1967–70 mortality and 4% interest that

$$s_{\overline{10|}} < s_{[50]:\overline{10|}} < s_{50:\overline{10|}} < s_{60:\overline{10|}} < \ddot{s}_{60:\overline{10|}}.$$

2.4 Assurances

The functions considered so far in this chapter have been dependent on the survival of a life; we now consider functions relating to payment contingent on death rather than on survivance. These are referred to as assurances, or, particularly in the USA, as insurances. The distinction is normally made in the United Kingdom between the *as*surance of life, whereas fire, marine, accident, aviation, etc., are *in*surance.

An assurance provides a payment of a specified amount (called the sum assured or insured) upon the death of the life assured. Although the actual practice is to pay a death benefit as soon as the death claim is made, or as soon as the legal formalities are completed, it is simpler initially to consider benefits which are paid at the end of the policy year of death, that is, on the first anniversary of effecting the policy, after the death.

The value of a benefit of 1 payable at the end of the year of death of a life aged x, no matter when the death occurs (called a whole life assurance) is given the symbol A_x. Then

$$A_x = \sum_{t=0}^{\infty} v^{t+1} \cdot {}_t|q_x = \frac{1}{l_x} \sum_{t=0}^{\infty} v^{t+1} \cdot d_{x+t},$$

the summation being stated to continue to ∞ although values after $t = \omega - x - 1$ will be zero.

This expression is simplified by the introduction of the commutation functions

$$C_x = v^{x+1} \cdot d_x \tag{2.4.1}$$

and

$$M_x = \sum_{t=0}^{\infty} C_{x+t}. \tag{2.4.2}$$

Then
$$A_x = \frac{1}{v^x l_x} \sum_{t=0}^{\infty} v^{x+t+1} \cdot d_{x+t} = \frac{1}{D_x} \sum_{t=0}^{\infty} C_{x+t} = \frac{M_x}{D_x}. \tag{2.4.3}$$

Note that in C_x the power of v is one greater than the suffix of d_x as the benefit is paid at the end of the year of death.

An assurance which provides a payment only if death occurs

within a limited period is known as a *term* or *temporary* assurance (or often as insurance) and the symbol for such a benefit for a life aged x with a term of n years is $A^1_{x:\,\overline{n}|}$, or alternatively as $_nA_x$, this being the symbol used in the tabulation of A1967–70.

The summation above will then be limited and

$$A^1_{x:\,\overline{n}|} = \frac{1}{l_x} \sum_{t=0}^{n-1} v^{t+1} . d_{x+t} = \frac{1}{D_x} \sum_{t=0}^{n-1} C_{x+t},$$

i.e.
$$A^1_{x:\,\overline{n}|} = \frac{M_x - M_{x+n}}{D_x}. \tag{2.4.4}$$

It will be seen that the symbol is very similar to that for a pure endowment, $A_{x:\,\overline{n}|}^{1}$ The 1 above the x in one case signifies that the life x must die before the expiry of the term for the benefit to be paid, and in the other the 1 above the $\overline{n}|$ signifies that the term certain must expire before the death of x for the benefit to be paid.

When the two benefits $A^1_{x:\,\overline{n}|}$ and $A_{x:\,\overline{n}|}^{1}$ are added together, the benefit is paid at the end of the policy year of death of x before the expiry of n years, that is before age $x+n$, or at age $x+n$ if the life has not previously died. This contract is called an n-year endowment assurance and is given the symbol $A_{x:\,\overline{n}|}$. It will be obvious that

$$A_{x:\,\overline{n}|} = A^1_{x:\,\overline{n}|} + A_{x:\,\overline{n}|}^{1},$$

i.e.
$$A_{x:\,\overline{n}|} = \frac{M_x - M_{x+n} + D_{x+n}}{D_x}. \tag{2.4.5}$$

If a death benefit is paid only if death occurs after a certain period, say m years, it is referred to as a deferred assurance, and given the symbol $_m|A_x$. It should be obvious that

$$_m|A_x = A_x - A^1_{x:\,\overline{m}|} = \frac{M_{x+m}}{D_x}. \tag{2.4.6}$$

Where the mortality table is select, if the duration t is less than the select period, symbols of the form $C_{[x]+t}$, $M_{[x]+t}$ will be used.

Some published tables give values of assurance functions though normally much less extensively than annuity values.

Example 2.3

Calculate by means of commutation functions on the basis of the A1967–70 table at 4% interest the values of

$$A_{30},\ A^1_{40:\,\overline{20}|},\ A_{[45]:\,\overline{15}|},\ _5|A_{50}.$$

Solution

$$A_{30} = \frac{M_{30}}{D_{30}}$$

$$= \frac{1,981 \cdot 96}{10,433 \cdot 3} = \cdot 1900.$$

$$A^1_{40 : \overline{20}|} = \frac{M_{40} - M_{60}}{D_{40}}$$

$$= \frac{1,909 \cdot 50 - 1,477 \cdot 08}{6,986 \cdot 50} = \cdot 0619.$$

$$A_{[45] : \overline{15}|} = \frac{M_{[45]} - M_{60} + D_{60}}{D_{[45]}}$$

$$= \frac{1,844 \cdot 06 - 1,477 \cdot 08 + 2,855 \cdot 60}{5,680 \cdot 37} = \cdot 5673.$$

$$_5|A_{50} = \frac{M_{55}}{D_{50}}$$

$$= \frac{1,645 \cdot 23}{4,597 \cdot 06} = \cdot 3579.$$

Exercise 2.11

Calculate by means of commutation functions on the basis of the A1967–70 mortality table at 4% interest the values of:

$$A_{[43]}, \quad A^1_{38 : \overline{14}|}, \quad A_{[31] : \overline{8}|}, \quad _3|A_{51}.$$

Exercise 2.12

If $l_x = 100 - x$ find the value of $A^1_{40 : \overline{15}|}$ at 2% interest given that v^{15} at 2% = $\cdot 74301$.

2.5 Net premiums

The premium or premiums for an assurance are the sum or sums paid, normally by the life assured, for the right to the sum assured in the event of death—or survivance in the case of an endowment assurance. Normally premiums are level, that is, each is of the same amount, and payable throughout the whole duration of the assurance. The notation for the premium is similar to that for assurance benefits, P being used instead of A. Thus

P_x is the annual premium for a whole life assurance effected on a life aged x;

$P^1_{[x]:\overline{n}|}$ is the annual premium for an n-year term assurance on a select life aged x;

$P_{x:\overline{n}|}$ is the annual premium for an n-year endowment assurance on a life aged x.

If the premium is paid for a shorter period than the whole term of the contract, a prefix is added to the symbol, thus

$_tP_{[x]}$ is the annual premium limited to t years for a whole life assurance on a select life aged x.

Sometimes, especially with more complicated benefits, for example those involving several lives, the symbol P is used with the relative assurance symbol in brackets, thus

$$P(A_{x:\overline{n}|}) = P_{x:\overline{n}|}.$$

When the assurance is purchased by a single premium the A symbol is normally used, for example,

$$_1P_{x:\overline{n}|} = A_{x:\overline{n}|}.$$

The normal method of finding formulae for premiums is to equate the present value of the benefits and the premiums, the value of the premiums being the premium multiplied by the relevant annuity value, using the same technique the student will have met in the study of compound interest.

For example:

$$P_x \cdot \ddot{a}_x = A_x$$

$$\therefore P_x = \frac{A_x}{\ddot{a}_x} = \frac{\dfrac{M_x}{D_x}}{\dfrac{N_x}{D_x}} = \frac{M_x}{N_x};$$

$$P_{[x]:\overline{n}|} \cdot \ddot{a}_{[x]:\overline{n}|} = A_{[x]:\overline{n}|}$$

$$\therefore P_{[x]:\overline{n}|} = \frac{A_{[x]:\overline{n}|}}{\ddot{a}_{[x]:\overline{n}|}} = \frac{M_{[x]} - M_{x+n} + D_{x+n}}{N_{[x]} - N_{x+n}};$$

$$_tP^1_{x:\overline{n}|} \cdot \ddot{a}_{x:\overline{t}|} = A^1_{x:\overline{n}|}$$

$$\therefore {_tP^1_{x:\overline{n}|}} = \frac{A^1_{x:\overline{n}|}}{\ddot{a}_{x:\overline{t}|}} = \frac{M_x - M_{x+n}}{N_x - N_{x+t}}.$$

No attempt should be made to remember any formulae for premiums as they are easily obtained from first principles as required.

When the premiums are not level they will normally be found by equating present values using the same technique.

Example 2.4

Find the annual premium halving after ten years for a whole life assurance for a select life aged 30 on the basis of the A1967–70 table of mortality and 4% interest.

Solution

If the premium is P reducing to $\frac{1}{2}P$, equating the present values of premium and benefits gives

$$P \cdot \ddot{a}_{[30]:\,\overline{10|}} + \tfrac{1}{2}P \cdot {}_{10|}\ddot{a}_{[30]} = A_{[30]}$$

$$\therefore\; P\,\frac{N_{[30]} - N_{40}}{D_{[30]}} + \tfrac{1}{2}P\,\frac{N_{40}}{D_{[30]}} = \frac{M_{[30]}}{D_{[30]}}$$

$$\therefore\; P = \frac{M_{[30]}}{N_{[30]} - \tfrac{1}{2}N_{40}} = \frac{1{,}978\cdot85}{219{,}731 - \tfrac{1}{2}(132{,}002)}$$

$$= \cdot0129.$$

So the premium per unit sum assured is ·0129 reducing to ·0065 after ten years.

Exercise 2.13

Calculate using the commutation columns of the A1967–70 mortality table at 4% interest:

$$P_{30},\; P_{[40]},\; P^{\,1}_{50:\,\overline{10|}},\; P^{\,\frac{1}{15|}}_{[45]:},\; P_{35:\,\overline{10|}},\; {}_{10}P_{[50]}.$$

Exercise 2.14

Find the annual premium payable for 10 years for a 20-year term assurance of £100 on the basis of the A1967–70 table of mortality and 4% interest for a select life aged 25.

Exercise 2.15

An insurance company offers an endowment assurance contract under which the annual premium for the first ten years is less than the annual premium in the subsequent years. If two alternative contracts for a certain life have a premium of 2·73 increasing to 7·45 and 1·36 increasing to 8·46, find the uniform annual premium.

2.6 Office premiums

The premiums considered in the previous section were *net* premiums, that is they take account only of interest and mortality, no allowance being made for the administrative expenses of the life assurance company. *Office* premiums include loadings for expenses and may also include margins to cover contingencies and profits.

Expenses are normally divided into:

(*a*) initial expenses—incurred when the policy is issued, and

(*b*) renewal expenses—incurred each year during the term of the policy.

An expense of either type may be:

(i) in direct proportion to the premium (e.g. renewal commission to an agent)

(ii) in direct proportion to the sum assured

(iii) independent of the premium or sum assured (e.g. cost of administration, medical fees).

At one time it was usual for initial commission to an agent to be of type (ii), in proportion to the sum assured, but this was changed more recently to type (i), in proportion to the premium (at a higher rate than the renewal commission).

Premium rates are normally quoted in the form of a premium per £100 or £1,000 sum assured, called per cent or per mil, symbolised by % or ‰, and can directly allow for expenses of types (i) and (ii). Expenses of type (iii) are normally now allowed for by making a fixed addition to the premium, called a *policy fee* or charge, not dependent on the sum assured or premium—the amount added to each premium being perhaps £2 or £3. At one time a system of *sliding scales* was used where the premium rate per cent was lower the higher the sum assured, for example the rate in the band £2,000 to £3,000 might be 10p% lower than in the band £1,000 to £2,000.

In this section we will be mainly concerned with expenses of types (i) and (ii) and while some formulae will be developed it is better not to attempt to memorise them, but to obtain any required expression from first principles using the equation of payments:

$$\begin{matrix} \text{Present value of} \\ \text{office premiums} \end{matrix} = \begin{matrix} \text{Present value of} \\ \text{benefits} \end{matrix} + \begin{matrix} \text{Present value of} \\ \text{expenses.} \end{matrix}$$

C

Often expenses will be a proportion of the office premium in which case the right-hand side will include the office premium. For example, if the expenses are k per unit of each office premium, c per unit sum assured each year, and additional initial expense of I, we obtain the following for the relationship between P the net premium and P'' the office premium (where $\ddot{a}$ is the annuity-due for the premium term and A is the value of the benefit)

$$P''\ddot{a} = A + kP''\ddot{a} + c\ddot{a} + I, \quad \text{and as} \quad A = P\ddot{a}$$

$$(1-k)P''\ddot{a} = (P+c)\ddot{a} + I$$

$$\therefore P'' = \frac{1}{1-k}\left(P + \frac{I}{\ddot{a}} + c\right). \tag{2.6.1}$$

The difference between the office and net premiums (i.e. $P'' - P$) is called the loading.

In practical examples it is important to be clear whether renewal expenses are considered as occurring in the first year or only in subsequent years, in the first case an $\ddot{a}$ annuity will be used and in the second an a will be applicable.

Example 2.5

Calculate on the basis of the A1967–70 select table of mortality at 4% interest the annual premium per cent for a 25-year endowment assurance on a life aged 40, allowing for initial expenses of £2% of the sum insured, renewal expenses including renewal commission of 5% of each premium including the first and 30p each year per £100 sum assured, and initial commission of 50% of the first year's gross premium.

Solution

Let £P'' be the required premium per cent.
Then

$$P''\ddot{a}_{[40]:\overline{25|}} = 100A_{[40]:\overline{25|}} + \cdot05P''\ddot{a}_{[40]:\overline{25|}} + \cdot3\ddot{a}_{[40]:\overline{25|}} + 2 + \cdot5P''$$

$$\therefore P'' = \frac{100A_{[40]:\overline{25|}} + \cdot3\ddot{a}_{[40]:\overline{25|}} + 2}{\cdot95\ddot{a}_{[40]:\overline{25|}} - \cdot5}$$

$$= \frac{100(\cdot39966) + \cdot3(15\cdot609) + 2}{(\cdot95)(15\cdot609) - \cdot5}$$

$$= 3\cdot26.$$

So premium required is £3·26%.

Example 2.6

Find the single premium for a 10-year term insurance with sum insured £500 for a life aged 30 on the A1967–70 select table at 4% interest. The premium paid is to be returned with the sum insured in the event of a claim. Expenses are £3% of the sum insured with a continuing administration cost of £1 each year.

Solution

If £P'' is the required single premium,

then
$$P'' = (500 + P'')A^1_{[30]:\overline{10}|} + 3(5) + 1 \cdot \ddot{a}_{[30]:\overline{10}|}$$

$$\therefore P'' = \frac{500A^1_{[30]:\overline{10}|} + 15 + \ddot{a}_{[30]:\overline{10}|}}{1 - A^1_{[30]:\overline{10}|}}$$

Now
$$A^1_{[30]:\overline{10}|} = \frac{M_{[30]} - M_{40}}{D_{[30]}} = \frac{1{,}978 \cdot 85 - 1{,}909 \cdot 50}{10{,}430 \cdot 0} = \cdot 00665$$

and
$$\ddot{a}_{[30]:\overline{10}|} = \frac{N_{[30]} - N_{40}}{D_{[30]}} = \frac{219{,}731 - 132{,}002}{10{,}430 \cdot 0} = 8 \cdot 411$$

so
$$P'' = \frac{500(\cdot 00665) + 15 + 8 \cdot 411}{1 - \cdot 00665}$$

$$= 26 \cdot 91.$$

So premium required is £26·91.

Example 2.7

A yearly annuity to a male aged 60 under which the first payment will be made one year hence has been purchased with £1,000. Assuming the $a(55)$ select male table of mortality and 4% interest is used with initial expenses of 2% of the purchase price and subsequent expenses of £1·50 each year, find the annual payment under the contract.

Solution

If £A is the annuity

$$1{,}000 = Aa_{[60]} + 1 \cdot 5a_{[60]} + 20,$$

$$\therefore A = \frac{980 - 1 \cdot 5a_{[60]}}{a_{[60]}}$$

$$= \frac{980}{a_{[60]}} - 1 \cdot 5$$

$$= \frac{980}{11\cdot691} - 1\cdot5$$

$$= 83\cdot83 - 1\cdot5 = 82\cdot33.$$

So the annuity payment is £82·33 each year.

Exercise 2.16

Find the annual premium for a 20-year endowment assurance with sum assured £1,500 for a life aged 40 on the A1967–70 select table at 4% interest. Expenses to be allowed for are initial expenses of £2·50% of the sum assured and 40% of the gross premium, renewal expenses of 3% of each premium exluding the first and expenses of paying the claim of £5.

Exercise 2.17

A yearly annuity to a male aged 65 under which the first payment is to be made immediately has been purchased to provide a pension of £200 per annum. The mortality table assumed is the $a(55)$ select male table with 4% interest. Expenses are $1\frac{1}{2}$% of the purchase price, and payment expenses of £1 at each payment. Find the purchase price.

Exercise 2.18

A deferred annuity is purchased by 20 annual premiums payable by a life aged 40 for a yearly annuity-due of £250 to commence at age 60. Find the premium on the basis of the A1967–70 select mortality table and 4% interest with expenses of 5% of each premium and 50p at each annuity payment.

Exercise 2.19

A single premium is paid for a 20-year temporary assurance with sum assured £2,000 for a life aged 40. Expenses are £2% of the sum assured, with a fixed addition of £15. Find the premium, half of which is returned with the sum assured in the event of a claim, on the A1967–70 select table at 4% interest.

2.7 Varying annuities and assurances

When an annuity or assurance varies in amount it will obviously be possible to evaluate it using suitable multiples of D_x or C_x. In cases where the annuity or assurance increases or decreases by an equal amount each year further commutation functions are useful.

Consider an annuity-due, given the symbol $(I\ddot{a})_x$, commencing at 1 immediately, increasing to 2 at the next payment one year hence, to 3 at duration 2, and so on indefinitely. Then

$$(I\ddot{a})_x = \frac{1}{D_x} (D_x + 2D_{x+1} + 3D_{x+2} + \dots)$$

$$= \frac{1}{D_x} (D_x + D_{x+1} + D_{x+2} + \dots$$
$$+ D_{x+1} + D_{x+2} + \dots$$
$$+ D_{x+2} + \dots$$
$$+ \dots)$$

$$= \frac{1}{D_x} (N_x + N_{x+1} + N_{x+2} + \dots),$$

i.e.
$$(I\ddot{a})_x = \frac{S_x}{D_x}, \tag{2.7.1}$$

where
$$S_x = \sum_{t=0}^{\infty} N_{x+t} \tag{2.7.2}$$

and S_x can be obtained by the successive summation of the N_x column from the highest age in the same way as N_x is obtained from D_x. As can be seen, S_x also equals $\sum_{t=0}^{\infty} (t+1)D_{x+t}$.

If the annuity is an immediate annuity commencing one year hence and increasing similarly it has the symbol

$$(Ia)_x = \frac{1}{D_x} (D_{x+1} + 2D_{x+2} + 3D_{x+3} + \dots)$$

$$= \frac{1}{D_x} (N_{x+1} + N_{x+2} + N_{x+3} + \dots),$$

i.e.
$$(Ia)_x = \frac{S_{x+1}}{D_x}. \tag{2.7.3}$$

The value of a temporary increasing annuity-due can also be obtained,

$$(I\ddot{a})_{x:\overline{n}|} = \frac{1}{D_x} (D_x + 2D_{x+1} + 3D_{x+2} + \dots + nD_{x+n-1})$$

$$= \frac{1}{D_x} (N_x - N_{x+n} + N_{x+1} - N_{x+n} + \dots + N_{x+n-1} - N_{x+n}),$$

i.e. $(I\ddot{a})_{x:\overline{n}|} = \frac{1}{D_x} (S_x - S_{x+n} - nN_{x+n}). \tag{2.7.4}$

It is important to note the subtraction of the N commutation function at the end of the term, multiplied by the difference between the suffices of the S factors. The need for this factor can also be demonstrated graphically, as shown in Figure 2.1.

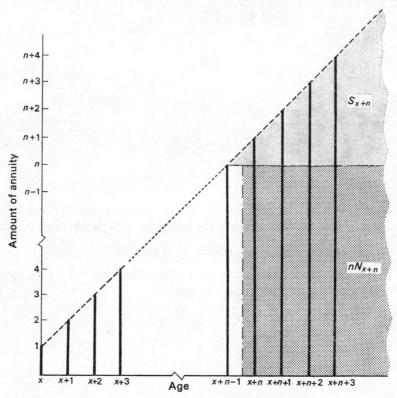

FIGURE 2.1. Pictorial representation of the function

$$(I\ddot{a})_{x:\overline{n}|} = \frac{S_x - S_{x+n} - nN_{x+n}}{D_x}.$$

The columns indicate the values that would be paid if $\dfrac{S_x}{D_x}$ were to be the benefit, the amount deducted by $\dfrac{S_{x+n}}{D_x}$ being indicated by the stippling in the top right showing clearly that nN_{x+n} must also be deducted.

A similar expression can be obtained for a decreasing annuity, commencing with n at age x and decreasing by 1 each year till zero,

$$(D\ddot{a})_{x:\overline{n}|} = \frac{1}{D_x}(nD_x + (n-1)D_{x+1} + \ldots + D_{x+n-1})$$

$$= \frac{1}{D_x}(N_x - N_{x+1} + N_x - N_{x+2} \ldots + N_x - N_{x+n})$$

$$= \frac{1}{D_x}(nN_x - S_{x+1} + S_{x+n+1}). \tag{2.7.5}$$

Again this can be demonstrated graphically as in Figure 2.2. The annuity commences at n giving the term nN_x and from this the annuity of 1 commencing one year hence, increasing by 1 each year must be deducted i.e. $-S_{x+1}$ (indicated by the stippling). After age $x+n$ the annuity would then become negative so S_{x+n+1} must be added, indicated by the shading.

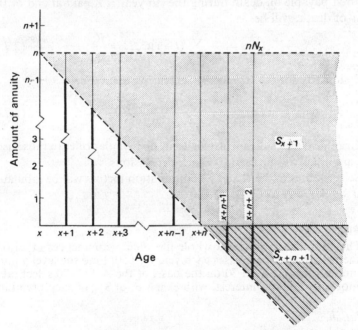

FIGURE 2.2. Pictorial representation of the function

$$(D\ddot{a})_{x:\overline{n}|} = \frac{nN_x - S_{x+1} + S_{x+n+1}}{D_x}$$

The rules for checking an expression involving S functions to evaluate temporary annuities are:

(a) the coefficients of the two S terms must be equal but opposite in sign,

(b) the coefficient of the N term (or sometimes when there is more than one N term—the sum of the coefficients of the N terms) must equal the coefficient of the S term at the older age multiplied by the difference between the suffices of the S terms.

Considering now assurances, similar methods will be applicable, the commutation function corresponding to S being R,

$$R_x = \sum_{t=0}^{\infty} M_{x+t} = \sum_{t=0}^{\infty} (t+1)C_{x+t} \qquad (2.7.6)$$

and similar formulae will result, for example, the value of an increasing whole-life assurance on the life of x under which the sum assured payable on death during the tth year is t, paid at end of the year of death, will be

$$(IA)_x = \frac{1}{D_x} \sum_{t=0}^{\infty} (t+1)C_{x+t} = \frac{R_x}{D_x}; \qquad (2.7.7)$$

and similarly for the temporary increasing assurance

$$(IA)^1_{x:\,\overline{n}|} = \frac{R_x - R_{x+n} - nM_{x+n}}{D_x}. \qquad (2.7.8)$$

Graphical methods can also be used, and similar rules to those used for annuities will be used to check expressions.

Select values of the R and S commutation factors will be tabulated in a similar way to C, D, M and N.

Example 2.8

The sum assured under a whole-life policy commences at £1,000 in the first year and increases each year by £50. Find the level annual premium for a life aged 50 on the basis of the A1967–70 select table of mortality and 4% interest, with expenses of 8% of each premium.

Solution

If P'' is the premium,

$$P'' \ddot{a}_{[50]} = 950A_{[50]} + \frac{50R_{[50]}}{D_{[50]}} + \cdot 08P'' \ddot{a}_{[50]},$$

the right-hand side being written this way rather than as

$$1{,}000A_{[50]} + \frac{50R_{[50]+1}}{D_{[50]}} + \ldots, \text{ as } R_{[50]+1} \text{ is not tabulated,}$$

$$= \frac{950(\cdot 38257) + 50\,\dfrac{39{,}142\cdot 9}{4{,}581\cdot 32}}{(\cdot 92)(16\cdot 053)}$$

$$= 53\cdot 53.$$

So premium required is £53·53.

Example 2.9

A yearly annuity to a life aged 40 commences at £100 and decreases each year by £4 till £20 at which it remains level until it ceases at the age of 80. Find the present value of the annuity on the A1967–70 ultimate table of mortality at 4% interest if the first payment is made immediately.

Solution

This example will be used to demonstrate a tabular technique similar to the pictorial representation previously described.

The annuity can be set out as follows:

Duration	0	1	2	3	..	18	19	20	21	22	..	39	40	41	42
Age	40	41	42	43	..	58	59	60	61	62	..	79	80	81	82
Required annuity	100	96	92	88	..	28	24	20	20	20	..	20	—	—	—
$100N_{40}$ gives	100	100	100	100	..	100	100	100	100	100	..	100	100	100	100
Subtract $4S_{41}$		−4	−8	−12	..	−72	−76	−80	−84	−88	..	−156	−160	−164	−168
gives	100	96	92	88	..	28	24	20	16	12	..	−56	−60	−64	−68
Add $4S_{61}$									4	8	..	76	80	84	88
gives	100	96	92	88	..	28	24	20	20	20	..	20	20	20	20
Subtract $20N_{80}$													−20	−20	−20
gives	100	96	92	88	..	28	24	20	20	20	..	20	—	—	—

as required.

So the value is $\dfrac{1}{D_{40}}(100N_{40} - 4S_{41} + 4S_{61} - 20N_{80})$,

which satisfies the rules for checking given previously—the coefficients of the S terms are equal and opposite in sign, and the sum of the coefficients of the N terms is 80 which equals the coefficient of the S term at the older age (4) multiplied by the difference between the suffices of the S terms (20).

The value is then

$$\frac{1}{6986\cdot 50}(100 \times 132{,}002 - 4 \times 1{,}799{,}542 + 4 \times 307{,}272 - 20 \times 3{,}151\cdot 31)$$

$$= 1{,}026.$$

i.e. value is £1,026.

Example 2.10

A 10-year term insurance provides a benefit of £1,000 at the end of the year of death together with the return without interest of the premiums paid. Allowing for expenses of 10% of each premium, find the annual premium for a life aged 50 on the basis of the A1967–70 ultimate table of mortality and 4% interest.

Solution

Let the gross premium be P'', then

$$P'' \frac{N_{50} - N_{60}}{D_{50}} = 1{,}000 \frac{M_{50} - M_{60}}{D_{50}} + P'' \frac{R_{50} - R_{60} - 10 M_{60}}{D_{50}}$$
$$+ 0 \cdot 1 P'' \frac{N_{50} - N_{60}}{D_{50}},$$

$$\therefore P'' \left(\cdot 9 \frac{73{,}567 \cdot 1 - 35{,}841 \cdot 3}{4{,}597 \cdot 06} - \frac{39{,}164 \cdot 1 - 22{,}644 \cdot 6 - 10 \times 1{,}477 \cdot 08}{4{,}597 \cdot 06} \right)$$

$$= 1{,}000 \frac{1{,}767 \cdot 56 - 1{,}477 \cdot 08}{4{,}597 \cdot 06}$$

$$\therefore P'' \, (7 \cdot 3859 - \cdot 3804) = 63 \cdot 1882$$

$$\therefore P'' = 9 \cdot 02.$$

So the annual premium is £9·02.

It will be noted that in the arithmetic of this question D_{50} was not cancelled throughout as it could have been. This was done so that a scrutiny could be put on the order of magnitude of the figures. (Some arithmetic could also have been saved by taking the tabulated values of $\ddot{a}_{50:\overline{10|}}$ and $_{10}A_{50}$).

Exercise 2.20

Show that $\qquad (Ia)_x = \dfrac{1}{D_x} \displaystyle\sum_{t=1}^{\infty} D_{x+t} \ddot{a}_{x+t}.$

Exercise 2.21

Calculate the annual premium for an assurance on a life aged 30 with sum assured £2,000 in the first year increasing by £200 each year, the benefit on survival to age 50 being £4,000. The mortality assumed is the A1967–70 ultimate table at 4% interest, with total expenses of £3% of the initial sum insured in the first year, and renewal expenses of £2 each year after the first.

Exercise 2.22

An annuity-due of £200 per annum is payable to a life aged 60. If the annuitant wishes to alter the annuity to one commencing at £100 and increasing by a level amount each year, find, on the basis of the A1967–70 ultimate table of mortality and 4% interest, the amount of the annual increase.

Exercise 2.23

A 20 year temporary assurance provides a benefit of £2,000 at the end of the year of death together with the return without interest of the premiums paid. Allowing for expenses of 12% of each premium, find the annual premium for a life aged 60 on the basis of the A1967–70 ultimate table and 4% interest.

2.8 Relations among the mortality functions

$$C_t = v^{t+1}d_t$$

$$= v^{t+1}(l_t - l_{t+1})$$

i.e. $\quad C_t = vD_t - D_{t+1}$ $\qquad\qquad$ (2.8.1)

$$= (1-d)D_t - D_{t+1}$$

$$= D_t - D_{t+1} - dD_t,$$

and summing from $t = x$ to ∞

$$M_x = D_x - dN_x, \qquad\qquad (2.8.2)$$

and dividing by D_x

$$A_x = 1 - d\ddot{a}_x. \qquad\qquad (2.8.3)$$

This is a most important equation; similar to the equivalent relationship in compound interest.

When the summation is from $t = x$ to $x+n-1$, instead of to ∞,

$$M_x - M_{x+n} = D_x - D_{x+n} - d(N_x - N_{x+n})$$

and dividing by D_x gives

$$A^1_{x:\overline{n}|} = 1 - A_{x:\overline{n}|} - d\ddot{a}_{x:\overline{n}|}$$

$$\therefore A_{x:\overline{n}|} = 1 - d\ddot{a}_{x:\overline{n}|}. \qquad\qquad (2.8.4)$$

Summing equation (2.8.1) from $t = x$ to $t = x+n-1$ gives

$$M_x - M_{x+n} = v(N_x - N_{x+n}) - (N_{x+1} - N_{x+n+1})$$

and dividing by D_x gives

$$A^1_{x:\overline{n}|} = v\ddot{a}_{x:\overline{n}|} - a_{x:\overline{n}|} \qquad\qquad (2.8.5)$$

Adding $A_{x:\overline{n}|}^1$ to each side gives

$$A_{x:\overline{n}|} = v\ddot{a}_{x:\overline{n}|} - a_{x:\overline{n-1}|}, \tag{2.8.6}$$

as

$$a_{x:\overline{n}|} = a_{x:\overline{n-1}|} + A_{x:\overline{n}|}^1,$$

If n is taken as ∞, the equation (2.8.6) becomes

$$A_x = v\ddot{a}_x - a_x. \tag{2.8.7}$$

Some of the above equations can be interpreted by general reasoning. For example, $A_x = 1 - d\ddot{a}_x$ can be interpreted as follows: A_x is the present value of a payment of 1 at the end of the year of death of (x); if the payment were now due its value would be 1, but as the payment is deferred, the value of the interest which it earns up to the time of death must be deducted—the value at the beginning of each year of this interest is d and the present value of this interest for each year that (x) enters upon is $d\ddot{a}_x$; hence $A_x = 1 - d\ddot{a}_x$.

Dividing both sides of equation (2.8.3) by $\ddot{a}_x$ gives

$$\frac{A_x}{\ddot{a}_x} = \frac{1}{\ddot{a}_x} - d$$

i.e.
$$P_x = \frac{1}{\ddot{a}_x} - d = \frac{1}{1 + a_x} - d. \tag{2.8.8}$$

This relation was used in the calculation of premiums before the advent of calculating machines, and special tables (known as annual premium conversion tables) were prepared so that at a given rate of interest the entry of a_x in the table enabled P_x to be found. Similar tables (known as single premium conversion tables) were also used for the single premium using the expression $A_x = 1 - d(1 + a_x)$.

The same tables are also used for endowment assurances as

$$P_{x:\overline{n}|} = \frac{1}{1 + a_{x:\overline{n-1}|}} - d$$

and

$$A_{x:\overline{n}|} = 1 - d(1 + a_{x:\overline{n-1}|}).$$

The relations are therefore often written without suffices as

$$P = \frac{1}{1 + a} - d \quad \text{or} \quad = \frac{1}{\ddot{a}} - d, \tag{2.8.9}$$

and

$$A = 1 - d(1 + a) \quad \text{or} \quad = 1 - d\ddot{a}. \tag{2.8.10}$$

Similar relationships that are sometimes useful which may easily be derived are:

$$\ddot{a} = \frac{1-A}{d} \qquad (2.8.11)$$

$$\ddot{a} = \frac{1}{P+d} \qquad (2.8.12)$$

$$A = \frac{P}{P+d} \qquad (2.8.13)$$

$$P = \frac{dA}{1-A}. \qquad (2.8.14)$$

It should be noted that these relationships apply to whole life and endowment assurances with level sum assured, and not to temporary or deferred assurances where the sum assured is not certainly payable, nor to limited premium assurances where the sum assured is not payable one year after the last premium payment.

Example 2.11

Demonstrate verbally the formula $A_{x:\overline{n}|} = v\ddot{a}_{x:\overline{n}|} - a_{x:\overline{n-1}|}$.

Solution

$v\ddot{a}_{x:\overline{n}|}$ represents a payment of v at the beginning of each year while (x) lives to a maximum of n, i.e. a payment of 1 at the end of each year that (x) enters upon; if $a_{x:\overline{n-1}|}$, a payment of 1 at the end of each year that (x) survives to, to a maximum of $n-1$ payments, is deducted the difference will be the payment of 1 at the end of the year which (x) enters but does not survive, i.e. the year of death, or at the end of n years if (x) survives, i.e. an endowment assurance. Therefore $v\ddot{a}_{x:\overline{n}|} - a_{x:\overline{n-1}|} = A_{x:\overline{n}|}$ as required.

Example 2.12

Prove and verify by general reasoning that $(IA)_x = \ddot{a}_x - d(I\ddot{a})_x$.

Solution

Summing formula (2.8.2) for $t = x$ to ∞ gives

$$R_x = N_x - dS_x, \text{ and dividing by } D_x \text{ gives}$$

$$(IA)_x = \ddot{a}_x - d(I\ddot{a})_x.$$

If (x) is entitled to an annuity-due of 1 payable yearly and he invests each payment the present value of the interest payable yearly in advance will be $d(I\ddot{a})_x$ and the present value of the invested payments on death will be $(IA)_x$, hence $\ddot{a}_x = d(I\ddot{a})_x + (IA)_x$.

Exercise 2.24

Explain the formula $A_{x:\overline{n}|} = 1 - d\ddot{a}_{x:\overline{n}|}$ by general reasoning.

Exercise 2.25

Find the rate of interest if $a_x = 12\cdot36$ and $A_x = \cdot738$.

Exercise 2.26

Given that

$$a_{x+1:\overline{9}|} = 7\cdot5,\ a_{x:\overline{9}|} = 7\cdot6,\ p_x = \cdot99,\ v = \cdot97,$$

calculate the annual premium for a 10-year temporary assurance to (x).

EXAMPLES AND EXERCISES ON CHAPTER 2

This chapter has introduced the six commutation functions, D, N, S, for annuities, and C, M, R, for assurances, together with the functions of A, a, $\ddot{a}$, P, which have similar meanings to the compound interest functions. The basis of the notation where prefixes and suffices are added to the symbol has been explained.

Example 2.13

Calculate the annual premium for a 20-year endowment assurance on a life aged 40, the sum assured of £800 at the end of the year of death being increased to £1,000 on survivance of the term. Mortality is assumed to follow the A1967–70 ultimate table during the first 10 years and the same table rated up five years subsequently. Interest is 4% per annum and expenses are initially 3% of the maturity sum assured and 5% of the premiums throughout.

Solution

Let P'' be the required premium, and mortality functions with one dash represent that experienced after age 50, undashed function represent A1967–70 mortality.

In a question of this type where either the mortality table or the rate of interest changes it is important to keep the commutation functions for the different age spans separate. The general principle is to use functions of the following type—where a death benefit after two changes of mortality table or interest rate is being evaluated:

$$\frac{D \text{ top age of first span}}{D \text{ bottom age of first span}} \cdot \frac{D \text{ top age of second span}}{D \text{ bottom age of second span}}$$

$$\cdot \frac{M - M \text{ for range considered}}{D \text{ bottom age of range considered}}.$$

The equation of value in this problem is then

$$\cdot 95 P'' \left(\frac{N_{40} - N_{50}}{D_{40}} + \frac{D_{50}}{D_{40}} \cdot \frac{N'_{50} - N'_{60}}{D'_{50}} \right)$$

$$= 800 \left(\frac{M_{40} - M_{50}}{D_{40}} + \frac{D_{50}}{D_{40}} \cdot \frac{M'_{50} - M'_{60}}{D'_{50}} \right) + 1,000 \frac{D_{50}}{D_{40}} \cdot \frac{D'_{60}}{D'_{50}} + 30.$$

As $N'_t = N_{t+5}$, $D'_t = D_{t+5}$, etc.,

$$\cdot 95 P'' \left(\frac{N_{40} - N_{50}}{D_{40}} + \frac{D_{50}}{D_{40}} \cdot \frac{N_{55} - N_{65}}{D_{55}} \right)$$

$$= 800 \left(\frac{M_{40} - M_{50}}{D_{40}} + \frac{D_{50}}{D_{40}} \cdot \frac{M_{55} - M_{65}}{D_{55}} \right) + 1,000 \frac{D_{50}}{D_{40}} \frac{D_{65}}{D_{55}} + 30,$$

$$\therefore \cdot 95 P'' \left(\frac{132,002 - 73,567 \cdot 1}{6,986 \cdot 50} + \frac{4,597 \cdot 06}{6,986 \cdot 50} \cdot \frac{52,502 \cdot 8 - 23,021 \cdot 4}{3,664 \cdot 57} \right)$$

$$= 800 \left(\frac{1,909 \cdot 50 - 1,767 \cdot 56}{6,986 \cdot 50} + \frac{4,597 \cdot 06}{6,986 \cdot 50} \cdot \frac{1,645 \cdot 23 - 1,258 \cdot 73}{3,664 \cdot 57} \right)$$

$$+ 1,000 \frac{4,597 \cdot 06}{6,986 \cdot 50} \cdot \frac{2,144 \cdot 17}{3,664 \cdot 57} + 30,$$

$$\therefore \cdot 95 P'' (8 \cdot 364 + 5 \cdot 294) = 800 (\cdot 0203 + \cdot 0694) + 1,000 (\cdot 3850) + 30$$

$$\therefore P'' = 37 \cdot 51.$$

So premium required is £37·51.

Example 2.14

Twenty years ago an assurance company issued a large number of annual premium 20-year pure endowment policies with sum assured £1,000 to lives then aged 40, assuming mortality according to the A1967–70 ultimate table at 4% per annum interest with expenses of 2% of each premium. If the assumption on interest was correct but expenses were 3% of each premium and the mortality experienced was A1967–70 rated down 10 years, find the average loss to the assurance company on each policy.

Solution

If P' is the premium paid,

$$\cdot 98P'\, \frac{N_{40}-N_{60}}{D_{40}} = 1{,}000\, \frac{D_{60}}{D_{40}}$$

$$\therefore P' = \frac{1{,}000 \times 2{,}855 \cdot 59}{\cdot 98(132{,}002 - 35{,}841 \cdot 3)}$$

$$= 30 \cdot 30.$$

The actual accumulated amount will be (two dashes representing the experienced mortality)

$$\cdot 97P'\ddot{s}''_{40\,:\,\overline{20|}}$$

$$= \cdot 97P'\ddot{s}_{30\,:\,\overline{20|}} \text{ on A1967–70}$$

$$= \cdot 97P'\, \frac{N_{30}-N_{50}}{D_{50}}$$

$$= \cdot 97(30 \cdot 30)\, \frac{219{,}735 - 73{,}567 \cdot 1}{4{,}597 \cdot 06}$$

$$= 934 \cdot 5.$$

So the loss on each policy is $1{,}000 - 934 \cdot 5$, i.e. £65·5.

Example 2.15

A yearly immediate annuity of £100 is purchased for a life aged 60. On death, if the payments of the annuity have not amounted to the purchase price, the difference is paid at the end of the year of death. Find the purchase price if mortality is A1967–70 ultimate with 4% interest and expenses are 5% of the purchase price.

Solution

The first step in a problem of this type is to find an approximate answer by ignoring the death benefit; if this premium is P''

$$\cdot 95P'' = 100a_{60}$$

$$\therefore P'' = \frac{100 \times 11 \cdot 551}{\cdot 95} = 1{,}216.$$

The actual purchase price will be greater than this, and if it is assumed that it is between 1,400 and 1,500 the equation of payment is (P' being the premium)

$$\cdot 95P' = 100a_{60} + P'\frac{C_{60}}{D_{60}} + (P'-100)\frac{C_{61}}{D_{60}} + (P'-200)\frac{C_{62}}{D_{60}} + \ldots$$
$$+ (P'-1,400)\frac{C_{74}}{D_{60}},$$

i.e. $\cdot 95P' = 100a_{60} + P'\frac{M_{60}-M_{75}}{D_{60}} - 100\frac{(R_{61}-R_{75}-14M_{75})}{D_{60}}.$

Similar expressions could also have been obtained by the pictorial or schedule methods.

Then $\qquad \cdot 95P' = 1,155\cdot 1 + P'\frac{1,477\cdot 08 - 703\cdot 04}{2,855\cdot 59}$

$$- 100\frac{21,167\cdot 5 - 5,501\cdot 0 - 14 \times 703\cdot 04}{2,855\cdot 59}$$

$$\therefore P'(\cdot 95 - \cdot 2711) = 1,155\cdot 1 - 203\cdot 9$$

$$\therefore P' = 1,401.$$

So the purchase price is £1,401.

If the answer had not been found to be within the range originally assumed. i.e. 1,400 to 1,500, then the calculation would require to be done again although the answer obtained would be very close to the correct answer, thus indicating the range, and only one further calculation should be necessary.

Example 2.16

Find the present value at rate of interest i of an annuity-due of 1 per annum accumulating during the life of (x) and until the end of the year of his death at rate of interest j.

Solution

Although an annuity is being considered, the benefit is not available until death. If death occurs between ages of $x+t$ and $x+t+1$, the present value of the accumulation would be $v^{t+1}\ddot{s}_{\overline{t+1}|}^{\,j}$ where v is at rate of interest i and $\ddot{s}_{\overline{t+1}|}^{\,j}$ is at rate of interest j. So multiplying by the probability of death occurring in the year and summing, the total present value will be

$$\sum_{t=0}^{\infty} v^{t+1}\ddot{s}_{\overline{t+1}|}^{\,j}\frac{d_{x+t}}{l_x}$$

$$= \sum_{t=0}^{\infty} v^{t+1}\frac{(1+j)^{t+1}-1}{d^j}\cdot\frac{d_{x+t}}{l_x}$$

where d^j is the rate of discount for rate of interest j

$$= \frac{1}{d^j} \sum_{t=0}^{\infty} \left(\frac{v'^{t+1} d_{x+t}}{l_x} - \frac{v^{t+1} d_{x+t}}{l_x} \right) \quad \text{where } v' = v(1+j)$$

$$= \frac{1+j}{j} (A'_x - A_x),$$

where A' is calculated at a rate of interest J such that $\dfrac{1}{1+J} = \dfrac{1+j}{1+i}$,

i.e. $J = \dfrac{i-j}{1+j}$ so that J may in fact be negative depending on the values of i and j, and is unlikely to be a rate of interest at which functions are tabulated.

Exercise 2.27

An assurance on a man aged 45 has a death benefit of £2,000 reducing by £50 each year to an endowment benefit of £1,000 on survivance to age 65. Find the annual premium, assuming interest at 4%, if the premium for the first ten years is half the subsequent premium, expenses are 5% of each premium and the life is considered to be subject to the A1967–70 ultimate table of mortality except that during the first ten years he is subject to extra mortality equivalent to the life being treated as five years older on that table.

Exercise 2.28

Find an expression for the present value at the rate of interest i per annum of an increasing annuity-due, commencing at 1 and increasing by 1 each year, which accumulates during the lifetime of a person aged x at the rate of interest of j per annum, the accumulation being paid at the end of the year of death of (x).

Exercise 2.29

Thirty years ago an assurance company issued a large number of annual premium 30-year pure endowment policies with sum assured £2,000 to lives then aged 30, assuming mortality according to the A1967–70 ultimate table at 4% per annum interest, with expenses of 3% of each premium. If the assumption on interest was correct, but expenses were 20% of the first premium and 2% of each subsequent premium, and the mortality experienced was the A1967–70 ultimate table rated up five years, find the average profit or loss to the assurance company on each policy.

Exercise 2.30

A yearly immediate annuity of £200 per annum is purchased for a life aged 65. On the death of the annuitant if the payments of the annuity have not amounted to the purchase price, the difference is paid at the end of the year of death. Find the purchase price if mortality is A1967–70 ultimate with 4% per annum interest and expenses are 2% of the purchase price.

CHAPTER THREE

FUNCTIONS OTHER THAN YEARLY

3.1 Annuities payable more frequently than once a year

In the previous chapter yearly annuities were considered. In this section we will find expressions for annuities payable at different frequencies, normally the resulting formulae being expressed as adjustments of the yearly formula.

The present value of an immediate life annuity of 1 payable m times a year to a life aged x is denoted by $a_x^{(m)}$, and consists of payments, each of $\frac{1}{m}$, at age $x + \frac{1}{m}$, $x + \frac{2}{m}$, $x + \frac{3}{m}$ .... The present value may be written

$$a_x^{(m)} = \frac{1}{m} \sum_{t=1}^{\infty} \frac{D_{x+\frac{t}{m}}}{D_x}.$$

The corresponding annuity-due is denoted $\ddot{a}_x^{(m)}$, and

$$\ddot{a}_x^{(m)} = \frac{1}{m} \sum_{t=0}^{\infty} \frac{D_{x+\frac{t}{m}}}{D_x}.$$

The only difference between $a_x^{(m)}$ and $\ddot{a}_x^{(m)}$ is the extra payment immediately of $\frac{1}{m}$.

Unless the mathematical formula for l_x is known, approximations will be required to evaluate these expressions. The approximation normally used is based on Woolhouse's formula which will be proved in the demonstration in the form most suitable for this purpose.

Let Δ denote differencing with interval 1.

   δ denote differencing with interval $\frac{1}{m}$.

   D denote differentiation

Σ denote summation at intervals of 1 within the range a to b, so that

$$\Sigma u_{x+t} = \sum_{t=a}^{b-1} u_{x+t}$$

and $\Sigma^{(m)}$ denote summation at intervals of $\dfrac{1}{m}$ within the range a to b, each term being multiplied by $\dfrac{1}{m}$, so that

$$\Sigma^{(m)} u_{x+t} = \sum_{t=a}^{b-1/m} {}^{(m)} \frac{1}{m} u_{x+t}.$$

Then in symbol notation

$$1 + \Delta = (1+\delta)^m = e^D$$

and

$$\Sigma = \frac{1}{e^D - 1} = \cfrac{1}{D + \dfrac{D^2}{2!} + \dfrac{D^3}{3!} + \ldots}$$

$$= \frac{1}{D} \left\{ 1 + \left(\frac{D}{2!} + \frac{D^2}{3!} + \frac{D^3}{4!} + \ldots \right) \right\}^{-1}$$

$$= \frac{1}{D} \left\{ 1 - \left(\frac{D}{2} + \frac{D^2}{6} + \frac{D^3}{24} + \frac{D^4}{120} + \ldots \right) \right.$$

$$\left. + \left(\frac{D^2}{4} + \frac{D^4}{36} + \frac{D^3}{6} + \frac{D^4}{24} + \ldots \right) - \left(\frac{D^3}{8} + \frac{D^4}{8} + \ldots \right) + \left(\frac{D^4}{16} + \ldots \right) \right\}$$

$$= \frac{1}{D} \left(1 - \frac{D}{2} + \frac{D^2}{12} - \frac{D^4}{720} \ldots \right),$$

i.e.

$$\Sigma = \frac{1}{D} - \frac{1}{2} + \frac{1}{12} D - \frac{1}{720} D^3 \ldots$$

Similarly,

$$\Sigma^{(m)} = \frac{1}{m} \cdot \frac{1}{\delta} = \frac{1}{m} \cdot \frac{1}{e^{\frac{D}{m}} - 1}$$

$$= \frac{1}{D} - \frac{1}{2m} + \frac{1}{12m^2} D - \frac{1}{720m^4} D^3 \ldots$$

Subtracting

$$\Sigma^{(m)} - \Sigma = \frac{m-1}{2m} - \frac{m^2-1}{12m^2} D + \frac{m^4-1}{720m^4} D^3 \ldots$$

Inserting the function $\dfrac{D_{x+t}}{D_x}$ and summing within the limit 0 and ∞ we obtain

$$\sum_{t=0}^{\infty}{}^{(m)} \frac{D_{x+t}}{D_x} = \sum_{t=0}^{\infty} \frac{D_{x+t}}{D_x} + \frac{m-1}{2m}\left[\frac{D_{x+t}}{D_x}\right]_{t=0}^{\infty} - \frac{m^2-1}{12m^2}\left[\frac{d}{dt}\frac{D_{x+t}}{D_x}\right]_{t=0}^{\infty} \cdots$$

Now
$$\frac{dD_x}{dx} = \frac{d}{dx}(v^x l_x)$$

$$= v^x(-l_x\mu_x) - l_x v^x \delta$$

i.e.
$$\frac{dD_x}{dx} = -D_x(\mu_x+\delta) \tag{3.1.1}$$

so
$$\frac{dD_{x+t}}{dt} = -D_{x+t}(\mu_{x+t}+\delta)$$

and as all the functions and derivatives will be zero at $t = \infty$, and if third and higher differential coefficients which are likely to be small are ignored, we obtain

$$\ddot{a}_x^{(m)} \fallingdotseq \ddot{a}_x - \frac{m-1}{2m} - \frac{m^2-1}{12m^2}(\mu_x+\delta) \tag{3.1.2}$$

or subtracting $\dfrac{1}{m}$ from each side

$$a_x^{(m)} \fallingdotseq a_x + \frac{m-1}{2m} - \frac{m^2-1}{12m^2}(\mu_x+\delta). \tag{3.1.3}$$

In most work the last term in each of these expressions is omitted giving

$$\ddot{a}_x^{(m)} \fallingdotseq \ddot{a}_x - \frac{m-1}{2m} \tag{3.1.4}$$

and
$$a_x^{(m)} \fallingdotseq a_x + \frac{m-1}{2m}. \tag{3.1.5}$$

The commonly used values of $\dfrac{m-1}{2m}$ will be ·250 for half-yearly, ·375 for quarterly and ·458 for monthly.

Formulae for deferred and temporary annuities can be obtained from these expressions, for example

$$_n|a_x^{(m)} = \frac{D_{x+n}}{D_x} \cdot a_{x+n}^{(m)}$$

$$\fallingdotseq \frac{D_{x+n}}{D_x}\left(a_{x+n} + \frac{m-1}{2m}\right)$$

$$= {}_n|a_x + \frac{m-1}{2m}\frac{D_{x+n}}{D_x},$$

and

$$a_{x:\overline{n}|}^{(m)} = a_x^{(m)} - {}_n|a_x^{(m)}$$

$$\fallingdotseq a_x + \frac{m-1}{2m} - \left({}_n|a_x + \frac{m-1}{2m}\cdot\frac{D_{x+n}}{D_x}\right)$$

i.e.

$$a_{x:\overline{n}|}^{(m)} \fallingdotseq a_{x:\overline{n}|} + \frac{m-1}{2m}\left(1 - \frac{D_{x+n}}{D_x}\right). \qquad (3.1.6)$$

Note the last term includes $\dfrac{D_{x+n}}{D_x}$ in this expression—it is often incorrectly omitted by students in practical work.

Obviously similar formulae apply for annuities-due, for example

$$\ddot{a}_{x:\overline{n}|}^{(m)} \fallingdotseq \ddot{a}_{x:\overline{n}|} - \frac{m-1}{2m}\left(1 - \frac{D_{x+n}}{D_x}\right). \qquad (3.1.7)$$

A simple diagrammatic method of obtaining formulae (3.1.4) or (3.1.5) in a particular case will be demonstrated for the expression

$$\ddot{a}_x^{(2)} \fallingdotseq \ddot{a}_x - \tfrac{1}{4}.$$

The value of $\ddot{a}_x^{(2)}$ may be demonstrated as shown in Figure 3.1. If the payments of $\frac{1}{2}$ paid half-way through the year are considered as

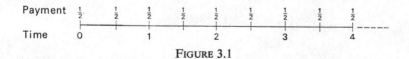

FIGURE 3.1

split into two payments of $\frac{1}{4}$, one six months earlier and one six months later, the payment will be represented as shown in Figure 3.2. This process has not changed the value of the annuity by much, and the value is now $\ddot{a}_x - \frac{1}{4}$.

While this method can by no means be considered as a proof of a formula it can be useful as a check on other methods.

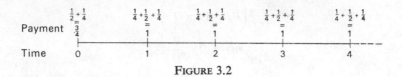

FIGURE 3.2

Example 3.1

Describe and find the values of $a_{60}^{(2)}$, $\ddot{a}_{60}^{(4)}$, $a_{[65]}^{(12)}$, $a_{70:\overline{10}|}^{(2)}$ on the $a(55)$ Males mortality table with 4% interest.

Solution

$a_{60}^{(2)}$, is a half-yearly immediate annuity, and using the normal approximation of formula (3.1.5), equals

$$a_{60} + \cdot25 = 11\cdot625 + \cdot25 = 11\cdot875.$$

$\ddot{a}_{60}^{(4)}$ is a quarterly annuity-due and similarly using formula (3.1.4) equals

$$\ddot{a}_{60} - \cdot375 = 12\cdot625 - \cdot375 = 12\cdot250.$$

$a_{[65]}^{(12)}$ is a monthly immediate annuity to a select life and equals

$$a_{[65]} + \cdot458 = 9\cdot883 + \cdot458 = 10\cdot341.$$

$a_{70:\overline{10}|}^{(2)}$ is a temporary half-yearly immediate annuity, and using formula (3.1.6) equals

$$\frac{N_{71} - N_{81}}{D_{70}} + \cdot25\left(1 - \frac{D_{80}}{D_{70}}\right)$$

$$= \frac{349,209 - 74,343}{43,852} + \cdot25\left(1 - \frac{15,791}{43,852}\right)$$

$$= 6\cdot268 + \cdot25(1 - \cdot360)$$

$$= 6\cdot428.$$

Example 3.2

Find the quarterly premium payable for 20 years by a man aged 40 for a deferred annuity of £500 per annum payable monthly in advance from his 60th birthday on the A1967–70 ultimate table of mortality at 4%. Expenses are 20p on each annuity payment and 5% of each premium.

Solution

Equating the present values of premiums, and benefit and expenses (where P' is the gross premium per annum) gives

$$\cdot 95 P' \ddot{a}_{40:\overline{20}|}^{(4)} = (500 + 12 \times \cdot 2)_{20|}\ddot{a}_{40}^{(12)},$$

i.e. $\qquad \cdot 95 P' \left\{ \ddot{a}_{40:\overline{20}|} - \cdot 375 \left(1 - \dfrac{D_{60}}{D_{40}} \right) \right\}$

$$= 502 \cdot 4 \, \frac{D_{60}}{D_{40}} \, (\ddot{a}_{60} - \cdot 458),$$

i.e. $\qquad \cdot 95 P' \left\{ 13 \cdot 764 - \cdot 375 \left(1 - \dfrac{2{,}855 \cdot 59}{6{,}986 \cdot 50} \right) \right\}$

$$= 502 \cdot 4 \, \frac{2{,}855 \cdot 59}{6{,}986 \cdot 50} \, (12 \cdot 551 - \cdot 458),$$

$$\therefore \ P' = 193 \cdot 02.$$

Each quarterly premium is thus £48·26.

Exercise 3.1

Find the values of $a_{60}^{(12)}$, $_{10|}\ddot{a}_{65}^{(4)}$ and $a_{[60]:\overline{15}|}^{(2)}$ on the basis of $a(55)$ Female mortality at 4% interest.

Exercise 3.2

Demonstrate and verify by general reasoning the formulae,

$$a_{x:\overline{n}|}^{(m)} \doteqdot \frac{m+1}{2m} \, a_{x:\overline{n}|} + \frac{m-1}{2m} \, \ddot{a}_{x:\overline{n}|}$$

$$\ddot{a}_{x:\overline{n}|}^{(m)} \doteqdot \frac{m+1}{2m} \, \ddot{a}_{x:\overline{n}|} + \frac{m-1}{2m} \, a_{x:\overline{n}|}.$$

Exercise 3.3

Find the percentage error involved in using formula (3.1.5) rather than (3.1.3) to evaluate $a_{60}^{(12)}$ and $a_{80}^{(12)}$ on the $a(55)$ Male mortality table and 4% interest.

Exercise 3.4

Find the purchase price of a quarterly annuity of £100 each payment payable in arrears to a man aged 65, assumed to be subject to the $a(55)$ Male mortality table and 4% interest. Expenses are 4% of the gross premium.

3.2 Continuous annuities

When the frequency of payment of an $m$thly annuity becomes infinite the resulting annuity is called a continuous annuity, payable momently throughout the year in such a way that the total annual payment is 1. This admittedly artificial concept has considerable importance in theoretical work and is useful as an approximation to payments made weekly, for example social insurance benefits. The symbol for a continuous annuity to a life aged x is $\bar{a}_x$. Making m tend to infinity in the formulae (3.1.3) or (3.1.5) gives the following approximations

$$\bar{a}_x \fallingdotseq a_x + \tfrac{1}{2} - \tfrac{1}{12}(\mu_x + \delta) \tag{3.2.1}$$

and
$$\bar{a}_x \fallingdotseq a_x + \tfrac{1}{2}, \tag{3.2.2}$$

the second normally being used.

An accurate formula will be expressed in integral form

$$\bar{a}_x = \int_0^\infty v^t {}_t p_x dt$$

$$= \int_0^\infty \frac{D_{x+t}}{D_x}\,dt. \tag{3.2.3}$$

Defining the continuous commutation functions

$$\bar{D}_x = \int_0^1 D_{x+t}dt \tag{3.2.4}$$

and
$$\bar{N}_x = \sum_{t=0}^\infty \bar{D}_{x+t} = \int_0^\infty D_{x+t}dt \tag{3.2.5}$$

we obtain
$$\bar{a}_x = \frac{\bar{N}_x}{D_x}. \tag{3.2.6}$$

If it is assumed that
$$\tfrac{1}{2}(D_x + D_{x+1}) \tag{3.2.7}$$

is an approximation to
$$\int_0^1 D_{x+t}.\,dt,$$

then
$$\bar{N}_x = \tfrac{1}{2}D_x + N_{x+1} = N_x - \tfrac{1}{2}D_x, \tag{3.2.8}$$

which obviously gives values of $\bar{a}_x$ consistent with formula (3.2.2).

Temporary and deferred annuities can be expressed in either integral or commutation function form:

$$\bar{a}_{x:\overline{n}|} = \int_0^n v^t \cdot {}_tp_x \cdot dt = \frac{\overline{N}_x - \overline{N}_{x+n}}{D_x} \qquad (3.2.9)$$

and

$$_n|\bar{a}_x = \int_n^\infty v^t \cdot {}_tp_x \cdot dt = \frac{\overline{N}_{x+n}}{D_x}.$$

Note that in these formulae while continuous functions appear in the numerator, the denominator remains D_x.

It is not usual for the functions $\overline{D}_x$ or $\overline{N}_x$ to be tabulated and normally if they are required the approximate formulae (3.2.7) or (3.2.8) are used, but population tables such as the English Life Tables will often have $\overline{N}_x$ calculated as they are used as a basis for Industrial Insurance premiums, that is life assurance where the premiums are collected at weekly intervals, and the continuous annuity is used as an approximation.

Example 3.3

An annuity is payable weekly to a widow aged 40 at the rate of £10 per week with a child's allowance of £5 per week till her child reaches age 18 five years hence. Find the present value of the benefit at 4% interest, assuming that the rate of mortality experienced by the widow will be the English Life Table No. 12 — Males and that the mortality experienced by the child is small enough to be ignored.

Solution

Because of the frequency of pension payments it is reasonable to assume that payments are continuous. In such a question it is usual to assume that there are 52·18 weeks in the year. The value of the benefit is then

$$(52·18)(10)\bar{a}_{40} + (52·18)(5)\bar{a}_{40:\overline{5}|}$$

$$= 521·8 \frac{\overline{N}_{40}}{D_{40}} + 260·9 \frac{\overline{N}_{40} - \overline{N}_{45}}{D_{40}}$$

$$= 521·8 \frac{338,786}{19,535} + 260·9 \frac{338,786 - 250,656}{19,535}$$

$$= 9,049 + 1,177$$

$$= 10,226.$$

The present value of the benefit is therefore £10,226.

Example 3.4

Show that
$$\bar{a}_x = \int_0^\infty {}_tp_x \cdot \mu_{x+t}\bar{a}_{\overline{t}|} \cdot dt$$

directly and using integration by parts.

Solution

As $\delta t \to 0$ the probability that (x) will die in the short interval of time $(x+t)$ to $(x+t+\delta t)$ tends to ${}_tp_x\mu_{x+t}\delta t$, and the value of the annuity paid until that time till be $\bar{a}_{\overline{t}|}$.

Hence
$$\bar{a}_x = \int_0^\infty {}_tp_x\mu_{x+t}\bar{a}_{\overline{t}|}dt.$$

Alternatively
$$\bar{a}_x = \int_0^\infty v^t {}_tp_x dt$$

$$= \int_0^\infty {}_tp_x \frac{d}{dt}\left(-\frac{v^t}{\delta}\right) dt, \quad \text{as} \quad \log_e v = -\delta,$$

$$= \left[{}_tp_x\left(-\frac{v^t}{\delta}\right)\right]_0^\infty - \int_0^\infty \left(-\frac{v^t}{\delta}\right)(-{}_tp_x\mu_{x+t})dt$$

$$= \frac{1}{\delta} + \frac{1}{\delta}\int_0^\infty \left(-\frac{v^t}{\delta}\right){}_tp_x\mu_{x+t}dt$$

and as
$$\int_0^\infty {}_tp_x\mu_{x+t}dt = {}_\infty q_x = 1,$$

this
$$= \int_0^\infty \frac{1-v^t}{\delta} {}_tp_x\mu_{x+t}dt$$

$$= \int_0^\infty {}_tp_x\mu_{x+t}\bar{a}_{\overline{t}|}dt, \text{ as required.}$$

Exercise 3.5

A formula commonly used in practice is
$$\bar{a}_{x:\overline{n}|} \doteqdot \tfrac{1}{2}(a_{x:\overline{n}|} + \ddot{a}_{x:\overline{n}|}).$$

Prove this formula.

Exercise 3.6

A pension is payable at the rate of £25 a week to a man aged 60, reducing to £20 at age 65 when the National Insurance Pension becomes payable. Find the value of the pension at 4% interest on the basis of

(i) English Life Table No. 12—Males

(ii) $a(55)$—Males, ultimate.

3.3 Assurances payable at the moment of death

So far we have considered assurances under which the sum assured is paid at the end of the year of death. In practice this would be unusual as the sum assured will be paid immediately death has been intimated and satisfactory evidence, such as a death certificate, produced. The symbol for the assurance payable at the moment of death is $\bar{A}_x$.

The probability of (x) dying between ages $x+t$ and $x+t+\delta t$ tends to ${}_tp_x\mu_{x+t}\delta t$ as $\delta t \to 0$, and discounting by the interest function v^t we obtain

$$\bar{A}_x = \int_0^\infty v^t {}_tp_x\mu_{x+t}dt. \qquad (3.3.1)$$

The continuous commutation functions are

$$\bar{C}_x = \int_0^1 D_{x+t}\mu_{x+t}dt \qquad (3.3.2)$$

and

$$\bar{M}_x = \sum_{t=0}^\infty \bar{C}_{x+t}. \qquad (3.3.3)$$

Hence

$$\bar{A}_x = \frac{\bar{M}_x}{D_x}, \qquad (3.3.4)$$

with similar expressions for temporary and deferred assurances,

$$\bar{A}^1_{x:\overline{n}|} = \frac{\bar{M}_x - \bar{M}_{x+n}}{D_x}$$

$$_n|\bar{A}_x = \frac{\bar{M}_{x+n}}{D_x}.$$

If it is assumed that there is a uniform distribution of deaths over the year of age, ${}_tp_x\mu_{x+t}$ is constant and equals q_x

$$\therefore \bar{A}^1_{x:\overline{1}|} \doteqdot q_x \int_0^1 v^t dt = q_x \bar{a}_{\overline{1}|} = q_x \frac{iv}{\delta};$$

and as
$$A^1_{x:\overline{1}|} = vq_x$$

$$\bar{A}^1_{x:\overline{1}|} \doteqdot \frac{i}{\delta} A^1_{x:\overline{1}|}$$

a convenient approximation as the continuous functions can be obtained easily from the normally tabulated 'end of year' functions.

Another approximation is based on the assumption that the assurance payment is made half a year earlier on average, so that

$$\bar{A}^1_{x:\overline{1}|} \doteqdot (1+i)^{\frac{1}{2}} A^1_{x:\overline{1}|}$$

or
$$\bar{A}^1_{x:\overline{1}|} \doteqdot \left(1 + \frac{i}{2}\right) A^1_{x:\overline{1}|}.$$

It is convenient that the constant factor is independent of the age x and as

$$\bar{A}^1_{x:\overline{n}|} = \sum_{n=0}^{n-1} v^t{}_t p_x \bar{A}_{\underset{x+t:\overline{1}|}{1}}$$

it follows that

$$\bar{A}^1_{x:\overline{n}|} \doteqdot \frac{i}{\delta} A^1_{x:\overline{n}|},$$

or
$$\bar{A}^1_{x:\overline{n}|} \doteqdot (1+i)^{\frac{1}{2}} A^1_{x:\overline{n}|},$$

or
$$\bar{A}^1_{x:\overline{n}|} \doteqdot \left(1 + \frac{i}{2}\right) A^1_{x:\overline{n}|}; \qquad (3.3.5)$$

the last being the most often used, although the whole life form $\bar{A}_x \doteqdot \frac{i}{\delta} A_x$ may be used, and when the function $\bar{C}_x$ is tabulated it is often obtained from $\bar{C}_x = v^{x+\frac{1}{2}} d_x$. In practice there is very little difference between the approximations, for example when

$$i = 4\%, \frac{i}{\delta} = 1{\cdot}019869, (1+i)^{\frac{1}{2}} = 1{\cdot}019804, 1 + \frac{i}{2} = 1{\cdot}02.$$

The adjustment to the year end functions is called *claim acceleration* and it will be noted that it only applies to the death benefit, for example with the endowment assurance no claim acceleration is applied to the maturity benefit so that

$$\bar{A}_{x:\overline{n}|} \neq \left(1 + \frac{i}{2}\right) A_{x:\overline{n}|}$$

and the formula will be

$$\bar{A}_{x\,:\,\overline{n}|} = \frac{\overline{M}_x - \overline{M}_{x+n} + D_{x+n}}{D_x}$$

$$\therefore \bar{A}_{x\,:\,\overline{n}|} \fallingdotseq \left(1 + \frac{i}{2}\right) A^1_{x\,:\,\overline{n}|} + A_{x\,:\,\frac{1}{n}|}. \qquad (3.3.6)$$

The function $\bar{A}_x$ may also be considered as the limiting case of $A_x^{(m)}$ when m tends to infinity, $A_x^{(m)}$ being an assurance payable at the end of the mth part of a year in which death occurs. While the related annuity $a_x^{(m)}$ is of considerable practical importance, $A_x^{(m)}$ is of little importance. The relationship between the functions is

$$A_x^{(m)} = 1 - d^{(m)} \ddot{a}_x^{(m)} \qquad (3.3.7)$$

with the approximate formula

$$A_x^{(m)} \fallingdotseq \frac{i}{i^{(m)}} A_x.$$

Example 3.5

Find the net single premium for a 20-year endowment assurance with sum assured £500 payable at the moment of death for a select life aged 40 subject to the mortality of the A1967–70 table of mortality and 4% interest.

Solution

$$500 \bar{A}_{[40]\,:\,\overline{20}|}$$

$$= 500 \left(1 \cdot 02 \frac{M_{[40]} - M_{60}}{D_{[40]}} + \frac{D_{60}}{D_{[40]}}\right)$$

$$= 500 \left(1 \cdot 02 \frac{1{,}904 \cdot 86 - 1{,}477 \cdot 08}{6{,}981 \cdot 60} + \frac{2{,}855 \cdot 59}{6{,}981 \cdot 60}\right)$$

$$= 235 \cdot 76,$$

i.e. the net single premium is £236.

Example 3.6

If a mortality table follows Gompertz law, show that $\bar{A}_x = \mu_x \bar{a}'_x$, where $\bar{a}'_x$ is calculated at rate $i' = \dfrac{1+i}{c} - 1$.

Solution

$$\bar{A}_x = \int_0^\infty v^t {}_t p_x \mu_{x+t} dt$$

$$= \int_0^\infty v^t {}_t p_x B c^{x+t} dt \quad \text{as} \quad \mu_{x+t} = B c^{x+t}$$

$$= B c^x \int_0^\infty (vc)^t {}_t p_x dt$$

$$= \mu_x \bar{a}'_x,$$

where $\bar{a}'_x$ is at rate of interest such that

$$v' = vc,$$

i.e. $$i' = \frac{1+i}{c} - 1.$$

Exercise 3.7

Find the net annual premium for a 35-year endowment assurance with sum insured £1,000 payable at the moment of death for a select life aged 30 subject to the mortality of the A1967–70 table of mortality and 4% interest. What is the proportionate increase in the premium compared to the assurance payable at the end of the year of death?

Exercise 3.8

If a mortality table follows Makeham's Law $\mu_x = A + B c^x$ show that

$$\bar{A}_x = A \bar{a}_x + (\mu_x - A) \bar{a}'_x$$

and determine the rate of interest at which $\bar{a}'_x$ is calculated.

3.4 Relations between continuous functions

$$\bar{A}_x = \int_0^\infty v^t {}_t p_x \mu_{x+t} dt$$

$$= \int_0^\infty v^t \frac{d}{dt} (-{}_t p_x) dt, \quad \text{using formula (1.6.12)}$$

$$= \left[-v^t {}_t p_x \right]_0^\infty - \int_0^\infty (-{}_t p_x) v^t \log_e v \, dt$$

i.e. $$\bar{A}_x = 1 - \delta \bar{a}_x, \tag{3.4.1}$$

as $$-\log_e v = \log_e (1+i) = \delta;$$

the formula obviously being analagous to $A_x = 1 - d\ddot{a}_x$. The formula is also consistent with formula (3.3.7) when m tends to ∞.

The equivalent relationship for the endowment assurance will be found using the limits of integration of 0 and n instead of 0 and ∞;

$$\bar{A}^1_{x:\,\overline{n}|} = \left[-v^t{}_tp_x \right]_0^n - \delta \int_0^n v^t{}_tp_x dt$$

$$= -A_{x:\,\frac{1}{n}|} + 1 - \delta \bar{a}_{x:\,\overline{n}|}$$

$$\therefore \bar{A}_{x:\,\overline{n}|} = 1 - \delta \bar{a}_{x:\,\overline{n}|}. \qquad (3.4.2)$$

The symbol for the annual premium for an assurance payable at the moment of death is $P(\bar{A}_x)$, and if the premium is paid continuously the symbol is $\bar{P}(\bar{A}_x)$. If the premium were to be paid continuously but the benefit paid at the end of the year of death the symbol is $\bar{P}(A_x)$. Obvious extensions to these symbols can be used for other benefits such as temporary insurances.

There will be similar relationships between $\bar{A}$, $\bar{a}$ and $\bar{P}(\bar{A})$ as demonstrated for the yearly functions in section 2.8:

$$\bar{P}(\bar{A}) = \frac{1}{\bar{a}} - \delta$$

$$\bar{a} = \frac{1 - \bar{A}}{\delta}$$

$$\bar{a} = \frac{1}{\bar{P}(\bar{A}) + \delta}$$

$$\bar{A} = \frac{\bar{P}(\bar{A})}{\bar{P}(\bar{A}) + \delta}$$

$$\bar{P}(\bar{A}) = \frac{\delta \bar{A}}{1 - \bar{A}}.$$

Example 3.7

Show that $\bar{C}_x + \delta \bar{D}_x = D_x - D_{x+1}$.

Solution

From the formula above (3.4.2) with $n = 1$

$$\bar{A}^1_{x:\,\overline{1}|} = -A_{x:\,\frac{1}{1}|} + 1 - \delta \bar{a}_{x:\,\overline{1}|}$$

$$\therefore \frac{\bar{C}_x}{D_x} = -\frac{D_{x+1}}{D_x} + 1 - \delta \frac{\bar{D}_x}{D_x}$$

$$\therefore \bar{C}_x + \delta \bar{D}_x = D_x - D_{x+1}.$$

Exercise 3.9

Prove directly, and by using a conversion table relationship, that if (x) is subject to a constant force of mortality of $\cdot 019803$,

$$\bar{A}^1_{x:\overline{1}|} \text{ at } 2\% = \tfrac{1}{2}\delta\bar{a}_{\overline{2t}|}.$$

3.5 Premiums payable m times a year

An assurance may be subject to premiums payable more frequently than once a year, sometimes referred to as fractional premiums. In any particular example it is normally best, as explained in sections 2.5 and 2.6, to equate the present value of the premiums to the present value of the benefits and expenses. The notation for fractional premiums includes the superscript (m)—thus $P^{(m)}_{[x]}$ is the total annual premium payable $m$thly (that is m times the $m$thly payment) for a whole life assurance to a select life aged x, so

$$P^{(m)}_{[x]} = \frac{A_{[x]}}{\ddot{a}^{(m)}_{[x]}}.$$

The premiums actually paid will then be $\dfrac{1}{m} P^{(m)}_{[x]}$ immediately, and the same amount at intervals of $\dfrac{1}{m}$ of a year till death.

While in any case a fractional premium will normally be obtained by equating present values, the relationships between fractional and annual premiums have theoretical interest and may be useful in practice.

As
$$P_x = \frac{A_x}{\ddot{a}_x},$$

$$P^{(m)}_x = \frac{A_x}{\ddot{a}^{(m)}_x} = P_x \cdot \frac{\ddot{a}_x}{\ddot{a}^{(m)}_x}$$

$$\doteqdot P_x \frac{\ddot{a}_x}{\ddot{a}_x - \dfrac{m-1}{2m}}$$

i.e.
$$P^{(m)}_x \doteqdot \frac{P_x}{1 - \dfrac{m-1}{2m}(P_x + d)}, \qquad (3.5.1)$$

using
$$\frac{1}{\ddot{a}_x} = P_x + d.$$

Similarly
$$P_{x:\overline{n}|}^{(m)} = P_{x:\overline{n}|} \frac{\ddot{a}_{x:\overline{n}|}}{\ddot{a}_{x:\overline{n}|}^{(m)}}$$

$$\doteqdot \frac{P_{x:\overline{n}|}}{1 - \dfrac{m-1}{2m}\left(1 - \dfrac{D_{x+n}}{D_x}\right)\dfrac{1}{\ddot{a}_{x:\overline{n}|}}}$$

$$= \frac{P_{x:\overline{n}|}}{1 - \dfrac{m-1}{2m}\left(1 - A_{x:\frac{1}{n}|}\right)\dfrac{1}{\ddot{a}_{x:\overline{n}|}}}$$

$$= \frac{P_{x:\overline{n}|}}{1 - \dfrac{m-1}{2m}\left(P_{x:\overline{n}|} + d - P_{x:\frac{1}{n}|}\right)}$$

i.e.
$$P_{x:\overline{n}|}^{(m)} \doteqdot \frac{P_{x:\overline{n}|}}{1 - \dfrac{m-1}{2m}\left(P_{x:\overline{n}|}^1 + d\right)}. \tag{3.5.2}$$

Note that the premium in the denominator is the temporary assurance and not the endowment assurance premium.

Formulae (3.5.1) and (3.5.2) may be explained verbally. When fractional premiums are paid there are two significant differences from the annual premium—the insurer earns less interest since he receives them on average $\dfrac{m-1}{2m}$ of a year late, and in the year of death the insurer receives less premium, the fractional premiums for the balance of the year not being collected after death has occurred. The amount of the balance will, on the assumption of a uniform distribution of deaths over the year of age, be

$$P_x^{(m)} \frac{1}{m}\left(\frac{m-1}{m} + \frac{m-2}{m} + \dots + \frac{1}{m} + 0\right) = \frac{m-1}{2m} P_x^{(m)},$$

there being $m-1$ payment outstanding if death occurs in the first mth of the year, and so on.

If formula (3.5.1) is written in the following form after multiplying by the denominator of the right-hand side:

$$P_x^{(m)} - \frac{m-1}{2m} P_x^{(m)}(P_x + d) \doteqdot P_x,$$

i.e.
$$P_x^{(m)} \doteqdot P_x + \frac{m-1}{2m} P_x^{(m)} d + \frac{m-1}{2m} P_x^{(m)} P_x, \tag{3.5.3}$$

the second term on the right-hand side represents the loss of interest on the instalment premium for the average delay of $\dfrac{m-1}{2m}$, and the third term represents the premium for the average balance of premiums not collected in the year of death. Similarly we can obtain and explain the expression

$$P^{(m)}_{x:\overline{n}|} \fallingdotseq P_{x:\overline{n}|} + \frac{m-1}{2m} P^{(m)}_{x:\overline{n}|} \cdot d + \frac{m-1}{2m} P^{(m)}_{x:\overline{n}|} \cdot P^1_{x:\overline{n}|} \qquad (3.5.4)$$

noting that a temporary assurance is required to cover the loss of premium on death.

Using this type of formula it is relatively easy to develop similar formulae for other classes—for example

$$_tP^{(m)}_x \fallingdotseq \ _tP_x + \frac{m-1}{2m} \ _tP^{(m)}_x(d + P^1_{x:\overline{t}|}),$$

noting that the temporary assurance is required only for the premium paying period, thus

$$_tP^{(m)}_x \fallingdotseq \frac{_tP_x}{1 - \dfrac{m-1}{2m}(P^1_{x:\overline{t}|} + d)}.$$

The fractional premiums so far discussed are referred to as *true* premiums, and cease with the last payment preceding death, and must be distinguished from *instalment* premiums which continue to be paid until the end of the policy year of death—in practice the balance of the year's instalments is deducted from the sum assured. Instalment premiums have a symbol of the type $P^{[m]}$. It will be seen that the difference between the yearly premium P and the $m$thly instalment premium $P^{[m]}$ is a matter of compound interest and the total number of years payments will be the same in each case. Hence

$$P^{[m]} = P \frac{d^{(m)}}{d}.$$

The ratio $\dfrac{d^{(m)}}{d}$ is not usually tabulated. It is however approximately equal to $\dfrac{i}{i^{(m)}}$ or to $1 + \dfrac{m-1}{2m} i$, giving the approximate formula

$$P^{[m]} \fallingdotseq P\left(1 + \frac{m-1}{2m} i\right), \qquad (3.5.5)$$

the formula being applicable to all classes of assurances.

Another method of finding a formula will be to use the verbal approach leading up to formula (3.5.3). In this case only the loss of interest term is required so that

$$P_x^{[m]} \fallingdotseq P_x + \frac{m-1}{2m} P_x^{[m]} \cdot d$$

or
$$P_x^{[m]} \fallingdotseq \frac{P_x}{1 - \dfrac{m-1}{2m} \cdot d} . \tag{3.5.6}$$

In practice, in addition to the loss of interest and perhaps premiums the additional administrative expenses of more frequent premium collection must be considered, and it is common for life offices to charge a fixed percentage addition in calculating half-yearly, quarterly and monthly true or instalment premiums, and in addition the policy fee may be increased.

Example 3.8
Find the percentage increase of the annual total of the gross monthly true premiums over the gross annual premium for a whole life assurance with sum assured £1,000 payable at the moment of death for a select life aged 50 on the A1967–70 table of mortality and 4% interest. Expenses are 4% of each premium, and 10p on each premium payment.

Solution
If the gross annual premium is P'

$$\cdot 96 P' \ddot{a}_{[50]} = 1{,}000 \bar{A}_{[50]} + \cdot 1 \ddot{a}_{[50]}$$

$$\therefore P' = \frac{(1 \cdot 02)(382 \cdot 57) + \cdot 1(16 \cdot 053)}{(\cdot 96)(16 \cdot 053)}$$

$$= 25 \cdot 43.$$

If the annual total of the gross monthly premiums is P'',

$$\cdot 96 P'' \ddot{a}_{[50]}^{(12)} = 1{,}000 \bar{A}_{[50]} + 1 \cdot 2 \ddot{a}_{[50]}^{(12)}$$

and as
$$\ddot{a}_{[50]}^{(12)} = \ddot{a}_{[50]} - \cdot 458 = 16 \cdot 053 - \cdot 458 = 15 \cdot 595$$

then
$$P'' = \frac{(1 \cdot 02)(382 \cdot 57) + 1 \cdot 2(15 \cdot 595)}{(\cdot 96)(15 \cdot 595)}$$

$$= 27 \cdot 31.$$

So percentage increase is $\dfrac{1 \cdot 88}{25 \cdot 43} \times 100\% = 7 \cdot 4\%$.

Example 3.9

An *apportionable* premium, which is given the symbol $P^{\{m\}}$, is one under which a pro-rata refund for the period from the date of death to the next premium date is made on a claim. Demonstrate that

$$P_x^{\{m\}} \doteqdot \frac{P_x}{1 - \dfrac{m-1}{2m} d - \tfrac{1}{2} P_x}.$$

Solution

Assuming a uniform distribution of deaths in the policy year the insurer will refund an average amount of $\dfrac{1}{2m} P^{\{m\}}$. Thus the sum insured will equivalently be increased to

$$1 + \frac{1}{2m} P_x^{\{m\}},$$

so

$$P_x^{\{m\}} \ddot{a}_x^{(m)} \doteqdot A_x \left(1 + \frac{1}{2m} P_x^{\{m\}}\right),$$

and as

$$\frac{A_x}{\ddot{a}_x^{(m)}} = P_x^{(m)} = \frac{P_x}{1 - \dfrac{m-1}{2m}(P_x + d)}$$

$$P_x^{\{m\}} \left(1 - \frac{m-1}{2m}(P_x + d)\right) \doteqdot P_x \left(1 + \frac{1}{2m} P_x^{\{m\}}\right)$$

giving

$$P_x^{\{m\}} \doteqdot \frac{P_x}{1 - \dfrac{m-1}{2m} d - \tfrac{1}{2} P_x}.$$

Exercise 3.10

Calculate, on the basis of the A1967–70 table of mortality and 4% interest,

$$P_{40}^{(2)}, \; P_{30:\overline{20}|}^{(12)}, \; P_{60}^{\{1\}}.$$

Exercise 3.11

As $m \to \infty$, determine which two of $P_x^{(m)}$, $P_x^{[m]}$, and $P_x^{\{m\}}$ tend to the same limit.

Exercise 3.12

Find an expression for $_tP^{(m)}_{x:\overline{n}|}$.

Exercise 3.13

Demonstrate algebraically and by general reasoning the approximate formula

$$P^{1\,(m)}_{x:\overline{n}|} = \frac{P^1_{x:\overline{n}|}}{1 - \dfrac{m-1}{2m}(P^1_{x:\overline{n}|}+d)}.$$

3.6 Complete and other special annuities

A complete or apportionable annuity, also referred to as an annuity with final proportion, is an annuity under which on the death of the annuitant an additional payment is made proportionate to the time elapsed since the last payment. The normal annuity without final proportion may also be referred to as curtate. The symbol for the complete annuity is $\mathring{a}_x$ or $\mathring{a}^{(m)}_x$ if $m$thly. The difference between $\mathring{a}_x$ and a_x is the final payment which assuming a uniform distribution of deaths in the year of age, will be $\frac{1}{2}$ on average, and multiplying by $\bar{A}_x$ to obtain the present value we obtain the approximate formula

$$\mathring{a}_x = a_x + \tfrac{1}{2}\bar{A}_x, \tag{3.6.1}$$

and for the $m$thly annuity

$$\mathring{a}^{(m)}_x = a^{(m)}_x + \frac{1}{2m}\bar{A}_x. \tag{3.6.2}$$

Using a diagrammatic method similar to that in section 3.1, we can consider the difference between $\mathring{a}^{(m)}_x$ and $\bar{a}_x$. The total amount payable will be the same, but in the case of $\mathring{a}^{(m)}_x$ each payment will be at the end of the period to which it relates, whereas in the case of $\bar{a}_x$ the payment is spread evenly. Each mth of a year's payment of the complete annuity is thus paid $\dfrac{1}{2m}$ of a year on average later than under the continuous annuity. It follows that

$$\mathring{a}^{(m)}_x \doteqdot v^{\frac{1}{2m}}\bar{a}_x,$$

which is normally expressed as

$$\mathring{a}^{(m)}_x \doteqdot \left(1 - \frac{\delta}{2m}\right)\bar{a}_x, \tag{3.6.3}$$

using
$$v^{\frac{1}{2m}} \fallingdotseq 1 - \frac{\delta}{2m}.$$

Formula (3.6.3) could have been obtained by substitution of

$$a_x^{(m)} \fallingdotseq a_x + \frac{m-1}{2m} \fallingdotseq \bar{a}_x - \frac{1}{2m},$$

and $\bar{A}_x = 1 - \delta\bar{a}_x$ in formula (3.6.2) as follows:

$$\ddot{a}_x^{(m)} \fallingdotseq \bar{a}_x - \frac{1}{2m} + \frac{1}{2m}(1 - \delta\bar{a}_x)$$

$$= \bar{a}_x\left(1 - \frac{\delta}{2m}\right).$$

When temporary annuities are considered, the formula used will be

$$\ddot{a}_{x:\overline{n}|}^{(m)} \fallingdotseq a_{x:\overline{n}|}^{(m)} + \frac{1}{2m}\bar{A}_{x:\overline{n}|}^1 \tag{3.6.4}$$

or
$$\ddot{a}_{x:\overline{n}|}^{(m)} \fallingdotseq \bar{a}_{x:\overline{n}|}\left(1 - \frac{\delta}{2m}\right). \tag{3.6.5}$$

An annuity may commence after a fractional period of deferment, for example a yearly annuity may commence after a fraction k of a year. This is normally evaluated by using first difference interpolation between $\ddot{a}_x$ (first payment deferred 0 years) and a_x (first payment deferred 1 year). Thus

$$_k|\ddot{a}_x \fallingdotseq (1-k)\ddot{a}_x + ka_x$$

$$= (1-k)\ddot{a}_x + k(\ddot{a}_x - 1),$$

i.e.
$$_k|\ddot{a}_x \fallingdotseq \ddot{a}_x - k. \tag{3.6.6}$$

Formulae for other types of annuity may be obtained by similar interpolation, for example (see example 3.11)

$$_k|\ddot{a}_{x:\overline{n}|} \fallingdotseq \ddot{a}_{x:\overline{n}|} - k\left(1 - \frac{D_{x+n}}{D_x}\right)$$

or
$$\fallingdotseq (1-k)\ddot{a}_{x:\overline{n}|} + ka_{x:\overline{n}|},$$

the second being more useful in practice if temporary annuities are tabulated.

In the case of an $m$thly annuity deferred for a part k of a year where k is less than $\dfrac{1}{m}$, we have

$$_0|\ddot{a}_x^{(m)} = \ddot{a}_x^{(m)}$$

and

$$_{\frac{1}{m}}|\ddot{a}_x^{(m)} = a_x^{(m)} = \ddot{a}_x^{(m)} - \frac{1}{m};$$

and interpolating $\quad _k|\ddot{a}_x^{(m)} \fallingdotseq \ddot{a}_x^{(m)} - k$

i.e.

$$_k|\ddot{a}_x^{(m)} \fallingdotseq \ddot{a}_x - \left(\frac{m-1}{2m} + k\right). \tag{3.6.7}$$

An annuity is frequently issued subject to the provision that payments will continue for at least a period of years even if the annuitant does not survive that period—such an annuity may be referred to as a 'term and life' annuity, or as a 'guaranteed' annuity. Normally the period is five or ten years. Such an annuity is an annuity certain followed by a deferred annuity, and is given the symbol $a_{\overline{x:\overline{n}|}}$, where x is the age of the life and n is the guaranteed term. Thus

$$a_{\overline{x:\overline{n}|}} = a_{\overline{n}|} + {}_n|a_x \tag{3.6.8}$$

and

$$a_{\overline{x:\overline{n}|}}^{(m)} = a_{\overline{n}|}^{(m)} + {}_n|a_x^{(m)}.$$

A different annuity is that payable during the lifetime of x and continuing n years after death. In this case the annuity will be paid during the first n years in any event and afterwards if the life was alive n years previously, i.e. a payment is made at time t if the life was alive at time $t-n$.

The yearly annuity will have value

$$a_{\overline{n}|} + \sum_{t=n+1}^{\infty} v^t \, {}_{t-n}p_x, \text{ and if } s = t - n,$$

$$= a_{\overline{n}|} + \sum_{s=1}^{\infty} v^{s+n} \, {}_sp_x,$$

$$= a_{\overline{n}|} + v^n a_x.$$

Similarly the continuous annuity is found,

$$\bar{a}_{\overline{n}|} + \int_r^{\infty} v_t^t \, {}_{t-n}p_x \, dt, \quad \text{and substituting } s = t-n,$$

$$= \bar{a}_{\overline{n}|} + \int_0^{\infty} v^{s+n} \, {}_sp_x \, dt$$

$$= \bar{a}_{\overline{n}|} + v^n \bar{a}_x.$$

All the annuities considered so far have assumed payments yearly or more frequently. If payment were at intervals of r years the value may be obtained

$$\frac{1}{D_x}(D_{x+r}+D_{x+2r}+D_{x+3r}+\ldots).$$

If r is small, this will be laborious to evaluate. By making $m = \dfrac{1}{r}$ in formula (3.1.3) we obtain the expression

$$a_x + \frac{1-r}{2} - \frac{1-r^2}{12}(\mu_x+\delta)$$

as the value of payments each of r, so that the value of payments of 1 each will be

$$\frac{1}{r}\left(a_x - \frac{r-1}{2} + \frac{r^2-1}{12}(\mu_x+\delta)\right) \qquad (3.6.9)$$

and in this case the last term may be significant and should not be ignored as it does not have r^2 in the denominator.

Example 3.10

Find the value of $\ddot{a}_{70}^{(2)}$ on the A1967–70 table of mortality with 4% interest by two different formulae.

Solution

Formula (3.6.2) gives

$$\ddot{a}_{70}^{(2)} = 7\cdot957 + \cdot25 + \frac{1}{(2)(2)}(1\cdot02)(\cdot65550)$$

$$= 8\cdot374.$$

Formula (3.6.3) gives

$$\ddot{a}_{70}^{(2)} = \left(1 - \frac{\cdot039221}{(2)(2)}\right)8\cdot457$$

$$= 8\cdot374.$$

Example 3.11

Prove the formula given in the previous section for $_k|\ddot{a}_{x:\overline{n}|}$, where $0 < k < 1$.

Solution

$$_0|\ddot{a}_{x:\overline{n}|} = \ddot{a}_{x:\overline{n}|}$$

$$_1|\ddot{a}_{x:\overline{n}|} = a_{x:\overline{n}|} = \ddot{a}_{x:\overline{n}|} - \left(1 - \frac{D_{x+n}}{D_x}\right).$$

By first difference interpolation

$$_k|\ddot{a}_{x:\overline{n}|} \doteqdot (1-k)\ddot{a}_{x:\overline{n}|} + ka_{x:\overline{n}|}$$

or

$$\doteqdot \ddot{a}_{x:\overline{n}|} - k\left(1 - \frac{D_{x+n}}{D_x}\right).$$

Example 3.12

Show that

$$\mathring{a}_x = a_x + \sum_{n=0}^{\infty} v^n {}_n p_x \int_0^1 tv^t {}_t p_{x+n} \mu_{x+n+t} dt,$$

and by assuming a uniform distribution of deaths over the year of age, derive the approximate formula

$$\mathring{a}_x \doteqdot a_x + A_x \left(\frac{i-\delta}{\delta^2}\right).$$

Solution

The payment on death at time $x+n+t$, where $0 \leq t < 1$ is t, the present value being $tv^{n+t} {}_{n+t}p_x$, so that the value of the payment on death, between ages $x+n$ and $x+n+1$ will be

$$\int_0^1 tv^{n+t} {}_{n+t}p_x \mu_{x+n+t} dt$$

$$= v^n {}_n p_x \int_0^1 tv^t {}_t p_{x+n} \mu_{x+n+t} dt.$$

Summing over n from 0 to ∞ gives the expression required when added to the yearly annuity.

If deaths are uniformly distributed over the year of age

$$_t p_{x+n} \mu_{x+n+t}$$

is constant and equals q_{x+n}, so the additional term becomes

$$\sum_{n=0}^{\infty} v^n {}_n p_x q_{x+n} \int_0^1 tv^t dt,$$

the integral being independent of n, and the first part being $A_x(1+i)$.

Now $\displaystyle\int_0^1 tv^t dt = \int_0^1 td\left(\frac{e^{-\delta t}}{-\delta}\right)$ and integrating by parts,

$$= \left[\frac{e^{-\delta t}}{-\delta}t\right]_0^1 - \int_0^1 \frac{e^{-\delta t}}{-\delta} \cdot dt$$

$$= \frac{v}{-\delta} - \left[\frac{e^{-\delta t}}{\delta^2}\right]_0^1$$

$$= \frac{-v\delta - v + 1}{\delta^2},$$

so the expression becomes

$$A_x \frac{(1+i)(1-v-v\delta)}{\delta^2}$$

$$= A_x\left(\frac{i-\delta}{\delta^2}\right).$$

Exercise 3.14

Demonstrate the approximate formula

$$\ddot{a}^{(m)}_{x:\overline{n}|} \doteqdot \bar{a}_{x:\overline{n}|}\frac{\delta}{i^{(m)}}$$

Exercise 3.15

Explain by general reasoning the relation

$$\bar{A}_x \doteqdot 1 - i\mathring{a}_x$$

showing why the formula is not exact.

Exercise 3.16

Find the values of $_{\frac{1}{4}|}\ddot{a}^{(2)}_{50:\overline{20}|}$ and $\mathring{a}^{(4)}_{60}$ on the A 1967-70 table of mortality and 4% interest.

Exercise 3.17

Show that

$$_k|\ddot{a}^{(m)}_{x:\overline{n}|} \doteqdot \ddot{a}^{(m)}_{x:\overline{n}|} - k\left(1 - \frac{D_{x+n}}{D_x}\right) \quad \text{where } 0 < k < \frac{1}{m}.$$

Exercise 3.18

Find the value of an annuity of 1 payable every three years commencing immediately to a life aged 60 on the A1967-70 table of mortality with 4% interest.

3.7 Family income benefit

Family Income Benefit, F.I.B. for short, is the name given to a form of decreasing temporary insurance which provides on death within a fixed period of the commencement of the policy, say n years, an income, normally payable monthly, for the balance of the n-year period. If the payments are made on the same day of the month as the day of issue, the value for a benefit of 1 per annum will be

$$a_{\overline{n}|}^{(12)} - a_{x:\overline{n}|}^{(12)} \tag{3.7.1}$$

the difference between the annuity certain and the temporary life annuity clearly giving the value of the benefits after death. Alternatively this expression could have been obtained from

$$\sum_{t=1}^{12n} v^{\frac{t}{12}} \left(1 - {}_{\frac{t}{12}}p_x\right),$$

each payment being made if the life has died.

The expression may be adapted if the benefit is paid other than monthly or on different days in the month—for example if the benefit commences immediately on death it will be paid on average half a month earlier and will have the approximate value

$$(1+i)^{\frac{1}{24}} (a_{\overline{n}|}^{(12)} - a_{x:\overline{n}|}^{(12)}).$$

Also of interest is the benefit paid continuously commencing at death, which will have the value

$$\int_0^n v^t {}_tp_x \mu_{x+t} \bar{a}_{\overline{n-t}|} dt \tag{3.7.2}$$

$$= \int_0^n v^t \frac{1-v^{n-t}}{\delta} \frac{d}{dt}(-{}_tp_x)dt$$

as $\dfrac{d}{dt}({}_tp_x) = -{}_tp_x \mu_{x+t}$, and integrating by parts,

$$= \left[v^t \bar{a}_{\overline{n-t}|}(-{}_tp_x) \right]_0^n + \frac{1}{\delta} \int_0^n {}_tp_x \frac{d}{dt}(v^t - v^n)dt$$

$$= 0 + \bar{a}_{\overline{n}|} + \frac{1}{\delta} \int_0^n {}_tp_x v^t(-\delta)dt$$

$$= \bar{a}_{\overline{n}|} - \bar{a}_{x:\overline{n}|},$$

which could obviously have been obtained using the general reasoning approach above.

Another formula can be obtained by re-writing expression (3.7.2) as

$$\int_0^n \frac{v^t - v^n}{\delta}\, {}_tp_x\mu_{x+t}dt$$

$$= \frac{1}{\delta}\, \bar{A}^1_{x:\,\overline{n}|} - \frac{v^n}{\delta}\, {}_nq_x. \tag{3.7.3}$$

The verbal interpretation of this expression is interesting—from a perpetuity of 1 commencing on death within n years is subtracted the perpetuity of payments made after the n years provided death occurred.

If the benefits, though paid monthly or quarterly, are in total proportionate to the period following the date of death so that a proportion is paid either on death or at the end of the term, an approximation based on the continuous benefit should be used (and sometimes as the inaccuracy is not large no adjustment to the continuous value is made). An alternative approach is to use a complete annuity—for example a quarterly benefit will approximately equal

$$a^{(4)}_{\overline{n}|} - \ddot{a}^{(4)}_{x:\,\overline{n}|}.$$

While at one time a family income benefit was only allowed by an insurance company if an endowment insurance was also effected, now it is normally issued on a separate contract. When issued with an endowment assurance some or all of the death benefit under the endowment assurance may be deferred until the end of the assurance period—an example is shown below.

Example 3.13

Find the net annual premium payable for fifteen years for a family income benefit of £10 per month with an income term of twenty years for a life aged 45 on the A1967–70 ultimate table of mortality and 4% interest. Each month's payment is made on the same day of the month as the policy was effected.

Solution

If the premium is P,

$$P\ddot{a}_{45:\,\overline{15}|} = 120(a^{(12)}_{\overline{20}|} - a^{(12)}_{45:\,\overline{20}|})$$

i.e. $P = \dfrac{120\left[(13\cdot5903)(1\cdot018204)-\left\{13\cdot488-\cdot542\left(1-\dfrac{2{,}144\cdot2}{5{,}689\cdot2}\right)\right\}\right]}{11\cdot235}$

$= \dfrac{120(13\cdot8377-13\cdot1503)}{11\cdot235}$

$= 7\cdot34.$

i.e. net annual premium is £7·34.

This example shows that, as the value of a family income benefit is found by the subtraction of the value of two almost equal annuities relatively small approximations or inaccuracies in the calculation of the annuities will make a large proportionate difference to the final answer.

Example 3.14

Find two expressions for the value of a combined endowment assurance of $2S$ and a family income benefit of I per annum for a life aged x, the terms of both benefits being n years, and show that they are equal. Half of the sum assured under the endowment assurance is deferred until the end of the term, if the life assured dies within the term, the other half being paid at the end of the year of death. The income benefit is paid yearly on each policy anniversary following death.

Solution

The benefit is

$$SA_{x:\,\overline{n}|}+Sv^{n}+I(a_{\overline{n}|}-a_{x:\,\overline{n}|}).$$

Alternatively, considering the endowment benefit as paid immediately, but reducing the income benefit by the interest which would be paid on half the sum assured, but noting that there will be no interest adjustment for the first payment of income benefit, the value is

$$2SA_{x:\,\overline{n}|}+(I-Si)(a_{\overline{n}|}-a_{x:\,\overline{n}|})+SiA^{1}_{x:\,\overline{n}|}.$$

This second expression is

$$SA_{x:\,\overline{n}|}+I(a_{\overline{n}|}-a_{x:\,\overline{n}|})+S(1+i)A_{x:\,\overline{n}|}-SiA_{x:\,\overline{n}|}^{\,\frac{1}{}}-Sia_{\overline{n}|}+Sia_{x:\,\overline{n}|}$$

$$= SA_{x:\,\overline{n}|}+I(a_{\overline{n}|}-a_{x:\,\overline{n}|})+S(1+i)A_{x:\,\overline{n}|}-S(1-v^{n})+Si\ddot{a}_{x:\,\overline{n}|}-Si$$

$$= SA_{x:\,\overline{n}|}+I(a_{\overline{n}|}-a_{x:\,\overline{n}|})+Sv^{n}+S(1+i)(A_{x:\,\overline{n}|}+d\ddot{a}_{x:\,\overline{n}|})-S(1+i)$$

which equals the first expression, the last two terms cancelling.

Example 3.15

Find an expression for the value of a family income benefit which is payable continuously and increases from the date of death at the rate of j per annum.

Solution

The value of the benefit at the time of death t is

$$\int_0^{n-t} v^s(1+j)^s ds$$

$$= \bar{a}'_{\overline{n-t}|} \text{ at rate of interest } i' \text{ where } \frac{1+j}{1+i} = \frac{1}{1+i'}$$

i.e. $i' = \dfrac{i-j}{1+j}.$

The value of the total benefit is then

$$\int_0^n v^t {}_tp_x\mu_{x+t}\bar{a}'_{\overline{n-t}|} dt$$

$$= \int_0^n v^t \frac{1-v'^{n-t}}{\delta} {}_tp_x\mu_{x+t} dt$$

$$= \frac{1}{\delta} \bar{A}^1_{x:\overline{n}|} - \frac{v'^n}{\delta} \bar{A}''^1_{x:\overline{n}|},$$

where A'' is at rate of interest such that

$$\frac{v}{v'} = v''$$

i.e. $\dfrac{1+i'}{1+i} = \dfrac{1}{1+i''}$

i.e. $\dfrac{1}{1+j} = \dfrac{1}{1+i''}$

i.e. $i'' = j.$

Exercise 3.19

Use two different formulae to calculate a family income benefit of £100 per quarter for a term of 25 years for a life aged 40, the first payment being in proportion to the period from the date of death to the date of payment. Mortality is A1967–70 and interest 4%.

Exercise 3.20

Find the annual premium payable for twenty years for a life aged 40 for a combined endowment assurance for £5,000 and family income benefit of £50 per month. The term of the endowment assurance is thirty years and of the assurance benefit is twenty years, and no endowment benefit is paid until income benefit ceases. The income benefit commences immediately on death and a final pro-portional payment is made. Assume A1967–70 mortality and 4% interest.

Exercise 3.21

Find an expression for a family income benefit which is payable continuously and under which the rate of payment at any time is equivalent to the rate of payment that would have been paid on death if this had occurred immediately the policy was effected increased at the rate of j per annum.

3.8 Increasing functions

The increasing commutation functions S_x and R_x were introduced in section 2.7 together with the symbols $(I\ddot{a})_x$, $(Ia)_x$ and $(IA)_x$. In this section increasing continuous functions will be considered. The value of an increasing continuous annuity under which the payments during the tth year are at the rate of t per annum is given the symbol $(I\bar{a})_x$. This annuity is a sum of continuous annuities deferred 0, 1, 2, ... years and will have value

$$(I\bar{a})_x = \sum_{t=0}^{\infty} {}_t|\bar{a}_x = \frac{1}{D_x} \sum_{t=0}^{\infty} \bar{N}_{x+t}$$

and if $\bar{S}_x$ is defined as $\sum_{t=0}^{\infty} \bar{N}_{x+t}$,

$$(I\bar{a})_x = \frac{\bar{S}_x}{D_x}. \tag{3.8.1}$$

It must be noted that the payments under this annuity, although made continuously, do not increase continuously. If the annuity increases continuously it is given the symbol $(\bar{I}\bar{a})_x$ and is defined as follows:

$$(\bar{I}\bar{a})_x = \int_0^{\infty} t v^t {}_t p_x dt \tag{3.8.2}$$

or

$$= \frac{1}{D_x} \int_0^{\infty} t D_{x+t} dt.$$

Similarly we may define the increasing assurance functions—first a benefit paid at the moment of death of amount 1 in the first year, 2 in the second etc.,

$$(I\bar{A})_x = \sum_{t=0}^{\infty} {}_t|\bar{A}_x = \frac{1}{D_x} \sum_{t=0}^{\infty} \bar{M}_{x+t}$$

and if $\bar{R}_x$ is defined as $\sum_{t=0}^{\infty} \bar{M}_{x+t}$

$$(I\bar{A})_x = \frac{\bar{R}_x}{D_x}. \tag{3.8.3}$$

It was proved in example 2.12 that

$$(IA)_x = \ddot{a}_x - d(I\ddot{a})_x. \tag{3.8.4}$$

To find the similar expression for $(I\bar{A})_x$, we multiply the expression $\bar{A}_x = 1 - \delta\bar{a}_x$ by D_x giving $\bar{M}_x = D_x - \delta\bar{N}_x$, and summing gives $\bar{R}_x = N_x - \delta\bar{S}_x$, and dividing by D_x gives

$$(I\bar{A})_x = \ddot{a}_x - \delta(I\bar{a})_x. \tag{3.8.5}$$

This formula can also be verified by general reasoning by assuming that (x) is entitled to an annuity-due of 1 payable yearly for the rest of his life, that he invests each payment as soon as it is made, and that he receives the interest payable continuously leaving the invested payments intact until death.

The value of a whole-life assurance with sum assured proportional to the duration so that the benefit at time t is t, is given the symbol

$$(\bar{I}\bar{A})_x = \int_0^{\infty} tv^t {}_tp_x\mu_{x+t}dt \tag{3.8.6}$$

or

$$= \frac{1}{D_x} \int_0^{\infty} tD_{x+t}\mu_{x+t}dt.$$

The latter expression

$$= \frac{1}{D_x} \int_0^{\infty} tD_{x+t}(\mu_{x+t}+\delta)dt - \frac{1}{D_x} \int_0^{\infty} tD_{x+t}.\delta dt$$

$$= -\frac{1}{D_x} \int_0^{\infty} t\frac{d}{dt}(D_{x+t})dt - \delta(\bar{I}\bar{a})_x \text{ using formula (3.1.1)}$$

$$= -\frac{1}{D_x} \left\{ \left[tD_{x+t} \right]_0^{\infty} - \int_0^{\infty} D_{x+t}dt \right\} - \delta(\bar{I}\bar{a})_x \text{ integrating by parts,}$$

i.e.

$$(\bar{I}\bar{A})_x = \bar{a}_x - \delta(\bar{I}\bar{a})_x \tag{3.8.7}$$

the first term vanishing at both limits.

This formula can obviously also be obtained by general reasoning.

The normal approximations used in evaluating increasing functions are as follows:

$$(I\bar{a})_x \doteqdot \frac{S_x - \frac{1}{2}N_x}{D_x} \qquad (3.8.8)$$

assuming that $\bar{S}_x \doteqdot S_x - \frac{1}{2}N_x$, which may be obtained by summing formula (3.2.8). The approximate formula

$$(\bar{I}\bar{a})_x \doteqdot (Ia)_x + \frac{1}{12} \qquad (3.8.9)$$

will be demonstrated in Example 3.18 below.

The formula for $(I\bar{A})_x$ is approximated to by using a normal claim acceleration approximation,

i.e. $\qquad (I\bar{A})_x \doteqdot \left(1 + \frac{i}{2}\right)(IA)_x \quad \text{or} \quad (1+i)^{\frac{1}{2}}(IA)_x. \qquad (3.8.10)$

In $(\bar{I}\bar{A})_x$ the sums assured in successive years are 1, 2, 3, 4 ... while the average sum assured with $(\bar{I}\bar{A})_x$ is $\frac{1}{2}$, $1\frac{1}{2}$, $2\frac{1}{2}$ ... so that

$$(\bar{I}\bar{A})_x \doteqdot (I\bar{A})_x - \frac{1}{2}\bar{A}_x$$

or $\qquad (\bar{I}\bar{A})_x \doteqdot \left(1 + \frac{i}{2}\right)\{(IA)_x - \frac{1}{2}A_x\}. \qquad (3.8.11)$

While whole-life functions have been considered in this section temporary and endowment functions can also be evaluated—for example

$$(I\bar{A})_{x:\overline{n}|} \doteqdot \left(1 + \frac{i}{2}\right)(IA)^1_{x:\overline{n}|} + nA_{x:\overline{n}|}^{\ 1}.$$

Example 3.16

On the basis of the A1967–70 table of mortality and 4% interest find values for

$$(I\bar{a})_{50}, (\bar{I}\bar{A})_{[60]}, (I\bar{a})_{40:\overline{10}|}.$$

Solution

$$(I\bar{a})_{50} \doteqdot \frac{S_{50} - \frac{1}{2}N_{50}}{D_{50}}$$

$$= \frac{894{,}480 - \frac{1}{2}(73{,}567 \cdot 1)}{4{,}597 \cdot 06}$$

$$= 186 \cdot 57.$$

$$(I\bar{A})_{[60]} \doteqdot (1 \cdot 02)\left(\frac{R_{[60]}}{D_{[60]}} - \tfrac{1}{2}A_{[60]}\right)$$

$$= (1 \cdot 02)\left(\frac{22{,}589 \cdot 9}{2{,}815 \cdot 30} - \tfrac{1}{2}(\cdot 51114)\right)$$

$$= 7 \cdot 924.$$

$$(I\bar{a})_{40:\overline{10}|} = (I\bar{a})_{40} - \frac{D_{50}}{D_{40}}\{(I\bar{a})_{50} + 10\bar{a}_{50}\}$$

$$\doteqdot \frac{S_{40} - \tfrac{1}{2}N_{40}}{D_{40}} - \frac{D_{50}}{D_{40}}\left(\frac{S_{50} - \tfrac{1}{2}N_{50} + 10(N_{50} - \tfrac{1}{2}D_{50})}{D_{50}}\right)$$

$$= \frac{1{,}931{,}544 - \tfrac{1}{2}(132{,}002)}{6{,}986 \cdot 50} - \frac{894{,}480 + (9\tfrac{1}{2})(73{,}567 \cdot 1) - (5)(4{,}597 \cdot 06)}{6{,}986 \cdot 50}$$

$$= 267 \cdot 02 - 224 \cdot 77$$

$$= 42 \cdot 25.$$

Example 3.17

A whole-life assurance policy for a life aged 60 provides a benefit immediately on death proportional to the duration so that the benefit on death exactly at duration 1 year is £200. The premiums are payable weekly and remain constant during each year, but increase each year so that the total premium paid in the first year is P, $2P$ in the second year, $3P$ in the third year etc. Find P on the basis of the A1967–70 mortality table and 4% interest with expenses of 10% of each premium.

Solution

$\cdot 9P(I\bar{a})_{60} = 200(I\bar{A})_{60}$, assuming that weekly payments are equivalent to continuous payments;

i.e. $\quad \cdot 9P\dfrac{S_{60} - \tfrac{1}{2}N_{60}}{D_{60}} = 200(1 \cdot 02)\left(\dfrac{R_{60}}{D_{60}} - \tfrac{1}{2}\dfrac{M_{60}}{D_{60}}\right)$

$$\therefore P = \frac{200(1 \cdot 02)(22{,}644 \cdot 6 - \tfrac{1}{2}(1{,}477 \cdot 08))}{\cdot 9(343{,}113 - \tfrac{1}{2}(35{,}841 \cdot 3))}$$

$$= 15 \cdot 27,$$

i.e. total premium paid in first year is £15·27.

Example 3.18

Demonstrate the approximate formula

$$(\bar{I}\bar{a})_x \fallingdotseq (Ia)_x + \tfrac{1}{12}.$$

Solution

If the operational identity

$$\sum = \frac{1}{D} - \tfrac{1}{2} + \tfrac{1}{12}D - \dots$$

discussed in section 3.1 is applied to the function $t\dfrac{D_{x+t}}{D_x}$ between the limits 0 and ∞ we obtain

$$\sum_{t=0}^{\infty} t\frac{D_{x+t}}{D_x} \fallingdotseq \int_0^{\infty} t\frac{D_{x+t}}{D_x}\,dt - \tfrac{1}{2}\left[t\frac{D_{x+t}}{D_x}\right]_0^{\infty} + \tfrac{1}{12}\left[\frac{d}{dt}\left(t\frac{D_{x+t}}{D_x}\right)\right]_0^{\infty},$$

and the last term will be $\dfrac{1}{12D_x}[D_{x+t} - tD_{x+t}(\mu_{x+t} + \delta)]_0^{\infty}$ using (3.1.1), so

$$(Ia)_x \fallingdotseq (\bar{I}\bar{a}_x)_x + \frac{1}{12}\frac{(-D_x)}{D_x}$$

as tD_{x+t} and $tD_{x+t}\mu_{x+t}$ are 0 when $t = 0$ and at the limit of life. Thus $(\bar{I}\bar{a})_x = (Ia)_x + \tfrac{1}{12}$ as required.

Exercise 3.22

Find values for $(\bar{I}\bar{A})_{[30]:\overline{30|}}$ and $(\bar{I}\bar{a})_{25:\overline{15|}}$ on the A1967–70 table with 4% interest.

Exercise 3.23

Demonstrate algebraically and by general reasoning a relationship between $(I\bar{A})_x$ and $(I\mathring{a})_x$.

Exercise 3.24

Assuming a uniform distribution of deaths over the year of age find an expression for $(\bar{I}\bar{A})^1_{x:\overline{1|}}$

Exercise 3.25

A whole-life assurance with premiums payable weekly for sum assured £1,000 also provides that the premiums will be returned at the moment of death. Find the premium for a life aged 40 on the A1967–70 table with 4% interest, expenses being 5% of each premium.

EXAMPLES AND EXERCISES ON CHAPTER 3

This chapter has introduced the notation and formulae for annuities payable at intervals other than once a year, assurances payable at the moment of death, and premiums based on these annuities and assurance. The introductory treatment on increasing functions in Chapter 2 has been expanded.

It may be opportune at this point to remind students of the forms of the formulae for integration by parts and double integration, one being more useful than another in some questions. These are

$$\int_a^b u\,dv = \left[uv \right]_a^b - \int_a^b v\,du, \tag{3.9.1}$$

$$\int_a^b u_t v_t dt = u_b \int_a^b v_t dt - \int_a^b \frac{du_t}{dt}\left(\int_a^t v_r dr \right) dt \tag{3.9.2}$$

or

$$\qquad\qquad = u_a \int_a^b v_t dt + \int_a^b \frac{du_t}{dt}\left(\int_t^b v_r dr \right) dt, \tag{3.9.3}$$

$$\int_a^b u_t \left(\int_a^t v_r dr \right) dt = \int_a^b v_t \left(\int_t^b u_r dr \right) dt. \tag{3.9.4}$$

Example 3.19

An endowment assurance policy is about to mature on a man's 65th birthday and he is considering various ways of applying the sum of £3,000 available. Find the following options:

(a) the sum payable in twenty half-yearly instalments, the first payable immediately, assuming interest at $2\frac{1}{2}\%$ per annum,

(b) the annuity, payable quarterly in advance, guaranteed for five years, assuming mortality on the A1967–70 table select and 4% interest, with an expense charge of 10p on each payment of the annuity,

(c) the annuity, payable half-yearly in arrears to his wife aged 62 exactly, with proportion to the date of death, assuming mortality on the $a(55)$ female table select and 4% interest with an expense charge of 3% of the purchase money.

Solution

(a) Let S be sum payable each year, then

$$S\ddot{a}_{\overline{10}|}^{(2)} = 3,000$$

$$\therefore S = \frac{3,000}{(8\cdot7521)(1\cdot018711)}$$

$$= 336\cdot48$$

each payment is £168·24, the total sum paid being £3,364·80.

(b) Let A be the annual amount of annuity, then

$$(A+0\cdot40)\left(\ddot{a}_{\overline{5}|}^{(4)} + \frac{D_{70}}{D_{[65]}}\,\ddot{a}_{70}^{(4)}\right) = 3{,}000,$$

i.e.

$$(A+0\cdot40)\left\{(4\cdot4518)(1\cdot0249) + \frac{1{,}517\cdot00}{2{,}087\cdot57}(8\cdot957 - \cdot375)\right\} = 3{,}000,$$

i.e.

$$A+0\cdot40 = \frac{3{,}000}{10\cdot843}$$

$$\therefore A = 276\cdot67.$$

So annual amount of annuity is £276·67 each payment being £69·17.

(c) Let W be the annual annuity, then

$$W(a_{[62]}^{(2)} + \tfrac{1}{4}(1\cdot02)(1 - d\ddot{a}_{[62]})) = (\cdot97)(3{,}000),$$

i.e. $$W\left\{(12\cdot643 + \cdot25) + \frac{1\cdot02}{4}\{1 - (\cdot03846)(13\cdot643)\}\right\} = 2{,}910,$$

i.e.

$$W = \frac{2{,}910}{13\cdot014}$$

$$= 223\cdot60$$

so total payment each year is £223·60, each payment being £111·80.

Example 3.20

A double endowment assurance is one in which the sum assured at maturity is twice the sum assured payable in the event of previous death, and is thus a combination of a normal endowment assurance and a pure endowment.

Find the net annual premium for a select life aged 40 on the A1967–70 table of mortality with 4% interest for such a policy with sum assured £1,000 increasing to £2,000 on survivance. The term of the policy is 25 years and the sum assured is payable at the moment of death.

Find also the additional premium which should be charged if the policy contains the additional benefit that on death the sum paid will not be less than the premiums paid.

Solution

Let P be the normal annual premium, then

$$P\ddot{a}_{[40]:\,\overline{25}|} = 1,000(1 \cdot 02)(A^{1}_{[40]:\,\overline{25}|}) + 2,000(A_{[40]:\,\overline{25}|} - A^{1}_{[40]:\,\overline{25}|})$$

i.e. $P(15 \cdot 609) = 1,020(\cdot 09255) + 2,000(\cdot 39966 - \cdot 09255)$

$$\therefore P = 45 \cdot 40$$

so annual premium is £45·40.

The additional premium for the final part of the question must be evaluated by finding the total premium for the total benefit. The additional premium is likely to be small as the period during which the larger benefit will be paid will be only the last few years. As a first guess assume the premium is £46, then as 1,000 divided by 46 is 21·7 the benefit would be greater than £1,000 after 22 premiums are paid, that is the extra benefit would be paid only during the last four years.

Thus if P' is the total premium—

$$P'\ddot{a}_{[40]:\,\overline{25}|} = 1,000(1 \cdot 02)A^{1}_{[40]:\,\overline{21}|}$$

$$+ (1 \cdot 02)(P') \frac{22C_{61} + 23C_{62} + 24C_{63} + 25C_{64}}{D_{[40]}} + 2,000A^{1}_{[40]:\,\overline{25}|}$$

$$\therefore P' \left\{ 15 \cdot 609 - \frac{1 \cdot 02}{6,981 \cdot 60} \left\{ 22(41 \cdot 668) + 23(43 \cdot 698) + 24(45 \cdot 701) \right. \right.$$

$$\left. \left. + 25(47 \cdot 657) \right\} \right\}$$

$$= 1,020 \left(\frac{1,904 \cdot 86 - 1,437 \cdot 46}{6,981 \cdot 60} \right) + 2,000(\cdot 39966 - \cdot 09255)$$

$$\therefore P'(14 \cdot 994) = 682 \cdot 51$$

$$\therefore P' = 45 \cdot 52.$$

Dividing 1,000 by 45·52 gives 21·97 so that after 22 premiums have been paid the benefit changes from £1,000 to the sum of the premiums as has been assumed. If the assumption had not been correct we would of course have had to assume a different number of years and recalculate.

The required additional premium is thus 12p per annum.

Example 3.21

A policy with sum assured £1,000 payable at the moment of death before age 60 also returns on death all premiums accumulated at 4% per annum compound interest. Find the net annual premium for a life aged 40, on the basis of the A1967–70 table of mortality and 4% interest.

Solution

The present value of the return of premiums benefit on death in the $(t+1)$th year is

$$v^t P s_{\overline{t+1}|} \int_0^1 (1+i)^r v^r {}_r p_{40+t} \mu_{40+t+r} dr,$$

and as all interest functions are at the same rate of interest this

$$= P \ddot{a}_{\overline{t+1}|t|} q_{40}$$

$$= P \ddot{a}_{\overline{t+1}|} \frac{l_{40+t} - l_{40+t+1}}{l_{40}}.$$

Summing from $t = 0$ to $t = 19$ gives the total return of premium benefit

$$\frac{P}{l_{40}} \sum_{t=0}^{19} \ddot{a}_{\overline{t+1}|}(l_{40+t} - l_{40+t+1})$$

$$= \frac{P}{l_{40}} [\ddot{a}_{\overline{1}|}l_{40} - \ddot{a}_{\overline{1}|}l_{41} + \ddot{a}_{\overline{2}|}l_{41} - \ddot{a}_{\overline{2}|}l_{42} + \ddot{a}_{\overline{3}|}l_{42} \ldots$$

$$- \ddot{a}_{\overline{19}|}l_{59} + \ddot{a}_{\overline{20}|}l_{59} - \ddot{a}_{\overline{20}|}l_{60}]$$

$$= \frac{P}{l_{40}} (l_{40} + v l_{41} + v^2 l_{42} + \ldots + v^{19} l_{59} - \ddot{a}_{\overline{20}|}l_{60})$$

$$= P(\ddot{a}_{40:\overline{20}|} - {}_{20}p_{40}\ddot{a}_{\overline{20}|}).$$

The equation of benefits and premiums is

$$P \ddot{a}_{40:\overline{20}|} = 1{,}000 \overline{A}^1_{40:\overline{20}|} + P \ddot{a}_{40:\overline{20}|} - P {}_{20}p_{40}\ddot{a}_{\overline{20}|},$$

i.e.

$$P = \frac{1{,}000 \overline{A}^1_{40:\overline{20}|}}{{}_{20}p_{40}\ddot{a}_{\overline{20}|}}$$

$$= \frac{1{,}000(1{\cdot}02)({\cdot}06189)}{\dfrac{30{,}039{\cdot}8}{33{,}542{\cdot}3} (14{\cdot}1339)}$$

$$= 4{\cdot}99.$$

So annual premium required is £4·99.

Example 3.22

A table of whole-life continuous annuity values with interest at 3% calculated on a mortality table following Gompertz Law is given. Find an expression for $\bar{a}_{30}$ at 4% interest according to a second Gompertz table whose constants (with dashes) are related to the first table as follows:

$$\log c' = 1 \cdot 327 \log c$$

$$\log g' = c^{\cdot 19} \log g.$$

Solution

$$\bar{a}'_{30} \text{ (at 4\%)} = \int_0^\infty v^t{}_t p'_{30} dt$$

$$= \int_0^\infty v^t g'^{c'^{30}(c'^t - 1)} dt \quad \text{from formula (1.9.3)}$$

$$= \int_0^\infty v^t g^{c^{\cdot 19} c^{(1 \cdot 327)(30)}(c^{1 \cdot 327 t} - 1)} dt$$

as $\qquad\qquad c' = c^{1 \cdot 327}$

and $\qquad\qquad g' = g^{c^{\cdot 19}};$

and substituting $1 \cdot 327 t = T$,

$$= \int_0^\infty v^{\frac{T}{1 \cdot 327}} g^{c^{\{\cdot 19 + (1 \cdot 327)(30)\}}(c^T - 1)} \frac{dT}{1 \cdot 327}$$

$$= \frac{1}{1 \cdot 327} \int_0^\infty v_{3\%}^T g^{c^{40}(c^T - 1)} dT, \text{ as } v_{4\%}^{\frac{1}{1 \cdot 327}} = v_{3\%}$$

$$= \frac{1}{1 \cdot 327} \bar{a}_{40} \text{ (at 3\%).}$$

Example 3.23

Prove and demonstrate by general reasoning the formula

$$(\bar{I}\bar{a})_x = \int_0^\infty {}_t p_x \mu_{x+t} (\bar{I}\bar{a})_{\bar{t}|} dt$$

Solution

$$(\bar{I}\bar{a})_x = \int_0^\infty t v^t {}_t p_x dt, \quad \text{which using formula (3.9.2)}$$

$$= {}_\infty p_x \int_0^\infty tv^t dt - \int_0^\infty (-{}_t p_x \mu_{x+t}) \int_0^t rv^r dr\,dt$$

$$= \int_0^\infty {}_t p_x \mu_{x+t} (I\bar{a})_{\bar{t}|} dt, \quad \text{as required.}$$

The probability that (x) will die between durations t and $t+\delta t$ is ${}_t p_x \mu_{x+t} \delta t$. The present value of the annuity which he will have received is $(I\bar{a})_t$. The value of the annuity is therefore obtained by integrating the product over all values of t. The similar result for the level annuity was shown in Example 3.4.

Exercise 3.26

A man aged 60 has available a sum of £2,000. He is offered the following alternatives:

(a) The sum of £2,700 if he survives to age 65, or

(b) an annuity of £160 payable half yearly in arrears with final proportion, or

(c) the sum of £3,150 if he survives to age 70, with £2,000 paid immediately on previous death.

If each is evaluated on the A1967–70 table of mortality and 4% interest which is the most valuable?

Exercise 3.27

Prove the formula in Example 3.23 commencing with the right-hand side of the formula.

Exercise 3.28

It is common practice for a life insurance office to offer to accept an impaired life at the normal rate of premium for a double endowment assurance because the premium for the same term of policy either decreases or increases little with age. Determine whether this is possible for a life aged 40 who is assessed to be subject to mortality ten years older than A1967–70 (which is assumed in the table of rates). The rate of interest is 4% and the term of the policy twenty years.

Exercise 3.29

A mortality table follows Makeham's Law. If the constant c is changed to c', find an expression for $\bar{a}_x$ on the new mortality in terms of an annuity value on the old table at a certain rate of interest showing how to find the rate of interest.

Exercise 3.30

If between ages x and $x+n$ the graph of l_{x+t} is assumed to follow a straight line find an expression for $\bar{a}_{x:\overline{n}|}$.

Exercise 3.31

Develop from first principles a formula, involving the first differential coefficient, for $a_x^{(m)}$ to be used in evaluating annuities on the mortality of the English Life Table No. 12 (for which continuous functions are tabulated).

CHAPTER FOUR

POLICY VALUES

4.1 Nature of reserve

At the outset of a whole-life or endowment assurance policy, if expenses are ignored, the present value of the benefits equals the present value of the premiums. As time passes and no claim has been made, the present value of the benefits will increase as the time for payment becomes nearer, and the value of the premiums still to be paid will reduce as the annuity value with which they are valued will decrease. It is therefore important for the insurance office to have on hand the difference between the present values of the benefit and the premiums and this amount is known as the *policy value* or *reserve*. This amount will have arisen because the death claims in the early years of a group of policies will be less than the premiums paid and interest received.

Consider as an example a group of 10,000 policies all effected at exactly the same time on lives of exact age 60. The policies are five year annual premium endowment assurances with benefit of £100 paid at the end of the year of death. The net premium ignoring expenses for each policy is £18·43 on the A1967–70 ultimate table and 4% interest. Assume that A1967–70 mortality is experienced, rounding the number of deaths in the group to whole numbers and round all sums to pounds.

The total premiums collected at the commencement of the policy will be $10,000 \times £18·43 = £184,300$; during the first year interest of 4% of £184,300 (i.e. £7,372) is added and there will be $10,000 \times q_{60}$ $(= ·01443)$ death claims—the number of the claims will be 144 for a sum of £14,400.

The fund at the end of the year is then

$$£184,300 + £7,372 - £14,400 = £177,272$$

to which will be added the premiums paid by the survivors, i.e. $9,856 \times £18·43 = £181,646$ giving a total fund of £358,918. Interest added during the second year will be 4% of £358,918 = £14,357 and death claims will be deducted for $9,856 \times q_{61} (= ·01601) = 158$ lives, i.e. £15,800 sum insured, giving a fund of £357,475.

The same calculation can then be done for each year and for simplicity the results are shown in tabular form (Table 4.1).

This demonstrates that allowing for the rounding of the figures in the calculation £100 is available at the end of the term for each survivor as would be expected. The other figures in column (8) give the policy value or reserve for each policy. These figures have not in fact been found from the description given in the first paragraph of this section—the method indicated there would give at the end of year one;

Present value of benefits − Present value of premiums

$$= 100A_{61:\overline{4}|} - (18\cdot43)\ddot{a}_{61:\overline{4}|}$$

$$= 100(\cdot85838) - (18\cdot43)(3\cdot682)$$

$$= 85\cdot84 - 67\cdot86$$

$$= 17\cdot98 \text{ compared to } 17\cdot99 \text{ in the table.}$$

Similarly the other figures can be found—at the end of the second year

$$100A_{62:\overline{3}|} - (18\cdot43)\ddot{a}_{62:\overline{3}|}$$

$$= 100(\cdot89097) - (18\cdot43)(2\cdot835)$$

$$= 36\cdot85 \text{ compared to } 36\cdot86 \text{ in the table,}$$

and so on.

Using the method in the table opposite but applying it to a group of l_{60} policies with unit sum assured, the total reserve at the end of the first year will be (P being the premium, and i the rate of interest)

$$l_{60}P(1+i) - d_{60}$$

which divided among the l_{61} survivors gives the reserve for each surviving life as

$$P\frac{(1+i)l_{60}}{l_{61}} - \frac{d_{60}}{l_{61}}$$

$$= P\frac{D_{60}}{D_{61}} - \frac{C_{60}}{D_{61}}$$

$$= P\frac{N_{60}-N_{61}}{D_{61}} - \frac{M_{60}-M_{61}}{D_{61}},$$

being written in this form to be consistent with subsequent formulae.

TABLE 4.1

(1) Year	(2) Premiums received	(3) Total fund at beginning of year $(2)+(6)$	(4) Interest added	(5) Death claims	(6) Fund at end of year $(3)+(4)-(5)$	(7) Number of survivors	(8) Fund per survivor $(6) \div (7)$
	£	£	£		£		£
1	184,300	184,300	7,372	14,400	177,272	9,856	17·99
2	181,646	358,918	14,357	15,800	357,475	9,698	36·86
3	178,734	536,209	21,448	17,200	540,457	9,526	56·73
4	175,564	716,021	28,641	18,700	725,962	9,339	77·73
5	172,118	898,080	35,923	20,300	913,703	9,136	100·01

The reserve at the end of the second year will be similarly

$$\frac{1}{l_{62}}\left\{l_{61}\left(P\frac{N_{60}-N_{61}}{D_{61}} - \frac{M_{60}-M_{61}}{D_{61}} + P\right)(1+i)-d_{61}\right\}$$

and as $\quad D_{61} = v^{61}l_{61}$, and $D_{62} = v^{62}l_{62}$, this

$$= P\frac{N_{60}-N_{61}+D_{61}}{D_{62}} - \frac{M_{60}-M_{61}+C_{61}}{D_{62}}$$

$$= P\frac{N_{60}-N_{62}}{D_{62}} - \frac{M_{60}-M_{62}}{D_{62}},$$

and the same process can be continued for each year. It will be seen that the formula becomes, when x is the entry age and t the duration

$$P\frac{N_x-N_{x+t}}{D_{x+t}} - \frac{M_x-M_{x+t}}{D_{x+t}}. \tag{4.1.1}$$

This formula can be formally proved by mathematical induction and does not depend on the class of assurance, provided the sum assured is level, although the premium will, of course vary.

Exercise 4.1

By considering a group of four-year endowment assurance policies with sum assured £100 payable at the end of the year of death on lives aged 56 effected at the same time, find the accumulated fund and hence the policy value at the end of each policy year. Check the answers by deducting the present value of the premiums from the present value of the benefits. Use the A1967–70 ultimate mortality table and 4% interest.

4.2 Prospective and retrospective reserves

The symbol given to a reserve at duration t is of the form $_tV$ with suffices to indicate the original term and type of insurance. Thus a whole-life insurance has the symbol $_tV_x$ and an endowment $_tV_{x:\overline{n}|}$.

Where there is no simple formula for the premium and brackets have to be used, brackets are used similarly, for example $_tV(\overline{A}_{x:\overline{n}|})$ is the reserve for an endowment assurance with benefit paid at the time of death.

Where there is already a prefix in the premium symbol it is raised so that the reserve for a whole life limited premium policy is denoted

$$_t^nV_x.$$

In the previous section we use two different methods to arrive at the reserve for a policy. These are called the prospective and retrospective methods.

The *prospective* reserve is that found from considering the difference between the present values of the future benefits and premiums. The *retrospective* reserve is found by considering the difference between the accumulation of the premiums paid and the accumulated cost of assurance.

While the formula for the accumulation of the premium in the retrospective reserve (formula 4.1.1)

$$P \frac{N_x - N_{x+t}}{D_{x+t}} \quad \text{or} \quad P\ddot{s}_{x:\overline{t}|}$$

is relatively easy to understand and has already been discussed in section 2.3, the significance of the accumulated cost of assurance may not be so easy to follow. In the discussion at the end of the previous section culminating in formula (4.1.1) it was found algebraically to be of the form

$$\frac{M_x - M_{x+t}}{D_{x+t}},$$

and is sometimes given the symbol $_t k_x$. This expression does not in general vary with class of assurance provided the sum assured is constant.

We will now consider the prospective and retrospective formulae for a whole life assurance for a life aged x at duration t and prove that they are equal.

The prospective formula is

$$_t V_x = A_{x+t} - P_x \ddot{a}_{x+t}. \tag{4.2.1}$$

The retrospective formula is

$$_t V_x = \frac{1}{D_{x+t}} \{ P_x (N_x - N_{x+t}) - (M_x - M_{x+t}) \}$$

$$= \frac{M_{x+t}}{D_{x+t}} - P_x \frac{N_{x+t}}{D_{x+t}} \quad \text{as } P_x N_x = M_x$$

$$= A_{x+t} - P_x \ddot{a}_{x+t}, \quad \text{the prospective value.}$$

This equality while always true is not necessarily as easy to prove in

E

any particular case for more complicated policies—a general method will be discussed in Example 4.1 below.

The equality of prospective and retrospective reserves may also be demonstrated by general reasoning. At any moment of time during the premium paying period of an assurance policy the value of all premiums past and future under the contract must be equal to the value of the policy benefit already provided and promised in the future. The value of all premiums, past and future, can be denoted

$$P\ddot{s} + P\ddot{a}$$

and the value of past and future benefit by

$$k + A.$$

We then have

$$P\ddot{s} + P\ddot{a} = k + A,$$

i.e. $\quad P\ddot{s} - k = A - P\ddot{a};$

the left-hand side being the retrospective reserve, and the right-hand side the prospective reserve.

While discussion has so far been limited to whole-life and endowment assurances, there is nothing in the argument which will restrict the reasoning from applying to other classes of assurance. For example, with a term or temporary insurance the prospective reserve will be

$$_tV^1_{x:\overline{n}|} = A^1_{x+t:\overline{n-t}|} - P^1_{x:\overline{n}|}\ddot{a}_{x+t:\overline{n-t}|},$$

and the retrospective reserve

$$_tV^1_{x:\overline{n}|} = P^1_{x:\overline{n}|}\frac{N_x - N_{x+t}}{D_{x+t}} - \frac{M_x - M_{x+t}}{D_{x+t}}.$$

In this case the reserve will not increase each year to 1 at the end of the term, but will increase and then decrease to 0 at the end of the term.

The same formulae are adaptable to limited premium policies, different expressions being used before and after the end of the premium payment period.

While some of the examples which follow will be concerned with both prospective and retrospective reserves, in practice only one is normally required and whichever is the more simple to evaluate should be used. While the prospective reserve is often used students should remember the possibility of working with the retrospective reserve in some questions, for example during a deferred period when no benefits have as yet been provided, or for a pure endowment policy.

The equality of prospective and retrospective policy values will hold only if both they and the premium are based on the same rates of interest and mortality and, for example, if the premium has been calculated using a select table, the select table must also be used in the valuation if the equality is to hold true.

Example 4.1

Give expressions for the reserve prospectively and retrospectively for a limited premium endowment assurance during the premium payment term and prove that they are equal.

Solution

If the entry age is x, the term n years, the premium term m years and the duration t, the prospective reserve is

$$A_{x+t:\overline{n-t}|} - {}_mP_{x:\overline{n}|}\ddot{a}_{x+t:\overline{m-t}|}$$

and the retrospective

$${}_mP_{x:\overline{n}|}\ddot{s}_{x:\overline{t}|} - \frac{M_x - M_{x+t}}{D_{x+t}}.$$

The easiest method of proving that these expressions are equal is to subtract them and prove that the result is zero. However, we will prove the equality more elegantly by commencing with the prospective reserve and by algebraic manipulation obtain the retrospective reserve.

The prospective reserve is

$$\frac{M_{x+t} - M_{x+n} + D_{x+n}}{D_{x+t}} - {}_mP_{x:\overline{n}|}\frac{N_{x+t} - N_{x+m}}{D_{x+t}}$$

and adding

$$\frac{1}{D_{x+t}}({}_mP_{x:\overline{n}|}(N_x - N_{x+m}) - (M_x - M_{x+n} + D_{x+n})); \text{ (which} = 0)$$

the expression $= {}_mP_{x:\overline{n}|}\dfrac{N_x - N_{x+m} - N_{x+t} + N_{x+m}}{D_{x+t}}$

$$+ \frac{M_{x+t} - M_{x+n} + D_{x+n} - M_x + M_{x+n} - D_{x+n}}{D_{x+t}}$$

$$= {}_mP_{x:\overline{n}|}\frac{N_x - N_{x+t}}{D_{x+t}} - \frac{M_x - M_{x+t}}{D_{x+t}}$$

which is the retrospective reserve.

This method of adding the formula for the premium will usually be found to be effective in solving questions of this type.

Example 4.2

An annual premium is paid for a ten-year policy issued to a life aged 40 in connection with a house purchase mortgage. The sum assured of £10,000 decreases each year by £1,000, the sum assured being paid at the instant of death. Find the reserve at the end of five years. Mortality is A1967–70 select with 4% interest.

Solution

If the premium for the policy is P

$$P \frac{N_{[40]} - N_{50}}{D_{[40]}} = \frac{1 \cdot 02}{D_{[40]}} \{11,000 M_{[40]} - 1,000 R_{[40]} + 1,000 R_{51}\},$$

i.e.

$$P \frac{131,995 - 73,567}{6,981 \cdot 60} = \frac{1,020}{6,981 \cdot 60} ((11)(1,904 \cdot 86) - 57,705 \cdot 4 + 37,396 \cdot 5)$$

i.e. $\qquad 8 \cdot 369 P = 94 \cdot 18$

$$\therefore P = 11 \cdot 25.$$

The reserve at the end of five years will be (prospectively)

$$\frac{1 \cdot 02}{D_{45}} (5,000 M_{45} - 1,000 R_{46} + 1,000 R_{51}) - 11 \cdot 25 \frac{N_{45} - N_{50}}{D_{45}}$$

$$= \frac{1,020}{5,689 \cdot 18} ((5)(1,852 \cdot 39) - 46,417 \cdot 0 + 37,396 \cdot 5)$$

$$- 11 \cdot 25 \frac{99,756 \cdot 5 - 73,567 \cdot 1}{5,689 \cdot 18}$$

$$= 43 \cdot 3 - 51 \cdot 8$$

$$= -8 \cdot 5.$$

The reserve is thus negative. In the case of decreasing temporary assurances, including family income benefits, this is not unusual and some insurance offices restrict the term of premium payments to some fraction, such as three-quarters, of the benefit term in order that a policyholder who lapses his policy will not cause a loss to the office. When negative reserves occur, assurance benefits have been provided to a greater extent than the premiums which have been paid.

Example 4.3

State the prospective reserve for a family income benefit policy and show that it equals the retrospective reserve.

Solution

Assuming that the income benefit for a life aged x is I per annum payable continuously for a term of n years the net premium (P) is

$$\frac{I(\bar{a}_{\overline{n}|} - \bar{a}_{x:\overline{n}|})}{\ddot{a}_{x:\overline{n}|}}.$$

The prospective policy value at duration t is

$$I(\bar{a}_{\overline{n-t}|} - \bar{a}_{x+t:\overline{n-t}|}) - P\ddot{a}_{x+t:\overline{n-t}|}$$

$$= I\left(\bar{a}_{\overline{n-t}|} - \frac{\bar{N}_{x+t} - \bar{N}_{x+n}}{D_{x+t}}\right) - P\frac{N_{x+t} - N_{x+n}}{D_{x+t}}$$

and adding

$$\frac{D_x}{D_{x+t}}\left[P\frac{N_x - N_{x+n}}{D_x} - I\left(\bar{a}_{\overline{n}|} - \frac{\bar{N}_x - \bar{N}_{x+n}}{D_x}\right)\right] \quad \text{which} = 0,$$

in a similar fashion to Example 4.1 the reserve

$$= P\frac{N_x - N_{x+n} - N_{x+t} + N_{x+n}}{D_{x+t}}$$

$$- I\left(\frac{D_x}{D_{x+t}}\bar{a}_{\overline{n}|} - \bar{a}_{\overline{n-t}|} - \frac{\bar{N}_x - \bar{N}_{x+n} - \bar{N}_{x+t} + \bar{N}_{x+n}}{D_{x+t}}\right)$$

$$= P\frac{N_x - N_{x+t}}{D_{x+t}} - I\left(\bar{a}_{\overline{n}|} - \bar{a}_{\overline{n-t}|}\frac{D_{x+t}}{D_x} - \bar{a}_{x:\overline{t}|}\right)\frac{D_x}{D_{x+t}}$$

$$= P\ddot{s}_{x:\overline{t}|} - I\left(\bar{a}_{\overline{t}|} + v^t\bar{a}_{\overline{n-t}|} - \bar{a}_{\overline{n-t}|}\frac{D_{x+t}}{D_x} - \bar{a}_{x:\overline{t}|}\right)\frac{D_x}{D_{x+t}}$$

$$= P\ddot{s}_{x:\overline{t}|} - I(\bar{a}_{\overline{t}|} - \bar{a}_{x:\overline{t}|})\frac{D_x}{D_{x+t}} - I(1 - {}_tp_x)v^t\bar{a}_{\overline{n-t}|}\frac{D_x}{D_{x+t}}$$

which is the *retro* prospective reserve—the second term representing the amount already paid in claims per policy still in force, and the third term is the amount which must be set aside to capitalise the benefits still to be paid for policies which have already become claims per policy still in force.

Exercise 4.2

Give expressions for the reserve prospectively and retrospectively for a limited premium endowment assurance after the premium payment term and prove that they are equal.

Exercise 4.3

Show that the product of the reserve after t years for an annual premium n-year pure endowment issued at age x, and the annual premium for a pure endowment of like amount issued at the same age but maturing in t years is constant for all values of t.

Exercise 4.4

A double endowment assurance with term 20 years was issued to a life aged 40 with sum assured £1,000 increasing to £2,000 at maturity. Mortality is A1967–70 ultimate and interest 4%. Find the first duration at which the reserve is greater than £1,000.

Exercise 4.5

A deferred annuity of £100 per annum payable half-yearly in arrears with final proportion from age 65 is purchased for a life aged 45 by twenty annual premiums. The death benefit before age 65 is the return without interest of the premiums paid, paid at the instant of death. Determine on the A1967–70 ultimate table of mortality and 4% interest the reserve at the end of 15 years.

4.3 Further expressions for reserves

There are various useful transformations of the basic reserve formulae. Considering the whole life reserve $_tV_x$,

$$_tV_x = A_{x+t} - P_x\ddot{a}_{x+t}$$

$$= 1 - d\ddot{a}_{x+t} - P_x\ddot{a}_{x+t}$$

$$= 1 - (P_x + d)\ddot{a}_{x+t},$$

and since
$$P_x + d = \frac{1}{\ddot{a}_x},$$

then
$$_tV_x = 1 - \frac{\ddot{a}_{x+t}}{\ddot{a}_x}. \qquad (4.3.1)$$

A similar formula will be true of any policy satisfying the premium conversion relationships, so

$$_tV_{x:\overline{n|}} = 1 - \frac{\ddot{a}_{x+t:\overline{n-t|}}}{\ddot{a}_{x:\overline{n|}}}. \qquad (4.3.2)$$

Other, perhaps less useful, relations are found as follows:

(i) substituting $\ddot{a}_x = \dfrac{1-A_x}{d}$ and $\ddot{a}_{x+t} = \dfrac{1-A_{x+t}}{d}$ in formula (4.3.1)

$$_tV_x = 1 - \frac{1-A_{x+t}}{1-A_x},$$

i.e. $_tV_x = \dfrac{A_{x+t}-A_x}{1-A_x};$ \hfill (4.3.3)

(ii) as $\qquad _tV_x = A_{x+t} - P_x\ddot{a}_{x+t}$

$$= A_{x+t}\left(1 - \frac{P_x \cdot \ddot{a}_{x+t}}{A_{x+t}}\right)$$

$$= A_{x+t}\left(1 - \frac{P_x}{P_{x+t}}\right)$$

$$_tV_x = (P_{x+t} - P_x)\ddot{a}_{x+t} \hfill (4.3.4)$$

or $\qquad\qquad _tV_x = \dfrac{P_{x+t}-P_x}{P_{x+t}+d}. \hfill (4.3.5)$

Similar formulae may be proved for endowment assurances.

Example 4.4

Demonstrate the formula $_tV_x = 1 - \dfrac{\ddot{a}_{x+t}}{\ddot{a}_x}$ by general reasoning.

Solution

If (x) invests 1 in an annuity due he will receive $\dfrac{1}{\ddot{a}_x}$ at the beginning

of the year. Now $\dfrac{1}{\ddot{a}_x} = P_x + d$, and P_x is the premium required to

ensure the return of the 1 invested, with d being the annual interest paid in advance on the unit. If therefore (x) at the same time purchases the annuity and effects the assurance, the annuity payment will keep the assurance in force and provide interest on his investment. At the end of any year the value of the two contracts will be unity and as the value of the remaining payments of the annuity is

$$\frac{\ddot{a}_{x+t}}{\ddot{a}_x}$$

the policy value of the assurance will be

$$1 - \frac{\ddot{a}_{x+t}}{\ddot{a}_x} \quad \text{as required.}$$

Exercise 4.6

Prove that

$$_tV_x = 1 - (1 - {_1}V_x)(1 - {_1}V_{x+1})(1 - {_1}V_{x+2})...(1 - {_1}V_{x+t-1}).$$

Exercise 4.7

Demonstrate formula (4.3.4) by general reasoning.

Exercise 4.8

Prove that

(a)
$$_tV_{x:\overline{n}|} = \frac{P_{x+t:\overline{n-t}|} - P_{x:\overline{n}|}}{P_{x+t:\overline{n-t}|} + d}$$

(b)
$$_tV_{x:\overline{n}|} = \frac{A_{x+t:\overline{n-t}|} - A_{x:\overline{n}|}}{1 - A_{x:\overline{n}|}}.$$

Exercise 4.9

If $P_x = \cdot02$, $_nV_x = \cdot06$, and $P_{x:\overline{n}|} = \cdot25$, find $P^1_{x:\overline{n}|}$.

4.4 Relationship between successive reserves: mortality profit

Adding P_x to the basic prospective reserve formula for a whole-life assurance—formula (4.2.1)—we obtain

$$_tV_x + P_x = A_{x+t} - P_x . a_{x+t},$$

and substituting $A_{x+t} = vq_{x+t} + vp_{x+t}A_{x+t+1}$

and $a_{x+t} = vp_{x+t}\ddot{a}_{x+t+1},$

gives $_tV_x + P_x = (vq_{x+t} + vp_{x+t}A_{x+t+1}) - P_x vp_{x+t}\ddot{a}_{x+t+1}$

$$= vq_{x+t} + vp_{x+t}(A_{x+t+1} - P_x\ddot{a}_{x+t+1})$$

or, $_tV_x + P_x = v(q_{x+t} + p_{x+t} . {_{t+1}}V_x)$

and multiplying by $1 + i$

$$(_tV_x + P_x)(1 + i) = q_{x+t} + p_{x+t} . {_{t+1}}V_x. \qquad (4.4.1)$$

This formula demonstrates that the reserve at the end of t years increased by the premium then due and by one year's interest provides insurance for the next year plus the reserve at the end of $t+1$ years. This is the principle used in the construction of the table in section 4.1.

If p_{x+t} is replaced by $1-q_{x+t}$, we obtain

$$({}_tV_x+P_x)(1+i) = {}_{t+1}V_x+q_{x+t}(1-{}_{t+1}V_x). \qquad (4.4.2)$$

In this form the relationship shows that the reserve with premium and interest provides the reserve at the end of $t+1$ years with the excess of the sum assured of 1 over the reserve in the case of death.

While the algebraic proof assumed a whole life assurance the explanation given is not restricted to this one class of assurance. Formulae (4.4.1) and (4.4.2) are general and are sometimes expressed in the following forms, where the sum assured is taken as S instead of unity and the reserves ${}_tV$, ${}_{t+1}V$ apply to the sum assured S.

$$({}_tV+P)(1+i) = qS+p_{t+1}V \qquad (4.4.3)$$

$$({}_tV+P)(1+i) = {}_{t+1}V+q(S-{}_{t+1}V). \qquad (4.4.4)$$

The difference $(S-{}_{t+1}V)$ is referred to as the 'death strain at risk', and when multiplied by the death rate, $q(S-{}_{t+1}V)$ is referred to as the 'cost of assurance'.

When formula (4.4.4) is summed over a group of policies we obtain

$$\sum ({}_tV+P)(1+i) = \sum {}_{t+1}V + \sum q(S-{}_{t+1}V) \qquad (4.4.5)$$

the summation implying summation over the group. This demonstrates that if an office has in effect a group of policies all renewable yearly on the same date, the total reserves on any renewal date, including the net premiums then due, accumulated for a year will provide the reserves at the end of the year for all the policies in force at the beginning of the year and also increase the reserves to the sums assured in respect of the death claims, provided that the claims are exactly in accordance with the valuation assumptions. The expression

$$\sum q(S-{}_{t+1}V) \qquad (4.4.6)$$

the sum of the 'cost of assurance' is referred to as the 'expected death strain'.

The amount which the office will actually need to have on hand will be

$$\sum {}_{t+1}V + \sum_{\text{claims}} (S-{}_{t+1}V), \qquad (4.4.7)$$

where the first term is the same as in formula (4.4.5), the summation being over all policies in force at the beginning of the year, but the second term is a summation in respect only of the policies which actually became claims during the year. The expression

$$\sum_{\text{claims}} (S - {}_{t+1}V) \tag{4.4.8}$$

is called the 'actual death strain'.

The profit made by the office during the year on the group of policies will be the difference between the amount the office expected to need to have in hand at the end of the year and the amount actually required—that is, the expected death strain less the actual death strain. If this difference is negative there is a mortality loss instead of a mortality profit.

If formula (4.4.3) is rewritten

$$_{t+1}V = \frac{({}_tV + P)(1 + i) - qS}{p}$$

and the substitutions $\dfrac{1+i}{p} = u_{x+t}\left(= \dfrac{D_{x+t}}{D_{x+t+1}}\right)$

and $\dfrac{q}{p} = k_{x+t}\left(= \dfrac{C_{x+t}}{D_{x+t+1}}\right)$ made,

$$_{t+1}V = ({}_tV + P)u_{x+t} - Sk_{x+t}. \tag{4.4.9}$$

This formula may be used to prepare reserve values on a continuous basis starting with the initial value $_0V = 0$. The functions u and k are called Fackler valuation functions. The use of such a continuous method means that intermediate values are checked if the reserve at the end of the term is 1 or 0 depending on the class of assurance.

Example 4.5

Calculate the profit or loss from mortality for the year to 31st December 1977 in respect of the business in table 4.2 assuming that all birthdays and renewal dates are 31st December. The deferred annuities are payable yearly from the 60th birthday and sums assured are paid at the end of the year.

Solution

By addition the business in force at 1.1.77 was £101,000 sum assured and £5,100 p.a. annuity.

TABLE 4.2

At 31.12.77				Year 1.1.77–31.12.77
Class	Age at entry	No. of years in force	Sum assured or annuity p.a.	Contracts ceasing by death: sum insured or annuity p.a.
Whole-life annual premium	40	10	£100,000	£1,000
Deferred annuity single premium without return	45	15	£5,000	£100

Basis: A1967–70 ultimate, 4% interest.

The death strain at risk during 1977 for the assurances will be, per unit

$$1 - {}_{10}V_{40}$$

$$= 1 - \left(1 - \frac{\ddot{a}_{50}}{\ddot{a}_{40}}\right) = \frac{\ddot{a}_{50}}{\ddot{a}_{40}}$$

$$= \frac{16 \cdot 003}{18 \cdot 894}$$

$$= \cdot 8470.$$

So the total death strain at risk will be $101,000 \times \cdot 8470 = 85,547$ and the expected death strain is $85,547 . q_{49}$

$$= (85,547)(\cdot 00426)$$

$$= 364.$$

The actual death strain is $1,000(\cdot 8470) = 847$. So for the assurances there is a loss from mortality of $847 - 364 = 483$.

For the annuities the reserve at the end of the year for the annuities in force at the start of the year will be $5,100 . \ddot{a}_{60}$

$$= (5,100)(12 \cdot 551)$$

$$= 64,010$$

and the expected release of reserve on death will be $64{,}010 . q_{59}$

$$= 64{,}010 \ (\cdot 01299)$$

$$= 831.$$

The actual release of reserve on death will be $100 . \ddot{a}_{60}$

$$= 1{,}255.$$

As the actual release is greater than the expected there will be a profit on the annuities of $1{,}255 - 831 = 424$.

The total loss on the year for the two groups is thus $483 - 424 = £59$.

Example 4.6

Use the Fackler valuation functions to evaluate ${}_1 V_{55 : \overline{10|}}$ and ${}_2 V_{55 : \overline{10|}}$ on the A1967–70 mortality table with 4% interest.

Solution

$$
{}_1 V_{55 : \overline{10|}} = ({}_0 V_{55 : \overline{10|}} + P) \frac{D_{55}}{D_{56}} - \frac{C_{55}}{D_{56}}
$$

$$
= (0 + \cdot 08584) \cdot \frac{3{,}664 \cdot 57}{3{,}493 \cdot 88} - \frac{29 \cdot 7439}{3{,}493 \cdot 88}
$$

$$
= \cdot 0900 - \cdot 0085
$$

$$
= \cdot 0815.
$$

$$
{}_2 V_{55 : \overline{10|}} = ({}_1 V_{55 : \overline{10|}} + P) \frac{D_{56}}{D_{57}} - \frac{C_{56}}{D_{57}}
$$

$$
= (\cdot 0815 + \cdot 08584) \cdot \frac{3{,}493 \cdot 88}{3{,}327 \cdot 86} - \frac{31 \cdot 6432}{3{,}327 \cdot 86}
$$

$$
= \cdot 1757 - \cdot 0095
$$

$$
= \cdot 1662.
$$

These figures may be checked by the more usual formula

$$
1 - \frac{\ddot{a}_{55 + t : \overline{10 - t|}}}{\ddot{a}_{55 : \overline{10|}}}
$$

which gives $\cdot 0815$ and $\cdot 1662$ when $t = 1$ and 2 respectively.

Exercise 4.10

Prove formula (4.4.2) for an endowment assurance.

Exercise 4.11

Calculate the profit or loss from mortality for the year to 31st December 1976 in respect of the undernoted annual premium business assuming that all birthdays and renewal dates are 31st December, and sums assured are paid at 31st December.

TABLE 4.3

At 31.12.76				Year 1.1.76–31.12.76
Class	Age at entry	No. of years in force	Sum assured	Sums assured paid
Whole-life	40	15	£150,000	£1,500
	40	20	£200,000	£2,000
Endowment assurance term 30 years	30	20	£100,000	£800

Basis: A1967–70 ultimate, 4% interest.

Exercise 4.12

Show that

$$P + d \cdot {}_tV = vq(1 - {}_tV) + vp({}_{t+1}V - {}_tV)$$

and give a verbal interpretation.

Exercise 4.13

Use the Fackler valuation functions to evaluate ${}_1V_{[50]}$ and ${}_2V_{[50]}$ on the A1967–70 mortality table with 4% interest.

Exercise 4.14

A certain reserve accumulation formula is

$$_{t+1}V = ({}_tV + P - c_{x+t})u_{x+t}.$$

How is c_{x+t} defined in this formula?

Exercise 4.15

Calculate the profit or loss from mortality for the year 1977 of a group of single premium deferred annuities originally effected on 1st January 1967 at exact age 50 without return on death on the basis of the $a(55)$—males ultimate table and 4% interest. The annuities are payable half-yearly in advance without final proportion from age 70. The annuities in force at 1st January 1977 were £6,000 per annum and annuities of £100 per annum ceased on death during the year.

4.5 Fractional premiums and fractional durations

So far reserves at the end of each policy year (that is terminal reserves) have been considered. The value at the commencement of the policy year will be the previous terminal reserve increased by the premium paid. During the policy year the value if accurately stated will be, for an annual premium whole life policy, at duration $t+k$ with t integral and $0 < k < 1$;

$$_{t+k}V_x = v^{1-k}(_{1-k}q_{x+t+k} + _{1-k}p_{x+t+k}A_{x+t+k}) - P_x._{1-k}\ddot{a}_{x+t+k}, \quad (4.5.1)$$

noting that it is not correct to use A_{x+t+k} for the insurance factor as this would provide for death payment at the end of years measured from time $t+k$ instead of at the end of the policy year.

Such an exact expression is not amenable to easy calculation and it is customary to obtain the value of $_{t+k}V$ by means of linear interpolation based on reserve values at integral duration, thus

$$_{t+k}V \fallingdotseq (1-k)(_tV+P) + k_{t+1}V. \quad (4.5.2)$$

In the early years of the assurance $_tV+P$ may be greater than $_{t+1}V$ but later once the interest on the reserve becomes appreciable the terminal reserve will usually become greater than the initial reserve— the first stage is sometimes referred to as 'falling values' and the second as 'rising values'. Figure 4.1 illustrates this and also the discontinuities in the reserve when the premium is paid.

The symbol $_tV^{(m)}$ is used to denote the reserve at the end of t years on a policy with true fractional premiums $P^{(m)}$. For a whole-life assurance at an integral duration.

$$_tV_x^{(m)} = A_{x+t} - P_x^{(m)}.\ddot{a}_{x+t}^{(m)}.$$

We can estimate how much $_tV_x^{(m)}$ differs from $_tV_x$ by substituting approximations for $P_x^{(m)}$ and $\ddot{a}_{x+t}^{(m)}$, then

$$_tV_x^{(m)} \fallingdotseq A_{x+t} - P_x^{(m)}\left(\ddot{a}_{x+t} - \frac{m-1}{2m}\right)$$

$$\fallingdotseq A_{x+t} - \left\{P_x + \frac{m-1}{2m}P_x^{(m)}(P_x+d)\right\}\ddot{a}_{x+t} + \frac{m-1}{2m}P_x^{(m)}$$

$$= (A_{x+t} - P_x \ddot{a}_{x+t}) + \frac{m-1}{2m} P_x^{(m)} \{1 - (P_x + d)\ddot{a}_{x+t}\}$$

i.e. $\quad {}_tV_x^{(m)} \doteqdot {}_tV_x \left(1 + \frac{m-1}{2m} P_x^{(m)}\right).$ $\qquad$ (4.5.3)

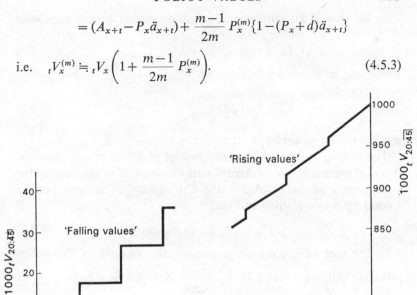

FIGURE 4.1. Policy values for £1,000 45-year endowment assurance effected at age 20 (A1967–70, 4%).

The reserve is larger when true fractional premiums are paid because there will be a loss of premium in the year of death if death occurs before all the fractional premiums are due. The average loss is approximately $\frac{m-1}{2m} P_x^{(m)}$ on the assumption of a uniform distribution of deaths (see section 3.5) and the reserve on the fractional premium basis is approximately equal to the reserve on an annual premium basis for an assurance with a benefit of 1 plus the average loss of premium.

The difference between ${}_tV_x^{(m)}$ and ${}_tV_x$ when t is integral is small within the ranges of values of x and t which occur in practice. For practical purposes it is not unusual to ignore the difference and assume that

$$_tV_x^{(m)} \doteqdot {}_tV_x \quad (t \text{ integral}). \qquad (4.5.4)$$

In the case of an endowment assurance subject to true premiums $P_{x:\overline{n}|}^{(m)}$

$$_tV_{x:\overline{n}|}^{(m)} = A_{x+t:\overline{n-t}|} - P_{x:\overline{n}|}^{(m)}\ddot{a}_{x+t:\overline{n-t}|}^{(m)} \tag{4.5.5}$$

which can be expressed in terms of $_tV_{x:\overline{n}|}$

$$_tV_{x:\overline{n}|}^{(m)} \fallingdotseq {}_tV_{x:\overline{n}|} + \frac{m-1}{2m} P_{x:\overline{n}|}^{(m)}{}_tV_{x:\overline{n}|}^1 \tag{4.5.6}$$

the algebra being similar to that shown above.

The reserve to cover the possible loss of premium arising from the fact that premiums are payable m times a year will in this case be for a temporary assurance. Again it is not unusual to assume that the second term is negligible and that

$$_tV_{x:\overline{n}|}^{(m)} \fallingdotseq {}_tV_{x:\overline{n}|} \quad (t \text{ integral}). \tag{4.5.7}$$

In the case of instalment premiums, the amount of the policy proceeds will, on average, be $1 - \dfrac{m-1}{2m} P_x^{[m]}$. We then have

$$_tV_x^{[m]} \fallingdotseq A_{x+t}\left(1 - \frac{m-1}{2m} P_x^{[m]}\right) - P_x^{[m]}\ddot{a}_{x+t}^{(m)}$$

$$\fallingdotseq A_{x+t} - \frac{m-1}{2m} P_x^{[m]}(1 - d\ddot{a}_{x+t}) - P_x^{[m]}\left(\ddot{a}_{x+t} - \frac{m-1}{2m}\right)$$

$$= A_{x+t} - \ddot{a}_{x+t}P_x^{[m]}\left(1 - \frac{m-1}{2m} d\right)$$

$$\fallingdotseq A_{x+t} - P_x\ddot{a}_{x+t} \text{ using formula (3.5.6);}$$

that is $_tV_x^{[m]} \fallingdotseq {}_tV_x$ (t integral). $\tag{4.5.8}$

This result could have been obtained by general reasoning since there is no loss of premium in the year of death, and hence also

$$_tV_{x:\overline{n}|}^{[m]} \fallingdotseq {}_tV_{x:\overline{n}|} \quad (t \text{ integral}). \tag{4.5.9}$$

So far consideration has been given only to integral durations. For non-integral $t+k$ interpolation between year ends is normally used. When k is a multiple of $\dfrac{1}{m}$ this means that the interpolation is between $_tV^{(m)}$ and $_{t+1}V^{(m)}$, there being no outstanding premiums to be allowed for. When k is not a multiple of $\dfrac{1}{m}$ interpolation should first be done between the year end values for the two *m*thly durations straddling the duration required with the fractional premium added to the lower of the durations. This is probably more clearly seen graphically as in Figures 4.2 and 4.3.

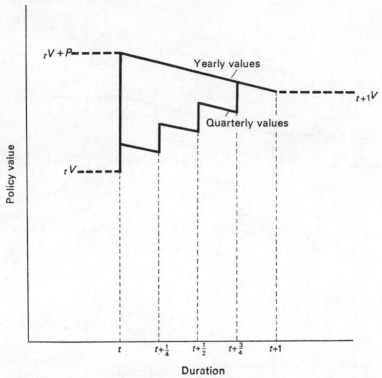

FIGURE 4.2. Graphical representation of policy values for quarterly premiums (falling values).

Formulae can of course be given for fractional durations but tend to look complicated, for example the approximate formula for $_{t+\frac{r}{m}+h}V^{(m)}$, where r is an integer and $h < \dfrac{1}{m}$ is

$$_{t+\frac{r}{m}+h}V^{(m)} = {}_tV^{(m)} + \left(\frac{r}{m} + h\right)\left({}_{t+1}V^{(m)} - {}_tV^{(m)}\right) + \left(\frac{1}{m} - h\right)P^{(m)}.$$

$$(4.5.10)$$

This expresses in symbols the general rule: interpolate between successive terminal reserves and add the amount of net premium for any period already paid beyond the date of valuation.

As previously mentioned, normally the values of the reserve at the integral durations would be assumed to be the same as yearly reserves.

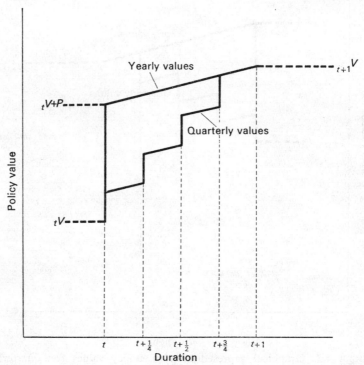

FIGURE 4.3. Graphical representation of policy values for quarterly premiums (rising values).

Example 4.7

Find the proportionate error introduced by using formula (4.5.4) rather than formula (4.5.3) to evaluate $_tV_{40}^{(4)}$ with $t = 10, 30, 50$ on A1967–70, 4%.

Solution

Considering formulae (4.5.3) and (4.5.4) it will be seen that the error does not in fact depend on duration.

Now
$$P_{40}^{(4)} \doteqdot \frac{P_{40}}{1 - \frac{3}{8}(P_{40} + d)}$$

$$= \frac{\cdot 01447}{1 - \frac{3}{8}(\cdot 01447 + \cdot 03846)}$$

$$= \frac{\cdot 01447}{\cdot 9802}$$

$$= \cdot 0148.$$

So
$$1 + \tfrac{3}{8}P_{40}^{(4)} = 1 \cdot 0056.$$

Referring to the difference between the formulae it will be seen that formula (4.5.4) understates the reserve by $\cdot 56\%$ at all durations.

Exercise 4.16

Demonstrate formula (4.5.6).

Exercise 4.17

Write approximate formulae for the following (t being an integer) in terms of reserves subject to annual premiums:

$$_tV_{x:\,\overline{n}|}^{\overset{(m)}{1}}, \quad _t^kV_{x:\,\overline{n}|}^{(m)}.$$

Exercise 4.18

Find values for $_{14\frac{1}{3}}^{20}V_{[30]}$, $_{14\frac{1}{3}}^{20}V_{[30]}^{(2)}$, $_{14\frac{1}{3}}^{20}V_{[30]}^{[2]}$ on A1967–70, 4%.

Exercise 4.19

Find an approximation for $_tV_x^{\{m\}}$ when t is the integral—the premium is apportionable (see Example 3.9).

4.6 Modified reserves

In the policy values so far discussed, which may be referred to as 'net level premium reserves', the premium valued is a net premium based on the same mortality table and rate of interest as are used for valuing the premiums and benefits. Policy values, however, may be calculated on the basis of a premium obtained in some other way, for example the mortality table and rate of interest used for calculating the net premium may be different from that used in valuing the benefit and premiums, or the premium valued may be an arbitrary percentage of the office premium. In these cases, which may be referred to as special or modified reserves, retrospective and prospective reserves are not necessarily equal and the prospective reserve just before payment of the first premium will not normally be zero.

The premium valued may allow for the actual expenses assumed in the premium calculation. If the office premium P'' for a whole life assurance was obtained by formula (2.6.1)

$$P'' = \frac{1}{1-k}\left(P_x + \frac{I}{\ddot{a}_x} + c\right),$$

the value of future office premiums at duration t will be

$$P''\ddot{a}_{x+t}$$

and the value of future expenses

$$(kP'' + c)\ddot{a}_{x+t}.$$

Hence the special policy value allowing for future expenses, given the symbol $_tV_x^{\text{mod.}}$, will be

$$_tV_x^{\text{mod.}} = A_{x+t} + (kP'' + c)\ddot{a}_{x+t} - P''\ddot{a}_{x+t}$$

$$= A_{x+t} - \left(P_x + \frac{I}{\ddot{a}_x}\right)\ddot{a}_{x+t} \qquad (4.6.1)$$

$$= _tV_x - I\frac{\ddot{a}_{x+t}}{\ddot{a}_x}$$

$$= _tV_x - I(1 - {_tV_x}). \qquad (4.6.2)$$

The special policy value just after payment of the first premium is $P_x - I$. If there are no additional initial expenses (i.e. $I = 0$) the special policy value is the same as the normal. Similar expressions, called Zillmerized policy values, apply to other classes of assurance.

The same method is also used assuming a value of I different from that used in the individual premium calculation as a convenient, though arbitrary, method of allowing for the additional initial expenses.

Special or modified reserves are used particularly in North America and Europe, but may be used in Britain by a recently established rapidly growing insurance company whose initial expenses will be heavy relative to the funds.

The most extreme modified reserve normally used is the *full preliminary term* under which it is assumed that the whole of the first premium is expended on the cost of the risk and expenses so that

$$_1V^{\text{mod.}} = 0.$$

For a whole-life insurance effected at age x with P' being the premium valued this means

$$A_{x+1} - P'\ddot{a}_{x+1} = 0$$

$$\therefore P' = \frac{A_{x+1}}{\ddot{a}_{x+1}} = P_{x+1}.$$

The reserve at a subsequent duration t will then be

$$_tV_x^{\text{mod.}} = A_{x+t} - P_{x+1}\ddot{a}_{x+t}$$

$$= {_{t-1}}V_{x+1}, \tag{4.6.3}$$

thus demonstrating that the modified reserve is the same as the net level premium reserve for a policy issued at an age one year older.

While the full preliminary term method may be used for a whole-life assurance a similar formula would in the case of an endowment assurance usually make too large a provision for initial expenses.

In countries where minimum valuation reserves are specified by legislation the minimum is often on a modified preliminary term basis under which reserves lower than the net level premium reserves are permitted on a stated basis. Examples of this are the Commissioners reserve valuation method specified in many American states, and the Canadian method. While both these methods give modified reserves over the full premium paying period of the policy some methods have special values for a limited period, say 20 years, after which the reserves are net level premium reserves.

In any modified reserve system of these types the sequence of net level premiums P is replaced by a reduced first year net premium α followed by a series of increased renewal premiums β, and if the modification period is less than the premium term the normal premium P is assumed after this period. If the policy is issued at age x with modification of premiums for k years

$$\alpha + \beta a_{x:\overline{k-1}|} = P\ddot{a}_{x:\overline{k}|}, \tag{4.6.4}$$

so that given either α or β the reserves can be found.

In some cases the difference $\beta - \alpha$ is known, in which case β is found from

$$\beta = P + \frac{\beta - \alpha}{\ddot{a}_{x:\overline{k}|}}. \tag{4.6.5}$$

It will be seen that for the full preliminary term reserve $\alpha = A_{x:\overline{1}|}^{1}$.

Example 4.8

The Commissioners reserve valuation method allows a modified reserve for certain policies in such a way that the difference between the first year and subsequent years' net premiums is the same as the full preliminary term method allows to a whole-life assurance with premiums limited to 20 years effected at the same age. Find the Commissioners reserve after 10 years on an endowment assurance at age 65 effected at age 40 on A1967–70 ultimate, 4%, and compare with the normal net level premium reserve.

Solution

The statement on the modification implies

$$\beta - \alpha = {}_{19}P_{41} - \frac{C_{40}}{D_{40}}$$

$$= \frac{1{,}899 \cdot 81}{125{,}015 - 35{,}841} - \frac{9 \cdot 6915}{6{,}986 \cdot 50}$$

$$= \cdot 0213 - \cdot 0014$$

$$= \cdot 0199.$$

From formula (4.6.5) $\beta = \cdot 02565 + \dfrac{\cdot 0199}{15 \cdot 599}$

$$= \cdot 02693.$$

The modified reserve

$${}_{10}V^{\text{mod.}}_{40\,:\,\overline{25|}} = A_{50\,:\,\overline{15|}} - \beta \ddot{a}_{50\,:\,\overline{15|}}$$

$$= \cdot 57711 - (\cdot 02693)(10 \cdot 995)$$

$$= \cdot 28101.$$

The normal reserve

$${}_{10}V_{40\,:\,\overline{25|}} = 1 - \frac{\ddot{a}_{50\,:\,\overline{15|}}}{\ddot{a}_{40\,:\,\overline{25|}}}$$

$$= 1 - \frac{10 \cdot 995}{15 \cdot 599}$$

$$= \cdot 29515.$$

As expected, the modified reserve is smaller than the normal reserve.

Exercise 4.20

Show that the prospective and retrospective special reserves are equal for a whole-life assurance when the modified method assumes the expenses used in the premium calculation.

Exercise 4.21

Where the modified reserve is on the full preliminary term basis prove that

$$_t^m V_{x\,:\,\overline{n}|}^{\text{mod.}} = _{t-1}^{m-1} V_{x+1\,:\,\overline{n-1}|}.$$

Exercise 4.22

The Canadian reserve valuation method allows a modified reserve for certain policies in such a way that the excess of the net level premium over the first year modified net premium is equal to the corresponding excess produced by the full preliminary term method applied to a whole-life assurance effected at the same age. Find the Canadian reserve after 15 years for a 30-year term endowment assurance effected at age 30 on A1967–70 ultimate, 4%, and compare the value with the normal net level premium reserve.

Exercise 4.23

The Illinois modified reserve method is similar to the Commissioners method except that when the premium payment period is more than 20 years the modified reserve is identical with the normal net level premium reserve after 20 years.

Find the Illinois reserve after 10 years for a 25-year term endowment assurance effected at age 35 on A1967–70 ultimate, 4%.

4.7 Variation in interest and mortality

If we are given two mortality tables referred to as normal and special in which the rates of mortality are q and q' respectively, the premiums on the tables at rates of interest i and i' being P and P' respectively, and the policy value on the two bases are identical we have from formula (4.4.2)

$$(_tV + P)(1+i) = {}_{t+1}V + q(1 - {}_{t+1}V)$$

and

$$(_tV + P')(1+i') = {}_{t+1}V + q'(1 - {}_{t+1}V).$$

Subtracting we have

$$(_tV + P)(i' - i) + (P' - P)(1 + i') = (q' - q)(1 - {}_{t+1}V). \qquad (4.7.1)$$

This equation is called the *equation of equilibrium* and has application in the study of extra risks, valuation and surplus. It may be explained verbally: the contrast of the special value with the normal shows that the excess premium accumulated on the special rate of interest together with the excess interest on the initial reserve must meet the extra death claims, or

$$\frac{\text{Excess}}{\text{interest}} + \frac{\text{excess premium}}{\text{accumulated}} = \frac{\text{excess death}}{\text{strain}}$$

Another way of considering reserves on two bases is to use formula (4.3.1) or (4.3.2), for example for a whole-life assurance, with reserves $_tV'_x$ and $_tV_x$ on the two bases

$$_tV'_x \gtreqless {_tV_x}$$

as
$$1 - \frac{\ddot{a}'_{x+t}}{\ddot{a}'_x} \gtreqless 1 - \frac{\ddot{a}_{x+t}}{\ddot{a}_x}$$

or
$$\frac{\ddot{a}'_{x+t}}{\ddot{a}'_x} \lesseqgtr \frac{\ddot{a}_{x+t}}{\ddot{a}_x}$$

or
$$\frac{\ddot{a}'_{x+t}}{\ddot{a}_{x+t}} \lesseqgtr \frac{\ddot{a}'_x}{\ddot{a}_x}.$$

Thus it is only necessary to calculate the values of $\dfrac{\ddot{a}'_x}{\ddot{a}_x}$ for all ages of x, and inspection then shows the ages at which the ordinary reserves exceed the special.

If the reserves are equal over an interval,

$$\ddot{a}_y = (1+k)\ddot{a}'_y,$$

where y is within the interval, and k is constant. Then if $i' = i$

$$1 + vp_y\ddot{a}_{y+1} = (1+k) + (1+k)vp'_y\ddot{a}'_{y+1},$$

and as
$$(1+k)\ddot{a}'_{y+1} = \ddot{a}_{y+1},$$

$$vp_y\ddot{a}_{y+1} = k + vp'_y\ddot{a}_{y+1};$$

$$\therefore p_y = \frac{k(1+i)}{\ddot{a}_{y+1}} + p'_y$$

$$\therefore q'_y = q_y + \frac{k(1+i)}{\ddot{a}_{y+1}}. \tag{4.7.2}$$

Now $\ddot{a}_{y+1}$ will decrease with increasing age so the mortality rates will differ by an amount which increases with age.

This result may also be obtained by putting $i' = i$ in formula (4.7.1), giving

$$(P' - P)(1+i) = (q' - q)(1 - {_{t+1}V})$$

$$\therefore \left(\frac{1}{\ddot{a}'_x} - \frac{1}{\ddot{a}_x}\right)(1+i) = (q'_y - q_y)\frac{\ddot{a}_{y+1}}{\ddot{a}_x}$$

and multiplying by $\ddot{a}_x$ and writing $1+k$ for $\dfrac{\ddot{a}_x}{\ddot{a}_x'}$ gives

$$k(1+i) = (q_y' - q_y)\ddot{a}_{y+1},$$

giving (4.7.2).

This proof demonstrates that if the policy values are equal the the difference between the rates of mortality must be inversely proportional to the death strain at risk.

A general theory on the effect of variations in interest and mortality is Lidstone's theorem (1905) which it is not intended to state or prove but which has two corollaries:

(1) Provided the reserves increase with duration, an increase in the rate of interest produces a decrease in reserves, and a decrease in the rate of interest produces an increase in reserves.

(2) Provided the reserves increase with duration, a constant increase in the rate of mortality produces a decrease in reserves, and a constant decrease in the rate of mortality produces an increase in reserves.

Exercise 4.24

Demonstrate that a decrease in the rate of interest gives larger reserves by comparing whole-life, and endowment assurance at age 65, reserves at age 40, 50 and 60 for a policy effected at age 30, on the A1967–70 table with 3% and 4% interest. (On A1967–70 3%, $\ddot{a}_{30} = 24 \cdot 747$, $\ddot{a}_{40} = 21 \cdot 678$, $\ddot{a}_{50} = 17 \cdot 894$, $\ddot{a}_{60} = 13 \cdot 667$, $\ddot{a}_{30:\overline{35}|} = 21 \cdot 421$, $\ddot{a}_{40:\overline{25}|} = 17 \cdot 169$, $\ddot{a}_{50:\overline{15}|} = 11 \cdot 671$, $\ddot{a}_{60:\overline{5}|} = 4 \cdot 572$).

Exercise 4.25

Determine the effect on whole-life reserves of multiplying each p_x by $(1+k)$ when k is a positive constant.

4.8 Continuous reserves

When the sum assured is paid immediately on death the prospective reserve under a whole-life policy will be,

$$_tV(\bar{A}_x) = \bar{A}_{x+t} - P(\bar{A}_x)\ddot{a}_{x+t}$$

$$\doteqdot \left(1 + \frac{i}{2}\right) A_{x+t} - \frac{\left(1 + \dfrac{i}{2}\right) A_x}{\ddot{a}_x}\ddot{a}_{x+t}$$

that is $\qquad _tV(\bar{A}_x) \doteqdot \left(1 + \dfrac{i}{2}\right) {}_tV_x.$ (4.8.1)

This formula can also be obtained by general reasoning by considering that the effective sum assured is $\left(1 + \dfrac{i}{2}\right)$ times greater when the sum assured is paid at the moment of death.

In the case of the endowment assurance the reserve must be increased only in respect of the death benefit so

$$_tV(\bar{A}_{x\,:\,\overline{n}|}) \doteqdot {}_tV^1_{x\,:\,\overline{n}|}\left(1 + \frac{i}{2}\right) + {}_tV_{x\,:\,\frac{1}{n|}}. \tag{4.8.2}$$

When we consider a whole-life assurance payable at the moment of death and purchased by continuous premiums $\bar{P}(\bar{A}_x)$, that is all functions are continuous, the reserve $_t\bar{V}(\bar{A}_x)$ will be a continuous function of the duration t, premiums are being paid continuously, interest is added momently and in the case of a modified reserve the expenses may be considered as deducted at each instant.

The reserve on a retrospective basis is then

$$_t\bar{V}(\bar{A}_x) = \bar{P}\,\frac{\bar{N}_x - \bar{N}_{x+t}}{D_{x+t}} - \frac{\bar{M}_x - \bar{M}_{x+t}}{D_{x+t}}. \tag{4.8.3}$$

This can also be obtained by considering the change in the reserve in a small interval of time δt for a group of l_x policies issued at age x of whom l_{x+t} survive to age $x+t$. Writing $_t\bar{V}$ for the reserve required, the total fund at age $x+t$ will be $l_{x+t}.\,_t\bar{V}$. In the small interval of time δt the following changes will occur in the fund:

premiums will be added—of amount $l_{x+t}\bar{P}.\delta t$
interest will be added—of amount $\delta.l_{x+t}.\,_t\bar{V}.\delta t$
death claims will be incurred—of amount $l_{x+t}.\mu_{x+t}.\delta t$.

The total change can then be expressed as

$$\delta(l_{x+t}.\,_t\bar{V}) \doteqdot (l_{x+t}.\bar{P} + \delta.l_{x+t}.\,_t\bar{V} - l_{x+t}\mu_{x+t})\delta t$$

and in the limit as $\delta t \to 0$

$$\frac{d}{dt}(l_{x+t}.\,_t\bar{V}) = l_{x+t}\bar{P} + \delta.l_{x+t}.\,_t\bar{V} - l_{x+t}\mu_{x+t}.$$

Multiplying by v^t and rearranging gives

$$v^t\,\frac{d(l_{x+t}.\,_t\bar{V})}{dt} - \delta v^t(l_{x+t}.\,_t\bar{V}) = v^t(\bar{P}l_{x+t} - l_{x+t}\mu_{x+t}).$$

Now the left side is $\dfrac{d}{dt}(v^t l_{x+t} \cdot {}_t\overline{V})$, so integrating from 0 to t gives

$$\left[v^t . l_{x+t} \cdot {}_t\overline{V} \right]_0^t = P l_x \int_0^t v^t {}_t p_x dt - l_x \int_0^t v^t {}_t p_x \mu_{x+t} dt,$$

i.e. $v^t l_{x+t} \cdot {}_t\overline{V} = \overline{P} l_x \bar{a}_{x:\overline{t}|} - l_x \overline{A}_{x:\overline{t}|}^1,$

then dividing by $v^t l_{x+t}$

$$_t\overline{V} = \overline{P} \frac{\overline{N}_x - \overline{N}_{x+t}}{D_{x+t}} - \frac{\overline{M}_x - \overline{M}_{x+t}}{D_{x+t}},$$

which is expression (4.8.3) as required. The reasoning above is not in fact restricted to a whole-life assurance and will apply to any class of policy. The expression could be transformed algebraically to the prospective formula if required. Formulae similar to those for discrete functions can also be obtained thus

$$_t\overline{V}(\overline{A}_x) = \overline{A}_{x+t} - \overline{P}(\overline{A}_x)\bar{a}_{x+t}$$
$$= 1 - (\overline{P}(\overline{A}_x) + \delta)\bar{a}_{x+t},$$

i.e. $_t\overline{V}(\overline{A}_x) = 1 - \dfrac{\bar{a}_{x+t}}{\bar{a}_x}$ (4.8.4)

and similarly $_t\overline{V}(\overline{A}_{x:\overline{n}|}) = 1 - \dfrac{\bar{a}_{x+t:\overline{n-t}|}}{\bar{a}_{x:\overline{n}|}}.$

Example 4.9

Find the values of $_{20}V(\overline{A}_{50})$, $_{30}\overline{V}(\overline{A}_{[40]})$ on A1967–70, 4%.

Solution

$$_{20}V(\overline{A}_{50}) \doteqdot (1{\cdot}02)\left(1 - \frac{\ddot{a}_{70}}{\ddot{a}_{50}}\right)$$

$$= (1{\cdot}02)\left(1 - \frac{8{\cdot}957}{16{\cdot}003}\right)$$

$$= {\cdot}4491.$$

$$_{30}\overline{V}(\overline{A}_{[40]}) = 1 - \frac{\bar{a}_{70}}{\bar{a}_{[40]}}$$

$$= 1 - \frac{8{\cdot}457}{18{\cdot}406}$$

$$= {\cdot}5405.$$

Exercise 4.26

Demonstrate formula (4.8.2) algebraically.

Exercise 4.27

Demonstrate the approximate formula

$$_t\overline{V}(\overline{A}_x) \fallingdotseq {}_tV_x(1 + \tfrac{1}{2}(\overline{P}(\overline{A}_x) + \delta)).$$

Exercise 4.28

Find values for

$$_{10}V(\overline{A}_{40\,:\,\overline{20|}}), \quad {}_{20}\overline{V}(\overline{A}_{30\,:\,\overline{35|}})$$

on A1967–70, 4%.

EXAMPLES AND EXERCISES ON CHAPTER 4

Example 4.10

A policy is issued at age 20 with a maturity value at age 50 of £1,500. The benefit paid at the end of the year of death is £1,000 or the terminal reserve on the premium basis, whichever is the greater. Prove that the annual premium ignoring expenses is

$$\frac{1,000(M_{20} - M_{20+a}) + 1,500v^{30-a}D_{20+a}}{N_{20} - N_{20+a} + D_{20+a}\ddot{a}_{\overline{30-a|}}},$$

where a is the greatest integer for which $\ddot{a}_{20\,:\,\overline{a|}} \leq 2\ddot{s}_{\overline{30-a|}}$

Solution

Let a be the last duration at which the death benefit is 1,000 so that after this time the death benefit is the reserve. During the time when the death benefit equals the reserve equation (4.4.3) becomes

$$(_tV + P)(1 + i) = {}_{t+1}V.$$

$$\therefore {}_tV = v_{t+1}V - P.$$

Now $$_{30}V = 1,500$$

so $$_{29}V = 1,500v - P$$

and $$_{28}V = (1,500v - P)v - P$$

$$= 1,500v^2 - P\ddot{a}_{\overline{2|}}$$

and continuing till

$$_aV = 1,500v^{30-a} - P\ddot{a}_{\overline{30-a|}}.$$

Now considering $_aV$ retrospectively with a constant sum assured of 1,000 gives

$$_aV = P\frac{N_{20}-N_{20+a}}{D_{20+a}} - 1,000\frac{M_{20}-M_{20+a}}{D_{20+a}}.$$

Equating the retrospective and prospective reserves and solving for P gives

$$P\left(\frac{N_{20}-N_{20+a}}{D_{20+a}} + \ddot{a}_{\overline{30-a}|}\right) = 1,000\frac{M_{20}-M_{20+a}}{D_{20+a}} + 1,500v^{30-a},$$

that is P equals the required expression.

To find a:

a is the greatest integer such that

$$_aV \leq 1,000,$$

that is

$$1,500v^{30-a} - P\ddot{a}_{\overline{30-a}|} \leq 1,000,$$

or substituting for P and multiplying by the denominator times $\dfrac{D_{20+a}}{D_{20}}$, and then dividing by 500

$$3v^{30-a}\left(\ddot{a}_{20:\overline{a}|} + \ddot{a}_{\overline{30-a}|}\frac{D_{20+a}}{D_{20}}\right) - 2\left(1 - \frac{D_{20+a}}{D_{20}} - d\ddot{a}_{20:\overline{a}|}\right)\ddot{a}_{\overline{30-a}|}$$

$$- 3v^{30-a}\frac{D_{20+a}}{D_{20}}\ddot{a}_{\overline{30-a}|} \leq 2\ddot{a}_{20:\overline{a}|} + 2\ddot{a}_{\overline{30-a}|}\frac{D_{20+a}}{D_{20}}.$$

Dividing by v^{30-a} gives

$$3\ddot{a}_{20:\overline{a}|} - 2\ddot{s}_{\overline{30-a}|} + 2\ddot{a}_{20:\overline{a}|}\ddot{s}_{\overline{30-a}|}d \leq 2(1+i)^{30-a}\ddot{a}_{20:\overline{a}|},$$

and substituting $\ddot{s}_{\overline{30-a}|}d = (1+i)^{30-a} - 1$, the expression simplifies to

$$\ddot{a}_{20:\overline{a}|} \leq 2\ddot{s}_{\overline{30-a}|} \quad \text{as required.}$$

Example 4.11

A life office issues a group of 100 fifteen-year endowment assurances by annual premium, each for a sum assured of £500 payable at the end of the year of death, to lives aged 45 exactly. As no medical evidence was obtained the A1967–70 ultimate table is used, instead of the normally used select table.

Medical evidence is later obtained for another purpose and it is found that of the 100 lives, 95 would have been charged the normal select premium but five would have been charged the select premium for a life five years older.

Calculate the expected death strain in the first year

(a) on the terms of the contract as issued, and

(b) on the terms that would have applied if medical evidence had been obtained.

Assume that the valuation basis in each case is exactly the same as the relevant premium basis and that 4% interest applies throughout.

Solution

(a) Expected death strain $= 500(100)q_{45}(1 - {}_1V_{45:\overline{15|}})$

$$= 50{,}000q_{45}\frac{\ddot{a}_{46:\overline{14|}}}{\ddot{a}_{45:\overline{15|}}}$$

$$= 50{,}000\ (\cdot 00264)\frac{10\cdot 672}{11\cdot 235}$$

$$= \pounds 125.$$

(b) Expected death strain

$$= 500(95)q_{[45]}(1 - {}_1V_{[45]:\overline{15|}}) + 500(5)q_{[50]}(1 - {}_1V_{[50]:\overline{15|}})$$

$$= 47{,}500q_{[45]}\frac{\ddot{a}_{[45]+1:\overline{14|}}}{\ddot{a}_{[45]:\overline{15|}}} + 2{,}500q_{[50]}\frac{\ddot{a}_{[50]+1:\overline{14|}}}{\ddot{a}_{[50]:\overline{15|}}}$$

$$= 47{,}500\ (\cdot 00174)\frac{10\cdot 250}{11\cdot 250}\cdot\frac{1\cdot 04\ (33{,}180\cdot 0)}{33{,}122\cdot 2}$$

$$+\ 2{,}500\ (\cdot 00286)\frac{10\cdot 028}{11\cdot 028}\cdot\frac{1\cdot 04\ (32{,}558\cdot 0)}{32{,}464\cdot 8}$$

using $\ddot{a}_{[x]+1:\overline{14|}} = a_{[x]:\overline{14|}}\cdot\dfrac{D_{[x]}}{D_{[x)+1}} = (\ddot{a}_{[x]:\overline{15|}} - 1)\dfrac{l_{[x]}}{l_{[x]+1}}\ (1+i)$

$$= 78\cdot 5 + 6\cdot 8$$

$$= \pounds 85.$$

The expected death strain on basis (b) is of course much smaller because of the use of the select rates of mortality.

Example 4.12

A special type of policy provides that the death benefit at the end of the year of death is the sum assured increased by the reserve that would have been held if death had not occurred. Find the annual premium for such a five-year endowment policy with sum assured £1,000 on the A1967–70 table with 4% interest for a life aged 40.

Solution

The death benefit in the $(t+1)$th year is $1{,}000 + {}_{t+1}V$ so that equation (4.4.4) gives

$$({}_tV + P)(1+i) = {}_{t+1}V + q1{,}000$$

and putting $t = 0, 1, 2, 3, 4, 5$, with ${}_0V = 0$ and ${}_5V = 1{,}000$ gives

$$P(1+i) = {}_1V + q_{40}\,.\,1{,}000$$

$$({}_1V + P)(1+i) = {}_2V + q_{41}\,.\,1{,}000$$

$$({}_2V + P)(1+i) = {}_3V + q_{42}\,.\,1{,}000$$

$$({}_3V + P)(1+i) = {}_4V + q_{43}\,.\,1{,}000$$

$$({}_4V + P)(1+i) = 1{,}000 + q_{44}\,.\,1{,}000.$$

Multiplying the first equation by v, the second by v^2 etc., gives

$$P = v\,{}_1V + vq_{40}\,.\,1{,}000$$

$$v\,{}_1V + vP = v^2\,{}_2V + v^2 q_{41}\,.\,1{,}000$$

$$v^2\,{}_2V + v^2 P = v^3\,{}_3V + v^3 q_{42}\,.\,1{,}000$$

$$v^3\,{}_3V + v^3 P = v^4\,{}_4V + v^4 q_{43}\,.\,1{,}000$$

$$v^4\,{}_4V + v^4 P = v^5 1{,}000 + v^5 q_{44}\,.\,1{,}000.$$

Adding all the equations will remove the intermediate values of ${}_tV$ giving

$$P\ddot{a}_{\overline{5}|} = v^5 1{,}000 + 1{,}000 \sum_{t=1}^{5} v^t q_{39+t}.$$

Note that the last term is not a normal insurance factor. If the term of the policy had been long it would probably be easiest to find the value of the summation by an approximate method but with a five-year term it can be calculated exactly:

$$vq_{40} = (\cdot 96154)(\cdot 00144) = \cdot 00138$$

$$v^2 q_{41} = (\cdot 92456)(\cdot 00162) = \cdot 00150$$

$$v^3 q_{42} = (\cdot 88900)(\cdot 00183) = \cdot 00163$$

$$v^4 q_{43} = (\cdot 85480)(\cdot 00207) = \cdot 00177$$

$$v^5 q_{44} = (\cdot 82193)(\cdot 00234) = \cdot 00192$$

$$\overline{\phantom{v^5 q_{44} = (\cdot 82193)(\cdot 0023)} \cdot 00820.}$$

Then $P(4 \cdot 6299) = 821 \cdot 93 + 8 \cdot 20$

$$\therefore P = 179 \cdot 30.$$

So premium required is £179·30.

This may be compared with the premium without the special benefit.

$$= 1,000 \, \frac{M_{40} - M_{45} + D_{45}}{N_{40} - N_{45}}$$

$$= 1,000 \, \frac{1,909 \cdot 50 - 1,852 \cdot 39 + 5,689 \cdot 18}{132,001 - 99,756}$$

$$= 178 \cdot 20.$$

Example 4.13

A proposer aged 45 effects with a life office an annual premium endowment assurance with a sum assured of £50,000 payable at the end of 20 years or the end of the year of death if earlier. The life office reassures the mortality risk on £20,000 of the sum assured with a reinsurance company on the 'risk premium' basis under which the reinsurance company undertakes to pay the original office the amount of the 'death strain at risk' on the policy reserve basis if the life dies during the term. Reinsurance premiums payable by the office to the reinsurance company at the beginning of each policy year are calculated by means of the following formula:

Premium at age x per unit of 'death strain at risk'

$$= 1 \cdot 2q_x + \cdot 002,$$

where q_x is the rate of mortality according to the English Life Table No. 12—Males.

The life office calculates premiums and maintains policy reserves on the basis of the A1967–70 ultimate table with 4% interest.

Calculate the rate of interest the original office must earn on the policy in the sixth year in order to make neither profit nor loss in that year.

Solution

The reserve at the end of 5 years $(_5V)$

$$= 50,000 \left(1 - \frac{\ddot{a}_{50 \,:\, \overline{15|}}}{\ddot{a}_{45 \,:\, \overline{20|}}} \right)$$

$$= 50,000 \left(1 - \frac{10 \cdot 995}{13 \cdot 488} \right)$$

$$= 9,242.$$

The reserve at the end of 6 years ($_6V$)

$$= 50{,}000 \left(1 - \frac{\ddot{a}_{51:\overline{14|}}}{\ddot{a}_{45:\overline{20|}}} \right)$$

$$= 50{,}000 \left(1 - \frac{10{\cdot}445}{13{\cdot}488} \right)$$

$$= 11{,}280.$$

The reserve on the reinsured portion will be two-fifths of this, i.e. 4,512, the remainder being 6,768.

The premium for the whole contract is 50,000 ($\cdot$03568) = 1,784.

The premium rate during the sixth year paid to the reinsuring office is $1{\cdot}2q_{50} + {\cdot}002$ on the English Life Table No. 12—Males.

$$= 1{\cdot}2 \, ({\cdot}00728) + {\cdot}002$$

$$= {\cdot}010736.$$

The premium paid will be $\cdot$010736 $(20{,}000 - 4{,}512)$

$$= 166.$$

The expected death strain on the part of the policy not reinsured

$$= q_{50} \, (30{,}000 - 6{,}768)$$

$$= ({\cdot}00479)(23{,}232)$$

$$= 111.$$

Now in the sixth year the initial reserve including the premium just paid less the premium paid to the reinsurance office accumulated for the year will equal the reserve at the end of the year plus the expected death strain on the part of the policy not reinsured—that is, if i' is the rate of interest earned,

$$(9{,}242 + 1{,}784 - 166)(1 + i') = 11{,}280 + 111$$

$$\therefore \; 1 + i' = \frac{11{,}391}{10{,}860} = 1{\cdot}049.$$

The office must earn 4$\cdot$9 % interest during the year to make no profit or loss.

Exercise 4.29

Find the generalised expression for the premium and the condition on the duration when the policy described in Example 4.10 is effected for a term of n years by a life aged x, the sum assured at maturity being $(1 + k)$ times the original sum assured on death.

F

Exercise 4.30

Ignoring expenses devise a formula for the single premium at age x for an n-year endowment assurance with maturity value $1+k$ and death benefit paid at the end of the year of death of 1 or the reserve if greater. Give a criterion for determining c, the number of years during which the death benefit is constant at 1.

Exercise 4.31

An annual premium policy provides a death benefit at the end of the year of death of the sum insured of £10,000 plus the terminal reserve. Find the premium for a 20-year term insurance on the A1967–70 table at 4% interest for a life aged 30.

Exercise 4.32

An insurance company has just issued 1,000 whole-life assurances each for a sum assured of £500 payable at the end of the year of death, with family income benefit of £100 per annum payable weekly if death occurs within the first 20 years, from the date of death until the 20th policy anniversary. The lives are all aged 35 and the benefits are being secured by half-yearly instalment premiums, any unpaid instalments being deducted from the sum assured paid on death. Find the total reserve the company expect to hold at the end of five years if premiums and reserves are on the A1967–70 select table with 4% interest.

Exercise 4.33

A proposer aged 40 effects with a life office an annual premium whole life assurance with a sum assured of £100,000 payable at the end of the year of death. The life office, which calculates premiums and reserves on the A1967–70 table with 4% interest, decides that if in any policy year the death strain at risk is greater than £50,000 the excess death strain will be reinsured with a reinsurance company which charges premiums at age x per unit

$$= 1 \cdot 1 q_x + \cdot 0015,$$

where q_x is the rate of mortality on the English Life Table No. 12— Males.

Calculate the reinsurance premiums in the first and tenth years of the contract.

If the office makes neither profit nor loss in the tenth year find the rate of interest which it must earn.

Exercise 4.34

A life office issues a group of 500 twenty-year endowment assurances by annual premium each with a sum assured of £1,000 (payable at the end of the year of death) to lives aged 40 exactly. No medical evidence was obtained and the A1967–70 ultimate table was used instead of the A1967–70 select table normally used.

Medical evidence is later obtained and it is found that of the lives 470 should have been charged the normal select premium but 25 should have been charged the select premium for a life five years older and 5 the select premium for a life ten years older.

If there is one death in the first year (one of the lives who would have been charged ordinary rates) compare the actual death strain with the expected death strain on the basis on which the policies were issued, and also on the basis which would have been used if the medical evidence had been obtained.

The valuation basis in each case is exactly the same as the premium basis and 4% interest is used throughout.

CHAPTER FIVE

SURRENDER AND PAID-UP VALUES: BONUS: SPECIAL POLICIES

5.1 Surrender values

After a certain number of premiums have been paid under a life assurance policy a life office will normally allow a cash payment called a surrender value (S.V.) or cash value if the policy is cancelled. However, certain classes such as temporary insurances where the reserve values are very small are not usually granted surrender values.

In Britain the provisions of the policy do not normally state the surrender values, but abroad most policies are required by statutory requirements to specify or tabulate them, and a minimum basis of calculation may be laid down by legislation. This latter is the case in Britain for Industrial assurance policies which are described in section 5.5.

The surrender value basis of a life office will normally be such that it will give values similar to but less than a modified reserve allowing for the expenses incurred. The reasons for the difference are that there may be selection against the office as incapacitated lives will tend to maintain their policies while the good lives will be more likely to surrender, and that surrenders may occur for financial reasons or changes in market rates of interest. The discontinuing policyholder should be paid a reasonable amount but the continuing policyholders should not be left in a less favourable financial position than if the policy had not been surrendered.

A term which is sometimes met is the *asset share* of a policy which is the accumulated excess at any time of the gross premiums paid, less expenses incurred and the cost of insurance, and increased by interest and it could be considered that this should be the surrender value. In practice it is very difficult to make these calculations and obtain ideal equity among the many policyholders of a company and it may be contrary to the 'pooling' concept of insurance risks. As there is no unique answer to a surrender value and as a change of basis causes problems if some of the new values are less than the old, a life office may not change its surrender value basis for long periods with the result that the basis may in practice use out-of-date mortality and an unrealistic rate of interest.

In the case of pure endowment policies and other benefits which are only due on survival, such as deferred annuities without return of premiums on death during the deferred period, payment of a surrender value would be dependent on evidence of good health. This would also be the case if an office is willing to allow a surrender value on an annuity in payment.

The surrender value forms the basis of another important right enjoyed by most policyholders; that is to a loan up to some proportion such as 80% or 90% of the surrender value at any time. If there is later a claim under a policy with a loan, the loan and any outstanding interest will be deducted from the policy proceeds.

Example 5.1

A life office calculates surrender values on the basis of the A1967–70 ultimate table of mortality with 4% interest allowing for initial expenses of £3%, with a minimum of half the office premiums paid. Find the duration during which the minimum will apply for a 30-year endowment assurance for a life aged 35. The gross premium for the policy is £24 per mil.

Solution

The surrender value is a modified reserve, and the gross premium is ignored for this purpose.

Surrender value per £1,000 sum assured

$$= 1,000_t V_{35:\overline{30|}} - 30(1 - _t V_{35:\overline{30|}}).$$

The duration required will be found by trial and error.

$$\text{S.V. at duration } 3 = 1,000\left(1 - \frac{16\cdot347}{17\cdot375}\right) - 30\left(\frac{16\cdot347}{17\cdot375}\right)$$

$$= 59\cdot2 - 28\cdot2.$$

$$= 31\cdot0.$$

The total of the premiums paid before duration 3 will be £72, of which half is £36, so that the guarantee will apply at least for 3 years.

Similarly, the surrender value at duration 4 can be found to be £52·7 compared with the minimum of £48.

Hence the guaranteed minimum applies for three years.

Exercise 5.1

A life office which previously calculated surrender values on the basis of the English Life Table No. 12—Males and 4% interest with an allowance for initial expenses of £2% is to alter the basis to the A1967–70 ultimate table and 4% interest with an allowance for initial expenses of £3%. Compare the values on the old and new basis at 10-year intervals for a whole-life assurance for a life aged 40.

5.2   Paid-up policies

A paid-up policy (PUP)—sometimes called a free policy—is a policy free from future premiums. While a single premium policy may thus be regarded as a paid-up policy, in practice the term is normally restricted to policies under which the sum assured has been reduced at the request of the policyholder because he did not wish to continue paying premiums but did not request payment of the surrender value.

Considering a whole-life assurance originally effected at age x which has been t years in force, the reserve will be ${}_tV_x$ and this will purchase if applied as a single premium a paid-up sum assured of

$$
{}_tW_x = \frac{{}_tV_x}{A_{x+t}}, \tag{5.2.1}
$$

where W is the symbol for a paid-up policy.

Alternatively, if a life aged $x+t$ effected a whole-life assurance with net premium P_x the sum assured would by proportion be P_x/P_{x+t}. This is the sum assured purchased by future premiums so the sum assured already purchased must be

$$
{}_tW_x = 1 - \frac{P_x}{P_{x+t}}. \tag{5.2.2}
$$

Formulae (5.2.1) and (5.2.2) give identical values as

$$
\frac{{}_tV_x}{A_{x+t}} = \frac{A_{x+t} - P_x \ddot{a}_{x+t}}{A_{x+t}}
$$

$$
= 1 - \frac{P_x}{P_{x+t}}.
$$

By similar reasoning the paid-up value of an n-year endowment assurance at duration t is

$$_tW_{x:\overline{n}|} = \frac{_tV_{x:\overline{n}|}}{A_{x+t:\overline{n-t}|}}$$

or

$$_tW_{x:\overline{n}|} = 1 - \frac{P_{x:\overline{n}|}}{P_{x+t:\overline{n-t}|}}. \qquad (5.2.3)$$

In order that the formula $1 - \dfrac{P}{P}$ may be used, often called the 'buying-back' method, the reasoning given must be appropriate; it will not be appropriate, for example, if the sum assured varies or if part of the benefit is a return of premiums.

Some cases where the formula applies are:

for a temporary assurance

$$_tW^1_{x:\overline{n}|} = 1 - \frac{P^1_{x:\overline{n}|}}{P^1_{x+t:\overline{n-t}|}},$$

—in practice because of the small reserves under temporary assurances it is unusual to allow paid-up policies;

for a pure endowment

$$_tW_{x:\frac{1}{\overline{n}|}} = 1 - \frac{P_{x:\frac{1}{\overline{n}|}}}{P_{x+t:\frac{1}{\overline{n-t}|}}};$$

and for a whole-life limited premium policy

$$^n_tW_x = 1 - \frac{_nP_x}{_{n-t}P_{x+t}}.$$

In the case of endowment and limited premium policies, it is usual to grant a paid-up policy for a sum assured proportionate to the premiums paid, that is ratioing the original sum assured by the number of premiums paid to the number which would have been paid—this is called a *proportionate paid-up* value. While this value is not strictly accurate—normally being less and occasionally more than the true value—it is used for the convenience of calculation and the appearance of equity.

While the values given above are the theoretical values, in practice an office may reduce them, particularly in the early years where the initial expenses have not been fully met. Some offices alternatively may calculate the paid-up policy by using the surrender value as a single premium, that is substituting the surrender value for $_tV_x$ in formula (5.2.1), thus giving a lower value.

Ultimate functions have been used throughout this section, but select functions should be inserted if appropriate in any particular case.

Example 5.2

On the A1967–70 table with 4% interest calculate

$$_{10}W_{[30]}, \quad _{20}W_{35:\overline{30}|}, \quad _{10}^{20}W_{40}$$

and compare the second and third values with the proportionate PUPs.

Solution

$$_{10}W_{[30]} = 1 - \frac{P_{[30]}}{P_{40}}$$

$$= 1 - \frac{\cdot 00901}{\cdot 01447}$$

$$= \cdot 377.$$

$$_{20}W_{35:\overline{30}|} = 1 - \frac{P_{35:\overline{30}|}}{P_{55:\overline{10}|}}$$

$$= 1 - \frac{\cdot 01909}{\cdot 08584}$$

$$= \cdot 778,$$

compared with the proportionate value of $\dfrac{20}{30} = \cdot 667$.

$$_{10}^{20}W_{40} = 1 - \frac{_{20}P_{40}}{_{10}P_{50}}$$

$$= 1 - \frac{A_{40}}{\ddot{a}_{40:\overline{20}|}} \cdot \frac{\ddot{a}_{50:\overline{10}|}}{A_{50}}$$

$$= 1 - \frac{\cdot 27331}{13 \cdot 764} \cdot \frac{8 \cdot 207}{\cdot 38450}$$

$$= \cdot 576$$

compared with the proportionate value of $\dfrac{10}{20} = \cdot 500$.

Exercise 5.2

On the A1967–70 table with 4% interest calculate

$$_{20}W_{60}, \quad _{15}W_{[30]:\,\overline{30|}}, \quad _{20}^{35}W_{25:\,\overline{40|}}$$

comparing where appropriate with the proportionate values.

5.3 Non-forfeiture provisions

The paid-up policy described in the previous section is one option available to a policyholder who is unable or unwilling to continue paying premiums. In some cases a policyholder who ceases to pay premiums may not indicate his wishes to the life office and in this event the office will have a practice to be followed, which may be stated in the policy, or which may be determined by legislation.

In the first few, perhaps two, years, where the surrender value is nil or small, no options will be available and on premiums ceasing the surrender value, if any, will be payable.

One option commonly used by the USA is *extended term insurance*, where the surrender value at the time the premiums cease is used to purchase temporary assurance for the full sum assured for a limited period, the period (n) being determined from

$$\text{surrender value} = (\text{original sum assured}) \, A^{1}_{x+t:\,\overline{n|}}, \qquad (5.3.1)$$

interpolation being required for n. In the case of an endowment assurance, if the surrender value is more than sufficient to purchase temporary assurance to the end of the endowment period a pure endowment is also available at maturity.

One common practice is to allow the full sum assured for a period of one year after the premium is unpaid and then to give a paid-up value reduced to allow for the extra cover and the unpaid premium—this is demonstrated in example 5.4 below.

When a loan has been granted on a policy the surrender value will be reduced by the amount of the loan and any outstanding interest in determining the extended term option or paid-up value.

Example 5.3

A 20-year term endowment assurance with sum assured £500 payable at the end of the year of death effected at age 45 has surrender values just before the fourth and eleventh premiums are due to be paid of £50 and £200 respectively. The non-forfeiture provisions of the policy state that if a premium is not paid the surrender value is applied to purchase extended term assurance for the full sum assured on the A1967–70 table with 4% interest and no allowance for expenses. Find the respective extended terms applicable if the fourth or eleventh and subsequent premiums are unpaid.

Solution

(a) Just before the fourth premium is due, three premiums have been paid, and the age is 48. If y is the age at which the extended term assurance ceases

$$50 = 500 \frac{M_{48} - M_y}{D_{48}}$$

$$\therefore \frac{50}{500}(5012{\cdot}42) = 1805{\cdot}46 - M_y$$

$$\therefore M_y = 1304{\cdot}22.$$

Interpolating between $M_{64} = 1{,}306{\cdot}39$ and $M_{65} = 1{,}258{\cdot}73$ to days gives $y = 64$ and 17 days. The extended term is thus 16 years and 17 days.

(b) Just before the eleventh premium is due, ten premiums have been paid, and the age is 55. If the age y is calculated as in (a) above it will be found to be greater than 65 so the extended term will be to age 65 and there will in addition be a pure endowment available at that age. If Y is the amount of pure endowment

$$200 = 500A^1_{55\,:\,\overline{10|}} + Y_{10}E_{55}$$

i.e. $$200 = 500({\cdot}10547) + Y({\cdot}69058 - {\cdot}10547)$$

$$\therefore Y = \frac{147{\cdot}27}{{\cdot}58511}$$

$$= 252.$$

The extended term is thus to the normal maturity date and there is in addition pure endowment of £252.

Example 5.4

A whole-life policy with annual premium £36 effected at age 40 with sum assured £2,000 has surrender values calculated as 95% of the reserve on the basis of the A1967–70 ultimate table with 4% interest. The assured fails to pay the eleventh premium. The non-forfeiture provision in the policy states that the full sum assured is paid during the first year after the premium is unpaid and the policy is then made paid-up—the theoretical paid-up policy on the A1967–70 ultimate table being reduced by the ratio of the surrender value less premium and fine for late payment at 6% interest, to the surrender value.

Solution

The change to paid-up policy is made at age 51.

The surrender value at age 51, eleven premiums having been paid, is

$$2,000(\cdot95)\left(1 - \frac{\ddot{a}_{51}}{\ddot{a}_{40}}\right)$$

$$= 2,000(\cdot95)\left(1 - \frac{15\cdot678}{18\cdot894}\right)$$

$$= 323\cdot4.$$

The premium and fine $= 36(1\cdot06) = 38\cdot2$.

The paid-up value after 11 premiums

$$= 2,000\left(1 - \frac{P_{40}}{P_{51}}\right)$$

$$= 2,000\left(1 - \frac{\cdot01447}{\cdot02532}\right)$$

$$= 857\cdot0.$$

The paid-up value to be allowed

$$= 857\frac{323\cdot4 - 38\cdot2}{323\cdot4}$$

$$= 756.$$

The paid-up value is thus £756.

The reasoning for the method of calculation is that the surrender value of the policy with the premiums unpaid should be the same as that if the premium is paid less the premium and the fine for late payment. The paid-up value of £857 is equivalent to the surrender value of £323·4, so the paid-up value equivalent to the reduced surrender value of £285·2 is found by proportion.

The paid-up value after 10 years is

$$2,000\left(1 - \frac{P_{40}}{P_{50}}\right)$$

$$= 2,000\left(1 - \frac{\cdot01447}{\cdot02403}\right)$$

$$= 795\cdot7.$$

The difference between this value and £756 is caused by the policy being on risk for the full sum assured during the eleventh policy year.

Exercise 5.3

Find the extended term applicable to the policy in Example 5.3 if the surrender value just before payment of the fifth premium which is unpaid is £50.

Exercise 5.4

If the policy in Example 5.4 had a loan of £100, find the paid-up value after ten years and after the subsequent one-year forfeiture period if the paid-up policy is to be free from loan and 6% p.a. interest is charged on the loan (and on the unpaid premium and interest), neither the interest nor premium being paid at the tenth policy anniversary.

5.4   Bonus: with-profit policies

In Britain when life assurance was first transacted on a long-term basis the premiums were more than sufficient to cover the expenses and mortality risk and it became the custom as there were no share-holders in the original office (the 'Equitable Society') for there to be a distribution of 'profits' or 'surplus' to the policyholders by increasing the sums assured. This means that there is no immediate distribution of cash during the term of the policy but when the policy becomes a claim the amount paid is greater than the sum assured by the *bonus* declared—the bonus is referred to as reversionary as it is not paid immediately. This practice has become almost universal with all offices, including those with shareholders where the profits are shared between the shareholders and policyholders.

It has now become the practice for most offices to offer both non-profit (or non-participating) and with-profit (or participating) policies except for temporary assurances which are normally non-profit. In the case of non-profit policies the office pays exactly the benefits stated, while a with-profit policyholder pays a larger premium for the same sum assured and expects to have his benefits increased by declarations of bonus, some of the profits contributing to the bonus perhaps arising from the non-profit business of the office.

While the reversionary bonus system is the normal system in Britain, in America the common method of profit distribution is for there to be a cash dividend each year which decreases the premiums after the first from those stated in the policy.

When an office transacts with-profit business on the reversionary bonus system it will increase the premium to allow for part of the bonus it expects to declare, this is called 'loading' for the bonus, and the difference between the resulting premium and that for the non-profit policy is referred to as the bonus loading. The bonus is now normally declared either annually or every three years (triennially) and may be simple (declared as a percentage of the sum assured) or compound (declared as a percentage of the sum assured plus any existing bonus). Where the bonus is declared triennially it is customary to allow an intermediate bonus, perhaps at a lower rate, on the policies becoming claims during the three-year period. In all cases bonus is declared in proportion to the number of premiums paid in the period since the last declaration of bonus and it is usual for all policies to be allowed the same rate of bonus, although some offices vary the rate according to the class, age, original term and duration. As bonus is added as soon as a premium is paid the benefit increases by one year's intermediate bonus immediately the policy is effected.

In recent years further bonuses, such as terminal bonus which is paid only on claims actually occurring, have been introduced. Such bonuses are outside the scope of this book.

If bonuses are declared on the simple reversionary system at rate b the formula (2.6.1) for the premium P'' becomes

$$P'' = \frac{1}{1-k}\left(P + \frac{I}{\ddot{a}} + c + b\frac{(IA)}{\ddot{a}}\right) \qquad (5.4.1)$$

If bonus is declared on the compound reversionary system at rate b each year the total benefit will increase each year by the fraction $(1+b)$ so the net single premium for the total benefit of sum assured and bonus of a whole-life policy will be

$$\frac{1}{l_x}\left\{(1+b)vd_x + (1+b)^2v^2d_{x+1} + \dots + (1+b)^{n+1}v^{n+1}d_{x+n} + \dots\right\} = A'_x$$

at a rate of interest i' such that

$$1 + i' = \frac{1}{(1+b)v}, \quad \text{i.e.} \quad i' = \frac{i-b}{1+b}$$

—in practice it is often calculated at $i-b$ as b is small in relation to 1. The net annual premium for the sum assured and bonus is therefore $\dfrac{A'_x}{\ddot{a}_x}$ with A' at rate i' and $\ddot{a}$ at rate i. Similarly for an n-year endowment assurance, the net annual premium for the sum assured and bonus is $\dfrac{A'_{x:\overline{n}|}}{\ddot{a}_{x:\overline{n}|}}$.

The symbolic formula for the gross premium for a policy with a compound reversionary bonus at the rate b is thus

$$P'' = \frac{1}{1-k}\left(\frac{A'}{\ddot{a}} + \frac{I}{\ddot{a}} + c\right). \qquad (5.4.2)$$

While it would be possible, though laborious, to calculate exact figures for bonus declared triennially it is customary to use the same expressions as above.

Some policies are described as guaranteed bonus policies under which the rate of bonus is guaranteed. If the policy does not participate in profits beyond the amount stated in the contract, although the sum payable increases, it is determined at the outset, and the policy is really non-participating.

When a with-profit assurance is surrendered it is necessary to calculate the surrender value of the bonus already allotted together with intermediate bonus for any premium paid since the last declaration. Normally the bonus will be valued by an assurance factor such as $A_{x+t:\overline{n-t}|}$, where x is the age at entry, n the original term and t the number of years in force.

When a with-profit assurance is paid-up, offices follow differing practices. Some allow the whole of the existing bonus without reduction to be added to the non-profit paid-up value and allow the paid-up policy to participate in profits in the future on the reduced sum, while some reduce the existing bonus or do not allow the policy to participate in future profits.

When a whole-life policy with a simple guaranteed bonus at rate b is valued at duration t, the formula for the reserve will be of the form (where P is the total premium including that for the bonus):

prospectively: $(1+tb)A_{x+t} + b(IA)_{x+t} - P\ddot{a}_{x+t}$

retrospectively:

$$\frac{1}{D_{x+t}}\left\{P(N_x - N_{x+t}) - (M_x - M_{x+t}) - b(R_x - R_{x+t} - tM_{x+t})\right\}.$$

Similar formulae will be used for endowment assurances.

The valuation of with-profit assurances raises problems which are outside the scope of this book and it is not normally considered appropriate to value using the retrospective method. One method used is to value prospectively using the equivalent non-profit premium and ignore bonuses that have not been declared, so that if S is the sum assured and B the bonus already declared the reserve is of the form

$$(S+B)A_{x+t} - SP_x\ddot{a}_{x+t}, \text{ } (SP_x \text{ being the non-profit premium})$$
$$= {}_tV_x + BA_{x+t}. \quad (5.4.3)$$

Another method is to use the net premium payable but allow for expected future bonus, giving, for a simple bonus at rate b

$$(S+B)A_{x+t} + Sb(IA)_{x+t} - SP\ddot{a}_{x+t}, \quad (5.4.4)$$

SP being the net premium payable including the bonus loading.

Expressions for endowment assurances and for policies with compound reversionary bonus can be obtained on similar lines.

Example 5.5

An office declares a compound bonus triennially at an annual rate of £4%. Calculate on the basis of the A1967–70 ultimate table with 4% interest the net annual premium for a 9-year endowment assurance with sum assured £1,000 to a life aged 56, both accurately and using the normal approximation. The office loads for the full amount of the bonus it declares.

Solution

The 'normal' formula involves the calculation of A' at the rate of interest of $i - b$, i.e. $\cdot04 - \cdot04 = 0$.

$$\therefore A' = 1.$$

The net annual premium is then $\dfrac{1,000(1)}{\ddot{a}_{56:\overline{9}|}}$

$$= \frac{1,000}{7\cdot389}$$

$$= 135\cdot3.$$

The 'accurate' value will allow for the effect of compounding triennially and is easiest set down in tabular form (Table 5.1); note that during each triennium the bonus is 'simple', the benefit increasing in the progression:

$$1+b; \text{ } 1+2b; \text{ } 1+3b; \text{ } (1+b)(1+3b); \text{ } (1+2b)(1+3b); \text{ } (1+3b)^2;$$
$$(1+b)(1+3b)^2; \text{ } (1+2b)(1+3b)^2; \text{ } (1+3b)^3.$$

If the net premium required is P, then

$$P\ddot{a}_{56:\overline{9}|} = \frac{1}{D_{56}} \sum_{x=56}^{64} \text{Benefit} \cdot C_x + 1404 \cdot 9_9 E_{56},$$

$$\therefore P7 \cdot 389 = \frac{438 \cdot 899}{3493 \cdot 88} + 1404 \cdot 9(\cdot 71580 - \cdot 10211)$$

$$= 125 \cdot 6 + 862 \cdot 2$$

$$\therefore P = \frac{987 \cdot 8}{7 \cdot 389} = 133 \cdot 7.$$

The comparison is thus between the more accurate value of £133·7 and the 'normal' formula of £135·3; the difference being of approximately the same proportion as the maturity values assumed: 1,404·9 in the accurate calculation and $1,000(1 \cdot 04)^9 = 1,423 \cdot 3$ when annual compounding is assumed.

TABLE 5.1

Age x	Benefit	C_x	$\dfrac{\text{Benefit} \times C_x}{1,000}$
56	1,040·0	31·643	32·909
57	1,080·0	33·590	36·277
58	1,120·0	35·577	39·846
59	1,164·8	37·593	43·788
60	1,209·6	39·628	47·934
61	1,254·4	41·668	52·268
62	1,304·6	43·698	57·008
63	1,354·8	45·701	61·916
64	1,404·9	47·657	66·953
		Total	438·899

Example 5.6

A life office calculates premiums on the basis of the A1967–70 table select and 4% interest with initial expenses of £3% and renewal expenses of 4% of each premium, and with a with-profit bonus loading for a reversionary bonus of 1%. Calculate the annual premium per cent for a whole-life assurance effected at age 40 and an endowment assurance to age 65 effected at age 35, on the basis of both a simple and compound bonus.

Solution

Let the premium for the whole-life assurance with simple bonus be P' then

$$\cdot 96P'\ddot{a}_{[40]} = A_{[40]} + \cdot 01 \frac{R_{[40]}}{D_{[40]}} + \cdot 03,$$

i.e. $$\cdot 96P'18\cdot 906 = \cdot 27284 + \cdot 01 \frac{57705\cdot 4}{6981\cdot 6} + \cdot 03$$

$$= \cdot 27284 + \cdot 08265 + \cdot 03$$

$$\therefore P' = \frac{\cdot 38549}{(\cdot 96)(18\cdot 906)} = \cdot 0212.$$

Let the premium for the whole life assurance with compound bonus be P'': then as rate of interest – rate of bonus $= 4\% - 1\% = 3\%$.

$$\cdot 96P''\ddot{a}_{[40]} = A^{3\%}_{[40]} + \cdot 03$$

$$\therefore \cdot 96P''18\cdot 906 = \cdot 36817 + \cdot 03$$

$$\therefore P'' = \frac{\cdot 39817}{(\cdot 96)(18\cdot 906)} = \cdot 0219.$$

Let the premium for the endowment assurance with simple bonus be P''' then

$$\cdot 96P'''\ddot{a}_{[35]:\,\overline{30|}} = A_{[35]:\,\overline{30|}} + \cdot 01 \frac{R_{[35]} - R_{65} - 30M_{65} + 30D_{65}}{D_{[35]}} + \cdot 03,$$

i.e. $\cdot 96P'''17\cdot 381 = \cdot 33148$

$$+ \cdot 01 \frac{67378\cdot 9 - 15675\cdot 8 - 30(1258\cdot 73) + 30(2144\cdot 17)}{8541\cdot 71}$$

$$+ \cdot 03$$

$$= \cdot 33148 + \cdot 09163 + \cdot 03$$

$$\therefore P''' = \frac{\cdot 45311}{(\cdot 96)(17\cdot 381)} = \cdot 0272.$$

Let the premium for the endowment assurance with compound bonus be P^{iv}; then

$$\cdot 96P^{iv}\ddot{a}_{[35]:\,\overline{30|}} = A^{3\%}_{[35]:\,\overline{30|}} + \cdot 03$$

i.e. $$\cdot 96P^{iv}17\cdot 381 = \cdot 43357 + \cdot 03$$

$$\therefore P^{iv} = \frac{\cdot 46357}{(\cdot 96)(17\cdot 381)} = \cdot 0278.$$

The required premiums per cent are then £2·12% with simple bonus and £2·19% with compound bonus for the whole-life assurance and £2·72% and £2·78% respectively for the endowment assurance.

Example 5.7

A deferred annuity contract effected at age 40 purchases a half-yearly annuity at age 60 payable in arrears on a with-profit basis before commencement, being loaded for a compound bonus of 2%. The basis is A1967–70 ultimate mortality with 4% interest and expenses of 3% of the premiums which are returned without interest on death before commencement.

Find the annual premium per £10 p.a. annuity.

Solution

In this case, as the profits cease at age 60, the only effect of the bonus is to increase the annuity assumed purchased. If P' is the required premium per 1 p.a. annuity,

$$\cdot 97P'\ddot{a}_{40:\,\overline{20|}} = (1\cdot02)^{20}\,_{20|}a_{40}^{(2)} + P'\,\frac{R_{40}-R_{60}-20M_{60}}{D_{40}},$$

i.e. $\cdot 97P'13\cdot764 = (1\cdot48595)\dfrac{2855\cdot59}{6986\cdot50}(11\cdot551+\cdot25)$

$$+ P'\,\frac{57711\cdot8-22644\cdot6-20(1477\cdot08)}{6986\cdot50}$$

i.e. $\quad 13\cdot351P' = 7\cdot167 + \cdot791P'$

$\therefore\; 12\cdot560P' = 7\cdot167$

$\therefore\; P' = \cdot571,$

so that the annual premium per £10 p.a. basic annuity will be £5·71.

Exercise 5.5

Show that $\dfrac{A'_{x:\,\overline{n|}}}{\ddot{a}_{x:\,\overline{n|}}}$ is an expression for the net annual premium for an n year with profit endowment assurance with compound reversionary bonus, stating the rate of interest used in calculating the numerator.

Exercise 5.6

A with-profit policy with sum assured £5,000 is loaded for an annual reversionary bonus of £1%. Compare the annual premiums for a 20-year endowment assurance on a life aged 40 on the A1967–70 select table with 4% interest if the bonus is simple or compound. Expenses are, initial 3%, of the sum assured, renewal £2 and 3% of each premium excluding the first.

$$(A^{3\%}_{[40]:\,\overline{20|}} = \cdot56571).$$

Exercise 5.7

Prove that the retrospective and prospective policy values are equal for an annual premium endowment assurance with a simple guaranteed bonus.

Exercise 5.8

An office calculates with-profit deferred annuities on the basis of the 1967–70 ultimate table and 4% interest, expenses of 4% of the premiums, and loading for a simple bonus of $2\frac{1}{2}$% per annum before commencing age. Calculate the annual premium for a life aged 50 for an annuity payable monthly in advance and guaranteed for 5 years commencing at age 65. On death before commencement the premiums are returned without interest.

5.5 Industrial assurance

Life assurance in Britain is conducted by assurance companies, institutions and societies and by friendly societies, the general term life office often being used to include all such bodies. Legally life assurance is divided into *ordinary* and *industrial* although an office may transact both classes. Industrial assurance business may be briefly defined as that for which premiums are received by means of collectors and payable at intervals of less than two months—at one time the collector usually made weekly visits to the home of the assured to collect the premiums. Ordinary assurance business is any not classified as industrial.

Office premiums for ordinary assurances have already been discussed, the normal formulae being described in section 2.6. In the case of industrial assurance almost all expenses are considered as in proportion to the premium with an additional percentage in the first year. Premiums are assumed to be payable continuously and claims paid at the moment of death.

If renewal expenses are k per unit premium and if the excess of the initial expenses over the renewal expenses is K per unit of the first year's premium, then if P'' is the gross premium for a whole-life assurance,

$$P''\bar{a} = \bar{A} + KP'' + kP''\bar{a}$$

$$\therefore P'' = \frac{\bar{A}}{(1-k)\bar{a} - K}. \tag{5.1.1}$$

The sum assured is often expressed as that obtained from a weekly payment of 5p, and would be

$$2 \cdot 60893 \frac{((1-k)\bar{a} - K)}{\bar{A}}, \tag{5.1.2}$$

$2 \cdot 60893$ being $\cdot 05 \times 365\frac{1}{4} \div 7$.

As the expenses of collection of premium are high and the sum assured low the figures for k and K will be very high relative to ordinary business; for weekly collected policies k might be 35% and K 40%.

Exercise 5.9

Find the whole-life sum assured purchased by a weekly premium of 10p on the English Life Table No. 12—Males at 4% interest for a life aged 30. Expenses are 35% of the premiums with an additional 30% in the first year.

5.6 Children's deferred assurances

A type of policy frequently issued is a child's deferred assurance under which there is no life assurance on the child's life until a selected age such as 18, 21 or 25 with the option at that age of selecting a whole-life or endowment assurance, either fully paid or subject to future premiums, or an immediate cash payment (*cash option*). On the death of the child before the selected age the premiums paid or a percentage of them, with or without interest, are returned. Some policies are written as life assurances on the child's father with premiums ceasing if the father dies before the child reaches the selected age, when premiums would recommence unless a paid-up option were chosen.

It is customary in calculating premiums for this type of policy to ignore the child's mortality before the selected age, using interest only functions and to quote the sums assured purchased by an annual premium such as £10 or £12. For the policy with no life assurance on the father the endowment option (Z) at age m purchased by an annual premium of £12 for a child aged x with a selected age of 21 might be

$$(1-k)12(\ddot{a}_{\overline{21-x}|}+v^{21-x}\ddot{a}_{21\,:\,\overline{m-21}|}) = Zv^{21-x}A_{21\,:\,\overline{m-21}|}, \quad (5.6.1)$$

where k is the expense loading. The equation for the paid-up option will be similar but have no life annuity factor. If the policy is to participate in profits from age 21, the assurance factor would be adjusted suitably.

When the premiums cease on the father's death before the child is 21, then if the father is aged y, the endowment option (Z') will be found from a formula of the type

$$(1-k)12(\ddot{a}_{[y]\,:\,\overline{21-x}|}+v^{21-x}\ddot{a}_{21\,:\,\overline{m-21}|}) = Z'v^{21-x}A_{21\,:\,\overline{m-21}|}, \quad (5.6.2)$$

the only difference being that the receipt of the premiums up to age 21 is dependent on the father's survival.

Exercise 5.10

Find on the basis of the A1967–70 table with 4% interest the endowment option at age 60, with premiums continuing or paid-up for a child's deferred assurance purchased for a child aged 5 with a selected age of 21 by an annual premium of £12. Expenses are 5% of each premium.

5.7 Options

Options have been mentioned in the previous section in connection with the choice available on a child's deferred assurance at the selected age. Mention was also made of a cash option which would be available if the policy ceased at the selected age. If a policy has guaranteed surrender values it could be considered to have cash options at all times but the more usual use of the term is to restrict it to child's deferred assurance and to the cash option often allowed at the end of the period of deferment under a deferred annuity. This last is usually calculated either by accumulating the whole or a percentage of the premiums paid with compound interest or alternatively by valuing the annuity prospectively. Because cash options are quoted in the policy document they are usually calculated on relatively favourable bases to the policyholder.

When an assurance matures there may be an option available to take the sum available over a period instead of in cash—this is called a *settlement option*. The common options are an annuity certain and a life annuity. The annuity certain is normally stated as a sum assured paid in instalments while the life annuity will normally be quoted as a minimum rate at which it is guaranteed the annuity may be purchased —if the office's current rate of annuity at maturity is greater then this will be available. Both options are normally calculated by equating the benefits at maturity

Occasionally there is an option that on a claim occurring the sum assured may be deposited with the office for a term of n years and interest at a rate of j per annum will be paid in the meantime, where j is a rate higher than the rate used in calculating the premiums (i). In this case the sum assured will be treated as $v^n + ja_{\overline{n}|} = 1 + (j-i)a_{\overline{n}|}$ where v^n and $a_{\overline{n}|}$ are calculated at rate i, and the premiums are thus obtained by increasing the normal premiums by this factor.

One of the most common types of option is a temporary assurance with the option to convert it into a whole-life or endowment assurance for the same sum assured at any time during the term of the policy at the normal rate of premium without regard to the state of health of the life assured. One method is to consider that if the option is exercised at the end of the term (n) of a temporary assurance originally effected at age x the net premium which should be charged is P_{x+n} and the premium actually to be charged is $P_{[x+n]}$. The value of the difference at the option date is

$$(P_{x+n} - P_{[x+n]})\ddot{a}_{x+n}$$

and the additional annual premium which should be charged is

$$P_{[x]:\,\overline{n}|}^{1}(P_{x+n} - P_{[x+n]})\ddot{a}_{x+n} = \frac{N_{x+n}}{N_{[x]} - N_{x+n}}(P_{x+n} - P_{[x+n]}). \qquad (5.7.1)$$

The expenses which should be allowed for in this calculation cause difficulties and there is the additional theoretical problem that the rates of mortality at which P_{x+n} is calculated should more properly be the mortality experienced by those lives effecting option policies which may not necessarily be the same as the ultimate rates of mortality; there is likely to be self-selection with the less healthy lives being more likely to use the option.

While the discussion above has been based on the conversion of a temporary assurance the option could in fact be granted without a basic policy or in addition to another policy; in the later case it is sometimes referred to as an *increase option* or *guaranteed insurability rider* allowing some multiple of the original sum assured to be effected as new assurances at various times during the term of the policy.

Example 5.8

A policy has an increase option added to it under which the life assured who is at present aged 55 may at the fifth and tenth policy anniversaries effect a whole-life policy with sum assured £1,000 without evidence of health. Find the additional annual premium payable for ten years for the option if there is an expense and contingency loading of 50%, mortality is A1967–70 select and interest is 4%.

Solution

If the level annual premium for the options is X, then

$$X\ddot{a}_{[55]:\,\overline{10}|} = 1{,}000\left(\frac{D_{60}}{D_{[55]}}\,(P_{60}-P_{[60]})\ddot{a}_{60}\right.$$
$$\left. + \frac{D_{65}}{D_{[55]}}\,(P_{65}-P_{[65]})\ddot{a}_{65}\right),$$

i.e. $\quad X(8{\cdot}093) = 1{,}000\left(\dfrac{2855{\cdot}59}{3638{\cdot}33}\,({\cdot}04121-{\cdot}04021)12{\cdot}551\right.$
$$\left. + \frac{2144{\cdot}17}{3638{\cdot}33}\,({\cdot}05468-{\cdot}05254)10{\cdot}737\right),$$

i.e. $\quad X(8{\cdot}093) = 1{,}000({\cdot}00985+{\cdot}01354)$

$$\therefore X = 2{\cdot}89.$$

Adding the loading of 50% gives an annual premium of £4·34.

The net premium should be compared with the premium for the five-year option by itself—if the annual premium for the five-year option is Y, then

$$Y\ddot{a}_{[55]:\,\overline{5}|} = 1{,}000({\cdot}00985),$$

i.e. $$Y = \frac{9{\cdot}85}{4{\cdot}569} = 2{\cdot}16.$$

This net premium is thus less than that for the combined option, indicating that the cost of the five-year option is met by the premium paid in the first five years. This, however, is not always the case and such a check should be made, and if the option premium for the earlier or earliest options is higher than the premium for the total the premium would normally be increased in the early years so that the premium is paid before the 'risk' expires.

Example 5.9

An endowment assurance maturing at age 65 with sum assured £2,000 has the following options:

    (i) the sum assured may be paid in 10 annual instalments of £240 commencing immediately at maturity;

    (ii) an annuity of £200 per annum payable half-yearly in advance from age 65 instead of the sum assured;

    (iii) the right on death before maturity, instead of the death benefit being payable immediately on death, to leave the sum assured on deposit for 5 years receiving interest at the rate of 5% per annum in the meantime.

Ignoring expenses, calculate the annual premium for the policy for a life aged 50 on the basis of the A1967–70 select table with 4% interest, allowing where necessary for each of the above options.

Solution

    The value at maturity of option (i) is

$$240\ddot{a}_{\overline{10}|} = 240(8\cdot4353)$$

$$= 2024\cdot5.$$

The value at maturity of option (ii) is

$$200\ddot{a}^{(2)}_{65} = 200(10\cdot487)$$

$$= 2097\cdot4.$$

The greater value of these options is 2,097·4, so the policy is considered as having a maturity value of £2,097·4.

    The value at death of the deposit option is

$$2,000(1+(\cdot05-\cdot04)a_{\overline{5}|})$$

$$= 2,000(1\cdot0445)$$

$$= 2089\cdot0.$$

The policy can thus be considered as having a death benefit of £2,089·0 and a maturity value of £2,097·4; the annual premium is then

$$\frac{1}{\ddot{a}_{[50]:\,\overline{15}|}}\left(2{,}089(1\cdot02)A^{\,1}_{[50]:\,\overline{15}|} + 2097\cdot4(A_{[50]:\,\overline{15}|} - A^{\,1}_{[50]:\,\overline{15}|})\right)$$

$$= \frac{1}{\ddot{a}_{[50]:\,\overline{15}|}}(2097\cdot4A_{[50]:\,\overline{15}|} + 33\cdot4A^{\,1}_{[50]:\,\overline{15}|})$$

$$= 2097\cdot4P_{[50]:\,\overline{15}|} + \frac{33\cdot4(\cdot10782)}{11\cdot028}$$

$$= 2097\cdot4(\cdot05222) + \cdot33$$

$$= 109\cdot9.$$

The required annual premium is thus £109·9.

Exercise 5.11

An endowment assurance maturing at age 60 with sum assured £3,000 has the following options available at maturity:

(i) the sum assured may be left on deposit indefinitely with the company, interest at the rate of $4\frac{1}{2}\%$ being paid in the meantime;

(ii) an annuity of £270 per annum payable monthly in advance from age 60.

Find the annual premium for a life aged 40 ignoring expenses on the basis of the A1967–70 select table with 4% interest.

Exercise 5.12

A guaranteed insurability rider is added to an assurance policy giving the right to effect a whole-life assurance for a sum assured of £5,000 at either the fourth or eighth policy anniversaries but not both, without evidence of good health. Find the annual premium for the option for a life aged 50 on the A1967–70 select table with 4% interest if there is an expense and contingency loading of 40%.

5.8 Alterations to policies

A life office may be asked to revise the terms of an existing assurance policy to make the policy more suitable to the present requirement of the policyholder. For example, he may wish to change a whole-life assurance to an endowment assurance or vice versa, or to change the maturity date of an endowment assurance. The principles of the calculations are the same in each case and only the first will be considered in detail.,

It will be assumed that the conversion of the policy makes no change in the mortality to be assumed, i.e. that the future mortality will be the same as that of those lives who continue their policies unaltered. If P is the net annual premium to be charged in future, the policy originally being effected at age x with premium $P_{[x]}$, the change taking place at duration t, to mature at age $x+m$, there are at least five methods of approaching the calculation of P:

(1) If the policy had originally been effected as an endowment assurance to mature at age $x+m$ with premiums $P_{[x]}$ for t years and P thereafter,

$$P_{[x]}\ddot{a}_{[x]:\overline{t}|} + P_t|\ddot{a}_{[x]:\overline{m-t}|} = A_{[x]:\overline{m}|} \qquad (5.8.1)$$

from which P can be found.

(2) If the reserve under the original policy is used as a single premium for part of the endowment assurance with term $m-t$ then

$$_tV_{[x]}+P\ddot{a}_{x+t:\,\overline{m-t}|} = A_{x+t:\,\overline{m-t}|} \qquad (5.8.2)$$

from which P can be found.

(3) The reserves on the policy before and after alteration must be identical as no cash is paid, so

$$_tV_{[x]} = A_{x+t:\,\overline{m-t}|} - P\ddot{a}_{x+t:\,\overline{m-t}|}, \qquad (5.8.3)$$

which is only slightly different from (5.8.2).

(4) If the policy had originally been effected to mature at age $x+m$ the reserve on hand would be $_tV_{[x]:\overline{m}|}$ and the excess of this over $_tV_{[x]}$ must be paid by the policyholder by adding to the premium for the endowment, $P_{[x]:\overline{m}|}$, the excess spread over the remaining term, that is

$$P = P_{[x]:\,\overline{m}|} + \frac{_tV_{[x]:\,\overline{m}|} - {_tV_{[x]}}}{\ddot{a}_{x+t:\,\overline{m-t}|}}. \qquad (5.8.4)$$

(5) The 'arrears' of premiums which have not been paid in the past $(P_{[x]:\overline{m}|} - P_{[x]})$ accumulated are spread over the remaining term, i.e.

$$P = P_{[x]:\,\overline{m}|} + \frac{(P_{[x]:\,\overline{m}|} - P_{[x]})\ddot{s}_{x:\,\overline{t}|}}{\ddot{a}_{x+t:\,\overline{m-t}|}}. \qquad (5.8.5)$$

It can be shown that all these formulae give identical results. In practice an office premium will be required and the office may also wish to charge expenses for the administration of the change. The above formulae should not be used in any case where office premiums are required without consideration of the actual expenses of the policy concerned.

When a with-profit policy is altered it is customary for the bonus to be kept unchanged in amount but allow for the change in the reserve value of the bonus in assessing the new premium.

Normally in any problem the above formulae should be ignored and the reserves immediately before and after the alteration to the individual policy should be equated (i.e. method (3) above).

Policy values of altered policies are usually most easily obtained by the prospective method.

Example 5.10

Ten years ago an office issued a 25-year endowment assurance policy to a life then aged 35 for a sum assured of £1,000 with guaranteed simple reversionary bonuses of 3% per annum added on the payment of each premium. The policyholder now wishes to convert the policy into an ordinary non-profit endowment assurance for £1,000 maturing in ten years with an additional sum payable if he survives the period. Existing bonus is to be cancelled and the annual premium is to be increased by 50%. Calculate the additional sum payable at maturity assuming that sums payable on death are payable at the end of the year of death. The basis is A1967–70 ultimate 4% throughout.

Solution

If P is the original premium

$$P(N_{35}-N_{60}) = 1,000M_{35}+30(R_{35}-R_{60})$$
$$-1,750M_{60}+1,750D_{60},$$

i.e. $P(171,493-35,841) = 1,000(1,949\cdot13)+30(67,383\cdot1-22,644\cdot6)$

$$+1,750(2,855\cdot59-1,477\cdot08),$$

i.e. $$P = \frac{5,703,678}{135,652} = 42\cdot05.$$

At duration 10 the retrospective reserve is

$$42\cdot05\frac{N_{35}-N_{45}}{D_{45}} - \frac{1}{D_{45}}(1,000M_{35}+30(R_{35}-R_{45})-1,300M_{45})$$

$$= 42\cdot05\frac{171,493-99,757}{5,689\cdot18} - \frac{1}{5,689\cdot18}(1,000(1,949\cdot13)$$

$$+30(67,383\cdot1-48,269\cdot4)-1,300(1,852\cdot39))$$

$$= 530\cdot2-20\cdot1 = 510\cdot1.$$

After the change the premium is 63·08 and if X is the extra sum then

$$510\cdot1+63\cdot08\,\ddot{a}_{45:\overline{10|}} = 1,000\,A_{45:\overline{10|}}+X_{10}E_{45}$$

i.e. $$510\cdot1+63\cdot08\left(\frac{99,756\cdot5-52,502\cdot8}{5,689\cdot18}\right)$$

$$= 1,000\left(\frac{1,852\cdot39-1,645\cdot23+3,664\cdot57}{5,689\cdot18}\right)+X\frac{3,664\cdot57}{5,689\cdot18}$$

i.e. $510 \cdot 1 + 523 \cdot 9 = 680 \cdot 4 + X(\cdot 64413)$

$$X = \frac{1{,}034 \cdot 0 - 680 \cdot 4}{\cdot 64413} = 549.$$

So extra 'pure endowment' sum at maturity is £549.

Exercise 5.13

Prove the identity of the values of P obtained in the equations (5.8.1), (5.8.2), (5.8.3), (5.8.4), (5.8.5).

Exercise 5.14

An m year annual premium endowment assurance effected at age x is changed after t years into a whole-life assurance. Show that the prospective reserve at age $x + r(r > t)$ is identical to the retrospective reserve.

Exercise 5.15

A policyholder who effected at age 30 a £1,000 40-year endowment assurance subject to annual premiums asks immediately before the 25th premium becomes due that the policy be converted to mature at age 65. Assuming that the office calculates premiums and maintains reserves on the basis of the A1967–70 ultimate table at 4%, find the revised premium. Expenses are assumed to be 10% of each premium. The sum assured is payable at the end of the year of death.

5.9 Return of premiums with interest on death

Particularly in the case of deferred annuities a death benefit before the annuity commences is often a return of the premium paid accumulated at a specified rate of interest. The simplest case to consider is when the specified rate of interest is the same as the rate assumed in the premium calculation and only net functions are used. The relationship between successive reserves on an annual premium (P) contract assuming the benefit is paid at the end of the year of death is then in the first year

$$(0 + P)(1 + i) = qP\ddot{s}_{\overline{1}|} + p_1 V$$

giving $_1V = P\ddot{s}_{\overline{1}|}$, i.e. the death benefit equals the reserve at the end of the year. Similarly in the second year

$$(_1V + P)(1 + i) = qP\ddot{s}_{\overline{2}|} + p_2 V$$

$$\therefore P\ddot{s}_{\overline{2}|} = qP\ddot{s}_{\overline{2}|} + p_2 V$$

and $_2V = P\ddot{s}_{\overline{2}|}$ and the death benefit and the reserve at the end of the year are equal.

Obviously the same relationship will hold good throughout the contract and may formally be proved by induction. The rates of mortality before the annuity commences have therefore no effect on the net premium which is calculated by assuming only an interest accumulation, the annual premium P then being

$$P\ddot{a}_{\overline{n}|} = v^n a'_{x+n}, \tag{5.9.1}$$

where n is the deferred period and a'_{x+n} is the value of the annuity when due to commence.

It will be seen that this reasoning will break down if the gross premium is considered. In practice, however, this approach is often used, but the actual rate of interest allowed on death is less than that assumed in the premium basis.

An accurate formula when the gross premium is to be returned can be found. If P' is the gross premium then the value of the return of premiums on death is:

$$\frac{1}{l_x} \sum_{t=0}^{n-1} v^{t+1} P' \ddot{s}_{\overline{t+1}|} d_{x+t}, \tag{5.9.2}$$

and as

$$v^{t+1} \ddot{s}_{\overline{t+1}|} = \ddot{a}_{\overline{t+1}|}$$

$$= \frac{1 - v^{t+1}}{d},$$

the expression equals

$$\frac{P'}{d} \sum_{t=0}^{n-1} \left(\frac{d_{x+t}}{l_x} - \frac{v^{x+t+1} d_{x+t}}{v^x l_x} \right)$$

$$= \frac{P'}{d} \left(\frac{l_x - l_{x+n}}{l_x} - \frac{M_x - M_{x+n}}{D_x} \right). \tag{5.9.3}$$

If it had been assumed that the benefit was payable on death rather than at the end of the year of death, formula (5.9.2) could have been used adapted to assume that on average death occurs at mid-year—

$$\frac{1}{l_x} \sum_{t=0}^{n-1} v^{t+\frac{1}{2}} P' s_{\overline{t+1}|}(1+i)^{\frac{1}{2}} d_{x+t},$$

which gives the same answer.

A similar approach can be used to obtain an accurate formula when the death benefit specifies a different rate of interest accumulation from the premium basis. Using accented interest functions for the specified rate of interest gives the value of the benefit when paid at the end of the year of death

$$= \frac{1}{l_x} \sum_{t=0}^{n-1} v^{t+1} P' \ddot{s}_{\overline{t+1}|} d_{x+t}$$

and as $v^{t+1} \ddot{s}_{\overline{t+1}|}$

$$= v^{t+1} \frac{(1+i')^{t+1} - 1}{d'}$$

$$= \frac{v''^{t+1} - v^{t+1}}{d'}, \quad \text{where} \quad v'' = v(1+i') = \frac{v}{v'} = \frac{1+i'}{1+i},$$

the expression equals

$$\frac{P'}{d'} \sum_{t=0}^{n-1} \left(\frac{v''^{x+t+1} d_{x+t}}{v''^x l_x} - \frac{v^{x+t+1} d_{x+t}}{v^x l_x} \right)$$

$$= \frac{P'}{d'} \left(\frac{M''_x - M''_{x+n}}{D''_x} - \frac{M_x - M_{x+n}}{D_x} \right) \qquad (5.9.4)$$

the double accented functions being calculated at the rate of interest

$$i'' = \frac{1+i}{1+i'} - 1 = \frac{i-i'}{1+i'}.$$

As i' is usually less than i but differs by a small amount such as 1% or 2% the accurate calculation of the formula requires the tabulation of commutation functions at lower rates of interest than may be available.

Example 5.11

A life office issues annual premium deferred annuity contracts under which the death benefit paid at the end of the year of death before the annuity commences is the return of the gross premiums paid accumulated with 4% interest. Calculate the annual premium on the A1967–70 ultimate table with 4% interest and expenses of 5% of the premium for a life aged 40 for an annuity of £200 p.a. payable half-yearly in advance from age 60.

Solution

Using formula (5.9.3) the equation for the premium P' is

$$\cdot 95 P' \ddot{a}_{40:\overline{20}|} = 200 \frac{D_{60}}{D_{40}} \ddot{a}_{60}^{(2)} + \frac{P'}{d} \left(\frac{l_{40} - l_{60}}{l_{40}} - \frac{M_{40} - M_{60}}{D_{40}} \right),$$

i.e. $\cdot 95P'(13\cdot764) = (200)\dfrac{2,855\cdot59}{6,986\cdot50}(12\cdot301)$

$$+ \frac{P'}{\cdot038462}\left(\frac{33,542\cdot3-30,039\cdot8}{33,542\cdot3} - \frac{1,909\cdot50-1,477\cdot08}{6,986\cdot50}\right),$$

i.e. $\qquad 13\cdot076P' = 1,005\cdot6 + P'(1\cdot106)$

$$\therefore P' = \frac{1,005\cdot6}{11\cdot970} = 84\cdot01.$$

The annual premium is thus £84.

Example 5.12

Calculate the annual premium for a deferred annuity of £500 per annum payable quarterly in advance from age 65 for a life aged 35 if the benefit on death, paid at the end of the year of death, before commencement is the return of premiums paid. No interest is added to the return until 16 premiums have been paid when 4% interest is allowed. The basis is A1967–70 ultimate with 4% interest and expenses are 6% of the premium.

Solution

In this case the value of the death benefit when interest is added during the second 15 years cannot be found directly from formula (5.9.3)—but can be found by taking the summation in formula (5.9.2) over different limits as follows:

$$\frac{1}{l_{35}}\sum_{t=15}^{29} v^{t+1}P'\ddot{s}_{\overline{t+1}|}d_{35+t}$$

$$= \frac{P'}{d}\sum_{t=15}^{29}\left(\frac{d_{35+t}}{l_{35}} - \frac{v^{35+t+1}d_{35+t}}{v^{35}l_{35}}\right)$$

$$= \frac{P'}{d}\left(\frac{l_{50}-l_{65}}{l_{35}} - \frac{M_{50}-M_{65}}{D_{35}}\right).$$

The equation for the premium is therefore

$$\cdot94P'\ddot{a}_{35:\,\overline{30}|} = 500\,\frac{D_{65}}{D_{35}}\,\ddot{a}^{(4)}_{65} + P'\,\frac{(R_{35}-R_{50}-15M_{50})}{D_{35}}$$

$$+ \frac{P'}{d}\left(\frac{l_{50}-l_{65}}{l_{35}} - \frac{M_{50}-M_{65}}{D_{35}}\right),$$

i.e. $\cdot 94P'(17\cdot375) = 500\dfrac{2,144\cdot17}{8,545\cdot01}(10\cdot362)$

$$+ P'\frac{67,383\cdot1 - 39,164\cdot1 - 15(1,767\cdot56)}{8,545\cdot01}$$

$$+ \frac{P'}{\cdot038462}\left(\frac{32,669\cdot9 - 27,442\cdot7}{33,719\cdot4} - \frac{1,767\cdot56 - 1,258\cdot73}{8,545\cdot01}\right),$$

i.e. $16.333P' = 1,300\cdot1 + P'(\cdot200) + P'(2\cdot482)$

$$\therefore P' = \frac{1,300\cdot1}{13\cdot651} = 95\cdot24$$

the premium required is thus £95·24.

Exercise 5.16

An annuity of £100 per annum is purchased by annual premiums for a life aged 40 to commence at age 65 payable monthly in advance and guaranteed for five years. On death before age 65 the benefit is £500 or the premiums paid accumulated at 4% interest whichever is the greater. Calculate the premium on the basis of the A1967–70 ultimate table with 4% interest and expense loadings of £2 per £100 of annuity paid and 5% of the gross premium. The death benefit is payable at the end of the year of death.

Exercise 5.17

An annuity of £500 per annum is purchased by annual premiums for a life aged 50 to commence at age 65 payable half-yearly in advance. On death before age 65, 95% of the premiums accumulated at 1% per annum compound interest are returned at the end of the year of death. Calculate the premium on the basis of the A1967–70 ultimate table with 4% interest and expenses of 3% of the gross premium.

$$(A^1_{50\,:\,\overline{15}|} \text{ at } 3\% = \cdot1209).$$

5.10   Extra risks

Not all proposers to life offices are acceptable at normal rates of premium, the impairment may for example be because of a medical condition or history of illness, or a hazardous occupation or pastime, or residence in an unhealthy climate.

Special terms should in theory be calculated on the basis of special mortality tables but in practice this would be too difficult as only a rough estimate of the probable extra mortality is likely to be available. In this section the term extra mortality will be used to indicate the addition to the normal rate (or sometimes force) of mortality. If accented symbols are used for the total mortality expected to be experienced by an impaired life, then the rate of extra mortality $q'-q$ (or $\mu'-\mu$) may be constant, or increase or decrease when the time increases.

While the normal method of allowing for an extra risk is to increase the premium there is the alternative that the death benefit may be reduced by an amount known as a debt or lien, which may be a fixed amount for a period of years or the duration of the contract but more usually reduces by a level amount each year as each premium is paid.

To find a debt the normal method of equating the values of premiums and benefits can be used for example for an n-year endowment assurance on a life aged x with annual premium P and a debt of $(n-1)D$ reducing by D each year so that there is no debt in the last year when no further premiums are payable,

$$P\ddot{a}'_{x:\,\overline{n}|} = A'_{x:\,\overline{n}|} - D\,\frac{(n-1)M'_x - R'_{x+1} + R'_{x+n}}{D'_x}. \qquad (5.10.1)$$

The equivalent relationship when the extra premium is payable is

$$P'\ddot{a}'_{x:\,\overline{n}|} = A'_{x:\,\overline{n}|}$$

and subtracting

$$(P'-P)\ddot{a}'_{x:\,\overline{n}|} = D\,\frac{(n-1)M'_x - R'_{x+1} + R'_{x+n}}{D'_x}, \qquad (5.10.2)$$

which express the relationship between the extra premium and debt that the *value of the extra premiums equals the value of the debt on the basis of the special mortality*, which result is also obtainable by general reasoning.

The above reasoning has been concerned with net premiums. The equivalent gross extra premium will be equal to the net premium increased by the factor for renewal expenses ($\frac{1}{1-k}$ in the usual notation).

It will be realised that the debt or extra premium cannot be obtained from the other unless full information on the special mortality is available, and the result of the calculation may vary considerably according to the incidence of the extra risk, and particularly on whether the extra mortality is constant, increasing or decreasing.

G

Constant extra mortality normally means a constant addition to μ_x, while a common assumption on increasing risks is to assume that the life is a certain number of years older than the actual age—often referred to as the *rated-up* age.

When a constant addition ξ is assumed to the normal force of mortality so that

$$\mu'_x = \mu_x + \xi$$

then $\qquad n p'_x = e^{-\int_0^n (\mu_{x+t} + \xi)dt}$

and $\qquad v^n {}_n p'_x = e^{-\int_0^n (\mu_{x+t} + \xi + \delta)dt}$

$$= e^{-\int_0^n (\xi+\delta)dt} \cdot e^{-\int_0^n \mu_{x+t}dt},$$

i.e. $\qquad v^n {}_n p'_x = v^{*n} \cdot {}_n p_x \left(\text{and } \dfrac{D'_{x+n}}{D'_x} = \dfrac{D^*_{x+n}}{D^*_x} \right),$

where v^* is calculated at force of interest $\delta + \xi$.

This is a particularly useful expression if commutation functions on the normal mortality are available (or can be interpolated) at the increased force of interest.

By summation it can then be seen that

$$a'_{x:\,\overline{n}|} = a^*_{x:\,\overline{n}|}, \tag{5.10.3}$$

where $'$ implies the normal rate of interest and special mortality and $*$ implies the increased rate of interest such that $\delta^* = \delta + \xi$ and the normal mortality.

While the annuity function takes this simple form the life assurance form is slightly more complicated, e.g.

$$\bar{A}'^1_{x:\,\overline{n}|} = \int_0^n v^t {}_t p'_x (\mu_{x+t} + \xi)dt$$

$$= \int_0^n v^{*t} {}_t p_x (\mu_{x+t} + \xi)dt,$$

i.e. $\qquad \bar{A}'^1_{x:\,\overline{n}|} = \bar{A}^{1*}_{x:\,\overline{n}|} + \xi \bar{a}^*_{x:\,\overline{n}|}, \tag{5.10.4}$

where the $*$ functions are on normal mortality and the increased force of interest as described above.

Now
$$\bar{A}^{1*}_{x:\overline{n}|} = 1 - \delta^*\bar{a}^*_{x:\overline{n}|} - \frac{D^*_{x+n}}{D^*_x}$$

so
$$\bar{A}'^{1}_{x:\overline{n}|} = 1 - (\delta^* - \zeta)\bar{a}^*_{x:\overline{n}|} - \frac{D^*_{x+n}}{D^*_x},$$

i.e.
$$\bar{A}'^{1}_{x:\overline{n}|} = 1 - \delta\bar{a}^*_{x:\overline{n}|} - \frac{D^*_{x+n}}{D^*_x}, \qquad (5.10.5)$$

which result could also be obtained by the usual premium conversion relationship

$$\bar{A}'^{1}_{x:\overline{n}|} = 1 - \delta\bar{a}'_{x:\overline{n}|} - \frac{D'_{x+n}}{D'_x}$$

i.e.
$$\bar{A}'^{1}_{x:\overline{n}|} = 1 - \delta\bar{a}^*_{x:\overline{n}|} - \frac{D^*_{x+n}}{D_x{}^*}, \quad \text{as before,}$$

it being important to note that while the commutation functions on the right-hand side are at the increased rate of interest, the δ is at the normal rate of interest.

The similar expression for the benefit payable at the end of the year of death will be

$$A'^{1}_{x:\overline{n}|} = 1 - d\ddot{a}^*_{x:\overline{n}|} - \frac{D^*_{x+n}}{D^*_x}. \qquad (5.10.6)$$

For the endowment assurance benefit

$$\bar{A}'_{x:\overline{n}|} = 1 - \delta\bar{a}^*_{x:\overline{n}|} \qquad (5.10.7)$$

and
$$A'_{x:\overline{n}|} = 1 - d\ddot{a}^*_{x:\overline{n}|}, \qquad (5.10.8)$$

again noting that δ and d are at a different rate of interest than the annuity.

Example 5.13

A life office calculates premium rates on the basis of the A1967–70 ultimate table with 3% interest. A proposer aged 50 is subject to a constant addition to the assumed force of mortality of $\cdot009662$. If he wishes to pay the normal annual premium of £113$\cdot$12, calculate the equivalent level debt for an endowment assurance with sum assured £2,000 payable at age 65 or the end of year of death if earlier—ignore expenses.

Solution

$$\delta \text{ at } 3\% \text{ interest} = \cdot029559$$
$$\text{plus} \qquad \cdot009662$$
$$\overline{}$$
$$= \cdot039221, \text{ which is } \delta \text{ at } 4\% \text{ interest.}$$

Then by formula (5.10.3) annuity functions on the special mortality table at 3% interest equal those on the normal mortality table at 4% interest. Using formula (5.10.6) if D is the debt and equating benefits and premiums gives

$$(113 \cdot 12)\ddot{a}_{50:\overline{15|}} = 2,000\{1 - (\cdot 029126)\ddot{a}_{50:\overline{15|}}\}$$
$$- D\{1 - (\cdot 029126)\ddot{a}_{50}\ _{\overline{15|}} - {}_{15}E_{50}\}$$

with the mortality functions on A1967–70 4%, ·029126 being d at 3%,

i.e. $(113 \cdot 12)(10 \cdot 995) = 2,000\{1 - (\cdot 029126)(10 \cdot 995)\}$
$$- D\{1 - (\cdot 029126)(10 \cdot 995) - (\cdot 57711 - \cdot 11058)\}$$

i.e. $1,243 \cdot 8 = 1,359 \cdot 5 - \cdot 2132D$

$$\therefore D = \frac{115 \cdot 7}{\cdot 2132} = 542 \cdot 7.$$

So level debt is £543.

Example 5.14

An impaired life aged 45 has been accepted for a 15-year endowment assurance with sum assured £3,000 subject to the payment of the rate of premium for a life five years older. On the assumption that each year the expected mortality will be that of a life five years older, calculate the alternative debt reducing uniformly each year to nil in the last year of insurance. The office calculates premiums on the basis of the A1967–70 select table with 4% interest. Expenses are 6% of each premium.

Solution

Premium paid for the policy

$$= \frac{1}{\cdot 94} \, 3,000 P_{[45]:\overline{15|}} = \frac{3,000(\cdot 05043)}{\cdot 94} = 160 \cdot 95.$$

Let the initial debt be $14D$ decreasing by D each year.

Then equating the present value of benefits and premiums and expenses using the mortality table 'rated-up' five years

$$(\cdot 94)(160 \cdot 95)\ddot{a}_{[50]:\overline{15|}} = 3,000 A_{[50]:\overline{15|}} - D \frac{15M_{[50]} - R_{[50]} + R_{65}}{D_{[50]}},$$

expressed in this way as $R_{[50]+1}$ is not tabulated in the Appendix, i.e. $(151 \cdot 29)(11 \cdot 028) = 3{,}000(\cdot 57584)$

$$-D\,\frac{15(1{,}752 \cdot 68) - 39142 \cdot 9 + 15{,}675 \cdot 8}{4581 \cdot 32},$$

i.e. $1{,}668 \cdot 4 = 1{,}727 \cdot 5 - D(\cdot 6162)$

$$\therefore D = 95 \cdot 9,$$

which multiplied by 14 is 1,342·6, so the initial debt is 1,342·60 reducing by £95·90 each year.

Example 5.15

A proposer aged 40 subject to the mortality of the A1967–70 ultimate table proposed to a life office which assumes lighter mortality for its premium tables and 4% per annum interest. As an alternative to the extra premium of £1 per £1,000 sum assured for an endowment assurance for a term of 25 years the proposer is offered a debt reducing on each anniversary by a level amount to nil in the last year of the policy. Ignoring expenses and assuming that the sum assured is payable at the end of the year of death, find the initial debt and the annual reduction.

Solution

The premium per unit sum assured which should be charged for the policy is ·02565, the extra premium is ·00100, so the tabular premium on the offices normal rate is ·02465.

If D is the annual reduction of the debt, the initial debt is $24D$ and applying formula (5.10.2) gives

$$(\cdot 001)\ddot{a}_{40:\,\overline{25|}} = D\,\frac{24M_{40} - R_{41} + R_{65}}{D_{40}}$$

the mortality being on the A1967–70 table which in this case is the special mortality;

i.e. $$D = \frac{(\cdot 001)(N_{40} - N_{65})}{24M_{40} - R_{41} + R_{65}}$$

$$= \frac{\cdot 001(132{,}002 - 23{,}021)}{24(1{,}909 \cdot 50) - 55{,}802 \cdot 3 + 15{,}675 \cdot 8}$$

$$= \frac{108 \cdot 98}{5{,}701 \cdot 5}$$

$$= \cdot 0191,$$

and multiplying by 24 gives the initial debt of ·4584. Per £1,000 sum insured the initial debt is then £458·40 with an annual reduction of £19·10.

Exercise 5.18

After 10 years the policyholder in Example 5.15 wishes to cancel the debt and pay an increased premium. Find the premium if the expected mortality is assumed to remain the same.

Exercise 5.19

A life office calculates premium rates on the basis of the A1967–70 select table with 2% interest. A life aged 45 effects a 20-year endowment assurance with sum assured £4,000 at the normal annual premium of £173·80, but because of an impairment equivalent to an addition to the normal force of mortality of ·019418 a level debt will be deducted on death before age 65. If expenses are ignored, find the debt.

Exercise 5.20

A proposed life aged 50 has been 'rated up' three years for a whole-life assurance. Find the debt decreasing uniformly over 30 years if the normal annual premium is paid, mortality is A1967–70 select with 4% interest and expenses are ignored. *Sum assured £1000.*

Exercise 5.21

Find the reserve after 10 years for the policy in Example 5.14 if the proposer accepts the alternative debt and compare it with the reserve if the extra premium is paid and with the reserve if the policy was on a normal life not subject to extra mortality.

EXAMPLES AND EXERCISES ON CHAPTER 5

Example 5.16

A life aged 45 effects a deferred annuity of £100 per annum payable half-yearly in advance from age 60 for ten years certain and life thereafter. Annual premiums are to be paid for a maximum of ten years. On death before age 60 the premiums previously paid are to be returned, without interest, by yearly instalments commencing at the end of the year of death, each instalment being equal to the premium. Ignoring expenses, derive an expression for the annual premium.

Solution

Value of return of premium benefits, where P is the premium

$$= \frac{P}{D_{45}} (C_{45}\ddot{a}_{\overline{1}|} + C_{46}\ddot{a}_{\overline{2}|} + C_{47}\ddot{a}_{\overline{3}|} + \ldots + C_{54}\ddot{a}_{\overline{10}|} + (M_{55} - M_{60})\ddot{a}_{\overline{10}|})$$

$$= \frac{P}{D_{45}.d}\left(C_{45}(1-v)+C_{46}(1-v^2)+C_{47}(1-v^3)+\ldots+C_{54}(1-v^{10})\right)$$

$$+ \frac{P}{D_{45}}(M_{55}-M_{60})\ddot{a}_{\overline{10}|}, \quad \text{using } \ddot{a}_{\overline{n}|} = \frac{1-v^n}{d},$$

$$= \frac{P}{D_{45}.d}\left(C_{45}-v^{47}d_{45}+C_{46}-v^{49}d_{46}+C_{47}-v^{51}d_{49}+\ldots\right.$$

$$\left.+C_{54}-v^{65}d_{54}\right)+ \frac{P}{D_{45}}(M_{55}-M_{60})\ddot{a}_{\overline{10}|}$$

$$= \frac{P}{d}\frac{(M_{45}-M_{55})}{D_{45}} - \frac{P}{dv^{90}l_{45}}(v^{92}d_{45}+v^{94}d_{46}+\ldots+v^{110}d_{54})$$

$$+ \frac{P}{D_{45}}(M_{55}-M_{60})\ddot{a}_{\overline{10}|}$$

$$= \frac{P}{d}\frac{(M_{45}-M_{55})}{D_{45}} - \frac{P}{d}\frac{(M'_{45}-M'_{55})}{D'_{45}} + \frac{P}{D_{45}}(M_{55}-M_{60})\ddot{a}_{\overline{10}|},$$

where accented functions are calculated at a rate of interest such that $v' = v^2$, i.e. $i' = 2i+i^2$.

Equating the value of benefits and premiums gives

$$P\ddot{a}_{45:\overline{10}|} = \frac{P}{d}\left\{\frac{M_{45}-M_{55}}{D_{45}} - \frac{M'_{45}-M'_{55}}{D'_{45}}\right\} + \frac{P}{D_{45}}(M_{55}-M_{60})\ddot{a}_{\overline{10}|}$$

$$+ 100\frac{D_{60}}{D_{45}}\left(\ddot{a}^{(2)}_{\overline{10}|} + \frac{D_{70}}{D_{60}}\ddot{a}^{(2)}_{70}\right)$$

and solving for P,

$$P = \frac{100(D_{60}\ddot{a}^{(2)}_{\overline{10}|}+D_{70}\ddot{a}^{(2)}_{70})}{(N_{45}-N_{55})-\frac{1}{d}\left\{M_{45}-M_{55}-\frac{D_{45}}{D'_{45}}(M'_{45}-M'_{55})\right\}-(M_{55}-M_{60})\ddot{a}_{\overline{10}|}};$$

the expression required, the accented functions being calculated at rate of interest $2i+i^2$.

Example 5.17

A region of a country is subject to earthquakes, and a life office transacting business in the rest of the country is considering extending to this region. It will assume that earthquakes occur at exactly five-year intervals and that at each occurrence out of 100 lives one will die, the probability of dying being independent of age. Normal premiums are calculated using the A1967–70 ultimate table 4%. Ignoring expenses and assuming that claims are paid at the end of the

year of death, calculate the additional annual premium per cent
required for a ten-year endowment assurance for a life aged 55 on
the assumption that an earthquake has just happened.

If the proposer wishes to pay the normal premium but reduce the
death benefit if death is due to an earthquake, calculate the percentage reduction in the sum assured.

Solution

The effect of the special mortality will be to reduce the value of l_x
by 1% each time an earthquake is assumed to happen, i.e. in five and
ten years' time, so the value of the annuity on the special mortality
will be (the earthquake ten years hence having no effect on the value)

$$\ddot{a}_{55:\overline{10|}} = \ddot{a}_{55:\overline{5|}} + \frac{99}{100}\,_{5|5}\ddot{a}_{55}$$

$$= \ddot{a}_{55:\overline{10|}} - \frac{1}{100}\,_5E_{55}\ddot{a}_{60:\overline{5|}}$$

$$= 8\cdot045 - \frac{1}{100}(\cdot82513 - \cdot04588)(4\cdot489)$$

$$= 8\cdot010.$$

Using the formula $P = \dfrac{1}{\ddot{a}} - d$ gives $\dfrac{1}{8\cdot010} - \cdot038462 = \cdot08638$. The
normal premium is $\cdot08584$, so the additional premium is $\cdot00054$, i.e.
5 pence per £100 sum assured.

The present value of the death benefit on earthquakes will be the
value of the benefit if death occurs on the earthquake five years hence
plus the value of the benefit if death occurs on the earthquake ten
years hence just before the policy matures, i.e.

$$\frac{1}{100}\,_5E_{55} + \frac{99}{100}\cdot\frac{1}{100}\cdot\,_{10}E_{55}$$

$$= \frac{1}{100}(\cdot82513 - \cdot04588) + \frac{99}{10{,}000}(\cdot69058 - \cdot10547)$$

$$= \cdot01358.$$

If D is the reduction in benefit on earthquakes

$$\text{(normal premium)}.\,\ddot{a}'_{55:\overline{10|}} = A'_{55:\overline{10|}} - D(\cdot01358),$$

i.e. $(\cdot08584)(8\cdot010) = \cdot69192 - D(\cdot01358)$

$$\therefore D = \cdot320.$$

Thus the percentage reduction required is 32%.

Exercise 5.22

On the basis of the A1967–70 ultimate table 4% calculate the annual premium limited to 20 years' payments to secure on a life aged 40 a policy providing, on survival to the end of the term of 25 years, a sum assured of £1,000 and in the event of death during the term, a sum assured of £500 if death occurs within the first 15 years and a return of premiums paid, accumulated with compound interest at a rate of 4% per annum, if death takes place thereafter. Assume that the benefit in the event of death is payable at the end of the year of death.

If after it has been in force for 5 years the policy is altered so that the payment in the event of death thereafter is a return of the premiums paid without interest, what adjustment will be made in the sum payable at maturity assuming no alteration is made in the annual premium or the period of payment? The basis of alteration is the same as the premium basis.

Exercise 5.23

Recalculate the premium and debt in Example 5.17 on the assumption that an earthquake is just about to happen.

Exercise 5.24

Five years ago an assurance company issued to a man then aged 30 a whole-life assurance for a sum assured of £1,000 with additional family income benefits, subject to level annual premiums limited to 30 payments. In the event of death during the first 30 years the income benefit is payable for the balance of the period in quarterly instalments, the first falling due 3 months after the date of death and ceasing with a proportionate payment at the end of the period. The annual rate of income benefit is £250 if death occurs during the first 15 years and £500 if death occurs thereafter, and payment of the whole sum assured is deferred until the end of the period. The company calculates premiums on the basis of the A1967–70 ultimate table at 4% interest.

The policyholder now requests that the policy should be altered so that the sum assured will be payable at age 60 in any event and if death occurs within the next 10 years the annual rate of income benefit will be increased to £500 for the last 15 years. Ignoring expenses, calculate the annual premium payable before and after the alteration.

Exercise 5.25

An office issues to an unmarried female life, aged 21, a 20-year endowment assurance for £1,000 by annual premiums. Included in the policy is an option at the end of five years if the assured is then married for her husband to effect an endowment policy to age 60 for the same sum assured without evidence of health. Calculate the additional premium paid for five years for the option, ignoring expenses, if females are assumed to experience mortality according to the A1967–70 select table with a deduction of four years, males experience the mortality of the A1967–70 select table and husbands are assumed to be two years older than their wives in half of the cases and eight years older in the other half. Interest is 4%. Assume that the probability of an unmarried female aged 21 being alive and married within five years is ·9, and that all married women exercise the option.

CHAPTER SIX

APPLICATIONS OF CALCULUS: POPULATION THEORY

6.1 Differential coefficients with respect to age

The following results have already been found:

$$\frac{d}{dx} l_x = -l_x \mu_x \qquad \text{(equation 1.6.3)}$$

$$\frac{d}{dt} ({}_t p_x) = -{}_t p_x \mu_{x+t} \qquad \text{(equation 1.6.12)}$$

$$\frac{d}{dx} ({}_t p_x) = {}_t p_x (\mu_x - \mu_{x+t}). \qquad \text{(equation 1.6.13)}$$

There will now be found the differential coefficients with respect to x of

$$D_x, \ \bar{N}_x, \ \bar{M}_x, \ \bar{a}_x, \ \bar{A}_x, \ {}_t\bar{V}(\bar{A}_x).$$

$$\frac{dD_x}{dx} = \frac{d(v^x l_x)}{dx}$$

$$= v^x(-l_x\mu_x) + l_x v^x \log_e v,$$

i.e.
$$\frac{dD_x}{dx} = -D_x(\mu_x + \delta). \qquad (6.1.1)$$

$$\bar{N}_x = \int_0^\infty D_{x+t} dt$$

$$\therefore \frac{d\bar{N}_x}{dx} = \int_0^\infty \frac{d(D_{x+t}) dt}{dx}$$

$$= \int_0^\infty \frac{d(D_{x+t}) dt}{dt} \qquad \text{as } D_{x+t} \text{ is symmetric in } x \text{ and } t$$

$$= [D_{x+t}]_{t=0}^{t=\infty},$$

i.e.
$$\frac{d\bar{N}_x}{dx} = -D_x. \qquad (6.1.2)$$

$$\bar{M}_x = \int_0^\infty D_{x+t} \mu_{x+t} dt$$

$$\therefore \frac{d\overline{M}_x}{dx} = \int_0^\infty \frac{d(D_{x+t}\mu_{x+t})dt}{dx}$$

$$= \int_0^\infty \frac{d(D_{x+t}\mu_{x+t})dt}{dt}$$

$$= [D_{x+t}\mu_{x+t}]_{t=0}^{t=\infty}$$

$$\therefore \frac{d\overline{M}_x}{dx} = -D_x\mu_x. \tag{6.1.3}$$

$$\frac{d\bar{a}_x}{dx} = \frac{d}{dx}\int_0^\infty v^t {}_t p_x dt$$

$$= \int_0^\infty v^t \frac{d}{dx}({}_t p_x)dt$$

$$= \int_0^\infty v^t {}_t p_x(\mu_x - \mu_{x+t})dt$$

$$= \mu_x \bar{a}_x - \overline{A}_x,$$

i.e. $$\frac{d\bar{a}_x}{dx} = \bar{a}_x(\mu_x + \delta) - 1. \tag{6.1.4}$$

$$\frac{d\overline{A}_x}{dx} = \frac{d}{dx}(1 - \delta\bar{a}_x)$$

$$= -\delta\frac{d\bar{a}_x}{dx}$$

$$= -\delta[\bar{a}_x(\mu_x + \delta) - 1]$$

$$= (\overline{A}_x - 1)(\mu_x + \delta) + \delta,$$

i.e. $$\frac{d\overline{A}_x}{dx} = \overline{A}_x(\mu_x + \delta) - \mu_x. \tag{6.1.5}$$

$$\frac{d}{dx}({}_t\overline{V}(\overline{A}_x)) = \frac{d}{dx}\left(1 - \frac{\bar{a}_{x+t}}{\bar{a}_x}\right)$$

$$= -\frac{1}{(\bar{a}_x)^2}\left(\bar{a}_x[\bar{a}_{x+t}(\mu_{x+t} + \delta) - 1]\right.$$
$$\left. - \bar{a}_{x+t}[\bar{a}_x(\mu_x + \delta) - 1]\right)$$

$$= -\frac{1}{(\bar{a}_x)^2}\{\bar{a}_x\bar{a}_{x+t}(\mu_{x+t} - \mu_x) - \bar{a}_x + \bar{a}_{x+t}\}$$

$$= -\frac{\bar{a}_{x+t}}{\bar{a}_x}\left\{\mu_{x+t} - \mu_x - \frac{1}{\bar{a}_{x+t}} + \frac{1}{\bar{a}_x}\right\},$$

i.e. $\dfrac{d}{dx}\left({}_t\overline{V}(\overline{A}_x)\right) = \{1 - {}_t\overline{V}(\overline{A}_x)\}\{\overline{P}(\overline{A}_{x+t}) - \overline{P}(\overline{A}_x) - \mu_{x+t} + \mu_x\}.$

(6.1.6)

We may also find the differential coefficient with respect to the duration (t):

$$\frac{d}{dt}{}_t\overline{V}(\overline{A}_x) = \frac{d}{dt}\left(1 - \frac{\bar{a}_{x+t}}{\bar{a}_x}\right), \quad \text{and using (6.1.4)}$$

$$= \frac{1}{\bar{a}_x}\{1 - (\delta + \mu_{x+t})\bar{a}_{x+t}\}. \tag{6.1.7}$$

Exercise 6.1

Prove formulae (6.1.4) and (6.1.5) by using formulae (6.1.1), (6.1.2) and (6.1.3).

Exercise 6.2

Prove that

$$\frac{d}{dx}(\bar{a}_{x:\overline{t}|}) = \bar{a}_{x:\overline{t}|}(\mu_x + \delta) - 1 + A_{x:\overline{t}|}^{1};$$

$$\frac{d}{dt}(\bar{a}_{x:\overline{t}|}) = A_{x:\overline{t}|}^{1}.$$

Exercise 6.3

Prove that

$$\frac{d}{dx}{}_t\overline{V}(\overline{A}_{x:\overline{n}|}) = \{1 - {}_t\overline{V}(\overline{A}_{x:\overline{n}|})\}\{\overline{P}(\overline{A}^1_{x+t:\overline{n-t}|}) - \overline{P}(\overline{A}^1_{x:\overline{n}|}) - (\mu_{x+t} - \mu_x)\};$$

$$\frac{d}{dt}{}_t\overline{V}(\overline{A}_{x:\overline{n}|}) = \overline{P}(\overline{A}_{x:\overline{n}|}) + \delta - (\mu_{x+t} + \delta)\{1 - {}_t\overline{V}(\overline{A}_{x:\overline{n}|})\}.$$

6.2   Differential coefficients with respect to the rate of interest

It is rare in practice that differential coefficients with respect to the rate of interest are required but the results have some importance as an approximate method of calculating increasing functions (as demonstrated below in the example).

$$\frac{dD_x}{di} = \frac{d}{di}(v^x l_x)$$

$$= l_x.x.v^{x-1}\frac{dv}{di}$$

$$= x.l_x.v^{x-1}(-v^2),$$

i.e. $$\frac{dD_x}{di} = -vxD_x.$$ (6.2.1)

$$\frac{dA_x}{di} = \frac{d}{di} \sum_{t=0}^{\infty} v^{t+1}{}_t|q_x$$

$$= - \sum_{t=0}^{\infty} (t+1)v^{t+2}{}_t|q_x,$$

i.e. $$\frac{dA_x}{di} = -v(IA)_x.$$ (6.2.2)

Similarly it may be proved that

$$\frac{da_x}{di} = -v(Ia)_x.$$ (6.2.3)

Example 6.1

Given the following values for A_{60} at various rates of interest

i	A_{60}
2%	·7331
$2\frac{1}{2}$%	·6819
3%	·6354
$3\frac{1}{2}$%	·5933

find the value of $(IA)_{60}$ at 2%.

Solution

From (6.2.2)

$$(IA)_x = -(1+i)\frac{dA_x}{di},$$

i.e. $$(IA)_x = -(1+i)\frac{1}{\Delta i}(\Delta - \tfrac{1}{2}\Delta^2 + \tfrac{1}{3}\Delta^3 ...)A_x.$$ (6.2.4)

The differences are found as follows:

i	A	Δ	Δ^2	Δ^3
·02	·7331			
		−·0512		
·025	·6819		·0047	
		−·0465		−·0003
·03	·6354		·0044	
		−·0421		
·035	·5933			

So $(IA)_{60} = -(1 \cdot 02) \dfrac{1}{\cdot 005} \{ -\cdot 0512 - \tfrac{1}{2}(\cdot 0047) + \tfrac{1}{3}(-\cdot 0003) \}$

$\qquad = 10 \cdot 94.$

The correct value on the mortality table concerned is in fact 10·99.

Exercise 6.4

Find $(\bar{I}\bar{a})_x$ at 3% interest given that

$$\begin{aligned} \bar{a}_x \text{ at } 3\% &= 14 \cdot 375, \\ \bar{a}_x \text{ at } 4\% &= 13 \cdot 018, \\ \bar{a}_x \text{ at } 5\% &= 11 \cdot 865, \\ \bar{a}_x \text{ at } 6\% &= 10 \cdot 882. \end{aligned}$$

Exercise 6.5

Given

$$\begin{aligned} \bar{a}_x \text{ at } 3\tfrac{1}{2}\% &= 10 \cdot 323, \\ \bar{a}_x \text{ at } 4\% &= 9 \cdot 948, \\ \bar{a}_x \text{ at } 4\tfrac{1}{2}\% &= 9 \cdot 597, \\ \bar{a}_x \text{ at } 5\% &= 9 \cdot 267. \end{aligned}$$

Calculate as accurately as possible the value at $3\tfrac{1}{2}\%$ p.a. interest of a continuous annuity to a life aged x where the payment at time t is at the rate of t^2 per annum.

6.3   Mortality table as a population model

The consideration of population statistics forms a branch of actuarial science known as demography. In general, this subject is outside the scope of this book but there are certain basic mortality functions which are common to demography and life assurance mathematics. Although demography is based on a mortality table the interpretation of the various functions differs somewhat from that already described—it is an interpretation in which the mortality table is considered as representing a stationary population.

It is assumed that a community free from emigration and immigration has always experienced the mortality of a life table represented by l_x. If $l_0 \delta t$ births occur in each short interval of time δt (implying a uniform distribution of births over every calendar year) then the number of survivors after x years will be $l_x \delta t$, and l_x lives will attain age x in any year—being the survivors of the l_0 births x years previously.

At any time the total population between ages x and $x+1$ will be

$$\int_0^1 l_{x+t}\,dt = L_x,$$

where $$L_x = \int_0^1 l_{x+t}\,dt, \qquad (6.3.1)$$

The total population over age x at any time is defined as T_x, so

$$T_x = \sum_{t=0}^{\infty} L_{x+t} = \int_0^{\infty} l_{x+t}\,dt. \qquad (6.3.2)$$

The population between ages x and $x+n$ will be

$$T_x - T_{x+n} = \sum_{t=0}^{n-1} L_{x+t} = \int_0^n l_{x+t}\,dt.$$

Figure 6.1 represents the part of the graph of l_x between x and $x+1$.

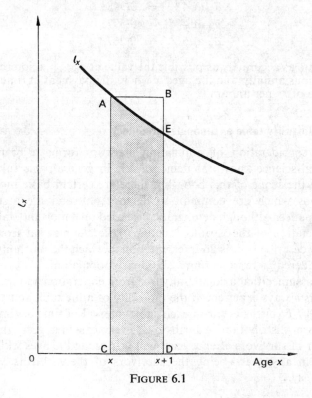

FIGURE 6.1

The rectangle ABDC represents l_x as an area since $AC = l_x$ and $CD = 1$.

The shape AEDC represents L_x since $L_x = \int_0^1 l_{x+t}dt$.

An approximation to L_x and T_x will be

$$L_x \fallingdotseq \tfrac{1}{2}(l_x + l_{x+1}) \tag{6.3.3}$$

and

$$T_x \fallingdotseq \tfrac{1}{2}l_x + \sum_{t=1}^{\infty} l_{x+t}. \tag{6.3.4}$$

On the assumption that there is a uniform distribution of deaths over the year of age x to $x+1$, AE becomes a straight line and the approximate formulae become exact.

It should be noted how this interpretation of the mortality table contrasts with the usual interpretation in which l_x represents the number of lives surviving to age x out of the original l_0 births. In the stationary population concept l_x represents the number of lives attaining age x in any year of time. Similarly d_x rather than being the number of deaths between age x and $x+1$ among the survivors out of the original l_0 births represents the number of deaths in any year of time. The functions L_x and T_x represent numbers living in the population at any moment of time—on a census enumeration of the population at any time the number of lives who would state that they were age x last birthday would be L_x. The number of deaths in the stationary population each year will be $\sum_{t=0}^{\infty} d_{x+t} = l_0$, which equality is obvious, as if the population is stationary the number of births must equal the number of deaths.

When the population being considered is not that represented by the whole life table but only by a part of it, for example the staff of a company, then the entrants each year will equal the sum of the exits (e.g. death, retiral, withdrawal).

If a stationary staff is supported by l_x entrants at exact age x and retirement takes place at exact age $x+n$, then the total staff at any time will be $T_x - T_{x+n}$. If, therefore, the employer wished to give Christmas presents to his staff he would require $T_x - T_{x+n} = \sum_{t=0}^{n-1} L_{x+t}$ presents. On the other hand, if he wished to give birthday presents he would require to give presents to those reaching each age during the year, that is $\sum_{t=1}^{n} l_{x+t}$ (assuming the presents are given to those reaching retirement but not to those just joined). Some students find this a helpful way to remember the distinction in the use of L_x and l_x when considering stationary populations.

So far consideration has been given to a population directly represented by the l_x column of the mortality table. However, in most examples the number of persons considered will not be consistent with the radix of the mortality table, and proportions of the tabular figures by a *reduction factor* or *scale factor*, usually represented by k, will be used. In examples information is given to enable k to be found—in some cases the main part of the question will be to find k.

The functions L_x and T_x are not given in many published mortality tables; L_x is then found by formula (6.3.3) and T_x from summation or from the relationship $T_x = l_x \mathring{e}_x$, where $\mathring{e}_x$ is tabulated. The meaning of $\mathring{e}_x$ and the proof of the identity will be given in the next section, the result is used in the arithmetic of the following examples and exercises.

Example 6.2

A large company has a staff maintained in a stationary condition by 500 annual entrants at exact age 20. If the staff retire at age 60 and English Life No. 12—Males mortality is experienced find:

(a) the size of the staff,

(b) the number of staff who retire each year,

(c) the number of pensioners.

Solution

If the reduction factor is k

$$kl_{20} = 500.$$

(a) The total staff

$$= k(T_{20} - T_{60})$$

$$= \frac{500}{l_{20}}(T_{20} - T_{60})$$

$$= \frac{500}{l_{20}}(l_{20}\mathring{e}_{20} - l_{60}\mathring{e}_{60})$$

$$= 500\left(\mathring{e}_{20} - \frac{l_{60}}{l_{20}}\mathring{e}_{60}\right)$$

$$= 500\left(50{\cdot}57 - \frac{78{,}924}{96{,}293}\,15{\cdot}06\right)$$

$$= 500(50{\cdot}57 - 12{\cdot}34)$$

$$= 19{,}115.$$

(b) The number of staff who retire each year

$$= kl_{60}$$

$$= \frac{500l_{60}}{l_{20}}$$

$$= 500\frac{78{,}924}{96{,}293}$$

$$= 410.$$

(c) The number of pensioners

$$= kT_{60}$$

$$= \frac{500}{l_{20}}\,T_{60}$$

$$= \frac{500}{l_{20}}\,l_{60}\mathring{e}_{60}$$

$$= \frac{500}{96{,}293}\,78924(15{\cdot}06)$$

$$= 6{,}172.$$

Example 6.3

An organisation has 20,000 workers and is kept in a stationary condition by admission of new entrants at exact age 25. A quarter of these reaching age 30 leave. Of the remaining employees who attain age 60 one-third retire at that age; the remainder retire on attaining age 65. If on the death of each member a benefit of £100 is paid find the total cost each year. Mortality is English Life Table No. 12—Males.

Solution

If the reduction factor is k,

$$k(T_{25} - \tfrac{1}{4}T_{30} - \tfrac{1}{4}T_{60} - \tfrac{1}{2}T_{65}) = 20{,}000.$$

The number of deaths each year

$=$ (no. of entrants)$-$(no. of withdrawals)$-$(no. of members

$\qquad\qquad\qquad\qquad\qquad\qquad\qquad\qquad\qquad$ retiring on pension)

$= kl_{25} - \tfrac{1}{4}kl_{30} - \tfrac{1}{4}kl_{60} - \tfrac{1}{2}kl_{65}$

$$= \frac{20{,}000(l_{25} - \tfrac{1}{4}l_{30} - \tfrac{1}{4}l_{60} - \tfrac{1}{2}l_{65})}{T_{25} - \tfrac{1}{4}T_{30} - \tfrac{1}{4}T_{60} - \tfrac{1}{2}T_{65}}$$

$$= \frac{20{,}000\{95{,}753 - \tfrac{1}{4}(95{,}265) - \tfrac{1}{4}(78{,}924) - \tfrac{1}{2}(68{,}490)\}}{95{,}753(45\cdot84) - \tfrac{1}{4}(95{,}265)(41\cdot06) - \tfrac{1}{4}(78{,}924)(15\cdot06) - \tfrac{1}{2}(68{,}490)(11\cdot95)}$$

$$= \frac{20{,}000(17{,}961)}{2{,}705{,}046}$$

$= 132\cdot8.$

Whilst the actual number of deaths must obviously be an integer, on average each year the number may be fractional.

Total cost on average each year $=$ £13,280.

Exercise 6.6

A company with a stationary staff employs 10,000 qualified tradesmen who serve a 5-year apprenticeship commencing on the 16th birthday. Find the number of apprentices who must be accepted for training each year if one-tenth fail the trade test at the end of the apprenticeship and tradesmen retire at age 65. Mortality is English Life Table No. 12—Males.

Exercise 6.7

A staff in a stationary condition is supported by 500 entrants each year at exact age 20. The withdrawals from the staff are so distributed that it may be assumed that one-tenth of those who reach 25 and one-tenth of those who reach 30 withdraw. All those who reach age 60 retire on pension. The staff is separated into two grades, A and B, and if 30% of the staff are in grade B and promotion is by seniority only find the age at which promotion takes place. Determine also the annual cost of giving Christmas boxes and birthday presents of £5 to each member of staff. Assume that those entering at 20 do not receive a birthday present, nor do those withdrawing at ages 25 and 30. Mortality is English Life Table No. 12—Males.

6.4   Expectation of life and average age at death

The expectation of life is defined in two forms e_x and $\mathring{e}_x$,

$$e_x = \frac{1}{l_x} \sum_{t=1}^{\infty} l_{x+t} = \sum_{t=1}^{\infty} {}_t p_x, \qquad\qquad (6.4.1)$$

$$\mathring{e}_x = \frac{1}{l_x} \int_0^\infty l_{x+t}dt = \int_0^\infty {}_tp_xdt = \frac{T_x}{l_x}. \qquad (6.4.2)$$

The functions may be interpreted as representing the average future lifetime of a life aged x, with e_x, called the curtate expectation counting only full years of future lifetime, and $\mathring{e}_x$, called the complete expectation counting the complete lifetime.

An approximation to the relationship between the two expectations can be based on general reasoning; that to ignore the fractional years of life on average ignores $\frac{1}{2}$ and gives

$$\mathring{e}_x \eqsim e_x + \tfrac{1}{2}. \qquad (6.4.3)$$

This relation is more exactly proved by considering formula (3.2.2), i.e.

$$\bar{a}_x \eqsim a_x + \tfrac{1}{2}$$

and making the rate of interest $i = 0$ gives formula (6.4.3) as the expectation of life is the special case of the life annuity when the rate of interest is zero.

A more exact form of the relationship will be found using formula (3.2.1):

$$\mathring{e}_x \eqsim e_x + \tfrac{1}{2} - \tfrac{1}{12}\mu_x \qquad (6.4.4)$$

but this expression is not normally used.

In mortality tables based on population mortality statistics $\mathring{e}_x$ is normally tabulated while in life insurance tables e_x is usually shown.

The average number of years lived after age x is $\mathring{e}_x$ so the average age at death of the persons who attain age x is

$$x + \mathring{e}_x = x + \frac{T_x}{l_x}. \qquad (6.4.5)$$

It should be noted that T_x can thus be interpreted in two different ways, depending on whether a stationary population is being considered where it represents the population over age x, or whether the normal model of the life table is considered where it is the total expected future lifetime of a group of persons l_x of identical age x.

This may be represented graphically as shown in Figure 6.2. T_x is equal to the area PNB, which can be divided by strips either parallel to OX or OY.

The division parallel to OY represents the definition of T_x by summing the population over age x. In considering the division parallel to OX the l_x lives aged x are considered as arranged along PN in order of longevity, then in the limit each strip represents the future lifetime of one individual.

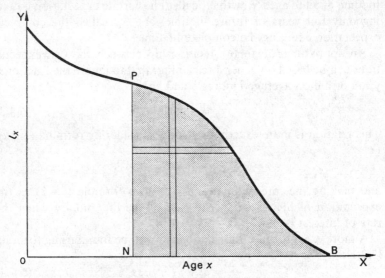

FIGURE 6.2. Representation of T_x.

In a stationary population the ratio of the annual number of births to the total population (the 'birth rate') is

$$\frac{l_0}{T_0} = \frac{1}{\mathring{e}_0},$$

which will also be the 'death rate'.

Temporary expectations of life

$$e_{x:\overline{n}|} = \sum_{t=1}^{n} {}_t p_x$$

and

$$\mathring{e}_{x:\overline{n}|} = \int_0^n {}_t p_x \, dt$$

are sometimes encountered; and

$$e_{x:\overline{n}|} = e_x - \frac{l_{x+n}}{l_x} e_{x+n}.$$

Example 6.4

Prove that

(i) $$\frac{dL_x}{dx} = -d_x,$$

(ii) $$\frac{dT_x}{dx} = -l_x,$$

(iii) $$\frac{d\mathring{e}_x}{dx} = \mu_x \mathring{e}_x - 1.$$

Solution

(i) $$L_x = \int_0^1 l_{x+t}\,dt$$

$$\therefore \frac{dL_x}{dx} = \int_0^1 \frac{dl_{x+t}}{dx}\,dt$$

$$= \int_0^1 \frac{dl_{x+t}}{dt}\,dt$$

$$= \left[l_{x+t}\right]_{t=0}^{t=1}$$

$$= l_{x+1} - l_x,$$

i.e. $$\frac{dL_x}{dx} = -d_x. \qquad (6.4.6)$$

(ii) $$T_x = \int_0^\infty l_{x+t}\,dt$$

$$\therefore \frac{dT_x}{dx} = \int_0^\infty \frac{dl_{x+t}}{dx}\,dt$$

$$= \int_0^\infty \frac{dl_{x+t}}{dt}\,dt$$

$$= \left[l_{x+t}\right]_{t=0}^{t=\infty}$$

i.e. $$\frac{dT_x}{dx} = -l_x. \qquad (6.4.7)$$

(iii) $$\mathring{e}_x = \frac{T_x}{l_x}$$

$$\therefore \frac{d\mathring{e}_x}{dx} = \frac{1}{l_x^2}\left(l_x(-l_x) - T_x(-\mu_x l_x)\right),$$

$$\text{i.e. } \frac{d\mathring{e}_x}{dx} = \mu_x\mathring{e}_x - 1, \tag{6.4.8}$$

which would also be found by putting $i = 0$ in equation (6.1.4).

Example 6.5

Show that the widely held belief that the value of an annuity certain for a term equal to the life expectancy is equal to the value of the life annuity at the same age is not true, and determine which is larger.

Solution

Let there be l_x quantities of which d_x are equal to v, d_{x+1} equal to v^2, d_{x+2} equal to v^3.... The arithmetic mean of these quantities is

$$\frac{1}{l_x} \sum_{t=0}^{\infty} v^{t+1} d_{x+t}$$

$$= A_x = 1 - d\ddot{a}_x.$$

The geometric mean is

$$\left(v^{d_x} v^{2d_{x+1}} v^{3d_{x+2}}\dots\right)^{\frac{1}{l_x}}$$

$$= v^{\frac{1}{l_x}(l_x + l_{x+1} + l_{x+2}\dots)}$$

$$= v^{1+e_x}$$

$$= 1 - d\ddot{a}_{\overline{1+e_x}}.$$

The arithmetic mean of a set of different positive quantities is greater than the geometric mean so

$$1 - d\ddot{a}_x > 1 - d\ddot{a}_{\overline{1+e_x}}$$

$$\therefore \ddot{a}_{\overline{1+e_x}} > \ddot{a}_x$$

$$\text{or } a_{\overline{e_x}} > a_x.$$

Thus the annuity certain for the life expectancy always exceeds the life annuity.

Example 6.6

Determine in two ways the average age at death of those who die between ages x and $x+n$.

Solution

Method 1. The number of years lived between ages x and $x+n$ by the l_x persons aged x

$$= \int_0^n l_{x+t}dt = T_x - T_{x+n},$$

which includes n years lived by each of the survivors to age $x+n$ so the number of years lived by those who die will be

$$T_x - T_{x+n} - nl_{x+n}.$$

The number of deaths is $l_x - l_{x+n}$. Thus the average age at death of those who die between ages x and $x+n$ will be

$$x + \frac{T_x - T_{x+n} - nl_{x+n}}{l_x - l_{x+n}}. \tag{6.4.9}$$

Method 2. During one year the number of persons who die between ages x and $x+n$ is

$$\int_x^{x+n} l_y\mu_y dy = l_x - l_{x+n}.$$

The total of the ages at death is

$$\int_x^{x+n} yl_y\mu_y dy$$

$$= \int_x^{x+n} y\frac{d}{dy}(-l_y)dy$$

$$= \left[-yl_y\right]_x^{x+n} - \int_x^{x+n} (-l_y)dy$$

$$= -(x+n)l_{x+n} + xl_x + T_x - T_{x+n}$$

$$= x(l_x - l_{x+n}) + T_x - T_{x+n} - nl_{x+n}.$$

Dividing by the number of deaths gives the average age at death as

$$x + \frac{T_x - T_{x+n} - nl_{x+n}}{l_x - l_{x+n}}.$$

Exercise 6.8

Find (i) $\dfrac{d}{dt}({}_tp_x\mathring{e}_{x+t})$, and (ii) $\dfrac{d}{dx}\mathring{e}_{x:\,\overline{n}|}$.

Exercise 6.9

Find the average age at death of persons dying between the ages of 50 and 60 by the English Life Table No. 12—Males.

Exercise 6.10

If between ages 1 and 11, $l_x = l_1(1 - \frac{1}{9} \log_{10} x)$, find

(a) the complete expectation of life at age 1 during the next 10 years,

(b) the average age at death of those who die between ages 1 and 11.

6.5 Stationary funds

An extension of the concept of a stationary population is a stationary fund, again a theoretical concept not attained in practice. Such a fund might be a society or company where each year income from contributions, premiums or fees and interest equals the outgo in benefits and/or expenses.

Usually in questions the problem is to find the amount of the fund which will normally be found from an expression of the form

$$\text{Contributions} + \delta.\text{Fund} = \text{Benefits} + \text{Expenses}. \qquad (6.5.1)$$

Example 6.7

For many years a Society has recruited 1,000 new members uniformly over each year at age 25. Mortality is in accordance with the A1967–70 ultimate table. Members pay at entry and annually thereafter level premiums to secure at age 65 annuities of £100 per annum payable continuously for 5 years certain and life thereafter. No payment is made on death before age 65. If the Society earns 4% interest and expenses are ignored, find the amount of the fund.

$$(e_{25} = 49 \cdot 255, \ e_{65} = 13 \cdot 745, \ e_{70} = 10 \cdot 623)$$

Solution

The amount of the annual premium for each member is

$$100 \frac{D_{65}\bar{a}_{\overline{5}|} + D_{70}\bar{a}_{70}}{N_{25} - N_{65}}$$

$$= 100 \frac{2,144 \cdot 17(4 \cdot 4518)(1 \cdot 019869) + 1,517 \cdot 00(8 \cdot 457)}{278,625 - 23,021}$$

$$= 8 \cdot 83.$$

The total premium collected each year will be the number of persons having a birthday during the year times the premium, i.e.

$$(8 \cdot 83)(1,000)\left(1 + e_{25} - \frac{l_{65}}{l_{25}}(1 + e_{65})\right)$$

$$= (8 \cdot 83)(1,000)\left(50 \cdot 255 - \frac{27,442 \cdot 7}{33,951 \cdot 8}(14 \cdot 745)\right)$$

$$= 338,514.$$

Annuities paid out each year $= \dfrac{(1,000)(100)}{l_{25}}(5l_{65} + l_{70}\mathring{e}_{70})$ allowing for the payments continuing for five years for each person reaching age 65,

$$= \frac{100,000}{33,951 \cdot 8}\{5(27,442 \cdot 7) + (23,622 \cdot 1)(11 \cdot 123)\}$$

$$= 1,178,029.$$

So using expression (6.5.1)

(total premiums in year) $+ \delta$ (Fund) $=$ (Annuities paid out in year)

$$338,514 + (\cdot 039221)\,(\text{Fund}) = 1,178,029$$

$$\therefore \text{Fund} = £21,405,000.$$

Example 6.8

A life assurance company has issued 1,000 whole-life policies for unit sum assured each year to proposers at exact age x. Premiums are payable continuously and benefit is payable at the instant of death, and the fund is now in a stationary condition. Ignoring expenses, prove in two ways that the amount of the fund is $\dfrac{1,000}{\delta}(1 - \bar{P}(\bar{A}_x)\mathring{e}_x)$.

Solution

First method. Let F be the fund. The reduction factor is $\dfrac{1,000}{l_x}$, and thus the premiums received each year

$$= \frac{1,000}{l_x}\bar{P}(\bar{A}_x)T_x$$

interest received each year $= \delta \, . \, F$

and claims $= 1,000$ as population is stationary

$$\therefore \delta F + \frac{1,000}{l_x} \bar{P}(\bar{A}_x) T_x = 1,000$$

$$\therefore F = \frac{1,000}{\delta} (1 - \bar{P}(\bar{A}_x)\mathring{e}_x).$$

Second method. The reserve of a policy effected t years ago is (writing $\bar{P}$ for $\bar{P}(\bar{A}_x)$)

$$1 - \frac{\bar{a}_{x+t}}{\bar{a}_x} = 1 - (\bar{P} + \delta)\bar{a}_{x+t}.$$

The fund will then be the sum of the reserves of all the policies now existing, i.e.

$$\int_0^\infty 1,000 \frac{l_{x+t}}{l_x} (1 - (\bar{P} + \delta)\bar{a}_{x+t}) dt$$

$$= 1,000 \left(\mathring{e}_x - (\bar{P} + \delta) \int_0^\infty {}_tp_x \bar{a}_{x+t} dt \right).$$

Now $\displaystyle\int_0^\infty {}_tp_x \bar{a}_{x+t} dt = \int_0^\infty (1+i)^t {}_t|\bar{a}_x dt$

$$= \int_0^\infty (1+i)^t \int_t^\infty v^r {}_rp_x \, dr \, dt,$$

and changing the order of integration,

$$= \int_0^\infty v^t {}_tp_x \int_0^t (1+i)^r dr \, dt$$

$$= \int_0^\infty v^t {}_tp_x \bar{s}_{\bar{t}|} dt, \text{ and substituting } \bar{s}_{\bar{t}|} = \frac{(1+i)^t - 1}{\delta},$$

$$= \int_0^\infty {}_tp_x \frac{(1 - v^t)}{\delta} dt$$

$$= \frac{1}{\delta} (\mathring{e}_x - \bar{a}_x).$$

The fund then is

$$1,000 \left(\mathring{e}_x - \frac{(\bar{P} + \delta)}{\delta} (\mathring{e}_x - \bar{a}_x) \right)$$

$$= \frac{1,000}{\delta} (\delta \mathring{e}_x - \bar{P} \mathring{e}_x - \delta \mathring{e}_x + 1) \text{ as } (\bar{P} + \delta)\bar{a}_x = 1$$

$$= \frac{1,000}{\delta} (1 - \bar{P}(\bar{A}_x)\mathring{e}_x).$$

Exercise 6.11

In a stationary community, all persons now aged x and over agree to contribute a single sum equally to a fund from which a unit will be paid at the death of each of them. Find the amount of the payment.

Exercise 6.12

For many years a fraternal society has recruited 500 new members uniformly over each year at age 30. Mortality is in accordance with the English Life Table No. 12—Males. The benefits paid by the society are a death benefit of £200 on death before age 60, a cash payment of £500 at age 60 and a pension of £52 per annum paid on the member's birthday commencing at age 61. If contributions are paid weekly, expenses are ignored and 4% interest is earned determine the amount of the fund.

Exercise 6.13

For many years a firm has recruited uniformly over the year 100 entrants to its staff at age 30 for service for ten years in a foreign country. At the end of the period of service a gratuity of £1,000 is paid but on death during service a grant of £2,000 is made. Each year the firm pays into a fund which accumulates at 5%, an amount sufficient to secure for each new entrant the benefits payable. If $_t|q_{30} = \cdot01$ for $0 \leq t \leq 9$ and the fund has reached a stationary condition, find the amount of the fund.

6.6   Central death rate

So far use has been made of two functions which provide a measure of the mortality assumed at any age—the rate of mortality q_x and the force of mortality μ_x. A further measure of mortality is the central death rate m_x defined by

$$m_x = \frac{\int_0^1 l_{x+t}\mu_{x+t}dt}{\int_0^1 l_{x+t}dt} = \frac{d_x}{L_x}. \qquad (6.6.1)$$

Thus m_x is the ratio of the expected deaths between age x and $x+1$ among the l_x lives attaining age x to the total number of years which the lives are expected to live between the two ages. The importance of m_x lies in its similarity to the form in which a measure of mortality of a group of actual persons is sometimes obtained in a mortality investigation.

If the assumption is made that the deaths are uniformly distributed over the year of age x to $x+1$ we have

$$m_x \fallingdotseq \frac{d_x}{l_x - \frac{1}{2}d_x}, \tag{6.6.2}$$

or

$$m_x \fallingdotseq \frac{q_x}{1 - \frac{1}{2}q_x}, \tag{6.6.2}$$

and

$$q_x \fallingdotseq \frac{m_x}{1 + \frac{1}{2}m_x}. \tag{6.6.3}$$

Now

$$m_x = \frac{d_x}{L_x}$$

$$= -\frac{1}{L_x}\frac{dL_x}{dx} \quad \text{using formula (6.4.6)}$$

$$\fallingdotseq -\frac{1}{l_{x+\frac{1}{2}}}\frac{dl_{x+\frac{1}{2}}}{dx}$$

i.e.

$$m_x \fallingdotseq \mu_{x+\frac{1}{2}}. \tag{6.6.4}$$

This important approximate relationship can also be demonstrated by considering formula (6.6.1) as a weighted mean value of the force of mortality and this will approximate to the value at the mid-age; and the relationship will be exact if there is a uniform distribution of deaths over the year of age (see Exercise 6.14).

Exercise 6.14

If the value of l_{x+t} for all values of t from $-\frac{1}{2}$ to $+\frac{1}{2}$ can be expressed in the form $A - Bt$, where A and B are independent of t, prove that $\mu_x = m_{x-\frac{1}{2}}$.

Exercise 6.15

Show that m_x is constant for all values of x if $l_x = ke^{-x}$.

Exercise 6.16

Show that $L_{x+1} = L_x e^{-\int_0^1 m_{x+t}dt}$.

EXAMPLES AND EXERCISES ON CHAPTER 6

Example 6.9

A profession was founded over a century ago and has had 500 students enrolling each year on their 20th birthday, and 250 on their

22nd birthday. Mortality has been experienced on the English Life Table No. 12—Males.

There are three grades of members—Student, Associate and Fellow. The Students sit the examination for Associateship on the 1st April following their 25th birthdays, one-half passing. Those who fail leave the profession immediately, while those who pass sit an oral examination for Fellowship on their 30th birthday, and, if they fail, remain Associates until they retire at 65. The number of Fellows between the ages of 50 and retirement at 65 is 2,000, this being the number of senior posts in the profession.

Find (*a*) the annual income from election fees of £5 per member charged to Associates on their transfer from Students on 1st April. (*b*) the pass rate at the Fellowship examinations.

Solution

(*a*) The problem is to find the number of Students who survive each year from those who enter at ages 20 and 22 to the 1st April following their 25th birthdays at which time they will be aged 25 to 26. Considering then the 500 entering at age 20, the number surviving to the examination will, assuming a uniform distribution of births over the calendar year, be

$$\frac{500}{l_{20}} L_{25}$$

$$\doteqdot \frac{500}{l_{20}} \frac{l_{25}+l_{26}}{2}$$

$$= \frac{500}{96,293} \frac{95,753+95,658}{2}$$

$$= 496 \cdot 9.$$

Similarly, the number of those entering at age 22 surviving to sit the examination is

$$\frac{250}{l_{22}} L_{25}$$

$$\doteqdot \frac{250}{96,065} \frac{95,753+95,658}{2}$$

$$= 249.1.$$

As half the students pass the examination, the total election fees will be

$$£5 . \tfrac{1}{2} . (496 \cdot 9 + 249 \cdot 1)$$

$$= £1,865.$$

It will be noted that the date in the year on which the examination takes place does not affect the answer.

(b) The number of Associates sitting the examination each year following the same reasoning as in (a) above will be

$$\tfrac{1}{2} \cdot \frac{500}{l_{20}} \cdot l_{30} + \tfrac{1}{2} \frac{250}{l_{22}} \cdot l_{30},$$

on this occasion l_{30} being used, not L_{30}, as the examination is sat on the birthday and not a fixed day. This equals

$$\tfrac{1}{2} \cdot \frac{500}{96,293} \cdot 95,265 + \tfrac{1}{2} \cdot \frac{250}{96,065} \cdot 95,265$$

$$= 247 \cdot 3 + 124 \cdot 0$$

$$= 371 \cdot 3.$$

The number of Fellows who qualify each year is determined by the number of Fellows who will eventually reach the age band 50 to 65, and will thus be

$$\frac{2,000}{T_{50} - T_{65}} \cdot l_{30}$$

$$= \frac{2,000}{l_{50}\overset{\circ}{e}_{50} - l_{65}\overset{\circ}{e}_{65}} \cdot l_{30}$$

$$= \frac{2,000}{90,085(22 \cdot 68) - 68,490(11.95)} \times 95,265$$

$$= 155 \cdot 6.$$

The pass rate is then $\dfrac{155 \cdot 6}{371 \cdot 3} = 41 \cdot 9\%$.

Example 6.10

A certain international company recruits 100 employees each year at age 20. At 25 half are chosen for overseas service and serve abroad until retirement at age 50. Employees remaining at home retire at age 60. Pensions of £200 per annum are paid continuously to each pensioner. All staff and pensioners experience the mortality of the English Life Table No. 12—Males except that employees on overseas service experience an addition to the normal force of mortality of ·039221. Find

(a) the number of employees serving overseas,

(b) the annual cost of pensions.

Solution

By similar reasoning to that in section 5.10 where the effect of an addition to the force of mortality was discussed we have

$$\mu'_x = \mu_x + \delta,$$

δ being ·039221, or δ at 4%, and the dash indicating the special mortality of overseas employees. Then

$$_np'_x = v^n{}_np_x$$

or
$$\frac{l'_{x+n}}{l'_x} = \frac{v^{x+n}l_{x+n}}{v^x l_x} = \frac{D_{x+n}}{D_x},$$

so that on the special mortality one may consider the D_x commutation column as the life table column of l'_x, and L'_x will be equivalent to $\bar{D}_x$ and T'_x will be equivalent to $\bar{N}_x$.

(*a*) The number of employees serving overseas will be

$$\frac{100}{l_{20}} \frac{l_{25}}{2} \frac{T'_{25} - T'_{50}}{l'_{25}}$$

$$= \frac{100}{l_{20}} \frac{l_{25}}{2} \frac{\bar{N}_{25} - \bar{N}_{50}}{D_{25}}$$

$$= \frac{100}{96,293} \frac{95,753}{2} \frac{742,891 - 179,605}{35,919}$$

$$= 779 \cdot 7, \quad \text{say } 780.$$

(*b*) the annual cost of pensions will be

$$£200 \left\{ \frac{100}{l_{20}} \cdot \frac{l_{25}}{2} \cdot \frac{l'_{50}}{l'_{25}} \cdot \frac{T_{50}}{l_{50}} + \frac{100}{l_{20}} \cdot \frac{1}{2} \cdot T_{60} \right\}$$

$$= £200 \left\{ \frac{100}{l_{20}} \cdot \frac{l_{25}}{2} \cdot \frac{D_{50}}{D_{25}} \cdot \mathring{e}_{50} + \frac{100}{l_{20}} \cdot \frac{1}{2} \cdot l_{60} \cdot \mathring{e}_{60} \right\}$$

$$= £200 \left\{ \frac{100}{96,293} \cdot \frac{95,753}{2} \cdot \frac{12,676}{35,919} \cdot (22 \cdot 68) + \frac{100}{96,293} \cdot \frac{78,924}{2} \cdot (15 \cdot 06) \right\}$$

$$= £203,000.$$

Example 6.11

Officer cadets for a country's air force are recruited each year on their 18th or 21st birthdays; the same number being recruited each birthday. After training till their 24th birthdays one-half of the

H

cadets become air crew officers, one-quarter become ground staff officers and one-quarter are discharged as unsuitable. At age 40 half the air crew officers are appointed as ground staff officers and half are retired. A proportion of ground staff officers are also retired at this age.

Air crew officers are subject to a constant force of mortality of ·024693; other officers and cadets are subject to the mortality of the English Life Table No. 12—Males.

The total number of air crew officers is 5,000 and for them the country's government agrees to pay the additional premiums required to cover aviation risks for a life insurance policy up to a sum insured of £2,000. The life office charges an extra premium of £5% for ten years.

Find: (a) The proportion of ground staff officers who are prematurely retired at age 40 if the government wish to state that the probability of a newly promoted officer serving after 40 is unaffected by whether he is appointed air crew or ground staff.

(b) The maximum cost per annum to the government of the extra premiums for aviation assuming that the policies are effected immediately on promotion.

(c) The number of officer cadets who enter each year.

Solution

(a) Considering the mortality of air crew officers,

$$\text{as} \quad 0{\cdot}024693 = \delta \quad \text{at } 2\tfrac{1}{2}\% \text{ interest,}$$

$$_tp'_{24} = e^{-\int_0^t \delta dt} = v^t \quad \text{at } 2\tfrac{1}{2}\% \text{ interest,}$$

using a dash to indicate the special mortality.

Thus the column of figures for v^t at $2\tfrac{1}{2}\%$ can be considered as a column of l'_{24+t} with the radix $l'_{24} = 1$. The probability of an air crew officer of 24 serving to 40

$$= {}_{16}p'_{24} = v^{16} = {\cdot}67362,$$

so the probability of an air crew officer serving after 40 is half this,

i.e. ·337.

The probability of a ground staff officer serving to 40

$$= \frac{l_{40}}{l_{24}} = \frac{93{,}790}{95{,}851} = {\cdot}978,$$

so if the proportion who serve after age 40 is X, and this is to equal the probability for an air crew officer then

$$\cdot 978X = {\cdot}337$$

$$\therefore X = {\cdot}345 \quad \therefore 1 - X = {\cdot}655.$$

So the proportion of ground staff officers who retire at 40, i.e. answer $(a) = \cdot655$.

(b) Each officer is refunded a premium of £100 paid on the 24, 25, ..., 33 birthdays.

If k is the reduction factor considering the population of air crew officers represented by the v^t column, then

$$k(T'_{24} - T'_{40}) = 5,000,$$

$$\text{i.e.} \quad k\bar{a}_{\overline{16}|} = 5,000.$$

Now the total premiums

$$= £100k(l'_{24} + l'_{25} + \dots l'_{33})$$

$$= £100 \frac{5,000}{\bar{a}_{\overline{16}|}} \ddot{a}_{\overline{10}|}$$

$$= £500,000 \frac{8\cdot9709}{(13\cdot055)(1\cdot012449)}$$

$$= £339,400\text{—answer } (b).$$

(c) No. of air crew officers appointed each year

$$= kl'_{24}$$

$$= \frac{5,000}{\bar{a}_{\overline{16}|}} 1 = 378\cdot3,$$

∴ total cadets finishing training is twice this, 756·6.

If C is the number of cadets joining each year, half at each of 18 and 21, then

$$\tfrac{1}{2}C\frac{l_{24}}{l_{18}} + \tfrac{1}{2}C\frac{l_{24}}{l_{21}} = 756\cdot6,$$

i.e. $$\tfrac{1}{2}C\left(\frac{95,851}{96,514} + \frac{95,851}{96,178}\right) = 756\cdot6,$$

giving $C = 760\cdot5$—answer (c).

Exercise 6.17

In a certain ancient civilisation the population had been stationary for many years, males being subject to the mortality of the English Life Table No. 12—Males and females to the A1967–70 ultimate table with an addition to the age of twenty years. Bigamy was practised, each man marrying his first wife on his 30th birthday and his second on his 40th birthday. All women married on their 20th birthday except for 5% who were selected to be sacred virgins and never married. Males aged 17 and over who were not yet married were in a special warrior class and were subject to an addition to the normal force of mortality of ·039221.

Find the percentage of the births who were male.

Exercise 6.18

A company has recruited 100 male employees throughout each year at exact age 25 for over 40 years, but it now wishes to reduce its labour force by one-quarter in the next five years by reducing the number of recruits to 25 per annum in each of these years and by reducing the retirement age from the 65th birthday as at present. Find the retirement age at the end of the five years. Mortality is according to the English Life Table No. 12—Males.

Exercise 6.19

The inhabitants of a country where the population is stationary experience mortality such that for all ages

$$_tp_x = \left(1 - \frac{t}{80 - x}\right)^{\frac{1}{2}}.$$

Obtain expression for μ_x and $\mathring{e}_x$ and calculate the average age at death of the inhabitants aged exactly 30.

Exercise 6.20

The staff of 20,000 of a large international company is maintained in a stationary condition by recruiting men on their 18th birthdays. Of those who reach their 19th birthdays, 20% resign immediately, and 5% of those who reach their 25th birthdays are transferred to the executive grade. Members of the executive grade retire on their 65th birthdays and the other members of the staff retire on their 60th birthdays. All members of staff experience the mortality of the English Life Table No. 12—Males with an addition to the force of mortality of ·039221.

A pension scheme for members of the executive grade provides an annuity payable continuously for life from the 65th birthday. A unit of pension of £20 per annum is earned in respect of each year of service in the grade. The unit of pension earned by a member is purchased from a life office each year by a single premium paid in advance on the member's birthday, the member contributing £1·50 for each £1 per annum pension and the employer paying the balance.

If the life office calculates its premiums on the English Life Table No. 12—Males with 4% interest without return of premium on death before retirement and expenses of 5% of the gross premium, what is the total amount of premiums paid by the employer in a year?

CHAPTER SEVEN

JOINT LIFE AND LAST SURVIVOR STATUSES

7.1 Joint life functions

In previous chapters the theory of life contingencies has been developed in terms of functions of a single life. If there are two lives (x) and (y) and the probabilities of their survival are independent, the probability that both lives will survive n years, denoted $_nP_{xy}$, will be

$$_nP_{xy} = {_nP_x} \cdot {_nP_y} \tag{7.1.1}$$

$$= \frac{l_{x+n}}{l_x} \cdot \frac{l_{y+n}}{l_y}.$$

If we write $l_{xy} = l_x \cdot l_y$

$$_nP_{xy} = \frac{l_{x+n:y+n}}{l_{x:y}},$$

the colon being used to separate lives in the suffix where there is any possibility of confusion.

The function l_{xy} may be treated similarly to l_x in the single life case.

If $_nq_{xy}$ denotes the probability that at least one of the two lives (x) and (y) die within n years, that is the failure of the joint-life status xy, then

$$_nq_{xy} = 1 - {_nP_{xy}},$$

i.e.

$$_nq_{xy} = \frac{l_{xy} - l_{x+n:y+n}}{l_{xy}}. \tag{7.1.2}$$

When $n = 1$,

$$q_{xy} = 1 - p_{xy} = \frac{d_{xy}}{l_{xy}},$$

where $d_{xy} = l_{xy} - l_{x+1:y+1}$, it being noted particularly that d_{xy} does *not* equal $d_x \cdot d_y$.

Extending the above reasoning to more than two lives, and denoting the m lives by $(x_1), (x_2), (x_3)...(x_m)$ gives

$$l_{x_1 : x_2 : x_3... : x_m} = l_{x_1} \cdot l_{x_2} \cdot l_{x_3} \cdot ... \cdot l_{x_m}, \tag{7.1.3}$$

$$_np_{x_1 x_2 x_3...x_m} = {_np_{x_1}} \cdot {_np_{x_2}} \cdot {_np_{x_3}} \cdots {_np_{x_m}}, \tag{7.1.4}$$

and $$_nq_{x_1 x_2 x_3...x_m} = 1 - {_np_{x_1 x_2 x_3...x_m}}, \tag{7.1.5}$$

The probability that the m-life joint status will fail in the $(n+1)$th year is

$$_n|q_{x_1 x_2 x_3...x_m} = {_np_{x_1 x_2 x_3...x_m}} - {_{n+1}p_{x_1 x_2 x_3...x_m}}.$$

The usual annuity and assurance functions may be defined for the joint life status. For example

$$a_{x_1 x_2 x_3...x_m} = \sum_{t=1}^{\infty} v^t {_tp_{x_1 x_2 x_3...x_m}}$$

represents an annuity payable as long as all the m lives are alive; and

$$A_{x_1 x_2 x_3...x_m} = \sum_{t=0}^{\infty} v^{t+1} {_t|q_{x_1 x_2...x_m}}$$

represents the joint life assurance payable at the end of the year of the first death of the m lives.

The total force of decrement for the joint life status will by analogy with formulae (1.6.1) and (1.6.2) be

$$\mu_{x_1+t : x_2+t : x_3+t : ... : x_m+t}$$

$$= -\frac{1}{l_{x_1+t : x_2+t : ... : x_m+t}} \frac{dl_{x_1+t : x_2+t : x_3+t : ... : x_m+t}}{dt} \tag{7.1.6}$$

$$= -\frac{d}{dt} \log_e l_{x_1+t : x_2+t : x_3+t : ... : x_m+t}$$

$$= -\frac{d}{dt} \log_e (l_{x_1+t} \cdot l_{x_2+t} \cdot l_{x_3+t} \cdot ... \cdot l_{x_m+t})$$

$$= -\frac{d}{dt} (\log_e l_{x_1+t} + \log_e l_{x_2+t} + ... + \log_e l_{x_m+t})$$

$$= \mu_{x_1+t} + \mu_{x_2+t} + ... + \mu_{x_m+t}.$$

Thus $$\mu_{x_1 : x_2 : x_3 : ... : x_m} = \mu_{x_1} + \mu_{x_2} + \mu_{x_3} ... + \mu_{x_m}. \tag{7.1.7}$$

Either using this expression or directly from (7.1.4) it can be seen that

$$_nP_{x_1x_2x_3...x_m} = e^{-\int_0^n (\mu_{x_1+t} + \mu_{x_2+t} + ... + \mu_{x_m+t})dt} \qquad (7.1.8)$$

Multiplying equation (7.1.6) by $l_{x_1+t : x_2+t : x_3+t : ... : x_m+t}$ and integrating from 0 to 1 gives

$$\int_0^1 l_{x_1+t : x_2+t : ... : x_m+t} \cdot \mu_{x_1+t : x_2+t : ... : x_m+t} dt$$

$$= [-l_{x_1+t : x_2+t : ... : x_m+t}]_0^1,$$

i.e. $$d_{x_1 : x_2 : x_3 : ... : x_m} = \int_0^1 l_{x_1+t : x_2+t : ... : x_m+t}\mu_{x_1+t : x_2+t : ... : x_m+t} dt$$

and $$q_{x_1 : x_2 : x_3 : ... : x_m} = \int_0^1 {_tP_{x_1x_2x_3...x_m}}\mu_{x_1+t : x_2+t : x_3+t : ... : x_m+t} dt.$$

q_{xy} may be obtained from $1 - p_{xy} = 1 - p_x \cdot p_y$

$$= 1 - (1 - q_x)(1 - q_y),$$

i.e. $$q_{xy} = q_x + q_y - q_x q_y.$$

In some cases x and y or $x_1, x_2...x_m$ are assumed to be subject to the same mortality table. This has no effect on the formulae which hold provided the mortality of each life is independent.

The formulae may also be applied to select lives, $l_{[x]:[y]}$ being equal to $l_{[x]} \cdot l_{[y]}$ and sometimes being written $l_{[xy]}$.

Commutation functions for the joint life status may be defined, thus

$$D_{x_1x_2...x_m} = v^{\frac{x_1+x_2+...+x_m}{m}} \cdot l_{x_1x_2...x_m},$$

and $$C_{x_1x_2...x_m} = v^{\frac{x_1+x_2+...+x_m}{m}+1} d_{x_1x_2...x_m}$$

it being noted that by using the expression $\dfrac{x_1+x_2+...+x_m}{m}$ the m lives enter the function symmetrically and each function will behave in a similar fashion to the single life counterpart, so that for example N, S, M, R functions are obtained by summation and

$$a_{x_1x_2...x_m} = \frac{N_{x_1+1 : x_2+1 : x_3+1 : ... : x_m+1}}{D_{x_1x_2x_3...x_m}}$$

$$A_{x_1x_2...x_m} = \frac{M_{x_1x_2x_3...x_m}}{D_{x_1x_2x_3...x_m}}.$$

While some joint life functions for two lives are published, particularly for annuity tables where it is common for an annuity to depend on the survivance of both a husband and wife, it is less usual for more than two life functions or for joint life commutation functions to be available and when they are they are usually for equal ages with all lives on the same mortality table. If for example l_{xx} or D_{xx} functions are published it is usual for the figures to be adjusted to make the figures more manageable (for example on A1949–52 $D_{xx} = vl_x l_x 10^{-6}$; on A1967–70 $l_{0:0}$ is chosen such that it equals l_0). If commutation functions or annuity values are not available on the required table (or tables as the mortality of the lives may be different) then they may be obtained by the use of an electronic computer or a method of approximate integration may be used—examples of this will be found in section 8.5 where contingent functions are also evaluated. In the special case where a mortality table follows Gompertz's or Makeham's Law evaluation of joint life functions is simplified (this is discussed fully in section 7.2) and sometimes one of these laws is assumed to apply in order that approximate values may be obtained.

Normally the only functions available where the ages are different are joint life annuities (and sometimes last survivor annuities which are discussed in section 7.3) for two lives on tables prepared from annuitants mortality. For example, the $a(55)$ tables give values of a_{xy} (x male, y female) but it will be noted if reference is made to the tables that values are only published for even ages x and y. If values at odd ages are required, interpolation by a straight line is normally used, e.g.

a_{xy} where x is even, y odd is taken as $\frac{1}{2}(a_{x:y-1} + a_{x:y+1})$

a_{xy} where x is odd, y even is taken as $\frac{1}{2}(a_{x-1:y} + a_{x+1:y})$

and it is probably best to take

a_{xy} where both x and y are odd as

$$\frac{1}{4}(a_{x-1:y-1} + a_{x-1:y+1} + a_{x+1:y-1} + a_{x+1:y+1}).$$

When x and y are both male or female, more extensive interpolation is required as the values are given only for every fifth age.

Similar expressions to those above can also be found for continuous functions $\bar{a}$ and $\bar{A}$ be defining continuous commutation functions similar to those used for single lives. Expressions may also be found in integral form, for example

$$\bar{a}_{xy} = \frac{1}{l_{xy}} \int_0^\infty v^t l_{x+t:y+t} dt$$

and

$$\bar{A}_{xy} = \frac{1}{l_{xy}} \int_0^\infty v^t l_{x+t:y+t} \mu_{x+t:y+t} dt.$$

The normal relationships between a, A and P functions will also hold, for example:

$$A_{xy:\overline{n}|} = 1 - d\ddot{a}_{xy:\overline{n}|}, \qquad (7.1.9)$$

where $A_{xy:\overline{n}|}$ is the endowment assurance payable on the first death within n years or at the end of n years if neither life has died, and $\ddot{a}_{xy:\overline{n}|}$ is a temporary joint life annuity, normally found from whole life annuities which are more likely to be tabulated:

$$\ddot{a}_{xy:\overline{n}|} = \ddot{a}_{xy} - \frac{D_{x+n:y+n}}{D_{x:y}} \ddot{a}_{x+n:y+n}$$

or

$$= \ddot{a}_{xy} - v^n \frac{l_{x+n}}{l_x} \frac{l_{y+n}}{l_y} \ddot{a}_{x+n:y+n},$$

and

$$\bar{P}(\bar{A}_{xy:\overline{n}|}) = \frac{1}{\bar{a}_{xy:\overline{n}|}} - \delta.$$

The joint expectation of life may also be defined, for example

$$\dot{e}_{xy} = \int_0^\infty {}_t p_{xy} dt$$

$$\fallingdotseq \sum_{t=1}^\infty {}_t p_{xy} + \tfrac{1}{2}$$

$$= e_{xy} + \tfrac{1}{2}.$$

Example 7.1

Express each of the following probabilities in terms of the single-life probabilities ${}_n p_x$ and ${}_n p_y$,

(a) both lives will survive n years
(b) at least one life will survive n years
(c) exactly one life will survive n years
(d) not more than one life will survive n years

(e) neither life will survive n years

(f) at least one life will die within n years

(g) not more than one life will die within n years.

Solution

(a) $_np_x \cdot _np_y$

(b) $_np_x \cdot _np_y + _np_x(1 - _np_y) + (1 - _np_x)_np_y = _np_x + _np_y - _np_x \, _np_y$

(c) $_np_x(1 - _np_y) + _np_y(1 - _np_x) = _np_x + _np_y - 2_np_x \cdot _np_y$

(d) $1 - _np_x \cdot _np_y$

(e) $(1 - _np_x)(1 - _np_y) = 1 - _np_x - _np_y + _np_x \cdot _np_y$

(f) Same as (d)

(g) Same as (b).

Example 7.2

Twenty years hence the sum of £20,000 is to be divided equally among a charitable trust and such of two lives now aged 30 and 40 as survive. Find the amount of the trust's expectation according to the A1967–70 ultimate table.

Solution

The probability of both lives living 20 years

$$= {}_{20}p_{30} \cdot {}_{20}p_{40}.$$

So the expectation in these circumstances

$$= \tfrac{1}{3}20{,}000 \, {}_{20}p_{30} \cdot {}_{20}p_{40}.$$

Similarly the expectation if one life lives

$$= \tfrac{1}{2}20{,}000 \, {}_{20}p_{30}(1 - {}_{20}p_{40}) + \tfrac{1}{2}20{,}000(1 - {}_{20}p_{30}){}_{20}p_{40},$$

and the expectation if both lives die

$$= 20{,}000(1 - {}_{20}p_{30})(1 - {}_{20}p_{40}).$$

Now
$${}_{20}p_{30} = \frac{l_{50}}{l_{30}} = \frac{32{,}669 \cdot 9}{33{,}839 \cdot 4} = \cdot 9654,$$

and
$${}_{20}p_{40} = \frac{l_{60}}{l_{40}} = \frac{30{,}039 \cdot 8}{33{,}542 \cdot 3} = \cdot 8956.$$

Total expectation $= 20{,}000(\tfrac{1}{3}(\cdot 9654)(\cdot 8956) + \tfrac{1}{2}(\cdot 9654)(\cdot 1044)$

$$+ \tfrac{1}{2}(\cdot 0346)(\cdot 8956) + (\cdot 0346)(\cdot 1044))$$

$$= 7{,}154, \quad \text{i.e.} \quad \text{£7,154.}$$

Example 7.3

Demonstrate by verbal reasoning Lidstone's approximation to the annual premium for a joint life endowment assurance:

$$P_{xy:\overline{n}|} \doteqdot P_{x:\overline{n}|} + P_{y:\overline{n}|} - P_{\overline{n}|}. \qquad (7.1.10)$$

Solution

The level annual premium for a single-life endowment assurance can be regarded as divided into

(a) the level annual premium for a capital redemption policy without life risk payable at the end of n years, and

(b) the level annual premium payable for a term of n years but ceasing on the death of the life assured for a reducing temporary assurance with sum assured equal to the difference between the endowment sum assured and the reserve under the capital redemption policy.

That is $P_{x:\overline{n}|} = P_{\overline{n}|} +$ (premium for reducing temporary assurance). When a second life is introduced it is necessary to add

(c) the level annual premium for a reducing temporary assurance on the second life similar to (b) less

(d) the level annual premium payable for a term of n years but ceasing on the death of the first of the two lives to die for a varying term assurance on the joint lives with sum payable to be the reserve on the policy under (c) if the first life is the first to die and the reserve on the policy under (b) if the second life is the first to die.

The sum assured under (d) will be small and thus the premium will be negligible and ignoring it will give the approximation

$$P_{xy:\overline{n}|} \doteqdot P_{\overline{n}|} + (P_{x:\overline{n}|} - P_{\overline{n}|}) + (P_{y:\overline{n}|} - P_{\overline{n}|})$$

$$= P_{x:\overline{n}|} + P_{y:\overline{n}|} - P_{\overline{n}|} \quad \text{as required.}$$

Example 7.4

Use Lidstone's approximation to determine the annual premium for a 30-year endowment assurance on two lives aged 35 on the A1967–70 ultimate table with 4% interest, and compare the answer with the accurate value.

Solution

$$P_{35:35:\overline{30}|} \doteqdot 2P_{35:\overline{30}|} - P_{\overline{30}|}$$

$$= 2(\cdot01909) - \left(\frac{1}{17\cdot98371} - \cdot038462\right)$$

$$= \cdot02104.$$

The accurate value will be found by first calculating

$$\ddot{a}_{35:35:\overline{30|}} = \ddot{a}_{35:35} - \frac{D_{65:65}}{D_{35:35}} \ddot{a}_{65:65}$$

$$= 18{\cdot}482 - \frac{1{,}706{\cdot}10}{8{,}345{\cdot}32}\, 8{\cdot}145$$

$$= 16{\cdot}819$$

then $$P_{35:35:\overline{30|}} = \frac{1}{16{\cdot}819} - {\cdot}038462$$

$$= {\cdot}02099.$$

Example 7.5

Derive an expression for an annuity of 1 per annum payable yearly in arrear so long as (x) and (y) both survive and for n years after the death of (y) if (x) is still alive.

Solution

During the first n years the annuity is payable if x is alive whether y is alive or not, so the value for these years is

$$a_{x:\overline{n|}}.$$

After the first n years the annuity is payable if (x) is alive and if (y) was alive n years earlier, with value

$$= \sum_{t=n+1}^{\infty} v^t\, {}_tp_x\, {}_{t-n}p_y$$

and substituting $t = n+s$

$$= \sum_{s=1}^{\infty} v^{n+s}\, {}_{n+s}p_x\, {}_sp_y$$

$$= v^n\, {}_np_x \sum_{s=1}^{\infty} v^s\, {}_sp_{x+n}\, {}_sp_y$$

$$= v^n\, {}_np_x a_{x+n:y}.$$

So total value $$= a_{x:\overline{n|}} + v^n\, {}_np_x a_{x+n:y}.$$

Exercise 7.1

Express in terms of ${}_n|q_x$, ${}_n|q_y$ and ${}_n|q_z$

(a) the probability that all three lives (x), (y) and (z) will die in the $(n+1)$th year,

(b) the probability that none of the lives will die in the $(n+1)$th year,

(c) the probability that at least one of the lives will die in the $(n+1)$th year.

Exercise 7.2

Derive an expression for the annuity in Example 7.5 if no payment is made after m years $(m > n)$.

Exercise 7.3

Use Lidstone's approximation to find approximations to

$$P_{30:40:\overline{20}|}, \quad P_{20:30:40:\overline{25}|}$$

on the A1967–70 ultimate table with 4% interest.

Exercise 7.4

A sum of £50,000 is to be divided in ten years equally among such of three lives now aged 60, 65 and 65 as survive. Find the expectation of the life aged 60 using the $a(55)$ female ultimate table.

7.2   Law of uniform seniority

When a life table follows Makeham's or Gompertz's Law considerable simplification is possible in evaluating joint life functions and it is not necessary to tabulate numerical values for joint tables to such an extent as is otherwise the case provided all lives are subject to the mortality of the same table. Even when a table does not follow either law accurately it is sometimes adequate to assume that it does for a certain range of ages thus enabling values to be estimated.

Considering first Makeham's Law the probability of survival of one life (x) was given in formula (1.9.6)

$$_tp_x = s^t g^{c^x(c^t-1)}.$$

The probability of joint survival of the m lives $x_1, x_2, x_3 \ldots, x_m$ will be

$$_tp_{x_1x_2x_3\ldots x_m}$$
$$= s^t g^{c^{x_1}(c^t-1)} s^t g^{c^{x_2}(c^t-1)} \ldots s^t g^{c^{x_m}(c^t-1)}$$
$$= s^{mt} g^{(c^{x_1}+c^{x_2}+\ldots+c^{x_m})(c^t-1)}$$

and substituting

$$c^{x_1} + c^{x_2} + \ldots + c^{x_m} = mc^w \tag{7.2.1}$$

we obtain $$_tp_{x_1x_2...x_m} = s^{mt}g^{mc^w(c^t-1)}.$$

In calculating probabilities based on survival the joint life status $(x_1x_2...x_m)$ involving m lives of different ages can thus be replaced by the simpler status $(ww...w)$ all being the same age; the calculation does not depend on the duration t. The age w is referred to as the *equivalent equal age*.

While the equation (7.2.1) could be used to determine w it is much easier to use a relationship involving the force of mortality. By multiplying equation (7.2.1) by B and adding mA to each side,

$$m(A+Bc^w) = (A+Bc^{x_1})+(A+Bc^{x_2})+...+(A+Bc^{x_m})$$

hence $$m\mu_w = \mu_{x_1}+\mu_{x_2}+...+\mu_{x_m}. \tag{7.2.2}$$

It is thus only necessary to tabulate joint life functions for equal ages to enable all functions to be evaluated, for annuities are directly dependent on the joint life probabilities of survival thus

$$a_{x_1x_2...x_m} = a_{ww...w}$$

and $$1-d\ddot{a}_{x_1x_2...x_m} = 1-d\ddot{a}_{ww...w},$$

i.e. $$A_{x_1x_2...x_m} = A_{ww...w},$$

and also by division

$$P_{x_1x_2...x_m} = P_{ww...w}.$$

In the case of the two life joint life status $(x:x+n)$ can be replaced by the equal age status $(x+t:x+t)$, where $x+t$ is substituted for w in the usual notation, and

$$2c^{x+t} = c^x+c^{x+n},$$

dividing by $2c^x$ gives

$$c^t = \tfrac{1}{2}(1+c^n)$$

hence $$t = \frac{\log(1+c^n)-\log 2}{\log c}.$$

The value of t is thus independent of x but dependent only on n, the difference between the respective ages. Thus a simple table may be constructed to show the value of t for each age difference n. When expressed in this way the method of equating ages is referred to as the *Law of Uniform Seniority*. An extract from a table of uniform seniority is given in Table 7.1.

TABLE 7.1

Difference in age	Addition to younger age
1	0·51
2	1·04
3	1·60
4	2·17
5	2·77
:	
10	6·04
:	
15	9·75
:	
20	13·83

When a mortality table follows Gompertz's Law an even simpler relationship can be found. From equation (1.9.3)

$$_tp_{x_1x_2x_3...x_m} = g^{c^{x_1}(c^t-1)}g^{c^{x_2}(c^t-1)}...g^{c^{x_m}(c^t-1)}$$
$$= g^{(c^{x_1}+c^{x_2}+...+c^{x_m})(c^t-1)},$$

and by substituting

$$c^w = c^{x_1}+c^{x_2}+...+c^{x_m},$$
$$_tp_{x_1x_2...x_m} = g^{c^w(c^t-1)} = {_tp_w}.$$

Thus the joint life status can be replaced by a single life, and joint life functions can be evaluated directly from single life tables, the age w being referred to as the *equivalent single age*. Multiplying the equation for c^w above by B,

$$\mu_w = \mu_{x_1}+\mu_{x_2}+\mu_{x_3}+...+\mu_{x_m}. \qquad (7.2.3)$$

It is important to realise that the w in the single life substitution in a Gompertz's table is different from the w used in the Makeham's table—in fact the equivalent single age in the Gompertz case is always greater than the oldest life while in the Makeham case the equivalent equal age is intermediate among the original ages.

The Law of Uniform Seniority can equally be used in this case. The joint life status $(x, x+n)$ being replaced by the one life status $x+n+t \ (= w)$, measuring t from the older age in this case,

i.e. $\qquad c^{x+n+t} = c^x + c^{x+n}$

$$\therefore t = \frac{\log(1+c^n)}{\log c} - n, \quad \text{independent of } x.$$

An extract from a table of uniform seniority is given in Table 7.2.

TABLE 7.2

Difference in age	Addition to older age
0	9·12
1	8·63
2	8·16
3	7·71
4	7·27
5	6·86
⋮	
10	5·05
⋮	
15	3·65
⋮	
20	2·60

Even if a mortality table does not follow Makeham's or Gompertz's Law it is sometimes possible to adopt a table of uniform seniority that will produce joint life values with sufficient accuracy for practical purposes.

While it is possible to use a table of uniform seniority by repeated application to evaluate functions involving more than two lives it is normally easier to use the basic method of finding an equivalent age by formula (7.2.2) or (7.2.3).

Example 7.6

Assuming that the A1967–70 table follows

(a) Makeham's Law

(b) Gompertz's Law

find, in each case, $\ddot{a}_{40:50:70}$ at 4% p.a. interest.

Solution

(*a*) $\qquad 3\mu_w = \mu_{40} + \mu_{50} + \mu_{70}$

$\qquad\qquad = \cdot00136 + \cdot00452 + \cdot03798 = \cdot04386$

$\therefore \ \mu_w = \cdot01462$

and interpolating between μ_{60} and μ_{61} gives $w = 60\cdot55$.

Now, referring to the tabulated values for lives of equal ages given

$$\ddot{a}_{60:60:60} = 8\cdot452$$

$$\ddot{a}_{61:61:61} = 8\cdot095,$$

and interpolating, gives $\ddot{a}_{40:50:70} \doteqdot 8\cdot256$.

(*b*) In this case $\mu_w = \cdot04386$, giving $w = 71\cdot47$ and referring to the single life tables $\ddot{a}_{71\cdot47} = 8\cdot452$.

We do not expect either of these answers to be accurate as the table does not follow either Makeham's or Gompertz's Law.

Example 7.7

Assuming that the table of uniform seniority given in section 7.2 applying to a Makeham's table can be used with the A1967–70 table, calculate $P_{30:50}$ at 4% p.a. interest.

Solution

The addition to the younger age given for a difference of 20 is $13\cdot83$ so we require

$$\ddot{a}_{43.83:43.83}.$$

Interpolating between $\qquad \ddot{a}_{43:43} = 16\cdot102$

and $\qquad\qquad\qquad\quad \ddot{a}_{44:44} = 15\cdot771$

gives $\qquad\qquad\qquad \ddot{a}_{43.83:43.83} = 15\cdot827,$

$$\therefore \ P_{30:50} = \frac{1}{15\cdot827} - \cdot038462$$

$$= \cdot02472.$$

Example 7.8

Assuming that the table of uniform seniority given in section 7.2 applying to a Gompertz table can be used with the *a*(55) males table, calculate $A_{55:65}$ at 4% p.a. interest.

Solution

The addition to the higher age given for a difference of 10 is 5·05 so we require $a_{70.05}$. Interpolating between

$$a_{70} = 7·963$$

and

$$a_{71} = 7·607$$

gives

$$a_{70.05} = 7·945$$

$$\therefore \ddot{a}_{70.05} = 8·945$$

and

$$A_{55:65} \fallingdotseq 1-(·038462)(8·945)$$

$$= ·656.$$

Example 7.9

A mortality table which follows Makeham's Law is used to obtain an immediate joint life annuity on m lives $x_1 x_2 \ldots x_m$. Prove that the value is a'_w at a rate of interest

$$\frac{1+i}{s^{m-1}} - 1,$$

and determine the method of finding w.

Solution

$$v^n{}_n p_{x_1 x_2 x_3 \ldots x_m}$$

$$= e^{-\delta n} e^{-\int_0^n (\mu_{x_1+t} + \mu_{x_2+t} + \mu_{x_3+t} + \ldots + \mu_{x_m+t})dt}$$

$$= e^{-\int_0^n (mA + Bc^t(c^{x_1} + c^{x_2} + \ldots + c^{x_m}) + \delta)dt}$$

$$= e^{-\int_0^n (A + Bc^{w+t} + (m-1)A + \delta)dt}, \quad \text{writing} \quad c^{x_1} + c^{x_2} + \ldots + c^{x_m} = c^w$$

$$= e^{-\int_0^n (\mu_{w+t} + \delta')dt}, \quad \text{where} \quad \delta' = (m-1)A + \delta$$

$$= v'^n{}_n p_w.$$

Thus summing over n gives the required result that the annuity value is a'_w provided that the condition on the rate of interest is satisfied. Now

$$\log_e (1+i') = -(m-1)\log_e s + \log_e (1+i) \quad \text{as} \quad A = -\log_e s$$

i.e.

$$1+i' = \frac{1+i}{s^{m-1}}$$

i.e.

$$i' = \frac{1+i}{s^{m-1}} - 1 \quad \text{as required.}$$

The condition on w is

$$c^w = c^{x_1} + c^{x_2} + c^{x_3} + \ldots + c^{x_m},$$

multiplying by B and adding mA to each side gives

$$(m-1)A + (A + Bc^w) = (A + Bc^{x_1}) + (A + Bc^{x_2}) + \ldots + (A + Bc^{x_m}),$$

i.e. $$(m-1)A + \mu_w = \mu_{x_1} + \mu_{x_2} + \ldots + \mu_{x_m}$$

$$\therefore \ \mu_w = \mu_{x_1} + \mu_{x_2} + \ldots + \mu_{x_m} - (m-1)A,$$

the equation required to find w.

Exercise 7.5

Assuming first the Makeham table of uniform seniority and secondly the Gompertz table both given in section 7.2, find the value of $a_{40:50}$ on the A1967–70 table at 4% p.a. interest and compare the values in each case with using the equivalent equal age or single age.

(Note that this exercise is given to test the use of the methods as none of the assumptions is accurate.)

Exercise 7.6

Two single-life tables, one for male and one for female lives, both follow Makeham's Law with the same value of c. A joint life table is constructed for one male life (x) and one female life (y). Prove that $a_{xy} = a_{ww}$ where

$$c^w = \frac{Bc^x + B'c^y}{B + B'},$$

where the dashed symbol applies to the female table.

7.3   Last survivor status

So far in dealing with functions based on two or more lives, it has been considered that the status fails on the death of the first of the lives; the failure of the joint life status. On the other hand the status could be considered to fail on the death of the last of the lives—this is referred to as the *last survivor* status often called in connection with annuities the joint-life-and-survivor status.

A bar is placed above the lives to denote the last survivor status, for example $_n p_{\overline{x_1 x_2 \ldots x_m}}$ is the probability that *at least* one of the m lives $x_1, x_2, \ldots, x_m$ is alive after n years. Note that in fact more than one life may be alive.

In the simplest two life case

$$_np_{\overline{xy}} = 1-(1-{}_np_x)(1-{}_np_y),$$

i.e.
$$_np_{\overline{xy}} = {}_np_x + {}_np_y - {}_np_{xy} \qquad (7.3.1)$$

by considering that the probability that one life is alive is the complement of the probability that both the lives are dead.

The annuity based on the last survivor status represented by

$$a_{\overline{xy}} = \sum_{t=1}^{\infty} v^t {}_tp_{\overline{xy}}$$

$$= \sum_{t=1}^{\infty} v^t {}_tp_x + \sum_{t=1}^{\infty} v^t {}_tp_y - \sum_{t=1}^{\infty} v^t {}_tp_{xy}$$

i.e.
$$a_{\overline{xy}} = a_x + a_y - a_{xy}. \qquad (7.3.2)$$

This formula may also be demonstrated by general reasoning, the following check perhaps appearing simple but being very useful with more complicated expressions. The right hand side $a_x + a_y - a_{xy}$ gives annuities which may be tabulated as shown in Table 7.3, the demonstration being correct as the summation line represents $a_{\overline{xy}}$.

TABLE 7.3

	x and y alive	x alive, y dead	x dead, y alive	x and y dead
a_x	1	1	0	0
a_y	1	0	1	0
$-a_{xy}$	-1	0	0	0
Summation	1	1	1	0

An assurance payable on the last death of (x) and (y) is equivalent to an assurance payable on the death of (x) together with an assurance payable on the death of (y) less an assurance payable on the first death of (x) and (y)—such an assurance is represented by the symbol $\overline{A}_{\overline{xy}}$ and is known as a last survivor assurance.

Then
$$\overline{A}_{\overline{xy}} = \overline{A}_x + \overline{A}_y - \overline{A}_{xy}.$$

Similarly
$$A_{\overline{xy}} = A_x + A_y - A_{xy}. \qquad (7.3.3)$$

Using the normal premium conversion relationship

$$A_{\overline{xy}} = (1 - d\ddot{a}_x) + (1 - d\ddot{a}_y) - (1 - d\ddot{a}_{xy})$$
$$= 1 - d(\ddot{a}_x + \ddot{a}_y - \ddot{a}_{xy})$$
$$\therefore \; A_{\overline{xy}} = 1 - d\ddot{a}_{\overline{xy}}. \qquad (7.3.4)$$

The annual premium for a last survivor assurance (with the sum assured paid at the end of the year of death) is

$$P_{\overline{xy}} = \frac{A_{\overline{xy}}}{\ddot{a}_{\overline{xy}}}$$
$$= \frac{1 - d\ddot{a}_{\overline{xy}}}{\ddot{a}_{\overline{xy}}},$$

i.e. $$P_{\overline{xy}} = \frac{1}{\ddot{a}_{\overline{xy}}} - d. \qquad (7.3.5)$$

It will be seen that as would be expected from general reasoning the premium conversion relationships apply, but note that $P_{\overline{xy}}$ does *not* equal $P_x + P_y - P_{xy}$. Expressions for temporary and endowment functions can also be found, for example

$$a_{\overline{xy} : \overline{n}|} = a_{x : \overline{n}|} + a_{y : \overline{n}|} - a_{xy : n|}$$
$$A_{\overline{xy} : \overline{n}|} = A_{x : \overline{n}|} + A_{y : \overline{n}|} - A_{xy : \overline{n}|}$$
$$A^{1}_{\overline{xy} : \overline{n}|} = A^{1}_{x : \overline{n}|} + A^{1}_{y : \overline{n}|} - A^{1}_{xy : \overline{n}|}.$$

In the last equation note the notation:

$A^{1}_{\overline{xy} : \overline{n}|}$ is the assurance payable on the failure of the last survivor status (xy) before n years, *while*

$A^{1}_{xy : \overline{n}|}$ with a bracket instead of a bar means the assurance payable on the first death if either (x) or (y) dics in n years.

Considering the more general last survivor functions involving m lives

$$_n p_{\overline{x_1 x_2 x_3 \ldots x_m}}$$
$$= 1 - (1 - {_n p_{x_1}})(1 - {_n p_{x_2}}) \ldots (1 - {_n p_{x_m}})$$
$$= ({_n p_{x_1}} + {_n p_{x_2}} + \ldots + {_n p_{x_m}}) - ({_n p_{x_1 x_2}} + {_n p_{x_1 x_3}} + \ldots + {_n p_{x_{m-1} x_m}})$$
$$+ ({_n p_{x_1 x_2 x_3}} + {_n p_{x_1 x_2 x_4}} + \ldots + {_n p_{x_{m-2} x_{m-1} x_m}})$$
$$- ({_n p_{x_1 x_2 x_3 x_4}} + \ldots) + \ldots + (-1)^{m+1} {_n p_{x_1 x_2 \ldots x_m}},$$

or expressed as summations

$$_nP_{\overline{x_1x_2x_3...x_m}}$$

$$= \Sigma_n p_{x_1} - \Sigma_n p_{x_1x_2} + \Sigma_n p_{x_1x_2x_3} ... + (-1)^{m+1}{}_n p_{x_1x_2...x_m}, \qquad (7.3.6)$$

where the summations cover all possible combinations of the lives, taken first one at a time, then two at a time and so on.

This expression may be extended to any function which is a *linear* combination of 'p's'. The obvious ones are annuity functions being a weighted sum of p's, assurance functions because of the single premium conversion relationship, and q functions because $q = 1 - p$. On the other hand, premiums are not linear combinations of p's and so the following expression does not apply to them.

The generalised expressions of formula (7.3.6) applying to a last survivor function $F(_t p_{\overline{x_1x_2x_3...x_m}})$ which is a linear combination of p's is

$$F(_t p_{\overline{x_1x_2x_3...x_m}})$$

$$= \Sigma F(_t p_{x_1}) - \Sigma F(_t p_{x_1x_2}) + ... + (-1)^{m+1} F(_t p_{x_1x_2...x_m}), \qquad (7.3.7)$$

where the summations are of all possible joint life functions of the number of lives indicated.

Whereas the policy value of a joint life assurance is found in exactly the same manner as a single life assurance, e.g.

$$_t V_{xy} = A_{x+t:y+t} - P_{xy} \ddot{a}_{x+t:y+t}$$

$$= 1 - \frac{\ddot{a}_{x+t:y+t}}{\ddot{a}_{x:y}},$$

in the last survivor case there is the complication that one of the lives may be dead at the time of valuation:

$$_t V_{\overline{xy}} = A_{\overline{x+t:y+t}} - P_{\overline{xy}} \ddot{a}_{\overline{x+t:y+t}}$$

$$= 1 - \frac{\ddot{a}_{\overline{x+t:y+t}}}{\ddot{a}_{\overline{x:y}}}$$

if both (x) and (y) are alive, but

$$= A_{x+t} - P_{\overline{xy}} \ddot{a}_{x+t} \quad \text{if only } (x) \text{ is alive}$$

$$= A_{y+t} - P_{\overline{xy}} \ddot{a}_{y+t} \quad \text{if only } (y) \text{ is alive.}$$

Example 7.10

Show algebraically that formula (7.3.7) applies to $_n|q_{\overline{xyz}}$.

Solution

$$_n|q_{\overline{xyz}} = {}_nP_{\overline{xyz}} - {}_{n+1}P_{\overline{xyz}}$$

$$= ({}_nP_x + {}_nP_y + {}_nP_z - {}_nP_{xy} - {}_nP_{xz} - {}_nP_{yz} + {}_nP_{xyz})$$

$$- ({}_{n+1}P_x + {}_{n+1}P_y + {}_{n+1}P_z - {}_{n+1}P_{xy} - {}_{n+1}P_{xz} - {}_{n+1}P_{yz} + {}_{n+1}P_{xyz})$$

$$= {}_n|q_x + {}_n|q_y + {}_n|q_z - {}_n|q_{xy} - {}_n|q_{xz} - {}_n|q_{yz} + {}_n|q_{xyz}$$

$$= \Sigma_n|q_x - \Sigma_n|q_{xy} + {}_n|q_{xyz}, \quad \text{as required.}$$

Exercise 7.7

Given that $P_{\overline{xy}:\,\overline{n}|} = \cdot 0379$, $P_{\overline{xy}} = \cdot 0083$, $i = \cdot 04$ find ${}_nP_{\overline{xy}}$.

Exercise 7.8

Show algebraically that formula (7.3.7) applies to $\bar{a}_{\overline{xyz}}$ and $A_{\overline{xyz}:\,\overline{n}|}$.

Exercise 7.9

Find the value of an annuity of 1 per annum payable annually, the first payment being deferred until the end of the year in which the failure of the joint lifetime of (x) and (y) occurs, to be payable thereafter until 10 years after the death of the survivor, with the provision that no payments are to be made after 20 years from the present.

7.4 The Z-method

The symbol ${}_nP^{[r]}_{\overline{x_1x_2\ldots x_m}}$ represents the probability that out of m lives *exactly* r lives will survive n years.

The probability that exactly r specified lives $x_1x_2\ldots x_r$ are alive and $x_{r+1}\ldots x_m$ are dead is

$$_nP_{x_1}\cdot {}_nP_{x_2}\cdot {}_nP_{x_3}\cdots {}_nP_{x_r}\cdot {}_nq_{x_{r+1}}\cdot {}_nq_{x_{r+2}}\cdots {}_nq_{x_m}.$$

The probability that exactly r unspecified lives will survive, ${}_nP^{[r]}_{\overline{x_1x_2\ldots x_m}}$ will be the sum of all possible such expressions which will be the coefficient of a^r in the expansion of

$$(_nP_{x_1}a + {}_nq_{x_1})({}_nP_{x_2}a + {}_nq_{x_2})\ldots({}_nP_{x_m}a + {}_nq_{x_m}).$$

Writing $_nq_x = 1 - {}_nP_x$ this expression can be written,

$$\{1 + {}_nP_{x_1}(a-1)\}\{1 + {}_nP_{x_2}(a-1)\}\ldots\{1 + {}_nP_{x_m}(a-1)\}$$

$$= 1 + (\Sigma_nP_{x_1})(a-1) + (\Sigma_nP_{x_1x_2})(a-1)^2 + \ldots + (\Sigma_nP_{x_1x_2\ldots x_m})(a-1)^m,$$

the summations being over all possible combinations of the number of lives indicated.

Now writing Z_1 for $\Sigma_n p_{x_1}$, Z_2 for $\Sigma_n p_{x_1 x_2}$, and so on this becomes

$$1 + Z_1(a-1) + Z_2(a-1)^2 + \ldots + Z_m(a-1)^m,$$

and the coefficient of a^r in this expression, i.e.

$$_n p^{[r]}_{\overline{x_1 x_2 \ldots x_m}} = Z_r - (r+1)Z_{r+1} + \binom{r+2}{2}Z_{r+2} - \binom{r+3}{3}Z_{r+3}$$

$$+ \ldots + (-1)^{m-r}\binom{m}{m-r}Z_m. \quad (7.4.1)$$

Now, comparing this expression with the binomial expansion

$$\frac{Z^r}{(1+Z)^{r+1}} = Z^r - (r+1)Z^{r+1} + \binom{r+2}{2}Z^{r+2} - \binom{r+3}{3}Z^{r+3} + \ldots,$$

we see that the expressions are identical if we replace the suffix in Z by a power and we regard Z_{m+1}, Z_{m+2}, ... as being zero. Formula (7.4.1) can then be expressed symbolically in the form

$$_n p^{[r]}_{\overline{x_1 x_2 \ldots x_m}} = \frac{Z^r}{(1+Z)^{r+1}}, \quad (7.4.2)$$

it being understood that the expression on the right-hand side is to be expanded by the binomial theorem as far as the term containing Z^m and the powers in the expression are replaced by suffices.

As an example we will find $_n p^{[1]}_{\overline{xy}}$, the probability that exactly one of two lives survives n years.

Here $m = 2$ and $r = 1$,

$$Z_1 = {_n p_x} + {_n p_y}, \quad Z_2 = {_n p_{xy}}.$$

$$\frac{Z}{(1+Z)^2} = Z - 2Z^2 + \ldots.$$

$$\therefore \; _n p^{[1]}_{\overline{xy}} = Z_1 - 2Z_2$$

$$= {_n p_x} + {_n p_y} - 2{_n p_{xy}}.$$

In practice the method would not be used for such a simple problem—the answer being found from first principles as

$$_n p_x(1 - {_n p_y}) + (1 - {_n p_x}){_n p_y} = {_n p_x} + {_n p_y} - 2{_n p_{xy}}.$$

The probability that out of m lives *at least* r will survive n years is represented by $_n p^r_{\overline{x_1 x_2 \ldots x_m}}$, with no brackets round the r. When $r = 1$ it may be omitted, this being the last survivor status described in the previous section.

Now the probability of at least r lives surviving will be the sum of the probability of exactly r lives, exactly $r+1$ lives and so on, that is

$$_n p_{\overline{x_1 x_2 x_3 \ldots x_m}}^{\,r} = {}_n p_{x_1 x_2 \ldots x_m}^{[r]} + {}_n p_{x_1 x_2 \ldots x_m}^{[r+1]} + \ldots + {}_n p_{x_1 x_2 \ldots x_m}^{[m]}$$

which may be expressed symbolically as

$$Z_r - \binom{r+1}{1} Z_{r+1} + \binom{r+2}{2} Z_{r+2} - \binom{r+3}{3} Z_{r+3} + \ldots + (-1)^{m-r} \binom{m}{m-r} Z_m$$
$$+ Z_{r+1} - \binom{r+2}{1} Z_{r+2} + \binom{r+3}{2} Z_{r+3} - \ldots + (-1)^{m-r-1} \binom{m}{m-r-1} Z_m$$
$$+ Z_{r+2} - \ldots$$
$$\ldots$$
$$\ldots \quad + Z_m.$$

The coefficient of Z_{r+s} (adding a vertical column) is

$$1 - \binom{r+s}{1} + \binom{r+s}{2} - \binom{r+s}{3} + \ldots + (-1)^s \binom{r+s}{s}$$
$$= -\binom{r+s-1}{1} + \binom{r+s}{2} - \binom{r+s}{3} + \ldots + (-1)^s \binom{r+s}{s}.$$

Now $\qquad \binom{r+s-1}{t} - \binom{r+s}{t+1}$

$$= \frac{(r+s-1)!}{t!(r+s-1-t)!} - \frac{(r+s)!}{(t+1)!(t+s-1-t)!}$$

$$= \frac{(r+s-1)!}{(t+1)!(r+s-1-t)!}(t+1-(r+s))$$

$$= -\frac{(r+s-1)!}{(t+1)!(r+s-2-t)!}$$

$$= -\binom{r+s-1}{t+1}.$$

i.e. $\qquad \binom{r+s}{t+1} = \binom{r+s-1}{t} + \binom{r+s-1}{t+1}.$

The coefficient of Z_{r+s} above, by successive applications of this expression, from the second term onwards, first with $t = 1$, then $t = 2$, and so on gives

$$-\binom{r+s-1}{1} + \binom{r+s-1}{1} + \binom{r+s-1}{2} - \binom{r+s-1}{2} - \binom{r+s-1}{3} + \ldots$$
$$+ (-1)^s \binom{r+s-1}{s-1} + (-1)^s \binom{r+s-1}{s}$$

in which all terms but the last will cancel leaving

$$(-1)^s \binom{r+s-1}{s}.$$

Substituting this coefficient of Z_{r+s} in the above expression for $_n p_{\overline{x_1 x_2 x_3 \ldots x_m}}^{\,r}$ gives

$$Z_r - \binom{r}{1} Z_{r+1} + \binom{r+1}{2} Z_{r+2} - \ldots + (-1)^{m-r} \binom{m-1}{m-r} Z_m.$$

Now the binomial expansion of $\dfrac{Z^r}{(1+Z)^r}$

$$= Z^r - \binom{r}{1}Z^{r+1} + \binom{r+1}{2}Z^{r+2} - \ldots + (-1)^{m-r}\binom{m-1}{m-r}Z^m \ldots$$

So using the same understanding as previously, that the powers in the expression are replaced by suffices and Z_{m+1}, Z_{m+2}, etc. $= 0$ we have

$$_np^r_{x_1x_2\ldots x_m} = \frac{Z^r}{(1+Z)^r}. \tag{7.4.3}$$

Annuities can also be considered based on the condition of at least or exactly a certain number of lives being alive. As annuities are linear summations of probabilities the expressions will be the same as those already found except that Z_r will now be a summation of annuities. Thus

$$a^r_{\overline{x_1x_2\ldots x_m}} = \frac{Z^r}{(1+Z)^r}.$$

An example of the use of this formula will be to find the annuity payable while at least three lives survive out of four lives.

Here $m = 4$ and $r = 3$,

$$\frac{Z^3}{(1+Z)^3} = Z^3 - 3Z^4 + \ldots$$

$$\therefore a^3_{\overline{x_1x_2x_3x_4}} = Z_3 - 3Z_4$$

$$= a_{x_1x_2x_3} + a_{x_1x_2x_4} + a_{x_1x_3x_4} + a_{x_2x_3x_4} - 3a_{x_1x_2x_3x_4}.$$

It is useful to check such expressions by considering one or more cases—for example if $x_1x_2x_3$ are alive and x_4 is dead, the right-hand side will pay $1 + 0 + 0 + 0 - 0 = 1$.

Assurances can also be considered based on the failure of the status of at least a certain number of lives being alive, and can be evaluated using the same expressions—note that it is not possible to have an assurance based on the 'exactly' status because at time $t = 0$ the status has already failed as no lives have died.

For example

$$\bar{A}^3_{\overline{x_1x_2x_3x_4}} = \bar{A}_{x_1x_2x_3} + \bar{A}_{x_1x_2x_4} + \bar{A}_{x_1x_3x_4} + \bar{A}_{x_2x_3x_4} - 3\bar{A}_{x_1x_2x_3x_4},$$

the assurance being payable when the status $\overline{x_1x_2x_3x_4}^3$ fails, i.e. when the second death occurs; in the general case $A_{\overline{x_1 x_2 \ldots x_m}}^{\;\;r}$ the benefit is payable on the $(m-r+1)$th death and not on the rth death.

It may be noted that when $r = 1$, that is the last survivor status, the expansion of the Z-method gives

$$\frac{Z}{(1+Z)} = Z - Z^2 + Z^3 - Z^4 + \ldots,$$

which is equation (7.3.7).

Example 7.11

Find an expression for the probability that of four lives (w), (x), (y) and (z) exactly two will survive n years.

Solution

Using formula (7.4.2) with $m = 4$ and $r = 2$

$$Z_1 = {}_nP_w + {}_nP_x + {}_nP_y + {}_nP_z$$

$$Z_2 = {}_nP_{wx} + {}_nP_{wy} + {}_nP_{wz} + {}_nP_{xy} + {}_nP_{xz} + {}_nP_{yz}$$

$$Z_3 = {}_nP_{wxy} + {}_nP_{wxz} + {}_nP_{wyz} + {}_nP_{xyz}$$

$$Z_4 = {}_nP_{wxyz}.$$

$$\frac{Z^2}{(1+Z)^3} = Z^2 - 3Z^3 + 6Z^4 + \ldots$$

$$\therefore {}_nP_{\overline{wxyz}}^{[2]} = Z_2 - 3Z_3 + 6Z_4$$

$$= {}_nP_{wx} + {}_nP_{wy} + {}_nP_{wz} + {}_nP_{xy} + {}_nP_{xz} + {}_nP_{yz}$$

$$- 3({}_nP_{wxy} + {}_nP_{wxz} + {}_nP_{wyz} + {}_nP_{xyz}) + 6{}_nP_{wxyz}.$$

Example 7.12

Find an expression for the probability that of four lives (w), (x), (y) and (z) at least two will survive n years.

Solution

The expressions for Z_1, Z_2, Z_3 and Z_4 are the same as in the previous example. Using formula (7.4.3)

$$\frac{Z^2}{(1+Z)^2} = Z^2 - 2Z^3 + 3Z^4 - \ldots$$

$$\therefore {}_nP_{\overline{wxyz}}^{\;2} = Z_2 - 2Z_3 + 3Z_4$$

$$= {}_nP_{wx} + {}_nP_{wy} + {}_nP_{wz} + {}_nP_{xy} + {}_nP_{xz} + {}_nP_{yz}$$

$$- 2({}_nP_{wxy} + {}_nP_{wxz} + {}_nP_{wyz} + {}_nP_{xyz}) + 3{}_nP_{wxyz}.$$

Example 7.13

Find an expression for $a_{\overline{xyz}}^{[1]}$.

Solution

$$\frac{Z}{(1+Z)^2} = Z - 2Z^2 + 3Z^3 - \ldots$$

so

$$a_{\overline{xyz}}^{[1]} = Z_1 - 2Z_2 + 3Z_3$$
$$= a_x + a_y + a_z - 2(a_{xy} + a_{xz} + a_{yz}) + 3a_{xyz}.$$

Under the annuity no payments are made until two of the lives are dead and payments are then made until all three lives are dead. A check can be made by assuming that various of the lives are alive or dead. If all are alive the payment is

$$1 + 1 + 1 - 2(1 + 1 + 1) + 3 = 0,$$

if x and y are alive and z is dead the payment is

$$1 + 1 + 0 - 2(1 + 0 + 0) + 0 = 0,$$

and if x is alive and y and z are dead the payment is

$$1 + 0 + 0 - 2(0 + 0 + 0) + 0 = 1.$$

Example 7.14

An annual last survivor immediate annuity is payable at the rate of £1,000 per annum while all of three lives x, y and z are alive. At the first death the annuity reduces to £800 per annum and at the second to £600 per annum. Find an expression for the value of the annuity.

Solution

The annuity is £1,000 if exactly three lives are alive i.e. $1,000a_{xyz}$; £800 if exactly two lives are alive and as

$$\frac{Z^2}{(1+Z)^3} = Z^2 - 3Z^3$$

this annuity is

$$800(a_{xy} + a_{xz} + a_{yz} - 3a_{xyz});$$

and £600 if exactly one life is alive and as

$$\frac{Z}{(1+Z)^2} = Z - 2Z^2 + 3Z^3 \ldots$$

this annuity is

$$600(a_x + a_y + a_z - 2(a_{xy} + a_{yz} + a_{xz}) + 3a_{xyz}).$$

Summing the parts of the annuity gives

$$600(a_x + a_y + a_z) - 400(a_{xy} + a_{xz} + a_{yz}) + 400a_{xyz},$$

as the answer. This answer may be checked by considering the payment made in various conditions, for example, x and y alive and z dead,

$$600(2) - 400 = 800 \quad \text{as required.}$$

Example 7.15

Find the single premium at 4% interest for an assurance of £1,000 payable at the end of the year of death of the second life to fail out of three lives aged 30, 40 and 50 given that

$$a_{30:40} = 16\cdot15,$$
$$a_{30:50} = 13\cdot93,$$
$$a_{40:50} = 13\cdot59,$$
$$a_{30:40:50} = 13\cdot08.$$

Solution

The death of the second life will be the failure of the status 'at least two lives alive', so we require $A\overset{2}{{}_{30:40:50}}$.

Now $a\overset{2}{{}_{30:40:50}}$ by the Z method is represented by

$$\frac{Z^2}{(1+Z)^2} = Z^2 - 2Z^3$$

and so

$$= 16\cdot15 + 13\cdot93 + 13\cdot59 - 2(13\cdot08)$$
$$= 17\cdot51.$$

$A\overset{2}{{}_{30:40:50}} = 1 - d\ddot{a}\overset{2}{{}_{30:40:50}}$ being the normal premium conversion relationship

$$= 1 - (\cdot038462)(18\cdot51)$$
$$= \cdot288.$$

So premium required = £288.

Exercise 7.10

Given
$$a_{xx} = 16\cdot42$$
$$a_{xxx} = 14\cdot18$$
$$a_{xxxx} = 12\cdot54,$$

find the value of an annuity payable as long as

(a) at least two lives are alive,

(b) exactly two lives are alive,

out of four persons all aged x.

Exercise 7.11

Find an expression for the single premium for a deferred annuity payable annually in arrear so long as one of three lives now aged 40, 45 and 50 is alive and over age 60. The annuity is to be £300 per annum while exactly one is over 60, £400 per annum while exactly two are over 60, and £500 per annum while all three are over 60.

Exercise 7.12

Given the following values of joint life annuities at 3% interest, find the net single premium for an insurance payable at the end of the year of death of the second life to fail out of four lives aged 30, 40, 50 and 60.

$$a_{30:40:50} = 12\cdot61$$

$$a_{30:40:60} = 9\cdot60$$

$$a_{30:50:60} = 9\cdot09$$

$$a_{40:50:60} = 8\cdot91$$

$$a_{30:40:50:60} = 8\cdot75.$$

Exercise 7.13

Assuming formula (7.4.2), prove formula (7.4.3) by mathematical induction.

7.5 Compound statuses

The functions considered so far in this chapter have depended on groups of single lives. The methods are also applicable when one or more of the lives is not a single life but is itself a status. For example, an annuity $a_{\overline{wx}:y:z}$ is payable while y and z and either (or both) of w and x are alive. Similarly, the benefit $A_{x:\overline{yz}}$ is payable on the death of x or on the last death of y and z if this should occur first.

Functions of this type can always be expressed in the form of functions of simple joint life functions, mainly through an expansion of equation (7.3.2)

i.e. $a_{\overline{xy}} = a_x + a_y - a_{xy},$

which applies whether x and y are lives or are themselves statuses or even a term certain. This is probably most easily seen (rewriting x

and y as u and v to indicate that they may be a status) by writing the equation

$$a_{\overline{uv}} + a_{uv} = a_u + a_v. \qquad (7.5.1)$$

The left-hand side will provide payments of two until one of the statuses $(\overline{uv})$ and (uv) fail when the payment reduces to one, and this is the same as the payments on the right-hand side.

Similar reasoning gives the analogous relationship for assurances

$$\bar{A}_{\overline{uv}} = \bar{A}_u + \bar{A}_v - \bar{A}_{uv}. \qquad (7.5.2)$$

It was mentioned above that the same formula can also be applied when a status is a term certain—for example, the most common annuity with a term certain is an annuity for a term certain (n) and then for the lifetime of the annuitant (x) thereafter, symbolised by

$$a_{\overline{x:\overline{n}|}} = a_x + a_{\overline{n}|} - a_{x:\overline{n}|} \quad \text{using (7.5.1)}$$

$$= a_{\overline{n}|} + {}_n|a_x \quad \text{as expected.}$$

A further useful expression is

$$a_{u:\overline{vw}} = a_{uv} + a_{uw} - a_{uvw}, \qquad (7.5.3)$$

which may be demonstrated by similar reasoning to that above, or by evaluating

$$a_{u:\overline{vw}} = \sum_{t=1}^{\infty} v^t {}_tp_u \, {}_tp_{\overline{vw}}$$

$$= \sum_{t=1}^{\infty} v^t {}_tp_u ({}_tp_v + {}_tp_w - {}_tp_{vw})$$

i.e. $$a_{u:\overline{vw}} = a_{uv} + a_{uw} - a_{uvw}.$$

The similar expression for the assurance is

$$\bar{A}_{u:\overline{vw}} = \bar{A}_{uv} + \bar{A}_{uw} - \bar{A}_{uvw}. \qquad (7.5.4)$$

Example 7.16

Find an expression in joint life annuities for

$$a_{\overline{wx}:\overline{yz}}.$$

Solution

Using equation (7.5.3) twice

$$a_{\overline{wx}:\overline{yz}} = a_{\overline{wx}:y} + a_{\overline{wx}:z} - a_{\overline{wx}:yz}$$

$$= (a_{wy} + a_{xy} - a_{wxy}) + (a_{wz} + a_{xz} - a_{wxz}) - (a_{wyz} + a_{xyz} - a_{wxyz})$$

$$= a_{wy} + a_{wz} + a_{xy} + a_{xz} - a_{wxy} - a_{wxz} - a_{wyz} - a_{xyz} + a_{wxyz}.$$

Example 7.17

Find an expression in terms of joint life assurances for

$$A_{\overline{wx} : \overline{yz}}.$$

Solution

$$A_{\overline{wx} : \overline{yz}} = A_{wx} + A_{\overline{yz}} - A_{wx : \overline{yz}} \quad \text{using equation (7.5.2)}$$

$$= A_{wx} + (A_y + A_z - A_{yz}) - (A_{wxy} + A_{wxz} - A_{wxyz})$$

$$\text{using equation (7.5.4)}$$

$$= A_y + A_z + A_{wx} - A_{yz} - A_{wxy} - A_{wxz} + A_{wxyz}.$$

It is possible in examples such as this and particularly more complicated ones to use a shorthand notation by omitting the assurance A or annuity a symbol in the working. Thus $A_{\overline{wx} : \overline{yz}}$ is written as $\overline{wx} : \overline{yz}$, which

$$= wx + \overline{yz} - wx : \overline{yz}$$

$$= wx + (y + z - yz) - wx(y + z - yz)$$

giving the same answer.

Exercise 7.14

Find an expression for the last survivor annuity with a certain period

$$a_{\overline{x : y : \overline{n}|}}.$$

Exercise 7.15

State the meaning of the symbol

$$A_{\overline{x : \overline{n}|}}$$

and find a simple expression for it.

Exercise 7.16

Express $a_{ab : \overline{xyz}}$ in terms of joint life annuities.

Exercise 7.17

Express $A_{\overline{ab} : \overline{xy} : z}$ in terms of joint life assurances.

Exercise 7.18

Prove formula (7.5.4).

EXAMPLES AND EXERCISES ON CHAPTER 7

Example 7.18

If $\mu_x = \dfrac{1}{100-x}$ calculate the complete last survivor expectation of life of two lives aged 40 and 50.

Solution

$$_np_x = e^{-\int_0^n \mu_{x+t}dt}$$

$$= e^{-\int_0^n \frac{1}{100-(x+t)}\,dt}$$

$$= e^{[\log_e(100-(x+t))]_0^n}$$

$$= \frac{100-(x+n)}{100-x}$$

$$= 1 - \frac{n}{100-x}.$$

Hence $$\mathring{e}_x = \int_0^{100-x}\left(1 - \frac{t}{100-x}\right)dt,$$

the upper limit being $100-x$ as 100 must be the limiting age of the table as $\mu_{100} = \infty$,

$$= \left[t - \frac{t^2}{2(100-x)}\right]_0^{100-x}$$

$$= \tfrac{1}{2}(100-x).$$

$\mathring{e}_{xy}$ (when $x > y$)

$$= \int_0^{100-x} {}_tp_x\,{}_tp_y\,dt$$

$$= \int_0^{100-x}\left(1 - \frac{t}{100-x}\right)\left(1 - \frac{t}{100-y}\right)dt$$

$$= \left[t - \frac{t^2}{2(100-x)} - \frac{t^2}{2(100-y)} + \frac{t^3}{3(100-x)(100-y)}\right]_0^{100-x}$$

$$= \tfrac{1}{2}(100-x) - \frac{(100-x)^2}{6(100-y)}.$$

I

The last survivor expectation has not been specifically defined but the meaning should be obvious and

$$\mathring{e}_{\overline{40:50}} = \mathring{e}_{40} + \mathring{e}_{50} - \mathring{e}_{40:50}$$

by considering the expectation as the same as an annuity at a zero rate of interest,

$$= 30 + 25 - (25 - 6 \cdot 94)$$

$$= 36 \cdot 94.$$

Example 7.19

Obtain a formula for the value of an annuity payable annually in arrear during the joint existence of (x) and the survivor of (y) and (z) continuing n years after the death of (x) should the survivor of (y) and (z) live so long.

Solution

During the first n years the annuity is paid whether or not (x) is alive and has value

$$a_{\overline{yz}:\overline{n}} = a_{y:\overline{n}} + a_{z:\overline{n}} - a_{yz:\overline{n}}.$$

After n years the annuity is paid if x was alive n years previously and if either y or z is alive and has value of

$$\sum_{t=n+1}^{\infty} v^t {}_{t-n}p_x({}_t p_{\overline{yz}}) = \sum_{t=n+1}^{\infty} v^t {}_{t-n}p_x({}_t p_y + {}_t p_z - {}_t p_{yz}),$$

and substituting $t = s + n$

$$= \sum_{s=1}^{\infty} v^{s+n} {}_s p_x({}_{s+n}p_y + {}_{s+n}p_z - {}_{s+n}p_{yz})$$

$$= v^n \left(\sum_{s=1}^{\infty} v^s {}_s p_x {}_n p_y {}_s p_{y+n} + \sum_{s=1}^{\infty} v^s {}_s p_x {}_n p_z {}_s p_{z+n} \right.$$

$$\left. - \sum_{s=1}^{\infty} v^s {}_s p_x {}_n p_{yz} {}_s p_{y+n:z+n} \right)$$

$$= v^n({}_n p_y a_{x:y+n} + {}_n p_z a_{x:z+n} - {}_n p_{yz} a_{x:y+n:z+n}),$$

to which must be added $a_{y:\overline{n}} + a_{z:\overline{n}} - a_{yz:\overline{n}}$ for the first n years to give the total answer.

Example 7.20

Given that ${}_{15}p_{60} = \frac{2}{5}$, ${}_5 p_{70} = \frac{2}{3}$ and that the probability of only one of three lives aged 65 surviving five years is one-seventh of the probability that at least one of the three will survive the five years, find the probability that of four lives aged 60, 60, 65 and 70 at least three will survive five years.

Solution

Let $p = {}_5p_{65}$ then the probability that only one specified of three lives aged 65 will survive is $p(1-p)^2$ so summing over the three lives the probability that only one lives is $3p(1-p)^2$.

Alternatively this expression could be found using the Z-method by finding $p_{\overline{65:65:65}}^{[1]}$ represented by

$$\frac{Z}{(1+Z)^2} = Z - 2Z^2 + 3Z^3,$$

i.e. $3p - 2(3p^2) + 3p^3$ which gives the same answer—noting that Z represents $p + p + p = 3p$, and so on.

The probability that at least one life aged 65 survives is

$$1 - (1-p)^3$$

which could also of course be found using the Z-method.

Using the information in the question

$$3p(1-p)^2 = \tfrac{1}{7}(1 - (1-p)^3),$$

i.e. $p(5p-6)(4p-3) = 0$, giving the usable solution $p = \tfrac{3}{4}$,

i.e. $\qquad\qquad\qquad\qquad {}_5p_{65} = \tfrac{3}{4}.$

The other probability needed is

$$_5p_{60} = \frac{{}_{15}p_{60}}{{}_5p_{65}\,{}_5p_{70}} = \frac{\tfrac{2}{5}}{\tfrac{3}{4}\cdot\tfrac{2}{3}} = \frac{4}{5}.$$

The probability required is

$$_5p_{\overline{60:60:65:70}}^{3}$$

represented by $\qquad\qquad \dfrac{Z^3}{(1+Z)^3} = Z^3 - 3Z^4$

and thus $= (\tfrac{4}{5})^2(\tfrac{3}{4}) + (\tfrac{4}{5})^2(\tfrac{2}{3}) + 2(\tfrac{4}{5})(\tfrac{3}{4})(\tfrac{2}{3}) - 3(\tfrac{4}{5})^2(\tfrac{3}{4})(\tfrac{2}{3})$

$\qquad = \tfrac{56}{75}.$

Exercise 7.19

A special last survivor deferred annuity providing yearly payments of £100 is to commence as soon as either of two lives now aged 35 and 40 attain age 60. Once payments have commenced they are to continue for ten years certain and thereafter until the death of the survivor.

Give an expression for the present value of the annuity in a simple form.

Exercise 7.20

Obtain a simple expression for an annuity of £100 p.a. payable during the joint lifetime and the lifetime of the survivor of (40) and (50) and subject to the provision that it will continue for at least 20 years after the first death and 10 years after the second death.

Exercise 7.21

Given that $_{10}p_{20} = \cdot9$, and $_{10}p_{30} = \cdot8$ find

(a) the probability that of four lives each aged 20, at least one will die between the ages of 30 and 40, and

(b) the probability that of four lives aged 20, 20, 30 and 30 respectively, at least two will die within the next 10 years.

CHAPTER EIGHT

CONTINGENT FUNCTIONS AND REVERSIONARY ANNUITIES

8.1 Contingent probabilities

In the functions dependent on more than one life described in the previous chapter the order in which the various deaths occurred was not considered—it was the number of lives that were alive that was important—for example the status $\overset{2}{xyz}$ ceases on the second death regardless of whether this is x, y or z. Much of the work in this chapter will concern functions in which the order of the deaths is significant. It is assumed that the probabilities of living and dying of the individual lives are independent and thus compound probabilities can be obtained by the multiplication rule.

The simplest probability to consider is the probability of x dying before y which is given the symbol $_\infty q^1_{xy}$. The probability that x and y will both survive t years and x will die within the short interval of time δt will tend to

$$_tp_{xy}\mu_{x+t}\delta t \quad \text{as} \quad \delta t \to 0.$$

It follows that

$$_\infty q^1_{xy} = \int_0^\infty {}_tp_{xy}\mu_{x+t}dt. \tag{8.1.1}$$

The probability that x dies before y, before the expiry of n years is given the symbol

$$_nq^1_{xy} = \int_0^n {}_tp_{xy}\mu_{x+t}dt, \tag{8.1.2}$$

and if $n = 1$ the figure may be omitted so

$$q^1_{xy} = \int_0^1 {}_tp_{xy}\mu_{x+t}dt.$$

It will be noted that whether y dies during the period is unimportant provided he does not die before x. On the other hand, if the probability is that y dies after x before the expiry of n years then this is given the symbol

$$_nq_{xy}^2 = \int_0^n (1 - {}_tp_x){}_tp_y\mu_{y+t}dt$$

$$= \int_0^n {}_tp_y\mu_{y+t}dt - \int_0^n {}_tp_x{}_tp_y\mu_{y+t}dt,$$

i.e. $\qquad _nq_{xy}^2 = {}_nq_y - {}_nq_{xy}^1.$ \hfill (8.1.3)

This equation may also be obtained by general reasoning in the form

$$_nq_y = {}_nq_{xy}^1 + {}_nq_{xy}^2$$

as if y dies within n years he must either die before or after x.

It must be noted that $_nq_{xy}^2$ does not equal $_nq_{xy}^1$, as in the first both x and y must die within the n years as described above, in the second y may be either alive or dead at the end of the n years.

However when $n = \infty$

$$_\infty q_{xy}^2 = \int_0^\infty (1 - {}_tp_x){}_tp_y\mu_{y+t}dt$$

$$= \int_0^\infty (1 - {}_tp_x)\frac{d}{dt}(-{}_tp_y)dt$$

$$= \left[(-{}_tp_y)(1 - {}_tp_x)\right]_0^\infty - \int_0^\infty (-{}_tp_y)({}_tp_x\mu_{x+t})dt$$

using integration by parts,

$$= 0 + {}_\infty q_{xy}^1,$$

i.e. $\qquad _\infty q_{xy}^2 = {}_\infty q_{xy}^1,$

which can also be obtained by general reasoning.

The normal technique in simplifying contingent functions will be demonstrated on the following probabilities depending on three lives. In each case an integral is considered, the small interval summed being taken at the instant of death of the life which has the number over the suffix in the symbol. If this life is x then the general form is as follows

$$\int_0^n \left\{\begin{array}{l}\text{probability depending on all lives}\\\text{other than } x \text{ at time of } x\text{'s death}\end{array}\right\} {}_tp_x\mu_{x+t}dt. \quad (8.1.4)$$

Thus

$$_nq^1_{xyz} = \int_0^n {}_tp_{yz} \cdot {}_tp_x\mu_{x+t}dt;$$

$$_nq^2_{xyz} = \int_0^n {}_tp^{[1]}_{yz} \cdot {}_tp_x\mu_{x+t}dt$$

$$= \int_0^n ({}_tp_y + {}_tp_z - 2{}_tp_{yz}){}_tp_x\mu_{x+t}dt$$

$$= {}_nq^1_{xy} + {}_nq^1_{xz} - 2{}_nq^1_{xyz}; \tag{8.1.5}$$

$$_nq^3_{xyz} = \int_0^n (1 - {}_tp_y)(1 - {}_tp_z){}_tp_x\mu_{x+t}dt$$

$$= {}_nq_x - {}_nq^1_{xy} - {}_nq^1_{xz} + {}_nq^1_{xyz}. \tag{8.1.6}$$

This also demonstrates that probabilities can normally be expressed in terms of probabilities depending on the first death and in practical examples it is used to express them in this form for ease of evaluation.

When lives are of the same age and subject to the same mortality table values can sometimes be found simply, often by general reasoning, for example $_\infty q^1_{xxx}$ is the probability of one of three identical lives dying first which by symmetry will be $\frac{1}{3}$.

Example 8.1

State the meaning of the symbols $_nq^1_{x\,:\,\overline{yz}}$ and $_nq^{1\,:\,2}_{x\,\,yz}$ and prove that they are equal.

Solution

$_nq^1_{x\,:\,\overline{yz}}$ is the probability that (x) dies within n years while one at least of (y) and (z) is still alive, so using formula (8.1.4)

$$_nq^1_{x\,:\,\overline{yz}} = \int_0^n {}_tp_{\overline{yz}} \cdot {}_tp_x\mu_{x+t}dt$$

$$= \int_0^n ({}_tp_y + {}_tp_z - {}_tp_{yz}){}_tp_x\mu_{x+t}dt$$

$$= {}_nq^1_{xy} + {}_nq^1_{xz} - {}_nq^1_{xyz}.$$

$_nq^{1\,:\,2}_{x\,\,yz}$ is the probability that (x) dies either first or second out of the three lives, and

$$_nq^{1\,:\,2}_{x\,\,yz} = {}_nq^1_{xyz} + {}_nq^2_{xyz}$$

$$= {}_nq^1_{xyz} + {}_nq^1_{xy} + {}_nq^1_{xz} - 2{}_nq^1_{xyz} \quad \text{using (8.1.5)}$$

$$= {}_nq^1_{xy} + {}_nq^1_{xz} - {}_nq^1_{xyz}, \quad \text{as above.}$$

It will also be obvious from the descriptions of the symbols that they are equal.

Exercise 8.1

Find a simple expression for $_\infty q_{wxyz}^{\,3}$.

Exercise 8.2

Find $_\infty q_{xyz}^3$ given that $_\infty q_{xy}^2 = \cdot 3$, $_\infty q_{xz}^2 = \cdot 4$ and $_\infty q_{xyz}^2 = \cdot 2$.

Exercise 8.3

Find an expression for the probability that two children aged respectively 6 and 8 will both die before age 25 in the lifetime of their mother aged 45.

8.2 Contingent assurances

The symbols for contingent assurances, that is benefits payable on the death of a certain life but only if other lives die before or after in a defined way, are similar to those for contingent probabilities. The simplest is the benefit payable on the death of (x) (the *life assured*) if he dies before (y) (the *counter life*) given the symbol

$$\bar{A}_{xy}^1 = \int_0^\infty v^t {}_t p_{xy} \mu_{x+t} dt, \qquad (8.2.1)$$

it being seen in comparison with the probability given in (8.1.1) that the compound interest factor has been introduced.

It will be seen either by formula or by general reasoning that

$$\bar{A}_{xy}^1 + \bar{A}_{xy}^{\,1} = \bar{A}_{xy}. \qquad (8.2.2)$$

While $_\infty q_{xy}^2 = {}_\infty q_{xy}^1$ the similar relationship does not hold for the assurance as while the deaths occur in the same order the benefit is paid on a different death. The formula for

$$\bar{A}_{xy}^2 = \int_0^\infty v^t (1 - {}_t p_x) {}_t p_y \mu_{y+t} dt,$$

i.e.
$$\bar{A}_{xy}^2 = \bar{A}_y - \bar{A}_{xy}^1. \qquad (8.2.3)$$

Then
$$\bar{A}_y = \bar{A}_{xy}^1 + \bar{A}_{xy}^2,$$

which is obviously correct as the sum of the benefit paid on y dying before or after x is a benefit paid no matter when x dies.

Similar expressions will be obtained for benefits payable at the end of the year of death of the specified life, and for temporary benefits, for example

$$A^1_{xy\,:\,\overline{n}|} = \sum_{t=0}^{n-1} v^{t+1}{}_t|q^1_{xy}.$$

When more than two lives are involved the normal technique is to use a similar formula to (8.1.4) but introducing the compound interest term v^t, thus

$$\bar{A}^1_{xyz} = \int_0^\infty v^t{}_tp_{xyz}\mu_{x+t}dt;$$

$$\bar{A}^2_{xyz} = \int_0^\infty v^t{}_tp^{[1]}_{yz}{}_tp_x\mu_{x+t}dt$$

$$= \int_0^\infty v^t({}_tp_y + {}_tp_z - 2{}_tp_{yz}){}_tp_x\mu_{x+t}dt, \qquad (8.2.4)$$

i.e. $$\bar{A}^2_{xyz} = \bar{A}^1_{xy} + \bar{A}^1_{xz} - 2\bar{A}^1_{xyz}; \qquad (8.2.5)$$

$$\bar{A}^3_{xyz} = \int_0^\infty v^t(1 - {}_tp_y)(1 - {}_tp_z){}_tp_x\mu_{x+t}dt$$

i.e. $$\bar{A}^3_{xyz} = \bar{A}_x - \bar{A}^1_{xy} - \bar{A}^1_{xz} + \bar{A}^1_{xyz}. \qquad (8.2.6)$$

This also demonstrates that benefits can normally be expressed in terms of benefits payable on the first death.

For example, referring to Example 8.1 it will be seen that introducing the compound interest function gives

$$\bar{A}^1_{x\,:\,\overline{yz}} = \bar{A}^{1\,:\,2}_{x\,:\,y\,:\,z}$$

and a simple expression is

$$\bar{A}^1_{xy} + \bar{A}^1_{xz} - \bar{A}^1_{xyz}.$$

$\bar{A}^1_{xy\,:\,z}$ represents an assurance payable on the failure of the joint life status xy provided this occurs before the death of z, i.e.

$$\bar{A}^1_{xy\,:\,z} = \int_0^\infty v^t{}_tp_{xyz}(\mu_{x+t} + \mu_{y+t})dt$$

$$= \bar{A}^1_{xyz} + \bar{A}^{1}_{xyz},$$

which again should be obvious by general reasoning.

On the other hand $\bar{A}^{1}_{xy:z}$ represents the benefit payable on the failure of the last survivor status xy before the death of z,

$$\bar{A}^{1}_{xy:z} = \int_{0}^{\infty} v^{t} {}_{t}p_{z}((1-{}_{t}p_{x}){}_{t}p_{y}\mu_{y+t}+(1-{}_{t}p_{y}){}_{t}p_{x}\mu_{x+t})dt$$

$$= \bar{A}^{1}_{yz} - \bar{A}^{1}_{xyz} + \bar{A}^{1}_{xz} - \bar{A}^{1}_{xyz},$$

which can also be expressed in terms only of benefits depending on z dying first,

$$= (\bar{A}_{yz} - \bar{A}^{1}_{yz}) + (\bar{A}_{xz} - \bar{A}^{1}_{xz}) + (\bar{A}_{xyz} - \bar{A}^{1}_{xyz}),$$

as $\bar{A}_{xyz} = \bar{A}^{1}_{xyz} + \bar{A}^{1}_{xyz} + \bar{A}^{1}_{xyz}$ either by expansion or by general reasoning.

When lives are subject to the same mortality and are of equal ages, formulae may often be simplified—for example as

$$\bar{A}^{1}_{xyz} + \bar{A}^{1}_{xyz} + \bar{A}^{1}_{xyz} = A_{xyz}$$

then
$$\bar{A}^{1}_{xxx} = \tfrac{1}{3}\bar{A}_{xxx}.$$

An expression for a temporary contingent assurance is normally found by altering the upper limit of integration from ∞ to n. Provided the benefit is payable on the first death the value can also be obtained by deducting the value of a deferred contingent assurance from the whole life assurance thus

$$\bar{A}^{1}_{xy:\overline{n}|} = \int_{0}^{n} v^{t} {}_{t}p_{xy}\mu_{x+t}dt$$

$$= \bar{A}^{1}_{xy} - v^{n} {}_{n}p_{xy}\bar{A}^{1}_{x+n:y+n}.$$

Example 8.2

Show that

$$\bar{A}^{1}_{xyz} + \bar{A}^{2}_{xyz} + \bar{A}^{3}_{xyz} = \bar{A}_{x}.$$

Solution

Adding formulae (8.2.5) and (8.2.6) gives

$$\bar{A}^{2}_{xyz} + \bar{A}^{3}_{xyz} = \bar{A}_{x} - \bar{A}^{1}_{xyz}$$

giving the required result. The result should also be obvious by general reasoning.

Example 8.3

Find expressions for $\bar{A}^2_{xy}$ by considering integrals based on the deaths of (x) and (y) respectively and prove that the values of the integrals are equal.

Solution

Considering the death of (x) the value of the benefit is

$$\int_0^\infty v^t(1 - {}_tp_y)\,{}_tp_x\mu_{x+t}dt,$$

and considering the death of (y) the value is

$$\int_0^\infty v^t\,{}_tp_{xy}\mu_{y+t}\bar{A}_{x+t}dt,$$

In the first integral $\quad 1 - {}_tp_y = {}_tq_y = \int_0^t {}_rp_y\mu_{y+r}dr,$

so $\qquad \bar{A}^2_{xy} = \int_0^\infty v^t\,{}_tp_x\mu_{x+t}\left(\int_0^t {}_rp_y\mu_{y+r}dr\right)dt$

which by formula (3.9.4)

$$= \int_0^\infty {}_tp_y\mu_{y+t}\left(\int_t^\infty v^r\,{}_rp_x\mu_{x+r}dr\right)dt$$

$$= \int_0^\infty {}_tp_y\mu_{y+t}\,{}_t|\bar{A}_xdt$$

$$= \int_0^\infty v^t\,{}_tp_{xy}\mu_{y+t}\bar{A}_{x+t}dt, \quad \text{as required.}$$

Exercise 8.4

Express $\bar{A}^3_{wxyz}$ in terms of assurances payable on the first death.

Exercise 8.5

Prove the equality in Example 8.3 commencing with the second integral.

8.3 Compound and special contingent functions

In the discussion in this chapter so far the order of the deaths when there are more than two lives is not fully specified. For example, in

$_\infty q^2_{xyz}$ or $\bar{A}^2_{xyz}$ either y or z may die first. When a further restriction is made the order of deaths is specified by a number or numbers *below* the suffices for example in $_\infty q^2_{\underset{1}{xyz}}$, y must die first and x second. In the case of insurances the benefit is paid on the death of the life which has a number *above* the suffix, for example, in $\bar{A}^2_{\underset{1}{xyz}}$ and $\bar{A}^3_{\underset{1}{xyz}}$ the order of the deaths is the same but the benefit is paid on different deaths. When there are more than three lives there may be several digits below the suffices although the order of the deaths may still not be completely specified, e.g. $\bar{A}_{\underset{23}{uvwxyz}}^{4}$.

Considering $_\infty q^2_{\underset{1}{xyz}}$ the value will most easily be found by considering the death of x, thus

$$_\infty q^2_{\underset{1}{xyz}} = \int_0^\infty (1 - {}_tp_y)\,{}_tp_{xz}\mu_{x+t}\,dt$$

$$= \int_0^\infty {}_tp_{xz}\mu_{x+t}\,dt - \int_0^\infty {}_tp_{xyz}\mu_{x+t}\,dt$$

i.e. $$_\infty q^2_{\underset{1}{xyz}} = {}_\infty q^1_{xz} - {}_\infty q^1_{xyz}, \qquad (8.3.1)$$

a result which may also be obtained by general reasoning.

The similar result will also be found for the assurance—

$$\bar{A}^2_{\underset{1}{xyz}} = \int_0^\infty v^t(1 - {}_tp_y)\,{}_tp_{xz}\mu_{x+t}\,dt,$$

so $$\bar{A}^2_{\underset{1}{xyz}} = \bar{A}^1_{xz} - \bar{A}^1_{xyz}. \qquad (8.3.2)$$

By general reasoning it will be obvious that

$$\bar{A}^2_{xyz} = \bar{A}^2_{\underset{1}{xyz}} + \bar{A}^2_{\underset{1}{xyz}}. \qquad (8.3.3)$$

While assurances of the type payable on the second death can be satisfactorily simplified as in (8.3.2) by the use of the normal method of integrating over the instant of death of the life on whose death the benefit is to be payable, when the benefit is payable on the third death this leads to more complicated expressions such as

$$\bar{A}^3_{\underset{1}{xyz}} = \int_0^\infty v^t\,{}_tq^2_{yz}\cdot{}_tp_x\mu_{x+t}\,dt,$$

which is difficult to evaluate. A simpler form though still not easy to calculate will be found by basing the integration on the second death—

$$\bar{A}^3_{\underset{1}{xyz}} = \int_0^\infty v^t(1 - {}_tp_y){}_tp_{xz}\mu_{z+t}\bar{A}_{x+t}dt.$$

Similarly, when evaluating functions of more than three lives it is best to choose the latest death that does not necessitate the inclusion of a contingent probability in the expression to be integrated; for example

$$\bar{A}^3_{\underset{12}{wxyz}} = \int_0^\infty v^t(1 - {}_tp_x){}_tp_{wyz}\mu_{y+t}\bar{A}_{w+t:z+t}^{\,1}dt.$$

Such expressions may also be written as a double integral, for example

$$\bar{A}^3_{\underset{12}{wxyz}} = \int_0^\infty (1 - {}_tp_x){}_tp_y\mu_{y+t}\left(\int_t^\infty v^s{}_sp_{wz}\mu_{w+s}ds\right)dt.$$

A contingent function may involve conditions other than the order of the deaths, for example a restriction may be placed on the time interval between deaths. As is demonstrated in the examples at the end of this section no new ideas are involved and questions should be approached from first principles. Normally it is not possible to give a simple symbol to such probabilities or assurances.

One of the simplest probabilities of this type is that (x) will be alive n years after the death of (y);

$$\int_0^\infty {}_{t+n}p_x\,{}_tp_y\mu_{y+t}dt$$

$$= {}_np_x\int_0^\infty {}_tp_{x+n:y}\mu_{y+t}dt$$

$$= {}_np_x\cdot{}_\infty q_{x+n:y}^{\,1}.$$

Similarly, the probability that (y) will be alive n years after the death of (x) is ${}_np_y\cdot{}_\infty q_{x:y+n}^{\,1}$ so the probability that at least n years will elapse between the deaths is

$${}_np_x\cdot{}_\infty q_{x+n:y}^{\,1}+{}_np_y\cdot{}_\infty q_{x:y+n}^{\,1}.$$

Thus the probability that (x) and (y) will die within n years of each other is

$$1-({}_np_x\cdot{}_nq_{x+n:y}^{\,1}+{}_np_y\cdot{}_\infty q_{x:y+n}^{\,1}).$$

When considering functions such as have been discussed in this section they should if possible be simplified to contingent functions based on the first death.

Example 8.4

Find an expression for the probability that (x) will die during the n years following the death of (y).

Solution

$$\text{Probability} = \int_0^\infty ({}_tp_x - {}_{t+n}p_x){}_tp_y\mu_{y+t}dt$$

$$= {}_\infty q_{xy}^{\;1} - {}_np_x \cdot {}_\infty q_{x+n:\overset{1}{y}}.$$

Example 8.5

Find an expression for the value of an assurance payable on the death of (x) if (y) has predeceased him by not more than ten years.

Solution

This question will be considered in some detail in order to show the method of approach.

First the value is expressed in the form of integrals. As the benefit is payable on the death of (x) and only two lives are involved the integration will be based on the death of (x).

The probability that y died in the ten years before time t will be $({}_{t-10}p_y - {}_tp_y)$ so the basic value of the integral will be

$$\int v^t({}_{t-10}p_y - {}_tp_y){}_tp_x\mu_{x+t}dt.$$

The limits of integration must now be inserted—the upper limit is obviously ∞, but the lower limit cannot be less than $t = 10$ as ${}_{t-10}p_y$ will be meaningless with $t < 10$. A separate integral will therefore be required for the interval $0 < t < 10$; considering y to die between time 0 (when he is known to be alive) and time t.

The total expression is thus

$$\int_0^{10} v^t(1 - {}_tp_y){}_tp_x\mu_{x+t}dt + \int_{10}^\infty v^t({}_{t-10}p_y - {}_tp_y){}_tp_x\mu_{x+t}dt.$$

The next step is to simplify these integrals. Often any integrals with the lower limit not 0 are simplified by making a substitution so that it becomes 0—in this case substitute $t = s + 10$.

The expression now becomes

$$\bar{A}^1_{x:\overline{10|}} - \bar{A}^1_{x:y:\overline{10|}}$$

$$+ \int_0^\infty v^{s+10}({}_sp_y - {}_sp_{y+10} \cdot {}_{10}p_y) \cdot {}_sp_{x+10} \cdot {}_{10}p_x\mu_{x+10+s}ds$$

using
$$_{s+10}p_x = {}_sp_{x+10} \cdot {}_{10}p_x$$

$$= \bar{A}^1_{x:\overline{10|}} - \bar{A}^1_{x:y:\overline{10|}} + v^{10} {}_{10}p_x \int_0^\infty v^s {}_sp_y {}_sp_{x+10}\mu_{x+10+s}ds$$

$$- v^{10} {}_{10}p_y {}_{10}p_x \int_0^\infty v^s {}_sp_{y+10} {}_sp_{x+10}\mu_{x+10+s}ds,$$

$$= \bar{A}^1_{x:\overline{10|}} - \bar{A}^1_{x:y:\overline{10|}} + v^{10} {}_{10}p_x \bar{A}^1_{x+10:y} - v^{10} {}_{10}p_{xy} \bar{A}^1_{x+10:y+10}$$

$$= \bar{A}^1_{x:\overline{10|}} + v^{10} {}_{10}p_x \bar{A}^1_{x+10:y} - \bar{A}^1_{x:y},$$

taking the second and fourth terms together; these could have been added earlier by taking the second term in each of the integrals together.

Example 8.6

Express in terms of contingent assurances payable on the first death, the value of a contingent assurance payable on the death of the survivor of (20) and (30) provided that he attains at least age 60 and dies at least 10 years after the death of (40). All lives are subject to the same mortality table.

Solution

The value of the assurance is obtained by considering separately the cases when the benefit is paid on the death of each of (20) and (30). If the benefit is paid on the death of (20) the value is

$$\int_{40}^\infty v^t (1 - {}_tp_{30})(1 - {}_{t-10}p_{40}){}_tp_{20}\mu_{20+t}dt$$

and if on the death of (30)

$$\int_{30}^\infty v^t (1 - {}_tp_{20})(1 - {}_{t-10}p_{40}){}_tp_{30}\mu_{30+t}dt.$$

Summing and simplifying using the substitution $t = 40+s$ in the first integral and $t = 30+r$ in the second, gives

$$v^{40} {}_{40}p_{20} \int_0^\infty v^s(1 - {}_{40+s}p_{30})(1 - {}_{30+s}p_{40}){}_sp_{60}\mu_{60+s}ds$$

$$+ v^{30} {}_{30}p_{30} \int_0^\infty v^r(1 - {}_{30+r}p_{20})(1 - {}_{20+r}p_{40}){}_rp_{60}\mu_{60+r}dr$$

$$= v^{40} {}_{40}p_{20} \left\{ \int_0^\infty v^s {}_sp_{60}\mu_{60+s}ds - {}_{40}p_{30} \int_0^\infty v^s {}_sp_{70} {}_sp_{60}\mu_{60+s}ds \right.$$

$$- {}_{30}p_{40} \int_0^\infty v^s \, {}_sp_{70} \, {}_sp_{60}\mu_{60+s}ds$$

$$+ {}_{40}p_{30} \cdot {}_{30}p_{40} \int_0^\infty v^s \, {}_sp_{70} \cdot {}_sp_{70} \cdot {}_sp_{60}\mu_{60+s}ds \Big\}$$

$$+ v^{30} \, {}_{30}p_{30} \Big\{ \int_0^\infty v^r \, {}_rp_{60}\mu_{60+r}dr - {}_{30}p_{20} \int_0^\infty v^r \, {}_rp_{50} \, {}_rp_{60}\mu_{60+r}dr$$

$$- {}_{20}p_{40} \int_0^\infty v^r \, {}_rp_{60} \, {}_rp_{60}\mu_{60+r}dr$$

$$+ {}_{30}p_{30} \, {}_{20}p_{40} \int_0^\infty v^r \, {}_rp_{50} \cdot {}_rp_{60} \, {}_rp_{60}\mu_{60+r}dr \Big\}$$

$$= \frac{D_{60}}{D_{20}} \{ \bar{A}_{60} - ({}_{40}p_{30} + {}_{30}p_{40})\bar{A}_{60:70}^{\,1} + {}_{40}p_{30} \cdot {}_{30}p_{40}\bar{A}_{60:70:70}^{\,1} \}$$

$$+ \frac{D_{60}}{D_{30}} \{ \bar{A}_{60} - {}_{30}p_{20}\bar{A}_{50:60}^{\,1} - {}_{20}p_{40} \cdot \tfrac{1}{2}\bar{A}_{60:60}$$

$$+ {}_{30}p_{20} \cdot {}_{20}p_{40}\bar{A}_{50:60:60}^{\,1} \}.$$

Example 8.7

Find by the English Life Table No. 12—Males the probability that three lives aged 40, 30 and 20 will die in that order, at least ten years separating any two deaths.

Solution

If the second death which must be (30) is considered, (40) must be dead ten years before and (20) must be alive ten years after the death of (30). The integral is thus

$$\int_{10}^\infty (1 - {}_{t-10}p_{40}) {}_{t+10}p_{20} \cdot {}_tp_{30}\mu_{30+t}dt,$$

—there being no integral for the interval $0 < t < 10$ as the conditions cannot be satisfied. Substituting $t = s + 10$ gives

$$\int_0^\infty (1 - {}_sp_{40}){}_sp_{40} \, {}_{20}p_{20} \, {}_sp_{40} \, {}_{10}p_{30}\mu_{40+s}ds$$

$$= {}_{20}p_{20} \cdot {}_{10}p_{30} \Big\{ \int_0^\infty {}_sp_{40} \, {}_sp_{40}\mu_{40+s}ds - \int_0^\infty {}_sp_{40} \, {}_sp_{40} \, {}_sp_{40}\mu_{40+s}ds \Big\}$$

$$= {}_{20}p_{20} \, {}_{10}p_{30}({}_\infty q_{40:40}^{\,1} - {}_\infty q_{40:40:40}^{\,1})$$

and as $_\infty q^1_{40\,:\,40} = \frac{1}{2}$ and $_\infty q^1_{40\,:\,40\,:\,40} = \frac{1}{3}$, this

$$= \frac{l_{40}}{l_{20}} \cdot \frac{l_{40}}{l_{30}} \left(\tfrac{1}{2} - \tfrac{1}{3} \right)$$

$$= \frac{93{,}790}{96{,}293} \cdot \frac{93{,}790}{95{,}265} \cdot \frac{1}{6}$$

$$= \cdot 160.$$

Exercise 8.6
Find an expression for the probability that (x) will die before (y) or within n years of his death.

Exercise 8.7
Find an expression for the value of an insurance payable on the death of (x) provided it occurs at least n years after the death of (y).

Exercise 8.8
The probability $_\infty q^2_{xyz}$ was simplified in formula (8.3.1) by considering the death of x. Show by changing the order of integration in double integrals that the following expressions obtained by considering the deaths of (y) and (z) respectively are equal to (8.3.1).

$$_\infty q^2_{xyz} = \int_0^\infty {}_t p_{xyz} \mu_{y+t} \cdot {}_\infty q^{\,1}_{x+t\,:\,\boldsymbol{z}+t}\, dt,$$

$$_\infty q^2_{xyz} = \int_0^\infty {}_t q^2_{xy}\, {}_t p_z \mu_{z+t}\, dt.$$

Exercise 8.9
Find an expression for the value of an assurance payable at the death of (25) if he dies before the survivor of (30) and (40) or within ten years after the death of the survivor, leaving another person (20) surviving.

Exercise 8.10
Express in terms of probabilities dependent on the first death the chance that either (x) will survive (y) and (z) will die within n years of the death of (y) or (x) will predecease (y) and (z) will die within n years of the death of (x).

8.4 Premiums for contingent assurances
A contingent assurance may terminate either by the occurrence of the event insured against or an occurrence (normally a death) which is

contrary to the conditions for the assurance to become payable in which case the contract ceases.

In the simple case of the assurance payable on the death of (x) if he predeceases (y) the death of either (x) or (y) will terminate the assurance, and the annual premium should be payable only during the joint lifetime of (x) and (y), giving a net annual premium of $\dfrac{\overline{A}^1_{xy}}{\ddot{a}_{xy}}$. If, for example, the premium was assumed payable during the lifetime of x giving the smaller premium $\dfrac{\overline{A}^1_{xy}}{\ddot{a}_x}$, then, in the cases in which (y) dies first, on the death of (y) the person paying the premiums will cease payment and the life office will not collect enough premium from these cases to pay the death claims in the cases in which (x) dies first. The life office will also consider whether medical evidence is required—in this case the life assured (x) should be medically examined but there is no need to examine the counter life (y) as his death causes the assurance to terminate.

In any contingent assurance, particularly those not payable on the first death very careful consideration is required on two related points: (i) the status during which the premiums are to be paid (unless it is known to be a single premium policy) and (ii) which of the lives should be medically examined.

Considering the assurance payable on the death of (x) provided he is predeceased by (y), that is $\overline{A}^2_{xy}$, the assurance does not terminate with the death of (y) if (x) is alive. On the death of (y) before (x) the value of the assurance increases because the sum insured will now certainly be payable. The net premium will thus be $\dfrac{\overline{A}^2_{xy}}{\ddot{a}_x}$. As the death of (y) increases the value of the policy, medical evidence is required on his life. It is probably necessary to obtain medical evidence on (x) although it is possible that if he is in fact an impaired life the premium should theoretically decrease—if for example (x) is considered to be subject to the mortality of a life n years older it is possible that $\dfrac{\overline{A}^2_{x+n:y}}{\ddot{a}_{x+n}}$ is less than $\dfrac{\overline{A}^2_{xy}}{\ddot{a}_x}$.

In more complicated cases the main principles to be borne in mind are

(a) that as the premiums will not be paid in respect of a policy no longer in force, premiums must cease on any death causing the assurance to terminate.

(b) that it is usually necessary to medically examine the person at whose death the sum assured is payable.

(c) that it is usually necessary to medically examine any person whose early death improves the value of the policy either by increasing the probability that the sum assured will ultimately become payable or by making the assurance paid-up.

Considering as an example the assurance for which the net single premium is $\bar{A}^2_{x\overset{1}{y}z}$, the net annual premium should be $\dfrac{\bar{A}^2_{x\overset{1}{y}z}}{\ddot{a}_{xz}}$ because the assurance will terminate as soon as either (x) or (z) dies but will not terminate on the death of (y). It is necessary to examine medically (y) because his early death increases the probability that the sum assured will ultimately become payable. It is probably also necessary to examine (x) but there is no point in examining (z) as his death during the term of the assurance causes it to terminate. If the policy were a single premium contract the medical requirements would be the same.

In some cases there is the possibility that on the death of one of the lives the assured will have the option of forfeiting the policy and effecting another providing the same benefit at a lower premium. Considering for example the benefit $\bar{A}^1_{x:\overline{yz}}$, it might seem that the annuity value should be based on the status $(x:\overline{yz})$ but on the death of say (y) it is possible that the annual premium for the benefit as it has become, i.e. $\bar{A}^{1}_{x+t:z+t}/\ddot{a}_{x+t:z+t}$ is less than the original premium so that if x is in good health the original policy will be forfeited. In this case it might be advisable to charge an increased premium during the joint life status (xyz) reducing after the death of (y) or (z) to a premium not greater than the premium payable for a new policy after the death of either y or z.

Office premiums are usually obtained by adding similar loadings to those for temporary assurances. In some cases where the probability of the benefit becoming payable is small, a minimum premium such as £1‰ may be quoted.

Policy values except in the simplest cases will depend on which lives are alive and should always be calculated by the prospective method.

The policy value of an assurance payable on the death of (x) after (y), will be

$$\bar{A}^{\,2}_{x+t:y+t} - P\ddot{a}_{x+t} \quad \text{if both } (x) \text{ and } (y) \text{ are alive}$$

or $\quad\quad \bar{A}_{x+t} - P\ddot{a}_{x+t} \quad\quad$ if (y) is dead.

Example 8.8

Find on the A1967–70 mortality table ultimate at 4% interest the net annual premium for a policy securing £1,000 on the death of a life aged 30 provided he dies after another person also aged 30.

Solution

$$\bar{A}^{2}_{30:30} = \bar{A}_{30} - \bar{A}^{1}_{30:30}$$

$$= \bar{A}_{30} - \tfrac{1}{2}\bar{A}_{30:30}$$

$$= (1{\cdot}02)({\cdot}18996) - \tfrac{1}{2}(1{\cdot}02)(1 - ({\cdot}038462)(19{\cdot}701))$$

$$= {\cdot}1938 - {\cdot}1236$$

$$= {\cdot}0702.$$

The premium term is based on $\ddot{a}_{30} = 21{\cdot}061$.

So net annual premium $\quad\quad\quad = \dfrac{{\cdot}0702}{21{\cdot}061}\, 1{,}000$

$$= 3{\cdot}33 \text{ i.e. £3.33.}$$

Exercise 8.11

An assurance is payable in the event that a life aged 20 dies before age 35, and a life aged 50 dies before age 60, the sum assured being payable on the second death. Give an expression for the level annual premium payable until the sum assured is payable or until it is known that it will not be paid.

Exercise 8.12

A policy with sum assured £5,000 is payable on the death of a person aged 40 provided he dies after another person aged 40 and before a third also aged 40. Find the net annual premium on the basis of the A1967–70 table with 4% interest.

Exercise 8.13

An insurance is payable if (x) dies second of the three lives x, y and z.

(a) State the term during which the premium should be payable and which lives should be medically examined.

(b) Give expressions for the reserve after t years.

8.5 Evaluation of contingent functions

The evaluation of functions has already been touched on in the simple cases where the lives are of equal age and are subject to the same mortality table. When the lives are not of equal age and also may be subject to different mortality tables calculations are more difficult and the methods that are used are

(1) commutation functions,
(2) approximate integration,
(3) methods based on Gompertz and Makeham Laws,
(4) other methods.

The discussion will concentrate on functions based on the first death as most other functions can be simplified to this form, and also on two life functions—the extension to more lives is often obvious. It will also refer to assurances but similar expressions will be obtained for probabilities by making the rate of interest zero.

(1) Commutation functions based on the same system as indicated in section 7.1 can be defined. On the assumption of a uniform distribution of deaths over the years of age

$$\bar{C}^1_{xy} \fallingdotseq v^{\frac{1}{2}(x+y)+\frac{1}{2}} d_x l_{y+\frac{1}{2}}, \tag{8.5.1}$$

and

$$\bar{M}^1_{xy} \fallingdotseq \sum_{t=0}^{\infty} \bar{C}^1_{x+t:y+t}. \tag{8.5.2}$$

The accurate formula for $\bar{C}^1_{xy}$ will be

$$\bar{C}^1_{xy} = v^{\frac{1}{2}(x+y)} \int_0^1 v^t l_{x+t:y+t} \mu_{x+t} dt. \tag{8.5.3}$$

It is unusual for such commutation functions to be available for published mortality tables but in any particular case they may be calculated particularly if a computer is available.

(2) Approximate integration may be used to evaluate an integral, one of the following formulae normally being used:

Hardy's '39a':

$$\int_0^\infty u_t dt = n(\cdot 28u_0 + 1 \cdot 62u_n + 2 \cdot 2u_{3n} + 1 \cdot 62u_{5n} + \cdot 56u_{6n} + 1 \cdot 62u_{7n}).$$

Repeated Simpson:

$$\int_0^\infty u_t dt = \frac{n}{3}(u_0 + 4u_n + 2u_{2n} + 4u_{3n} + 2u_{4n} + \ldots).$$

This was the normal method used in practice before the advent of electronic computers and was also used as mentioned in section 7.1 for joint life functions for which commutation functions were not available; the examples and exercises will also cover these functions.

(3) When Gompertz's Law holds

$$\bar{A}_{xy}^1 = \int_0^\infty v^t {}_t p_{xy} Bc^{x+t} dt$$

$$= \frac{c^x}{c^x + c^y} \int_0^\infty v^t {}_t p_{xy} Bc^t (c^x + c^y) dt$$

$$= \frac{\mu_x}{\mu_x + \mu_y} \int_0^\infty v^t {}_t p_{xy} (\mu_{x+t} + \mu_{y+t}) dt,$$

i.e. $$\bar{A}_{xy}^1 = \frac{\mu_x}{\mu_x + \mu_y} \bar{A}_{xy} = \frac{\mu_x}{\mu_w} \bar{A}_w. \qquad (8.5.4)$$

where $\mu_x + \mu_y = \mu_w$.

It follows that as $\ddot{a}_{xy} = \ddot{a}_w$ from section 7.2

$$P(\bar{A}_{xy}^1) = \frac{\mu_x}{\mu_w} P(\bar{A}_w). \qquad (8.5.5)$$

When Makeham's Law holds

$$\bar{A}_{xy}^1 = \int_0^\infty v^t {}_t p_{xy} (A + Bc^{x+t}) dt$$

$$= A\bar{a}_{xy} + \frac{c^x}{c^x + c^y} \int_0^\infty v^t {}_t p_{xy} Bc^t (c^x + c^y) dt$$

$$= A\bar{a}_{xy} + \frac{c^x}{2c^w} \int_0^\infty v^t {}_t p_{ww} 2Bc^{w+t} dt,$$

where $c^x + c^y = 2c^w$ or $\mu_x + \mu_y = 2\mu_w$;

$$\therefore \bar{A}_{xy}^1 = A\bar{a}_{ww} + \frac{c^x}{2c^w} \int_0^\infty v^t {}_t p_{ww} (2\mu_{w+t} - 2A) dt,$$

i.e. $$\bar{A}_{xy}^1 = A\bar{a}_{ww} + \frac{c^x}{2c^w}(\bar{A}_{ww} - 2A\bar{a}_{ww}). \qquad (8.5.6)$$

When neither Gompertz's nor Makeham's Law applies, a rough approximation can be obtained by assuming that one or other does hold but finding the equivalent equal age or ages by using ages $x+n$ and $y+n$ rather than x and y choosing n to give an intermediate age within the range. For example, it has been suggested that assuming Gompertz's Law

$$\bar{A}^1_{xy} \doteqdot \frac{\mu_{x+n}}{\mu_{w+n}} \bar{A}_w,$$

where n is taken approximately equal to a_y and w such that

$$\mu_{x+n} + \mu_{y+n} = \mu_{w+n}.$$

(4) Two other methods will be described, the first is based on the approximation

$$\mu_{x+t} \doteqdot \frac{l_{x+t-1} - l_{x+t+1}}{2l_{x+t}};$$

then $\quad \bar{A}^1_{xy} = \displaystyle\int_0^\infty v^t {}_tp_{xy}\mu_{x+t}dt$

$$\doteqdot \int_0^\infty v^t {}_tp_{xy} \frac{l_{x+t-1} - l_{x+t+1}}{2l_{x+t}}\, dt$$

$$= \tfrac{1}{2}\left\{ \frac{l_{x-1}}{l_x} \int_0^\infty \frac{v^t l_{x+t-1}}{l_{x-1}}\, {}_tp_y dt - \frac{l_{x+1}}{l_x} \int_0^\infty \frac{v^t l_{x+t+1}}{l_{x+1}}\, {}_tp_y dt \right\}$$

$$\therefore \bar{A}^1_{xy} \doteqdot \tfrac{1}{2}\left(\frac{\bar{a}_{x-1:y}}{p_{x-1}} - p_x \bar{a}_{x+1:y} \right). \tag{8.5.7}$$

The second method is based on the differentiation of $\bar{a}_{xy}$ with respect to x keeping y constant;

$$\frac{d}{dx} \bar{a}_{xy} = \frac{d}{dx} \int_0^\infty v^t {}_tp_{xy}dt$$

$$= \int_0^\infty v^t {}_tp_y \frac{d}{dx} ({}_tp_x)dt$$

$$= \int_0^\infty v^t {}_tp_y\, {}_tp_x(\mu_x - \mu_{x+t})dt \quad \text{using equation (1.6.13)}$$

$$= \mu_x \bar{a}_{xy} - \bar{A}^1_{xy}.$$

$$\therefore \bar{A}^1_{xy} = \mu_x \bar{a}_{xy} - \frac{d}{dx} \bar{a}_{xy}$$

$$\therefore \bar{A}^1_{xy} \doteqdot \mu_x \bar{a}_{xy} + \tfrac{1}{2}(\bar{a}_{x-1:y} - \bar{a}_{x+1:y}) \tag{8.5.8}$$

Example 8.9

Calculate the values of $\bar{A}^1_{40\,:\,60}$ and $\ddot{a}_{40\,:\,60}$ the life aged 40 being subject to the mortality of the $a(55)$ males table and the life aged 60 being subject to the mortality of the $a(55)$ females table. The rate of interest is 4%. Hence calculate the annual premium for a contingent assurance with sum assured £2,000 payable on the death of (40) before (60) allowing for expenses of 10% of each premium with an additional £20 in the first year.

Solution

It is desirable to set out an approximate integration in tabular form in order to reduce the possibility of error. In this example logarithms will be used in order to show the 'classical' method of calculation although it would often be more convenient to use a modern calculating machine in practice. It is usual to use an interval in the approximate integration of between 5 and 10 years giving perhaps 6 to 8 ordinates. In this case the value of the functions will become negligible after about 44 years and the repeated Simpson formula will be used with an interval between ordinates of 8.

The formulae used will be

$$\bar{A}^1_{40\,:\,60} = \frac{1}{D_{40}l_{60}} \int_0^\infty D_{40+t}l_{60+t}\mu_{40+t}dt$$

$$\bar{a}_{40\,:\,60} = \frac{1}{D_{40}l_{60}} \int_0^\infty D_{40+t}l_{60+t}dt.$$

The functions D, l and μ are extracted from the relevant mortality tables remembering that the two lives are subject to different tables, and the logarithms to the base 10 are inserted as shown in Table 8.1. Summing the 'antilog total' gives ·033658 and the sum of the 'antilog subtotal' gives 4·9039. These totals have been obtained in this way so as most conveniently to calculate both the assurance and the annuity. Now

$$\bar{A}^1_{40\,:\,60} = \tfrac{8}{3}(\cdot033658) = \cdot08975,$$

and $\bar{a}_{40\,:\,60} = \tfrac{8}{3}(4\cdot9039) = 13\cdot077$ and adding ·5 gives

$$\ddot{a}_{40\,:\,60} = 13\cdot577,$$ compared with the tabular value of 13·576.

If the required annual premium is P',

$$P'\ddot{a}_{40\,:\,60} = 2{,}000\bar{A}^1_{40\,:\,60} + \cdot1P'\ddot{a}_{40\,:\,60} + 20,$$

i.e. $\cdot9P'(13\cdot577) = 2{,}000(\cdot08975) + 20$

$$\therefore P' = £16\cdot33.$$

TABLE 8.1

t	0	8	16	24	32	40
$\log D_{40+t}$	5·30581	5·15864	4·99995	4·81570	4·57271	4·19841
$\log l_{60+t}$	5·95279	5·90984	5·81201	5·58448	5·07403	4·03751
$\log$ coefficient	0·00000	0·60206	0·30103	0·60206	0·30103	0·60206
$-\log D_{40}l_{60}$	$\overline{12}$·74140	$\overline{12}$·74140	$\overline{12}$·74140	$\overline{12}$·74140	$\overline{12}$·74140	$\overline{12}$·74140
Subtotal	0·00000	0·41194	$\bar{1}$·85439	$\bar{1}$·74364	$\bar{2}$·68917	$\bar{3}$·57938
$\log \mu_{40+t}$	$\bar{3}$·34635	$\bar{3}$·63949	$\bar{3}$·96142	$\bar{2}$·30061	$\bar{2}$·65109	$\bar{2}$·99524
Total	$\bar{3}$·34635	$\bar{2}$·05143	$\bar{3}$·81581	$\bar{2}$·04425	$\bar{3}$·34026	$\bar{4}$·57462
Antilog total	0·002220	0·011258	0·006544	0·011071	0·002189	0·000376
Antilog subtotal	1·0000	2·5819	0·7151	0·5542	0·0489	0·0038

Exercise 8.14

Find $_\infty q^1_{50:70}$ if the mortality table follows Makeham's Law with $A = \cdot003$, $c^{10} = 2$ and $\mathring{e}_{50:70} = 10$.

Exercise 8.15

Obtain the approximation

$$\bar{A}^1_{x:\overline{yz}} = \mu_x \bar{a}_{x:\overline{yz}} + \tfrac{1}{2}(\bar{a}_{x-1:\overline{yz}} - \bar{a}_{x+1:\overline{yz}}).$$

Exercise 8.16

A mortality table follows Makeham's Law. Show that $\bar{A}^1_{xy}$ may be expressed in terms of $\bar{a}_{xy}$ and $\bar{a}'_{xy}$ (this annuity being at a special rate of interest) and hence that it may be expressed in the form

$$\frac{\mu_{x+n}}{\mu_{x+n} + \mu_{y+n}} \bar{A}_{xy}, \quad \text{and find } n.$$

Exercise 8.17

Use an approximate integration method to verify that on the English Life Table No. 12—Males

(1) $_\infty q_{50:60} = \displaystyle\int_0^\infty {_t}p_{50:60}(\mu_{50+t} + \mu_{60+t})dt = 1$

(2) $_\infty q^1_{50:50} = \displaystyle\int_0^\infty {_t}p_{50:50}\mu_{50+t}dt = \tfrac{1}{2}.$

Exercise 8.18

Use an approximate integration method to calculate $\bar{A}^1_{70:70}$ on the A1967–70 ultimate table at 4% interest verifying the result by the use of the available table of $\ddot{a}_{xx}$.

8.6   Reversionary annuities

An annuity which commences on the failure of a given status if a second status is then in existence and which continues during the existence of the second status is referred to as a reversionary annuity. The simplest reversionary annuity is one which commences on the death of (x) if (y) is then living and continues thereafter during the remaining lifetime of (y); the life (x) is referred to as the *failing* or *counter* life and (y) is the *annuitant*. If the annuity is payable yearly commencing at the end of the year of death of (x) it is given the symbol $a_{x|y}$. Considering the condition under which each payment is made, that x is dead and y is alive, the value of the annuity can be found,

$$a_{x|y} = \sum_{t=1}^{\infty} v^t(1-{}_tp_x){}_tp_y$$

i.e. $\qquad a_{x|y} = a_y - a_{xy}.$ $\qquad\qquad$ (8.6.1)

The basic formula applies when (x) and (y) are themselves statuses rather than simply lives, so that

$$a_{u|v} = a_v - a_{uv}, \qquad\qquad (8.6.2)$$

where u and v are statuses.

Applying this formula, for example, to

$$a_{x|yz} = a_{yz} - a_{xyz};$$

$$a_{\overline{xy}|z} = a_z - a_{\overline{xy}:z}$$

$$= a_z - (a_{xz} + a_{yz} - a_{xyz}).$$

In the first of these the annuity is paid while both y and z are alive after the death of x, and in the second the annuity is paid while z is alive after both x and y are dead.

When a reversionary annuity is payable continuously, the normal bar is placed above the symbol so that the annuity payable continuously to (y) after (x) is dead is $\bar{a}_{x|y}$ and

$$\bar{a}_{x|y} = \int_0^{\infty} v^t(1-{}_tp_x){}_tp_y dt \qquad\qquad (8.6.3)$$

i.e. $\qquad \bar{a}_{x|y} = \bar{a}_y - \bar{a}_{xy}, \qquad\qquad (8.6.4)$

which could also be obtained by general reasoning.

A second method, which emphasises the basic assurance nature of the function since payment is made following the failure of a status, is to consider the value of the benefit at the death of x at time t, i.e. $\bar{a}_{y+t}$, so

$$\bar{a}_{x|y} = \int_0^{\infty} v^t{}_tp_{xy}\mu_{x+t}\bar{a}_{y+t} dt. \qquad\qquad (8.6.5)$$

The equivalence of the formulae is shown as follows—commencing with the second formula

$$= \int_0^{\infty} {}_tp_x\mu_{x+t}\left(\int_t^{\infty} v^r{}_rp_y dr\right) dt,$$

and changing the order of integration using formula (3.9.4),

$$= \int_0^\infty v^t {}_tp_y \left(\int_0^t {}_rp_x\mu_{x+r}dr \right) dt,$$

$$= \int_0^\infty v^t {}_tp_y(1 - {}_tp_x)dt, \quad \text{which is formula (8.6.3).}$$

Substituting formula (3.2.1) and the similar joint life formula in equation (8.6.4) gives

$$\bar{a}_{x|y} \doteqdot (a_y + \tfrac{1}{2} - \tfrac{1}{12}(\mu_y + \delta)) - (a_{xy} + \tfrac{1}{2} - \tfrac{1}{12}(\mu_x + \mu_y + \delta))$$

$$= a_y - a_{xy} + \tfrac{1}{12}\mu_y,$$

and normally the last term is ignored giving

$$\bar{a}_{x|y} = a_y - a_{xy}, \tag{8.6.6}$$

which is the same expression as formula (8.6.1).

The annuity could be paid at other than yearly intervals. By general reasoning

$$a_{x|y}^{(m)} = a_y^{(m)} - a_{xy}^{(m)}$$

$$\doteqdot \left(a_y + \frac{m-1}{2m} - \frac{m^2-1}{12m^2}\mu_y \right) - \left(a_{xy} + \frac{m-1}{2m} - \frac{m^2-1}{12m^2}(\mu_x + \mu_y) \right),$$

i.e.

$$a_{x|y}^{(m)} \doteqdot a_y - a_{xy} + \frac{m^2-1}{12m^2}\mu_x \tag{8.6.7}$$

or ignoring the last term whose value is small

$$a_{x|y}^{(m)} \doteqdot a_y - a_{xy}, \tag{8.6.8}$$

which is again the same formula as (8.6.1).

Under this annuity payments are made at intervals measured from the time the annuity is effected. When the payments are made at intervals measured from the date of (x)'s death the sign $\wedge$ is added above the annuity symbol, thus $\hat{a}_{x|y}^{(m)}$ is payable at intervals of one mth of a year from the death of x.

$$\hat{a}_{x|y}^{(m)} = \int_0^\infty v^t {}_tp_{xy}\mu_{x+t} a_{y+t}^{(m)}dt$$

$$\doteqdot \int_0^\infty v^t {}_tp_{xy}\mu_{x+t} \left(\bar{a}_{y+t} - \frac{1}{2m} \right) dt$$

$$\left(\text{substituting} \quad a^{(m)}_{y+t} \doteqdot a_{y+t} + \frac{m-1}{2m} \doteqdot \bar{a}_{y+t} - \frac{1}{2m}\right)$$

$$= \bar{a}_{x|y} - \frac{1}{2m} \bar{A}^1_{xy}$$

i.e.
$$\hat{a}^{(m)}_{x|y} \doteqdot a_y - a_{xy} + \tfrac{1}{12}\mu_y - \frac{1}{2m} \bar{A}^1_{xy}. \tag{8.6.9}$$

In practice again the last two terms are often ignored and the value taken as $a_y - a_{xy}$, which is then the approximate value for almost any reversionary annuity no matter the frequency of payment or the time of commencement following death, even if the annuity is payable continuously. Because of this approximate equality between the annuity payable continuously and with periodic payments the normal method of finding values when suitable functions are not tabulated is by approximate integration. It is particularly appropriate to use a formula based on (8.6.5), where of course x and y may be statuses not lives, if the rate of interest or the mortality assumption changes at the failure of the x status.

Reversionary annuities may be issued subject to annual premiums. Normally the premiums will be payable during the joint status so that the annual premium for a reversionary annuity to (v) after the failure of (u) is

$$\frac{a_{u|v}}{\ddot{a}_{uv}}. \tag{8.6.10}$$

Example 8.10

A complete reversionary annuity is one in which one proportional instalment is paid on the death of the annuitant. Find expressions for the value of complete annuities payable $m$thly where the first payment is made (i) at the first $m$thly interval measured from the commencement of the policy and (ii) one mth of a year after the death of the failing life.

Solution

(i) The annuity is given the symbol $\hat{a}^{(m)}_{x|y}$. The difference between $\hat{a}^{(m)}_{x|y}$ and $a^{(m)}_{x|y}$ is the fractional payment made on the death of y. Assuming that on average this is $\dfrac{1}{2m}$ and assuming the usual approximation for $a^{(m)}_{x|y}$ gives

$$\hat{a}^{(m)}_{x|y} \doteqdot a_y - a_{xy} + \frac{1}{2m} \bar{A}^2_{xy}$$

or
$$\hat{a}_{x|y}^{(m)} \doteqdot a_y - a_{xy} + \frac{1}{2m}(\bar{A}_y - \bar{A}_{xy}^1).$$

(ii) The annuity is given the symbol $\hat{\bar{a}}_{x|y}^{(m)}$. Then

$$\hat{\bar{a}}_{x|y}^{(m)} = \int_0^\infty v^t {}_t p_{xy} \mu_{x+t} \hat{a}_{y+t}^{(m)} dt$$

and replacing $\hat{a}_{y+t}^{(m)}$ by $\bar{a}_{y+t} - \frac{1}{2m} + \frac{1}{2m} \bar{A}_{y+t}$ gives

$$\hat{\bar{a}}_{x|y}^{(m)} \doteqdot \bar{a}_{x|y} - \frac{1}{2m} \bar{A}_{xy}^1 + \frac{1}{2m} \bar{A}_{xy}^2,$$

$$\doteqdot a_y - a_{xy} - \frac{1}{2m}(\bar{A}_{xy}^1 - \bar{A}_y + \bar{A}_{xy}^1) \quad \text{using (8.6.6),}$$

$$= a_y - a_{xy} - \frac{1}{2m}(\bar{A}_{xy} - \bar{A}_y).$$

Example 8.11

A continuous reversionary annuity of 1 per annum payable to (y) after the death of (x) is effected by annual premiums. Give an expression for the net annual premium reserve at the end of t years if (x) is still alive.

Solution

The annual premium will by (8.6.10) be

$$\frac{\bar{a}_{x|y}}{\ddot{a}_{xy}}.$$

At the end of t years the value of the benefit is

$$\bar{a}_{x+t|y+t}$$

and the value of future premiums is

$$\frac{\bar{a}_{x|y}}{\ddot{a}_{xy}} \ddot{a}_{x+t:y+t}$$

so the reserve is

$$\bar{a}_{x+t|y+t} - \frac{\bar{a}_{x|y}}{\ddot{a}_{xy}} \ddot{a}_{x+t:y+t}.$$

Using the normal approximation $\bar{a}_{x|y} \doteqdot a_y - a_{xy} = \ddot{a}_y - \ddot{a}_{xy}$, the reserve becomes

$$\ddot{a}_{y+t} - \ddot{a}_{x+t:y+t} - (\ddot{a}_y - \ddot{a}_{xy}) \frac{\ddot{a}_{x+t:y+t}}{\ddot{a}_{xy}}$$

$$= \ddot{a}_{y+t} - \ddot{a}_y \frac{\ddot{a}_{x+t:y+t}}{\ddot{a}_{xy}}.$$

Example 8.12

Fund A gives an income of £1,000 per annum. The lives (v) and (w) are entitled to the income during their joint lifetime, and the survivor is entitled to one-half of the income during the remainder of his lifetime.

Fund B produces an income of £700 per annum reducing on the death of (v) to £500 per annum in perpetuity; (x) is entitled to the whole of the income from this fund during his lifetime.

Subject to the interests of (v), (w) and (x), (z) is entitled to the income from both funds during his lifetime.

Give an expression in terms of single and joint life annuities for the value of (z)'s interest if all payments are made yearly the next payment being due a year hence.

Solution

The solution to this question will be given by three different methods to exemplify the approaches that can be made to this type of question.

Method 1

The annual share of (z) in fund A is £500 following the death of (v) and £500 following the death of (w), i.e.

$$500 a_{v|z} + 500 a_{w|z}.$$

The annual share of (z) in fund B is £700 if (v) is alive and £500 if (v) is dead, each only so long as (x) is dead, i.e.

$$700 a_{x|vz} + 500 a_{\overline{vx}|z}.$$

The total amount is thus

$$500 a_z - 500 a_{vz} + 500 a_z - 500 a_{wz} + 700 a_{vz} - 700 a_{vxz}$$

$$+ 500 a_z - 500 a_{xz} - 500 a_{vz} + 500 a_{vxz}$$

$$= 1{,}500 a_z - 300 a_{vz} - 500 a_{wz} - 500 a_{xz} - 200 a_{vxz}.$$

Method 2

The total value of the income is a perpetuity of 1,500 plus an annuity of 200 during (v)'s lifetime;

the value of (v)'s and (w)'s interests $= 500a_v + 500a_w$ and
the value of (x)'s interest $= 500a_x + 200_{vx}$.

The value of all interest other than those of (v), (w) and (x) is then the total value less the value of the interest of those three lives. The interest of (z) is the difference provided he is alive so the value of his interest, adding z to the lives in each of the annuities, is

$$1{,}500a_z + 200a_{vz} - 500a_{vz} - 500a_{wz} - 500a_{xz} - 200a_{vxz}$$

$$= 1{,}500a_z - 300a_{vz} - 500a_{wz} - 500a_{xz} - 200a_{vxz}.$$

Method 3

In this method each combination of living and dead persons is taken, together with the probability that the condition will be in force at time t and then summing or integrating to give annuities. It is often convenient to use a tabular form (Table 8.2). Multiplying each of the last column by v^t and summing $t = 1$ to ∞ gives the total value of (z)'s share:

$$500a_{wxz} - 500a_{vwxz} + 500a_{vxz} - 500a_{vwxz}$$

$$+ 700a_{vwz} - 700a_{vwxz} + 1{,}200a_{vz} - 1{,}200a_{vwz} - 1{,}200a_{vxz}$$

$$+ 1{,}200a_{vwxz} + 1{,}000a_{wz} - 1{,}000a_{vwz} - 1{,}000a_{wxz} + 1{,}000a_{vwxz}$$

$$+ 1{,}000a_{xz} - 1{,}000a_{vxz} - 1{,}000a_{wxz} + 1{,}000a_{vwxz}$$

$$+ 1{,}500a_z - 1{,}500a_{vz} - 1{,}500a_{wz} - 1{,}500a_{xz}$$

$$+ 1{,}500a_{vwz} + 1{,}500a_{wxz} + 1{,}500a_{vxz} - 1{,}500a_{vwxz}$$

$$= 1{,}500a_z - 300a_{vz} - 500a_{wz} - 500a_{xz} - 200a_{vxz}.$$

TABLE 8.2

Lives dead	Lives alive	Total income	(z)'s share	Expressions for obtaining value
		£	£	
—	$vwxz$	1,700	—	not necessary
v	wxz	1,500	500	$(1 - {}_tp_v){}_tp_{wxz}$
w	vxz	1,700	500	$(1 - {}_tp_w){}_tp_{vxz}$
x	vwz	1,700	700	$(1 - {}_tp_x){}_tp_{vwz}$
wx	vz	1,700	1,200	$(1 - {}_tp_w)(1 - {}_tp_x){}_tp_{vz}$
vx	wz	1,500	1,000	$(1 - {}_tp_v)(1 - {}_tp_x){}_tp_{wz}$
vw	xz	1,500	1,000	$(1 - {}_tp_v)(1 - {}_tp_w){}_tp_{xz}$
vwx	z	1,500	1,500	$(1 - {}_tp_v)(1 - {}_tp_w)(1 - {}_tp_x){}_tp_z$

In such questions it is advisable to check the solution, perhaps by adding the various shares in the fund, or by testing the answer by a combination of survivals and deaths to ensure that it provides the correct payment. For example if (v), (x) and (z) are alive and (w) is dead the answer gives a payment (in hundreds) of

$$15 - 3 - 0 - 5 - 2 = 5$$

which is correct since (z) in these circumstances receives 5 from fund A and nothing from fund B.

Exercise 8.19
State the meaning of the symbol

$$\hat{a}_{x|y}^{(m)}$$

and find an expression for its value.

Exercise 8.20
Find expressions for

$$a_{wx|\overline{yz}} \quad \text{and} \quad a_{\overline{wx}|yz}.$$

Exercise 8.21
Show that $_tV(a_{x|y})$ is negative if

$$\frac{\ddot{a}_{y+t}}{\ddot{a}_y} < \frac{\ddot{a}_{x+t:y+t}}{\ddot{a}_{xy}}.$$

Exercise 8.22
A reversionary annuity of £100 is to be payable so long as at least two of three lives aged 30, 35 and 55 survive after the death of a life aged 60. The annuity is to be payable annually, the first payment to be made at the end of the year of death of (60). The whole annuity is to be paid to (55) so long as he survives with either or both of (30) and (35) but if (55) dies before these two, the payments are to be divided equally between them.

Obtain expressions in terms of joint life annuities for the present values of the interests of (30), (35) and (55), checking the answers by summation.

Exercise 8.23
Annual payments are to be made of £500 at the end of each of the next 20 years, and £300 thereafter, provided at least one of three lives (30), (42) and (50) is alive. While all three lives survive, (50) is to receive 40% of each payment and (42) and (30) are to receive 30% each.

K

If (50) dies first, subsequent payments will be divided equally between (42) and (30) so long as they are both alive; if (42) dies first, then while (50) and (30) are both alive (50) is to receive 60% of each payment and (30) the balance; if (42) and (50) both predecease (30), (30) will be entitled to half of each payment, the remainder of the payment passing elsewhere.

Set down and simplify a formula for the present value of the annuity on the life of (30) which would be needed to ensure that in conjunction with the above payments, (30)'s income would not fall below £300 per annum.

8.7 Special and contingent reversionary annuities

When one or both of the statuses in a reversionary annuity involves a term certain it is not normally satisfactory to use the approximation (8.6.1) which was used for most annuities in the previous section. While this formula does apply in the simplest case

$$a_{\overline{n}|x} = a_x - a_{x:\overline{n}},$$

the single life deferred annuity normally given the symbol $_n|a_x$, it does not apply if this annuity is payable at other than yearly intervals—

$$a_{\overline{n}|x}^{(m)} = a_x^{(m)} - a_{x:\overline{n}}^{(m)}$$

$$\doteqdot \left(a_x + \frac{m-1}{2m}\right) - \left(a_{x:\overline{n}} + \frac{m-1}{2m}\left(1 - \frac{D_{x+n}}{D_x}\right)\right),$$

i.e.
$$a_{\overline{n}|x}^{(m)} \doteqdot a_x - a_{x:\overline{n}} + \frac{m-1}{2m}\frac{D_{x+n}}{D_x} \tag{8.7.1}$$

and the last term cannot be ignored.

When a reversionary annuity is payable to (y) following the death of (x) within n years it is important to distinguish the cases

    (a) in which no payment is made after the n years,   and

    (b) in which once payments commence they continue during (y)'s lifetime.

The value of (a) paid continuously is

$$\int_0^n v^t(1 - {}_tp_x){}_tp_y\,dt$$

$$= \bar{a}_{y:\overline{n}} - \bar{a}_{xy:\overline{n}}. \tag{8.7.2}$$

The value of (b) paid continuously is

$$\int_0^n v^t {}_t p_{xy} \mu_{x+t} \bar{a}_{y+t} dt$$

$$= \int_0^\infty v^t {}_t p_{xy} \mu_{x+t} \bar{a}_{y+t} dt - v^n {}_n p_{xy} \int_0^\infty v^t {}_t p_{x+n:y+n} \mu_{x+n+t} \bar{a}_{y+n+t} dt$$

$$= \bar{a}_y - \bar{a}_{xy} - v^n {}_n p_{xy} (\bar{a}_{y+n} - \bar{a}_{x+n:y+n}). \tag{8.7.3}$$

When the reversionary annuity is payable for a temporary period of n years following the death of (x) the value will be, in the case of the annuity payable yearly

$$\sum_{t=1}^n v^t (1 - {}_t p_x) {}_t p_y + \sum_{t=n+1}^\infty v^t ({}_{t-n} p_x - {}_t p_x) {}_t p_y,$$

and first taking together the second term in each summation and then substituting $t = s+n$ in the first term of the second summation,

$$= a_{y:\overline{n}|} + v^n {}_n p_y \sum_{s=1}^\infty v^s {}_s p_x {}_s p_{y+n} - a_{xy}$$

$$= a_{y:\overline{n}|} + v^n {}_n p_y a_{x:y+n} - a_{xy}.$$

When payment of a reversionary annuity depends on the order of the death of lives in the (u) status it is called a contingent reversionary annuity. An example is the annuity payable continuously to (z) after the death of x provided y is then alive, represented by the symbol $\bar{a}^1_{xy|z}$, which is only conveniently evaluated by considering the death of (x).

$$\bar{a}^1_{xy|z} = \int_0^\infty v^t {}_t p_{xyz} \mu_{x+t} \bar{a}_{z+t} dt.$$

The annuity payable to (z) after the death of (y) provided this occurs after the death of (x) is $\bar{a}^2_{xy|z}$, and

$$\bar{a}^2_{xy|z} = \int_0^\infty v^t (1 - {}_t p_x) {}_t p_{yz} \mu_{y+t} \bar{a}_{z+t} dt$$

$$= \bar{a}_{y|z} - \bar{a}^1_{xy|z}.$$

Normally approximate integration is the most convenient method to evaluate contingent reversionary annuities.

If $\bar{a}^1_{xy|z}$ and $a^2_{xy|z}$ are compared, the order of the deaths required for payment is the same but payment commences on the death of x in the first case and additional payments are made until the death of y. These additional payments are $\bar{a}_{x|yz}$ so

$$\bar{a}^1_{xy|z} = \bar{a}^2_{xy|z} + \bar{a}_{x|yz}$$

$$= \bar{a}_{y|z} - \bar{a}^1_{xy|z} + a_{x|yz},$$

i.e. $$\bar{a}^1_{xy|z} + \bar{a}^1_{xy|z} = \bar{a}_{y|z} + \bar{a}_{x|yz}$$

$$= \bar{a}_z - \bar{a}_{yz} + \bar{a}_{yz} - \bar{a}_{xyz}$$

$$= \bar{a}_z - \bar{a}_{xyz},$$

i.e. $$\bar{a}^1_{xy|z} + \bar{a}^1_{xy|z} = \bar{a}_{xy|z},$$

an obvious result by general reasoning.

When more lives are involved a notation similar to that for compound contingent assurances is used, for example $\bar{a}^2_{xyz|w}$ represents an annuity to (w) commencing on the death of (x) provided that (x) dies before (z) and after (y)—

$$\bar{a}^2_{\underset{1}{xyz}|w} = \int_0^\infty v^t {}_tp_{wxz}(1 - {}_tp_y)\mu_{x+t}\bar{a}_{w+t}dt$$

$$= \bar{a}^1_{xz|w} - \bar{a}^1_{xyz|w}.$$

As with simple reversionary annuities the values of annuities payable at yearly or $m$thly intervals are normally taken as approximately the same as that for the continuous functions so that normally whichever is the most convenient to evaluate will be found no matter what the method of payment.

Example 8.13

Describe the function given the symbol $a_{\overline{y : \overline{n}}|x}$ and find its value.

Solution

$a_{\overline{y : \overline{n}}|x}$ is an annuity to (x) after the second to occur of the events— the death of (y) and the passing of n years.

$$a_{\overline{y : \overline{n}}|x} = a_x - a_{x : \overline{y : \overline{n}}} \qquad \text{by formula (8.6.2)}$$

$$= a_x - a_{xy} - a_{x : \overline{n}} + a_{xy : \overline{n}} \qquad \text{by formula (7.5.3)}$$

which is ${}_n|a_x - {}_n|a_{xy}$ so that an alternative symbol is ${}_n|a_{y|x}$, a reversionary annuity deferred n years.

Example 8.14

Three persons (x), (y) and (z) have purchased an immediate annuity of 1 per annum payable annually until the death of the last survivor. The annuity is to be paid to (x) during his lifetime and to his estate for n years after his death if one at least of (y) and (z) are living. After the n years the annuity is to be paid to (y) if living during the remainder of his lifetime. When the interests of (x) and (y) have both ceased, the annuity is to be paid to (z) if living.

Find expressions for the share of each in the annuity.

Solution

(x)'s share

$$= a_x + \sum_{t=1}^{n} v^t (1 - {}_t p_x)\, {}_t p_{\overline{yz}} + \sum_{t=n+1}^{\infty} v^t ({}_{t-n} p_x - {}_t p_x)\, {}_t p_{\overline{yz}}$$

$$= a_x + \sum_{t=1}^{n} v^t\, {}_t p_{\overline{yz}} - \sum_{t=1}^{\infty} v^t\, {}_t p_{x:\overline{yz}} + \sum_{t=n+1}^{\infty} v^t\, {}_{t-n} p_x\, {}_t p_{\overline{yz}},$$

and substituting $t = s + n$ in the last term,

$$= a_x + a_{\overline{yz}:\overline{n}|} - a_{x:\overline{yz}} + v^n \sum_{s=1}^{\infty} v^s\, {}_s p_x\, {}_{s+n} p_{yz}$$

$$= a_x + a_{\overline{yz}:\overline{n}|} - a_{x:\overline{yz}} + v^n \sum_{s=1}^{\infty} v^s\, {}_s p_x ({}_{s+n} p_y + {}_{s+n} p_z - {}_{s+n} p_{yz})$$

$$= a_x + a_{y:\overline{n}|} + a_{z:\overline{n}|} - a_{yz:\overline{n}|} - a_{xy} - a_{xz} + a_{xyz}$$

$$\qquad + v^n \{ {}_n p_y a_{x:y+n} + {}_n p_z a_{x:z+n} - {}_n p_{yz} a_{x:y+n:z+n} \}.$$

(y)'s share

$$= \sum_{t=n+1}^{\infty} v^t\, {}_t p_y (1 - {}_{t-n} p_x), \text{ and substituting } t = s + n,$$

$$= \sum_{s=1}^{\infty} v^{s+n}\, {}_{s+n} p_y (1 - {}_s p_x)$$

$$= v^n\, {}_n p_y (a_{y+n} - a_{x:y+n}).$$

(z)'s share

$$= \sum_{t=n+1}^{\infty} v^t\, {}_t p_z (1 - {}_t p_y)(1 - {}_{t-n} p_x)$$

$$= v^n \sum_{s=1}^{\infty} v^s\, {}_{s+n} p_z (1 - {}_{s+n} p_y)(1 - {}_s p_x)$$

$$= v^n \{ {}_n p_z (a_{z+n} - a_{x:z+n}) - {}_n p_{yz} (a_{y+n:z+n} - a_{x:y+n:z+n}) \}.$$

A check on the answers can be made to ensure that the sum of the three shares is $a_{\overline{xyz}}$.

Exercise 8.24

Show that an alternative expression for (8.7.3) is

$$\int_0^n v^t(1 - {}_tp_x)\,{}_tp_y\,dt + \int_n^\infty v^t(1 - {}_np_x)\,{}_tp_y\,dt$$

and prove that it reduces to the same expression.

Exercise 8.25

Find an expression for $\bar{a}^1_{xx|y}$.

Exercise 8.26

Show that $\bar{A}^2_{xy} = \bar{A}^1_{xy} - \delta\bar{a}_{y|x}$.

Exercise 8.27

Give integral expressions for

$$\bar{a}^2_{yz|wx}, \quad \bar{a}_{x\,:\,y\,:\,z|w}^{2:3}_{1}$$

Exercise 8.28

Find the value of an annuity of 1 per annum payable annually, the first payment being deferred until the end of the year in which the failure of the joint lifetime of (30) and (40) occurs, to be payable thereafter for a term of 20 years or until 10 years after the death of the survivor, whichever is the longer period.

EXAMPLES AND EXERCISES ON CHAPTER 8

Example 8.15

The probability that three lives aged 50, 40 and 30 will die in that order and that the time elapsing between deaths will be at least 10 years is ·0972. The probability that a life now aged 40 will die before or within not more than 10 years after the second to die of two lives now aged 50 is ·73. On the basis of the same mortality table find the probability that of three lives A, B and C all aged 30, A will die within 10 years from now and will be survived by only one of B and C.

Solution

The probability that 50, 40 and 30 will die in that order with at least 10 years between death is

$$\int_{10}^{\infty} (1 - {}_{t-10}p_{50}){}_{t}p_{40}\mu_{40+t} \cdot {}_{t+10}p_{30} dt$$

and substituting $t = s + 10$

$$= \int_{0}^{\infty} (1 - {}_{s}p_{50}){}_{s}p_{50} \cdot {}_{10}p_{40}\mu_{50+s} \cdot {}_{s}p_{50} \cdot {}_{20}p_{30} dt$$

$$= {}_{10}p_{40} \cdot {}_{20}p_{30} \left\{ \int_{0}^{\infty} {}_{s}p_{50}^{2}\mu_{50+t} dt - \int_{0}^{\infty} {}_{s}p_{50}^{3}\mu_{50+t} dt \right\}$$

$$= {}_{10}p_{40} \cdot {}_{20}p_{30} ({}_{\infty}q_{50:50}^{1} - {}_{\infty}q_{50:50:50}^{1})$$

$$= {}_{10}p_{40} \cdot {}_{20}p_{30} (\tfrac{1}{2} - \tfrac{1}{3})$$

$$= \tfrac{1}{6}{}_{10}p_{40} \cdot {}_{20}p_{30}, \quad \text{which is stated to be } \cdot 0972$$

$$\therefore \; {}_{20}p_{30} \cdot {}_{10}p_{40} = \cdot 5832.$$

The probability that a life aged 40 dies before or within not more than 10 years after the second to die of two lives now aged 50 is

$$\int_{10}^{\infty} {}_{t-10}p_{\overline{50:50}} \, {}_{t}p_{40}\mu_{40+t} dt + \int_{0}^{10} {}_{t}p_{40}\mu_{40+t} dt$$

and substituting $t = s + 10$ in the first integral

$$= \int_{0}^{\infty} (2{}_{s}p_{50} - {}_{s}p_{50}^{2}){}_{s}p_{50} \cdot {}_{10}p_{40}\mu_{50+s} ds + (1 - {}_{10}p_{40})$$

$$= 2{}_{10}p_{40} \, {}_{\infty}q_{50:50}^{1} - {}_{10}p_{40} \, {}_{\infty}q_{50:50:50}^{1} + (1 - {}_{10}p_{40})$$

$$= {}_{10}p_{40}(2 \cdot \tfrac{1}{2} - \tfrac{1}{3} - 1) + 1$$

$$= 1 - \tfrac{1}{3}{}_{10}p_{40} \quad \text{which is stated to be } \cdot 73$$

$$\therefore \; {}_{10}p_{40} = \cdot 81,$$

and substituting in the expression previously found

$$ {}_{20}p_{30} = \frac{\cdot 5832}{\cdot 81} = \cdot 72$$

$$\therefore \; {}_{10}p_{30} = \frac{\cdot 72}{\cdot 81} = \frac{8}{9}.$$

The probability required is that of three lives A, B and C all aged 30, A will die within 10 years from now and will be survived by only one of B and C, i.e.

$$\int_0^{10} 2\,_tp_{30}(1-\,_tp_{30})\,_tp_{30}\mu_{30+t}dt$$

$$= 2\,_{10}q^{1}_{30:30} - 2\,_{10}q^{1}_{30:30:30}$$

$$= 2.\tfrac{1}{2}(1-(\,_{10}p_{30})^2) - 2.\tfrac{1}{3}(1-(\,_{10}p_{30})^3)$$

$$= 1-(\tfrac{8}{9})^2 - \tfrac{2}{3}(1-(\tfrac{8}{9})^3)$$

$$= \cdot0114.$$

Example 8.16

A fund of £30,000 is held on trust for the following purposes:

(a) if a life aged x dies within 10 years it will be divided equally between such of three lives aged w, y and z as survive him, or if all predecease him it will be paid to the estate of the last of the three lives to die;

(b) if (x) survives 10 years, one-half of the fund will be divided at that time equally between such of (w), (y) and (z) as also survive and the balance of the fund will, at (x)'s death, be divided equally between such of (w), (y) or (z) as survive him but if all three lives predecease (x) the fund or the balance of the fund will be paid to charity.

If each of the lives (x), (w), (y) and (z) is aged 60 calculate on the A1967–70 ultimate table the probability that (y) or his estate will receive more than £10,000.

Solution

If (x) dies within 10 years, then (y) will receive more than £10,000 if either or both of (w) or (z) are dead, and (y) is alive on the death of (x), or all of (w), (y) and (z) are dead on the death of x and y was the last to die.

Considering the first condition the probability required is

$$\int_0^{10} \,_tp_y(1-\,_tp_{wz})\,_tp_x\mu_{x+t}dt$$

$$= \int_0^{10} \,_tp_{60:60}\mu_{60+t}dt - \int_0^{10} \,_tp_{60:60:60:60}\mu_{60+t}dt$$

$$= \,_{10}q^{1}_{60:60} - \,_{10}q^{1}_{60:60:60:60}$$

$$= \tfrac{1}{2}\,_{10}q_{60:60} - \tfrac{1}{4}\,_{10}q_{60:60:60:60}$$

$$= \tfrac{1}{2}(1-(\,_{10}p_{60})^2) - \tfrac{1}{4}(1-(\,_{10}p_{60})^4).$$

*

The second condition was that all the lives will die in the 10 years the probability of which is $(1 - {}_{10}p_{60})^4$. The four lives can die in 4! different orders all being equally likely by symmetry as all lives are the same age and subject to the same mortality, and of the 24 orders two, namely (w), (z), (y), (x) and (z), (w), (y), (x) satisfy the condition. The probability is thus

$$\tfrac{1}{12}(1 - {}_{10}p_{60})^4. \qquad *$$

If (x) survives 10 years then (y) must also survive the 10 years to get a share in the fund and then:

(i) if (w) and (z) do not survive 10 years, then (y) will immediately receive £15,000 and the required probability is

$$(1 - {}_{10}p_w){}_{10}p_x\,{}_{10}p_y(1 - {}_{10}p_z)$$
$$= ({}_{10}p_{60})^2(1 - {}_{10}p_{60})^2; \qquad *$$

(ii) if (w) survives 10 years and (z) does not, then (y) will receive £7,500 immediately but must be alive at (x)'s death to receive more, and he will then receive enough to give at least £10,000, and it does not matter when (w) dies after the 10 years. The probability of $(x+10)$ predeceasing $(y+10)$ is $\tfrac{1}{2}$ as the ages are the same so the probability required is

$$_{10}p_w\,{}_{10}p_x\,{}_{10}p_y(1 - {}_{10}p_z)\tfrac{1}{2}$$
$$= \tfrac{1}{2}({}_{10}p_{60})^3(1 - {}_{10}p_{60}); \qquad *$$

(iii) if (z) survives 10 years and (w) does not, then the reasoning will be the same as in (ii), giving the same answer

$$\tfrac{1}{2}({}_{10}p_{60})^3(1 - {}_{10}p_{60}); \qquad *$$

(iv) if both (y) and (z) survive 10 years, then y will receive £5,000 immediately and will only receive more than £5,000 on (x)'s death if he is alive then and either or both of (w) and (z) are dead.

This probability is

$$_{10}p_{wxyz}\int_0^\infty {}_tp_{y+10}(1 - {}_tp_{w+10\,:\,z+10}){}_tp_{x+10}\mu_{x+10+t}\,dt$$
$$= ({}_{10}p_{60})^4\left\{\int_0^\infty {}_tp_{70\,:\,70}\mu_{70+t}\,dt - \int_0^\infty {}_tp_{70\,:\,70\,:\,70}\mu_{70+t}\,dt\right\}$$
$$= ({}_{10}p_{60})^4({}_\infty q^{\,1}_{70\,:\,70} - {}_\infty q^{\,1}_{70\,:\,70\,:\,70\,:\,70})$$
$$= ({}_{10}p_{60})^4(\tfrac{1}{2} - \tfrac{1}{4})$$
$$= \tfrac{1}{4}({}_{10}p_{60})^4. \qquad *$$

For the total probability the six separate probabilities which are marked * are added giving

$$\tfrac{1}{3} - \tfrac{1}{3}{}_{10}p_{60} + ({}_{10}p_{60})^2 - \tfrac{4}{3}({}_{10}p_{60})^3 + \tfrac{7}{12}({}_{10}p_{60})^4,$$

and substituting

$$_{10}p_{60} = \frac{23{,}622 \cdot 1}{30{,}039 \cdot 8} = \cdot 7864,$$

gives $\cdot 3333 - \cdot 2621 + \cdot 6184 - \cdot 6484 + \cdot 2231$

$$= \cdot 2643.$$

Example 8.17

If a mortality table follows Gompertz's Law prove that

$$_{\infty}q_{\underset{1}{40}:\underset{2}{50}:\overset{3}{60}:70} = \frac{1}{1+c^{10}} \; _{\infty}q_{\underset{1}{40}:\overset{2}{50}:60:70}.$$

Hence, or otherwise evaluate

$$_{\infty}q_{\underset{1}{40}:50:60:\overset{4}{70}} \quad \text{given that} \quad c^{10} = 2.$$

Solution

$$_{\infty}q_{\underset{1}{40}:\underset{2}{50}:\overset{3}{60}:70} = \int_0^\infty (1 - {}_tp_{40}){}_tp_{50:60:70}\,\mu_{50+t}\; _{\infty}q_{\overset{1}{60}+t:70+t}\,dt.$$

Now $\; _{\infty}q_{\overset{1}{60}+t:70+t} = \displaystyle\int_0^\infty {}_sp_{60+t:70+t}\,Bc^{60+t+s}ds$

$$= \frac{c^{60+t}}{c^{60+t}+c^{70+t}} \int_0^\infty {}_sp_{60+t:70+t}\,Bc^s(c^{60+t}+c^{70+t})ds$$

$$= \frac{1}{1+c^{10}} \; _{\infty}q_{60+t:70+t}$$

$$= \frac{1}{1+c^{10}}, \quad \text{as} \quad _{\infty}q_{60+t:70+t} = 1.$$

So $\; _{\infty}q_{\underset{1}{40}:\underset{2}{50}:\overset{3}{60}:70} = \dfrac{1}{1+c^{10}} \displaystyle\int_0^\infty (1 - {}_tp_{40}){}_tp_{50:60:70}\,\mu_{50+t}\,dt$

$$= \frac{1}{1+c^{10}} \; _{\infty}q_{\underset{1}{40}:\overset{2}{50}:60:70} \quad \text{as required.}$$

$$\infty q_{\substack{40:50:60:70 \\ 1}}^{\;\;\;\;\;\;\;\;4} = \infty q_{\substack{40:50:60:70 \\ 1 \;\; 2}}^{\;\;\;\;\;\;\;\;3} + \infty q_{\substack{40:50:60:70 \\ 1 \;\; 2}}^{\;\;\;\;\;\;\;\;3}$$

$$= \frac{1}{1+c^{10}} \; \infty q_{\substack{40:50:60:70 \\ 1}}^{\;\;\;\;\;\;\;\;2} + \frac{1}{1+c^{20}} \; \infty q_{\substack{40:50:60:70 \\ 1}}^{\;\;\;\;\;\;\;\;2}$$

by the above result and an obvious extension with the lives 50 and 60 interchanged,

$$= \frac{1}{1+c^{10}} \left(\infty q_{\substack{50:60:70 \\ 1}}^{\;\;\;1} - \infty q_{\substack{40:50:60:70 \\ 1}}^{\;\;\;\;\;\;\;\;1} \right)$$

$$+ \frac{1}{1+c^{20}} \left(\infty q_{\substack{50:60:70 \\ 1}}^{\;\;\;1} - \infty q_{\substack{40:50:60:70 \\ 1}}^{\;\;\;\;\;\;\;\;1} \right)$$

using an extension of formula 8.3.1.

Now,
$$\infty q_{wxyz}^{1} = \int_0^\infty {}_t p_{wxyz} B c^{w+t} dt$$

$$= \frac{c^w}{c^w + c^x + c^y + c^z} \int_0^\infty {}_t p_{wxyz} B c^t (c^w + c^x + c^y + c^z) dt$$

$$= \frac{c^w}{c^w + c^x + c^y + c^z} \; \infty q_{wxyz}$$

$$= \frac{c^w}{c^w + c^x + c^y + c^z} \quad \text{as} \quad \infty q_{wxyz} = 1.$$

Similarly
$$\infty q_{wxy}^{1} = \frac{c^w}{c^w + c^x + c^y}.$$

So
$$\infty q_{\substack{40:50:60:70 \\ 1}}^{\;\;\;\;\;\;\;\;4} = \frac{1}{1+c^{10}} \left(\frac{1}{1+c^{10}+c^{20}} - \frac{c^{10}}{1+c^{10}+c^{20}+c^{30}} \right)$$

$$+ \frac{1}{1+c^{20}} \left(\frac{c^{10}}{1+c^{10}+c^{20}} - \frac{c^{20}}{1+c^{10}+c^{20}+c^{30}} \right),$$

and substituting $c^{10} = 2$ gives the answer ·0070.

Example 8.18

Calculate the value of an annuity of £480 per annum payable quarterly in arrears during the joint lifetime of A and B both aged x and continuing during the lifetime of the survivor with proportion to the date of death of the survivor but reducing by one-third on the death of A, should he die first.

(Given $\bar{A}_{xx} = ·5089$, $\bar{A}_x = ·4144$, $i = ·04$.)

Solution

The value of the annuity disregarding the proportion to the date of death will be (using A and B initially instead of x to indicate the life being considered)

$$480a_A^{(4)} + 320a_{A|B}^{(4)}.$$

$$= 480a_A^{(4)} + 320a_B^{(4)} - 320a_{AB}^{(4)}.$$

Proportions are paid on the death of A if he dies second of an average amount of $\dfrac{480}{4.2} = 60$ and on the death of B if he dies second of an average of $\dfrac{320}{4.2} = 40$, so the value of the proportion is

$$60\bar{A}_{AB}^2 + 40\bar{A}_{AB}^2.$$

The total value is thus

$$800a_x^{(4)} - 320a_{xx}^{(4)} + 100\bar{A}_{xx}^2.$$

Now $$\bar{a}_x = \frac{1 - \cdot4144}{\cdot039221} = 14\cdot931, \quad \text{i.e.} \quad a_x^{(4)} = 14\cdot806$$

$$\bar{a}_{xx} = \frac{1 - \cdot5089}{\cdot039221} = 12\cdot521, \quad \text{i.e.} \quad a_{xx}^{(4)} = 12\cdot396$$

$$\bar{A}_{xx}^2 = \bar{A}_x - \bar{A}_{xx}^1 = \cdot4144 - \tfrac{1}{2}(\cdot5089) = \cdot1600.$$

So the value is

$$800(14\cdot806) - 320(12\cdot396) + 100(\cdot16)$$

$$= £7,894.$$

It will be seen that the adjustment for the proportion is in fact very small.

Exercise 8.29

(*a*) Calculate the net level annual premium limited to 20 years' payments to secure in the event of a male life aged 40 dying before age 60 an annuity of £100 per annum for a period of 10 years, and in the event of survival to age 60 an annuity of £150 per annum for a period of 10 years certain and during the subsequent lifetime. The basis of calculation is the A1967–70 ultimate table with 4% interest, the annuity being assumed to be payable continuously.

(*b*) Calculate the additional single premium to be paid to secure that, in the event of the male life being survived by his wife now aged 30 and also subject to the same mortality table, the annuity will continue after the certain period during her lifetime at the rate of £100 per annum.

(Given $\ddot{a}_{60:70} = 7{\cdot}770$.)

Exercise 8.30

You are given that

(a) the probability that a life aged 60 will die before a life aged 40 is $\frac{4}{5}$;

(b) the probability that at least two of three lives aged 50 will die within 10 years, a specified life being the second to die, equals four times the probability that three lives aged 50 will all die within 10 years, a specified life being the second to die; and

(c) the probability that a life aged 40 is alive 20 years after the death of a life aged 60 equals the probability that the life aged 40 will die before the life aged 60.

Find the probability that two lives aged 40 and 50 will die within 10 years of each other.

Exercise 8.31

The probability that at least two out of three lives aged 55, 65 and 75 respectively survive 10 years is $\frac{1}{6}$. The probability that at least one dies within 10 years is $\frac{59}{60}$. The reciprocal of the probabilities $_{10}p_{55}$, $_{10}p_{65}$ and $_{10}p_{75}$ are in arithmetical progression. Given that $_{\infty}q^{1}_{55:75}$ is $\frac{1}{5}$, calculate the probability that two lives aged 55 and 65 will die at least ten years apart.

Exercise 8.32

If a mortality table follows Gompertz's Law, show that

$$\bar{a}^{1}_{xy|z} = {}_{\infty}q^{1}_{xy}\bar{a}_{xy|z}.$$

Exercise 8.33

The annual income of £15,000 from a trust fund is payable subject to the conditions stated below in equal shares to two lives aged x so long as they both survive and after the first death to the survivor. The income is payable yearly and the first instalment falls due in one year's time.

The conditions are:

(a) after the first five years and until five years after the death of the first to die of the lives (x), a third life (y) will, so long as he survives be entitled to share in the income but his share will be limited to one-half of the share payable to each life (x) or to the survivor of them.

(b)   after five years have elapsed since the first death of the two lives (x), (y) will be entitled to share the income equally with the surviving life (x) so long as they both survive.

Derive an expression in terms of single and joint life annuities for the value of the benefits payable to one of the lives (x).

CHAPTER NINE

MULTIPLE-DECREMENT TABLES

9.1 The multiple-decrement table

The theory developed so far in this book can be extended to a more general theory involving the effect of several causes of decrement on a particular body of lives. One example would be the valuation of a pension scheme where there are several causes of decrement—death, disability, withdrawal and retirement all operating at the same time. A similar problem is to consider separately various causes of death, for example accidental deaths might be separated from other deaths. The mathematical model of such analyses is referred to as a multiple-decrement table, or if there are only two decrements, a double-decrement table.

The multiple-decrement table considers a large number of lives subject to several independent causes of decrement. It is very similar to the mortality or single-decrement table described in Chapter 1 except that the l_x column is reduced by several d_x's rather than one. The notation in this work varies with the type of table considered—for example a specialised notation is used in pension fund work. In this chapter the most general notation will normally be used in which a letter, normally a, is prefixed to the symbol which is enclosed in brackets so that the number of active lives is given the symbol $(al)_x$, the individual decrements (m in number) are $(ad)_x^k$ with total decrement $(ad)_x$, so that

$$(ad)_x = \sum_{k=1}^{m} (ad)_x^k \qquad (9.1.1)$$

$$(ad)_x = (al)_x - (al)_{x+1}. \qquad (9.1.2)$$

An example of a multiple-decrement table with three decrements is given in Table 9.1. The decrements instead of being denoted by numbers are given indicating letters. The radix $(al)_{18}$ is of course arbitrary as in the single-decrement table. The functions shown are those usually shown in any multiple-decrement table, if $(ad)_x$ is required it must be found using formula (9.1.1) or (9.1.2). Many tables continue with age to a high limiting age of the table, but in this case all the members leave at age 21 and $(al)_{21}$ is really another decrement (promotion) at exact age 21. The table represents a population of apprentices who start to learn a trade at their 18th birthday and become fully trained at their 21st birthday provided that they have not left due to death $(ad)_x^d$; voluntary withdrawal $(ad)_x^w$; or failure $(ad)_x^f$.

TABLE 9.1

Age x	$(al)_x$	$(ad)_x^d$	$(ad)_x^w$	$(ad)_x^f$
18	100,000	2,000	5,000	3,000
19	90,000	2,100	4,000	3,900
20	80,000	2,200	2,500	5,300
21	70,000			

Similar probabilities of survival and decrement will apply to those in a single-decrement table, and will be exemplified using this table. The probability that a life aged 18 exactly will survive to finish the apprenticeship will be

$$_3(ap)_{18} = \frac{(al)_{21}}{(al)_{18}} = \frac{70,000}{100,000} = \cdot 7.$$

The probability that a life aged 18 exactly will not be an apprentice after one year is

$$(aq)_{18} = \frac{(ad)_{18}}{(al)_{18}} = \frac{(al)_{18}-(al)_{19}}{(al)_{18}} = \frac{10,000}{100,000} = \cdot 1.$$

The probability that a life aged exactly 20 will withdraw in the next year is

$$(aq)_{20}^w = \frac{(ad)_{20}^w}{(al)_{20}} = \frac{2,500}{80,000} = \cdot 03125.$$

The probability that a life aged exactly 19 will be failed before the end of the apprenticeship is

$$_2(aq)_{19}^f = \frac{(ad)_{19}^f+(ad)_{20}^f}{(al)_{19}} = \frac{3,900+5,300}{90,000} = \cdot 1022.$$

While it would be possible to construct a multiple-decrement table on a select basis, and this would probably accord with experience, the additional labour involved is normally considered to be disproportionate to any resulting gain in accuracy.

Exercise 9.1

Using the table given in the above section, find

(a) the probability that an apprentice aged 18 exactly will withdraw before completing his training,

(b) the probability that an apprentice aged 19 exactly will die between his 20th and 21st birthdays,

(c) the number of new apprentices that should be admitted each year if 1,000 newly qualified tradesmen are required each year.

9.2 Forces of decrement

The total force of decrement in a multiple-decrement table is defined as

$$(a\mu)_x = -\frac{1}{(al)_x}\frac{d(al)_x}{dx} \tag{9.2.1}$$

$$= -\frac{d}{dx}\log_e(al)_x. \tag{9.2.2}$$

This function is mathematically the same as μ_x in a single-decrement table and similar relationships will apply, for example considering formula (1.6.6) we obtain

$$_n(ap)_x = e^{-\int_0^n (a\mu)_{x+t}dt} \tag{9.2.3}$$

and considering formula (1.6.11)

$$(aq)_x = \int_0^1 {}_t(ap)_x(a\mu)_{x+t}dt \tag{9.2.4}$$

or

$$(ad)_x = \int_0^1 (al)_{x+t}(a\mu)_{x+t}dt. \tag{9.2.5}$$

In order to define the forces of decrement for the individual causes of decrement the new functions $(al)_x^k$ are introduced where

$$(al)_x^k = \sum_{t=0}^{\infty} (ad)_{x+t}^k \tag{9.2.6}$$

and $1 \leq k \leq m$, there being m causes of decrement. This function is the total of the number of lives at age x that will eventually leave by cause k.

The ratio which the rate of decrease of $(al)_x^k$ bears to the value of

(al_x) (not $(al)_x^k$) at that age is denoted by the symbol $(a\mu)_x^k$ and is referred to as the force of decrement by cause k at age x,

$$(a\mu)_x^k = -\frac{1}{(al)_x}\frac{d(al)_x^k}{dx}. \qquad (9.2.7)$$

The functions $(al)_x^k$ are rarely encountered in practice and are used merely to define the partial forces of decrement.

Adding the values of $(al)_x^k$ for all k will give the sum of all the decrements for ages subsequent to x so that

$$(al)_x = \sum_{k=1}^{m}(al)_x^k. \qquad (9.2.8)$$

Differentiating with respect to x and dividing throughout by $-(al)_x$ gives

$$(a\mu)_x = \sum_{k=1}^{m}(a\mu)_x^k. \qquad (9.2.9)$$

Integrating formula (9.2.7) gives

$$(al)_x^k = \int_0^{\infty}(al)_{x+t}(a\mu)_{x+t}^k dt \qquad (9.2.10)$$

so that by subtraction,

$$(ad)_x^k = \int_0^1 (al)_{x+t}(a\mu)_{x+t}^k dt. \qquad (9.2.11)$$

The symbol $_n(ap)_x^k$ is not used, being meaningless, but $_n(aq)_x^k$ represents the probability that a life aged x will leave by decrement k between ages x and $x+n$, i.e.

$$_n(aq)_x^k = \frac{(al)_x^k-(al)_{x+n}^k}{(al)_x} = \frac{\sum\limits_{t=0}^{n-1}(ad)_{x+t}^k}{(al)_x}, \qquad (9.2.12)$$

and

$$(aq)_x^k = \int_0^1 {}_t(ap)_x(a\mu)_{x+t}^k dt = \frac{(ad)_x^k}{(al)_x}. \qquad (9.2.13)$$

An important distinction between the forces of decrement and probabilities of decrement will be noticed. The probabilities involve an interval of time during which all the causes of decrement are operative, so that the number of decrements due to any cause will not be independent of the size of the other decrements—for example if all other decrements increased, there would be fewer exposed to the decrement being considered and that probability of decrement would decrease. On the other hand, the force of each decrement is not based on a time interval and is not effected by any variation in the other decrements.

When values of $(a\mu)_x^k$ are required it is normal to use the approximation based on the same assumption as formula (1.7.4), i.e.

$$(a\mu)_x^k \doteqdot \frac{(ad)_{x-1}^k + (ad)_x^k}{2(al)_x}.$$

Example 9.1

Find expressions for $(al)_x$ and $(ad)_x^1$ for a double-decrement table in which

$$(a\mu)_x^1 = \frac{1}{1,000-x}$$

$$(a\mu)_x^2 = 1$$

and

$$(al)_0 = 1,000.$$

Solution

$$(a\mu)_x = \frac{1}{1,000-x} + 1.$$

From formula (9.2.3)

$$(al)_x = (al)_0 e^{-\int_0^x \left(\frac{1}{1,000-t} + 1\right) dt}$$

$$= 1,000 e^{[\log_e (1,000-t)]_0^x} e^{-x}$$

$$= 1,000 e^{\log_e (1,000-x) - \log_e (1,000)} e^{-x}$$

$$= 1,000 \frac{1,000-x}{1,000} \cdot e^{-x}$$

i.e. $\quad (al)_x = (1,000-x)e^{-x}.$

$$(ad)_x^1 = \int_0^1 (al)_{x+t}(a\mu)_{x+t}^1 dt$$

$$= \int_0^1 (1,000-x-t)e^{-x-t} \frac{1}{(1,000-x-t)} dt$$

$$= [-e^{-x-t}]_0^1$$

i.e. $\quad (ad)_x^1 = e^{-x} - e^{-x-1}.$

Exercise 9.2

Find the value of $(ad)_x^2$ in example 9.1.

9.3 Central rates

The central rate of decrement from all causes is defined similarly to formula (6.6.1) as

$$(am)_x = \frac{\int_0^1 (al)_{x+t}(a\mu)_{x+t}dt}{\int_0^1 (al)_{x+t}dt}, \qquad (9.3.1)$$

i.e.

$$(am)_x = \frac{(ad)_x}{(aL)_x} \qquad (9.3.2)$$

using formula (9.2.5) and defining

$$(aL)_x = \int_0^1 (al)_{x+t}dt.$$

The central rate of decrement from cause k is

$$(am)_x^k = \frac{\int_0^1 (al)_{x+t}(a\mu)_{x+t}^k dt}{\int_0^1 (al)_{x+t}dt}, \qquad (9.3.3)$$

i.e.

$$(am)_x^k = \frac{(ad)_x^k}{(aL)_x} \qquad (9.3.4)$$

using formula (9.2.11).

From formula (9.1.1) and the above expression it will be seen that

$$(am)_x = \sum_{k=1}^m (am)_x^k. \qquad (9.3.5)$$

In order to evaluate $(am)_x^k$ from the double-decrement table it is often assumed (similarly to section 6.6) that the total decrement is uniformly distributed over the year of age, i.e.

$$(al)_{x+t} \fallingdotseq (al)_x - t(ad)_x, \quad 0 < t < 1,$$

so that

$$(aL)_x \fallingdotseq \int_0^1 ((al_x - t(ad)_x)dt$$

$$\fallingdotseq (al)_x - \tfrac{1}{2}(ad)_x.$$

Thus from formula (9.3.4)

$$(am)_x^k \fallingdotseq \frac{(ad)_x^k}{(al)_x - \frac{1}{2}(ad)_x} \qquad (9.3.6)$$

or
$$(am)_x^k \fallingdotseq \frac{(aq)_x^k}{1 - \frac{1}{2}(aq)_x}. \qquad (9.3.7)$$

The reverse problem of determining $(aq)_x^k$ given values of $(am)_x^k$ using the same assumption on distribution of decrements gives

$$(aq)_x^k = \frac{(ad)_x^k}{(al)_x} \fallingdotseq \frac{(am)_x^k (aL)_x}{(aL)_x + \frac{1}{2}(ad)_x}$$

$$\therefore (aq)_x^k \fallingdotseq \frac{(am)_x^k}{1 + \frac{1}{2}(am)_x}. \qquad (9.3.8)$$

The assumption that decrements are distributed uniformly over the year of age implies that the product $(al)_{x+t}(a\mu)_{x+t}\delta t$, being the total decrement in the interval t to $t + \delta t$, is constant for $0 < t < 1$. The value being constant can be taken at any point in the range such as $x + \frac{1}{2}$ so that formula (9.3.1) becomes

$$(am)_x \fallingdotseq \frac{(al)_{x+\frac{1}{2}}(a\mu)_{x+\frac{1}{2}}}{(al)_{x+\frac{1}{2}}},$$

i.e.
$$(am)_x \fallingdotseq (a\mu)_{x+\frac{1}{2}}, \qquad (9.3.9)$$

a relationship analogous to (6.6.4).

If in addition it is assumed that decrements of cause k are uniformly distributed over the year of age, identical reasoning using formula (9.3.3) will give

$$(am)_x^k \fallingdotseq (a\mu)_{x+\frac{1}{2}}^k, \qquad (9.3.10)$$

a relationship of considerable practical importance.

Exercise 9.3

Find values for $(am)_{18}^d$, $(am)_{19}^w$, $(am)_{20}^f$, $(a\mu)_{19}^w$, $(a\mu)_{20}^w$ using the table in section 9.1.

9.4 The associated single-decrement tables

For each of the causes of decrement in a multiple-decrement table a single-decrement table can be defined which shows the operation of that decrement independent of the others. Each table represents a group of lives reduced continuously by only one decrement. While this may appear unrealistic, particularly for example in considering a group subject to, say, withdrawal but not to death, the study is useful both in theory and practice.

The associated single-decrement table is indicated by using functions without brackets but with a superfix showing the decrement—for example l^k_x, μ^k_x. In the single-decrement table the function q^k_x is both an annual rate and a probability of decrement. In the context of the multiple-decrement table it is desirable to distinguish between the rate and probability—q^k_x is a *rate* of decrement while $(aq)^k_x$ is the *probability* of decrement and is dependent on the other rates of decrement. An alternative way of distinguishing the functions is to refer to q^k_x as the *independent rate* and $(aq)^k_x$ as the *dependent rate*.

The assumption is normally made that lives removed by other decrements are exposed to the operation of decrement k for one-half of the year on average. The number of such lives is $(ad)_x - (ad)^k_x$ given the symbol $(ad)^{(-k)}_x$. The lives exposed during a year to decrement k will then be $(al)_x - \frac{1}{2}(ad)^{(-k)}_x$. Thus

$$q^k_x \doteqdot \frac{(ad)^k_x}{(al)_x - \frac{1}{2}(ad)^{(-k)}_x}, \qquad (9.4.1)$$

and

$$q^k_x \doteqdot \frac{(aq)^k_x}{1 - \frac{1}{2}(aq)^{(-k)}_x}, \qquad (9.4.2)$$

where $\qquad (aq)^{(-k)}_x = (aq)_x - (aq)^k_x.$

When there are two decrements 1 and 2, this formula becomes

$$q^1_x \doteqdot \frac{(aq)^1_x}{1 - \frac{1}{2}(aq)^2_x}, \qquad q^2_x \doteqdot \frac{(aq)^2_x}{1 - \frac{1}{2}(aq)^1_x}. \qquad (9.4.3)$$

These formulae are sometimes expanded using the binomial theorem

$$q^1_x \doteqdot (aq)^1_x\{1 + \frac{1}{2}(aq)^2_x + \frac{1}{4}((aq)^2_x)^2 + \ldots\}$$

and assuming that the decrements are not large

$$q^1_x \doteqdot (aq)^1_x(1 + \frac{1}{2}(aq)^2_x) \qquad (9.4.4)$$

and similarly $\qquad q^2_x \doteqdot (aq)^2_x(1 + \frac{1}{2}(aq)^1_x).$

These formulae can also be used in cases where there are more than two decrements by assuming that the second decrement includes all the other modes of decrement not being considered—this can also be seen from formula (9.4.2).

While alternative formulae can be obtained on other assumptions or using different approximations the formulae already given are normally used, the difference in practical examples being usually negligible.

As was mentioned at the end of section 9.2, the force of decrement in the multiple-decrement table is not based on a time interval and is not effected by the other decrements, giving

$$(a\mu)_x^k = \mu_x^k. \tag{9.4.5}$$

From this formula and (6.6.4) and (9.3.10) we have

$$(am)_x^k \doteqdot (a\mu)_{x+\frac{1}{2}}^k = \mu_{x+\frac{1}{2}}^k \doteqdot m_x^k. \tag{9.4.6}$$

The approximate equality of dependent and independent central rates can also be seen by considering the formulae

$$(am)_x^k = \frac{\int_0^1 (al)_{x+t}(a\mu)_{x+t}^k dt}{\int_0^1 (al)_{x+t} dt}$$

and

$$m_x^k = \frac{\int_0^1 l_{x+t}^k \mu_{x+t}^k dt}{\int_0^1 l_{x+t}^k dt},$$

showing that the central rates are weighted means of the forces and as the dependent and independent forces are equal and the effect of the weights being proportional to $(al)_{x+t}$ and l_{x+t}^k will make little difference thus

$$(am)_x^k \doteqdot m_x^k.$$

An expression for q_x^k may be required in terms of central rates. On the assumption that the decrements in the single-decrement table are uniformly distributed over the year of age, formula (6.6.3)

$$q_x^k \doteqdot \frac{m_x^k}{1+\frac{1}{2}m_x^k},$$

and as

$$m_x^k \doteqdot (am)_x^k$$

$$q_x^k \doteqdot \frac{(am)_x^k}{1+\frac{1}{2}(am)_x^k} \tag{9.4.7}$$

Example 9.2

Find values for the independent rates of decrement at age 18 for the table in section 9.1.

Solution

Using formula (9.4.1)

$$q_x^d = \frac{2,000}{100,000 - \frac{1}{2}(5,000 + 3,000)} = \cdot 0208$$

$$q_x^w = \frac{5,000}{100,000 - \frac{1}{2}(2,000 + 3,000)} = \cdot 0513$$

$$q_x^f = \frac{3,000}{100,000 - \frac{1}{2}(2,000 + 5,000)} = \cdot 0311.$$

Example 9.3

Determine an expression for q_x^k by assuming that each decrement is uniformly distributed over the year of age.

Solution

The assumption that each decrement $(ad)_x^k$ is uniformly distributed over the year of age implies

$$(al)_{x+t}^k \fallingdotseq (al)_x^k - t(ad)_x^k \quad \text{for} \quad 0 < t < 1$$

and $(al)_{x+t} \fallingdotseq (al)_x - t(ad)_x.$

Differentiating the first gives

$$\frac{d(al)_{x+t}^k}{dt} \fallingdotseq -(ad)_x^k$$

and therefore

$$(a\mu)_{x+t}^k = -\frac{1}{(al)_{x+t}} \frac{d(al)_{x+t}^k}{dt}$$

$$\fallingdotseq \frac{(ad)_x^k}{(al)_{x+t}}$$

$$= \frac{(ad)_x^k}{(al)_x - t(ad)_x}.$$

Now in the associated single-decrement table formula (1.6.8) will apply,

$$q_x^k = 1 - e^{-\int_0^1 \mu_{x+t}^k \, dt}$$

and as $\mu^k_{x+t} = (a\mu)^k_{x+t}$, so that

$$\int_0^1 \mu^k_{x+t} dt = \int_0^1 (a\mu)^k_{x+t} dt \doteqdot \int_0^1 \frac{(ad)^k_x}{(al)_x - t(ad)_x} dt$$

$$= \left[\frac{-(ad)^k_x}{(ad)_x} \log_e \{(al)_x - t(ad)_x\} \right]_0^1$$

$$= \frac{-(ad)^k_x}{(ad)_x} \log_e (ap)_x.$$

Thus $q^k_x \doteqdot 1 - ((ap)_x)^{\frac{(ad)^k_x}{(ad)_x}}$

$$= 1 - (1 - (aq)_x)^{\frac{(ad)^k_x}{(ad)_x}}$$

which using the binomial expansion

$$= 1 - \left(1 - \frac{(ad)^k_x}{(ad)_x} (aq)_x + \frac{1}{2} \frac{(ad)^k_x}{(ad)_x} \left(\frac{(ad)^k_x}{(ad)_x} - 1 \right) ((aq)_x)^2 - \ldots \right)$$

and this ignoring the terms not given and simplifying gives

$$q^k_x \doteqdot (aq)^k_x (1 + \tfrac{1}{2}((aq)_x - (aq)^k_x))$$

$$= (aq)^k_x (1 + \tfrac{1}{2}(aq)^{(-k)}_x),$$

which can be seen to be the same as (9.4.4).

Exercise 9.4

Using the table in section 9.1, find values for q^w_{19}, q^f_{20}, m^d_{19}.

9.5 Construction of a multiple-decrement table

In the previous section the problem of establishing the independent rates of decrement from the multiple-decrement table was considered. In this section the problem is the reverse one of constructing the multiple-decrement table given the single-decrement tables. A practical example would be when it is desired to alter the rate of one decrement (or more) in a multiple-decrement table. The associated single-decrement table would first be obtained and the multiple-decrement table constructed after the single-decrement tables had been adjusted in the required manner.

If m decrements are involved from formulae (9.2.9) and (9.4.5),

$$(a\mu)_x = \sum_{k=1}^m \mu^k_x$$

then $\quad\quad {}_n(ap)_x = e^{-\int_0^n (a\mu)_{x+t}dt}$

$$= e^{-\int_0^n \sum\limits_{t=1}^m \mu_{x+t}^k dt}$$

$$= e^{-\int_0^n \mu_{x+t}^1 dt} \cdot e^{-\int_0^n \mu_{x+t}^2 dt} \cdots e^{-\int_0^n \mu_{x+t}^m dt},$$

i.e. $\quad\quad {}_n(ap)_x = {}_np_x^1 \cdot {}_np_x^2 \cdot {}_np_x^3 \cdots {}_np_x^m.$ $\quad\quad$ (9.5.1)

This formula is analgous to the product rule of probability.

It will be seen that

$$(al)_x = kl_x^1 . l_x^2 . l_x^3 \ldots l_x^m,$$ $\quad\quad$ (9.5.2)

where k is a constant to give a suitable radix to the multiple-decrement table.

While these formulae give an exact basis for constructing the $(al)_x$ column of the table the individual decrements $(ad)_x^k$ require to be found using approximate methods.

Formula (9.2.13) gives

$$(aq)_x^1 = \int_0^1 {}_t(ap)_x (a\mu)_{x+t}^1 dt$$

$$= \int_0^1 \frac{{}_t(ap)_x}{{}_tp_x^1} {}_tp_x^1 \mu_{x+t}^1 dt$$

$$\doteqdot q_x^1 \int_0^1 \frac{{}_t(ap)_x}{{}_tp_x^1} dt;$$

if the assumption is made that the decrements in the single-decrement table are uniformly distributed over the year of age, i.e. ${}_tp_x^1\mu_{x+t}^1$ is constant and equals q_x^1, then as

$$_t(ap)_x = {}_tp_x^1 \cdot {}_tp_x^2 \cdots {}_tp_x^m,$$

$$(aq)_x^1 \doteqdot q_x^1 \int_0^1 {}_tp_x^2 \cdot {}_tp_x^3 \cdots {}_tp_x^m dt$$

and if there is a uniform distribution of decrements in each single-decrement table over the year of age so that ${}_tq_x^k = tq_x^k$

$$(aq)_x^1 \doteqdot q_x^1 \int_0^1 (1 - tq_x^2)(1 - tq_x^3)\ldots(1 - tq_x^m)dt$$

$$= q_x^1 \int_0^1 (1 - t\Sigma q_x^k + t^2\Sigma q_x^k q_x^l - \ldots)dt,$$

where the summations are over all decrements except 1.

$$\therefore (aq)_x^1 \doteqdot q_x^1(1 - \tfrac{1}{2}\Sigma q_x^k + \tfrac{1}{3}\Sigma q_x^k q_x^l \ldots). \tag{9.5.3}$$

When there are two modes of decrement, this formula becomes

$$\left. \begin{aligned} (aq)_x^1 &\doteqdot q_x^1(1 - \tfrac{1}{2}q_x^2) \\ \text{and} \qquad (aq)_x^2 &\doteqdot q_x^2(1 - \tfrac{1}{2}q_x^1). \end{aligned} \right\} \tag{9.5.4}$$

These formulae have been obtained by the assumption that the decrements in each *single*-decrement table are uniformly distributed over each year of age. Formula (9.4.4) on the other hand could be obtained on the assumption that the decrements in the *multiple*-decrement table are uniformly distributed over the year of age—see Example 9.3. If the two equations (9.4.4) are treated as simultaneous equations in the dependent rates and solved,

$$\left. \begin{aligned} (aq)_x^1 &\doteqdot \frac{q_x^1(1 - \tfrac{1}{2}q_x^2)}{1 - \tfrac{1}{4}q_x^1 q_x^2}, \\ (aq)_x^2 &\doteqdot \frac{q_x^2(1 - \tfrac{1}{2}q_x^1)}{1 - \tfrac{1}{4}q_x^1 q_x^2}. \end{aligned} \right\} \tag{9.5.5}$$

The application of any of formulae (9.5.3), (9.5.4) or (9.5.5) is likely to give a sum of the decrements at age x, $\Sigma(ad)_x^k$, different from $(ad)_x$ found using (9.5.2) and subtraction. As this last formula is exact proportional adjustments should be made in the individual decrements found.

An alternative method is to obtain central rates and use the approximate equality of independent and dependent central rates, formula (9.4.6), and substituting in formula (9.3.8)

$$(aq)_x^k \doteqdot \frac{m_x^k}{1 + \tfrac{1}{2}(m_x^1 + m_x^2 + \ldots m_x^k)}. \tag{9.5.6}$$

Example 9.4

In a multiple-decrement table with three forces, death (d), withdrawal (w) and retirement (r) show that

$$(aq)_x^d \doteqdot q_x^d(1 - \tfrac{1}{2}(q_x^w + q_x^r) + \tfrac{1}{3}q_x^w q_x^r),$$

stating the assumptions made.

Hence find the number who die, withdraw and retire from 1,000 persons alive and in service at age 50 given that

$$(aq)_{50}^r = \cdot 00416, \quad m_{50}^w = \cdot 07469, \quad q_{50}^d = \cdot 006431.$$

Solution

Formula (9.5.3) gives the answer required on the assumption of a uniform distribution of decrements in the associated single-decrement table over each year of age.

$$q_{50}^w \fallingdotseq \frac{m_{50}^w}{1 + \frac{1}{2}m_{50}^w} = \frac{\cdot07469}{1\cdot0373} = \cdot0720.$$

Now $(aq)_{50}^r = q_{50}^r \{1 - \frac{1}{2}(q_{50}^d + q_{50}^w) + \frac{1}{3}q_{50}^d q_{50}^w\}$

$\therefore \cdot00416 = q_{50}^r \{1 - \frac{1}{2}(\cdot006431 + \cdot0720) + \frac{1}{3}(\cdot006431)(\cdot0720)\}$

$\therefore q_{50}^r = \cdot00433$ and each of the independent rates is now known.

$(aq)_{50}^d = q_{50}^d \{1 - \frac{1}{2}(q_{50}^r + q_{50}^w) + \frac{1}{3}q_{50}^r q_{50}^w\}$

$= \cdot00619$

and similarly

$(aq)_{50}^w = q_{50}^w \{1 - \frac{1}{2}(q_{50}^d + q_{50}^r) + \frac{1}{3}q_{50}^d q_{50}^r\}$

$= \cdot07161.$

Applying these rates to $(al)_{50} = 1,000$ gives

$$(ad)_{50}^d = 6, \quad (ad)_{50}^w = 72 \quad \text{and} \quad (ad)_{50}^r = 4.$$

(Hence $(ad)_{50} = 82$ and $(al)_{51} = 918$, which agrees with

$$1,000(1 - q_{50}^r)(1 - q_{50}^d)(1 - q_{50}^w) = 918\cdot0.)$$

Example 9.5

A service table of which an extract is given in Table 9.2a, is based on the experience of a large organisation. Recent changes in working conditions are estimated to have reduced the annual independent

TABLE 9.2a

Age (x)	No. in service $(al)_x$	Deaths $(ad)_x^d$	Retirement $(ad)_x^r$
60	10,000	299	919
61	8,782	278	897
62	7,607		

rates of mortality by ·005 at all ages. Assuming that the annual independent rates of retirement are unaltered, prepare a revised service table.

Solution

A question of this type should be solved by first finding the independent rates of decrement from the service table, adjusting them as required, and then constructing the table using these rates.

TABLE 9.2b

x	$(aq)^d_x$	$(aq)^r_x$	$1-\frac{1}{2}(aq)^r_x$	q^d_x	$1-\frac{1}{2}(aq)^d_x$	q^r_x
60	·0299	·0919	·95405	·0313	·98505	·0933
61	·0317	·1021	·94895	·0334	·98415	·1037

Using formula (9.4.3), that is

$$q^d_x \doteqdot \frac{(aq)^d_x}{1-\frac{1}{2}(aq)^r_x}, \quad q^r_x \doteqdot \frac{(aq)^r_x}{1-\frac{1}{2}(aq)^d_x},$$

Table 9.2b gives adjusted death rates $q'^d_{60} = ·0263$, $q'^d_{61} = ·0284$. The new table (Table 9.2c) can be found using the formula (9.5.4), that is $(aq')^d_x \doteqdot q'^d_x(1-\frac{1}{2}q^r_x)$, $(aq')^r_x \doteqdot q^r_x(1-\frac{1}{2}q'^d_x)$, and the required table is shown in Table 9.2d.

TABLE 9.2c

x	q'^d_x	q^r_x	$1-\frac{1}{2}q'^d_x$	$(aq')^r_x$	$1-\frac{1}{2}q^r_x$	$(aq')^d_x$
60	·0263	·0933	·98685	·0921	·95335	·0251
61	·0284	·1037	·98580	·1022	·94815	·0269

TABLE 9.2d

Age (x)	$(al')_x$	$(ad')^d_x$	$(ad')^r_x$
60	10,000	251	921
61	8,828	237	902
62	7,689		

It will have been noticed that the two formulae used in this question are not entirely consistent—it would have been more consistent to use formula (9.5.5) which means dividing the previous

$$(aq')_x \text{ by } (1 - \tfrac{1}{4} q_x'^d q_x^r)$$

that is at age 60 by

$$\{1 - \tfrac{1}{4}(\cdot0263)(\cdot0933)\} = \cdot9994 \quad \text{giving} \quad (aq')_{60}^d = \cdot0251$$

$$\text{and} \quad (aq')_{60}^r = \cdot0921,$$

and at age 61 by

$$\{1 - \tfrac{1}{4}(\cdot0284)(\cdot1037)\} = \cdot9993 \quad \text{giving} \quad (aq')_{61}^d = \cdot0269$$

$$\text{and} \quad (aq')_{61}^r = \cdot1023,$$

a difference of 1 in the $(al')_x$ column (Table 9.2e).

TABLE 9.2e

Age (x)	$(al')_x$	$(ad')_x^d$	$(ad')_x^r$
60	10,000	251	921
61	8,828	237	903
62	7,688		

It may be desirable to check the values of $(al')_{61}$ and $(al')_{62}$ by using the relationship

$$(al')_{61} = (al')_{60}(1 - q_{60}'^d)(1 - q_{60}^r)$$

$$= 10,000(\cdot9737)(\cdot9067)$$

$$= 8828\cdot5$$

and

$$(al)_{62} = (8828\cdot5)(\cdot9716)(\cdot8963)$$

$$= 7688\cdot3.$$

The second table found would thus probably be the more desirable to use, but as can be seen the differences are rarely large even with relatively high rates of decrement such as the rates of retirement in this case.

Exercise 9.5

A double-decrement table, the decrements being death and retirement, has dependent rates of mortality and retirement at a certain age of $\cdot01$ and $\cdot3$ respectively. What would be the approximate value of the dependent rate of mortality if the independent rate of retirement were reduced by ·12 while the independent rate of mortality remained unchanged?

Exercise 9.6

Use the mortality of the A1967–70 ultimate table and withdrawal and disablement rates as shown in Table 9.3 to complete a multiple decrement table for ages 50 and 51.

TABLE 9.3

Age	Rate of withdrawal	Rate of disablement
50	·08	·003
51	·09	·003

9.6 Combined tables

In the tables considered so far in this chapter consideration has been given to the experience of persons so long as they remain members of a certain class, and has not included the subsequent experience of those lives who are removed by a cause or causes other than death. Such history is considered in a combined table such as a combined mortality and marriage table or a combined mortality and disablement table.

Table 9.4 is an extract from a combined mortality and marriage table. For the purpose of this table married men include widowers and divorced men—the symbol $(bh)_x$ is used rather than $(bm)_x$ as

TABLE 9.4

(1) Age x	(2) Bachelors $(bl)_x$	(3) Bachelors dying $(bd)_x$	(4) Bachelors marrying $(bh)_x$	(5) Married men $(ml)_x$	(6) Married men dying $(md)_x$
⋮	⋮	⋮	⋮	⋮	⋮
24	6,135	20	541	4,372	14
25	5,574	19	502	4,899	16
26	5,053	17	465	5,385	18
27	4,571	16	430	5,832	20
⋮	⋮	⋮	⋮	⋮	⋮

m being the second letter inside the brackets implies a central rate (h stands for husband). It will be seen that the columns (2), (3) and (4) form a double-decrement table of bachelors with decrements of death and marriage. The columns (4), (5) and (6) form another table in respect of married men with the decrement of death, and the increment, or 'negative decrement' of bachelors marrying. The formulae which have been used earlier in this chapter can be applied to both tables provided that it is remembered that the married men table contains a negative decrement.

The relations among the various functions will be

$$(bl)_{x+1} = (bl)_x - (bd)_x - (bh)_x,$$

and $\qquad (ml)_{x+1} = (ml)_x - (md)_x + (bh)_x.$

The use of this table will first be demonstrated by evaluating some simple probabilities.

The probability that a bachelor aged 24 marries within a year is

$$\frac{(bh)_{24}}{(bl)_{24}} = \frac{541}{6,135} = \cdot088.$$

The probability that a bachelor aged 25 marries between his 26th and 28th birthday is

$$\frac{(bh)_{26} + (bh)_{27}}{(bl)_{25}} = \frac{465 + 430}{5,574} = \frac{895}{5,574} = \cdot161.$$

The central rate of marriage for bachelors aged 25 is, from formula (9.3.6),

$$(bm)_{25}^m \doteqdot \frac{(bh)_{25}}{(bl)_{25} - \frac{1}{2}(bd)_{25} - \frac{1}{2}(bh)_{25}}$$

$$= \frac{502}{5,574 - \frac{1}{2}(19) - \frac{1}{2}(502)} = \cdot094.$$

In considering the table for married men it must be remembered that marriage of bachelors is a negative decrement. For example, the central rate of mortality for married men aged 26 is

$$(mm)_{26} = \frac{(md)_{26}}{(ml)_{26} - \frac{1}{2}(md)_{26} + \frac{1}{2}(bh)_{26}}$$

$$= \frac{18}{5,385 - \frac{1}{2}(18) + \frac{1}{2}(465)} = \cdot0032.$$

The probability that a married man aged x will die within a year is not $\dfrac{(md)_x}{(ml)_x}$ because some of the $(md)_x$ deaths occurred among the men who married between the ages of x and $x+1$ and are not included in $(ml)_x$. It is necessary for this probability to find the mortality of married men and a possible approximation would be

$$(mq)_x \doteqdot \frac{(md)_x}{(ml)_x + \frac{1}{2}(bh)_x}, \qquad (9.6.1)$$

assuming that the $(bh)_x$ lives are exposed to the risk of death for one half year on average.

The probability that a bachelor aged x will be alive and married n years later will be found by deducting from $(ml)_{x+n}$ the lives who were already married at age x, that is

$$\frac{(ml)_{x+n} - (ml)_x \cdot {}_n(mp)_x}{(bl)_x}, \qquad (9.6.2)$$

where $_n(mp)_x$ is found from the table representing the mortality of married men by using (9.6.1) and $(mp)_x = 1 - (mq)_x$.

Exercise 9.7

Using the table in section 9.6, find

(a) the probability that a bachlor aged 25 dies a bachelor within two years,

(b) the rate of mortality for a married man aged 25,

(c) the probability that a bachelor aged 25 dies within two years.

9.7 Monetary functions

Commutation functions can be constructed by combining compound interest functions with multiple decrement tables. For example, if

$$(aD)_x = v^x (al)_x$$

and

$$(aN)_x = \sum_{t=0}^{\infty} (aD)_{x+t},$$

the value of an annuity due to (x), payable so long as he remains a member of the (al) class is

$$\frac{(aN)_x}{(aD)_x}.$$

L

Similarly if $(aC)_x^d = v^{x+1}(ad)_x^d$

and $(aM)_x^d = \sum\limits_{t=0}^{\infty} (aC)_{x+t}^d$

the value of an insurance of 1 payable at the end of the year of death
of (x) if he dies while in the (al) class is

$$\frac{(aM)_x^d}{(aD)_x}.$$

The main purpose for which monetary functions are required is in
the valuation of pension schemes and the techniques used are further
discussed in Chapter 10.

There is an obvious analogy between multiple-decrement and
joint-life theory—$(al)_x$ represents a status subject to m causes of
decrement as the joint life function $l_{x_1 x_2 \cdots x_m}$ represents a status
subject to the failure of any one of the m lives. While this is of some
theoretical interest it has little practical value.

Example 9.6

A certain firm employs a large number of unmarried female
workers between the ages of 20 and 25 and in addition to their wages
pays to an insurance company an annual premium yearly in advance
to secure on behalf of each the following benefits:

   (a) £25 on death in service,
   (b) £50 as a marriage dowry,
   (c) £75 on leaving service at age 25.

No benefit is paid on leaving service except on marriage.

Complete the multiple-decrement table (Table 9.5a) given that at
each age the central rate of mortality is ·01, the central rate of

TABLE 9.5a

Age x	$(al)_x$
20	1,000
21	860
22	730
23	610
24	500
25	400

marriage is ·1, and calculate the net annual premium required at 4% interest in respect of a new entrant at age 20.

Solution

The superfix m will denote marriage, d death and w withdrawal. The table is easily completed as using the approximation

$$(aL)_x = \tfrac{1}{2}((al)_x + (al)_{x+1})$$

and as

$$(am)_x^m = \frac{(ad)_x^m}{(aL)_x}, \quad \text{and} \quad (am)_x^d = \frac{(ad)_x^d}{(aL)_x},$$

$$(ad)_x^m = \tfrac{1}{2}((al)_x + (al)_{x+1})(·1)$$

and

$$(ad)_x^d = \tfrac{1}{2}((al)_x + (al)_{x+1})(·01).$$

The number of withdrawals will be found by subtraction,

$$(ad)_x^w = (al)_x - (al)_{x+1} - (ad)_x^m - (ad)_x^d.$$

The calculation is set down in tabular form in Table 9.5b.

TABLE 9.5b

x	$(al)_x$	$(aL)_x$	$(ad)_x^d$	$(ad)_x^m$	$(ad)_x^w$
20	1,000	930	9	93	38
21	860	795	8	80	42
22	730	670	7	67	46
23	610	555	6	56	48
24	500	450	5	45	50
25	400				

To calculate the required premium (assuming death and marriage benefits payable on death or marriage)—value of benefit on marriage

$$= \frac{50(1·02)}{1,000} (93v + 80v^2 + 67v^3 + 56v^4 + 45v^5) = 15·7.$$

As the number of deaths in any year is one-tenth of the number of marriages, the value of the benefit on death

$$= \frac{25}{50} \frac{(15·7)}{10} = 0·8.$$

The value of the benefit on leaving service at age 25 is

$$75 \frac{400}{1,000} v^5 = 24 \cdot 7.$$

The value of the premium annuity is

$$1 + \frac{1}{1,000} (860v + 730v^2 + 610v^3 + 500v^4) = 3 \cdot 47.$$

The required premium is thus $\dfrac{15 \cdot 7 + 0 \cdot 8 + 24 \cdot 7}{3 \cdot 47} = 11 \cdot 87$, i.e. £11.87.

Exercise 9.8

In Example 9.6 calculate the premium if the central rate of marriage is altered to ·08 at age 20 and 24, ·1 at age 21 and 23 and ·12 at age 22.

Exercise 9.9

A firm which employs only single girls and recruits 1,000 each year at exact age 18 provides a dowry on marriage of £10 for each completed year of service and a benefit of £100 on death in service. Mortality follows the A1967–70 ultimate table, the independent annual rate of marriage at all ages is 5% and the total exits from all causes are equivalent to a central rate of 10% per annum. Find the benefits paid each year in respect of the girls aged 22 last birthday.

EXAMPLES AND EXERCISES ON CHAPTER 9

Example 9.7

In a pension scheme providing for retirement between ages 60 and 62 it is assumed that one-quarter of the members retire at exact age 60, and the independent rate of retiral at age 60 is ·2 and at 61 is ·3. If mortality is according to the A1967–70 ultimate table, find the number of employees who retire at exact age 62 based on 1,000 active lives just reaching their 60th birthdays.

Solution

It will be seen that as well as the retirals at age 60 last birthday some employees retire at exact age 60—of the 1,000, one-quarter, that is 250, retire immediately so that while $(al)_{60} = 1,000$,

$$(al)_{60+} = 750,$$

where the '+' indicates that the age considered is just after the retirals at exact age 60.

There is given $q_{60}^d = \cdot01443$, $q_{61}^d = \cdot01601$. and also the independent rates of retiral

$$q_{60}^r = \cdot2, \quad q_{61}^r = \cdot3.$$

It is not necessary to find the individual decrements as $(al)_{62}$ is required—all the remaining employees retiring then.

$$(al)_{62} = (al)_{60+}(1-q_{60}^d)(1-q_{60}^r)(1-q_{61}^d)(1-q_{61}^r)$$

$$= 750(\cdot98557)(\cdot8)(\cdot98399)(\cdot7)$$

$$= 407.$$

The number of employees who retire at exact age 62 is thus 407.

Example 9.8

The employees of a firm are subject to mortality in accordance with the English Life Table No. 12—Males. Of those reaching age 60, 5% retire immediately. Between ages 60 and 65 a force of retiral of $\cdot039221$ operates continuously and all those still in service at age 65 retire then. Construct the multiple decrement table applicable, distinguishing the two types of retiral, from age 59 onwards. Use a radix such that 5,351 persons retire at exact age 65.

Solution

As $\quad \mu_x^r = \cdot039221 = \delta_{\cdot04}, \quad p_x^r = v$ at 4% interest

$\therefore (ap)_x$ for ages 60 to 65 $= vp_x^d$ at 4%,

and as the radix given is in fact D_{65} on English Life Table No. 12,

$$(al)_{64} = 5{,}351 \div vp_{64} = D_{64} = 5{,}758,$$

$$(al)_{63} = 5{,}758 \div vp_{63} = D_{63} = 6{,}176,$$

$$(al)_{62} = 6{,}176 \div vp_{62} = D_{62} = 6{,}607,$$

$$(al)_{61} = 6{,}607 \div vp_{61} = D_{61} = 7{,}049,$$

$$(al)_{60} = 7{,}049 \div vp_{60} = D_{60} = 7{,}503.$$

Now 5% of the employees retire at exact age 60 so

$$(al)_{59} = \frac{7{,}503}{\cdot95 p_{59}^d} = \frac{7{,}503}{(\cdot95)(\cdot97935)} = 8{,}064.$$

The multiple decrement table can be calculated between 60 and 65 by using the formula $(aq)_x^d = q_x^d(1 - \frac{1}{2}q_x^r)$, and as $q_x^r = 1 - v$ at 4%,

$$= q_x(1 - \tfrac{1}{2}(1 - v)), \quad q_x \text{ on English Life Table No. 12}$$

$$= (1 + \tfrac{1}{2}i) . vq_x$$

$$= \frac{\bar{C}_x}{D_x}.$$

Thus
$$(ad)_x^d = (aq)_x^d(al)_x = \frac{\bar{C}_x}{D_x} . D_{x.} = \bar{C}_x$$

so that $(ad)_x^d$ can be taken directly from the commutation columns of $\bar{C}_x$ as $(al)_x$ can be taken from D_x. $(ad)_x^r$ will be found by subtraction, and

$$(ad)_{60 \text{ (exact)}}^r = \cdot 05 . \frac{7,503}{\cdot 95} = 395.$$

The required table (using the '+' after an age to show the position immediately after the operation of retirals which occur exactly on the birthday) is shown in Table 9.6.

TABLE 9.6

Age x	Lives $(al)_x$	$(ad)_x^d + (ad)_x^r$	Deaths $(ad)_x^d$	Retirals $(ad)_x^r$
59	8,064		166	—
60	7,898		—	395
60+	7,503	454	168	286
61	7,049	442	175	267
62	6,607	431	180	251
63	6,176	418	185	233
64	5,758	407	189	218
65	5,351		—	5,351
65+	0			

Example 9.9

A certain employment is subject to a special accident risk such that, out of 100,000 lives entering employment at exact age 25, 500 die from all causes in each of the first 3 years. Thereafter the accident risk is such that the force of mortality due to accident is ·004820. Assuming that the mortality of the employees from causes other than accident is in accordance with the A1967–70 table ultimate, show how you would calculate at $3\frac{1}{2}\%$ interest the annual premium to secure an insurance for £1,000 payable in the event of death before age 65, the sum insured to be increased to £2,000 in the event of death as a result of an accident.

Solution

Let accented functions represent the special mortality and un-accented functions the A1967–70 ultimate table, and accented interest functions to represent $3\frac{1}{2}\%$ interest and unaccented 4% interest. From age 28 onwards,

$$v'^{t}{}_{t}p'_{x} = e^{-\int_0^t \mu'_{x+r}+\delta' dr} = e^{-\int_0^t \mu_{x+r}+\delta'+\cdot 00482 dr}$$

$$= e^{-\int_0^t \mu_{x+r}+\delta dr} = v^t{}_t p_x,$$

$$\therefore \bar{a}'_x \text{ at } 3\tfrac{1}{2}\% \text{ interest} = \bar{a}_x \text{ at } 4\% \text{ interest}$$

and $\qquad \ddot{a}'_x$ at $3\frac{1}{2}\%$ interest $= \ddot{a}_x$ at 4% interest.

$$\bar{A}'_x \text{ at } 3\tfrac{1}{2}\% = \int_0^\infty v'^t \cdot {}_t p'_x \cdot \mu'_{x+t} dt$$

$$= \int_0^\infty v^t \cdot {}_t p_x \cdot (\mu_{x+t} + \cdot 00482) dt$$

$$= \bar{A}_x + (\cdot 00482)\bar{a}_x \text{ at } 4\%.$$

If the premium is P,

value of premiums $= P(1 + \cdot 995v' + \cdot 99v'^2 + \cdot 985v'^3 \ddot{a}_{28\,:\,\overline{37|}})$,
the annuity value being $\ddot{a}_{28\,:\,\overline{37|}}$ at 4%,
and the value of the benefits if £2,000 is payable in any event

$$= 2,000(\cdot 005v'^{\frac{1}{2}} + \cdot 005v'^{1\frac{1}{2}} + \cdot 005v'^{2\frac{1}{2}} + \cdot 985v'^3 \bar{A}'^{\,1}_{28\,:\,\overline{37|}}),$$

the insurance value $= \bar{A}^{\,1}_{28\,:\,\overline{37|}} + (\cdot 00482)\bar{a}_{28\,:\,\overline{37|}}$ at 4%.
The value of benefit overprovided for, i.e. £1,000 on non-accidental death

$$= \frac{1,000}{100,000}\{(ad)^d_{25}v'^{\frac{1}{2}} + (ad)^d_{26}v'^{1\frac{1}{2}} + (ad)^d_{27}v'^{2\frac{1}{2}} + 98,500v'^3 \bar{A}^{\,1}_{28\,:\,\overline{37|}}\}$$

the insurance value being $\bar{A}^{\,1}_{28\,:\,\overline{37|}}$ at 4%.
The values of $(ad)^d_x$ for $x = 25$, 26, 27 are found from

$$(ad)^d_x = \tfrac{1}{2}\{(al)_x + (al)_{x+1}\}(am)^d_x$$

$$\doteqdot \tfrac{1}{2}\{(al)_x + (al)_{x+1}\}\mu^d_{x+\frac{1}{2}}$$

the $(al)_x$ being known.

Equating the value of premiums to the value of benefits gives the required annual premium.

Example 9.10

The following functions are available at a given rate of interest based on a combined mortality and marriage table:

$(sl)_x$ = number of spinsters expected to attain age x,

$(ml)_x$ = number of married women expected to attain age x,

$(sD)_x = v^x(sl)_x$,

$$(sN)_x = \sum_{t=0}^{\infty} (sD)_{x+t},$$

$(mD)_x = v^x(ml)_x$,

$$(mN)_x = \sum_{t=0}^{\infty} (mD)_{x+t}, \quad \text{and}$$

a_x = value of an annuity payable during the future lifetime of a married woman aged x.

Using only these functions, demonstrate how the annual premium at the given rate of interest for a policy would be calculated to provide the following benefits for a spinster aged 20:

(a) £1,000 on death as a spinster, payable at the end of the year of death if this occurs before age 45, and

(b) £500 at the end of the year of marriage if this occurs within 25 years, with a further £500 payable at the end of the year of subsequent death if this also occurs within that term.

The premium is payable for 25 years, but ceases when a benefit is paid.

Solution

Considering the benefits (a) and (b) together, it can be seen that the benefits can also be regarded as a benefit of £500 on death and £500 on the first of death or marriage—the benefits are considered in this way so that statuses can be determined at the end of which the benefits are paid. As annuity functions are available the benefits can be evaluated on the basis of a formula of the form

$$A = v\ddot{a} - a.$$

The annuity-due during spinsterhood for a life aged 20 with term 25 years is

$$(s\ddot{a})_{20\,:\,\overline{25|}} = \frac{(sN)_{20} - (sN)_{45}}{(sD)_{20}},$$

and the immediate annuity

$$(sa)_{20\,:\,\overline{25|}} = \frac{(sN)_{21} - (sN)_{46}}{(sD)_{20}}.$$

The benefit payable on the first of death and marriage is then $500(v(s\ddot{a})_{20\,:\,\overline{25|}} - (sa)_{20\,:\,\overline{25|}})$.

The problem in evaluating the benefit for a spinster on death whether as a spinster or married is that when the table is considered as a whole some of the deaths of married women will be of those who were spinsters at age 20 but some will have been married at that age. The annuity-due for all the women aged 20, i.e. $(sl)_{20} + (ml)_{20}$ in all

$$= \{(sl)_{20} + ml)_{20}\} \cdot \frac{(sN)_{20} - (sN)_{45} + (mN)_{20} - (mN)_{45}}{(sD)_{20} + (mD)_{20}}.$$

From this we wish to deduct the annuity for the $(ml)_{20}$ married women, i.e.

$$(ml)_{20}\{\ddot{a}_{20} - p_{20} \cdot p_{21} \cdot p_{22} \ldots p_{44} \cdot \ddot{a}_{45}\}$$

being expressed in this way as the data regarding married women's mortality is available in the form of a_x, the p_x will be found from $a_x = vp_x\ddot{a}_{x+1}$. Deducting the expression for the annuity to the women married at 20 from that already found and dividing the answer by $(sl)_{20}$ gives the required annuity-due ceasing on death for a spinster aged 20.

It will be obvious that the similar immediate annuity can also be calculated and hence the insurance factor multiplied by 500 in the same way as the benefit on the first of death or marriage. The total benefit is then the sum of these two benefits.

The annuity for the premium by which the resulting value should be divided will be the value $(s\ddot{a})_{20\,:\,\overline{25|}}$ as the premium ceases as soon as any benefit is paid.

Exercise 9.10

In a large staff of women there are three modes of exit, namely withdrawal, marriage and death. The probability that an employee aged 30 will remain in service for one year is ·8. The probability that she will withdraw in that year is ·11 and that she will withdraw in the following year is ·08. Mortality is in accordance with the A1967–70 ultimate table and the central rate of marriage at age 31 is ·0833.

Calculate the central rate of marriage at age 30 and the probability that an employee in service at age 31 will still be in service at age 32.

Exercise 9.11

The employees covered by a pension scheme may retire on their 65th birthdays or on any subsequent birthday provided retirement is not deferred beyond their 70th birthdays. At each age the mortality experience of employees and pensioners taken together is in accordance with the A1967–70 ultimate table but in the two years following retirement the force of mortality of those retiring before age 70 is ·024693 greater than the force of mortality according to that table. Otherwise the mortality experience of pensioners is in accordance with that table. The probability of a member in service on any birthday from the 65th to 69th inclusive retiring immediately is ·2.

Describe how the value of a death benefit of £1,000 payable on the death in service of an employee now aged 65 should be calculated. Assume interest at 3% per annum.

Exercise 9.12

Using only the information given below and the tables mentioned, show how you would calculate:

(a) the net purchase price of an annuity of £200 payable yearly in arrear to a bachelor, aged x. On his marriage the annuity increases to £400 per annum for 10 years certain and so long thereafter as he may live,

(b) the probability that, on a bachelor now aged x dying between ages z and $z+1$, the annuity will continue for exactly two payments.

The mortality applicable to male lives whether married or single is English Life Table No. 12, and you have the following columns from a table combining that mortality with the appropriate rates of marriage:

$(bl)_x$ = number of bachelors attaining age x,

$(hl)_x$ = number of married men (including widowers) attaining age x,

$(ha)_x$ = value of immediate annuity of £1 during the lifetime of a married man aged x.

The rate of interest in the annuity value is not known directly.

Exercise 9.13

Show how, using only the functions stated below, you would calculate at a given rate of interest the annual premium for a policy for a term of 20 years to provide, in the case of a bachelor aged 25:

- (i) £200 on survival to the end of the term,
- (ii) £200 on death as a bachelor during the term, payable at the end of the year of death,
- (iii) £100 on marriage during the term payable at the end of the year of marriage, and
- (iv) £100 on death during the term, marriage having previously taken place, payable at the end of the year of death.

In the event of marriage during the term the amount of the annual premium payable after marriage is to be one-half of the amount of the annual premium payable during bachelorhood.

It is to be assumed that the following functions from a combined mortality and marriage table are tabulated:

$(bl)_x$ = the number of bachelors expected to attain age x

$(hl)_x$ = the number of married men expected to attain age x

$(bD)_x = v^x(bl)_x$

$(bN)_x = \sum_{t=0}^{\infty} (bD)_{x+t}$

$(hD)_x = v^x(hl)_x$

$(hN)_x = \sum_{t=0}^{\infty} (hD)_{x+t}$

a_x = the value of an immediate annuity payable during the future lifetime of a married man aged x.

Exercise 9.14

For over 40 years there has been, on 1 January, a constant number of entrants at exact age 20 to the life insurance scheme of a large company and the membership has reached a stationary condition. Mortality has been in accordance with the A1967–70 table ultimate. Withdrawals have taken place only during the first ten years of membership, during which period the central annual rate of withdrawal has been constant at ·014528. Members can retire at any time after the 58th birthday but those who remain in service until the 60th birthday must retire on that date. Of each year's retirals 30% take place at age 58 last birthday, 10% at age 59 last birthday and 60% at exact age 60.

Assuming that retirals at ages 58 and 59 last birthday are evenly distributed over the calendar year show how to calculate on the basis of the above experience with interest at $2\frac{1}{2}\%$ the sum payable yearly in advance during membership to secure, for each entrant at age 20, £1,000 payable on retirement at age 60 or at the end of the year of death or retirement before that age. No benefit is payable on withdrawal.

CHAPTER TEN

PENSION FUND FUNCTIONS

10.1 Service tables and salary scales

In this chapter will be discussed the valuation of benefits and contributions for the members of a pension fund scheme, or plan (the terms will be treated as having the same meaning). Normally the members are the employees of a single employer and the benefits that may be provided are pensions on retiral (due to attainment of a certain age or on ill-health), benefits on death (either as a lump sum or as a widow's pension) and benefits on withdrawal from service (either in the form of a preserved or paid-up pension or of a return of the employee's contributions). The cost of the fund may be shared between the employer and employees (a contributory fund) or may be paid for entirely by the employer (a non-contributory fund).

The benefits that may be provided by a fund depend on the country in which the employer is situated. The supervision exercised by a Government, either directly or indirectly (through taxation requirements and the provision of any State Pension Scheme), will have a major influence on the level and type of benefits and contributions.

Different funds may vary considerably as regards the nature of the benefits, the relationship between contributions and benefits, the conditions that have to be fulfilled in order that a member may be entitled to benefit, and so on. However, in all cases the problems of valuation of the future benefits and contributions are those of applying monetary functions based on a multiple-decrement table (such as those described in section 9.7 of the previous chapter) with the slight additional complication of a salary scale.

While there is no standard notation for pension fund work (all the previous functions met in this book have followed the International Notation, see Appendix II) and special funds may require special consideration, the functions that will be described in this chapter are those generally accepted and can be used to value most benefits that will occur. The methods used can be applied to value any other benefits or contributions.

The multiple-decrement table is normally referred to as a service table and the following symbols will be used (those according to the normal multiple-decrement conventions are given in brackets):

l_x = number of active members surviving in service at exact age x, $((al)_x)$,

w_x = number of withdrawals from service in the year of age, x to $x+1$, $((ad)_x^w)$,

d_x = number of deaths in service in the year of age x to $x+1$, $((ad)_x^d)$,

i_x = number of retirements due to ill-health in the year of age x to $x+1$, $((ad)_x^i)$,

r_x = number of retirements due to attainment of retirement age, $((ad)_x^r)$.

While at one time it was common for the benefit on withdrawal from a fund to be a return of the employees' contributions, more recently (partly because of statutory requirements on 'preservation' or 'vesting') the benefit (usually after satisfying requirements on age and length of membership) is tending to become a preserved 'paid-up' pension at retirement. In this event it may be appropriate to treat the withdrawals as two separate decrements, one giving a return of contributions and one a preserved pension. The preserved pension may or not be a fixed amount; for example, it may increase with increases in national average earnings or by a fixed amount each year till retirement. If the value of the benefit on withdrawal with a preserved pension is equal to, or nearly equal to, the actual reserve held then it may not be necessary to introduce a separate decrement. Another approach would be to use a 'select' approach for withdrawals—that is those who withdraw within a specified period (perhaps 5 years) being entitled to a return of contributions and those after that period being entitled to a preserved pension benefit.

In most pension schemes special provision is made for retirements due to ill-health, and as indicated a separate decrement is normally used for these compared to age retirements. While age retirement may occur at one fixed age such as 65 so that the only r_x is r_{65} (which will be the same as l_{65}), it is more usual for there to be a range depending on age and/or service, for example retirement may occur at any time after age 60 provided forty years' service have been completed but with retirement at age 65 no matter the service completed (although there may be a maximum age such as 50 for entry to the fund so that the minimum service would be fifteen years).

As an example it will be seen that in the service table given in Appendix III table 5, which is used in some of the examples and exercises in this chapter, retirement takes place between ages 60 and 65 and ill-health retirement after attainment of age 31. Employees age 18 may join the fund and withdrawals are assumed to take place up to age 44. The actual rates of decrement are not given in this case but may be found using the methods of Chapter 9.

It is normal to assume that all forces of decrement are continuous throughout the range of ages over which they operate except that age retirements may be discontinuous at ages such as 60 or 65 where retirements may take place on the birthday. Rates of withdrawal may be a function of duration as well as age so that particularly at the younger ages it might be desirable to use select rates of withdrawal. The development of formulae based on select rates may, as mentioned above, also be appropriate when different benefits are paid depending on duration of membership because of preservation requirements.

Special circumstances may arise with pension funds which are 'contracted-out' of State pension schemes—in effect replacing part of the State scheme provided that various minimum levels of benefit are provided in the private scheme. The benefit may for example be the greater of the normal scheme benefit or a guaranteed minimum benefit based on the benefit which would have been paid in the State scheme if the private scheme had not contracted-out. Such provisions may complicate the formulae (a simple example is shown in Example 10.24 below).

A separate mortality table will be required for pensioners after retirement and it is usual to have two different tables, one for ill-health pensioners and one for normal retirements. In the case of ill-health pensioners there is likely to be particularly heavy mortality in the first one or two years after retirement so that a select table showing reverse selection may be appropriate.

While there are some pension funds which provide a benefit which does not depend on salary, for example a fixed amount of pension for each year of service, in most funds pensions and contributions depend on salary. Because of this a salary scale is introduced which is given the symbol s_x, and is such that s_{x+t}/s_x represents the ratio of the member's earnings in the year of age $x+t$ to $x+t+1$ to his earnings in the year of age x to $x+1$. The assumption implicit in this is that salaries on average increase with age as is normally the case in an organisation where with promotion and experience higher salaries are given. Some companies in fact have salary scales for clerical staff which depend on age. In the last few years it has also become more customary in pension fund work to recognise that salaries increase with inflation and that it may be unrealistic not to allow for possible future inflation.

The salary scales given in Appendix III table 5 in column s_x show a typical scale used assuming that there is no inflation. The increase in salary each year is proportionally much more at the earlier years, $\frac{1 \cdot 10}{1 \cdot 00} - 1 = 10\%$ at age 18 reducing to $\frac{3 \cdot 68}{3 \cdot 58} - 1 = 3\%$ at age 40 and $\frac{5 \cdot 29}{5 \cdot 24} - 1 = 1\%$ at age 60. The effect of adding an inflation assumption, for example 5% each year will be to redefine the salary scale as $s_x(1.05)^x$, such an alteration does not however introduce any changes in the formulae.

It will be found that the 'radix' of the s_x table is arbitrary and that the same values will result if each figure is multiplied or divided by the same factor. It is customary for the lowest age to have $s_x = 100$ or $1 \cdot 00$. It is of course impossible to predict the future earnings of any individual, and the scale is a means of estimating the average annual earnings in future of the members at a certain age whose present salaries are known. There is no standard practice in granting salary increases among different companies, some grant increases on one day each year, some grant increases on the anniversary of joining the company or the birthday of the individual employee, some give increases separately for cost-of-living from the annual increase due to a salary scale. Slight adjustments may occasionally be required to the usual valuation factors because of these practices, and this is discussed further in section 10.10.

It is common for the benefits under a scheme to differ for female and male staff, the most common difference being in the retirement age, this may be 60 or earlier for females but be 65 or between 60 and 65 for males. Because of this and also because the rates of decrement are likely to differ, separate service tables and commutation functions are prepared for females. There may also be separate schemes in a company for clerical staff and for manual workers, in which case separate service tables and salary scales may be appropriate. This book is not concerned with the problems arising in the choice of suitable bases so that attention will be confined to obtaining formulae for the various benefits and contributions assuming a service table, salary scale and pensioner mortality tables are given.

When a pension fund is started it is necessary to fix rates of contributions by the employee (if the fund is contributory) and by the employer. At intervals, often three or five years, though in some cases annually, a valuation is made of the expected future benefits and contributions and compared with the assets in the fund.

The following summarises the items which are commonly likely to require valuation in a fund or scheme:

(1) Contributions:
Value of future contributions by the

  (a) Members,

  (b) The employer—which could be a fixed cash amount, a proportion of the members' contributions or salaries or a combination of each. The fixed sum often arises in addition to a contribution based on salary in order to meet the liability which arises when a fund is started where some credit is given for service already completed ('past service pension').

(2) Benefits:

  (a) on age retirement,

  (b) on ill-health retirement (often at a younger age than is permitted for normal age retirement),

  (c) on early retirement other than on ill-health, or late retirement—this may sometimes be ignored in practice if the benefit is thought to approximate to the actuarial value of the pension that would be available on normal age retirement,

  (d) on withdrawal—often a return of the members' contributions with or without interest, or particularly after a period of service has been completed a preserved pension which will commence at the normal retiring age, and which might increase with inflation until retirement,

  (e) on death—a cash sum based on the contributions paid and/or a lump sum, and/or a pension to the widow (or sometimes widower) and perhaps orphans.

The calculations for pension funds will thus involve assumptions on the rate of mortality, rates of retirement due to age and ill-health, withdrawal rates and salary scales. There is likely to be considerably less data for any individual fund from which to obtain the necessary tables compared to life office valuations so there is not much point in introducing too many refinements into the calculations when so much judgment may be required from the actuary in determining the bases. Decrements, for example, are often assumed to occur half way through the scheme year.

To value the fund there should be available:

(a) A service table—it will be assumed in this chapter for the purposes of illustration that the final retirement age is 65.

(b) A salary scale, except in the few cases where the benefits do not depend on salary.

(c) Annuity values for the values of a pension of 1 per annum following ill-health retirement and age retirement, the annuity being paid in accordance with the rules of the fund—for example, the pension may be payable monthly and may have a guaranteed period of a certain number of years or be subject to the condition that on death the member's contributions are returned less the pension payments made. It may also increase ('escalate') perhaps in line with cost-of-living increases or national average earnings or at some fixed percentage rate such as 3% each year—where the pension increase is not at a fixed rate an assumption on the long-term average rate of inflation will be required, similar to any allowance for inflation in the salary scale. The values of the annuities will be given the symbols $\bar{a}_y^i$ and $\bar{a}_y^r$ for ill-health and age retirement respectively.

There should also be available information on the members of the fund; commonly the following may be needed—it will be seen that normally grouping of members is done by the age nearest birthday:

$(TPS)_x$ = The total of past salaries up to the valuation date for members aged x nearest birthday.

$(AS)_x$ = Total salaries expected to be received in the following year for members at present aged x nearest birthday.

$(nS)_x$ = Total value for members aged x nearest birthday of the product of the number of years past service and salary expected to be received in the following year.

$(AC)_x$ = The total annual contributions in force in the year following the valuation date for the members aged x nearest birthday. In many funds this is a fixed percentage of salary so is not separately required being found as a proportion of $(AS)_x$.

$(TPC)_x = $ The total of past contributions accumulated to the valuation date for the members aged x nearest birthday with compound interest at whatever rate is allowed on the return of contributions on leaving service (alternatively on death if this differs).

In some funds service before the fund commenced is allowed less than full credit (for example it may be counted as half service) in which case adjustments may be made in $(TPS)_x$ and $(nS)_x$.

10.2 Pensions not dependent on salary

Although it is now unusual to have a fund which provides a fixed amount of annual pension for each year of service, the development of formulae for such a benefit provides a convenient introduction to the methods used for pensions based on salary. It will be assumed that the pension for each year of service is P per annum and that allowance is made for fractional years of service in determining pension.

The value at age x of a pension of 1 per annum commencing on ill-health retirement at age y last birthday, assumed to occur on the average at age $y+\frac{1}{2}$, is

$$v^{y+\frac{1}{2}-x} \frac{i_y}{l_x} \bar{a}^i_{y+\frac{1}{2}}$$

$$= \frac{v^{y+\frac{1}{2}} i_y \bar{a}^i_{y+\frac{1}{2}}}{v^x l_x}$$

$$= \frac{C^{ia}_y}{D_x}, \tag{10.2.1}$$

where $\qquad C^{ia}_y = v^{y+\frac{1}{2}} \cdot i_y \bar{a}^i_{y+\frac{1}{2}} \quad (y \text{ being } <65). \tag{10.2.2}$

To be consistent with assurance functions the symbol C should have a bar above—however, all pension fund functions are 'mid-year' benefits and the bar has a different significance which will be discussed below.

The value at age x of a pension of 1 per annum commencing at any age will be the sum of the values of the expression in (10.2.1) over all ages of $y \geqq x$ with, of course, a limit of 64, i.e.

$$\frac{1}{D_x} \sum_{y=x}^{64} C_y^{ia}$$

$$= \frac{1}{D_x} M_x^{ia} \tag{10.2.3}$$

where
$$M_x^{ia} = \sum_{y=x}^{64} C_y^{ia};$$

more usually this is written

$$M_x^{ia} = \sum_{t=0}^{64-x} C_{x+t}^{ia}, \quad \text{where } y = x+t. \tag{10.2.4}$$

The annual pension arising in respect of past service, that is service by a member already completed at the time of valuation, will be nP, where n is the number of years past service (including fractions) for the individual member. The value at age x of the pension if it commences at any future age will be

$$nP \frac{M_x^{ia}}{D_x} \tag{10.2.5}$$

and summing over all members of the fund aged x nearest birthday gives

$$(\Sigma n)P \frac{M_x^{ia}}{D_x}, \tag{10.2.6}$$

(P being constant) as the total value of the past service ill-health retiral pensions.

To value the pension benefit arising from future service for a member aged exactly x, we first consider the benefit arising from service between ages y and $y+1$. The probability that the member will retire due to ill-health during the actual year will be $\dfrac{i_y}{l_x}$ assumed to take place on average half-way through the year and thus gives rise to $\frac{1}{2}P$ as an amount of pension. The probability that the member will retire during the next year, i.e. from age $y+1$ to $y+2$ is $\dfrac{i_{y+1}}{l_x}$ and the amount of pension in this case is based on the full year from y to $y+1$.

Similarly, in each future year the pension entitlement from service for age y to $y+1$ will be a full year. The total value of the pension at age x from future service between ages y and $y+1$ is thus found by summation:

$$\tfrac{1}{2}Pv^{y+\frac{1}{2}-x}\,\frac{i_y}{l_x}\,\bar{a}^i_{y+\frac{1}{2}}+Pv^{y+1\frac{1}{2}-x}\,\frac{i_{y+1}}{l_x}\,\bar{a}^i_{y+1\frac{1}{2}}+\ldots+Pv^{64\frac{1}{2}-x}\,\frac{i_{64}}{l_x}\,\bar{a}^i_{64\frac{1}{2}}$$

$$=\frac{P}{D_x}\,(\tfrac{1}{2}C^{ia}_y+C^{ia}_{y+1}+\ldots+C^{ia}_{64})$$

$$=\frac{P}{D_x}\,\overline{M}^{ia}_y, \tag{10.2.7}$$

where $\qquad \overline{M}^{ia}_y = M^{ia}_y - \tfrac{1}{2}C^{ia}_y;$ $\hfill$ (10.2.8)

as mentioned above, the bar having a different significance from that in assurance functions.

The total values of the pension arising from future service will be the sum of formula (10.2.7) for all values of y from x to 64, i.e.

$$\frac{P}{D_x}\sum_{y=x}^{64}\overline{M}^{ia}_y$$

or writing $y = x+t$

$$=\frac{P}{D_x}\sum_{t=0}^{64-x}\overline{M}^{ia}_{x+t}$$

$$=\frac{P}{D_x}\,\overline{R}^{ia}_x \tag{10.2.9}$$

where $\qquad \overline{R}^{ia}_x = \sum_{t=0}^{64-x}\overline{M}^{ia}_{x+t}.$ $\hfill$ (10.2.10)

The total future pension entitlement for the members aged x nearest birthday is then

$$\sum_{\text{(members)}}P\;\frac{\overline{R}^{ia}_x}{D_x}.$$

It might be thought that an easier approach to the problem would be to evaluate directly the pension commencing payment on retirement a certain number of years hence, giving an expression

$$\frac{P}{D_x}\,(\tfrac{1}{2}C^{ia}_x+1\tfrac{1}{2}C^{ia}_{x+1}+2\tfrac{1}{2}C^{ia}_{x+2}+\ldots).$$

It will be found that this expression is in fact $\dfrac{P}{D_x}\,\bar{R}_x^{ia}$. The different approach has been used as it is more easily adaptable to the more complicated cases where pensions are based on salary.

For the pension payable on age retirement, similar expressions will be found with the replacement of r_y for i_y, substituting r for i in the symbols, and the addition of the pension at exact age 65.

The value at age x of a pension of 1 per annum from age 65 will be

$$v^{65-x}\frac{r_{65}}{l_x}\,\bar{a}_{65}^r = \frac{C_{65}^{ra}}{D_x}, \tag{10.2.11}$$

the symbol having a different definition from (10.2.2) because 65 is the final retirement age.

If C_{65}^{ra} is added in the definition of M_x^{ra} and thus $\bar{M}_x^{ra}$ and $\bar{R}_x^{ra}$ identical expressions to those already found are obtained with the superfix ia replaced by ra. It will be noted that while the summation of the C to find $\bar{M}$ now extends to 65, the summation of $\bar{M}$ to find $\bar{R}$ ceases at 64 as no further pension accrues after age 65.

In some cases it might be that the ill-health and age-retirement benefits could be combined as the benefit provided is the same, so using a total C_y^{ra} covering both types of retirement

$$C_y^{ra} = v^{y+\frac{1}{2}}(i_y\bar{a}_{y+\frac{1}{2}}^i + r_y\bar{a}_{y+\frac{1}{2}}^r)$$

—the superfix ra on the left-hand side function in this case covering total retirement.

Example 10.1

Using the tables in Appendix III table 5, find the present values of the following pensions for a member aged 40 who joined the fund at age 30:

(a) Pension of £1,000 per annum on age or ill-health retirement.

(b) Pension of £100 per annum for each year of future service, on retirement due to age.

(c) Pension of £50 per annum for each year of membership of the fund on retirement due to ill-health.

(d) Pension of £100 per annum for each year of future service with an additional pension of £200 per annum if retirement does not occur till age 65.

Solution

(a) Using formula (10.2.3) the value of the pension will be

$$\frac{1,000}{D_{40}} (M_{40}^{ia} + M_{40}^{ra})$$

$$= \frac{1,000}{5,204} (1,688 + 16,742)$$

$$= 3,542, \text{ i.e. } £3,542.$$

(b) Using formula (10.2.9) the value of the pension will be

$$\frac{100}{D_{40}} \bar{R}_{40}^{ra}$$

$$= \frac{100}{5,204} 384,530$$

$$= 7,389, \text{ i.e. } £7,389.$$

(c) There are ten years' past service pension accrued, the value from formula (10.2.5) being

$$\frac{(10)(50)}{D_{40}} M_{40}^{ia}.$$

The value of the future service pension using formula (10.2.9) is

$$\frac{50}{D_{40}} \cdot \bar{R}_{40}^{ia},$$

so the value of the total pension is

$$\frac{50}{5,204} \{10(1,688) + 29,034\}$$

$$= 441, \text{ i.e. } £441.$$

(d) As no specific reason for retirement is given, both ill-health and age retirement are meant.

The value of the normal pension using formula (10.2.9) is

$$\frac{100}{D_{40}} (\bar{R}_{40}^{ia} + \bar{R}_{40}^{ra})$$

and adding the additional pension for retirement at age 65 from formula (10.2.11) of $\dfrac{200}{D_{40}} C_{65}^{ra}$, gives a total of

$$\frac{100}{5,204} (29,034 + 384,530 + 2(6,675))$$

$$= 8,204, \text{ i.e. } £8,204.$$

Example 10.2

In the fund discussed in the previous section an additional benefit is added so that the minimum pension on retirement due to ill-health is to be $10P$ per annum. Find an expression for the value of this additional benefit for a member aged x with fewer than ten years' service.

Solution

If the past service of the member is n then the additional benefit over that previously valued is a pension of $10 - (n + \frac{1}{2})$ on retirement in the first year (assuming retirement half way through the year) $10 - (n + 1\frac{1}{2})$ in the second year and so on.

Thus from formula (10.2.1) the value of the additional pension will be

$$\frac{P}{D_x} ((10 - (n + \tfrac{1}{2}))C_x^{ia} + (10 - (n + 1\tfrac{1}{2}))C_{x+1}^{ia} + \ldots)$$

the number of terms depending on n, the pension valued having of course to be positive. As the summation is over very few terms it is probably unnecessary to express the answer in terms of M's.

Exercise 10.1

Using the tables in Appendix III table 5, find the present value of the following pensions for an employee aged 45 who joined a scheme at age 40:

(a) Pension of £1,000 per annum on ill-health retirement, and £2,000 per annum on age retirement.

(b) Pension of £150 per annum for each year of service.

(c) Pension of £100 per annum for each year of future service with an additional pension of £250 per annum if retirement takes place after age 60.

Exercise 10.2

In the fund discussed in the previous section the benefit on ill-health retirement is based on the number of years of service which would have been completed by age 65 rather than on actual service. Find an expression for the value of the ill-health retirement benefit for a new member aged x, and evaluate it using the tables in the appendix if x is 35; the benefit is £100 per annum for each year of service.

10.3   Pensions based on average salary

As was seen in the previous section, the valuation of ill-health and age-retirement pensions is very similar and it is intended initially to develop formulae for ill-health retirement pension—the formulae for age-retirement pension will normally be found in a similar manner, adding the term at the final age of the service table (65 in the case of the table used for demonstrations in this chapter).

When the pension is based on average salary it is normally a fraction such as 1/60th, 1/80th or 1/100th of the average earnings throughout service for each year of service. In this section the formulae will be based on the general fraction of $1/K$th.

A pension of $1/K$th of the average salary throughout service for each year of service is equal to $1/K$th of the total salary received throughout service. Each payment of salary can be considered as giving an entitlement to $1/K$th of that salary as a pension each year.

The value of the pension accrued to a member aged x from past service is then $1/K$th of the salary already received, i.e.

$$\frac{(\text{past salary})}{K} \frac{M_x^{ia}}{D_x} \tag{10.3.1}$$

from formula (10.2.3).

Summing over all members aged x nearest birthday gives the total value of the past service pensions as

$$\frac{1}{K} (TPS)_x \frac{M_x^{ia}}{D_x}. \tag{10.3.2}$$

To value the pension which will accrue from future service the salary scale must be introduced to estimate future earnings. If the salary in the next year for a member aged x is S, the salary assumed to be received in the year of age y to $y+1$ is estimated using the definition of the salary scale in section 10.1 as $S\dfrac{s_y}{s_x}$,

The value at the present time of the pension due on retirement in respect of salary received in the year y to $y+1$ will, from formula (10.2.7), be

$$\frac{1}{K} \frac{1}{D_x} S \frac{s_y}{s_x} \overline{M}_y^{ia}$$

$$= \frac{S}{K} \frac{{}^s\overline{M}_y^{ia}}{{}^sD_x}, \tag{10.3.3}$$

where $\qquad {}^s\overline{M}_y^{ia} = s_y \overline{M}_y^{ia} \tag{10.3.4}$

and $\qquad {}^sD_x = s_x D_x. \tag{10.3.5}$

The value of the pension for all future years of service is

$$\frac{S}{K} \sum_{y=x}^{64} \frac{{}^s\overline{M}_y^{ia}}{{}^sD_x}$$

$$= \frac{S}{K} \frac{{}^s\overline{R}_x^{ia}}{{}^sD_x} \tag{10.3.6}$$

where $\qquad {}^s\overline{R}_x^{ia} = \sum_{y=x}^{64} {}^s\overline{M}_y^{ia}. \tag{10.3.7}$

The total value of the future service pension for members whose nearest birthday is x will be found by summing over all these members giving

$$\frac{(AS)_x}{K} \frac{{}^s\overline{R}_x^{ia}}{{}^sD_x}. \tag{10.3.8}$$

The values of the age-retirement pensions will be found similarly, r replacing i in the symbols, and C_{65}^{ra} already having been added into the definition of M_x^{ra} before the introduction of the salary scale in ${}^s\overline{M}_x^{ra}$ in (10.3.4).

Example 10.3

A member aged 50 of a pension scheme providing a pension of 1/80th of average salary for each year of service joined the scheme at age 40 and has a salary of £3,000. Find the present value of his pension if his total past salary is £18,000. Use the tables in the Appendix.

Solution

Using formulae (10.3.1) and (10.3.6) the value will be

$$\frac{18,000}{80} \cdot \frac{M_{50}^{ia} + M_{50}^{ra}}{D_{50}} + \frac{3,000}{80} \cdot \frac{{}^s\overline{R}_{50}^{ia} + {}^s\overline{R}_{50}^{ra}}{{}^sD_{50}}$$

$$= \frac{18,000}{80} \cdot \frac{1,421+16,742}{3,222} + \frac{3,000}{80} \cdot \frac{65,879+1,083,936}{14,693}$$

$$= 1,268+2,935, \text{ i.e. } £4,203.$$

Exercise 10.3

The members of a scheme whose nearest age is 55 have total current salaries of £15,000 and past salaries of £200,000. Find the present value of their pensions using the tables in the Appendix if the benefit is 1/60th of average salary for each year of service.

Exercise 10.4

The pension benefit in a scheme is 1/100th of total salary received with a minimum benefit on ill health of B per annum. Find an expression for the benefit for a member aged x.

10.4 Pensions based on final salary

When a pension is based on final salary it means that the pension for each year of service is a fraction such as 1/60th, 1/80th or 1/100th of the salary near retiral, in general $1/K$th. While it is possible for the salary rate at the time of retiral to be used it is usual for the rules of the scheme to provide that the salary be averaged over the last few years, such as the last three or five years of service, or perhaps the average of the highest three of the five consecutive years before retirement. The salaries taken may be the salary over a year or the salary rate at the yearly anniversary of the commencement of the scheme. The formulae used for demonstration in this section will assume a final average salary based on the average of the last m years before retirement using the salary over each year. The average of the final salaries on which the pension for a person retiring at age x is based is given the symbol z_x. In this case

$$z_x = \frac{1}{m}(s_{x-m}+s_{x-m+1}+\dots+s_{x-1}). \qquad (10.4.1)$$

The tables in Appendix III table 5 have $m = 3$ so that

$$z_x = \tfrac{1}{3}(s_{x-3}+s_{x-2}+s_{x-1}).$$

The salary on which the pension is based for a member aged x whose present salary is S if he retires at age last birthday $x+t$ (assumed to be at $x+t+\tfrac{1}{2}$) will be

$$S\frac{z_{x+t+\frac{1}{2}}}{s_x}.$$

The present value of the pension on ill-health retirement during the year from age $x+t$ to $x+t+1$ if past service is n years will be

$$\frac{n}{K} S \frac{z_{x+t+\frac{1}{2}}}{s_x} \frac{C^{ia}_{x+t}}{D_x}$$

$$= \frac{n}{K} S \frac{{}^zC^{ia}_{x+t}}{{}^sD_x}, \tag{10.4.2}$$

where

$${}^zC^{ia}_x = z_{x+\frac{1}{2}} C^{ia}_x. \tag{10.4.3}$$

Summing over the future years of possible retirement, the total value of the past service pension is

$$\frac{n}{K} \frac{S}{{}^sD_x} \sum_{t=0}^{64-x} {}^zC^{ia}_{x+t}$$

$$= \frac{n}{K} \frac{S}{{}^sD_x} {}^zM^{ia}_x, \tag{10.4.4}$$

where

$${}^zM^{ia}_x = \sum_{t=0}^{64-x} {}^zC^{ia}_{x+t}, \quad \text{or} \quad = \sum_{y=x}^{64} {}^zC^{ia}_y. \tag{10.4.5}$$

The total value of past service pension for members at present aged x nearest birthday is then

$$\frac{(nS)_x}{K} \cdot \frac{{}^zM^{ia}_x}{{}^sD_x}. \tag{10.4.6}$$

For future service pensions the amount of pension accruing in respect of service in the year from age $x+t$ to $x+t+1$ will be $1/K$ of the final salary on retirement after $x+t+1$ and half of that on retirement in that year. The total value of his pension is then

$$\frac{S}{K^sD_x} \{\tfrac{1}{2}{}^zC^{ia}_{x+t} + {}^zC^{ia}_{x+t+1} + {}^zC^{ia}_{x+t+2} + \ldots\}$$

$$= \frac{S}{K^sD_x} \{{}^zM^{ia}_{x+t} - \tfrac{1}{2}{}^zC^{ia}_{x+t}\}$$

$$= \frac{S}{K^sD_x} {}^z\overline{M}^{ia}_{x+t}, \tag{10.4.7}$$

where

$${}^z\overline{M}^{ia}_{x+t} = {}^zM^{ia}_{x+t} - \tfrac{1}{2}{}^zC^{ia}_{x+t}. \tag{10.4.8}$$

Summing this expression for all future years of service gives the value of the total future service pension as

$$\frac{S}{K^s D_x} \sum_{t=0}^{64-x} {}^z\overline{M}^{ia}_{x+t}$$

$$= \frac{S}{K^s D_x} {}^z\overline{R}^{ia}_x, \qquad (10.4.9)$$

where
$$\qquad {}^z\overline{R}^{ia}_x = \sum_{t=0}^{64-x} {}^z\overline{M}^{ia}_{x+t}. \qquad (10.4.10)$$

The total value of future service pension for members at present age x nearest birthday is then

$$\frac{1}{K}(AS)_x \frac{{}^z\overline{R}^{ia}_x}{{}^s D_x}. \qquad (10.4.11)$$

For pensions based on age retirement the expression will be similar with the addition of the term ${}^z C^{ra}_{65} = z_{65} v^{65} r_{65} \overline{a}^r_{65}$ in the value of ${}^z M^{ra}_x$. The summation of ${}^z \overline{M}^{ra}_x$ to give ${}^z \overline{R}^{ra}_x$ will be to 64 as in the case of ill-health retirement as no pension accrues after age 65.

It may be helpful to note the steps which are taken in the computation of the commutation functions used in evaluating pensions and to see particularly the difference in the treatment of average and final salary pensions in the previous and this section. In both an 'M' function is found for evaluating past service pensions, in the case of the average salary function the entitlement to pension from past service does not depend on future salaries and no salary scale requires to be introduced, whereas in the final salary scheme the pension entitlement for past service will depend on future salary progression to that a salary scale is required. For future service pensions '$\overline{M}$', relative to the benefit accruing for one year of membership, is found for each year of future service (up to 64) by deducting $\frac{1}{2}C$ and '$\overline{M}$' is summed for all years of future service to give the '$\overline{R}$' function. For average salary pensions the salary scale is introduced into the '$\overline{M}$' function as the benefit no matter when retirement takes place is based on the salary for that year of membership, but for final salary pensions the salary scale is introduced into the 'C' function before summing to give 'M' as the benefit is based on salary at the time of retiral rather than at the time the service is completed.

Example 10.4

A pension fund provides a pension of 1/80th of final salary for each year of service for a member aged 50 who joined the fund at age 40 and has a salary of £3,000. Find the present value of his pension assuming that the tables in the Appendix are appropriate to the fund.

Solution

Using formulae (10.4.4) and (10.4.9) the value will be

$$\frac{10}{80} \cdot \frac{3,000\,(^z M^{ia}_{50} + {}^z M^{ra}_{50})}{{}^s D_{50}} + \frac{3,000}{80} \frac{(^z \bar{R}^{ia}_{50} + {}^z \bar{R}^{ra}_{50})}{{}^s D_{50}}$$

$$= \frac{10}{80} \cdot \frac{3,000(7,197 + 88,345)}{14,693} + \frac{3,000}{80} \frac{(69,159 + 1,148,580)}{14,693}$$

$$= 2,438 + 3,108$$

$$= 5,546, \text{ i.e. £5,546.}$$

As expected, this gives a larger answer than the average salary pension calculated in Example 10.3.

Exercise 10.5

The four members of a scheme whose nearest birthday is 45 have the following salaries and years of past service

A	£5,000	20
B	£2,000	10
C	£4,000	5
D	£3,000	10

Find the total present value of a pension of 1/100th of final salary for each year of service for these members using the tables in the Appendix.

10.5 Contributions

When the pension benefit does not depend on salary, the contributions payable by the members of the fund will normally be a fixed amount each year. It is usual to assume that contributions are payable continuously although strictly they will be payable by deduction from wages or salary each week or each month.

The present value of future contributions of C each year paid by a member aged x from age $x+t$ to $x+t+1$ will be $Cv^{t+\frac{1}{2}} \frac{l_{x+t+\frac{1}{2}}}{l_x}$ assuming on average that they are paid midway through the year, i.e.

$$C \frac{D_{x+t+\frac{1}{2}}}{D_x} \quad \text{or} \quad C \frac{\bar{D}_{x+t}}{D_x},$$

$\bar{D}_x$ in practice being found from

$$\bar{D}_x = \tfrac{1}{2}(D_x + D_{x+1}).$$

Summing over the ages from x to the end of the service table gives the total value of the contributions as

$$C\frac{\bar{N}_x}{D_x}, \quad \text{where} \quad \bar{N}_x = \sum_{t=0}^{64-x} \bar{D}_{x+t}. \tag{10.5.1}$$

The present value of the contributions by all the members' nearest birthday x whose total present contributions are $(AC)_x$ per annum is then

$$(AC)_x\frac{\bar{N}_x}{D_x}.$$

In the more normal case where benefit and contributions depend on salary the salary scale will be introduced to estimate the salary on which contributions are based, so that the contribution in the year from age y to $y+1$ is then

$$C\frac{s_y}{s_x}, \bullet$$

where C is the present contribution. The present value of the contributions paid in this year can then be taken as

$$\frac{1}{D_x}C\frac{s_y}{s_x}\frac{D_y + D_{y+1}}{2}$$

$$= C\frac{{}^s\bar{D}_y}{{}^sD_x} \tag{10.5.2}$$

where

$${}^s\bar{D}_y = s_y\frac{(D_y + D_{y+1})}{2}. \tag{10.5.3}$$

Summing gives the value of all future contributions as

$$C\frac{{}^s\bar{N}_x}{{}^sD_x}, \quad \text{where} \quad {}^s\bar{N}_x = \sum_{t=0}^{64-x} {}^s\bar{D}_{x+t}, \tag{10.5.4}$$

$\dfrac{{}^s\bar{N}_x}{D_x}$ sometimes being written ${}^s\bar{a}_x$.

The value of the future contributions for all members at present nearest birthday x is then

$$(AC)_x\frac{{}^s\bar{N}_x}{{}^sD_x}. \tag{10.5.5}$$

If the contributions of the employer are a proportion of the members' contribution then they will be found by a similar formula—often the employers' contributions are payable at the end of the year so that slightly different formulae may be obtained or an adjustment of the members' formulae such as multiplying by $v^{\frac{1}{2}}$ might be suitable.

Example 10.5

Contributions to a pension fund by an employee are made at a rate of 2% of salary to age 30, 3% from age 30 to 40 and 4% over age 40. Find an expression for the present value of the future contributions by a member aged 25 whose salary is £1,500, and evaluate it using the tables in Appendix III.

Solution

The value will be similar to an increasing annuity, i.e.

$$\frac{1,500}{{}^sD_{25}}(\cdot02\,{}^s\overline{N}_{25}+\cdot01\,{}^s\overline{N}_{30}+\cdot01\,{}^s\overline{N}_{40}).$$

Entering the values from Appendix III gives

$$\frac{1,500}{35,222}(\cdot02(693,135)+\cdot01(540,020)+\cdot01(317,121))$$

$$=955,\text{ i.e. }£955.$$

Example 10.6

Employee contributions to a pension fund are at the rate of 5% of salary with a deduction from salary of £500 to allow for other pension arrangements. Find an expression for the present value of the future contributions by a member age x with salary S.

Solution

The contributions in the year y to $y+1$ will be

$$\frac{1}{D_x}\cdot05\left(S\frac{s_y}{s_x}-500\right)\overline{D}_y$$

(it being important to note that it is the total salary to which the salary scale is applied and not the salary after the fixed deduction)

$$=\cdot05S\frac{s_y}{s_x}\frac{\overline{D}_y}{D_x}-25\frac{\overline{D}_y}{D_x}$$

$$=\cdot05S\frac{{}^s\overline{D}_y}{{}^sD_x}-25\frac{\overline{D}_y}{D_x}$$

and summing over all future years gives the total value of contributions as

$$\cdot05S\,\frac{{}^{s}\overline{N}_x}{{}^{s}D_x} - 25\,\frac{\overline{N}_x}{D_x}.$$

Exercise 10.6

In a special pension fund all members contribute a percentage of salary at a rate such that the present value of the contributions they are expected to make are equal at the time of entry using the tables in Appendix III. If the rate of contribution by a member aged 40 at entry is 5% of salary what is the rate by members entering at age 30 and 50 (all new entrants are assumed to have the same salary).

Exercise 10.7

Contributions to a pension fund by an employee are made at a rate of $2\frac{1}{2}\%$ of salary for those aged under 35, $3\frac{1}{2}\%$ from age 35 to 45, and 5% for those aged over 45. Find an expression for the present value of the future contributions by an employee aged 30 whose salary is £2,000 and evaluate it using the tables in Appendix III.

Exercise 10.8

Employees contribute to a pension scheme at a rate of 6% of salary with a deduction from salary of £300 to allow for other pension arrangements. Find the present value of future contributions by a member age 30 whose salary is £2,500 using the tables in Appendix III.

10.6 Capital sums on retirement and death

Lump or capital sum benefits on retirement may be provided in a fund either as a separate benefit or as a right to commute part of the pension. When the benefit is separate the formulae to be used in valuation will be formulated in exactly the same way as the fund pension benefit except that the annuity value is omitted. Symbols for these benefits would be the same as for pension with the 'a' omitted, e.g. C_x^r instead of C_x^{ra}. Examples of these commutation functions where the benefit does not depend on salary are given in Appendix III.

A capital sum payable on death is likely to be based on the rate of salary at the date of death, and is commonly a fraction such as one or two times that salary although it is possible to have a scale based on

M

a fraction such as 1/20th of salary for each year of membership. The next section will deal with death benefits equal to a return of contributions.

The present value of a benefit equal to the then current salary for a member aged x with present salary S will be

$$\frac{S}{s_x l_x} \sum_{t=0}^{64-x} s_{x+t} v^{t+\frac{1}{2}} d_{x+t}$$

$$= \frac{S}{{}^s D_x} {}^s M_x^d, \tag{10.6.1}$$

where $\qquad\qquad {}^s C_x^d = s_x v^{x+\frac{1}{2}} d_x \tag{10.6.2}$

and $\qquad\qquad {}^s M_x^d = \sum_{t=0}^{64-x} {}^s C_{x+t}^d. \tag{10.6.3}$

The total value of the death benefit for members aged x is then

$$(AS)_x \frac{{}^s M_x^d}{{}^s D_x}. \tag{10.6.4}$$

Examples of these commutation functions are not given in the Appendix.

In some funds the death benefit varies with the marital status of the member. For example the benefit might double if the member is married or treble if he has children; and the proportion of members married at each age (h_x) will then be introduced into the formulae, and similarly the proportion with children might also be used. Strictly the proportion should be the proportion of members dying who are married rather than the proportion of all the members of that age. In using this method (the 'collective' method considered in more detail for widows benefits in section 10.8) it is important to realise that the method can only be applied to the group of members of a certain age and not to an individual member who is known either to be married or not married at age x and whose probability of being married in future years will depend considerably on his present marital status. The value of the benefit which is doubled for married men will then be found by introducing the factor $(1+h_x)$ to the commutation function ${}^s C_x^d$ as follows:

$$ {}^{sm} C_x^d = s_x (1+h_x) v^{x+\frac{1}{2}} d_x \quad \text{or} \quad (1+h_x) {}^s C_x^d, $$

and the other commutation functions will be found by summation as before.

Example 10.7

Develop the formulae for the present value of a cash benefit on age retirement of 1/40th of salary two years before retirement for each year of service for an employee aged x whose salary is S.

Solution

The formula will be found using the methods of section 10.4 as the benefit is based on a salary near to retirement. In this case z_x will be s_{x-2} rather than as used in that section. Using the same method as in section 10.4 (omitting the annuity value) the value of the past service benefit based on past service of n years will be

$$\frac{n}{40} S \frac{^zM_x^r}{^sD_x},$$

where

$$^zM_x^r = \sum_{t=0}^{65-x} {}^zC_{x+t}^r,$$

$$^zC_x^r = z_{x+\frac{1}{2}} v^{x+\frac{1}{2}} r_x \quad \text{for } x \leqq 64,$$

and

$$^zC_{65}^r = v^{65} z_{65} r_{65}.$$

It is appropriate to retain the symbol z_y in the formulae rather than s_{y-2} because as explained at the end of section 10.4 the salary function is introduced differently into the commutation functions for 's' cases (average salary benefits) and 'z' cases (final salary benefits).

For future service the amount of cash benefit will accrue each year—similarly to the pension accrual method leading to formula (10.4.9)—i.e.

$$\frac{S}{40^sD_x} {}^z\bar{R}_x^r,$$

where

$$^z\bar{R}_x^r = \sum_{t=0}^{64-x} ({}^zM_{x+t}^r - \tfrac{1}{2} {}^zC_{x+t}^r).$$

Example 10.8

Using the tables in the Appendix, find the present value of the benefit on ill-health or age retirement of £100 for each year of service for a member aged 40 who joined the scheme at age 30.

Solution

The present value will be found by adding the benefit from past service, £1,000, to that from £100 for each year of future service.

Adapting the pension benefit in formulae (10.2.5) and (10.2.9) to lump sums gives

$$1,000 \frac{M_{40}^i + M_{40}^r}{D_{40}} + 100 \frac{\bar{R}_{40}^i + \bar{R}_{40}^r}{D_{40}}$$

$$= 1,000 \frac{177 + 1,524}{5,204} + 100 \frac{3,111 + 35,191}{5,204}$$

$$= 327 + 736, \ i.e. \ £1,063.$$

Exercise 10.9

Using the tables in the Appendix, find the present value of the benefit on ill-health or age retirement of £200 for each year of service for a member aged 45 who joined the scheme at age 40.

Exercise 10.10

Find the formulae for the value of a benefit on death in service of 1/40th of salary at the date of death for each year of service for a member of a pension fund of age x whose salary is S, and whose past service is n.

Exercise 10.11

Find formulae for a capital sum benefit on age retirement of 1/30th of total salary received throughout service for a member aged x whose salary is S, and who has received a total of (PS) in salary in the past.

Exercise 10.12

Develop formulae for a group of members aged x for a benefit on death in service of 1/20th of the salary received up to the time of death, the benefit being increased by half if the member is married and also by half if the member has a child under age 18.

10.7 Return of contributions

On death or withdrawal from the fund a benefit is often paid equal to the member's contributions either with or without the addition of interest; this may be referred to as a 'return of contributions'. When interest is allowed it will usually be at a lower rate (j) than the valuation rate of interest (i).

The benefit equal to the contributions already paid for a member aged x, with interest at rate j on death between ages $x+t$ and $x+t+1$, will, assuming death on average in the middle of the year, be

$(PC)(1+j)^{t+\frac{1}{2}}$, where (PC) is the past contributions with interest at rate j added to the date of valuation. The present value at age x is

$$(PC)v^{t+\frac{1}{2}}(1+j)^{t+\frac{1}{2}}\frac{d_{x+t}}{l_x}$$

$$= (PC)\frac{(1+j)^{x+t+\frac{1}{2}}v^{x+t+\frac{1}{2}}d_{x+t}}{(1+j)^x v^x l_x}$$

$$= (PC)\frac{{}^jC^d_{x+t}}{{}^jD_x}, \tag{10.7.1}$$

where $\qquad {}^jD_x = \dfrac{l_x}{(1+J)^x} \quad$ or $\quad (1+j)^x D_x, \tag{10.7.2}$

and $\qquad {}^jC^d_x = \dfrac{d_x}{(1+J)^{x+\frac{1}{2}}} \quad$ or $\quad (1+j)^{x+\frac{1}{2}}C^d_x; \tag{10.7.3}$

in effect the functions being calculated at a rate of interest J such that $1+J = \dfrac{1+i}{1+j}$.

So, summing over future years of service gives the present value of the death benefit from contributions already paid as

$$(PC)\frac{{}^jM^d_x}{{}^jD_x}, \tag{10.7.4}$$

where $\qquad {}^jM^d_x = \displaystyle\sum_{t=0}^{64-x} {}^jC^d_{x+t}. \tag{10.7.5}$

The function $\dfrac{{}^jM^d_x}{{}^jD_x}$ is sometimes written ${}^jA^d_x$ although it will be noted that it is not a whole-life function.

In practice the introduction of the rate J may not facilitate the calculation as it may be a rate not available in commutation tables, and with the alternative of electronic calculators or computers it may not be used explicitly.

The total value of death benefit for all the members of the fund aged x nearest birthday will then be

$$(TPC)_x\frac{{}^jM^d_x}{{}^jD_x}. \tag{10.7.6}$$

In determining the value of the death benefit of the return of future contributions the case where the contribution does not vary with salary will first be considered—the contribution is taken as C each year. If the member dies in the year of age $x+t$ to $x+t+1$ on average only one-half of the contribution will have been paid in that year but in subsequent years the whole contribution with the addition of interest at the rate of $j\%$ will be returned, and the number of years for which the interest is assumed to accumulate will be a whole number on average as the contribution will be made on average half-way through the year and the accumulation is on average to the mid-year. The present value at age $x+t$ of the return of the contributions paid in the year of age $x+t$ to $x+t+1$ on subsequent death will then be

$$\frac{C}{l_{x+t}}\left(\tfrac{1}{2}v^{\frac{1}{2}}d_{x+t}+v^{1\frac{1}{2}}(1+j)d_{x+t+1}+v^{2\frac{1}{2}}(1+j)^2 d_{x+t+2}+\cdots\right),$$

and the present value at age x will be found by multiplying by

$$v^t \frac{l_{x+t}}{l_x}, \quad \text{and also by} \quad \frac{(1+j)^{x+t+\frac{1}{2}}v^x}{(1+j)^{x+t+\frac{1}{2}}v^x}=1, \quad \text{giving}$$

$$\frac{C}{(1+j)^{x+t+\frac{1}{2}}v^x l_x}\{\tfrac{1}{2}(1+j)^{x+t+\frac{1}{2}}v^{x+t+\frac{1}{2}}d_{x+t}$$

$$+(1+j)^{x+t+1\frac{1}{2}}v^{x+t+1\frac{1}{2}}d_{x+t+1}+\cdots\}$$

$$=\frac{C}{D_x}\cdot\frac{1}{(1+j)^{x+t+\frac{1}{2}}}\{\tfrac{1}{2}{}^{j}C^d_{x+t}+{}^{j}C^d_{x+t+1}+\cdots+{}^{j}C^d_{64}\}$$

$$=\frac{C}{D_x}\cdot\frac{{}^{j}\overline{M}^d_{x+t}}{(1+j)^{x+t+\frac{1}{2}}}, \tag{10.7.7}$$

where ${}^{j}M^d_x$ is defined in formula (10.7.5)

and

$$\qquad\qquad {}^{j}\overline{M}^d_x = {}^{j}M^d_x - \tfrac{1}{2}{}^{j}C^d_x. \tag{10.7.8}$$

Summing the contributions for each future year gives the total present value of the future return of contributions on death as

$$\frac{C}{D_x}\sum_{t=0}^{64-x}\frac{{}^{j}\overline{M}^d_{x+t}}{(1+j)^{x+t+\frac{1}{2}}}$$

$$=\frac{C}{D_x}{}^{j}\overline{R}^d_x, \tag{10.7.9}$$

where

$$\qquad\qquad {}^{j}\overline{R}^d_x = \sum_{t=0}^{64-x}\frac{{}^{j}\overline{M}^d_{x+t}}{(1+j)^{x+t+\frac{1}{2}}}. \tag{10.7.10}$$

The unusual structure of this function will be noted, being caused by the fact that interest accumulation on future contributions only commences from the date of payment and not from the present age x. It will also be seen that the denominator of (10.7.9) includes D_x without the introduction of the rate j unlike formula (10.7.1) for the value of the return of past contributions, which has denominator ${}^j D_x$.

The formulae for the present value of the benefits on withdrawal will be exactly the same as the above with the symbol 'd' replaced by 'w'—it is possible that the rate of interest allowed may be higher on death. As withdrawals normally are assumed to occur only in the earlier years the summations extend only to the highest age at which withdrawals take place. Examples of the commutation functions ${}^j C_x^d$, ${}^j M_x^d$, ${}^j \bar{R}_x^d$, ${}^j C_x^w$, ${}^j M_x^w$ and ${}^j \bar{R}_x^w$ with j at 3% are given in Appendix III table 5.

When the contribution depends on salary the salary scale will be introduced so that if the contribution is $C\%$ of salary the contribution in the year $x+t$ to $x+t+1$ will now be $\cdot 01CS \frac{s_{x+t}}{s_x}$ and with this replacing C in the reasoning leading to formula (10.7.7) will give the present value of the return on death of the contributions to be made in the year $x+t$ to $x+t+1$ as

$$
\cdot 01CS \frac{s_{x+t}}{s_x} \cdot \frac{1}{D_x} \cdot \frac{{}^j \overline{M}_{x+t}^d}{(1+j)^{x+t+\frac{1}{2}}} \qquad (10.7.11)
$$

$$
= \frac{\cdot 01CS}{{}^s D_x} \frac{{}^{sj} \overline{M}_{x+t}^d}{(1+j)^{x+t+\frac{1}{2}}},
$$

where $\qquad {}^{sj}\overline{M}_x^d = s_x {}^j \overline{M}_x^d.$

Summing over each future year gives the total present value of the future return of contributions on death as

$$
\frac{\cdot 01CS}{{}^s D_x} \sum_{t=0}^{64-x} \frac{{}^{sj}\overline{M}_{x+t}^d}{(1+j)^{x+t+\frac{1}{2}}}
$$

$$
= \frac{\cdot 01CS}{{}^s D_x} {}^{sj}\overline{R}_x^d, \qquad (10.7.12)
$$

where $\qquad {}^{sj}\overline{R}_x^d = \sum_{t=0}^{64-x} \frac{s_{x+t}}{(1+j)^{x+t+\frac{1}{2}}} {}^j \overline{M}_{x+t}^d. \qquad (10.7.13)$

Again the functions for returns on withdrawal will be the same with the replacement of 'd' by 'w'. Examples of the functions $^{sj}\bar{R}_x^d$ and $^{sj}\bar{R}_x^w$ are given in Appendix III table 5.

When the rate of interest used to calculate the return on death or withdrawal is either nil or the same as the valuation rate of interest, simplification of the formulae is possible, and this is demonstrated in the examples and exercises which follow.

Example 10.9

Using the tables in Appendix III, find the present value of the return of contributions on death and withdrawal for a member of a pension scheme aged 40 whose present salary is £4,000. The rate of contribution is 2% of salary and past contributions accumulated at 3%, the rate of interest added to contributions returned on death and withdrawal, amount to £500.

Solution

Using formula (10.7.6), the present value of the return of past contributions on death and withdrawal will be

$$\frac{500}{{}^jD_{40}} ({}^jM_{40}^d + {}^jM_{40}^w)$$

and with ${}^jD_{40} = (1\cdot03)^{40}D_{40}$, this

$$= \frac{500}{(3\cdot262)(5,204)} (2,338 + 735)$$

$$= 91.$$

Using formula (10.7.12), the present value of the return of future contributions will be

$$\frac{\cdot02(4,000)}{{}^sD_{40}} ({}^{sj}\bar{R}_{40}^d + {}^{sj}\bar{R}_{40}^w)$$

$$= \frac{80}{18,629} (36,298 + 1,424)$$

$$= 162,$$

so that the total present value of the return of contributions is

$$91 + 162, \text{ i.e. } £253.$$

Example 10.10

Obtain formulae for the present values of the return of contributions on death if the rate of interest used to determine the present value is the same as the rate of interest (j) allowed on the return of contributions. Contributions are a percentage of salary.

Solution

If $i = j$ in formulae (10.7.2) and (10.7.3)

$$^jD_x = l_x, \quad ^jC_x^d = d_x,$$

so that the value of the return of past contributions (10.7.6) becomes

$$\frac{(TPC)_x}{l_x} \sum_{t=0}^{64-x} d_{x+t}.$$

Considering future contributions formula (10.7.11) for the present value of the return on death of the contributions to be made in the year $x+t$ to $x+t+1$ will become

$$\frac{\cdot 01CSs_{x+t}}{s_x} \cdot \frac{1}{D_x} \cdot \frac{\left(\frac{1}{2}d_{x+t} + \sum\limits_{r=1}^{64-x} d_{x+t+r} \right)}{(1+j)^{x+t+\frac{1}{2}}},$$

$$= \frac{\cdot 01CSs_{x+t}}{s_x} \frac{v^{t+\frac{1}{2}}}{l_x} \left(\frac{1}{2}d_{x+t} + \sum_{r=1}^{64-x} d_{x+t+r} \right)$$

and this is then summed for $t = 0$ to $64 - x$, as in (10.7.12), to give the total value of the return of future contributions. The main simplification in the formulae is thus with past contributions.

Exercise 10.13

Using the tables in Appendix III, find the present value of the return of contributions of £1 per week on death with interest at 3% for a member aged 35 who joined at age 30.

Exercise 10.14

Using the tables in Appendix III, find the present value of the return of contributions of 4% salary with interest at 3% for the following:

(a) On death for a member aged 50 where present salary is £3,000 and past contributions accumulated with interest are £800.

(b) On withdrawal for a member aged 30 whose present salary is £2,000 and past contributions accumulated with interest are £500.

Exercise 10.15

The contributions to a pension fund by members are at a rate of 5% of salary less £250. Obtain formulae for the present value of the return of past and future contributions on subsequent death of the member if interest at a rate of $2\frac{1}{2}$% per annum compound is added on death.

Exercise 10.16

Obtain formulae for the present value of the return of contributions (which are made as a percentage of salary) to a member on withdrawal if no interest is added.

10.8 Widows' pensions: collective method

Widows' pensions may be valued using two different methods referred to as the collective method and the reversionary method. In the collective method the proportion of members married is introduced into the formulae in a similar way to the death benefit depending on marital status described in section 10.6. In the reversionary method, separate functions are prepared for application separately to the members at present married and not married.

The widow's pension benefit may be a fixed amount or it may depend on either or both of salary and service, and service may be that already completed or total service assuming the employee survived in employment to normal retirement date.

In the simplest case when a fixed benefit is provided the value of a pension of 1 per annum on the death in service of a member aged x will be

$$\frac{1}{D_x} \sum_{t=0}^{64-x} v^{x+t+\frac{1}{2}} d_{x+t} h_{x+t+\frac{1}{2}} \bar{a}''_{y+t+\frac{1}{2}}, \qquad (10.8.1)$$

where $\bar{a}''_{y+t+\frac{1}{2}}$ is the weighted average annuity value payable in accordance with the rules of the fund (it may for example cease on remarriage) to the wife of a man dying at age $x+t$ last birthday and $h_{x+t+\frac{1}{2}}$ is the proportion married at age $x+t+\frac{1}{2}$—strictly it should be the proportion married among those dying at that age, which could differ.

It will be seen that the formula does not depend on whether the member is married at age x and is applied to the group of all members of that age whether married or not. It is likely that the chance of being married in future depends on the marital status now so that it is not appropriate to apply this method to individuals but only to the group of members of whom it may be expected that proportions will be married and unmarried. It is for this reason that this method of valuing widow's pensions is called the collective method—members must not be treated individually but as a collective group.

If
$$C_x^{dwa} = v^{x+\frac{1}{2}} d_x h_{x+\frac{1}{2}} \bar{a}''_{y+\frac{1}{2}}$$

and
$$M_x^{dwa} = \sum_{t=0}^{64-x} C_{x+t}^{dwa}$$

the value of the pension of 1 per annum will be written

$$\frac{M_x^{dwa}}{D_x}. \tag{10.8.2}$$

If the pension depends on salary it would normally be based on a fraction such as $\frac{1}{5}$, $\frac{1}{4}$ or $\frac{1}{3}$ (in general P) of the salary at the time of death. If the current salary of a member aged x is S and the salary scale is introduced the present value of the pension will be

$$\frac{PS}{s_x D_x} \sum_{t=0}^{64-x} s_{x+t} C_{x+t}^{dwa}$$

$$= \frac{PS}{{}^s D_x} {}^s M_x^{dwa}, \tag{10.8.3}$$

where
$${}^s C_x^{dwa} = s_x C_x^{dwa}$$

and
$${}^s M_x^{dwa} = \sum_{t=0}^{64-x} {}^s C_{x+t}^{dwa}.$$

It will be seen that formulae for widows' pensions based on service can be obtained in a similar fashion to death benefits in section 10.6 example 10.7 but with the inclusion of proportions married and the annuity value to the widow in the benefit.

Widowers' pensions and orphans' benefits will be valued in a similar fashion to widows' pensions and an example of the latter is given below.

Example 10.11

Obtain an expression for the value of a widow's pension of 1 per annum on death after either ill-health or age retirement if the marriage took place before retirement.

Solution

In this case the relevant proportion married will be at the time of retirement when the benefit will be a reversionary annuity to the wife following the death of the member. The value of the benefit will therefore be

$$\frac{1}{D_x}\left\{ \sum_{t=0}^{64-x} v^{x+t+\frac{1}{2}}(i_{x+t}+r_{x+t})h_{x+t+\frac{1}{2}}\bar{a}''_{x+t+\frac{1}{2}|y+t+\frac{1}{2}} \right.$$
$$\left. +v^{65}r_{65}h_{65}\bar{a}''_{65|y+65-x}\right\}$$

and the reversionary annuities are average values, $y+t$ perhaps depending on $x+t$.

Example 10.12

An orphan's pension of £200 per annum is payable for the benefit of each child under age 18 until that age on the death of a member of a pension fund. Derive an expression to be used in valuing this benefit.

Solution

The value of the 'average' benefit on death will be found by using the collective method by introducing the proportions of men dying who have children, and the number and average age of these children. The 'annuity' value on death at age x last birthday will then take the following form:

$$(Oa)_x = 200(\tfrac{1}{2}c_x\bar{a}_{\overline{17\frac{1}{2}}|} + 1\tfrac{1}{2}c_x\bar{a}_{\overline{16\frac{1}{2}}|} + \cdots {}_{17\frac{1}{2}}c_x\bar{a}_{\overline{\frac{1}{2}}|})$$

where ${}_{t+\frac{1}{2}}c_x$ is the proportion of married men aged x (including widowers) who have a child aged t last birthday. This also assumes that child mortality can be ignored; if this is not so the annuity values may be adjusted.

This value is then introduced into the normal type of benefit formula

$$\frac{1}{D_x}\sum_{t=0}^{64-x} v^{x+t+\frac{1}{2}}d_{x+t}(h_{x+t+\frac{1}{2}}+w_{x+t+\frac{1}{2}})(Oa)_{x+t+\frac{1}{2}},$$

where $w_{x+t+\frac{1}{2}}$ is the proportion of widowers at age $x+t+\frac{1}{2}$.

Example 10.13

On the basis of the rates of death, withdrawal and retirement in in Appendix III table 5, and assuming 4% per annum interest, calculate the present value of pensions of £1,000 per annum to the widows of 20 lives aged 60, if the pensions are payable in the event of death while in active service. Table 10.1a gives the proportions married and the value of a widow's annuity at each age.

TABLE 10.1a

Age of husband	Proportion married	Average value of widow's annuity if death occurs during year of age
60 to 61	·80	14·0
61 to 62	·79	13·5
62 to 63	·78	13·0
63 to 64	·77	12·5
64 to 65	·76	12·0

Solution

The value of the pension will be

$$20\,\frac{1,000}{D_{60}}\sum_{x=60}^{64}C_x^d h_{x+\frac{1}{2}}\bar{a}''_{y+\frac{1}{2}},$$

where $h_{x+\frac{1}{2}}$ and $\bar{a}''_{y+\frac{1}{2}}$ are given in the table in the question; and as C_x^d is not given in the tables it will required to be calculated from $v^{x+\frac{1}{2}}d_x$, and to simplify calculation the value is

$$20\,\frac{1,000v^{\frac{1}{2}}}{l_{60}}\sum_{x=60}^{64}v^{x-60}d_x h_{x+\frac{1}{2}}\bar{a}''_{y+\frac{1}{2}}.$$

TABLE 10.1b

Age x	v^{x-60}	d_x	$h_{x+\frac{1}{2}}$	$\bar{a}''_{y+\frac{1}{2}}$	Product
60	1·000	297	·80	14·0	3,326
61	·962	253	·79	13·5	2,596
62	·925	228	·78	13·0	2,139
63	·889	216	·77	12·5	1,848
64	·855	203	·76	12·0	1,583
					11,492

The calculations are set out in tabular form in Table 10.1b. Hence the value of the pensions is

$$20 \frac{(1,000)(\cdot 981)}{20,306} (11,492)$$

$$= 11,104, \text{ i.e. say } £11,100.$$

Exercise 10.17

Find formulae to value a widow's pension benefit of 1/80th of salary at the date of death for each completed year of service.

Exercise 10.18

An orphan's benefit of £500 per annum is paid on the death prior to retirement of widowed members of a pension fund for each child with a maximum of three. Devise an expression for valuing the benefit if it is payable for children under age 16 till that age.

Exercise 10.19

Using the same basis as in example 10.13 and with the salary scale in table 5, find the value of the widows' pensions of one-quarter of the average of the salary received in the three years before death if the members have total salaries of £70,000.

10.9 Widows' pensions: reversionary method

The alternative method of valuing widows' pensions referred to in the first paragraph of section 10.8—the reversionary method—treats separately the present members who are married from those who are not. The main part of the liability will arise for members who are married at present, and the valuation factors relative to these members are determined first and those for present unmarried men are built up in chain fashion.

The value of a widow's benefit of 1 per annum for a married man at present age x whose wife is aged y will be

$$_m B_{xy} = \sum_{t=0}^{64-x} \frac{d_{x+t}}{l_x} \frac{D_{y+t+\frac{1}{2}}}{D_y} \bar{a}'_{y+t+\frac{1}{2}}, \qquad (10.9.1)$$

where the functions involving the symbol y will be based on wife's mortality (or widow's for the annuity value if this is considered to be different).

Normally this formula will not be applied individually to each member but it is not uncommon to group wife's ages in perhaps five-year intervals rather than use one factor for each age of member by assuming an average value for the annuity value, as this would lose some of the 'exactness' of the reversionary method compared to the collective method.

The formulae for the benefit for the present bachelors will require the introduction of a double decrement table involving death and marriage, or possibly a triple decrement table with withdrawal added. If $(bl)_x$ is the number of unmarried men and $(bh)_x$ is the number marrying at age x last birthday, the value of the widow's pension to an unmarried member aged x will be

$$\sum_{t=0}^{64-x} \frac{v^{x+t+\frac{1}{2}}(bh)_{x+t}}{v^x(bl)_x} \, _mB_{[x+t+\frac{1}{2}]:y+t+\frac{1}{2}}, \qquad (10.9.2)$$

where the select brackets imply the value for a newly married member—in this case an average estimated value of y will have to be used.

A similar formula might be used for present widowers or they might be included with bachelors.

Further formulae for the benefit for future wives of men at present married whose present wives die first could also be obtained in a chain fashion.

In practice the reversionary method is not often used.

Example 10.14

If 16 of the members in Example 10.13 are married, use the reversionary method to find the present value of the pensions to the present married members, using the same annuity values for the widow's annuity. Wives are assumed to be the same age as their husbands and experience mortality on the $a(55)$ ultimate females table.

Solution

Using formula (10.9.1), the value of the benefit will be

$$\frac{16(1,000)}{l_{60}D_{60}^f} \sum_{t=0}^{4} d_{60+t}D_{60+t+\frac{1}{2}}^f \bar{a}''_{60+t+\frac{1}{2}},$$

where D_x^f is on $a(55)$ ultimate. The calculation is set out in tabular form in Table 10.2.

Hence the value of the pensions is

$$\frac{16(1,000)}{(20,306)(85,269)} (1,201 \times 10^6)$$

$$= 11,098, \text{ i.e. say } £11,100.$$

It will be seen that the answer is the same as that found in Example 10.13. It is to be expected that the answers will be similar, particularly when there is a short period such as five years for the risk to be operative so that the result of ignoring in the reversionary method benefits for men at present unmarried will not be significant. However, if the number of those married had been different at age 60, say 14 rather than 16, this would have made no difference to the answer to Example 10.13 (except to the extent that it might be considered that the h_x table should be altered). The answer to this question on the other hand would be altered considerably being multiplied by 14/16.

TABLE 10.2

Age x	d_{60+t}	$D^f_{60+t+\frac{1}{2}}$	$\ddot{a}''_{60+t+\frac{1}{2}}$	Product $\times 10^{-6}$
60	297	83,279	14·0	346
61	253	79,359	13·5	271
62	228	75,555	13·0	224
63	216	71,862	12·5	194
64	203	68,273	12·0	166
				1,201

Exercise 10.20

Find a formula for the benefit for the widow's annuity to future wives of men at present married whose present wives die first.

10.10 Alternative salary and benefit assumptions

So far in this chapter it has been assumed that it was appropriate to base the projections of salary implicit in a salary scale on the expected salary to be received in the year following the valuation date, $(AS)_x$ being defined in this way. This is particularly appropriate when the valuation date coincides with the date on which the employer grants salary increases. In other cases, particularly when salaries are assumed to be increased at varying dates throughout the year (sometimes referred to as salary increases taking place continuously), it may be better to base the salary assumption on the total rate of salaries being received at the valuation date, in which case the total salaries might be given by symbol $(A\bar{S})_x$.

When salary increases are spread throughout the year it is possible to think of s_x as a continuous function, s_{x+t}/s_x continuing to be defined as before as the ratio of salaries expected in the year of age $x+t$ to $x+t+1$ compared with the year x to $x+1$. While an individual's salary will increase by a discrete amount, for a group it is reasonable to think of s_x as continuous. If it increases evenly over the year, then s_x will represent the actual rate of salary at age $x+\frac{1}{2}$, so that the rate of salary at x can be based on $x-\frac{1}{2}$. The functions previously found would then include $\dfrac{(A\bar{S})_x}{s_{x-\frac{1}{2}}}$ rather than $\dfrac{(AS)_x}{s_x}$ so that the formulae might be multiplied by $\dfrac{s_x}{s_{x-\frac{1}{2}}}$ before multiplying by the total present salary. A similar adjustment will be made for any pensions based on past service.

A further alternative would be to base the projection on the salary received in the previous year, in this case the total salaries might be given the symbol $(AS)'_x$ and the functions would include $\dfrac{(AS)'_x}{s_{x-1}}$ so that the previous formulae would be multiplied by $\dfrac{s_x}{s_{x-1}}$ before multiplying by the total present salary.

Although in most of the work in this chapter in order to demonstrate the method of building up the commutation functions only one definition of final salary has been used (average salary over the last three years of membership; $z_x = \frac{1}{3}(s_{x-3}+s_{x-2}+s_{x-1})$) it was mentioned in section 10.4 that there are numerous different possibilities. Example 10.7 has shown that the use of a different benefit rule has no effect on the formula except on the way in which z_x is defined. If, for example, final salary was to be defined as the actual rate of salary at retirement, s_x might be used rather than $z_{x+\frac{1}{2}}$ for those aged x last birthday on retirement.

In some schemes the pension is not based on total service including fractions of a year as has been assumed so far in this chapter but only complete years of service are counted, and an example is given below.

Example 10.15

A pension scheme has a pension benefit of 1% of final salary for each year of service, final salary being defined as the salary at the previous annual valuation date of the scheme of 1st January. Obtain expressions to find the present value of this pension, assuming that salary increases are spread during the year.

Solution

The formulae for past and future service pensions will be built up in the same way as in section 10.4, but the definition of the salary on which the pension is based ($z_{x+\frac{1}{2}}$ in the previous formulae) will, assuming retirement half-way through the scheme year, be $s_{x-\frac{1}{2}}$, being the rate of salary at age x, 6 months before retirement at age $x+\frac{1}{2}$. It seems likely that the information available will be the annual rates of salary rather than the expected salary in the year following the valuation date. This implies being given $(A\bar{S})_x$, and the formulae found otherwise would then be multiplied by $\dfrac{(A\bar{S})_x}{s_{x-\frac{1}{2}}}$. Similarly the past service information is likely to be $(n\bar{S})_x$ using the rate of salary at age x in the product rather than the total salary expected in the following year.

The past service pension will then be found by using $\dfrac{(n\bar{S})_x}{s_{x-\frac{1}{2}}}$ in the functions rather than $\dfrac{(nS)_x}{s_x}$.

As different functions from those previously given in this chapter will be required, it might be desirable to base them on different initial definitions, but the simplest approach is probably to think of the previous functions being adapted, so that the past service ill-health pension is valued as in (10.4.6) as

$$\cdot 01(n\bar{S})_x \, \frac{s_x}{s_{x-\frac{1}{2}}} \cdot \frac{{}^z M_x^{ia}}{{}^s D_x},$$

where $z_{x+\frac{1}{2}}$ is defined as $s_{x-\frac{1}{2}}$ so that

$$^z M_x^{ia} = \sum_{t=0}^{64-x} {}^z C_{x+t}^{ia}$$

and
$$^z C_{x+\frac{1}{2}}^{ia} = s_x C_{x+t}^{ia}.$$

For future service ill-health pension the value will be

$$\cdot 01(A\bar{S})_x \, \frac{s_x}{s_{x-\frac{1}{2}}} \cdot \frac{{}^z \bar{R}_x^{ia}}{{}^s D_x},$$

where
$$^z \bar{R}_x^{ia} = \sum_{t=0}^{64-x} {}^z \bar{M}_{x+t}^{ia},$$

and
$$^z \bar{M}_{x+t}^{ia} = {}^z M_{x+t}^{ia} - \tfrac{1}{2} {}^z C_{x+t}^{ia}$$

exactly as in section 10.4.

(margin annotation: /c)

(handwritten margin note top right: inconsistent with earlier assumps)

The age retirement formulae will be identical with r instead of i in the functions, except that attention should be given to the definition of ${}^z D^{ra}_{65}$. As on average the 1st January will be six months before retiral at exact age 65, the salary on which the pension for retiral at exact age 65 would be based would be the rate of salary six months earlier at $64\frac{1}{2}$ which will be s_{64}, thus ${}^z C^{ra}_{65} = s_{64} C^{ra}_{65}$—this will then be included in the definition of ${}^z M^{ra}_x$.

(handwritten margin note: $\hookrightarrow s_{63\frac{1}{2}}$)

Example 10.16

Obtain formulae for pensions of P for each year of service when only complete years of service count for pension.

Solution

The value of pension in respect to past salaries on ill-health retiral can be found in exactly the same way as previously, i.e. using formula (10.2.5)

$$\frac{nP}{D_x} M^{ia}_x,$$

where n is the number of years' past service including fractions. Unless there is evidence to the contrary it can be assumed that entries to the service were uniformly over the year so that on average past service for each member aged x from date of entry will be an integer plus $\frac{1}{2}$. As will be reasonable in a continuing fund, the formula overstates the strict past service pension liability in the sense that on immediate retiral at the valuation date only an integral number of years' pension would be allowed. Keeping this in mind, it will be seen that on retiral within the year x to $x+1$ a further pension of P will accrue at age $x+\frac{1}{2}$, but that on retiral before then from x to $x+\frac{1}{2}$ too much pension will have been assumed in the past service calculation. On average then no pension will accrue on retirement in the first year after the valuation date and in general no pension will accrue in the year of retirement. Considering the reasoning leading up to formula (10.2.7) therefore the value of the pension will be such that the first terms will be omitted thus giving the value of the future service pension as

$$\frac{P}{D_x} (C^{ia}_{y+1} + \ldots + C^{ia}_{64}) = \frac{P}{D_x} M^{ia}_{y+1}.$$

It will be necessary to introduce new symbols to signify the summation of the M as previously only $\bar{R}$ being the summation of $\bar{M}$ has been used. If

$$R^{ia}_x = \sum_{t=0}^{64} M^{ia}_{x+t},$$

then the value of the future ill-health pension will be

$$P \cdot \frac{R^{ia}_{x+1}}{D_x}.$$

Similarly, values for the age retirement pensions will be found giving the total pension for a member aged x as

$$\frac{nP}{D_x}(M^{ia}_x + M^{ra}_x) + \frac{P}{D_x}(R^{ia}_{x+1} + R^{ra}_{x+1}).$$

I think 65

It will also be possible to express the future service in terms of an R function as

$$R^{ia}_{x+1} = \bar{R}^{ia}_{x+1} + \tfrac{1}{2}C^{ia}_{x+1}$$

but because the summation of R extends to 64 rather than 65 in the case of age retirement

$$R^{ra}_{x+1} = \bar{R}^{ra}_{x+1} + \tfrac{1}{2}(M^{ra}_{x+1} - C^{ra}_{65}).$$

Exercise 10.21

Obtain formulae for the pensions of P for each complete year of service as in Example 10.16 basing the past service on complete years.

Exercise 10.22

Obtain formulae for pensions based on $1/K$th of final salary for each year of service when only complete years of service are to count. Final salary is defined as the salary earned in the year preceding retirement.

Exercise 10.23

Outline how the formulae previously found in this chapter should be adapted to the case where the pensions are based on the average of the salaries on the last two valuation dates of the scheme before retiral and the information provided is based on the salaries paid in the year before the valuation date, salary increases being granted on the valuation date.

10.11 Individual member approach

Commutation functions were introduced partly in order to make calculations manageable. With the advent of electronic computers and powerful small hand-calculators the burden of calculation has altered considerably from the days of logarithms. Earlier, to carry out valuations on the basis of individual members would have been a huge task and out of proportion to the accuracy obtained by not grouping similar members together, perhaps in age groups, but with the complication of the types of benefits now required in schemes, for example to contract-out of State schemes, it is becoming increasingly difficult not to give consideration to the individual member.

The approach will be essentially similar to that described earlier in this chapter except that consideration is required of the benefits and their value for the individual member in the light of his own circumstances. In many cases it will be appropriate to value benefits without introducing commutation functions as such by tabulating the value of the benefit—essentially the formula is the same as when commutation functions are used but the tabulation of the function involves the division of the denominator D_x or ^sD_x into the numerator. In some cases the functions will not be tabulated but will be held in the memory store of an electronic computer and are available to be applied when required.

The use of such methods may also simplify such problems as maximum and minimum benefit levels as separate functions can be held and used when a suitable test indicates that a limitation applies. The extra power of computers may also be useful perhaps in introducing separate salary scales for different groups of members of a scheme, or in using averages less often—for example the value of the weighted average annuity value $a''_{y+t+\frac{1}{2}}$ in formula (10.8.1) may in more simple cases be tabulated simply by assuming an average age difference between husband and wife whereas it is more desirable to calculate it from a formula of the type

$$\sum b_{(x-z)} p_{(x+t,\, z+t)} a''_{z+t+\frac{1}{2}},$$

where $p_{(x+t,\, z+t)}$ is the proportion of married men aged $x+t$ nearest birthday whose wives are aged $z+t$ nearest birthday, and the summation is over all appropriate ages. This also allows for the introduction of smaller benefits if the age difference is large, for example if the wife is more than ten years younger, and $b_{(x-z)}$ will then be less than 1 for some age differences.

Example 10.17

The contributions to a pension scheme are a percentage (p) of salary with a maximum salary to count of M. Outline a method of introducing the maximum in the valuation of the benefits.

Solution

When the facilities are available the value of each member's future contributions can be found, the calculation of each future year's contribution ensuring that the contribution is not assumed to be greater than the appropriate amount. Thus the formula will be of the form

$$p \sum_{t=0}^{64-x} \frac{\bar{D}_{x+t}}{D_x} \left(S \frac{s_{x+t}}{s_x} \right)$$

with the expression in the brackets replaced by M if this is smaller.

Exercise 10.24

The widow's pension in a pension arrangement is $\frac{1}{4}$ of salary at the time of death with a minimum of M_1, and a maximum of M_2. Outline a method of valuing the benefit.

EXAMPLES AND EXERCISES ON CHAPTER 10

It is most important to remember that there is unfortunately at present no International Notation in Pension Fund work. Thus although a certain notation is used in this book in an examination the student will have to define any function he uses—the same is also true in the practical work of valuing pension funds. Because of the lack of a standard notation it is also necessary in an examination to derive from first principles any formulae which are used, although this is not done in the examples which follow except in Example 10.23. Unless otherwise stated, salaries are assumed to be reviewed at the valuation date.

Example 10.18

On the basis of the rates of death, retirement and withdrawal and the salary scale in Appendix III with 4% interest value the age retirement pension benefit for a group of employees aged 55 with total salaries £20,000, the pension being $1\frac{1}{2}\%$ of average annual salary throughout service for each year of service except for retirement at age 64 last birthday when the proportion is increased to 1·6%, and on retirement at exact age 65 the percentage becomes 1·7%. Total salaries received to date are £100,000.

Solution

The valuation factor for past service pensions will be

$$\frac{100,000}{D_{55}(100)} \{1 \cdot 5 M_{55}^{ra} + \cdot 1 C_{64}^{ra} + \cdot 2 C_{65}^{ra}\}$$

$$= \frac{1,000}{2,535} (1 \cdot 5(16,742) + (\cdot 1)(814) + (\cdot 2)(6,675))$$

$$= 10,465.$$

For future service the $\overline{M}$ commutation columns will need to include not only the salary scale but also be of the extended form as above i.e. the pension in respect of the salary received in the year y to $y+1$ will be

$$\frac{20,000}{D_{55}(100)} \cdot \frac{s_y}{s_{55}} (1 \cdot 5\overline{M}_y^{ra} + \cdot 1C_{64}^{ra} + \cdot 2C_{65}^{ra})$$

and summing from 55 to 64 gives the total pension as

$$= \frac{200}{{}^sD_{55}} \sum_{y=55}^{64} \{1 \cdot 5{}^s\overline{M}_y^{ra} + s_y(\cdot 1C_{64}^{ra} + \cdot 2C_{65}^{ra})\}$$

$$= \frac{200}{{}^sD_{55}} \left\{ 1 \cdot 5{}^s\overline{R}_{55}^{ra} + \left(\sum_{y=55}^{64} s_y \right)\left(\cdot 1C_{64}^{a} + \cdot 2C_{65}^{ra} \right)\right\}$$

$$= \frac{200}{12,549} (1 \cdot 5(688,322) + (51 \cdot 98)(\cdot 1(814) + \cdot 2(6,675)))$$

$$= 17,629.$$

So the total value of the pensions is $10,465 + 17,629 = 28,094$, say £28,100.

Example 10.19

A pension fund has the following features:

(i) The pension is based on 1/80th of the average of salary over the final three years' service for each year of service.

(ii) Members contribute 5% of salary each month.

(iii) The death and withdrawal benefit is a refund of members' contributions with interest at 3%.

Using the tables in Appendix III, find the contribution by the employer paid as a percentage of salary annually at the beginning of the year, if 4% interest is assumed, for a new entrant at age 30 whose salary is £2,000.

Solution

The value of the pension benefit using formula (10.4.9)

$$= \frac{2,000}{80^sD_{30}} ({}^z\overline{R}_{30}^{ia} + {}^z\overline{R}_{30}^{ra})$$

$$= \frac{25}{28,043} (231,941 + 2,915,486)$$

$$= 2,806.$$

The value of the employee's contributions which commence at 100 using formula (10.5.4)

$$= 100 \, \frac{{}^{s}\overline{N}_{30}}{{}^{s}D_{30}}$$

$$= 100 \, \frac{540{,}020}{28{,}043}$$

$$= 1{,}926.$$

The value of the return of contributions on death and withdrawal using formula (10.7.12)

$$= \frac{100}{{}^{s}D_{30}} \, ({}^{sj}\overline{R}_{30}^{d} + {}^{sj}\overline{R}_{30}^{w})$$

$$= \frac{100}{28{,}043} \, (63{,}288 + 38{,}289)$$

$$= 362.$$

Then if the initial employer's contribution is C and it is assumed that the value of this contribution can be found from the value of the employee's contribution by proportion and by multiplying by 1·02 as on average it is paid half a year earlier it will be

$$\frac{C}{100} (1 \cdot 02)(1926) = 19 \cdot 65C.$$

Then equating the values of contributions and benefits

$$\begin{pmatrix} \text{Value of} \\ \text{employer's} \\ \text{contributions} \end{pmatrix} + \begin{pmatrix} \text{Value of} \\ \text{employee's} \\ \text{contributions} \end{pmatrix} = \begin{pmatrix} \text{Value of} \\ \text{Pension} \\ \text{Benefits} \end{pmatrix} + \begin{pmatrix} \text{Value of return} \\ \text{of contributions} \\ \text{on death} \\ \text{or withdrawal} \end{pmatrix}$$

i.e. $\quad 19 \cdot 65C \quad + \quad 1{,}926 \quad = \quad 2{,}806 \quad + \quad 362$

$$\therefore C = \frac{1{,}242}{19 \cdot 65} = 63 \cdot 21,$$

that is the contribution as a percentage of salary is $\dfrac{63 \cdot 21}{2{,}000} = 3 \cdot 2\%$.

Example 10.20

The scheme in Example 10.19 is to be altered so that an additional lump sum benefit of £100 is to be provided on retirement for each year of service. The employee's contribution is to be unchanged except that it will not exceed £200 in any year. On death a benefit will be provided in another scheme and no return of contributions will be made. Determine the altered employer's contribution which will be based on the full salary for the same employee.

Solution

The value of the additional lump sum benefit will be

$$\frac{100}{D_{30}} (\bar{R}^i_{30} + \bar{R}^r_{30})$$

$$= \frac{100}{10,997} (4,952 + 50,430)$$

$$= 504.$$

Assuming that the salary of the member increases in accordance with the salary scale, the initial contribution of 100 will become 200 at age y, where

$$\frac{s_y}{s_{30}} 100 \text{ first exceeds } 200$$

i.e. $$s_y = 2(2 \cdot 55) = 5.10$$

That is, y is 58.

The value of the contribution will thus be

$$100 \frac{{}^s\bar{N}_{30} - {}^s\bar{N}_{58}}{{}^sD_{30}} + 200 \frac{N_{58}}{D_{30}}$$

$$= 100 \frac{540,020 - 51,001}{28,043} + 200 \frac{9,722}{10,997}$$

$$= 1,921.$$

The value of the return of contributions on withdrawal will not alter as the change in contribution is made at a higher age than withdrawals occur. As there is now no death return, the separate withdrawal benefit must be found, as the combined death and withdrawal benefit was previously found, as follows:

$$\frac{100^{sj}\bar{R}^w_{30}}{{}^sD_{30}} = \frac{100(38,289)}{28,043} = 137.$$

If the employee's contributions are altered to C', then equating the value of the contributions to the value of the benefits:

$$\left(\begin{array}{c}\text{Value of}\\\text{employer's}\\\text{contributions}\end{array}\right) + \left(\begin{array}{c}\text{Value of}\\\text{employee's}\\\text{contributions}\end{array}\right) = \left(\begin{array}{c}\text{Value of}\\\text{Pension}\\\text{Benefit}\end{array}\right) + \left(\begin{array}{c}\text{Value of return}\\\text{of contributions}\\\text{on withdrawal}\end{array}\right) + \left(\begin{array}{c}\text{Value of}\\\text{lump sum}\\\text{benefit}\end{array}\right)$$

i.e. $19 \cdot 65C'$ $+$ $1,921$ $=$ $2,806$ $+$ 137 $+$ 504

$$\therefore C' = \frac{1,526}{19\cdot65} = 77\cdot7$$

that is, the contribution as a percentage of salary is $\dfrac{77\cdot7}{2,000} = 3\cdot9\%$.

Example 10.21

A pension fund provides for members withdrawing with at least five years' service a pension from the normal retirement date, the 65th birthday, based on 1 % of the salary at the time of leaving for each year of service.

Obtain formulae of the present value of this benefit.

Solution

If n is the number of years' past service for a member aged x whose salary is S, then if $n \geqq 5$ the value of the withdrawal benefits will be

$$\frac{(\cdot01)nS}{{}_sD_x} \sum_{t=0}^{64-x} v^{x+t+\frac{1}{2}} s_{x+t} w_{x+t} \, {}_{65-(x+t+\frac{1}{2})|}\bar{a}'_{x+t+\frac{1}{2}},$$

the annuity value being the value of a deferred pension of 1 per annum on withdrawal at age $x+t+\frac{1}{2}$. This might be given the symbol

$$\frac{(\cdot01)nS}{{}^sD_x} \sum_{t=0}^{64-x} {}^zC^{wa}_{x+t}$$

or
$$\frac{(\cdot01)nS}{{}^sD_x} {}^zM^{wa}_x,$$

z being used in the symbol rather than s because the benefit is based on salary at date of leaving rather than on average salary during the service. When $n < 5$, it would be necessary to commence the summation after five years' membership, and the value of the benefit from past service will be

$$\frac{(\cdot01)nS}{{}^sD_x} {}^zM^{wa}_{x+5-n}.$$

Considering future service if $n \geqq 5$, then the pension accruing in respect of service for the year from age $x+t$ to $x+t+1$ will (compare formula 10.4.7) be

$$\frac{(\cdot01)S}{{}^sD_x} \{\tfrac{1}{2}{}^zC^{wa}_{x+t} + {}^zC^{wa}_{x+t+1} + \ldots\}$$

i.e.
$$= \frac{(\cdot01)S}{{}^sD_x} {}^z\overline{M}^{wa}_{x+t},$$

and summing this for future years of service gives the total value for the future service as

$$\frac{(\cdot 01)S}{{}^{s}D_{x}} \sum_{t=0}^{64-x} {}^{z}\overline{M}_{x+t}^{wa}$$

given the symbol

$$\frac{(\cdot 01)S}{{}^{s}D_{x}} {}^{z}\overline{R}_{x}^{wa}.$$

When $n < 5$, then withdrawals before age $x + 5 - n$ will not receive a deferred pension, and the value of pension from service between ages $x + t$ and $x + t + 1$ before that age will be

$$\frac{(\cdot 01)S}{{}^{s}D_{x}} {}^{z}\overline{M}_{x+5-n}^{wa}$$

so that in summing over future years of service the total value will become

$$\frac{(\cdot 01)S}{{}^{s}D_{x}} \{(5-n){}^{z}\overline{M}_{x+5-n}^{wa} + {}^{z}\overline{R}_{x+5-n}^{wa}\}.$$

The values of all members will be found by grouping those of nearest birthday considering separately those for whom $n \geq 5$ and those from whom $n < 5$. For the second group further grouping by n will be required the extent to which this is done depending on the size of the scheme.

Example 10.22

A non-contributory fund provides pension for employees on retirement between ages 60 and 65. On the basis of the tables in Appendix III calculate the alternative rates of contribution by the employer as a percentage of salary (S) for a new entrant at 1st January aged 20 nearest birthday where the pension is

  (i) 1/60th of total earnings during service,
 (ii) 1/60th of total earnings during service with a maximum of 40 years to count, the earliest years of service being disregarded,
(iii) 1/60th of total earnings during service with a maximum of 40/60ths of the average salary throughout service,

in all cases fractions of a year counting for pension.

Solution

  (i) Using formula (10.3.6), the value of the pension is

$$\frac{S}{60} \frac{{}^{s}\overline{R}_{20}^{ra}}{{}^{s}D_{20}} = \frac{S}{60} \cdot \frac{2,567,780}{44,651} = \cdot 9585S$$

and the value of the contributions of $C\%$ of salary is

$$(\cdot01)CS\frac{^s\overline{N}_{20}}{^sD_{20}} = \cdot01CS \cdot \frac{903,883}{44,651} = \cdot2024CS.$$

Equating the values of the pension and the contributions,

$$C = \frac{\cdot9585}{\cdot2024} = 4\cdot74,$$

i.e. employers' contribution is $4\cdot74\%$ of salary.

(ii) From the value of the benefit in (i) above there will be deducted the value of the pension based on salary s_{20} on retirement for ages 60 to 65, s_{21} on retirement for ages 61 to 65..., i.e.

$$\frac{S}{60s_{20}D_{20}}\{s_{20}\overline{M}_{60}^{ra} + s_{21}\overline{M}_{61}^{ra} + s_{22}\overline{M}_{62}^{ra} + s_{23}\overline{M}_{63}^{ra} + s_{24}\overline{M}_{64}^{ra}\}$$

$$= \frac{S}{60(44,651)}(1\cdot21(14,482) + 1\cdot33(10,993) + 1\cdot46(9,135)$$

$$+ 1\cdot59(7,997) + 1\cdot73(7,082))$$

$$= \cdot0263S$$

so that if C' is the percentage contribution

$$C' = \frac{\cdot9585 - \cdot0263}{\cdot2024} = 4\cdot61,$$

i.e. the employers' contribution is 4.61% of salary.

(iii) In this case special commutation functions with the symbol (m) added will be found so that on retirement at each age after 60 the correct average pension is given—for example on retirement between ages 60 and 61 pension will be reduced on average in the proportion $\dfrac{40}{40\frac{1}{2}}$. The special values of $^{(m)}C$ will then be found as follows for retirement:

between ages 60 and 61,

$$^{(m)}C_{60}^{ra} = \frac{40}{40\frac{1}{2}}C_{60}^{ra} = \frac{40}{40\frac{1}{2}}\,4,520 = 4,464$$

between ages 61 and 62,

$$^{(m)}C_{61}^{ra} = \frac{40}{41\frac{1}{2}}C_{61}^{ra} = \frac{40}{41\frac{1}{2}}\,2,459 = 2,370$$

between ages 62 and 63,

$$^{(m)}C_{62}^{ra} = \frac{40}{42\frac{1}{2}} C_{62}^{ra} = \frac{40}{42\frac{1}{2}} 1{,}258 = 1{,}184$$

between ages 63 and 64,

$$^{(m)}C_{63}^{ra} = \frac{40}{43\frac{1}{2}} C_{63}^{ra} = \frac{40}{43\frac{1}{2}} 1{,}016 = 934$$

between ages 64 and 65,

$$^{(m)}C_{64}^{ra} = \frac{40}{44\frac{1}{2}} C_{64}^{ra} = \frac{40}{44\frac{1}{2}} 814 = 732$$

and at age 65 will be

$$^{(m)}C_{65}^{ra} = \frac{40}{45} C_{65}^{ra} = \frac{40}{45} 6{,}675 = 5{,}933.$$

Summing gives $^{(m)}M_x^{ra}$ and $^{(m)}\overline{M}_x^{ra}$, $^{(m)s}\overline{M}_x^{ra}$ and $^{(m)s}\overline{R}_x^{ra}$ are found in the same way as in section 10.3 (see Table 10.3).

TABLE 10.3

Age	$^{(m)}C_x^{ra}$	$^{(m)}M_x^{ra}$	$^{(m)}\overline{M}_x^{ra}$	$^{(m)s}M_x^{ra}$	$^{(m)s}\overline{R}_x^{ra}$
60	4,464	15,617	13,385	70,137	238,840
61	2,370	11,153	9,968	52,731	168,703
62	1,184	8,783	8,191	43,658	115,972
63	934	7,599	7,132	38,299	72,314
64	732	6,665	6,299	34,015	34,015
65	5,933	5,933			

As there are no age retirements before age 60, the value of

$$^{(m)}\overline{M}_x^{ra} = {}^{(m)}\overline{M}_{59}^{ra} \quad \text{for all } x < 60,$$

and

$$^{(m)s}\overline{M}_x^{ra} = s_x . {}^{(m)}\overline{M}_{59}^{ra} \quad \text{for } x < 60,$$

and as there are no retirals at age 59

$$^{(m)}\overline{M}_{59}^{ra} = {}^{(m)}M_{59}^{ra} = {}^{(m)}M_{60}^{ra} = 15{,}617.$$

Then $$^{(m)s}\overline{R}^{ra}_{20} = \left(\sum_{t=0}^{39} s_{20+t} \right) {}^{(m)}\overline{M}^{ra}_{59} + {}^{(m)s}\overline{R}^{ra}_{60}$$

$$= (137 \cdot 61)(15,617) + 238,840$$

$$= 2,381,895.$$

The value of the pension benefit is $\dfrac{S}{60} \cdot \dfrac{^{(m)s}\overline{R}^{ra}_{20}}{^{s}D_{20}}$

$$= \frac{S}{60} \cdot \frac{2,387,895}{44,651}$$

$$= \cdot 8913S.$$

Then if C'' is the percentage contribution

$$C'' = \frac{\cdot 8913}{\cdot 2024} = 4 \cdot 40,$$

i.e. employer's contribution is 4.40% of salary.

The relative answers show the unsatisfactory nature of the rules under (iii), where the pension of an employee who enters at a higher age, up to 25 at least, is likely to be greater than that of an employee who enters at age 20.

Example 10.23

A pension fund provides an age retirement pension, from age 65, of 1% of average pensionable salary earned by a member up to the anniversary immediately preceding retirement of his entry to service. Pensionable salary is defined as annual salary in excess of £500. The salary of a member is reviewed on each anniversary of his entry to service, and the following information is available for each member:

  (i) his annual rate of salary at the valuation date,

 (ii) his total salary received up to the last salary review,

(iii) dates of birth and entry to service.

Develop formulae for valuing the future and past service age retirement pensions.

Solution

(This solution is given more fully to indicate the amount of explanation required in an examination.)

It is assumed that there is available a suitable multiple decrement service table:

l_x = number of active members surviving at age x

w_x = number of withdrawals from service in year of age x to $x+1$

i_x = number of retirements due to ill-health between ages x and $x+1$

r_{65} = number retiring at age 65 (also = l_{65}).

There will also be required:

(a) a salary scale s_x defined so that s_{x+t}/s_x is the ratio of the salary expected to be received between ages $x+t$ and $x+t+1$ to that received between age x to $x+1$,

(b) annuity value $\bar{a}^r_{65}$ being the value of a pension of 1 per annum on retirement at age 65.

Adding the figures for members aged x nearest birthday (n_x) we are given:

(i) the total annual rate of salary at the valuation date for the member's nearest birthday x; given the symbol $(A\bar{S})_x$,

(ii) the total salaries received up to the last salary review for the member's nearest birthday x; given the symbol $(TPS)_x$.

The past salary has been given up to the last salary review date and it will be convenient to define past service pension as based on the figure given, the future service pension being the total pension less the past service pension.

The past service pension can be calculated directly, after adjusting for the deduction of 500 from salary to give pensionable salary. This adjustment will be 500m, where m is the curtate duration of the individual's membership of the scheme, so that the total past pensionable salary for the members aged x will be

$$(TPPS)_x = (TPS)_x - 500\Sigma m,$$

the summation being over members n_x.

It may be possible that a member at some time had a salary less then £500, in which case only the salary should be deducted rather than £500 for that year. It is most unlikely that past salaries have followed the salary scale, but if no further information is available then the present salary should be projected backwards to see if £500 is reached and if it is (say l years ago) the deduction for the individual member might be 500 for l years and the assumed salaries for previous years.

The value of the past service age retirement pension for the members aged x will be

$$\frac{(TPPS)_x}{100} \frac{v^{65} r_{65} \bar{a}^r_{65}}{v^x l_x}$$

$$= \frac{(TPPS)_x}{100} \frac{C^{ra}_{65}}{D_x},$$

where
$$C^{ra}_{65} = v^{65} r_{65} \bar{a}^r_{65}.$$

For future service age retirement pension it is assumed that on average the last salary review was at age $x-\frac{1}{2}$, so that we wish to find the benefit arising from salaries earned between ages $x-\frac{1}{2}$ to $x+\frac{1}{2}$, $x+\frac{1}{2}$ to $x+1\frac{1}{2}$, ...

The salaries data is based on the rate of salary at the date of the valuation, so that if s_x represents the salary received between ages x and $x+1$, and salaries are reviewed at intervals throughout the year of age, for the members aged x nearest birthday s_x will also represent the rate of salary at age $x+\frac{1}{2}$ and thus the rate of salary at age x is represented by $s_{x-\frac{1}{2}}$.

The benefit from salary earned between $x+t-\frac{1}{2}$ and $x+t+\frac{1}{2}$ is based on the salaries received during the year following $x+t-\frac{1}{2}$ (i.e. $s_{x+t-\frac{1}{2}}$) and the total projected pensionable salary during that year is

$$(A\bar{S})_x \frac{s_{x+t-\frac{1}{2}}}{s_{x-\frac{1}{2}}} - 500n_x$$

as the deduction of 500 is not projected.

The age retirement benefit from this salary is then

$$\frac{(A\bar{S})_x s_{x+t-\frac{1}{2}} C^{ra}_{65}}{100 s_{x-\frac{1}{2}} D_x} - \frac{500}{100} n_x \frac{C^{ra}_{65}}{D_x}.$$

Summing over all future service from age $x-\frac{1}{2}$ up to the last anniversary of entry on average at age $64\frac{1}{2}$ gives

$$\frac{(A\bar{S})_x}{100} \frac{s_x C^{ra}_{65}}{s_{x-\frac{1}{2}}{}^s D_x} \sum_{t=0}^{64\frac{1}{2}-x} s_{x+t-\frac{1}{2}} - 5n_x \frac{(65-x)C^{ra}_{65}}{D_x},$$

where
$$^s D_x = s_x D_x.$$

Example 10.24

The benefit in a pension fund is the greater of a pension based on 1/60ths of average salary during the last 3 years of membership and 1/80ths of earnings throughout membership, each year's earnings being increased until the year of retirement by the increase in national average earnings. The relationship of earnings (which includes overtime and bonus in addition to salary) and salary varies for each individual member of the fund.

Value the alternative pension benefits that are available at the normal retirement age of 65 to a new member of the fund aged 40 whose salary is £5,000 and whose expected earnings in the next year are £6,000. Use the tables in the Appendix and assume earnings increase at the same rate as salary and that national average earnings increase at 2% per annum.

Solution

As there is no stable relationship between earnings (E) and salary (S), it would seem necessary as indicated in the question to value the benefit for each member individually as the greater of the two possible benefits.

The formula for the pension based on 1/60ths of salary at retirement will be found in the same way as in section 10.4 with the same definition of z_x, giving the formula for the individual member's benefit as

$$S \frac{25}{60} \cdot \frac{z_{65}}{s_{40}} v^{25} \frac{r_{65}}{l_{40}} \bar{a}^r_{65}$$

$$= S \frac{25}{60} \cdot \frac{{}^z C^{ra}_{65}}{{}^s D_{40}}$$

$$= (5,000) \frac{25}{60} \cdot \frac{35,846}{18,629}$$

$$= 4,009.$$

The value of the benefits based on earnings will be similar to the formulae in section 10.3. If national average earnings increase at the rate of 2%, then the value of the pension benefit would be

$$\frac{E}{80} \sum_{x=40}^{64} \frac{s_x}{s_{40}} (1 \cdot 02)^{64\frac{1}{2}-x} v^{65} \times \frac{r_{65}}{l_{40}} \bar{a}^r_{65}$$

$$= \frac{E}{(80)(s_{40})} \frac{C^{ra}_{65}}{D_{40}} \frac{1}{(1 \cdot 02)^{\frac{1}{2}}} \sum_{x=40}^{64} s_x (1 \cdot 02)^{65-x}$$

Carrying out the calculation of the summation using the salary scale and compound interest tables at 2% gives

$$\frac{6,000}{(80)(3 \cdot 58)} \cdot \frac{6,675}{5,204} \frac{148 \cdot 84}{1 \cdot 01}$$

$$= 3,959.$$

The value of the two benefits in this case are found to be close and the slightly larger of £4,009 based on the 60ths of salary would be used in the valuation.

Exercise 10.25

On withdrawal from a pension fund, which is contracted-out of a State pension scheme, if less than five years' membership has been completed a lump sum of 7% of salary received during membership is paid to the State scheme. After five years the withdrawal benefit is

N

a 'preserved' pension based on 1/80ths of salary at the time of leaving service for each year of service increased by $8\frac{1}{2}\%$ per annum till retirement at age 65.

Derive formulae to value the withdrawal benefits for a member aged 30 with three years' membership.

Exercise 10.26

A pension fund provides pension for members withdrawing with at least ten years' service a pension from the normal retiring date of the 65th birthday based on 1/80th of the total salary received during service. Develop formulae for this benefit.

Exercise 10.27

A non-contributory pension fund has hitherto provided the following benefits:

(a) on retirement due to ill-health before age 60 a pension of 1/80th of average salary throughout service for each year of service,

(b) on retirement at or after age 60 for any reason a pension of 1/60th of average salary throughout service for each year of service.

It is now proposed to make retiral compulsory at age 60, the scale of benefits remaining otherwise unaltered. Using 4% interest and the tables in Appendix III, calculate the present value of the additional liability undertaken for a new entrant to the fund at age 20 whose salary is £1,500 per annum. (The value of a pension of 1 per annum at exact age 60 is $12\cdot119$ and $\sum\limits_{x=20}^{59} s_x = 137\cdot61$).

Exercise 10.28

The employees' contributions to a pension scheme are at the rate of 4% of salary in excess of £500. On the death of a member in service there is payable

(a) a refund of contributions with interest at $2\frac{1}{2}\%$,

(b) 10% of the salary without deduction at the date of death for each complete year of membership with a maximum of ten years' service to count.

Derive the commutation functions to evaluate the death benefit, assuming a rate of interest of 5%, assuming each member has an integral number of years past service.

Exercise 10.29

A company has a non-contributory scheme for its female employees. The benefits are to be amended to give a sum of £5,000 payable on death rather than £100 for each complete year of service provided five years' service have been completed, to introduce a bonus of £200 payable after completion of each 3 years' service, and to have a gratuity of £250 on withdrawal due to marriage.

Assuming that a fixed percentage of all withdrawals at each age are due to marriage, obtain formulae to calculate the additional cost of the proposals for a new entrant at age 20. No benefits are payable after age 60.

Exercise 10.30

A widows' pension fund provides a widow's pension equal to 1% of the member's final salary for each complete year of service. You are given that:

(a) the pension commences on the death of the member before or after retirement,

(b) retirement takes place either at age 65 or earlier on account of ill-health,

(c) no pension is payable in respect of marriages which take place after retirement,

(d) the pension ceases on the death or remarriage of the widow,

(e) unmarried members pay weekly contributions during service at the rate of $\frac{1}{2}$% of salary and married members pay weekly contributions during service at the rate of of 1% of salary,

(f) all salary revisions take place and all new members enter service on 1st January.

Using the collective method, develop formulae and commutation functions suitable for valuing benefits and contributions in respect of a new member aged x nearest birthday.

Exercise 10.31

How will the formulae and commutation functions you have developed in Exercise 10.30 be modified if the pension is 30% of the member's final salary irrespective of length of service?

CHAPTER ELEVEN

MISCELLANEOUS TOPICS

11.1 Sickness benefits

In Britain sickness insurance is provided under the National Insurance Scheme, by some Insurance Companies and by Friendly Societies. There has been a recent growth in hospitalisation benefit schemes which are similar. In this section we will be concerned mainly with the benefits granted by Friendly Societies, but the principles can also be applied to the other types of benefit. As in Pension Fund work there is no International Notation for sickness benefits.

A Friendly Society is a mutual association which gives financial assistance to its members at time of distress, especially in sickness and old age. It operates on insurance principles, accumulating a fund from contributions paid by the members in order to pay out future benefits. It is regulated by rules which may be amended by votes of the members, and is administered by a committee elected by them. Friendly Societies grew with the Industrial Revolution, but since the National Insurance Scheme commenced in 1946 many of their functions have been taken over by that scheme, and although there are still many millions of members the importance of the Societies has declined.

A sickness benefit is a rather less exact concept than the death and pension benefits already discussed. In any application the definition of what is meant by sickness must be clearly stated and in this section it will mean sickness as defined by the rules of a particular Society. Normally the benefit is paid weekly to members who can produce evidence of incapacity. For the first period of sickness, perhaps 26 or 52 weeks, the benefit may be at a full rate, which then reduces to a fraction such as one-half and may reduce further maybe to one-quarter or cease after perhaps two years.

Spells of sickness commencing within a certain period after a previous benefit may be treated as continuous in determining the rate of benefit—this period is the 'off-period', and may be one year. The 'waiting period' is the period, often six months, which must elapse before a new member is entitled to benefits.

It will be seen that a strict or lax definition of sickness (particularly in determining when a member has recovered), variation in the amount and the period during which benefit is paid, the waiting period, and the off-period can affect considerably the amount of benefit that a Society will pay, and the sickness rates that should be assumed in the calculations of the contributions.

The basic measure of sickness is the 'force of sickness', $\bar{z}_x$, which is the probability that a member aged x is sick, meaning that he is eligible for sickness benefit under the rules of the Society.

Sickness rates could also be expressed in the form of the ratio that the expected number of weeks' sickness in the year of age x to $x+1$ bears to the number of lives attaining age x. This is referred to as the annual rate of sickness, s_x. If 52·18 is the average number of weeks in the year

$$s_x = \frac{52 \cdot 18}{l_x} \int_0^1 l_{x+t} \bar{z}_{x+t} dt \qquad (11.1.1)$$

$$= 52 \cdot 18 \int_0^1 {}_t p_x \bar{z}_{x+t} dt. \qquad (11.1.2)$$

Although this has affinities with a rate of decrement it is important to realise that it is not a rate but a ratio which when multiplied by the number of persons attaining age x and by the amount of weekly benefit gives the expected amount of the claims for sickness benefit between ages x and $x+1$.

As ${}_t p_x$ and $\bar{z}_{x+t}$ only change slowly for $0 \leqq t \leqq 1$, formula (11.1.2) gives

$$s_x \fallingdotseq 52 \cdot 18 \, {}_{\frac{1}{2}} p_x \bar{z}_{x+\frac{1}{2}}. \qquad (11.1.3)$$

If the denominator in formula (11.1.1) is altered from l_x to

$$\int_0^1 l_{x+t} dt,$$

we obtain z_x, the central rate of sickness at age x (the average number of weeks' sickness experienced by members between ages x and $x+1$).

$$z_x = 52 \cdot 18 \frac{\int_0^1 l_{x+t} \bar{z}_{x+t} dt}{\int_0^1 l_{x+t} dt}, \qquad (11.1.4)$$

and dividing the numerator and denominator by l_x gives

$$z_x \doteq \frac{52 \cdot 18 \, {}_{\frac{1}{2}}p_x \bar{z}_{x+\frac{1}{2}}}{{}_{\frac{1}{2}}p_x},$$

i.e.
$$z_x \doteq 52 \cdot 18 \bar{z}_{x+\frac{1}{2}}, \tag{11.1.5}$$

corresponding to $m_x \doteq \mu_{x+\frac{1}{2}}$.

From formulae (11.1.3) and (11.1.5)

$$s_x \doteq {}_{\frac{1}{2}}p_x . z_x. \tag{11.1.6}$$

As the benefit paid by a Society often reduces after a certain period or periods it is necessary to break down the values of the sickness rates to show the values applied to the separate periods of sickness. If n is the period (in weeks) which is being considered during which the benefit is paid, and m is the number of weeks which must have elapsed before the period is reached, the sickness functions are denoted by $\bar{z}_x^{m/n}$, $s_x^{m/n}$ and $z_x^{m/n}$. The symbol for the first n weeks is z_x^n and for all sickness after the first m weeks the symbol is $z_x^{m/\text{all}}$. If, for example, the periods during which benefit is to be separately considered are 26 weeks and a subsequent period of $1\frac{1}{2}$ years, the total sickness rate will be the sum of the separate rates so that

$$z_x = z_x^{26} + z_x^{26/78} + z_x^{104/\text{all}}.$$

Sometimes the figures in the superfix are shown in months rather than weeks—which is meant in any case should be obvious. Considering first the simplest case when there is no reduction during prolonged sickness, the value at age x of a benefit of £1 per week received during the year of age x to $x+1$ is

$$52 \cdot 18 \int_0^1 v^t {}_tp_x \bar{z}_{x+t} dt$$

$$\doteq 52 \cdot 18 v^{\frac{1}{2}} {}_{\frac{1}{2}}p_x \bar{z}_{x+\frac{1}{2}}$$

$$\doteq v^{\frac{1}{2}} {}_{\frac{1}{2}}p_x z_x \quad \text{from formula (11.1.5)}.$$

For practical calculation commutation functions H_x and K_x defined as follows are used:

$$H_x = 52 \cdot 18 \int_0^1 v^{x+t} l_{x+t} \bar{z}_{x+t} dt \tag{11.1.7}$$

$$\doteq 52 \cdot 18 v^{x+\frac{1}{2}} l_{x+\frac{1}{2}} \bar{z}_{x+\frac{1}{2}}$$

$$\doteq \bar{D}_x z_x, \quad \text{from formula (11.1.5)};$$

$$K_x = \sum_{t=0}^{\infty} H_{x+t} = 52 \cdot 18 \int_0^{\infty} v^{x+t} l_{x+t} \bar{z}_{x+t} dt. \qquad (11.1.8)$$

It is important to remember that the H_x and K_x functions already include the factor $52 \cdot 18$ and thus value units of 1 per week directly.

Similar symbols are used for the separate period sickness functions

$$K_x^{m/n} = 52 \cdot 18 \int_0^{\infty} v^{x+t} l_{x+t} \bar{z}_{x+t}^{m/n} dt.$$

It will be seen that one way of thinking of a sickness benefit is of a varying annuity the amount of the annuity being the proportion of persons sick.

The value of any benefit will be found by dividing the relevant K_x functions by D_x. Thus if the benefit is £3 per week for the first 26 weeks, £2 per week thereafter until 2 years and £1 per week subsequently, the value of the benefit will be

$$\frac{1}{D_x} (3K_x^{26} + 2K_x^{26/78} + K_x^{104/\text{all}}),$$

if the benefit continues throughout life, or

$$\frac{1}{D_x} \left(3(K_x^{26} - K_{65}^{26}) + 2(K_x^{26/78} - K_{65}^{26/78}) + (K_x^{104/\text{all}} - K_{65}^{104/\text{all}}) \right)$$

if the benefit ceases at age 65.

In considering the sickness rates divided into periods, it must be realised that as for instance $z_x^{52/52}$ represents sickness for which benefit is payable experienced in the year starting at age x, earlier sickness must have been experienced before age x.

The sickness rates used in the examples and exercises which are given in Appendix III are those for Occupation Group AHJ of the experience of the Manchester Unity (a Friendly Society) in 1893–7: the functions tabulated being

$$z^{13}, z^{13/13}, z^{26/26}, z^{52/52}, z^{104/\text{all}}, z.$$

These rates are also combined with the mortality of the English Life Table No. 12—Males to give the K commutation functions at 4% interest.

When an annual premium is required the value of the benefit will be divided by $\bar{a}_{x:\overline{65-x}|}$ if the premium is payable continuously (in practice weekly) and ceasing at age 65.

In considering a new member of a Society there will probably be some selection as the member will normally produce some evidence of good health before being allowed to join. This makes only a relatively minor alteration in contribution rates and select rates are never prepared. On the other hand there are other considerations which affect new members particularly the 'waiting period' during which no benefit will be paid. Moreover, a member who entered a Society less than t years ago cannot experience at the present time sickness which would be classified under the rules as being of duration greater than t years. For example, if the waiting period is six months a member will not experience sickness classified as after 1 year until he has been a member for $1\frac{1}{2}$ years.

As sickness rates are in aggregate form, there is no way of allowing directly for this. A possible adjustment although not entirely theoretically correct which will make some allowance is to increase the age in the K functions by the waiting period and the previous periods of sickness—for example, the value of the benefits previously considered for a member entering at age x, with a waiting period of six months, might be taken as

$$\frac{1}{D_x}(3K_{x+\frac{1}{2}}^{26}+2K_{x+1}^{26/78}+K_{x+2\frac{1}{2}}^{104/\text{all}}),$$

the functions being found by interpolation.

Because of the relatively small alteration which this adjustment makes and as it reduces the contribution it is usual to ignore it and use age x for all the commutation functions.

According to the same principles as life assurance, assets will be built up in a Friendly Society and reserves can be calculated in a similar way, normally on the prospective basis. For example, for a benefit of B a week throughout life the annual contributions being k the reserve at age x will be

$$B\frac{K_x}{D_x} - k\bar{a}_x. \tag{11.1.9}$$

Example 11.1

A Friendly Society grants a sickness benefit of £4 per week for the first 26 weeks of sickness, £2 per week for the rest of the first year and £1 per week subsequently with benefit ceasing at age 60. Find the weekly contributions that should be paid until that age by a new member aged 40 on the basis of the tables in Appendix III table 6 at 4% interest if the waiting period is six months and compare the answer with the contribution calculated ignoring the special considerations for new entrants.

Solution

The value of the benefits ignoring the waiting period is

$$\frac{1}{D_{40}}\left(4(K_{40}^{26}-K_{60}^{26})+2(K_{40}^{26/26}-K_{60}^{26/26})+(K_{40}^{52/\text{all}}-K_{60}^{52/\text{all}})\right)$$

and as
$$K_x^{26}=K_x^{13}+K_x^{13/13},$$

and
$$K_x^{52/\text{all}}=K_x^{52/52}+K_x^{104/\text{all}}$$

this $= \dfrac{1}{19,535}\left(4(385,490+130.449-136,170-68,315)+2(144,315\right.$

$$\left.-89,993)+(172,341+700,172-124,022-552,353))\right.$$

$$=\frac{1,550,598}{19,535}$$

$$=79{\cdot}4.$$

Allowing for the waiting period and the special consideration of new entrants gives the value of the benefits as

$$\frac{1}{D_{40}}\left(4(K_{40\frac12}^{26}-K_{60}^{26})+2(K_{41}^{26/26}-K_{60}^{26/26})+(K_{41\frac12}^{52/\text{all}}-K_{60}^{52/\text{all}})\right)$$

$$=\frac{1}{19,535}\left(4(378,180+129,081-136,170-68,315)+2(142,229\right.$$

$$\left.-89,993)+(169,832+693,996-124,022-552,353))\right.$$

$$=\frac{1,503,029}{19,535}$$

$$=76{\cdot}9.$$

The value of the weekly contribution of 1 will be

$$52{\cdot}18\,\frac{\overline{N}_{40}-\overline{N}_{60}}{D_{40}}$$

$$=\frac{52{\cdot}18}{19,535}(338,876-79,735)$$

$$=692{\cdot}0.$$

Equating the values of benefits and contributions the weekly contribution using the 'accurate' formula will then be

$$\frac{76\cdot9}{692\cdot0} = \cdot111, \text{ say 11p per week,}$$

and on the 'usual' formula

$$\frac{79\cdot4}{692\cdot0} = \cdot115, \text{ say } 11\tfrac{1}{2}\text{p per week.}$$

Example 11.2

Demonstrate the relationship between successive prospective reserves for a sickness benefit of £1 per annum throughout life, if the reserve and premium bases are the same.

Solution

The reserve at age y, when the annual contribution is k_x is

$$_{y-x}V_x = \frac{K_y}{D_y} - k_x \bar{a}_y$$

$$\doteqdot v^{\frac{1}{2}} {}_{\frac{1}{2}}p_y z_y + v p_y \cdot \frac{K_{y+1}}{D_{y+1}} - k_x v^{\frac{1}{2}} {}_{\frac{1}{2}}p_y - k_x v p_y \bar{a}_{y+1}$$

$$\therefore \;_{y-x}V_x(1+i) + {}_{\frac{1}{2}}p_y(k_x - z_y)(1+i)^{\frac{1}{2}} \doteqdot p_y \cdot {}_{y+1-x}V_x.$$

This shows that the reserve accumulated for the year with the addition of the contributions and the deduction of the expected claims during the year gives the reserve at the end of the year provided the life is still alive.

Example 11.3

A life office offers a waiver of premium benefit on a life assurance policy if the policyholder is sick. Assuming that the combined sickness and mortality table in Appendix III is used with 4% interest, determine the percentage by which the weekly premium for a whole-life proposer aged 50 should be increased in order to provide this benefit if there is an expense loading of 20% of the gross premium for the waiver of premium benefit.

Solution

If P is the normal total premium for a year for the assurance and p is the proportional increase for the additional benefit

$$\cdot8p \, P\bar{a}_{50} = \frac{P}{52\cdot18} \frac{K_{50}}{D_{50}}$$

i.e.
$$p = \frac{K_{50}}{\overline{N}_{50}(\cdot 8)(52\cdot 18)}$$

$$= \frac{1,277,305}{179,605(\cdot 8)(52\cdot 18)}$$

$$= \cdot 170,$$

i.e. percentage required is about 17%.

Exercise 11.1

Determine as accurately as possible the weekly contribution which should be paid by a new member of a Friendly Society aged 45 who is granted sickness benefit of £10 per week for the first 3 months, £5 per week for the remainder of the first year and £3 per week thereafter, up to age 65 with a waiting period of one year. Basis: Manchester Unity AHJ sickness rates with English Life Table No. 12—Male mortality; 4% interest.

Exercise 11.2

A Friendly Society has a sickness benefit which provides for male members a weekly income without a waiting period of £4 for married men and £2 for others. Benefits and contributions, which do not vary with marital status, cease at age 65. It is also assumed that mortality and sickness rates do not vary with marital status.

If the proportions of men married are at the 25th birthday 70%, at the 26th 75%, at the 27th 80% and at the 28th and thereafter 85%, calculate the weekly contributions payable throughout membership for a member aged 25.

Exercise 11.3

A man aged 30 effects a without-profit endowment assurance by weekly premiums for £1,000 sum assured maturing at age 60 or immediately on previous death which provides in addition the following sickness benefits:

(a) premiums to be waived during period of sickness,

(b) an insurance benefit to be payable during sickness at the rate of £5 per week for the first six months, reducing to £3 per week for the next six months and to £2 per week thereafter, but ceasing at age 60 in any event.

Assuming no waiting period and the combined tables of sickness and mortality given in Appendix III table 6 with interest at 4%, calculate the weekly premium under the policy, allowing for initial expenses of 20% of the first year's premiums and renewal expenses of 4% of the premiums after the first year.

11.2   Alternative approaches to sickness benefits

There was discussed in the previous section the 'classical' method for the evaluation of sickness benefits. There are however alternative approaches, particularly for employee benefit schemes.

One which has been used particularly when the benefit is only paid when there is unlikely to be recovery is usually referred to as disability benefit. Total and permanent disability may for example be described as the loss of two limbs or the sight of both eyes or the loss of one of each, or evidence that an impairment is such that no work has been possible for two years and the person is unlikely to be able ever to follow any occupation. Disability benefit occurred at one time particularly in connection with life assurance policies where premiums may be waived on disability, or the sum assured may be payable on disability prior to death.

To value disability benefits a double decrement table with decrements of death and permanent disablement might be used, and, if the benefit is in the form of an income, annuity values based on the provision of the benefit, the mortality being that of a disabled person. It is also possible for the value of the annuity to be adjusted to allow for recovery, or to postpone the commencement of the benefit for a deferred period; and the annuity may cease at some age.

Another different approach may be used particularly for the increasingly important 'permanent health insurance' (or 'PHI' or 'Φ') benefits provided to cover sickness of groups of employees rather than an individual. These may also be referred to as salary continuation schemes and may be thought of as a means of phasing benefits for the chronically sick and disabled into retirement benefits payable from the normal retirement age. These are often insured by the employer with an assurance office normally on the single premium method under which the premium paid in any year covers benefits for those members of the scheme who become sick during the year, the benefit being payable, after the deferred period, for the duration of the disability which may of course extend for many years after the premium is paid—thus even if the policy is terminated the benefit may continue to be payable in respect of those sick at the time of the premiums ceasing. For this type of single premium contract it may be appropriate that a rate of inception of becoming sick be introduced rather than the proportion sick discussed in the previous section. A double decrement approach is not necessarily used and the mortality table is in the usual form, with $_{(k)}i_x$ the number of those becoming disabled during the year (relative to the conditions of the scheme particularly the deferred period of k) out of l_x lives at the start of the year. The effect of the deferred period is that claims are included in $_{(k)}i_x$ if the initial inception of sickness is during the year of age and the life is still disabled at the end of the deferred period.

The net single premium for a person aged x where the waiting period is k for an annual benefit of B will be of the form

$$Bv^{k+\frac{1}{2}}\,\frac{_{(k)}i_x}{l_x}\,\bar{a}'_{x+\frac{1}{2}+k},$$

where the annuity value is of an annuity during sickness (as defined in the scheme or contract) after the appropriate deferred period and allows for recovery.

Exercise 11.4

A permanent health plan provides from a single premium a benefit of B per annum on sickness occurring during the next three years. Find an expression for the net premium for this benefit.

11.3 Benefits dependent on marriage

Various benefits and contributions dependent on marital status have already been discussed and the methods used in this section do not introduce any new techniques. They are discussed partly to exemplify the differences between formulae for benefits which are payable *on* the occurrence of an event compared to those for benefits payable *during* a certain condition.

In considering a status, such as marriage, it is important to ensure that the condition is clearly known; for example there are really four groups—single, married, widowed and divorced—so that if two categories are used, married and unmarried, there must be a clear understanding of which group the last two are in. Normally widowed and divorced persons are classified as unmarried.

If h_x is the proportion of lives aged x who are married it is assumed that this is, as with l_x, a continuous and differentiable function of x. The number l_x in the normal mortality table may be considered as being split into $h_x l_x$ and $(1-h_x)l_x$, being the numbers married and unmarried. This procedure involves the implicit assumption that mortality is independent of marital status or alternatively that the mortality table has been specially constructed so that the mortality at age x is the weighted average of the married and unmarried rates of mortality with weights $h_x : 1 - h_x$. Because of the lack of data the assumption is normally accepted in practice, and if greater accuracy is possible the techniques of double decrement tables as in Chapter 9 are used.

If annuities of 1 per annum are payable to a large number of lives, N, of age x provided they are married at the time of payment the total present value would be

$$\sum_{t=1}^{\infty} v^t N h_{x+t} {}_t p_x \quad \text{if the annuity is yearly}$$

and $$\int_0^{\infty} v^t N h_{x+t} {}_t p_x dt \quad \text{if it is continuous.}$$

For purposes of calculation it is convenient to treat the annuity as a varying annuity where h_{x+t} is treated as the amount of the annuity in that year rather than as the proportion representing the condition, and the value of the annuity for the N lives will be

$$N \sum_{t=1}^{\infty} v^t h_{x+t} {}_t p_x. \tag{11.3.1}$$

Similarly, the value of the assurances payable on the death of the N persons if they be married would be

$$N \int v^t h_{x+t} {}_t p_x \mu_{x+t} dt. \tag{11.3.2}$$

Similar formulae may be used for valuing children's benefits, for example while a person has a child under age 16, or a benefit on the death of a member while an elderly dependent relative is alive, by the introduction of suitable proportions.

Benefits payable on marriage may be valued by the use of the function v_x which is defined so that the number of marriages in the time δx among l_x lives attaining age x is $l_x v_x \delta x$. As a proportion of the l_x are already married it is not appropriate to consider v_x as a force of marriage—it is merely a measure of the rate at which marriages take place.

The value of a benefit of 1 payable on marriage for a life aged x will be

$$\int_0^{\infty} v^t {}_t p_x v_{x+t} dt. \tag{11.3.3}$$

A practical question which arises is whether a person who marries more than once is to be entitled to more than one benefit. If he is, then v_x must include remarriages while if he is not then v_x will not include them.

Benefit payable in the event of maternity may be valued by means of an issue rate which may depend on the number of married men, married women, all men or all women. For example, considering the number of children born to $h_x l_x$ married men the value will be

$$l_x \int_0^\infty v^t h_{x+t\,t} p_x i^h_{x+t} dt,$$

where i^h_x is defined so that the number of births in the time δx to wives of $h_x l_x$ married men age x is $h_x l_x i^h_x \delta x$.

In general, a benefit payable on an event happening that is a change in state will include a rate of change (somewhat similar to the force of mortality) such as v_x or i_x. In some cases a further proportion may be included as only a certain proportion of the cases will qualify for a benefit. This type of benefit is similar to an assurance. When the benefit is payable during the continuation of a certain status it is similar to an annuity and no change of status rate will appear in the formula.

It is of course possible to define commutation functions to evaluate the formulae in this section on similar lines to Chapter 10, particularly if sufficient cases arise to make the construction of commutation columns worthwhile.

Example 11.4

A group of men is subject to the mortality of the A1967–70 ultimate table and has the following proportion married at various ages:

20% at age 20 increasing linearly to
70% at age 30 increasing linearly to
90% at age 50 decreasing linearly to
75% at age 65.

The proportions include those who have remarried but exclude widowers.

Find the value at 4% p.a. compound interest of an annuity of £1,000 per annum payable yearly in arrear to a life aged 20, ceasing at age 65 or earlier death, to be paid only while the life is married. The contract ceases on the death of the spouse, but starts again on remarriage.

Solution

The benefit can for the purposes of valuation be considered as a varying annuity giving the value

$$\frac{1}{D_{20}}[250N_{21}+50(S_{22}-S_{31})+10(S_{31}-S_{51})-10(S_{51}-S_{66})-750N_{66}]$$

$$=\frac{1}{D_{20}}[250N_{21}+50S_{22}-40S_{31}-20S_{51}+10S_{66}-750N_{66}]$$

$$=\frac{1}{15,557\cdot4}[250(334,979)+50(5,893,434)-40(3,485,461)$$

$$-20(820,913)+10(167,965)-750(20,877\cdot3)]$$

$$=13,408\cdot5 \quad \text{i.e.} \quad £13,409.$$

Exercise 11.5

Calculate on the basis of the A1967–70 ultimate table at 4% per annum interest, the value of an annuity payable yearly in arrear and ceasing on death or remarriage to a woman aged 30 who has just become a widow; it may be assumed that mortality is independent of marital status, and that of women becoming widows at age 30 the proportion of women who are still widows at subsequent ages is as shown in Table 11.1.

TABLE 11.1

Age	Proportion
31	·9
32	·8
33	·7
34 and over	·6

Exercise 11.6

Obtain a formula for the valuation of a benefit paid on the death of a person who dies unmarried but leaving a dependant female relative the benefit being doubled if the beneficiary is the widowed mother of the member.

11.4   Standard deviations

It is important to remember that a rate of mortality is a probability and that when applied to a group of lives it represents the mean of a statistical distribution. Consider a group of n lives aged x, each of whom is taken at random from an indefinitely large number of lives who are assumed to experience, as a whole, the mortality of the single-life mortality table.

The expected number of survivors to age $x+1$ is np_x and the expected number of deaths between ages x and $x+1$ is nq_x. The probability that exactly r lives will die before attaining age $x+1$ is

$$\binom{n}{r} p_x^{n-r} q_x^r.$$

Since we are concerned with a theoretical model we can imagine a very large number of groups similarly taken at random. The number of deaths will vary from group to group, but the mean number of deaths among the groups will be the same as the expected number for one group, i.e. nq_x and the expected relative frequency of groups with r deaths will be the same expression as above.

The moments of the binomial distribution are given in textbooks on statistics. The first two moments are

$$\mu_1' = nq$$

and
$$\mu_2' = nq + n(n-1)q^2.$$

$$\therefore \ \mu_2 = nq - nq^2 = npq.$$

It follows that the expected number of deaths is nq_x and that the standard deviation of the number of deaths among the groups is

$$\sigma = \sqrt{\mu_2} = \sqrt{(np_x q_x)}. \tag{11.4.1}$$

In applying this formula to an actual experience there must be kept in mind the underlying assumption that each unit in the investigation is taken at random independently of all the others—an assumption which may not always be fulfilled in practical conditions. The unit in an investigation of the mortality of assured lives or annuitants may be a policy and not a life.

Example 11.5

Develop an expression for the standard deviation of $\bar{a}_x$.

Solution

Consider the distribution of $\bar{a}_x$ by time of death of x, the probability of death occurring in the small interval δt after t years is

$\dfrac{l_{x+t}}{l_x}\mu_{x+t}\delta t$ and the present value of the annuity if death occurs at that time is $\bar{a}_{\bar{t}|}$

Hence
$$\mu'_1 = \frac{1}{l_x}\int_0^\infty \bar{a}_{\bar{t}|}l_{x+t}\mu_{x+t}dt$$

$$= \bar{a}_x \quad \text{as expected,}$$

and
$$\mu'_2 = \frac{1}{l_x}\int_0^\infty (\bar{a}_{\bar{t}|})^2 l_{x+t}\mu_{x+t}dt.$$

Now
$$(\bar{a}_{\bar{t}|})^2 = \delta^{-2}(1-v^t)^2$$

$$= \delta^{-2}(1-2v^t+v^{2t})$$

$$= \frac{1}{\delta}\left\{\frac{2(1-v^t)}{\delta} - \frac{2(1-v^{2t})}{2\delta}\right\}$$

$$= \frac{2}{\delta}(\bar{a}_{\bar{t}|}-\bar{a}'_{\bar{t}|}),$$

where
$$v' = v^2.$$

Thus
$$\mu'_2 = \frac{2}{\delta l_x}\int_0^\infty (\bar{a}_{\bar{t}|}-\bar{a}'_{\bar{t}|})l_{x+t}\mu_{x+t}dt$$

$$= \frac{2}{\delta}(\bar{a}_x-\bar{a}'_x).$$

Hence the standard deviation, σ, is given by

$$\sigma^2 = \mu'_2 - \mu'^2_1 = \frac{2}{\delta}(\bar{a}_x-\bar{a}'_x)-\bar{a}^2_x.$$

11.5 Calculation of tables

Under modern conditions tables of commutation functions, premiums and reserves are normally prepared by using a computer but first the methods used where computers are not available will be discussed. These methods are also required, for example, when independent checks are needed when a computer program is being tested.

Although a computer may not be used, in most cases desk electronic calculating machines will be available so that familiarity in the use of tables of logarithms is no longer really required. Such calculating machines as well as carrying out the simple calculations of addition, subtraction, multiplication and division may also have a memory or memories where answers to part of a calculation can be held till needed at a later stage. In carrying out any calculation the number of significant figures to be retained will require to be decided —there is no point in having more than are justified by the accuracy of the initial data but often more figures are retained during the calculation and the reduction is made at the end.

Normally the basic function from which the mortality table is constructed is q_x, and any other function can be calculated by means of the formulae developed earlier, but if a set of tables is required the method should give accurate and reliable figures with the expenditure of the least labour.

One convenient approach is to use a 'continued process' whereby each value is found from a previous value and the final value is checked by another method thus checking the whole table—even when this is done it is however advisable for two persons to make duplicate calculations. The great advantage of a continued process is that when the final value is checked by an independent calculation this automatically verifies the whole table. This advantage, however, has its limitations. For example, if an error is made in calculating one value of the function, this error will be transmitted to all subsequent values until an independent check is applied. In order that an error of this kind may be detected before it has affected many subsequent values, it is usual to calculate, say, every twentieth value in advance by an independent formula.

An independent summation check is also desirable—this means a calculation of $\Sigma f(x)$ by a formula which is independent of the working and a comparison of this with the figure obtained by adding up the calculated values of $f(x)$. A summation check which is not independent is frequently useful. For example, if a process of calculation includes adding a figure in one column to a figure in a second column and recording the sum of the two in a third column it will probably be worth while to add all three columns and to make sure that

$$\Sigma_{(col. 1)} + \Sigma_{(col. 2)} = \Sigma_{(col. 3)},$$

but this does not provide an *independent* check. If the figures in column 1 or column 2 have for example been obtained by multiplication, the summation check suggested will not pick up any errors which may have been made in copying the figures from the machine to the working sheet. This may seem obvious, but the point is mentioned because the difference between the effects of the two types of summation check is not always appreciated.

A continued process normally requires the following:

(1) a formula for the initial value,
(2) a working formula by which each value is obtained from the previous one,
(3) a formula for calculating intermediate check values and the final value, and
(4) (desirable though not essential) an independent summation check formula to detect errors in transcription.

Formula (3) will usually be similar to formula (1).

For the construction of tables of many of the simpler functions a satisfactory continued process will at once be apparent. When this is not the case it is worth while going to a little trouble to ascertain whether a suitable working formula can be found. It is advisable to tackle this problem systematically.

A working formula for the calculation of $f(x)$ will be available if either $\Delta f(x)$ or $\dfrac{f(x+1)}{f(x)}$ is

(a) a constant, or
(b) a function which has already been tabulated (or is worth tabulating), or
(c) a function which can itself be calculated by a continued process.

The non-monetary functions do not normally lend themselves to a continued process, but to demonstrate what is meant it can be seen that if q_x is known the simple method would be to calculate p_x as $1-q_x$. A continued process would be to calculate first the earliest value of $p_\alpha = 1-q_\alpha$ and then as $\Delta p_x = -\Delta q_x$ successively subtract Δq_x. The summation check is to sum all values of p_x and q_x which should give the range of ages considered.

Functions which are summations for example N_x and M_x are found by the continued process of summations of D_x and C_x. There is an important check in

$$M_y = D_y - dN_y.$$

In the days when logarithms were the main calculating tool, approximate integration was frequently used to calculate functions not available in published tables and examples of this application to contingent functions were given in section 8.5.

When an electronic computer is available the approach to calculation will depend on whether the computer is to be used as an extremely fast and accurate calculating machine, in which case it will be carrying out much the same calculations as would be done without it, or whether the whole method of calculation is to be altered—remembering that commutation functions were originally introduced to make calculation by hand feasible, and may then not be the most appropriate method in the changed circumstances. If the traditional methods are to be used it is possible to reduce the data held—for example, if commutation functions are needed, N_x might be input to the computer and stored for the use of the subsequent calculations and if other functions are required they would be found from

$$D_x = N_x - N_{x+1}$$
$$C_x = vN_x - (1+v)N_{x+1} + N_{x+2}$$
$$M_x = vN_x - N_{x+1}.$$

If R_x and S_x are likely to be required they could be calculated by summations, but it might be better to input S_x if it is available and all the other values would then be calculated from it, as long summations tend to be time consuming.

Where commutation functions are not already available they might of course be calculated by the computer from the basic input of the table of mortality, probably in the form of q_x, and the rate of interest.

Commutation functions are not really useful when the rate of interest is assumed to vary. With the fluctuations in the rate of interest there have been it is not unusual to assume a basis in which the rate of interest varies, normally reducing from a higher value to a lower which is assumed to be the average long-term rate of interest. It is of course possible to carry out calculations on such a basis using commutation columns by dividing the term of the function being considered into spans and using the method described in Example 2.13—which will become particularly laborious if the rate of interest varies each year, but if a computer is available the calculation will be easier done without introducing commutation functions. An example in the evaluation of annuities might be to use the formula

$$\ddot{a}_{x+r:\overline{n-r}|} = vp_x \ddot{a}_{x+r+1:\overline{n-r-1}|} + 1,$$

v varying perhaps with n or r.

A particularly useful application of computer calculation is where there are two unknowns related to each other and successive trial calculations have to be carried out—for example, the annuity with a refund on death of the excess of the purchase price over the actual payments made, where the term of the guarantee and the purchase price are both unknown.

In most cases the computer program will be written in one of the 'higher level' computer languages such as Algol or Fortran, which can be applied on many different manufacturers' machines.

It is desirable for the program to include if possible spot checks and summation checks similar to those used in manual calculations.

It is also possible to obtain standard 'packages' of actuarial programs (probably written in one of these languages) which will calculate the common commutation functions, assurances and annuity values, premiums, and reserves.

Example 11.6

Discuss the possible manual methods of obtaining numerical values of $a_{x:\overline{n}|}$, assuming that the normal commutation columns are available.

Solution

If x is regarded as the variable, there is no obvious continued process found from the rules suggested in the above section but there is the useful relationship

$$a_{x:\overline{n}|} = vp_x(1 + a_{x+1:\overline{n-1}|})$$

so that starting at $a_{x+n:\overline{0}|} = 0$ successive values can be found. There is however no independent summation check. The column headings for this calculation would be

x	p_x	$1 + a_{x+1:\overline{n-1}|}$	$a_{x:\overline{n}|}$	n

with v being held as a constant in the memory of the calculator.

If n rather than x is regarded as the variable,

$$\Delta a_{x:\overline{n}|} = D_{x+n+1}/D_x$$

and a continued process is available:

initial value $\qquad a_{x:\overline{1}|} = \dfrac{D_{x+1}}{D_x}$

working formula $a_{x:\overline{n}|} = a_{x:\overline{n-1}|} + \dfrac{D_{x+n}}{D_x}$

intermediate check formula

$$a_{x:\overline{n}|} = \frac{N_{x+1} - N_{x+n+1}}{D_x}$$

summation check formula

$$\sum_{n=1}^{t} a_{x:\overline{n}|} = \frac{tN_{x+1} - (S_{x+2} - S_{x+t+2})}{D_x}.$$

The column headings might be

n	D_{x+n}	$a_{x:\overline{n}|}$

with D_x held in the memory of the calculator.

Exercise 11.7

Determine a continued process to calculate the values of $_tV_{x:\overline{n}|}$ giving the column headings which would be used.

EXAMPLE AND EXERCISE ON CHAPTER 11

Example 11.7

A company offers a whole-life assurance under which the premiums would be waived if the life assured is sick, there being no waiting period. Premiums are payable weekly.

Using Appendix III tables 3 and 6, calculate at 4% interest the annual premium required for a life aged 40 at entry and find if the reserve at the end of 20 years is greater or less than under the policy without the waiver of premium benefit. Ignore expenses.

Solution

Let the annual premium for a sum assured of 100 be P payable continuously.

Then $\qquad P\bar{a}_{40} = 100\bar{A}_{40} + \dfrac{P}{52\cdot18}\dfrac{K_{40}}{D_{40}}$

and
$$K_{40} = K_{40}^{13} + K_{40}^{13/13} + K_{40}^{26/26} + K_{40}^{52/52} + K_{40}^{104/\text{all}}$$

$$= 385{,}490 + 130{,}449 + 144{,}315 + 172{,}341 + 700{,}172$$

$$= 1{,}532{,}767$$

$$\therefore P \frac{338{,}786}{19{,}535} = 100 \frac{6{,}247 \cdot 6}{19{,}535} + \frac{P}{52 \cdot 18} \frac{1{,}532{,}767}{19{,}535}$$

$$\therefore 17 \cdot 34P = 31 \cdot 98 + 1 \cdot 50P$$

$$\therefore P = \frac{31 \cdot 98}{15 \cdot 84} = 2 \cdot 02.$$

The prospective reserve after 20 years

$$= 100\bar{A}_{60} + \frac{P}{52 \cdot 18} \frac{K_{60}}{D_{60}} - P\bar{a}_{60}$$

and evaluating K_{60} similarly to K_{40} this

$$= 100 \frac{4{,}375 \cdot 3}{7{,}502 \cdot 5} + \frac{2 \cdot 02}{52 \cdot 18} \cdot \frac{970{,}853}{7{,}502 \cdot 5} - 2 \cdot 02 \frac{79{,}734 \cdot 6}{7{,}502 \cdot 5}$$

$$= 41 \cdot 9.$$

The reserve for the policy without waiver of premium benefit

$$= 100 \left(1 - \frac{\bar{a}_{60}}{\bar{a}_{40}} \right)$$

$$= 100 \left(1 - \frac{10 \cdot 63}{17 \cdot 34} \right)$$

$$= 38 \cdot 7.$$

Hence the reserve for the policy with a waiver is greater than for a policy without a waiver.

Exercise 11.8

An endowment assurance policy with premiums payable monthly maturing at age 65 includes a provision that premiums will be waived if the life assured is sick, there being no waiting period.

Using the tables 3 and 6 in Appendix III, calculate at 4% interest the annual premium required for a life aged 30 at entry, and find if the reserve at the end of 20 years is greater or less under the policy without the waiver of premium benefit. Ignore expenses. The sum assured is payable immediately on death.

ANSWERS TO EXERCISES

Normally only the answer to the exercise is given though in a few cases the line of approach is also indicated.

Chapter 1

1.1   ·8956, ·0668, ·3876

1.2   ·4739

1.3 $_{10}p_{56} = ·7785$, $_{10}p_{60} = ·7941$
       Therefore brother aged 60 is more likely to survive. This result is due to the lightness of the mortality of $a(55)$ when compared to ELT No. 12—Males. Normally, of course, the younger life is more likely to survive a given period

1.5   ·1455 (using 5% compound interest tables—which are not given in the Appendix)

1.6   Formulae (1.7.3) gives ·09905; (1.7.4) ·09874; (1.7.5) ·09888; (1.7.6) ·09891
       Tabulated value: ·09891

1.7   ·03125

1.8   (a) ·00129, (b) ·05726

1.9 $l_x = k\left(\dfrac{e}{x}\right)^{Ax}$

1.10 $A = 1·126 \times 10^{-4}$, $B = 1·135 \times 10^{-5}$, c = 1·126

1.11 $a = \dfrac{\log 2}{\log c}$

1.12   ·9760, ·0141, ·0268

1.13   77,344

1.14 $\dfrac{1}{x}$

1.16 $l_x = kg_1^{b^x}g_2^{d^x}$, where $\log_e g_1 = -\dfrac{a}{\log_e b}$, $\log_e g_2 = -\dfrac{c}{\log_e d}$

1.17   ·4647

1.18   877,015

1.19   1·263

Chapter 2

2.1 £351·24
2.2 £1,737·7
2.3 12·551, 8·330, 8·520, 9·267, 1·855, 7·240
2.4 £1,445·50
2.8 15·766
2.9 £49·12
2.10 $12·006 < 12·599 < 12·601 < 13·787 < 14·669$
2.11 ·3031, ·0268, ·7313, ·3803
2·12 ·2142
2.13 ·0090, ·0144, ·0077, ·0447, ·0807, ·0465
2.14 £0·1524
2.15 5·45
2.16 £57·38
2.17 £2,220·79
2.18 £98·29
2.19 £183·15
2.21 £138·29
2.22 £11·66
2.23 £123·21
2.25 2%
2.26 ·0209
2.27 £32·16 for first ten years then £64·32 for ten years
2.28 $\dfrac{1}{d_j^2}(A_x^J - A_x^i) - \dfrac{1}{d_j}(IA)_x^i$, where $\dfrac{1}{1+J} = \dfrac{1+j}{1+i}$
2.29 Profit of £150
2.30 £2,388

Chapter 3

3.1 13·752, 4·478, 10·242
3.3 At age 60, ·04%; at age 80, ·22%
3.4 £4,236
3.6 (i) £12,204, (ii) £13,794
3.7 ·5%
3.8 Rate of interest is $\dfrac{1+i}{c} - 1$
3.10 ·0147, ·0335, ·0421
3.11 $P_x^{(m)}$ and $P_x^{\{m\}} \to \bar{P}_x$

3.12 $$\dfrac{{}_tP_{x:\overline{n}|}}{1-\dfrac{m-1}{2m}\,(P^1_{x:\overline{t}|}+d)}$$

3.16 12·657, 11·992

3.18 3·529

3.19 £271

3.20 £138·92

3.21 $\bar{a}_{\overline{n}|}-\bar{a}_{x:\overline{n}|}$ at rate of interest $\dfrac{i-j}{1+j}$

3.22 9·193, 76·203

3.23 $(I\bar{A})_x \fallingdotseq \ddot{a}_x - i(I\mathring{a})_x$

3.24 $\dfrac{i-\delta}{\delta^2}\dfrac{C_x}{D_x}$

3.25 £30·33 p.a.

3.26 (a) 2,027 (most valuable), (b) 1,909, (c) 2,018

3.28 (40) Premium ·0638, (50) Premium ·0635
As premium for 'rated-up' age less, it is possible

3.29 $\dfrac{1}{k}\,\bar{a}_{x'}$, where $x' = kx - \dfrac{\log k}{\log c}$, at rate of interest such that

$\delta' = \dfrac{1}{k}(\delta - \log_e s) + \log_e s$ where $k = \dfrac{\log c'}{\log c}$

3.30 $\bar{a}_{\overline{n}|} - \dfrac{b}{\delta}(\bar{a}_{\overline{n}|} - nv^n)$, where $l_{x+t} = l_x(1-bt)$

3.31 $a_x^{(m)} \fallingdotseq \bar{a}_x - \dfrac{1}{2m} + \dfrac{1}{12m^2}(\mu_x+\delta)$

Chapter 4

4.1 Policy values at end of years are 23·21, 47·57, 73·11, 100·00

4.3 $\dfrac{D_{x+n}}{N_x-N_{x+n}}$, does not depend on t

4.4 13 years

4.5 £664·42

4.7 Reserve is equivalent to the present value of the difference between the premiums at the attained age and the premiums actually being paid

4.9 ·005

4.11 Loss of £26

4.13 ${}_1V_{[50]} = \cdot02198$, ${}_2V_{[50]} = \cdot04392$

4.14 vq_{x+t}

4.15 Profit of £78

4.17 $_tV^{1(m)}_{x:\,\overline{n}|} = \left\{1 + \dfrac{m-1}{2m} P^{1(m)}_{x:\,\overline{n}|}\right\} {}_tV^1_{x:\,\overline{n}|}$

$_t^kV^{(m)}_{x:\,\overline{n}|} = {}_t^kV_{x:\,\overline{n}|} + \dfrac{m-1}{2m} {}_kP^{(m)}_{x:\,\overline{n}|} {}_tV^1_{x:\,\overline{k}|}$ if $t < k$

and $_t^kV_{x:\,\overline{n}|}$ if $t \geqq k$

4.18 ·258, ·251, ·251

4.19 $_tV^{\{m\}}_x = (1 + \tfrac{1}{2}P^{\{m\}}_x){}_tV_x$

4.22 $_{15}V^{\text{mod}}_{30:\,\overline{30}|} = \cdot 3570,\ {}_{15}V_{30:\,\overline{30}|} = \cdot 3626$

4.23 ·282

4.24 Whole-life reserves are 3%: 124, 277, 448
                                4%: 103, 240, 404
     Endowment reserves are 3%: 198, 455, 787
                                4%: 173, 417, 762

4.25 Reserves are increased

4.28 ·4043, ·4188

4.29 $P = \dfrac{M_x - M_{x+a} + (1+k)v^{n-a}D_{x+a}}{N_x - N_{x+a} + D_{x+a}\ddot{a}_{\overline{n-a}|}}$

where a is the greatest integer for which $k\ddot{a}_{x:\,\overline{a}|} \leqq \ddot{s}_{\overline{n-a}|}$

4.30 $A = \dfrac{M_x - M_{x+c} + v^{n-c}(1+k)D_{x+c}}{D_x}$

where c is the greatest integer for which $(1+k) \leqq (1+i)^{n-c}$

4.31 £14·75

4.32 £34,473

4.33 £198·69, £297·86, ~~4·65%~~ 5·09%

4.34 Actual as issued   £966
     Expected as issued   £697
     With evidence of health:
     Actual   £965
     Expected   £517

Chapter 5

5.1 Per 1,000 sum assured

Age	ELT No. 12	A1967–70
50	161	128
60	364	316
70	554	512
80	715	684
90	818	808

5.2 ·692, ·639 (cf. proportional ·500); ·721 (cf. proportional ·571)

5.3 14 years, 360 days

5.4 £506, £458 the difference due to the life cover and extra interest on the loan

5.5 A' calculated at $\dfrac{i-b}{1+b}$

5.6 £222·24 (simple bonus); £224·37 (compound bonus)

5.8 £70·9 per £100 p.a. annuity

5.9 £290

5.10 £2,115, £1,124 (paid-up)

5.11 £113·59

5.12 The premium for the first option is greater than for the second so charge £10·67 (which could be reduced after four years to £8·87) 4·25 8·94

5.15 £29·42

5.16 £26·97 (£500 is payable on death in first 13 years, return of premiums thereafter)

5.17 £253·3 (extrapolate for assurance function at 2·97%)

5.18 £1·14

5.19 £1,659

5.20 Initial £391·5. Decrease £13·5

5.21 Reserve with Debt £1,789
Reserve with Extra Premium £1,779
Normal Reserve £1,787

5.22 £27·11. Sum assured increases to £1,080

5.23 15p per £100 more than normal premium; 68% deduction from sum assured

5.24 Before £17·98
After £29·88

5.25 6p option premium

Chapter 6

6.4 151·4

6.5 1,076·6

6.6 272 apprentices

6.7 Promotion at 47
Annual Christmas presents cost £80,895
Birthday present cost £80,240 per annum

6.8 (i) $-{}_t p_x$, (ii) $\mu_x \overset{\circ}{e}_{x:\overline{n}|} - 1 + \dfrac{l_{x+n}}{l_x}$

6.9 55·85

6.10 (*a*) 9·210, (*b*) 4·172

6.11 $\dfrac{\bar{a}_x}{\overset{\circ}{e}_x}$

6.12 Fund is £7,778,600

6.13 Fund is £797,700

6.15 $m_x = 1$ for all x

6.17 45·1%

6.18 Very close to age 58

6.19 $\mu_x = \dfrac{1}{2(80-x)}$; $\overset{\circ}{e}_x = \frac{2}{3}(80-x)$. Average age 63.3

6.20 £19,520 per annum

Chapter 7

7.1 (*a*) $_n|q_x \cdot _n|q_y \cdot _n|q_z$; (*b*) $(1 - _n|q_x)(1 - _n|q_y)(1 - _n|q_y)$; (*c*) $1 - (b)$

7.2 $a_{x:\overline{n}|} + v^n {_np_x} a_{x+n:y:\overline{m-n}|}$

7.3 ·0348, ·0270

7.4 £18,133

7.5 Makeham   (i) 14·077 (table in section 7.2)
               (ii) 13·957 (equivalent equal ages)

    Gompertz   (i) 13·310 (table in section 7.2)
              (ii) 14·262 (equivalent single age)

7.7 ·0136

7.9 $a_{\overline{10}|} - a_{xy:\overline{20}|} + v^{10} a_{\overline{xy}:\overline{10}|}$

7.10 (a) 22·70, (b) 3·60

7.11 $300(a_{50} - a_{50:\overline{10}|} + a_{45} - a_{45:\overline{15}|} + a_{40} - a_{40:\overline{20}|})$

$- 200(a_{45:50} - a_{45:50:\overline{15}|} + a_{40:50} - a_{40:50:\overline{20}|}$

$+ a_{40:45} - a_{40:45:\overline{20}|})$

$+ 200(a_{40:45:50} - a_{40:45:50:\overline{20}|})$

7.12 ·564

7.14 $a_{\overline{n}|} + (a_x - a_{x:\overline{n}|}) + (a_y - a_{y:\overline{n}|}) - (a_{xy} - a_{xy:\overline{n}|})$

7.15 An assurance payable on the death of x after n years, but if the death of x takes place before n years the assurance is payable at the end of the nth year.

or $A_x - A_{x:\overline{n}|} + v^n$

7.16 $a_{abx} + a_{aby} + a_{abz} - a_{abxy} - a_{abyz} - a_{abzx} + a_{abxyz}$

7.17 The suffices of A read as follows, using the shorthand notation mentioned in Example 7.17:

$a + b + x + y + z - ab - ax - ay - az - bx - by - bz - xy$

$- yz - zx + abx + aby + abz + axy + ayz + azx + bxy + byz$

$+ bzx + xyz - abxy - abyz - abzx - axyz - bxyz + abxyz$

7.19 $100\{(\ddot{a}_{\overline{10}|} + {}_{10}|\ddot{a}_{60})(v^{20}{}_{20}p_{40} + v^{25}(1 - {}_{20}p_{40}){}_{25}p_{35})$
$\qquad\qquad + v^{20}{}_{20}p_{40}\,{}_{20}p_{35}({}_{10}|\ddot{a}_{55} - {}_{10}|\ddot{a}_{55:60})\}$

7.20 $100\{a_{\overline{20}|} + v^{20}a_{40:50} + v^{20}{}_{10}p_{50}a_{60} - v^{20}{}_{10}p_{50}a_{40:60}$
$\qquad\qquad\qquad + v^{20}{}_{10}p_{40}a_{50} - v^{20}{}_{10}p_{40}a_{50:50}\}$

7.21 (a) ·5479, (b) ·1072

Chapter 8

8.1 ${}_{\infty}q^1_{yw} + {}_{\infty}q^1_{yx} + 2{}_{\infty}q^1_{yz} - 2{}_{\infty}q^1_{ywx} - 2{}_{\infty}q^1_{ywz} - {}_{\infty}q^1_{yxz} + 3{}_{\infty}q^1_{ywxz}$

8.2 ·25

8.3 ${}_{17}q^1_{8:45} + {}_{19}q^1_{6:45} - {}_{17}q_{6:8:45}$
$\qquad - {}_{17}q^1_{6:8:45} - {}_{17}p_{6:8:45} \times {}_{2}q^1_{23:62}$

8.4 $A^1_{yw} + A^1_{yx} + A^1_{yz} - 2A^1_{ywx} - 2A^1_{ywz} - 2A^1_{yxz} + 3A^1_{ywxz}$
(compare with Exercise 1)

8.6 $1 - {}_{n}p_{x}\,{}_{\infty}q^1_{y:x+n}$

8.7 $\dfrac{D_{x+n}}{D_x}(\bar{A}_{x+n} - \bar{A}^1_{x+n:y})$

8.9 $A^1_{25:20:\overline{10}|} + \dfrac{D_{35}}{D_{25}} \cdot \dfrac{l_{30}}{l_{20}}(A^1_{35:30:30} + A^1_{35:30:40} - A^1_{35:30:30:40})$

8.10 $1 - {}_{n}p_{xy}\,{}_{\infty}q_{x+n:y+n:\overset{1}{z}} - {}_{n}p_{z}(1 - {}_{\infty}q_{x:y:\overset{1}{z+n}})$

8.11 $P = A/\ddot{a}$ where

$$A = A^1_{50:\overline{10}|} - A_{\overline{50:20}:\overline{10}|} + A^1_{20:\overline{15}|} - \dfrac{D_{30:60}}{D_{20:50}}A^1_{30:\overline{5}|}$$

$$\ddot{a} = \ddot{a}_{20:\overline{15}|} + \ddot{a}_{50:\overline{10}|} - \ddot{a}_{20:50:\overline{10}|} - \dfrac{D_{30:60}}{D_{20:50}}\ddot{a}_{30:\overline{5}|}$$

8.12 £12·55

8.13 (a) Premium annuity $\ddot{a}_{x:\overline{yz}}$; all lives require to be medically examined.

(b) If both alive: $A^2_{x+t:y+t:z+t} - P\ddot{a}_{x+t:\overline{y+t:z+t}}$
If z dead: $\quad A^1_{x+t:y+t} - P\ddot{a}_{x+t:y+t}$
If y dead: $\quad A^1_{x+t:z+t} - P\ddot{a}_{x+t:z+t}$
where $P = A^2_{xyz}/\ddot{a}_{x:\overline{yz}}$

8.14 ·218

8.16 $A\bar{a}_{xy} + Bc^x\bar{a}'_{xy}$
n is such that $\bar{a}'_{xy} = c^n\bar{a}_{xy}$

where $\bar{a}'$ is calculated at a rate of interest $i' = \dfrac{1+i}{c} - 1$

8.18 ·3825

8.19 $a_y - a_{xy} + \dfrac{1}{2m} A_{xy}^1$; annuity to y payable $m$thly on the death of x with first payment immediately on death.

8.20 $a_y + a_z - a_{yz} - a_{wxy} - a_{wxz} + a_{wxyz}$; $a_{yz} - a_{yzw} - a_{xyz} + a_{xyzw}$

8.22 Interest of 55:
$100(a_{30\,:\,55} + a_{35\,:\,55} - a_{30\,:\,35\,:\,55} - a_{30\,:\,55\,:\,60} - a_{35\,:\,55\,:\,60}$
$+ a_{30\,:\,35\,:\,55\,:\,60})$

Interests of 30 and 35 each:
$50(a_{30\,:\,35} - a_{30\,:\,35\,:\,55} - a_{30\,:\,35\,:\,60} + a_{30\,:\,35\,:\,55\,:\,60})$

8.23 $150a_{30} - 100a_{30\,:\,\overline{20|}} + 30a_{30\,:\,50} + 20a_{30\,:\,50\,:\,\overline{20|}} + 30a_{30\,:\,42\,:\,50}$
$+ 20a_{30\,:\,42\,:\,50\,:\,\overline{20|}}$

8.25 $\frac{1}{2}(\bar{a}_y - \bar{a}_{xxy})$

8.27 $\displaystyle\int_0^\infty v^t{}_tp_{wxy}(1 - {}_tp_z)\mu_{y+t}\bar{a}_{w+t\,:\,x+t}dt$;

$\displaystyle\int_0^\infty v^t{}_tp_{wxyz}\mu_{z+t}(\bar{a}_{w+t} - \bar{a}_{y+t\,:\,w+t})dt$

8.28 $a_{\overline{20|}} - (1 - v^{20})a_{30\,:\,40} + v^{20}{}_{10}p_{40}(a_{50} - a_{30\,:\,50})$
$+ v^{20}{}_{10}p_{30}(a_{40} - a_{40\,:\,40})$

8.29 (a) £60·65, (b) £214·68

8.30 ·5

8.31 13/60

8.33 $15{,}000a_x - 7{,}500a_{xx} + 3{,}500\,{}_5|a_{xxy} - 7{,}500\,{}_5|a_{xy}$
$+ 2{,}500\,\dfrac{D_{x+5\,:\,y+5}}{D_{x\,:\,y}} \cdot a_{x\,:\,x+5\,:\,y+5}$

Chapter 9

9.1 (a) ·1150, (b) ·0244, (c) 1,429 apprentices

9.2 $(1{,}000 - x - 1)(e^{-x} - e^{-x-1}) + e^{-x-1}$

9.3 ·0211, ·0471, ·0707, ·0500, ·0406

9.4 ·0460, ·0683, ·0247

9.5 ·0107

9.6

x	$(al)_x$	$(ad)_x^d$	$(ad)_x^w$	$(ad)_x^v$
50	10,000	46	797	29
51	9,128	47	818	26

9.7 (a) ·0065, (b) ·0031, (c) ·0070

9.8 £11·65

9.9 £1,359

9.10 ·0993, ·823

9.11 Combined table of retirement and mortality of both in service lives $(sl)_x$ and pensioners $(rl)_x$, with total $l_x (=(sl)_x+(rl)_x)$ and $d_x (=(sd)_x+(rd)_x)$ with values found successively, and $r_x = \cdot 2(sl)_x, d_x = l_x q_x$ (q_x on A1967–70 ult) to be constructed.

An example of $(rd)_x$ is

$$(rd)_{68} = r_{65}.vp_{65}.vp_{66}.p_{67}.q_{68} + r_{66}.vp_{66}.vp_{67}.q_{68}$$
$$+ r_{67}.vp_{67}(1-vp_{68}) + r_{68}(1-vp_{68})$$

where v is at $2\frac{1}{2}\%$.

Value required $= \dfrac{v^{\frac{1}{2}} \sum\limits_{t=0}^{4} v^t (sd)_{65+t}}{(sl)_{65}}$, where v is now at 3%.

9.12 i found from $p_x \dfrac{1+(ha)_{x+1}}{(ha)_x} = 1$

$(bh)_x = \dfrac{(bl)_x(1-q_x)-(bl)_{x+1}}{1-\frac{1}{2}q_x}$, p_x and q_x on ELT 12

answer (a) is $200 \sum\limits_{t=1}^{\infty} v^t \dfrac{(bl)_{x+t}}{(bl)_x}$

$$+ 400 \sum\limits_{t=0}^{\infty} v^t \dfrac{(bh)_{x+t}}{(bl)_x} (a_{\overline{10|}} + v^{10}\,{}_9\!\frac{1}{2}p_{x+t+\frac{1}{2}}(ha)_{x+t+10})$$

(b) $\dfrac{(bh)_{z-8}}{(bl)_x} \cdot \dfrac{d_z}{l_{z-7\frac{1}{2}}}$, the second factor being on ELT 12

9.13 Find p_x from $a_x = vp\ddot{a}_{x+1}$

Value of (i) is $200 \dfrac{v^{20}}{(bl)_{25}} \left((bl)_{45} + (hl)_{45} - (hl)_{25} \prod\limits_{t=0}^{19} p_{25+t} \right)$

Values of (ii), (iii), (iv) combine to £100 on death and £100 on first of death or marriage.

Value of temporary annuity-due of a bachelor during bachelor-hood is $\dfrac{(bN)_{25}-(bN)_{45}}{(bD)_{25}}$ and value of annuity-due whether married or single

$$\frac{1}{(bl)_{25}} \left\{ ((bl)_{25}+(hl)_{25}) \frac{(bN)_{25}-(bN)_{45}+(hN)_{25}-(hN)_{45}}{(bD)_{25}+(hD)_{25}} \right.$$
$$\left. -(hl)_{25} \left(\ddot{a}_{25} - \prod\limits_{t=0}^{19} p_{25+t} v^{20} \ddot{a}_{45} \right) \right\}$$

Similar values are found for immediate annuities and values of benefits found using the $A = v\ddot{a}-a$ relationship for each annuity; multiplying each by 100 and adding the value of (i). The premium is found by dividing by the average of the annuities-due found.

O

9.14 From age 20 to 30 service table functions will be A1967–70 functions plus $\cdot014528$ (i.e. $\delta^{4\%}-\delta^{2\frac{1}{2}\%}$) in the force of interest. Find $(al)_{58}$, $(al)_{59}$ and $(al)_{60}$ using double decrement formulae.

Find value of benefits including a benefit of £1000 on withdrawal and deduct the withdrawal benefit, which will be

$$\frac{1,000}{(1\cdot025)^{\frac{1}{2}}}(\cdot014528)(a\bar{a})_{20\,:\,\overline{10|}}$$

the last factor being also $\bar{a}_{20\,:\,\overline{10|}}$ at 4%.

Chapter 10

10.1 (a) £8,716, (b) £15,413, (c) £9,085

10.2 $P(65-x)\dfrac{M_x^{ia}}{D_x}$; £736

10.3 £37,967

10.4 $\dfrac{B(M_x^{ia}-M_{x+n}^{ia})}{D_x}+\dfrac{S^s\bar{R}_{x+n}^{ia}}{100^sD_x}+\dfrac{TS}{100}\dfrac{M_{x+n}^{ia}}{{}^sD_x}$,

where $TS=\dfrac{S}{S_x}\displaystyle\sum_{t=0}^{n-1}s_{x+t}$,

and n is the lowest number for which

$\dfrac{S}{100s_x}\left(\displaystyle\sum_{t=0}^{n-1}s_{x+t}+\tfrac{1}{2}s_{x+n}\right)>B.$

10.5 £24,440

10.6 Age 30, 4·4%
Age 50, 8·1%

10.7 £1,508

10.8 £2,648

10.9 £1,903

10.10 $\dfrac{S}{40}\dfrac{{}^z\bar{R}_x^d}{{}^sD_x}+\dfrac{nS}{40}\dfrac{{}^zM_x^d}{{}^sD_x}$,

where z_x is s_x

10.11 $\dfrac{S}{30}\dfrac{{}^s\bar{R}_x^r}{{}^sD_x}+\dfrac{(PS)}{30}\dfrac{M_x^r}{D_x}$

10.12 $\dfrac{(AS)_x}{20}\dfrac{{}^s\bar{R}_x^{d(h)}}{{}^sD_x}+\dfrac{(TPS)_x}{20}\dfrac{M_x^{d(h)}}{D_x}$

using $C_x^{d(h)}=v^{x+\frac{1}{2}}d_x(1+\tfrac{1}{2}h_x+\tfrac{1}{2}g_x)$,

where h_x and g_x are proportions of members married and those with a child under age 18, respectively.

10.13 £125·04

10.14   (*a*) £216, (*b*) £260

10.15   Past Contributions: $(PC)\dfrac{^jM_x^d}{^jD_x}$

       Future Contributions: $\dfrac{(\cdot05)S}{^sD_x}\,{}^{sj}\bar{R}_x^d - 12\cdot5\,\dfrac{^j\bar{R}_x^d}{D_x}$

10.16 $(PC)\dfrac{M_x^w}{D_x} + (\cdot01)CS\dfrac{^s\bar{R}_x^w}{^sD_x}$

10.17 $\dfrac{S}{80}\dfrac{^s\bar{R}_x^{dwa}}{^sD_x} + \dfrac{(nS)}{80}\dfrac{^sM_x^{dwa}}{^sD_x}$,

       where ${}^sC_x^{dwa} = v^{x+\frac{1}{2}}s_x d_x h_{x+\frac{1}{2}}\bar{a}''_{y+\frac{1}{2}}$

10.18 $\dfrac{1}{D_x}\displaystyle\sum_{t=0}^{64-x} v^{x+t+\frac{1}{2}}d_{x+t}w_{x+t+\frac{1}{2}}(Oa)_{x+t+\frac{1}{2}}$,

       where w_x is the proportion of members at age x who are widowers,

       $(Oa)_x = \{\frac{1}{2}c_x\bar{a}_{\overline{15\frac{1}{2}}|} + \dots{}_{15\frac{1}{2}}c_x\bar{a}_{\overline{\frac{1}{2}}|}\}$,

       ${}_{t+\frac{1}{2}}c_x$ being the proportion of widowers who have a child aged t last birthday, ignoring the oldest children over three in number.

10.19   £9,716

10.20 $\displaystyle\sum_{t=0}^{64-x}\dfrac{v^{x+t+\frac{1}{2}}(hd)_{x+t}}{v^x(hl)_x}$ {factor of the form of formula (10.9.2)}

       where $(hd)_x$ is the number of married men becoming widowers between x and $x+1$.

10.21   Let n represent complete past years of service.

       Past Service: $nP\dfrac{(M_x^{ia}+M_x^{ra})}{D_x}$

       Future Service: $\dfrac{P(R_{x+\frac{1}{2}}^{ia}+R_{x+\frac{1}{2}}^{ra})}{D_x}$

10.22   Past Service: $\dfrac{nS}{K}\dfrac{(^zM_x^{ia}+^zM_x^{ra})}{^sD_x}$ (n includes fractions)

       Future Service: $S\dfrac{(^zR_{x+1}^{ia}+^zR_{x+1}^{ia})}{^sD_x}$

       z_x is s_{x-1}

10.23   Formulae multiplied by $\dfrac{s_x}{s_{x-1}}$, commutation functions being based on final salary of $\frac{1}{2}(s_{x-1}+s_x)$ and for retirement at 65, $\frac{1}{2}(s_{63}+s_{64})$.

10.24 $\dfrac{1}{D_x}\displaystyle\sum_{t=0}^{64-x} v^{x+t+\frac{1}{2}}d_{x+t}h_{x+t+\frac{1}{2}}\bar{a}''_{y+t+\frac{1}{2}}\left(\frac{1}{4}S\,\dfrac{S_{x+t}}{S_x}\right),$

where the bracket is given a minimum value of M_1 and maximum of M_2.

10.25 $\dfrac{\cdot 07(PS)}{l_{30}}\{v^{\frac{1}{2}}w_{30}+v^{\frac{3}{2}}w_{31}\}$

$+\dfrac{\cdot 07}{l_{30}}\dfrac{S}{s_{30}}\{\tfrac{1}{2}s_{30}v^{\frac{1}{2}}w_{30}+s_{30}v^{\frac{3}{2}}w_{31}+\tfrac{1}{2}s_{31}v^{\frac{3}{2}}w_{31}\}$

$+\dfrac{S}{80^sD_{30}}\{5^zM_{32}^{wa}+{}^z\bar{R}_{32}^{wa}\}$

being based on ${}^zC_x^{wa}=v^{x+\frac{1}{2}}s_xw_x(1\cdot 085)^{64\frac{1}{2}-x}{}_{64\frac{1}{2}-x|}a_{x+\frac{1}{2}}.$

10.26 If completed 10 years service:

$\dfrac{(PS)}{80}\dfrac{M_x^{wa}}{D_x}+\dfrac{S}{80}\dfrac{{}^s\bar{R}_x^{wa}}{{}^sD_x}$

based on $C_x^{wa}=v^{x+\frac{1}{2}}w_x\,{}_{64\frac{1}{2}-x|}a'_{x+\frac{1}{2}}$

with the salary scale introduced into the ${}^sM_x^{wa}$ function after summation of the C_x^{wa} to give M_x^{wa}.

If service completed (n) is less than 10 years:

$\left\{\dfrac{(PS)}{80}+\dfrac{1}{80}\dfrac{S}{s_x}\displaystyle\sum_{t=0}^{9-n}s_{x+t}\right\}\dfrac{M_{x+10-n}^{wa}}{D_x}+\dfrac{S}{80}\dfrac{{}^s\bar{R}_{x+10-n}^{wa}}{{}^sD_x}$

10.27 £302

10.28 (a) $\dfrac{(\cdot 04)S}{{}^sD_x}{}^{sj}\bar{R}_x^d-20\dfrac{{}^j\bar{R}_x^d}{D_x}+(PC)\dfrac{{}^jM_x^d}{{}^jD_x}$

(b) $S\dfrac{{}^sM_x^d}{{}^sD_x}$ if service >10 years; otherwise with service $n<10$,

$\dfrac{1}{{}^sD_x}\left\{\dfrac{n}{10}\dfrac{{}^sC_x^d}{{}^sD_x}+\dfrac{n+1}{10}{}^sC_{x+1}^d\ldots+{}^sM_{x+10-n}^d\right\}$

10.29 Former benefit: $\dfrac{1}{D_{20}}(400\,M_{25}^d+100R_{25}^d)$

New benefit: $5{,}000\dfrac{M_{20}^d}{D_{20}}+\dfrac{200}{D_{20}}\displaystyle\sum_{t=1}^{13}D_{20+3t}+250(p)\dfrac{M_{20}^w}{D_{20}},$

where (p) is the proportion of withdrawals due to marriage.

10.30 Contributions: $\dfrac{1}{200}\dfrac{S}{{}^sD_x}[{}^s\bar{N}_x+{}^{sh}\bar{N}_x]$

Benefits: $\dfrac{S}{100}\dfrac{{}^{z}R_{x+1}^{dwa}}{{}^{s}D_{x}} + S\dfrac{(65-x)}{100}\dfrac{{}^{z}C_{65}^{rwa}}{{}^{s}D_{x}} + \dfrac{S}{100}\dfrac{{}^{z}R_{x+1}^{iwa}}{{}^{s}D_{x}}$

where ${}^{z}C_{x}^{dwa} = v^{x+\frac12}z_{x}d_{x}h_{x}\bar{a}_{y+\frac12}''$, ${}^{z}C_{x}^{iwa} = v^{x+\frac12}z_{x}i_{x}h_{x}\bar{a}_{x+\frac12|y+\frac12}''$

10.31 $\dfrac{\cdot 3S}{{}^{s}D_{x}}\{{}^{z}M_{x}^{dwa}+{}^{z}C_{65}^{rwa}+{}^{z}M_{x}^{iwa}\}$

Chapter 11

11.1 33p per week

11.2 £0·12 per week

11.3 54p per week

11.4 $\dfrac{B}{l_{x}}\displaystyle\sum_{t=0}^{2} v^{t+k+\frac12}{}_{(k)}i_{x+t}\bar{a}_{x+t+\frac12+k}'$

11.5 12·598

11.6 $B\displaystyle\int_{0}^{\infty} v^{t}\{(uf)_{x+t}+(ufm)_{x+t}\}{}_{t}p_{x}\mu_{x+t}dt$, B being the benefit,

and $(uf)_{x}$ is the proportion of those who die at age x who have a dependant female relative
and $(ufm)_{x}$ is the proportion of those who die at age x who have a dependant widowed mother.

11.7 $_{t+1}V_{x:\,\overline{n}|} = \dfrac{1}{p_{x+t}}\{(_{t}V_{x:\,\overline{n}|}+P)(1+i)-q_{x+t}\}$

with $_{0}V_{x:\,\overline{n}|} = 0$.
Column headings: t; $(_{t}V+P)(1+i)$; q_{x+t}; p_{x+t}; $_{t+1}V$,

final check $_{n}^{*}V_{x:\,\overline{n}|} = 1$.

11.8 Premium 16·50
Reserve with waiver 432·3; greater than reserve without waiver 426·0.

NOTATION

1 The actuarial notation which had been used by the Institute of Actuaries was adopted with minor modifications as the International Actuarial Notation by the Second International Congress of Actuaries in London in 1898. A number of changes which had already been introduced by the Institute and Faculty of Actuaries in 1950 and by the Society of Actuaries (the principal professional organisation in North America) were adopted internationally by the Fourteenth International Congress in Madrid in 1954. This notation, which has been used in this book, does not cover multiple decrement tables; pension fund, sickness and disability functions. The full statement of the present notation appears in the *Journal of the Institute of Actuaries*, Vol. LXXV, p. 121, and the *Transactions of the Faculty of Actuaries*, Vol. XIX, p. 89, and a summary of the principles is given in paragraph 3 below.

At the present time there is discussion on whether there should be a new or alternative notation because of the problems of reproduction by typewriter and in printing of the present notation and also to facilitate the use of computer programming languages— the intention being that the symbols be linearised, that is they should all be on the same line rather than a 'halo' of symbols round a central symbol as now. The extension to other functions such as these mentioned earlier is also under consideration.

2 The principal change introduced in 1950 which may cause confusion when reading or referring to earlier textbooks and published tables is that earlier the symbol N_x was used to denote $\sum_{t=1}^{\infty} D_{x+t}$ which is N_{x+1} in the present notation. The simplest test when examining a table is to see whether

$$N_x = D_x + N_{x+1} \text{ (new definition)}$$

or $\qquad N_x = D_{x+1} + N_{x+1} \text{ (old definition)}.$

In some earlier tables and books the symbol N_x was used to denote $\sum_{t=0}^{\infty} D_{x+t}$, i,e. N_x on the present notation. Similarly S_x was formerly used to represent $\sum_{t=1}^{\infty} N_{x+t}$ and S_x to represent $\sum_{t=0}^{\infty} N_{x+t}$.

3 The general principles on which the system is based are as follows:

(*a*) To each fundamental symbolic letter are attached signs and letters each having its own signification.

The lower space to the left is reserved for signs indicating the conditions relative to the duration of the operations and to their position with regard to time.

The lower space to the right is reserved for signs indicating the conditions relative to ages and the order of succession of the events.

The upper space to the right is reserved for signs indicating the periodicity of the events.

The upper space to the left is free, and in it can be placed signs corresponding to other notions.

(*b*) A letter or number enclosed in a right angle, thus $\overline{n|}$ or $\overline{15|}$, denotes a term-certain of years, others, perhaps in brackets ( ), [ ], indicate persons.

(*c*) The fundamental symbolic letters are *interest:* i, v, d, δ, a, s; *mortality:* l, d, p, q, μ, m, a, s, e, A, E, P, π, V, W.

(*d*) The two-dot symbol (diaeresis or trema) above the letters a and s is used as a symbol of acceleration of payments.

(*e*) It is always understood (unless otherwise expressed) that the annual payment of an annuity is 1, that the sum assured in any case is 1, and that symbols indicate present values.

(*f*) A letter or number at the lower left corner of the principal symbol denotes the number of years involved in the probability or benefit in question. When this number is 1 it is customary to omit it.

(*g*) If a letter or number comes before a perpendicular bar it shows that a period of deferment is meant.

(*h*) A letter or number in brackets at the upper right corner of the principal symbol shows the number of intervals into which the year is to be divided.

(*i*) If the interval tends to ∞, then instead of writing (∞) a bar is placed over the principal symbol.

(*j*) A small circle placed over the principal symbol shows that the benefit is to be complete.

(*k*) If there are two or more letters or numbers in a suffix without any distinguishing mark, joint lives are intended.

If a perpendicular bar separates the letters in the suffix, then the status after the bar is to follow the status before the bar.

If a horizontal bar appears above the suffix then survivors of the lives, and not joint lives, are intended. The number of survivors can be denoted by a letter or number over the bar. If that letter, say r, is not distinguished by any mark, then the meaning is at least r survivors; but if it is enclosed in square brackets, $[r]$, then the meaning is exactly r survivors. If no letter or number appears over the bar, then unity is supposed and the meaning is at least one survivor.

(*l*) When numerals are placed above or below the letters of the suffix, they designate the order in which the lives are to fail. The numeral placed over the suffix points out the life whose failure will finally determine the event; and the numerals placed under the suffix indicate the order in which the other lives involved are to fail.

(*m*) Sometimes to make quite clear that a joint-life status is involved a symbol $\frown$ is placed above the lives included. (Thus $A\frac{1}{\overline{xy}:\overline{n}|}$ = a joint-life temporary assurance on (*x*) and (*y*).)

(*n*) The symbols P, V, W with the appropriate suffix or suffixes are used in simple cases, where no misunderstanding can occur, to denote an annual premium, reserve or paid-up value respectively. Otherwise they may be used with symbols for the benefit in brackets.

(*o*) (Ia), (IA) denote increasing benefits, (Da), (DI), decreasing and (Va), (VA) varying.

(*p*) Commutation functions are denoted by D, N, S, C, M, R. If benefits are payable continuously in the case of annuities, or at the moment of death in the case of assurances, a bar is placed above.

(*q*) If the suffix to a symbol which denotes the age is enclosed in a square bracket it indicates the age at which the life was selected. To this may be added, outside the bracket, the number of years which have elapsed since selection, so that the total suffix denotes the present age.

TABLES

The following tables are used in the examples in this book and are also required for many of the exercises. While the life and sickness tables are extracts of published tables the pension fund tables are not and the rates of decrement have been arbitrarily determined so that the tables cannot be regarded as suitable for practical use in connection with the valuation of any actual fund.

1. Compound Interest Table: 4% interest.
2. Life Assurance Table: A1967–70: 4% interest.
3. Population Life Table: English Life Table No. 12—Males (based on the 1961 census) as adapted by the Industrial Life Offices Association: 4% interest.
4. Annuity Table: $a(55)$ males and females—from age 60 only (the initial age of the published table is 20): 4% interest.
5. Pension Fund Tables: 4% interest.
6. Sickness Table: Manchester Unity Experience 1893–7; Occupation Group AHJ (and combined with English Life Table No. 12—Males): 4% interest.

TABLE 1

COMPOUND INTEREST TABLE

Rate of interest 4%

Constants			n	$(1+i)^n$	v^n	$s_{\overline{n}|}$	$a_{\overline{n}|}$
Function	**Value**		1	1·04000	·96154	1·0000	0·9615
			2	1·08160	·92456	2·0400	1·8861
i	·04		3	1·12486	·88900	3·1216	2·7751
$i^{(2)}$	·039608		4	1·16986	·85480	4·2465	3·6299
$i^{(4)}$	·039414		5	1·21665	·82193	5·4163	4·4518
$i^{(12)}$	·039285						
δ	·039221		6	1·26532	·79031	6·6330	5·2421
			7	1·31593	·75992	7·8983	6·0021
$(1+i)^{1/2}$	1·019804		8	1·36857	·73069	9·2142	6·7327
$(1+i)^{1/4}$	1·009853		9	1·42331	·70259	10·5828	7·4353
$(1+i)^{1/12}$	1·003274		10	1·48024	·67556	12·0061	8·1109
			11	1·53945	·64958	13·4864	8·7605
v	·961538		12	1·60103	·62460	15·0258	9·3851
$v^{1/2}$	·980581		13	1·66507	·60057	16·6268	9·9856
$v^{1/4}$	·990243		14	1·73168	·57748	18·2919	10·5631
$v^{1/12}$	·996737		15	1·80094	·55526	20·0236	11·1184
			16	1·87298	·53391	21·8245	11·6523
d	·038462		17	1·94790	·51337	23·6975	12·1657
$d^{(2)}$	·038839		18	2·02582	·49363	25·6454	12·6593
$d^{(4)}$	·039029		19	2·10685	·47464	27·6712	13·1339
$d^{(12)}$	·039157		20	2·19112	·45639	29·7781	13·5903
			21	2·27877	·43883	31·9692	14·0292
$i/i^{(2)}$	1·009902		22	2·36992	·42196	34·2480	14·4511
$i/i^{(4)}$	1·014877		23	2·46472	·40573	36·6179	14·8568
$i/i^{(12)}$	1·018204		24	2·56330	·39012	39·0826	15·2470
i/δ	1·019869		25	2·66584	·37512	41·6459	15·6221
			26	2·77247	·36069	44·3117	15·9828
$i/d^{(2)}$	1·029902		27	2·88337	·34682	47·0842	16·3296
$i/d^{(4)}$	1·024877		28	2·99870	·33348	49·9676	16·6631
$i/d^{(12)}$	1·021537		29	3·11865	·32065	52·9663	16·9837
			30	3·24340	·30832	56·0849	17·2920
$\log_{10}(1+i)$	·0170333		31	3·37313	·29646	59·3283	17·5885
			32	3·50806	·28506	62·7015	17·8736
			33	3·64838	·27409	66·2095	18·1476
			34	3·79432	·26355	69·8579	18·4112
			35	3·94609	·25342	73·6522	18·6646
			36	4·10393	·24367	77·5983	18·9083
			37	4·26809	·23430	81·7022	19·1426
			38	4·43881	·22529	85·9703	19·3679
			39	4·61637	·21662	90·4091	19·5845
			40	4·80102	·20829	95·0255	19·7928
			41	4·99306	·20028	99·8265	19·9931
			42	5·19278	·19257	104·8196	20·1856
			43	5·40050	·18517	110·0124	20·3708
			44	5·61652	·17805	115·4129	20·5488
			45	5·84118	·17120	121·0294	20·7200
			46	6·07482	·16461	126·8706	20·8847
			47	6·31782	·15828	132·9454	21·0429
			48	6·57053	·15219	139·2632	21·1951
			49	6·83335	·14634	145·8337	21·3415
			50	7·10668	·14071	152·6671	21·4822
			60	10·51963	·09506	237·9907	22·6235
			70	15·57162	·06422	364·2905	23·3945
			80	23·04980	·04338	551·2450	23·9154
			90	34·11933	·02931	827·9833	24·2673
			100	50·50495	·01980	1237·6237	24·5050

Table 2

LIFE ASSURANCE TABLE: A1967–70

MORTALITY FUNCTIONS

Age [x]	$l_{[x]}$	$l_{[x]+1}$	l_{x+2}	Age x+2
			344 89· 000	0
			344 63· 823	1
0	344 81· 408	344 61· 409	344 40· 388	2
1	344 56· 927	344 38· 320	344 18· 690	3
2	344 33· 841	344 16· 624	343 98· 727	4
3	344 12· 836	343 97· 007	343 80· 496	5
4	343 93· 221	343 78· 776	343 63· 650	6
5	343 75· 681	343 62· 274	343 48· 186	7
6	343 59· 181	343 46· 811	343 33· 760	8
7	343 44· 063	343 32· 386	343 20· 026	9
8	343 29· 638	343 18· 653	343 06· 985	10
9	343 15· 907	343 05· 612	342 94· 291	11
10	343 03· 210	342 92· 919	342 81· 602	12
11	342 90· 518	342 80· 230	342 68· 918	13
12	342 77· 830	342 67· 547	342 55· 210	14
13	342 64· 461	342 53· 497	342 39· 110	15
14	342 50· 070	342 37· 055	342 18· 225	16
15	342 32· 259	342 15· 485	341 90· 508	17
16	342 09· 439	341 87· 202	341 54· 424	18
17	341 79· 680	341 51· 017	341 20· 378	19
18	341 43· 368	341 16· 899	340 88· 257	20
19	341 09· 166	340 84· 731	340 57· 937	21
20	340 76· 957	340 54· 389	340 29· 283	22
21	340 46· 610	340 25· 734	340 02· 148	23
22	340 17· 983	339 98· 619	339 76· 374	24
23	339 90· 921	339 72· 879	339 51· 787	25
24	339 65· 254	339 48· 338	339 28· 197	26
25	339 40· 795	339 24· 799	339 05· 397	27
26	339 17· 341	339 02· 051	338 83· 161	28
27	338 94· 668	338 79· 860	338 61· 242	29
28	338 72· 531	338 57· 972	338 39· 370	30
29	336 50· 662	338 36· 106	338 17· 250	31
30	338 28· 764	338 13· 958	337 94· 559	32
31	338 06· 514	337 91· 191	337 70· 942	33
32	337 83· 557	337 67· 439	337 46· 015	34
33	337 59· 503	337 42· 299	337 19· 354	35
34	337 33· 924	337 15· 331	336 90· 498	36
35	337 06· 352	336 86· 054	336 58· 943	37
36	336 76· 272	336 53· 938	336 24· 136	38
37	336 43· 122	336 18· 409	335 85· 478	39
38	336 06· 286	335 78· 835	335 42· 311	40
39	335 65· 089	335 34· 529	334 93· 920	41
40	335 18· 794	334 84· 739	334 39· 528	42
41	334 66· 599	334 28· 646	333 78· 285	43
42	334 07· 624	333 65· 360	333 09· 271	44
43	333 40· 915	332 93· 909	332 31· 486	45
44	332 65· 431	332 13· 241	331 43· 847	46
45	331 80· 042	331 22· 213	330 45· 181	47
46	330 83· 523	330 19· 589	329 34· 221	48
47	329 74· 549	329 04· 032	328 09· 601	49
48	328 51· 686	327 74· 102	326 69· 855	50
49	327 13· 392	326 28· 250	325 13· 405	51
50	325 58· 008	324 64· 813	323 38· 568	52
51	323 83· 756	322 82· 013	321 43· 546	53
52	321 88· 740	320 77· 958	319 26· 430	54

Age [x]	$l_{[x]}$	$l_{[x]+1}$	l_{x+2}	Age x+2
53	319 70· 942	318 50· 639	316 85· 203	55
54	317 28· 226	315 97· 933	314 17· 739	56
55	314 58· 342	313 17· 610	311 21· 815	57
56	311 58· 931	310 07· 338	307 95· 116	58
57	308 27· 543	306 64· 702	304 35· 255	59
58	304 61· 645	302 87· 215	300 39· 787	60
59	300 58· 648	298 72· 344	296 06· 239	61
60	296 15· 936	294 17· 538	291 32· 138	62
61	291 30· 898	289 20· 265	286 15· 051	63
62	286 00· 975	283 78· 059	280 52· 632	64
63	280 23· 708	277 88· 571	274 42· 681	65
64	273 96· 808	271 49· 632	267 83· 206	66
65	267 18· 225	264 59· 331	260 72· 500	67
66	259 86· 236	257 16· 097	253 09· 230	68
67	251 99· 536	249 18· 797	244 92· 529	69
68	243 57· 348	240 66· 835	236 22· 102	70
69	234 59· 538	231 60· 273	226 98· 338	71
70	225 06· 732	221 99· 940	217 22· 421	72
71	215 00· 445	211 87· 559	206 96· 450	73
72	204 43· 198	201 25· 863	196 23· 545	74
73	193 38· 635	190 18· 696	185 07· 942	75
74	181 91· 617	178 71· 109	173 55· 074	76
75	170 08· 294	166 89· 418	161 71· 618	77
76	157 96· 140	154 81· 232	149 65· 496	78
77	145 63· 940	142 55· 427	137 45· 841	79
78	133 21· 717	130 22· 064	125 22· 890	80
79	120 80· 592	117 92· 241	113 07· 812	81
80	108 52· 568	105 77· 865	101 12· 467	82
			894 9·0 836	83
			782 9·8 752	84
			676 6·5 922	85
			577 0·0 459	86
			484 9·6 219	87
			401 2·8 253	88
			326 4·8 949	89
			260 8·5 274	90
			204 3·7 464	91
			156 7·9 405	92
			117 6·0 783	93
			861 ·08 935	94
			614 ·37 801	95
			426 ·42 117	96
			287 ·38 847	97
			187 ·72 094	98
			118 ·61 237	99
			72· 353 686	100
			42· 523 157	101
			24· 028 676	102
			13· 027 677	103
			6·7 627 284	104
			3·3 540 934	105
			1·5 860 118	106
			·71 350 781	107
			·30 474 896	108
			·12 332 121	109

TABLE 2 (continued)

MORTALITY FUNCTIONS

Age [x]	$d_{[x]}$	$d_{[x]+1}$	d_{x+2}	Age x+2
			25· 176 970	0
			23· 435 400	1
0	19· 999 217	21· 021 460	21· 697 444	2
1	18· 606 740	19· 629 842	19· 962 840	3
2	17· 216 920	17· 896 644	18· 231 325	4
3	15· 829 905	16· 510 563	16· 846 443	5
4	14· 445 153	15· 126 662	15· 463 642	6
5	13· 406 516	14· 088 533	14· 426 238	7
6	12· 369 305	13· 051 788	13· 733 504	8
7	11· 676 981	12· 359 659	13· 041 610	9
8	10· 985 484	11· 668 342	12· 693 584	10
9	10· 294 772	11· 320 852	12· 688 888	11
10	10· 290 963	11· 316 663	12· 684 193	12
11	10· 287 155	11· 312 476	13· 707 567	13
12	10· 283 349	12· 336 317	16· 099 949	14
13	10· 964 628	14· 386 469	20· 885 857	15
14	13· 015 027	18· 830 380	27· 716 762	16
15	16· 773 807	24· 977 304	36· 083 978	17
16	22· 236 135	32· 778 690	34· 045 471	18
17	28· 662 738	30· 638 927	32· 120 924	19
18	26· 468 621	28· 641 478	30· 320 482	20
19	24· 434 783	26· 794 348	28· 654 305	21
20	22· 568 487	25· 106 258	27· 134 610	22
21	20· 876 020	23· 586 299	25· 773 968	23
22	19· 364 397	22· 244 956	24· 587 343	24
23	18· 042 041	21· 092 742	23· 590 041	25
24	16· 916 055	20· 140 870	22· 800 087	26
25	15· 995 957	19· 402 610	22· 235 837	27
26	15· 289 937	18· 890 223	21· 918 678	28
27	14· 807 903	18· 618 338	21· 871 653	29
28	14· 559 430	18· 601 570	22· 120 120	30
29	14· 555 107	18· 856 185	22· 691 713	31
30	14· 805 835	19· 399 406	23· 616 313	32
31	15· 323 141	20· 249 033	24· 927 346	33
32	16· 118 473	21· 424 089	26· 660 702	34
33	17· 204 181	22· 945 101	28· 856 012	35
34	18· 593 127	24· 833 027	31· 555 531	36
35	20· 298 639	27· 110 873	34· 806 376	37
36	22· 334 104	29· 801 908	38· 658 678	38
37	24· 713 228	32· 931 249	43· 166 743	39
38	27· 450 286	36· 524 371	48· 390 486	40
39	30· 559 671	40· 608 638	54· 392 787	41
40	34· 055 430	45· 211 429	61· 242 823	42
41	37· 952 462	50· 361 593	69· 013 943	43
42	42· 264 654	56· 088 838	77· 784 809	44
43	47· 006 022	62· 422 750	87· 639 072	45
44	52· 189 802	69· 394 085	98· 666 249	46
45	57· 828 832	77· 032 663	110· 96 010	47
46	63· 934 240	85· 368 516	124· 61 914	48
47	70· 516 402	94· 430 954	139· 74 659	49
48	77· 583 527	104 ·24 754	156· 44 940	50
49	85· 141 837	114 ·84 459	174· 83 759	51
50	93· 195 017	126 ·24 462	195 ·02 226	52
51	101 ·74 264	138 ·46 756	217 ·11 551	53
52	110 ·78 141	151 ·52 826	241 ·22 717	54

Age [x]	$d_{[x]}$	$d_{[x]+1}$	d_{x+2}	Age x+2
53	120 ·30 282	165 ·43 636	267 ·46 367	55
54	130 ·29 323	180 ·19 385	295 ·92 431	56
55	140 ·73 267	195 ·79 456	326 ·69 876	57
56	151 ·59 350	212 ·22 166	359 ·86 126	58
57	162 ·84 064	229 ·44 710	395 ·46 749	59
58	174 ·42 947	247 ·42 777	433 ·54 803	60
59	186 ·30 410	266 ·10 433	474 ·10 129	61
60	198 ·39 834	285 ·39 954	517 ·08 729	62
61	210 ·63 300	305 ·21 436	562 ·41 852	63
62	222 ·91 514	325 ·42 710	609 ·95 119	64
63	235 ·13 712	345 ·88 962	659 ·47 534	65
64	247 ·17 647	366 ·42 582	710 ·70 576	66
65	258 ·89 480	386 ·83 065	763 ·27 009	67
66	270 ·13 861	406 ·86 723	816 ·70 101	68
67	280 ·73 896	426 ·26 792	870 ·42 676	69
68	290 ·51 252	444 ·73 322	923 ·76 451	70
69	299 ·26 511	461 ·93 488	975 ·91 662	71
70	306 ·79 264	477 ·51 848	102 5·9 708	72
71	312 ·88 565	491 ·10 898	107 2·9 056	73
72	317 ·33 547	502 ·31 798	111 5·6 028	74
73	319 ·93 915	510 ·75 392	115 2·8 673	75
74	320 ·50 791	516 ·03 434	118 3·4 569	76
75	318 ·87 523	517 ·80 072	120 6·1 218	77
76	314 ·90 742	515 ·73 651	121 9·6 548	78
77	308 ·51 288	509 ·58 574	122 2·9 514	79
78	299 ·65 297	499 ·17 412	121 5·0 778	80
79	288 ·35 166	484 ·42 902	119 5·3 452	81
80	274 ·70 314	465 ·39 868	116 3·3 830	82
			111 9·2 085	83
			106 3·2 830	84
			996 ·54 635	85
			920 ·42 398	86
			836 ·79 658	87
			747 ·93 036	88
			656 ·36 749	89
			564 ·78 102	90
			475 ·80 596	91
			391 ·86 219	92
			314 ·98 893	93
			246 ·71 135	94
			187 ·95 684	95
			139 ·03 270	96
			99· 667 530	97
			69· 108 564	98
			46· 258 687	99
			29· 830 529	100
			18· 494 482	101
			11· 000 998	102
			6·2 649 489	103
			3·4 086 350	104
			1·7 680 816	105
			·87 250 397	106
			·40 875 886	107
			·18 142 775	108
			·07 613 658	109

TABLE 2 (continued)

MORTALITY FUNCTIONS

Age [x]	$q_{[x]}$	$q_{[x]+1}$	q_{x+2}	Age x+2	Age [x]	$q_{[x]}$	$q_{[x]+1}$	q_{x+2}	Age x+2
			·00 073 000	0	53	·00 376 288	·00 519 413	·00 844 128	55
			·00 068 000	1	54	·00 410 654	·00 570 271	·00 941 902	56
0	·00 058 000	·00 061 000	·00 063 000	2	55	·00 447 362	·00 625 190	·01 049 742	57
1	·00 054 000	·00 057 000	·00 058 000	3	56	·00 486 517	·00 684 424	·01 168 566	58
2	·00 050 000	·00 052 000	·00 053 000	4	57	·00 528 231	·00 748 245	·01 299 373	59
3	·00 046 000	·00 048 000	·00 049 000	5	58	·00 572 620	·00 816 938	·01 443 246	60
4	·00 042 000	·00 044 000	·00 045 000	6	59	·00 619 802	·00 890 805	·01 601 356	61
5	·00 039 000	·00 041 000	·00 042 000	7	60	·00 669 904	·00 970 168	·01 774 972	62
6	·00 036 000	·00 038 000	·00 040 000	8	61	·00 723 057	·01 055 365	·01 965 464	63
7	·00 034 000	·00 036 000	·00 038 000	9	62	·00 779 397	·01 146 756	·02 174 310	64
8	·00 032 000	·00 034 000	·00 037 000	10	63	·00 839 065	·01 244 719	·02 403 101	65
9	·00 030 000	·00 033 000	·00 037 000	11	64	·00 902 209	·01 349 653	·02 653 550	66
10	·00 030 000	·00 033 000	·00 037 000	12	65	·00 968 982	·01 461 982	·02 927 491	67
11	·00 030 000	·00 033 000	·00 040 000	13	66	·01 039 545	·01 582 150	·03 226 890	68
12	·00 030 000	·00 036 000	·00 047 000	14	67	·01 114 064	·01 710 628	·03 553 846	69
13	·00 032 000	·00 042 000	·00 061 000	15	68	·01 192 710	·01 847 909	·03 910 594	70
14	·00 038 000	·00 055 000	·00 081 000	16	69	·01 275 665	·01 994 514	·04 299 507	71
15	·00 049 000	·00 073 000	·00 105 538	17	70	·01 363 115	·02 150 990	·04 723 096	72
16	·00 065 000	·00 095 880	·00 099 681	18	71	·01 455 252	·02 317 912	·05 184 008	73
17	·00 083 859	·00 089 716	·00 094 140	19	72	·01 552 279	·02 495 883	·05 685 022	74
18	·00 077 522	·00 083 951	·00 088 947	20	73	·01 654 404	·02 685 536	·06 229 041	75
19	·00 071 637	·00 078 611	·00 084 134	21	74	·01 761 844	·02 887 534	·06 819 083	76
20	·00 066 228	·00 073 724	·00 079 739	22	75	·01 874 822	·03 102 569	·07 458 263	77
21	·00 061 316	·00 069 319	·00 075 801	23	76	·01 993 572	·03 331 366	·08 149 779	78
22	·00 056 924	·00 065 429	·00 072 366	24	77	·02 118 334	·03 574 679	·08 896 883	79
23	·00 053 079	·00 062 087	·00 069 481	25	78	·02 249 357	·03 833 295	·09 702 855	80
24	·00 049 804	·00 059 328	·00 067 201	26	79	·02 386 900	·04 108 032	·10 570 968	81
25	·00 047 129	·00 057 193	·00 065 582	27	80	·02 531 227	·04 399 741	·11 504 443	82
26	·00 045 080	·00 055 720	·00 064 689	28				·12 506 403	83
27	·00 043 688	·00 054 954	·00 064 592	29				·13 579 820	84
28	·00 042 983	·00 054 940	·00 065 368	30				·14 727 448	85
29	·00 042 998	·00 055 728	·00 067 101	31				·15 951 762	86
30	·00 043 767	·00 057 371	·00 069 882	32				·17 254 883	87
31	·00 045 326	·00 059 924	·00 073 813	33				·18 638 498	88
32	·00 047 711	·00 063 446	·00 079 004	34				·20 103 786	89
33	·00 050 961	·00 068 001	·00 085 577	35				·21 651 335	90
34	·00 055 117	·00 073 655	·00 093 663	36				·23 281 066	91
35	·00 060 222	·00 080 481	·00 103 409	37				·24 992 160	92
36	·00 066 320	·30 088 554	·00 114 973	38				·26 782 990	93
37	·00 073 457	·00 097 956	·00 128 528	39				·28 651 074	94
38	·00 081 682	·00 108 772	·00 144 267	40				·30 593 028	95
39	·00 091 046	·00 121 095	·00 162 396	41				·32 604 550	96
40	·00 101 601	·00 135 021	·00 183 145	42				·34 680 421	97
41	·00 113 404	·00 150 654	·00 206 673	43				·36 814 521	98
42	·00 126 512	·00 168 105	·00 233 523	44				·38 999 883	99
43	·00 140 986	·00 187 490	·00 263 723	45				·41 228 762	100
44	·00 156 889	·00 208 935	·00 297 691	46				·43 492 729	101
45	·00 174 288	·00 232 571	·00 335 783	47				·45 782 791	102
46	·00 193 251	·00 258 539	·00 378 388	48				·48 089 531	103
47	·00 213 851	·00 286 989	·00 425 932	49				·50 403 251	104
48	·00 236 163	·00 318 079	·00 478 880	50				·52 714 144	105
49	·00 260 266	·00 351 979	·00 537 740	51				·55 012 452	106
50	·00 286 243	·00 388 866	·00 603 064	52				·57 288 631	107
51	·00 314 178	·00 428 931	·00 675 456	53				·59 533 510	108
52	·00 344 162	·00 472 375	·00 755 572	54				·61 738 430	109

TABLE 2 (*continued*)

MORTALITY FUNCTIONS

Age [x]	$\mu_{[x]}$	$\mu_{[x]+1}$	μ_{x+2}	Age x+2
			·00 075 528	0
			·00 070 525	1
0	·00 056 516	·00 059 518	·00 065 521	2
1	·00 052 514	·00 055 515	·00 060 518	3
2	·00 049 012	·00 051 013	·00 055 515	4
3	·00 045 010	·00 047 011	·00 051 013	5
4	·00 041 008	·00 043 009	·00 047 011	6
5	·00 038 007	·00 040 008	·00 043 509	7
6	·00 035 006	·00 037 007	·00 041 008	8
7	·00 033 005	·00 035 006	·00 039 008	9
8	·00 031 005	·00 033 005	·00 037 507	10
9	·00 028 504	·00 031 505	·00 037 007	11
10	·00 028 504	·00 031 505	·00 037 007	12
11	·00 028 504	·00 031 505	·00 038 507	13
12	·00 027 004	·00 033 005	·00 043 510	14
13	·00 027 003	·00 037 007	·00 054 015	15
14	·00 029 503	·00 046 511	·00 071 026	16
15	·00 037 005	·00 061 019	·00 108 623	17
16	·00 049 569	·00 080 473	·00 102 612	18
17	·00 080 963	·00 086 825	·00 096 902	19
18	·00 074 335	·00 080 769	·00 091 525	20
19	·00 068 174	·00 075 153	·00 086 512	21
20	·00 062 499	·00 070 000	·00 081 897	22
21	·00 057 330	·00 065 339	·00 077 721	23
22	·00 052 686	·00 061 195	·00 074 024	24
23	·00 048 586	·00 057 599	·00 070 853	25
24	·00 045 052	·00 054 581	·00 068 259	26
25	·00 042 105	·00 052 174	·00 066 298	27
26	·00 039 767	·00 050 413	·00 065 030	28
27	·00 038 061	·00 049 333	·00 064 523	29
28	·00 037 011	·00 048 974	·00 064 849	30
29	·00 036 639	·00 049 376	·00 066 089	31
30	·00 036 971	·00 050 582	·00 068 332	32
31	·00 038 033	·00 052 639	·00 071 673	33
32	·00 039 850	·00 055 594	·00 076 218	34
33	·00 042 449	·00 059 499	·00 082 084	35
34	·00 045 857	·00 064 407	·00 089 397	36
35	·00 050 104	·00 070 377	·00 098 296	37
36	·00 055 216	·00 077 468	·00 108 934	38
37	·00 061 224	·00 085 744	·00 121 477	39
38	·00 068 157	·00 095 273	·00 136 110	40
39	·00 076 047	·00 106 128	·00 153 032	41
40	·00 084 923	·00 118 382	·00 172 463	42
41	·00 094 819	·00 132 118	·00 194 644	43
42	·00 105 765	·00 147 419	·00 219 837	44
43	·00 117 795	·00 164 376	·00 248 332	45
44	·00 130 942	·00 183 083	·00 280 444	46
45	·00 145 239	·00 203 641	·00 316 519	47
46	·00 160 720	·00 226 156	·00 356 935	48
47	·00 177 419	·00 250 741	·00 402 107	49
48	·00 195 371	·00 277 514	·00 452 487	50
49	·00 214 609	·00 306 603	·00 508 572	51
50	·00 235 168	·00 338 138	·00 570 903	52
51	·00 257 082	·00 372 263	·00 640 073	53
52	·00 280 386	·00 409 125	·00 716 731	54

Age [x]	$\mu_{[x]}$	$\mu_{[x]+1}$	μ_{x+2}	Age x+2
53	·00 305 114	·00 448 882	·00 801 584	55
54	·00 331 298	·00 491 701	·00 895 406	56
55	·00 358 972	·00 537 759	·00 999 042	57
56	·00 388 168	·00 587 241	·01 113 415	58
57	·00 418 918	·00 640 345	·01 239 532	59
59	·00 451 252	·00 697 279	·01 378 490	60
59	·00 485 198	·00 758 264	·01 531 487	61
60	·00 520 785	·00 823 531	·01 699 826	62
61	·00 558 039	·00 893 329	·01 884 929	63
62	·00 596 984	·00 967 916	·02 088 340	64
63	·00 637 642	·01 047 567	·02 311 742	65
64	·00 680 033	·01 132 573	·02 556 959	66
65	·00 724 174	·01 223 241	·02 825 977	67
66	·00 770 079	·01 319 893	·03 120 944	68
67	·00 817 760	·01 422 872	·03 444 192	69
68	·00 867 223	·01 532 538	·03 798 242	70
69	·00 918 471	·01 649 272	·04 185 823	71
70	·00 971 505	·01 773 476	·04 609 876	72
71	·01 026 318	·01 905 571	·05 073 576	73
72	·01 082 900	·02 046 006	·05 580 336	74
73	·01 141 235	·02 195 249	·06 133 825	75
74	·01 201 302	·02 353 796	·06 737 977	76
75	·01 263 071	·02 522 169	·07 397 000	77
76	·01 326 508	·02 700 916	·08 115 389	78
77	·01 391 572	·02 890 614	·08 897 929	79
78	·01 458 213	·03 091 870	·09 749 701	80
79	·01 526 373	·03 305 322	·10 676 087	81
80	·01 595 988	·03 531 639	·11 682 766	82
			·12 775 710	83
			·13 961 178	84
			·15 245 697	85
			·16 636 045	86
			·18 139 225	87
			·19 762 432	88
			·21 513 014	89
			·23 398 425	90
			·25 426 170	91
			·27 603 745	92
			·29 938 569	93
			·32 437 911	94
			·35 108 808	95
			·37 957 989	96
			·40 991 786	97
			·44 216 050	98
			·47 636 075	99
			·51 256 512	100
			·55 081 304	101
			·59 113 622	102
			·63 355 815	103
			·67 809 369	104
			·72 474 882	105
			·77 352 058	106
			·82 439 707	107
			·87 735 768	108
			·93 237 342	109

TABLE 2 (continued)

4% interest

	SELECT			ULTIMATE			
Age [x]	$D_{[x]}$	$N_{[x]}$	$S_{[x]}$	D_x	N_x	S_x	Age x
0	344 81· 408	835 833 ·48	180 511 94·	344 89· 000	835 843 ·39	180 512 06·	0
1	331 31· 660	801 345 ·85	172 153 52·	331 38· 291	801 354 ·39	172 153 63·	1
2	318 36· 022	768 208 ·21	164 139 98·	318 42· 074	768 216· 10	164 140 08·	2
3	305 92· 886	736 367 ·35	156 457 84·	305 98· 090	736 374 ·03	156 457 92·	3
4	293 99· 470	705 769 ·82	149 094 10·	294 04· 176	705 775 ·94	149 094 18·	4
5	282 54· 304	676 366 ·72	142 036 36·	282 58· 262	676 371 ·76	142 036 42·	5
6	271 54· 560	648 108 ·92	135 272 65·	271 58· 091	648 113 ·50	135 272 70·	6
7	260 98· 665	620 951 ·27	128 791 52·	261 01· 798	620 955 ·41	128 791 57·	7
8	250 84· 331	594 849 ·63	122 581 96·	250 87· 342	594 853 ·61	122 582 01·	8
9	241 09· 901	569 762 ·45	116 633 43·	241 12· 795	569 766 ·27	116 633 48·	9
10	231 74· 019	545 650 ·03	110 935 77·	231 76· 570	545 653 ·47	110 935 81·	10
11	222 74· 466	522 473 ·60	105 479 24·	222 76· 917	522 476 ·90	105 479 28·	11
12	214 09· 831	500 196 ·81	100 254 47·	214 12· 188	500 199 ·99	100 254 51·	12
13	205 78· 348	478 784 ·13	952 524 6·5	205 81· 024	478 787 ·80	952 525 1·1	13
14	197 78· 562	458 202 ·67	904 645 8·1	197 81· 530	458 206 ·77	904 646 3·3	14
15	190 07· 958	438 419 ·98	858 824 9·8	190 11· 763	438 425 ·24	858 825 6·6	15
16	182 64· 699	419 407 ·09	814 982 3·2	182 69· 390	419 413 ·48	814 983 1·3	16
17	175 46· 933	401 136 ·85	773 040 8·9	175 52· 492	401 144 ·09	773 041 7·8	17
18	168 54· 126	383 584 ·49	732 926 5·0	168 59· 584	383 591 ·60	732 927 3·7	18
19	161 89· 657	366 725 ·08	694 567 3·6	161 94· 979	366 732 ·02	694 568 2·1	19
20	155 52· 279	350 530 ·32	657 894 1·8	155 57· 436	350 537 ·04	657 895 0·1	20
21	149 40· 797	334 973 ·13	622 840 5·1	149 45· 767	334 979 ·60	622 841 3·1	21
22	143 54· 071	320 027 ·63	589 342 5·8	143 58· 839	320 033 ·83	589 343 3·5	22
23	137 91· 012	305 669 ·08	557 339 2·4	137 95· 567	305 674 ·99	557 339 9·6	23
24	132 50· 575	291 873 ·80	526 771 7·7	132 54· 913	291 879 ·43	526 772 4·6	24
25	127 31· 763	278 619 ·17	497 583 8·6	127 35· 886	278 624 ·51	497 584 5·2	25
26	122 33· 620	265 883 ·55	469 721 4·5	122 37· 535	265 888 ·63	469 722 0·7	26
27	117 55· 233	253 646 ·27	443 132 6·2	117 58· 953	253 651 ·09	443 133 2·1	27
28	112 95· 726	241 887 ·55	417 767 5·3	112 99· 271	241 892 ·14	417 768 1·0	28
29	108 54· 263	230 588 ·47	393 578 3·4	108 57· 655	230 592 ·87	393 578 8·8	29
30	104 30· 039	219 730 ·97	370 519 0·7	104 33· 310	219 735 ·21	370 519 6·0	30
31	100 22· 288	209 297 ·76	348 545 5·7	100 25· 471	209 301 ·91	348 546 0·8	31
32	963 0·2 713	199 272 ·34	327 615 3·8	963 3·4 073	199 276 ·43	327 615 8·9	32
33	925 3·2 832	189 638 ·91	307 687 7·3	925 6·4 185	189 643 ·03	307 688 2·4	33
34	889 0·6 463	180 382 ·40	288 723 4·2	889 3·8 327	180 386 ·61	288 723 9·4	34
35	854 1·7 111	171 488 ·40	270 684 7·3	854 5·0 060	171 492 ·78	270 685 2·8	35
36	820 5·8 542	162 943 ·13	253 535 4·2	820 9·3 206	162 947 ·77	253 536 0·0	36
37	788 2·4 775	154 733 ·45	237 240 5·9	788 6·1 842	154 738 ·45	237 241 2·2	37
38	757 1·0 065	146 846 ·80	221 766 6·9	757 5·0 280	146 852 ·27	221 767 3·8	38
39	727 0·8 899	139 271 ·20	207 081 3·9	727 5·3 065	139 277 ·24	207 082 1·5	39
40	698 1·5 977	131 995 ·19	193 153 5·7	698 6·4 959	132 001 ·93	193 154 4·3	40
41	670 2·6 211	125 007 ·87	179 953 2·7	670 8·0 930	125 015 ·43	179 954 2·4	41
42	643 3·4 709	118 298 ·80	167 451 6·0	643 9·6 147	118 307 ·34	167 452 6·9	42
43	617 3·6 773	111 858 ·07	155 620 7·2	618 0·5 970	111 867 ·73	155 621 9·6	43
44	592 2·7 885	105 676 ·20	144 433 7·8	593 0·5 940	105 687 ·13	144 435 1·9	44
45	568 0·3 705	997 44· 168	133 864 8·8	568 9·1 776	997 56· 536	133 866 4·7	45
46	544 6·0 064	940 53· 378	123 889 0·2	545 5·9 365	940 67· 358	123 890 8·2	46
47	521 9·2 958	885 95· 648	114 482 0·5	523 0·4 756	886 11· 422	114 484 0·8	47
48	499 9·8 546	833 63· 190	105 620 6·5	501 2·4 160	833 80· 946	105 622 9·4	48
49	478 7·3 144	783 48· 597	972 822 ·67	480 1·3 938	783 68· 530	972 848 ·46	49
50	458 1·3 224	735 44· 823	894 451 ·04	459 7·0 607	735 67· 136	894 479 ·93	50
51	438 1·5 413	689 45· 176	820 880 ·53	439 9·0 830	689 70· 076	820 912 ·79	51
52	418 7·6 496	645 43· 296	751 906 ·81	420 7·1 417	645 70· 993	751 942 ·72	52
53	399 9·3 411	603 33· 143	687 331 ·90	402 0·9 326	603 63· 851	687 371 ·72	53
54	381 6·3 261	563 08· 985	626 963 ·84	384 0·1 664	563 42· 918	627 007 ·87	54

TABLE 2 (continued)

4% interest

| | | SELECT | | | | ULTIMATE | |
Age [x]	$D_{[x]}$	$N_{[x]}$	$S_{[x]}$	D_x	N_x	S_x	Age x
55	363 8·3 307	524 65· 379	570 616 ·44	366 4·5 684	525 02· 752	570 664 ·95	55
56	346 5·0 983	487 97· 161	518 108 ·94	349 3·8 796	488 38· 184	518 162 ·20	56
57	329 6·3 898	452 99· 429	469 265 ·73	332 7·8 564	453 44· 304	469 324 ·02	57
58	313 1·9 850	419 67· 525	423 916 ·16	316 6·2 716	420 16· 448	423 979 ·71	58
59	297 1·6 826	387 97· 026	381 894 ·20	300 8·9 150	388 50· 176	381 963 ·27	59
60	281 5·3 028	357 83· 721	343 038 ·30	285 5·5 942	358 41· 261	343 113 ·09	60
61	266 2·6 874	329 23· 597	307 191 ·14	270 6·1 356	329 85· 667	307 271 ·83	61
62	251 3·7 020	302 12· 820	274 199 ·42	256 0·3 853	302 79· 531	274 286 ·16	62
63	236 8·2 373	276 47· 715	243 913 ·74	241 8·2 107	277 19· 146	244 006· 63	63
64	222 6·2 106	252 24· 747	216 188 ·40	227 9·5 016	253 00· 935	216 287 ·48	64
65	208 7·5 676	229 40· 498	190 881 ·28	214 4·1 713	230 21· 434	190 986 ·55	65
66	195 2·2 839	207 91· 642	167 853 ·75	201 2·1 584	208 77· 262	167 965 ·12	66
67	182 0·3 664	187 74· 923	146 970 ·55	188 3·4 277	188 65· 104	147 087 ·85	67
68	169 1·8 542	168 87· 127	128 099 ·77	175 7·9 716	169 81· 676	128 222 ·75	68
69	156 6·8 197	151 25· 055	111 112 ·76	163 5·8 114	152 23· 705	111 241 ·07	69
70	144 5·3 689	134 85· 489	958 84· 189	151 6·9 972	135 87· 893	960 17· 369	70
71	132 7·6 401	119 65· 170	822 91· 992	140 1·6 093	120 70· 896	824 29· 475	71
72	121 3·8 036	105 60· 758	702 17· 476	128 9·7 567	106 69· 287	703 58· 579	72
73	110 4·0 584	926 8·8 080	595 45· 368	118 1·5 772	937 9·5 300	596 89· 293	73
74	998 ·62 904	808 5·7 327	501 63· 928	107 7·2 347	819 7·9 528	503 09· 763	74
75	897 ·76 009	700 7·7 767	419 65· 084	976 ·91 702	712 0·7 181	421 11· 810	75
76	801 ·70 978	603 0·9 878	348 44· 587	880 ·83 121	614 3·8 011	349 91· 092	76
77	710 ·74 161	515 1· 932	287 02· 194	789 ·19 865	526 2·9 698	288 47· 291	77
78	625 ·11 472	436 3·9 811	234 41· 874	702 ·24 821	447 3·7 712	235 84· 321	78
79	545 ·07 270	366 4·6 888	189 72· 017	620 ·20 821	377 1·5 230	191 10· 550	79
80	470 ·83 137	304 8·3 988	152 05· 661	543 ·29 713	315 1·3 148	153 39· 027	80
81				471 ·71 326	260 8·0 176	121 87· 712	81
82				405 ·62 366	213 6·3 044	957 9·6 944	82
83				345 ·15 280	173 0·6 807	744 3·3 900	83
84				290 ·37 173	138 5·5 279	571 2·7 093	84
85				241 ·28 824	109 5·1 562	432 7·1 814	85
86				197 ·83 908	853 ·86 794	323 2·0 252	86
87				159 ·88 487	656 ·02 886	237 8·1 572	87
88				127 ·20 858	496 ·14 399	172 2·1 284	88
89				99· 518 086	368 ·93 541	122 5·9 844	89
90				76· 453 060	269 ·41 733	857 ·04 898	90
91				57· 596 108	192 ·96 427	587 ·63 165	91
92				42· 487 615	135 ·36 816	394 ·66 739	92
93				30· 643 310	92· 880 543	259 ·29 923	93
94				21· 573 188	62· 237 233	166 ·41 869	94
95				14· 800 229	40· 664 045	104 ·18 145	95
96				9·8 772 987	25· 863 816	63· 517 408	96
97				6·4 008 172	15· 986 518	37· 653 592	97
98				4·0 201 797	9·5 857 004	21· 667 074	98
99				2·4 424 709	5·5 655 208	12· 081 374	99
100				1·4 326 059	3·1 230 498	6·5 158 530	100
101				·80 957 713	1·6 904 439	3·3 928 032	101
102				·43 987 495	·88 086 681	1·7 023 592	102
103				·22 931 531	·44 099 186	·82 149 243	103
104				·11 446 024	·21 167 655	·38 050 057	104
105				·05 458 515	·09 721 631	·16 882 401	105
106				·02 481 832	·04 263 116	·07 160 770	106
107				·01 073 573	·01 781 284	·02 897 654	107
108				·00 440 902	·00 707 711	·01 116 370	108
109				·00 171 555	·00 266 810	·00 408 659	109

TABLE 2 (continued)

4% interest

| | SELECT | | | | ULTIMATE | | |
Age [x]	$C_{[x]}$	$M_{[x]}$	$R_{[x]}$	C_x	M_x	R_x	Age x
0	19· 230 016	233 3·9 667	141 556 ·80	24· 208 625	234 1·1 771	141 566 ·24	0
1	17· 202 977	231 0·6 661	139 216 ·93	21· 667 344	231 6·9 685	139 225 ·07	1
2	15· 305 780	228 9·5 518	136 900 ·58	19· 288 949	229 5·3 012	136 908 ·10	2
3	13· 531 469	227 1·0 650	134 606 ·44	17· 064 320	227 6·0 122	134 612 ·80	3
4	11· 872 863	225 4·4 768	132 330 ·95	14· 984 821	225 8·9 479	132 336 ·79	4
5	10· 595 364	224 0·1 995	130 073 ·03	13· 313 989	224 3·9 631	130 077 ·84	5
6	9·3 996 553	222 7·2 934	127 829 ·51	11· 751 097	223 0·6 491	127 833 ·87	6
7	8·5 322 559	221 5·9 239	125 599 ·29	10· 541 111	221 8·8 980	125 603 ·23	7
8	7·7 182 555	220 5·4 984	123 380 ·54	9·6 489 777	220 8·3 569	123 384 ·33	8
9	6·9 547 791	219 5·9 605	121 172 ·33	8·8 104 444	219 8·7 079	121 175 ·97	9
10	6·6 848 133	218 7·4 797	118 973 ·99	8·2 455 103	218 9·8 975	118 977 ·26	10
11	6·4 253 268	217 9·3 280	116 784 ·22	7·9 254 418	218 1·6 520	116 787 ·36	11
12	6·1 759 129	217 1·4 928	114 602 ·69	7·6 177 975	217 3·7 265	114 605 ·71	12
13	6·3 317 993	216 3·5 733	112 428 ·50	7·9 157 785	216 6·1 087	112 431 ·99	13
14	7·2 267 823	215 5·3 826	110 261 ·97	8·9 397 301	215 8·1 929	110 265 ·88	14
15	8·9 556 726	214 5·6 514	108 102 ·68	11· 151 130	214 9·2 532	108 107 ·68	15
16	11· 415 437	213 3·6 569	105 952 ·35	14· 229 044	213 8·1 021	105 958 ·43	16
17	14· 148 733	211 8·5 928	103 813 ·43	17· 812 066	212 3·8 730	103 820 ·33	17
18	12· 563 131	210 0·8 767	101 689 ·68	16· 159 425	210 6·0 610	101 696 ·46	18
19	11· 151 716	208 4·8 463	995 83· 793	14· 659 570	208 9·9 015	995 90· 395	19
20	9·9 038 106	207 0·3 430	974 94· 098	13· 305 646	207 5·2 420	975 00· 494	20
21	8·8 087 489	205 7·2 146	954 19· 091	12· 090 838	206 1·9 363	954 25· 252	21
22	7·8 566 457	204 5·3 162	933 57· 410	11· 009 226	204 9·8 455	933 63· 316	22
23	7·0 385 877	203 4·5 090	913 07· 832	10· 054 978	203 8·8 363	913 13· 470	23
24	6·3 454 964	202 4·6 596	892 69· 268	9·2 231 254	202 8·7 813	892 74· 634	24
25	5·7 695 696	201 5·6 408	872 40· 757	8·5 086 738	201 9·5 582	872 45· 853	25
26	5·3 028 036	200 7·3 292	852 21· 458	7·9 074 481	201 1·0 495	852 26· 294	26
27	4·9 381 019	199 9·6 067	832 10· 651	7·4 151 508	200 3·1 420	832 15· 245	27
28	4·6 685 019	199 2·3 589	812 07· 727	7·0 282 551	199 5·7 269	812 12· 103	28
29	4·4 876 113	198 5·4 752	792 12· 185	6·7 434 391	198 8·6 986	792 16· 376	29
30	4·3 893 417	197 8·8 483	772 23· 632	6·5 577 364	198 1·9 552	772 27· 677	30
31	4·3 679 829	197 2·3 740	752 41· 776	6·4 684 530	197 5·3 975	752 45· 722	31
32	4·4 179 796	196 5·9 506	732 66· 423	6·4 730 939	196 8·9 290	732 70· 325	32
33	4·5 341 977	195 9·4 789	712 97· 477	6·5 696 540	196 2·4 559	713 01· 396	33
34	4·7 117 861	195 2·8 615	693 34· 935	6·7 562 343	195 5·8 863	693 38· 940	34
35	4·9 461 435	194 6·0 035	673 78· 886	7·0 313 075	194 9·1 300	673 83· 054	35
36	5·2 328 101	193 8·8 107	654 29· 508	7·3 933 615	194 2·0 987	654 33· 924	36
37	5·5 675 303	193 1·1 908	634 87· 070	7·8 413 694	193 4·7 054	634 91· 825	37
38	5·9 462 976	192 3·0 525	615 51· 924	8·3 742 663	192 6·8 640	615 57· 120	38
39	6·3 652 446	191 4·3 053	596 24· 513	8·9 911 596	191 8·4 897	596 30· 256	39
40	6·8 205 510	190 4·8 595	577 05· 359	9·6 915 462	190 9·4 986	577 11· 766	40
41	7·3 086 927	189 4·6 262	557 95· 072	10· 474 687	189 9·8 070	558 02· 267	41
42	7·8 260 699	188 3·5 169	538 94· 344	11· 340 223	188 9·3 323	539 02· 460	42
43	8·3 692 506	187 1·4 437	520 03· 950	12· 287 681	187 7·9 921	520 13· 128	43
44	8·9 348 112	185 8·3 192	501 24· 747	13· 316 636	186 5·7 044	501 35· 136	44
45	9·5 194 271	184 4·0 564	482 57· 676	14· 426 606	185 2·3 878	482 69· 431	45
46	10· 119 675	182 8·5 688	464 03· 756	15· 617 146	183 7·9 612	464 17· 044	46
47	10· 732 227	181 1·7 709	445 64· 092	16· 887 546	182 2·3 440	445 79· 082	47
48	11· 353 660	179 3·5 781	427 39· 865	18· 236 904	180 5·4 565	427 56· 738	48
49	11· 980 530	177 3·9 068	409 32· 340	19· 664 108	178 7·2 196	409 51· 282	49
50	12· 609 341	175 2·6 753	391 42· 860	21· 167 697	176 7·5 555	391 64· 062	50
51	13· 236 384	172 9·8 038	373 72· 848	22· 745 797	174 6·3 878	373 96· 507	51
52	13· 857 979	170 5·2 151	356 23· 803	24· 395 920	172 3·6 420	356 50· 119	52
53	14· 470 232	167 8·8 356	338 97· 301	26· 115 030	169 9·2 461	339 26· 477	53
54	15· 069 130	165 0·5 959	321 94· 991	27· 899 252	167 3·1 310	322 27· 231	54

TABLE 2 (*continued*)
4% interest

| | SELECT | | | ULTIMATE | | | |
Age [x]	$C_{[x]}$	$M_{[x]}$	$R_{[x]}$	C_x	M_x	R_x	Age x
55	15· 650 489	162 0·4 315	305 18· 593	29· 743 892	164 5·2 318	305 54· 100	55
56	16· 209 896	158 8·2 844	288 69· 894	31· 643 194	161 5·4 879	289 08· 868	56
57	16· 742 839	155 4·1 041	272 50· 747	33· 590 294	158 3·8 447	272 93· 380	57
58	17· 244 589	151 7·8 494	256 63· 058	35· 576 898	155 0·2 544	257 09· 536	58
59	17· 710 143	147 9·4 893	241 08· 788	37· 593 298	151 4·6 775	241 59· 281	59
60	18· 134 448	143 9·0 058	225 89· 941	39· 628 125	147 7·0 842	226 44· 604	60
61	18· 512 257	139 6·3 952	211 08· 554	41· 668 139	143 7·4 561	211 67· 520	61
62	18· 838 191	135 1·6 705	196 66· 689	43· 698 194	139 5·7 879	197 30· 063	62
63	19· 106 779	130 4·8 637	182 66· 418	45· 701 021	135 2·0 897	183 34· 276	63
64	19· 312 570	125 6·0 280	169 09· 809	47· 657 146	130 6·3 887	169 82· 186	64
65	19· 450 149	120 5·2 408	155 98· 910	49· 544 810	125 8·7 316	156 75· 797	65
66	19· 514 298	115 2·6 054	143 35· 728	51· 340 028	120 9·1 868	144 17· 065	66
67	19· 500 045	109 8·2 540	131 22· 210	53· 016 515	115 7·8 467	132 07· 879	67
68	19· 402 802	104 2·3 493	119 60· 213	54· 545 971	110 4·8 302	120 50· 032	68
69	19· 218 626	985 ·08 688	108 51· 487	55· 898 285	105 0·2 843	109 45· 202	69
70	18· 944 269	926 ·69 620	979 7·6 356	57· 041 926	994 ·38 597	989 4·9 175	70
71	18· 577 412	867 ·44 125	880 0·0 931	57· 944 508	937 ·34 404	890 0·5 315	71
72	18· 116 940	807 ·62 055	786 0·0 861	58· 573 508	879 ·39 953	796 3·1 875	72
73	17· 563 064	747 ·56 578	697 8·6 016	58· 897 169	820 ·82 603	708 3·7 880	73
74	16· 917 582	687 ·63 932	615 6·3 509	58· 885 607	761 ·92 886	626 2·9 619	74
75	16· 184 042	628 ·23 021	539 3·7 350	58· 512 079	703 ·04 325	550 1·0 331	75
76	15· 367 944	569 ·74 871	469 0·8 114	57· 754 434	644 ·53 117	479 7·9 898	76
77	14· 476 809	512 ·61 880	404 7·2 626	56· 596 645	586 ·77 674	415 3·4 587	77
78	13· 520 252	457 ·26 930	346 2·3 705	55· 030 459	530 ·18 009	356 6·6 819	78
79	12· 509 942	404 ·12 313	293 4·9 958	53· 056 922	475 ·14 963	303 6·5 018	79
80	11· 459 433	353 ·58 526	246 3·5 657	50· 687 819	422 ·09 271	256 1·3 522	80
81				47· 946 787	371 ·40 489	213 9·2 595	81
82				44· 869 945	323 ·45 811	176 7·8 546	82
83				41· 505 962	278 ·58 816	144 4·3 965	83
84				37· 915 345	237 ·08 220	116 5·8 083	84
85				34· 168 847	199 ·16 685	928 ·72 613	85
86				30· 345 019	164 ·99 801	729 ·55 928	86
87				26· 526 872	134 ·65 299	564 ·56 127	87
88				22· 797 854	108 ·12 612	429 ·90 828	88
89				19· 237 407	85· 328 262	321 ·78 217	89
90				15· 916 450	66· 090 855	236 ·45 390	90
91				12· 893 258	50· 174 405	170 ·36 305	91
92				10· 210 166	37· 281 148	120 ·18 864	92
93				7·8 915 333	27· 070 981	82· 907 496	93
94				5·9 432 212	19· 179 448	55· 836 514	94
95				4·3 536 905	13· 236 227	36· 657 066	95
96				3·0 965 854	8·8 825 365	23· 420 839	96
97				2·1 344 523	5·7 859 511	14· 538 303	97
98				1·4 230 864	3·6 514 989	8·7 523 514	98
99				·91 592 385	2·2 284 124	5·1 008 525	99
100				·56 792 853	1·3 124 886	2·8 724 401	100
101				·33 856 460	·74 456 006	1·5 599 515	101
102				·19 364 137	·40 599 545	·81 539 145	102
103				·10 603 525	·21 235 408	·40 939 600	103
104				·05 547 277	·10 631 884	·19 704 191	104
105				·02 766 740	·05 084 606	·09 072 308	105
106				·01 312 805	·02 317 866	·03 987 702	106
107				·00 591 380	·01 005 062	·01 669 835	107
108				·00 252 389	·00 413 682	·00 664 774	108
109				·00 101 842	·00 161 293	·00 251 092	109

TABLE 2 (*continued*)

4% interest

SELECT

Age [x]	$\ddot{a}_{[x]}$	$A_{[x]}$	$P_{[x]}$	Age [x]	$\ddot{a}_{[x]}$	$A_{[x]}$	$P_{[x]}$
0	24·240	·06769	·00279	55	14·420	·44538	·03089
1	24·187	·06974	·00288	56	14·082	·45837	·03255
2	24·130	·07192	·00298	57	13·742	·47146	·03431
3	24·070	·07424	·00308	58	13·400	·48463	·03617
4	24·006	·07668	·00319	59	13·056	·49786	·03813
5	23·939	·07929	·00331	60	12·710	·51114	·04021
6	23·867	·08202	·00344	61	12·365	·52443	·04241
7	23·792	·08491	·00357	62	12·019	·53772	·04474
8	23·714	·08792	·00371	63	11·674	·55099	·04720
9	23·632	·09108	·00385	64	11·331	·56420	·04979
10	23·546	·09439	·00401	65	10·989	·57734	·05254
11	23·456	·09784	·00417	66	10·650	·59039	·05544
12	23·363	·10143	·00434	67	10·314	·60331	·05850
13	23·266	·10514	·00452	68	9·981	·61610	·06172
14	23·167	·10898	·00470	69	9·653	·62872	·06513
15	23·065	·11288	·00489	70	9·330	·64115	·06872
16	22·963	·11682	·00509	71	9·012	·65337	·07250
17	22·861	·12074	·00528	72	8·701	·66536	·07647
18	22·759	·12465	·00548	73	8·395	·67711	·08065
19	22·652	·12878	·00569	74	8·097	·68858	·08504
20	22·539	·13312	·00591	75	7·806	·69978	·08965
21	22·420	·13769	·00614	76	7·523	·71067	·09447
22	22·295	·14249	·00639	77	7·248	·72124	·09951
23	22·164	·14752	·00666	78	6·981	·73150	·10478
24	22·027	·15280	·00694	79	6·723	·74141	·11027
25	21·884	·15832	·00723	80	6·475	·75098	·11599
26	21·734	·16408	·00755				
27	21·577	·17010	·00788				
28	21·414	·17638	·00824				
29	21·244	·18292	·00861				
30	21·067	·18973	·00901				
31	20·883	·19680	·00942				
32	20·692	·20414	·00987				
33	20·494	·21176	·01033				
34	20·289	·21965	·01083				
35	20·077	·22782	·01135				
36	19·857	·23627	·01190				
37	19·630	·24500	·01248				
38	19·396	·25400	·01310				
39	19·155	·26328	·01375				
40	18·906	·27284	·01443				
41	18·651	·28267	·01516				
42	18·388	·29277	·01592				
43	18·119	·30313	·01673				
44	17·842	·31376	·01759				
45	17·559	·32464	·01849				
46	17·270	·33576	·01944				
47	16·975	·34713	·02045				
48	16·673	·35873	·02152				
49	16·366	·37054	·02264				
50	16·053	·38257	·02383				
51	15·735	·39479	·02509				
52	15·413	·40720	·02642				
53	15·086	·41978	·02783				
54	14·755	·43251	·02931				

Table 2 (*continued*)

4% interest

SELECT

$\ddot{a}_{[x]:\overline{n}}$	$_nA_{[x]}$	$A_{[x]:\overline{n}}$	$P_{[x]:\overline{n}}$	n	$\ddot{a}_{[x]:\overline{n}}$	$_nA_{[x]}$	$A_{[x]:\overline{n}}$	$P_{[x]:\overline{n}}$	Age [x]
	$x+n=60$					$x+n=65$			
1·000	·00596	·96154	·96154	1	1·000	·00868	·96154	·96154	64
1·956	·01302	·92477	·47278	2	1·953	·01948	·92487	·47345	63
2·869	·02336	·88964	·31006	3	2·861	·03697	·88997	·31108	62
3·739	·03209	·85619	·22899	4	3·719	·05170	·85697	·23044	61
4·569	·03940	·82426	·18040	5	4·533	·06403	·82565	·18213	60
5·363	·04547	·79372	·14799	6	5·309	·07429	·79582	·14991	59
6·124	·05045	·76446	·12483	7	6·049	·08273	·76734	·12685	58
6·854	·05448	·73639	·10744	8	6·758	·08960	·74007	·10950	57
7·555	·05768	·70941	·09390	9	7·439	·09511	·71390	·09597	56
8·230	·06016	·68347	·08305	10	8·093	·09941	·68874	·08511	55
8·879	·06200	·65849	·07416	11	8·722	·10268	·66452	·07619	54
9·505	·06330	·63444	·06675	12	9·329	·10504	·64117	·06873	53
10·108	·06412	·61125	·06047	13	9·915	·10662	·61864	·06239	52
10·689	·06454	·58889	·05509	14	10·481	·10751	·59688	·05695	51
11·250	·06460	·56732	·05043	15	11·028	·10782	·57584	·05222	50
11·791	·06437	·54650	·04635	16	11·557	·10761	·55550	·04807	49
12·313	·06388	·52642	·04275	17	12·069	·10697	·53582	·04440	48
12·817	·06317	·50704	·03956	18	12·564	·10596	·51678	·04113	47
13·303	·06230	·48834	·03671	19	13·043	·10463	·49835	·03821	46
13·772	·06127	·47029	·03415	20	13·507	·10304	·48051	·03558	45
14·225	·06013	·45288	·03184	21	13·955	·10123	·46325	·03320	44
14·662	·05890	·43608	·02974	22	14·390	·09925	·44655	·03103	43
15·083	·05761	·41988	·02784	23	14·810	·09711	·43040	·02906	42
15·489	·05627	·40426	·02610	24	15·216	·09487	·41477	·02726	41
15·881	·05490	·38921	·02451	25	15·609	·09255	·39966	·02561	40
16·258	·05351	·37471	·02305	26	15·988	·09016	·38506	·02408	39
16·621	·05213	·36014	·02170	27	16·355	·08775	·37095	·02268	38
16·971	·05076	·34729	·02046	28	16·709	·08531	·35733	·02138	37
17·307	·04942	·33434	·01932	29	17·051	·08288	·34418	·02018	36
17·631	·04811	·32189	·01826	30	17·381	·08046	·33148	·01907	35
17·942	·04684	·30992	·01727	31	17·700	·07807	·31925	·01804	34
18·241	·04562	·29842	·01636	32	18·006	·07573	·30745	·01707	33
18·528	·04445	·28737	·01551	33	18·302	·07344	·29609	·01618	32
18·804	·04334	·27677	·01472	34	18·586	·07121	·28515	·01534	31
19·069	·04230	·26659	·01398	35	18·860	·06904	·27462	·01456	30
19·322	·04132	·25683	·01329	36	19·123	·06695	·26450	·01383	29
19·565	·04042	·24748	·01265	37	19·376	·06495	·25477	·01315	28
19·798	·03959	·23853	·01205	38	19·619	·06303	·24543	·01251	27
20·021	·03883	·22996	·01149	39	19·852	·06119	·23646	·01191	26
20·234	·03815	·22176	·01096	40	20·076	·05945	·22786	·01135	25
20·438	·03754	·21392	·01047	41	20·290	·05780	·21962	·01082	24
20·633	·03701	·20644	·01001	42	20·495	·05625	·21173	·01033	23
20·818	·03656	·19930	·00957	43	20·691	·05480	·20418	·00987	22
21·000	·03595	·19229	·00916	44	20·879	·05344	·19695	·00943	21
21·179	·03517	·18540	·00875	45	21·059	·05219	·19005	·00903	20
				46	21·230	·05103	·18347	·00864	19
				47	21·393	·04997	·17719	·00828	18
				48	21·549	·04900	·17120	·00794	17
				49	21·702	·04790	·16530	·00762	16
				50	21·854	·04666	·15946	·00730	15

TABLE 2 (continued)

4% interest

ULTIMATE

Age x	$\ddot{a}_x$	A_x	P_x	Age x	$\ddot{a}_x$	A_x	P_x
0	24·235	·06788	·00280	55	14·327	·44896	·03134
1	24·182	·06992	·00289	56	13·978	·46238	·03308
2	24·126	·07208	·00299	57	13·626	·47594	·03493
3	24·066	·07438	·00309	58	13·270	·48962	·03690
4	24·003	·07682	·00320	59	12·912	·50340	·03899
5	23·935	·07941	·00332	60	12·551	·51726	·04121
6	23·864	·08214	·00344	61	12·189	·53118	·04358
7	23·790	·08501	·00357	62	11·826	·54515	·04610
8	23·711	·08803	·00371	63	11·463	·55913	·04878
9	23·629	·09118	·00386	64	11·099	·57310	·05163
10	23·543	·09449	·00401	65	10·737	·58705	·05468
11	23·454	·09793	·00418	66	10·376	·60094	·05792
12	23·361	·10152	·00435	67	10·016	·61476	·06138
13	23·264	·10525	·00452	68	9·660	·62847	·06506
14	23·163	·10910	·00471	69	9·307	·64206	·06899
15	23·061	·11305	·00490	70	8·957	·65550	·07318
16	22·957	·11703	·00510	71	8·612	·66876	·07765
17	22·854	·12100	·00529	72	8·272	·68183	·08242
18	22·752	·12492	·00549	73	7·938	·69469	·08751
19	22·645	·12905	·00570	74	7·610	·70730	·09294
20	22·532	·13393	·00592	75	7·289	·71966	·09873
21	22·413	·13796	·00616	76	6·975	·73173	·10491
22	22·288	·14276	·00641	77	6·669	·74351	·11149
23	22·157	·14779	·00667	78	6·371	·75498	·11851
24	22·020	·15306	·00695	79	6·081	·76611	·12598
25	21·877	·15857	·00725	80	5·800	·77691	·13394
26	21·727	·16433	·00756	81	5·529	·78735	·14241
27	21·571	·17035	·00790	82	5·267	·79743	·15141
28	21·408	·17662	·00825	83	5·014	·80714	·16097
29	21·238	·18316	·00862	84	4·772	·81648	·17111
30	21·061	·18996	·00902	85	4·539	·82543	·18186
31	20·877	·19704	·00944	86	4·316	·83400	·19324
32	20·686	·20439	·00988	87	4·103	·84219	·20525
33	20·488	·21201	·01035	88	3·900	·84999	·21793
34	20·282	·21991	·01084	89	3·707	·85741	·23128
35	20·069	·22810	·01137	90	3·524	·86446	·24531
36	19·849	·23657	·01192	91	3·350	·87114	·26002
37	19·621	·24533	·01250	92	3·186	·87746	·27541
38	19·386	·25437	·01312	93	3·031	·88342	·29146
39	19·144	·26370	·01377	94	2·885	·88904	·30817
40	18·894	·27331	·01447	95	2·748	·89433	·32550
41	18·637	·28321	·01520	96	2·619	·89929	·34343
42	18·372	·29339	·01597	97	2·498	·90394	·36193
43	18·100	·30385	·01679	98	2·384	·90829	·38093
44	17·821	·31459	·01765	99	2·279	·91236	·40040
45	17·534	·32560	·01857	100	2·180	·91615	·42026
46	17·241	·33687	·01954	101	2·088	·91969	·44045
47	16·941	·34841	·02057	102	2·003	·92298	·46090
48	16·635	·36020	·02165	103	1·923	·92604	·48154
49	16·322	·37223	·02281	104	1·849	·92887	·50227
50	16·003	·38450	·02403	105	1·781	·93150	·52302
51	15·678	·39699	·02532	106	1·718	·93393	·54370
52	15·348	·40969	·02669	107	1·659	·93618	·56423
53	15·012	·42260	·02815	108	1·605	·93826	·58453
54	14·672	·43569	·02970	109	1·555	·94018	·60453

TABLE 2 (continued)

4% interest

ULTIMATE

$\ddot{a}_{x:\overline{n}}$	$_nA_x$	$A_{x:\overline{n}}$	$P_{x:\overline{n}}$	n	$\ddot{a}_{x:\overline{n}}$	$_nA_x$	$A_{x:\overline{n}}$	$P_{x:\overline{n}}$	Age x
	$x+n=60$					$x+n=65$			
1·000	·01249	·96154	·96154	1	1·000	·02091	·96154	·96154	64
1·950	·02311	·92499	·47428	2	1·943	·03861	·92528	·47630	63
2·856	·03208	·89017	·31173	3	2·835	·05353	·89097	·31430	62
3·720	·03961	·85693	·23036	4	3·682	·06604	·85838	·23312	61
4·547	·04588	·82513	·18148	5	4·489	·07646	·82733	·18429	60
5·339	·05105	·79466	·14885	6	5·261	·08506	·79767	·15163	59
6·099	·05525	·76543	·12551	7	5·999	·09207	·76926	·12823	58
6·829	·05860	·73735	·10798	8	6·708	·09769	·74200	·11062	57
7·531	·06122	·71035	·09433	9	7·389	·10211	·71580	·09687	56
8·207	·06319	·68436	·08339	10	8·045	·10547	·69058	·08584	55
8·857	·06459	·65934	·07444	11	8·667	·10791	·66627	·07678	54
9·484	·06551	·63522	·06697	12	9·287	·10956	·64281	·06922	53
10·089	·06601	·61196	·06066	13	9·876	·11051	·62016	·06279	52
10·672	·06614	·58954	·05524	14	10·445	·11085	·59827	·05728	51
11·235	·06597	·56790	·05055	15	10·995	·11068	·57711	·05249	50
11·777	·06553	·54703	·04645	16	11·527	·11007	·55664	·04829	49
12·301	·06487	·52689	·04283	17	12·042	·10907	·53685	·04458	48
12·806	·06402	·50746	·03963	18	12·540	·10776	·51769	·04128	47
13·294	·06302	·48871	·03676	19	13·022	·10617	·49916	·03833	46
13·764	·06189	·47062	·03419	20	13·488	·10435	·48123	·03568	45
14·217	·06067	·45318	·03187	21	13·939	·10235	·46389	·03328	44
14·655	·05938	·43635	·02978	22	14·375	·10019	·44711	·03110	43
15·077	·05803	·42013	·02787	23	14·797	·09793	·43089	·02912	42
15·483	·05664	·40449	·02612	24	15·205	·09557	·41521	·02731	41
15·875	·05524	·38943	·02453	25	15·599	·09315	·40005	·02565	40
16·252	·05384	·37491	·02307	26	15·980	·09068	·38540	·02412	39
16·616	·05244	·36094	·02172	27	16·347	·08820	·37126	·02271	38
16·965	·05106	·34748	·02048	28	16·702	·08572	·35761	·02141	37
17·302	·04970	·33454	·01934	29	17·045	·08324	·34443	·02021	36
17·626	·04839	·32209	·01827	30	17·375	·08080	·33172	·01909	35
17·937	·04712	·31012	·01729	31	17·694	·07839	·31947	·01806	34
18·236	·04590	·29862	·01638	32	18·001	·07603	·30767	·01709	33
18·523	·04474	·28758	·01553	33	18·296	·07372	·29630	·01619	32
18·799	·04363	·27698	·01473	34	18·581	·07148	·28536	·01536	31
19·063	·04259	·26681	·01400	35	18·854	·06932	·27483	·01458	30
19·316	·04162	·25706	·01331	36	19·118	·06723	·26471	·01385	29
19·559	·04072	·24771	·01266	37	19·370	·06523	·25499	·01316	28
19·792	·03989	·23876	·01206	38	19·613	·06331	·24565	·01252	27
20·015	·03913	·23020	·01150	39	19·846	·06148	·23669	·01193	26
20·228	·03845	·22200	·01097	40	20·070	·05974	·22810	·01137	25
20·432	·03784	·21417	·01048	41	20·284	·05810	·21986	·01084	24
20·626	·03731	·20668	·01002	42	20·489	·05655	·21197	·01035	23
20·812	·03685	·19954	·00959	43	20·685	·05510	·20442	·00988	22
20·995	·03618	·19249	·00917	44	20·873	·05374	·19720	·00945	21
21·176	·03536	·18556	·00876	45	21·052	·05248	·19031	·00904	20
				46	21·223	·05132	·18372	·00866	19
				47	21·387	·05026	·17744	·00830	18
				48	21·542	·04929	·17145	·00796	17
				49	21·697	·04813	·16550	·00763	16
				50	21·850	·04684	·15962	·00731	15

TABLE 2 (continued)

4% interest

MULTIPLE LIFE FUNCTIONS

Age	D_{xx}	N_{xx}	$\ddot{a}_{xx}$	$\ddot{a}_{[xx]}$	$\ddot{a}_{xxx}$	$\ddot{a}_{xxxx}$	Age
10	230 54· 255	524 240· 96	22·739	22·744	22·149	21·662	10
11	221 51· 152	501 186 ·70	22·626	22·630	22·019	21·520	11
12	212 83· 426	479 035 ·55	22·507	22·512	21·884	21·372	12
13	204 49· 692	457 752 ·12	22·384	22·390	21·743	21·219	13
14	196 47· 438	437 302 ·43	22·257	22·264	21·599	21·061	14
15	188 74· 013	417 654 ·99	22·129	22·137	21·453	20·903	15
16	181 25· 956	398 780 ·98	22·001	22·011	21·310	20·749	16
17	174 00· 580	380 655 ·02	21·876	21·889	21·174	20·606	17
18	166 96· 030	363 254 ·44	21·757	21·770	21·048	20·477	18
19	160 21· 886	346 558 ·41	21·630	21·644	20·912	20·337	19
20	153 76· 667	330 536 ·53	21·496	21·509	20·767	20·186	20
21	147 58· 966	315 159 ·86	21·354	21·367	20·613	20·024	21
22	141 67· 445	300 400 ·89	21·204	21·217	20·449	19·852	22
23	136 00· 827	286 233 ·45	21·045	21·058	20·275	19·669	23
24	130 57· 899	272 632 ·62	20·879	20·892	20·092	19·475	24
25	125 37· 507	259 574 ·72	20·704	20·716	19·899	19·269	25
26	120 38· 549	247 037 ·22	20·521	20·533	19·696	19·053	26
27	115 59· 975	234 998 ·67	20·329	20·341	19·483	18·826	27
28	111 00· 786	223 438 ·69	20·128	20·140	19·260	18·587	28
29	106 60· 028	212 337 ·91	19·919	19·931	19·028	18·338	29
30	102 36· 789	201 677 ·88	19·701	19·713	18·785	18·079	30
31	983 0·2 025	191 441 ·09	19·475	19·486	18·533	17·808	31
32	943 9·4 371	181 610 ·89	19·240	19·251	18·271	17·528	32
33	906 3·7 007	172 171 ·45	18·996	19·008	17·999	17·237	33
34	870 2·2 359	163 107 ·75	18·743	18·756	17·719	16·936	34
35	835 4·3 183	154 405 ·51	18·482	18·495	17·429	16·626	35
36	801 9·2 555	146 051 ·20	18·213	18·227	17·130	16·307	36
37	769 6·3 850	138 031 ·94	17·935	17·950	16·822	15·979	37
38	738 5·0 728	130 335 ·55	17·649	17·666	16·506	15·643	38
39	708 4·7 124	122 950 ·48	17·354	17·374	16·182	15·299	39
40	679 4·7 234	115 865 ·77	17·052	17·074	15·850	14·947	40
41	651 4·5 505	109 071 ·05	16·743	16·768	15·511	14·589	41
42	624 3·6 624	102 556 ·50	16·426	16·454	15·166	14·225	42
43	598 1·5 514	963 12· 833	16·102	16·135	14·813	13·855	43
44	572 7·7 324	903 31· 282	15·771	15·809	14·456	13·481	44
45	548 1·7 428	846 03· 549	15·434	15·477	14·092	13·102	45
46	524 3·1 420	791 21· 807	15·091	15·140	13·724	12·720	46
47	501 1·5 113	738 78· 665	14·742	14·799	13·352	12·335	47
48	478 6·4 540	688 67· 153	14·388	14·453	12·976	11·948	48
49	456 7·5 960	640 80· 699	14·029	14·104	12·598	11·559	49

TABLE 2 (continued)

4% interest

MULTIPLE LIFE FUNCTIONS

Age	D_{xx}	N_{xx}	$\ddot{a}_{xx}$	$\ddot{a}_{[xx]}$	$\ddot{a}_{xxx}$	$\ddot{a}_{xxxx}$	Age
50	435 4·5 857	595 13· 103	13·667	13·751	12·217	11·171	50
51	414 7·0 953	551 58· 518	13·301	13·396	11·835	10·783	51
52	394 4·8 212	510 11· 422	12·931	13·039	11·452	10·396	52
53	374 7·4 856	470 66· 601	12·560	12·680	11·070	10·011	53
54	355 4·8 379	433 19· 116	12·186	12·321	10·687	9·629	54
55	336 6·6 558	397 64· 278	11·811	11·962	10·307	9·251	55
56	318 2·7 480	363 97· 622	11·436	11·603	9·928	8·877	56
57	300 2·9 555	332 14· 874	11·061	11·246	9·553	8·508	57
58	282 7·1 537	302 11· 918	10·686	10·890	9·181	8·145	58
59	265 5·2 552	273 84· 765	10·313	10·538	8·814	7·788	59
60	248 7·2 117	247 29· 510	9·943	10·188	8·452	7·439	60
61	232 3·0 160	222 42· 298	9·575	9·843	8·095	7·097	61
62	216 2·7 040	199 19· 282	9·210	9·502	7·745	6·764	62
63	200 6·3 563	177 56· 578	8·850	9·167	7·402	6·440	63
64	185 4·0 990	157 50· 222	8·495	8·837	7·067	6·125	64
65	170 6·1 037	138 96· 123	8·145	8·514	6·739	5·820	65
66	156 2·5 867	121 90· 019	7·801	8·198	6·421	5·525	66
67	142 3·8 067	106 27· 432	7·464	7·890	6·111	5·241	67
68	129 0·0 608	920 3·6 255	7·134	7·590	5·811	4·967	68
69	116 1·6 793	791 3·5 647	6·812	7·298	5·521	4·704	69
70	103 9·0 172	675 1·8 854	6·498	7·014	5·241	4·452	70
71	922 ·44 485	571 2·8 682	6·193	6·740	4·972	4·211	71
72	812 ·33 548	479 0·4 233	5·897	6·476	4·713	3·981	72
73	709 ·05 081	397 8·0 879	5·610	6·220	4·465	3·763	73
74	612 ·92 481	326 9·0 371	5·334	5·975	4·227	3·555	74
75	524 ·24 609	265 6·1 122	5·067	5·740	4·000	3·358	75
76	443 ·23 962	213 1·8 662	4·810	5·515	3·784	3·172	76
77	370 ·04 897	168 8·6 265	4·563	5·299	3·579	2·997	77
78	304 ·72 013	131 8·5 776	4·327	5·094	3·385	2·831	78
79	247 ·18 848	101 3·8 574	4·102	4·899	3·201	2·676	79
80	197 ·27 014	766 ·66 895	3·886	4·713	3·027	2·531	80
81	154 ·65 931	569 ·39 881	3·682		2·863	2·394	81
82	118 ·93 229	414 ·73 950	3·487		2·709	2·267	82
83	89· 559 028	295 ·80 722	3·303		2·564	2·149	83
84	65· 921 727	206 ·24 819	3·129		2·429	2·039	84
85	47· 339 707	140 ·32 646	2·964		2·302	1·936	85
86	33· 098 686	92· 986 754	2·809		2·184	1·842	86
87	22· 481 984	59· 888 068	2·664		2·075	1·755	87
88	14· 800 829	37· 406 084	2·527		1·973	1·674	88
89	9·4 208 615	22· 605 255	2·399		1·878	1·601	89
90	5·7 824 207	13· 184 393	2·280		1·791	1·533	90

TABLE 3

POPULATION LIFE TABLE: ENGLISH LIFE TABLE
No. 12—Males

Age x	l_x	d_x	p_x	q_x	μ_x	$\overset{\circ}{e}_x$	Age x
0	100 000	2 449	·97551	·02449		68·09	0
1	97 551	153	·99843	·00157	·00210	68·80	1
2	97 398	96	·99901	·00099	·00134	67·90	2
3	97 302	67	·99931	·00069	·00079	66·97	3
4	97 235	60	·99938	·00062	·00063	66·02	4
5	97 175	55	·99943	·00057	·00059	65·06	5
6	97 120	51	·99948	·00052	·00054	64·09	6
7	97 069	47	·99952	·00048	·00050	63·13	7
8	97 022	43	·99956	·00044	·00046	62·16	8
9	96 979	40	·99959	·00041	·00043	61·18	9
10	96 939	38	·99961	·00039	·00040	60·21	10
11	96 901	37	·99962	·00038	·00039	59·23	11
12	96 864	37	·99962	·00038	·00038	58·25	12
13	96 827	40	·99959	·00041	·00039	57·28	13
14	96 787	45	·99953	·00047	·00043	56·30	14
15	96 742	57	·99941	·00059	·00052	55·33	15
16	96 685	75	·99922	·00078	·00067	54·36	16
17	96 610	96	·99901	·00099	·00089	53·40	17
18	96 514	108	·99888	·00112	·00107	52·45	18
19	96 406	113	·99883	·00117	·00115	51·51	19
20	96 293	115	·99881	·00119	·00119	50·57	20
21	96 178	113	·99882	·00118	·00119	49·63	21
22	96 065	110	·99886	·00114	·00116	48·69	22
23	95 955	104	·99892	·00108	·00112	47·74	23
24	95 851	98	·99898	·00102	·00105	46·80	24
25	95 753	95	·99901	·00099	·00100	45·84	25
26	95 658	94	·99902	·00098	·00098	44·89	26
27	95 564	96	·99900	·00100	·00099	43·93	27
28	95 468	99	·99896	·00104	·00102	42·98	28
29	95 369	104	·99891	·00109	·00106	42·02	29
30	95 265	110	·99885	·00115	·00112	41·06	30
31	95 155	115	·99879	·00121	·00118	40·11	31
32	95 040	122	·99872	·00128	·00125	39·16	32
33	94 918	129	·99864	·00136	·00132	38·21	33
34	94 789	137	·99855	·00145	·00140	37·26	34
35	94 652	147	·99845	·00155	·00150	36·31	35
36	94 505	158	·99833	·00167	·00161	35·37	36
37	94 347	171	·99819	·00181	·00174	34·43	37
38	94 176	185	·99804	·00196	·00189	33·49	38
39	93 991	201	·99786	·00214	·00205	32·55	39
40	93 790	220	·99765	·00235	·00224	31·62	40
41	93 570	242	·99741	·00259	·00246	30·70	41
42	93 328	268	·99713	·00287	·00273	29·77	42
43	93 060	297	·99681	·00319	·00303	28·86	43
44	92 763	330	·99644	·00356	·00337	27·95	44
45	92 433	369	·99601	·00399	·00377	27·05	45
46	92 064	412	·99552	·00448	·00423	26·15	46
47	91 652	463	·99495	·00505	·00476	25·27	47
48	91 189	520	·99430	·00570	·00538	24·40	45
49	90 669	584	·99356	·00644	·00607	23·53	49
50	90 085	656	·99272	·00728	·00687	22·68	50
51	89 429	736	·99177	·00823	·00777	21·84	51
52	88 693	825	·99070	·00930	·00878	21·02	52
53	87 868	923	·98949	·01051	·00993	20·21	53
54	86 945	1 029	·98816	·01184	·01121	19·42	54

TABLE 3 (*continued*)

Age x	l_x	d_x	p_x	q_x	μ_x	$\overset{\circ}{e}_x$	Age x
55	85 916	1 144	·98669	·01331	·01263	18·65	55
56	84 772	1 265	·98508	·01492	·01420	17·89	56
57	83 507	1 393	·98332	·01668	·01590	17·16	57
58	82 114	1 526	·98141	·01859	·01776	16·44	58
59	80 588	1 664	·97935	·02065	·01978	15·74	59
60	78 924	1 805	·97713	·02287	·02197	15·06	60
61	77 119	1 947	·97475	·02525	·02433	14·40	61
62	75 172	2 088	·97222	·02778	·02684	13·76	62
63	73 084	2 228	·96951	·03049	·02953	13·14	63
64	70 856	2 366	·96661	·03339	·03243	12·54	64
65	68 490	2 499	·96352	·03648	·03553	11·95	65
66	65 991	2 625	·96022	·03978	·03884	11·39	66
67	63 366	2 745	·95668	·04332	·04239	10·84	67
68	60 621	2 856	·95288	·04712	·04622	10·31	68
69	57 765	2 959	·94878	·05122	·05036	9·79	69
70	54 806	3 051	·94434	·05566	·05487	9·29	70
71	51 755	3 130	·93953	·06047	·05976	8·81	71
72	48 625	3 195	·93430	·06570	·06509	8·35	72
73	45 430	3 243	·92861	·07139	·07092	7·90	73
74	42 187	3 273	·92241	·07759	·07730	7·47	74
75	38 914	3 282	·91566	·08434	·08432	7·05	75
76	35 632	3 266	·90833	·09167	·09200	6·66	76
77	32 366	3 225	·90037	·09963	·10042	6·28	77
78	29 141	3 154	·89176	·10824	·10962	5·92	78
79	25 987	3 054	·88248	·11752	·11964	5·57	79
80	22 933	2 923	·87253	·12747	·13053	5·25	80
81	20 010	2 763	·86192	·13808	·14231	4·94	81
82	17 247	2 576	·85066	·14934	·15503	4·66	82
83	14 671	2 365	·83878	·16122	·16863	4·39	83
84	12 306	2 137	·82634	·17366	·18311	4·14	84
85	10 169	1 897·4	·81341	·18659	·19849	3·90	85
86	8 271·6	1 654·1	·80003	·19997	·21468	3·68	86
87	6 617·5	1 414·1	·78631	·21369	·23165	3·48	87
88	5 203·4	1 184·6	·77235	·22765	·24928	3·30	88
89	4 018·8	971·6	·75823	·24177	·26748	3·13	89
90	3 047·2	779·9	·74407	·25593	·28616	2·97	90
91	2 267·3	612·2	·72997	·27003	·30518	2·83	91
92	1 655·1	470·0	·71604	·28396	·32429	2·70	92
93	1 185·1	352·73	·70236	·29764	·34372	2·58	93
94	832·37	258·83	·68904	·31096	·36294	2·47	94
95	573·54	185·74	·67615	·32385	·38197	2·38	95
96	387·80	130·39	·66377	·33623	·40066	2·29	96
97	257·41	89·59	·65194	·34806	·41886	2·21	97
98	167·82	60·30	·64071	·35929	·43651	2·14	98
99	107·52	39·771	·63011	·36989	·45354	2·07	99
100	67·749	25·733	·62017	·37983	·46972	2·00	100
101	42·016	16·349	·61088	·38912	·48512		101
102	25·667	10·209	·60224	·39776	·49967		102
103	15·458	6·2721	·59425	·40575	·51335		103
104	9·1859	3·7949	·58688	·41312			104
105	5·3910						105

TABLE 3 (*continued*)

4% interest

Age x	D_x	$\bar{N}_x$	$\bar{C}_x$	$\bar{M}_x$	$\bar{R}_x$	Age x
1	93 799	2 190 962	144·3	7 867·9	441 230·1	1
2	90 050	2 099 056	87·4	7 723·6	433 362·2	2
3	86 501	2 010 796	58·2	7 636·2	425 638·6	3
4	83 117	1 925 999	50·2	7 578·0	418 002·4	4
5	79 871	1 844 516	45·0	7 527·8	410 424·4	5
6	76 755	1 766 215	39·6	7 482·8	402 896·6	6
7	73 764	1 690 965	34·6	7 443·2	395 413·8	7
8	70 893	1 618 645	31·0	7 408·6	387 970·6	8
9	68 136	1 549 140	26·9	7 877·6	380 562·0	9
10	65 489	1 482 337	25·7	7 350·7	373 184·4	10
11	62 945	1 418 129	23·5	7 325·0	365 833·7	11
12	60 501	1 356 414	22·5	7 301·5	358 508·7	12
13	58 152	1 297 095	23·8	7 279·0	351 207·2	13
14	55 892	1 240 080	25·8	7 255·2	343 928·2	14
15	53 717	1 185 282	30·5	7 229·4	336 673 0	15
16	51 621	1 132 620	39·3	7 198·9	329 443·6	16
17	49 597	1 082 016	48·4	7 159·6	322 244·7	17
18	47 642	1 033 403	52·6	7 111·2	315 085·1	18
19	45 758	986 708	52·1	7 058·6	307 973·9	19
20	43 947	941 862	51·7	7 006·5	300 915·3	20
21	42 206	898 791	48·6	6 954·8	293 908·8	21
22	40 535	857 426	45·9	6 906·2	286 954·0	22
23	38 931	817 699	40·4	6 860·3	280 047·8	23
24	37 394	779 541	37·6	6 819·9	273 187·5	24
25	35 919	742 891	35·2	6·782·3	266 367·6	25
26	34 503	707 684	33·6	6 747·1	259 585·3	26
27	33 143	673 866	32·9	6 713·5	252 838·2	27
28	31 836	641 381	32·1	6 680·6	246 124·7	28
29	30 580	610 176	32·5	6 648·5	239 444·1	29
30	29 372	580 204	33·0	6 616·0	232 795·6	30
31	28 210	551 417	33·6	6 583·0	226 179·6	31
32	27 092	523 770	34·7	6 549·4	219 596·6	32
33	26 016	497 219	34·0	6 514·7	213 047·2	33
34	24 982	471 723	35·9	6 480·7	206 532·5	34
35	23 986	447 243	36·1	6 444·8	200 051·8	35
36	23 028	423 738	38·1	6 408·7	193 607·0	36
37	22 105	401 175	39·5	6 370·6	187 198·3	37
38	21 216	379 517	40·8	6 331·1	180 827·7	38
39	20 360	358 731	42·7	6 290·3	174 496·6	39
40	19 535	338 786	44·5	6 247·6	168 206·3	40
41	18 740	319 650	47·1	6 203·1	161 958·7	41
42	17 973	301 296	50·8	6 156·0	155 755·6	42
43	17 232	283 696	54·2	6 105·2	149 599·6	43
44	16 516	266 824	57·9	6 051·0	143 494·4	44
45	15 824	250 656	61·6	5 993·1	137 443·4	45
46	15 155	235 168	66·3	5 931·5	131 450·3	46
47	14 507	220 339	72·5	5 865·2	125 518·8	47
48	13 878	206 148	76·7	5 792·7	119 653·6	48
49	13 269	192 576	84·2	5 716·0	113 860·9	49

TABLE 3 (continued)

4% interest

Age x	D_x	$\overline{N}_x$	$\overline{C}_x$	$\overline{M}_x$	$\overline{R}_x$	Age x
50	12 676	179 605	90·2	5 631·8	108 144·9	50
51	12 100	167 218	97·5	5 541·6	102 513·1	51
52	11 539	155 400	105·2	5 444·1	96 971·5	52
53	10 992	144 136	113·4	5 338·9	91 527·4	53
54	10 458	133 412	121·4	5 225·5	86 188·5	54
55	9 936·7	123 216	129·7	5 104·1	80·963·0	55
56	9 427·3	113 535	138·0	4 974·4	75 858·9	56
57	8 929·4	104 358	146·0	4 836·0	70 884·5	57
58	8 442·7	95 672·6	153·8	4 690·4	66 048·1	58
59	7 967·2	87 468·5	161·3	4 536·6	61 357·7	59
60	7 502·5	79 734·6	168·2	4 375·3	56 821·1	60
61	7 049·0	72 459·7	174·5	4 207·1	52 445·8	61
62	6 606·8	65 632·8	179·9	4 032·6	48 238·7	62
63	6 176·2	59 242·3	184·6	3 852·7	44 206·1	63
64	5 757·6	53 276·4	188·5	3 668·1	40 353·4	64
65	5 351·3	47 723·0	191·5	3 479·6	36 685·3	65
66	4 957·7	42 569·5	193·4	3 288·1	33 205·7	66
67	4 577·4	37 803·1	194·4	3 094·7	29 917·6	67
68	4 210·7	33 410·1	194·5	2 900·3	26 822·9	68
69	3 858·0	29 376·9	193·8	2 705·8	23 922·6	69
70	3 519·6	25 689·3	192·1	2 512·0	21 216·8	70
71	3 195·8	22 332·8	189·5	2 319·9	18 704·8	71
72	2 887·1	19 292·6	186·0	2 130·4	16 384·9	72
73	2 593·6	16 553·6	181·5	1 944·4	14 254·5	73
74	2 315·8	14 100·1	176·31	1 762·9	12 310·1	74
75	2 054·0	11 916·5	169·87	1 586·59	10 547·2	75
76	1 808·4	9 986·67	162·52	1 416·72	8 960·61	76
77	1 579·5	8 294·09	154·37	1 254·20	7 543·89	77
78	1 367·4	6 822·05	145·14	1 099·83	6 289·69	78
79	1 172·5	5 553·50	135·12	954·69	5 189·86	79
80	994·93	4 471·22	124·38	819·57	4 235·17	80
81	834·73	3 557·84	113·05	695·19	3 415·60	81
82	691·80	2 796·00	101·35	582·14	2 720·41	82
83	565·84	2 168·59	89·48	480·79	2 138·27	83
84	456·37	1 658·82	77·751	391·31	1 657·48	84
85	362·61	1 250·61	66·372	313·559	1 266·17	85
86	283·61	928·677	55·642	247·187	952·611	86
87	218·17	678·864	45·745	191·545	705·424	87
88	164·95	488·263	36·846	145·800	513·879	88
89	122·50	345·372	29·064	108·954	368·079	89
90	89·310	240·177	22·432	79·890	259·125	90
91	63·896	164·163	16·9339	57·458	179·235	91
92	44·849	110·265	12·5002	40·5241	121·777	92
93	30·878	72·7745	9·0209	28·0239	81·2529	93
94	20·854	47·1948	6·3654	19·0030	53·2290	94
95	13·817	30·0737	4·3934	12·6376	34·2260	95
96	8·9827	18·8297	2·9652	8·2442	21·5884	96
97	5·7331	11·5823	1·9593	5·2790	13·3442	97
98	3·5940	6·9951	1·2679	3·3197	8·0652	98
99	2·2141	4·1426	·8044	2·0518	4·7455	99
100	1·3414	2·3989	·5003	1·2474	2·6937	100

TABLE 4

ANNUITY TABLE: $a(55)$ Males and Females

MORTALITY FUNCTIONS (FEMALES)

Age [x]	SELECT			ULTIMATE				Age x
	$q_{[x]}$	$e_{[x]}$	$l_{[x]}$	l_x	μ_x	d_x	q_x	
60	·00513	21·144	893 918	897 001	·00819	7 669	·00855	60
61	·00563	20·330	885 969	889 332	·00900	8 351	·00939	61
62	·00619	19·526	877 320	880 981	·00989	9 092	·01032	62
63	·00682	18·733	867 895	871 889	·01088	9 913	·01137	63
64	·00752	17·953	857 616	861 976	·01200	10 809	·01254	64
65	·00831	17·185	846 412	851 167	·01326	11 789	·01385	65
66	·00919	16·430	834 193	839 378	·01466	12 851	·01531	66
67	·01017	15·690	820 865	826 527	·01623	14 010	·01695	67
68	·01126	14·965	806 345	812 517	·01799	15 251	·01877	68
69	·01248	14·256	790 549	797 266	·01995	16 583	·02080	69
70	·01384	13·563	773 377	780 683	·02214	18 010	·02307	70
71	·01535	12·887	754 741	762 673	·02459	19 517	·02559	71
72	·01703	12·229	734 568	743 156	·02731	21 098	·02839	72
73	·01891	11·590	712 785	722 058	·03035	22 752	·03151	73
74	·02099	10·970	689 313	699 306	·03375	24 462	·03498	74
75	·02329	10·370	664 120	674 844	·03753	26 191	·03881	75
76	·02609	9·788	637 350	648 653	·04172	27 931	·04306	76
77	·02923	9·226	608 873	620 722	·04639	29 646	·04776	77
78	·03272	8·686	578 715	591 076	·05158	31 297	·05295	78
79	·03660	8·167	549 961	559 779	·05732	32 837	·05866	79
80	·04092	7·669	513 739	526 942	·06369	34 225	·06495	80
81	·04591	7·192	479 326	492 717	·07073	35 397	·07184	81
82	·05144	6·736	443 850	457 320	·07850	36 302	·07938	82
83	·05755	6·302	407 594	421 018	·08705	36 881	·08760	83
84	·06431	5·890	370 897	384 137	·09646	37 092	·09656	84
85	·07174	5·500	334 132	347 045	·10679	36 884	·10628	85
86	·07988	5·131	297 722	310 161	·11810	36 221	·11678	86
87	·08876	4·782	262 120	273 940	·13043	35 086	·12808	87
88	·09843	4·455	227 785	238 854	·14387	33 490	·14021	88
89	·10890	4·147	195 163	205 364	·15845	31 454	·15316	89
90	·12020	3·859	164 670	173 910	·17424	29 033	·16694	90
91	·13069	3·596	136 407	144 877	·19126	26 297	·18151	91
92	·14172	3·352	110 965	118 580	·20953	23 341	·19684	92
93	·15328	3·126	88 535	95 239	·22908	20 275	·21289	93
94	·16531	2·916	69 190	74 964	·24991	17 212	·22960	94
95	·17775	2·723	52 896	57 752	·27200	14 258	·24688	95
96	·19055	2·544	39 512	43 494	·29530	11 511	·26465	96
97	·20362	2·379	28 803	31 983	·31976	9 045	·28280	97
98	·21689	2·228	20 467	22 938	·34531	6 910	·30124	98
99	·23028	2·087	14 164	16 028	·37183	5 126	·31983	99
100				10 902	·39922	3 690	·33846	100
101				7 212	·427	2 575	·357	101
102				4 637	·456	1 744	·376	102
103				2 893	·488	1 146	·396	103
104				1 747	·521	728	·417	104

TABLE 4 (*continued*)

MONETARY FUNCTIONS: 4% (FEMALES)

Age x	$a_{[x]}$	D_x	N_x	a_x	Age x
60	13·340	85 269	1 218 809	13·294	60
61	12·994	81 289	1 133 540	12·945	61
62	12·643	77 428	1 052 251	12·590	62
63	12·286	73 682	974 823	12·230	63
64	11·926	70 042	901 141	11·866	64
65	11·562	66 504	831 099	11·497	65
66	11·194	63 060	764 595	11·125	66
67	10·824	59 707	701 535	10·750	67
68	10·452	56 437	641 828	10 372	68
69	10·079	53 248	585 391	9·994	69
70	9·705	50 135	532 143	9·614	70
71	9·332	47 095	482 008	9·235	71
72	8·960	44 124	434 913	8·857	72
73	8·590	41 223	390 789	8·480	73
74	8·224	38 388	349 566	8·106	74
75	7·861	35 621	311 178	7·736	75
76	7·501	32 921	275 557	7·370	76
77	7·146	30 292	242 636	7·010	77
78	6·798	27 736	212 344	6·656	78
79	6·457	25 257	184 608	6·309	79
80	6·124	22 861	159 351	5·971	80
81	5·798	20 554	136 490	5·641	81
82	5·482	18 344	115 936	5·320	82
83	5·175	16 238	97 592	5·010	83
84	4·879	14 246	81 354	4·711	84
85	4·594	12 375	67 108	4·423	85
86	4·320	10 635	54 733	4·147	86
87	4·058	9 031·4	44 098	3·883	87
88	3·808	7 571·8	35 067	3·632	88
89	3·570	6 259·8	27 495	3·393	89
90	3·344	5 097·1	21 235	3·167	90
91	3·137	4 082·9	16 138	2·953	91
92	2·941	3 213·2	12 055	2·753	92
93	2·758	2 481·5	8 842	2·564	93
94	2·587	1 878·1	6 360	2·388	94
95	2·428	1 391·2	4 482	2·224	95
96	2·280	1 007·5	3 091	2·071	96
97	2·142	712·3	2 084	1·929	97
98	2·014	491·2	1 371	1·797	98
99	1·895	330·0	880	1·674	99
100		215·9	550	1·560	100
101		137·3	334	1·453	101
102		84·9	197	1·350	102
103		50·9	112	1·249	103
104		29·6	61	1·151	104

TABLE 4 (*continued*)

MORTALITY FUNCTIONS (MALES)

Age [x]	SELECT $q_{[x]}$	SELECT $e_{[x]}$	SELECT $l_{[x]}$	ULTIMATE l_x	ULTIMATE μ_x	ULTIMATE d_x	ULTIMATE q_x	Age x
60	·00841	17·520	855 051	859 916	·01344	12 056	·01402	60
61	·00928	16·773	842 571	847 860	·01482	13 108	·01546	61
62	·01024	16·041	829 000	834 752	·01637	14 241	·01706	62
63	·01130	15·323	814 262	820 511	·01808	15 450	·01883	63
64	·01248	14·622	798 279	805 061	·01998	16 745	·02080	64
65	·01378	13·936	780 970	788 316	·02209	18 108	·02297	65
66	·01523	13·268	762 269	770 208	·02443	19 548	·02538	66
67	·01682	12·617	742 101	750 660	·02702	21 041	·02803	67
68	·01858	11·984	720 415	729 619	·02989	22 589	·03096	68
69	·02052	11·370	697 156	707 030	·03307	24 180	·03420	69
70	·02266	10·774	672 300	682 850	·03658	25 784	·03776	70
71	·02502	10·199	645 825	657 066	·04047	27 400	·04170	71
72	·02761	9·643	617 745	629 666	·04478	28 977	·04602	72
73	·03045	9·107	588 112	600 689	·04952	30 485	·05075	73
74	·03357	8·592	556 999	570 204	·05474	31 903	·05595	74
75	·03698	8·098	524 517	538 301	·06050	33 181	·06164	75
76	·04112	7·622	491 034	505 120	·06684	34 277	·06786	76
77	·04567	7·166	456 555	470 843	·07381	35 139	·07463	77
78	·05067	6·731	421 330	435 704	·08143	35 723	·08199	78
79	·05615	6·317	385 645	399 981	·08979	35 990	·08998	79
80	·06212	5·923	349 829	363 991	·09891	35 893	·09861	80
81	·06898	5·547	314 365	328 098	·10887	35 418	·10795	81
82	·07645	5·192	279 519	292 680	·11973	34 530	·11798	82
83	·08458	4·856	245 697	258 150	·13151	33 234	·12874	83
84	·09339	4·539	213 296	224 916	·14428	31 540	·14023	84
85	·10291	4·241	182 695	193 376	·15807	29 482	·15246	85
86	·11314	3·961	154 234	163 894	·17293	27 110	·16541	86
87	·12412	3·698	128 198	136 784	·18889	24 498	·17910	87
88	·13581	3·453	104 795	112 286	·20599	21 723	·19346	88
89	·14824	3·223	84 158	90 563	·22421	18 881	·20849	89
90	·16137	3·009	66 318	71 682	·24360	16 066	·22413	90
91	·17303	2·818	51 090	55 616	·26414	13 366	·24032	91
92	·18503	2·640	38 519	42 250	·28580	10 858	·25699	92
93	·19732	2·477	28 391	31 392	·30852	8 603	·27405	93
94	·20983	2·326	20 436	22 789	·33225	6 641	·29143	94
95	·22250	2·186	14 351	16 148	·35695	4 990	·30903	95
96	·23525	2·058	9 823	11 158	·38256	3 646	·32673	96
97	·24800	1·941	6 548	7 512	·40896	2 588	·34445	97
98	·26070	1·832	4 249	4 924	·43594	1 783	·36209	98
99	·27325	1·731	2 682	3 141	·46333	1 192	·37952	99
100				1 949	·49106	773	·39668	100
101				1 176	·519	487	·414	101
102				689	·550	298	·432	102
103				391	·582	176	·450	103
104				215	·620	101	·469	104

TABLE 4 (continued)

MONETARY FUNCTIONS: 4% (MALES)

Age x	$a_{[x]}$	D_x	N_x	a_x	Age x
60	11·691	81 744	1 032 009	11·625	60
61	11·333	77 498	950 265	11·262	61
62	10·972	73 365	872 767	10·896	62
63	10·610	69 340	799 402	10·529	63
64	10·246	65 418	730 062	10·160	64
65	9·883	61 593	664 644	9·791	65
66	9·520	57 864	603 051	9·422	66
67	9·158	54 226	545 187	9·054	67
68	8·799	50 679	490 961	8·688	68
69	8·442	47 221	440 282	8·324	69
70	8·088	43 852	393 061	7·963	70
71	7·739	40 573	349 209	7·607	71
72	7·395	37 386	308 636	7·255	72
73	7·057	34 294	271 250	6·910	73
74	6·726	31 301	236 956	6·570	74
75	6·402	28 414	205 655	6·238	75
76	6·083	25 637	177 241	5·914	76
77	5·773	22 978	151 604	5·598	77
78	5·472	20 445	128 626	5·291	78
79	5·180	18 047	108 181	4·994	79
80	4·898	15 791	90 134	4·708	80
81	4·625	13 687	74 343	4·432	81
82	4·363	11 740	60 656	4·167	82
83	4·111	9 956·5	48 916	3·913	83
84	3·871	8 341·0	38 960	3·671	84
85	3·642	6 895·6	30 619	3·440	85
86	3·423	5 619·5	23 723	3·222	86
87	3·217	4 509·6	18 104	3·015	87
88	3·021	3 559·5	13 594	2·819	88
89	2·836	2 760·5	10 034	2·635	89
90	2·662	2 100·9	7 274	2·463	90
91	2·505	1 567·3	5 173	2·301	91
92	2·358	1 144·9	3 606	2·150	92
93	2·222	817·9	2 461	2·009	93
94	2·095	570·9	1 643	1·879	94
95	1·977	389·0	1 072	1·757	95
96	1·868	258·5	683	1·645	96
97	1·767	167·3	424	1·541	97
98	1·674	105·5	257	1·444	98
99	1·587	64·7	152	1·355	99
100		38·6	87	1·271	100
101		22·4	48	1·190	101
102		12·6	26	1·113	102
103		6·9	13	1·037	103
104		3·6	6	·961	104

TABLE 4 (continued)

JOINT LIFE ANNUITIES (MALES and FEMALES)

Ultimate: a_{xy}: 4%

Age of female	Age of male										
	60	62	64	66	68	70	72	74	76	78	80
60	9·852	9·380	8·875	8·343	7·790	7·223	6·651	6·080	5·519	4·976	4·458
62	9·547	9·111	8·641	8·141	7·619	7·080	6·531	5·982	5·440	4·912	4·406
64	9·203	8·804	8·371	7·907	7·418	6·910	6·389	5·865	5·344	4·834	4·344
66	8·818	8·459	8·064	7·639	7·186	6·712	6·223	5·726	5·229	4·741	4·269
68	8·396	8·076	7·722	7·336	6·922	6·484	6·029	5·563	5·095	4·631	4·179
70	7·938	7·657	7·343	6·998	6·625	6·226	5·808	5·376	4·938	4·501	4·073
72	7·451	7·208	6·933	6·629	6·296	5·937	5·558	5·162	4·758	4·351	3·949
74	6·940	6·732	6·496	6·231	5·938	5·621	5·281	4·923	4·554	4·179	3·806
76	6·413	6·238	6·037	5·810	5·556	5·279	4·978	4·660	4·327	3·987	3·645
78	5·878	5·732	5·564	5·372	5·156	4·916	4·655	4·375	4·080	3·774	3·465
80	5·345	5·225	5·085	4·925	4·743	4·540	4·315	4·073	3·814	3·544	3·267
82	4·821	4·724	4·609	4·477	4·326	4·156	3·966	3·759	3·535	3·300	3·056
84	4·316	4·237	4·145	4·037	3·913	3·772	3·614	3·439	3·249	3·046	2·834
86	3·836	3·774	3·700	3·613	3·512	3·396	3·266	3·120	2·960	2·788	2·606
88	3·388	3·339	3·280	3·210	3·129	3·035	2·928	2·808	2·675	2·530	2·376
90	2·977	2·938	2·891	2·836	2·771	2·695	2·608	2·510	2·400	2·280	2·150
92	2·604	2·574	2·537	2·493	2·441	2·381	2·310	2·231	2·141	2·041	1·933
94	2·272	2·248	2·219	2·184	2·143	2·094	2·038	1·973	1·900	1·818	1·728
96	1·980	1·961	1·938	1·910	1·877	1·839	1·793	1·741	1·681	1·614	1·539
98	1·725	1·710	1·692	1·670	1·644	1·613	1·576	1·533	1·485	1·430	1·368
100	1·504	1·492	1·477	1·460	1·439	1·414	1·384	1·350	1·310	1·265	1·214

Age of female	Age of male										
	80	82	84	86	88	90	92	94	96	98	100
60	4·458	3·969	3·515	3·099	2·723	2·387	2·090	1·831	1·606	1·413	1·246
62	4·406	3·928	3·483	3·074	2·703	2·371	2·077	1·821	1·598	1·407	1·240
64	4·344	3·879	3·443	3·043	2·678	2·351	2·062	1·808	1·589	1·399	1·234
66	4·269	3·818	3·395	3·004	2·648	2·327	2·043	1·793	1·576	1·389	1·226
68	4·179	3·746	3·337	2·958	2·611	2·298	2·019	1·774	1·561	1·377	1·216
70	4·073	3·660	3·268	2·903	2·567	2·263	1·991	1·752	1·543	1·362	1·203
72	3·949	3·559	3·186	2·837	2·514	2·220	1·957	1·724	1·520	1·343	1·189
74	3·806	3·441	3·090	2·759	2·451	2·169	1·916	1·691	1·493	1·321	1·170
76	3·645	3·307	2·980	2·669	2·377	2·110	1·868	1·652	1·461	1·295	1·149
78	3·465	3·156	2·854	2·565	2·293	2·041	1·811	1·605	1·423	1·263	1·123
80	3·267	2·989	2·714	2·449	2·197	1·962	1·746	1·552	1·379	1·227	1·092
82	3·056	2·808	2·561	2·320	2·090	1·873	1·673	1·491	1·328	1·185	1·057
84	2·834	2·616	2·397	2·181	1·973	1·775	1·591	1·423	1·271	1·137	1·017
86	2·606	2·417	2·225	2·034	1·847	1·669	1·502	1·348	1·208	1·084	·972
88	2·376	2·214	2·048	1·881	1·716	1·557	1·407	1·267	1·140	1·025	·922
90	2·150	2·013	1·870	1·726	1·582	1·442	1·308	1·183	1·068	·964	·869
92	1·933	1·817	1·696	1·572	1·448	1·325	1·207	1·096	·993	·899	·814
94	1·728	1·632	1·529	1·424	1·317	1·210	1·107	1·009	·917	·833	·757
96	1·539	1·459	1·373	1·283	1·192	1·100	1·010	·924	·843	·768	·700
98	1·368	1·301	1·229	1·153	1·075	·996	·918	·843	·771	·705	·644
100	1·214	1·158	1·098	1·034	·967	·899	·832	·766	·704	·646	·591

TABLE 5

PENSION FUND TABLES

Service table and salary scale

Age x	l_x	w_x	d_x	i_x	r_x	s_x	Age x
18	100 000	10 000	80			1·00	18
19	89 920	8 992	72			1·10	19
20	80 856	8 085	65			1·21	20
21	72 706	6 907	58			1·33	21
22	65 741	5 917	59			1·46	22
23	59 765	5 080	54			1·59	23
24	54 631	4 371	49			1·73	24
25	50 211	3 766	50			1·87	25
26	46 395	3 248	46			2·02	26
27	43 101	2 802	47			2·16	27
28	40 252	2 415	44			2·29	28
29	37 793	2 079	45			2·42	29
30	35 669	1 784	46			2·55	30
31	33 839	1 557	47	3		2·67	31
32	32 232	1 354	49	3		2·78	32
33	30 826	1 171	49	3		2·88	33
34	29 603	1 007	50	6		2·98	34
35	28 540	856	51	6		3·08	35
36	27 627	746	52	6		3·18	36
37	26 823	644	54	8		3·28	37
38	26 117	548	55	8		3·38	38
39	25 506	459	56	8		3·48	39
40	24 983	375	57	10		3·58	40
41	24 541	295	61	10		3·68	41
42	24 175	218	65	12		3·78	42
43	23 880	143	69	12		3·88	43
44	23 656	71	76	14		3·98	44
45	23 495		82	14		4·08	45
46	23 399		92	16		4·18	46
47	23 291		100	19		4·28	47
48	23 172		108	21		4·38	48
49	23 043		120	23		4·47	49
50	22 900		130	28		4·56	50
51	22 742		143	32		4·65	51
52	22 567		156	39		4·73	52
53	22 372		170	44		4·81	53
54	22 158		184	53		4·88	54
55	21 921		200	61		4·95	55
56	21 660		217	71		5·01	56
57	21 372		236	83		5·07	57
58	21 053		254	99		5·13	58
59	20 700		276	118		5·19	59
60	20 306		297	146	4 061	5·24	60
61	15 802		253	153	2 370	5·29	61
62	13 026		228	178	1 303	5·33	62
63	11 317		216	217	1 132	5·37	63
64	9 752		203	265	975	5·40	64
65	8 309				8 309		65

TABLE 5 (*continued*)

Contribution functions: 4% per annum interest

Age	D_x	$\overline{D}_x =$ $\frac{1}{2}(D_x + D_{x+1})$	$\overline{N}_x$ $= \Sigma\overline{D}_x$	${}^s\overline{D}_x$ $= s_x\overline{D}_x$	${}^s\overline{N}_x$ $= \Sigma{}^s\overline{D}_x$	${}^sD_x$ $= s_xD_x$	Age
18	49 363	46 021	438 252	46 021	973 119	49 363	18
19	42 680	39 791	392 231	43 770	927 098	46 948	19
20	36 902	34 404	352 440	41 629	883 328	44 651	20
21	31 906	29 823	318 037	39 665	841 699	42 435	21
22	27 740	25 994	288 214	37 951	802 034	40 500	22
23	24 248	22 780	262 220	36 220	764 083	38 554	23
24	21 313	20 074	239 440	34 728	727 863	36 871	24
25	18 835	17 785	219 366	33 258	693 135	35 222	25
26	16 734	15 841	201 581	31 999	659 877	33 803	26
27	14 948	14 186	185 740	30 642	627 878	32 288	27
28	13 423	12 771	171 555	29 246	597 236	30 739	28
29	12 118	11 558	158 784	27 970	567 990	29 326	29
30	10 997	10 515	147 226	26 813	540 020	28 043	30
31	10 032	9 610	136 711	25 659	513 207	26 785	31
32	9 188	8 819	127 102	24 517	487 548	25 542	32
33	8 449	8 126	118 283	23 403	463 031	24 334	33
34	7 802	7 518	110 157	22 404	439 628	23 249	34
35	7 232	6 982	102 640	21 505	417 224	22 276	35
36	6 732	6 508	95 658	20 695	395 719	21 407	36
37	6 284	6 084	89 150	19 956	375 024	20 613	37
38	5 884	5 704	83 066	19 280	355 068	19 887	38
39	5 525	5 364	77 362	18 667	335 788	19 227	39
40	5 204	5 059	71 997	18 111	317 121	18 629	40
41	4 915	4 785	66 938	17 609	299 010	18 087	41
42	4 656	4 539	62 153	17 157	281 401	17 598	42
43	4 422	4 317	57 614	16 750	264 244	17 157	43
44	4 212	4 117	53 297	16 386	247 494	16 763	44
45	4 022	3 937	49 180	16 063	231 108	16 411	45
46	3 852	3 769	45 243	15 754	215 045	16 100	46
47	3 687	3 607	41 474	15 438	199 291	15 778	47
48	3 527	3 449	37 867	15 107	183 853	15 447	48
49	3 372	3 297	34 418	14 738	168 746	15 073	49
50	3 222	3 150	31 121	14 364	154 008	14 693	50
51	3 077	3 006	27 971	13 978	139 644	14 308	51
52	2 936	2 867	24 965	13 561	125 666	13 886	52
53	2 799	2 732	22 098	13 141	112 105	13 461	53
54	2 665	2 600	19 366	12 688	98 964	13 006	54
55	2 535	2 472	16 765	12 236	86 276	12 549	55
56	2 409	2 347	14 294	11 758	74 040	12 068	56
57	2 285	2 225	11 947	11 281	62 282	11 586	57
58	2 165	2 106	9 722	10 804	51 001	11 105	58
59	2 046	1 988	7 616	10 318	40 197	10 621	59
60	1 930	1 687	5 628	8 840	29 879	10 115	60
61	1 444	1 295	3 940	6 851	21 039	7 641	61
62	1 145	1 051	2 646	5 602	14 188	6 102	62
63	956	874	1 595	4 693	8 586	5 136	63
64	792	721	721	3 893	3 893	4 279	64
65	649						65

TABLE 5 (*continued*)

4% per annum interest

FUNCTIONS FOR PAYMENTS ON DEATH WITH INTEREST ACCUMULATED AT 3% PER ANNUM

Age x	$jC_x^d = v^{x+\frac{1}{2}}(1+j)^{x+\frac{1}{2}}d_x$	$jM_x^d = \Sigma^j C_x^d$	$j\overline{R}_x^d = \Sigma \dfrac{jM_x^d - \frac{1}{2}jC_x^d}{(1+j)^{x+t+\frac{1}{2}}}$	$sj\overline{R}_x^d = \Sigma \dfrac{s_x(jM_x^d - \frac{1}{2}jC_x^d)}{(1+j)^{x+t+\frac{1}{2}}}$	Age x
20	53	3 110	31 397	87 726	20
25	39	2 881	23 699	76 546	25
30	35	2 701	17 504	63 288	30
35	36	2 525	12 495	49 451	35
40	39	2 338	8 474	36 298	40
45	53	2 120	5 288	24 285	45
50	80	1 803	2 859	13 927	50
55	117	1 332	1 177	5 999	55
56	125	1 215	930	4 776	56
57	135	1 090	713	3 690	57
58	145	955	526	2 743	58
59	155	810	369	1 940	59
60	165	655	243	1 285	60
61	140	490	147	783	61
62	124	350	79	423	62
63	117	226	34	181	63
64	109	109	8	43	64

All summations are based on accumulating from age 64 although only quinquennial values are shown up to age 55.

FUNCTIONS FOR PAYMENTS ON WITHDRAWAL WITH INTEREST ACCUMULATED AT 3% PER ANNUM

Age x	$jC_x^w = v^{x+\frac{1}{2}}(1+j)^{x+\frac{1}{2}}w_x$	$jM_x^w = \Sigma^j C_x^w$	$j\overline{R}_x^w = \Sigma \dfrac{jM_x^w - \frac{1}{2}jC_x^d}{(1+j)^{x+t+\frac{1}{2}}}$	$sj\overline{R}_x^w = \Sigma \dfrac{s_x(jM_x^d - \frac{1}{2}jC_x^d)}{(1+j)^{x+t+\frac{1}{2}}}$	Age x
20	6 633	43 550	119 400	207 911	20
25	2 944	19 045	42 211	98 740	25
30	1 328	8 041	13 391	38 289	30
35	608	3 007	3 281	10 741	35
36	524	2 399	2 334	7 826	36
37	448	1 875	1 608	5 516	37
38	378	1 427	1 063	3 729	38
39	313	1 049	666	2 389	39
40	253	735	389	1 424	40
41	197	482	205	766	41
42	144	285	93	352	42
43	94	140	32	124	43
44	46	46	6	24	44

All summations are based on annual values from age 44, the highest age at which withdrawals are assumed to take place although only quinquennial values are shown up to age 35.

TABLE 5 (continued)

ILL-HEALTH RETIREMENT FUNCTIONS: 4% per annum interest

Age x	$C_x^i = v^{x+\frac{1}{2}} i_x$	$M_x^i = \Sigma C_x^i$	$\bar{R}_x^i = \Sigma(M_x^i - \frac{1}{2}C_x^i)$	$C_x^{ia} = v^{x+\frac{1}{2}} i_x \bar{a}_{x+\frac{1}{2}}$	$M_x^{ia} = \Sigma C_x^{ia}$	$\bar{R}_x^{ia} = \Sigma(M_x^{ia} - \frac{1}{2}C_x^{ia})$	Age x
20		189	6 841		1 821	64 923	20
25		189	5 897		1 821	55 820	25
30		189	4 952		1 821	46 718	30
35	1	185	4 016	15	1 774	37 699	35
40	2	177	3 111	22	1 688	29 034	40
45	2	166	2 254	25	1 572	20 873	45
50	4	151	1 459	39	1 421	13 367	50
55	7	127	757	69	1 170	6 831	55
56	8	120	634	77	1 100	5 696	56
57	9	112	518	85	1 023	4 634	57
58	10	103	410	96	938	3 653	58
59	11	93	312	109	842	2 763	59
60	14	82	224	127	733	1 975	60
61	14	68	149	126	606	1 306	61
62	15	54	88	139	480	763	62
63	18	39	41	159	341	353	63
64	21	21	11	182	182	91	64

Age x	$^s\bar{M}_x^{ia} = s_x(M_x^{ia} - \frac{1}{2}C_x^{ia})$	$^s\bar{R}_x^{ia} = \Sigma \, ^s\bar{M}_x^{ia}$	$^zC_x^{ia} = z_{x+\frac{1}{2}}C_x^{ia}$	$^zM_x^{ia} = \Sigma \, ^zC_x^{ia}$	$^z\bar{R}_x^{ia} = \Sigma(^zM_x^{ia} - \frac{1}{2}\,^zC_x^{ia})$	Age x
20	2 203	215 088		8 636	318 302	20
25	3 404	201 761		8 636	275 122	25
30	4 642	182 173		8 636	231 941	30
35	5 441	157 184	45	8 513	188 977	35
40	6 004	128 781	75	8 243	147 045	40
45	6 361	97 957	98	7 819	106 825	45
50	6 391	65 879	173	7 197	69 159	50
55	5 618	35 026	335	6 036	35 759	55
56	5 320	29 408	377	5 700	29 891	56
57	4 972	24 089	424	5 323	24 379	57
58	4 566	19 117	484	4 899	19 268	58
59	4 088	14 550	554	4 415	14 611	59
60	3 509	10 462	657	3 861	10 472	60
61	2 871	6 953	658	3 204	6 940	61
62	2 187	4 082	729	2 546	4 064	62
63	1 404	1 895	844	1 817	1 882	63
64	491	491	974	974	487	64

All summations are based on annual values from age 64 although only quinquennial values are shown up to age

$$z_x = \tfrac{1}{3}(s_{x-3} + s_{x-2} + s_{x-1})$$

TABLE 5 (*continued*)

AGE RETIREMENT FUNCTIONS: 4% per annum interest

Age x	$C_x^r = v^{x+\frac{1}{2}} r_x$ ($v^x r_x$ at 65)	$M_x^r = \Sigma C_x^r$	$\bar{R}_x^r = \Sigma(M_x^r - \frac{1}{2}C_x^r)$	$C_x^{ra} = v^{x+\frac{1}{2}} r_x \bar{a}_{x+\frac{1}{2}}^r$ ($v^x r_x \bar{a}_x^r$ at 65)	$M_x^{ra} = \Sigma C_x^{ra}$	$\bar{R}_x^{ra} = \Sigma(M_x^{ra} - \frac{1}{2}C_x^{ra})$	Age x
20		1 524	65 669		16 742	719 370	20
25		1 524	58 049		16 742	635 660	25
30		1 524	50 430		16 742	551 950	30
35		1 524	42 810		16 742	468 240	35
40		1 524	35 191		16 742	384 530	40
45		1 524	27 571		16 742	300 820	45
50		1 524	19 951		16 742	217 110	50
55		1 524	12 332		16 742	133 399	55
56		1 524	10 808		16 742	116 657	56
57		1 524	9 284		16 742	99 915	57
58		1 524	7 760		16 742	83 173	58
59		1 524	6 236		16 742	66 431	59
60	379	1 524	4 712	4 520	16 742	49 689	60
61	212	1 145	3 378	2 459	12 222	35 207	61
62	112	933	2 339	1 258	9 764	24 214	62
63	94	821	1 462	1 016	8 505	15 079	63
64	78	727	688	814	7 489	7 082	64
65	649	649		6 675	6 675		65

Age x	$^s\bar{M}_x^{ra} = s_x(M_x^{ra} - \frac{1}{2}C_x^{ra})$	$^s\bar{R}^{ra} = \Sigma {^s\bar{M}_x^{ra}}$	$^zC_x^{ra} = z_{x+\frac{1}{2}} C_x^{ra}$ ($z_x C_x^{ra}$ at 65)	$^zM_x^{ra} = \Sigma {^zC_x^{ra}}$	$^z\bar{R}_x^{ra} = \Sigma({^zM_x^{ra}} - \frac{1}{2}{^zC_x^{ra}})$	Age x
20	20 258	2 567 780		88 345	3 798 939	20
25	31 308	2 445 228		88 345	3 357 212	25
30	42 692	2 265 084		88 345	2 915 486	30
35	51 565	2 033 040		88 345	2 473 760	35
40	59 936	1 758 471		88 345	2 032 033	40
45	68 307	1 442 047		88 345	1 590 307	45
50	76 344	1 083 936		88 345	1 148 580	50
55	82 873	688 322		88 345	706 854	55
56	83 877	605 450		88 345	618 509	56
57	84 882	521 572		88 345	530 163	57
58	85 886	436 690		88 345	441 818	58
59	86 891	350 804		88 345	353 473	59
60	75 887	263 913	23 321	88 345	265 127	60
61	58 152	188 026	12 811	65 024	188 443	61
62	48 686	129 874	6 618	52 213	129 824	62
63	42 944	81 187	5 397	45 596	80 920	63
64	38 243	38 243	4 352	40 199	38 022	64
65			35 846	35 846		65

ummations are based on annual values (from age 64 or age 65 as appropriate) although only quinquennial
s are shown up to age 55.

$$z_x = \tfrac{1}{3}(s_{x-3} + s_{x-2} - s_{x-1})$$

TABLE 6

SICKNESS TABLE

MANCHESTER UNITY EXPERIENCE 1893–7
OCCUPATION GROUP AHJ
Rates of sickness (in weeks per annum)

Age	First 3 months	Second 3 months	Second 6 months	Second 12 months	After 2 years	All periods	Age
16	·816	·048	·017	·000	·000	·881	16
17	·796	·050	·020	·000	·000	·866	17
18	·766	·054	·024	·004	·000	·848	18
19	·732	·059	·029	·009	·000	·829	19
20	·698	·065	·035	·013	·004	·815	20
21	·670	·071	·041	·019	·009	·810	21
22	·651	·075	·046	·026	·016	·814	22
23	·640	·078	·050	·031	·024	·823	23
24	·635	·080	·053	·034	·032	·834	24
25	·633	·082	·056	·035	·039	·845	25
26	·633	·084	·058	·036	·045	·856	26
27	·635	·085	·060	·038	·049	·867	27
28	·638	·086	·062	·041	·054	·881	28
29	·643	·088	·064	·044	·059	·898	29
30	·649	·090	·066	·048	·065	·918	30
31	·656	·093	·068	·052	·072	·941	31
32	·663	·096	·070	·055	·082	·966	32
33	·670	·100	·073	·055	·093	·991	33
34	·677	·105	·077	·056	·105	1·020	34
35	·685	·110	·081	·058	·118	1·052	35
36	·696	·115	·086	·062	·132	1·091	36
37	·709	·121	·091	·068	·147	1·136	37
38	·726	·128	·096	·074	·166	1·190	38
39	·744	·136	·102	·080	·187	1·249	39
40	·764	·143	·109	·087	·210	1·313	40
41	·784	·151	·116	·092	·235	1·378	41
42	·803	·159	·124	·098	·259	1·443	42
43	·821	·166	·133	·105	·283	1·508	43
44	·839	·174	·141	·112	·308	1·574	44
45	·858	·182	·148	·120	·335	1·643	45
46	·879	·190	·156	·129	·363	1·717	46
47	·904	·201	·165	·138	·396	1·804	47
48	·932	·215	·176	·148	·436	1·907	48
49	·962	·232	·189	·161	·486	2·030	49
50	·994	·249	·206	·177	·551	2·177	50
51	1·027	·268	·225	·196	·631	2·347	51
52	1·061	·288	·247	·219	·724	2·539	52
53	1·096	·309	·272	·244	·829	2·750	53
54	1·134	·330	·300	·275	·939	2·978	54
55	1·175	·353	·332	·310	1·051	3·221	55
56	1·218	·378	·368	·352	1·165	3·481	56
57	1·262	·405	·407	·400	1·285	3·759	57
58	1·308	·435	·449	·455	1·418	4·065	58
59	1·356	·471	·495	·516	1·575	4·413	59
60	1·409	·510	·547	·585	1·770	4·821	60

TABLE 6 (*continued*)

MANCHESTER UNITY EXPERIENCE 1893–7
OCCUPATION GROUP AHJ
Rates of sickness (in weeks per annum)

Age	First 3 months	Second 3 months	Second 6 months	Second 12 months	After 2 years	All periods	Age
61	1·466	·555	·607	·665	2·017	5·310	61
62	1·526	·602	·674	·759	2·332	5·893	62
63	1·587	·653	·747	·865	2·718	6·570	63
64	1·650	·707	·824	·980	3·174	7·335	64
65	1·715	·761	·906	1·106	3·695	8·183	65
66	1·779	·820	·997	1·244	4·277	9·117	66
67	1·841	·882	1·100	1·406	4·924	10·153	67
68	1·893	·945	1·213	1·596	5·655	11·302	68
69	1·929	1·008	1·332	1·803	6·487	12·559	69
70	1·948	1·064	1·449	2·017	7·435	13·913	70
71	1·952	1·110	1·554	2·224	8·506	15·346	71
72	1·947	1·147	1·646	2·427	9·679	16·846	72
73	1·940	1·178	1·725	2·592	10·974	18·409	73
74	1·932	1·205	1·793	2·756	12·350	20·036	74
75	1·921	1·228	1·856	2·906	13·802	21·713	75
76	1·901	1·247	1·913	3·031	15·305	23·397	76
77	1·871	1·260	1·956	3·118	16·856	25·061	77
78	1·824	1·266	1·990	3·180	18·428	26·688	78
79	1·764	1·259	1·973	3·216	20·053	28·265	79
80	1·696	1·238	1·932	3·219	21·692	29·777	80
81	1·625	1·206	1·864	3·193	23·313	31·201	81
82	1·559	1·161	1·784	3·133	24·819	32·456	82
83	1·497	1·107	1·707	3·042	26·134	33·487	83
84	1·436	1·055	1·648	2·926	27·246	34·311	84
85	1·365	1·006	1·607	2·811	28·183	34·972	85
86	1·278	·965	1·580	2·701	29·027	35·551	86
87	1·177	·935	1·560	2·601	29·846	36·119	87
88	1·078	·910	1·544	2·522	30·645	36·699	88
89	1·078	·910	1·544	2·522	31·177	37·231	89
90	1·078	·910	1·544	2·522	31·610	37·664	90
91	1·078	·910	1·544	2·522	31·891	37·945	91
92	1·078	·910	1·544	2·522	31·891	37·945	92
93	1·078	·910	1·544	2·522	31·891	37·945	93
94	1·078	·910	1·544	2·522	31·891	37·945	94
95	1·078	·910	1·544	2·522	31·891	37·945	95
96	1·078	·910	1·544	2·522	31·891	37·945	96
97	1·078	·910	1·544	2·522	31·891	37·945	97
98	1·078	·910	1·544	2·522	31·891	37·945	98
99	1·078	·910	1·544	2·522	31·891	37·945	99
100	1·078	·910	1·544	2·522	31·891	37·945	100

TABLE 6 (*continued*)

MORTALITY RATES OF ENGLISH LIFE TABLE No. 12—Males
SICKNESS RATES OF MANCHESTER UNITY EXPERIENCE 1893-7
OCCUPATION GROUP AHJ
Commutation columns *K* for sickness benefit values: 4% interest

Age	K_x^{13}	$K_x^{13/13}$	$K_x^{26/26}$	$K_x^{52/52}$	$K_x^{104/all}$	Age
16	934 156	194 925	186 421	198 447	738 483	16
17	892 859	192 496	185 561	198 447	738 483	17
18	854 158	190 065	184 588	198 447	738 483	18
19	818 386	187 543	183 467	198 260	738 483	19
20	785 554	184 896	182 167	197 857	738 483	20
21	755 486	182 096	180 659	197 297	738 311	21
22	727 768	179 159	178 963	196 511	737 939	22
23	701 901	176 179	177 135	195 477	737 303	23
24	677 477	173 202	175 227	194 294	736 387	24
25	654 200	170 270	173 284	193 048	735 214	25
26	631 912	167 383	171 312	191 816	733 841	26
27	610 502	164 541	169 351	190 598	732 319	27
28	589 870	161 780	167 401	189 363	730 727	28
29	569 959	159 096	165 466	188 084	729 041	29
30	550 684	156 458	163 548	186 765	727 273	30
31	531 998	153 867	161 647	185 383	725 401	31
32	513 859	151 295	159 767	183 945	723 410	32
33	496 253	148 746	157 908	182 485	721 233	33
34	479 168	146 196	156 047	181 082	718 861	34
35	462 592	143 625	154 161	179 711	716 291	35
36	446 490	141 039	152 257	178 347	713 517	36
37	430 783	138 444	150 317	176 948	710 538	37
38	415 425	135 823	148 345	175 475	707 354	38
39	400 332	133 162	146 350	173 937	703 903	39
40	385 490	130 449	144 315	172 341	700 172	40
41	370 869	127 712	142 229	170 676	696 153	41
42	356 477	124 940	140 099	168 987	691 839	42
43	342 342	122 141	137 917	167 262	687 280	43
44	328 488	119 340	135 672	165 490	682 505	44
45	314 921	116 527	133 392	163 679	677 524	45
46	301 631	113 707	131 100	161 820	672 335	46
47	288 594	110 889	128 786	159 907	666 951	47
48	275 764	108 037	126 444	157 949	661 331	48
49	263 113	105 118	124 055	155 940	655 413	49
50	250 633	102 109	121 604	153 851	649 108	50
51	238 319	·99 023·9	119 052	151 658	642 282	51
52	226 180	95 856·3	116 392	149 342	634 824	52
53	214 228	92 611·9	113 610	146 875	626 668	53
54	202 473	89 297·8	110 692	144 258	617 777	54
55	190 909	85 932·6	107 633	141 453	608 201	55
56	179 533	82 514·8	104 419	138 452	598 025	56
57	168 353	79 045·3	101 041	135 221	587 332	57
58	157 391	75 527·4	97 505·6	131 746	576 170	58
59	146 659	71 958·2	93 821·5	128 013	564 536	59
60	136 170	68 315·0	89 992·7	124 022	552 353	60

TABLE 6 (*continued*)

MORTALITY RATES OF ENGLISH LIFE TABLE No. 12—Males
SICKNESS RATES OF MANCHESTER UNITY EXPERIENCE 1893-7
OCCUPATION GROUP AHJ
Commutation columns K for sickness benefit values: 4% interest

Age	K_x^{13}	$K_x^{13/13}$	$K_x^{26/26}$	$K_x^{52/52}$	$K_x^{104/all}$	Age
61	125 918	64 604·3	86 012·7	119 765	539 475	61
62	115 908	60 814·7	81 868·1	115 225	525 702	62
63	106 155	56 967·0	77 560·2	110 374	510 797	63
64	96 685·4	53 070·6	73 102·9	105 212	494 579	64
65	87 520·4	49 143·5	68 526·0	99 768·8	476 949	65
66	78 680·3	45 220·9	63 855·9	94 067·8	457 903	66
67	70 198·6	41 311·4	59 102·6	88 136·8	437 512	67
68	62 109·0	37 435·8	54 269·0	81 958·8	415 875	68
69	54 471·9	33 623·2	49 375·3	75 519·8	393 060	69
70	47 356·1	29 904·9	44 461·7	68 868·1	369 131	70
71	40 815·2	26 332·2	39 596·3	62 096·1	344 166	71
72	34 878·1	22 956·1	34 869·8	55 331·8	318 294	72
73	29 542·4	19 812·8	30 359·0	48 680·7	291 770	73
74	24 780·1	16 921·0	26 124·4	42 317·8	264 830	74
75	20 558·6	14 288·1	22 206·7	36 296·0	237 846	75
76	16 848·7	11 916·5	18 622·3	30 683·7	211 190	76
77	13 628·4	9 804·08	15 381·6	25 549·1	185 263	77
78	10 871·5	7 947·48	12 499·5	20 954·8	160 426	78
79	8 554·97	6 339·66	9 972·18	16 916·2	137 023	79
80	6 643·24	4 975·23	7 833·95	13 430·8	115 290	80
81	5 091·68	3 842·65	6 066·48	10 486·0	95 445·5	81
82	3 851·37	2 922·15	4 643·75	8 048·87	77 651·5	82
83	2 871·03	2 192·09	3 521·92	6 078·75	62 044·7	83
84	2 105·89	1 626·29	2 649·45	4 523·95	48 687·3	84
85	1 517·86	1 194·27	1 974·61	3 325·78	37 530·2	85
86	1 076·82	869·22	1 455·37	2 417·51	28 424·0	86
87	756·18	627·11	1 058·97	1 739·86	21 141·4	87
88	530·71	448·01	760·13	1 241·61	15 424·2	88
89	375·78	317·22	538·22	879·14	11 019·7	89
90	261·61	220·84	374·70	612·05	7 717·90	90
91	179·03	151·13	256·43	418·85	5 296·46	91
92	120·42	101·65	172·48	281·72	3 562·44	92
93	79·60	67·20	114·01	186·23	2 354·93	93
94	51·72	43·66	74·08	121·00	1 530·03	94
95	33·03	27·88	47·31	77·28	977·20	95
96	20·74	17·51	29·71	48·53	613·65	96
97	12·81	10·81	18·35	29·97	379·00	97
98	7·78	6·57	11·15	18·21	230·28	98
99	4·65	3·93	6·67	10·89	137·67	99
100	2·74	2·31	3·92	6·40	80·98	100

BIBLIOGRAPHY

BIZLEY, M. T. L. (1957) *Probability*. London: Cambridge University Press.

DONALD, D. W. A. (1970) *Compound Interest and Annuities-Certain*, 2nd Edition. London: Heinemann.

FREEMAN, H. (1949) *Mathematics for Actuarial Students*. London: Cambridge University Press.

FREEMAN, H. (1960) *Finite Differences for Actuarial Students*. London: Cambridge University Press.

HOOKER, P. F. AND LONGLEY-COOK, L. H. *Life and Other Contingencies*, Volumes I (1953) & II (1957). London: Cambridge University Press.

JORDAN, C. W. Jr (1967) *Life Contingencies*, 2nd Edition. Chicago: Society of Actuaries.

KELLISON, S. G. (1970) *The Theory of Interest*. Illinois: Richard D. Irwin.

KING, G. (1902) *Institute of Actuaries' Text Book*, Part II, 2nd Edition. London: Charles and Edwin Layton.

SPURGEON, E. F. (1932) *Life Contingencies*, 3rd Edition. London: Cambridge University Press.

INDEX